INTELLECTUAL AMERICA

IDEAS ON THE MARCH

Oscar Cargill

COOPER SQUARE PUBLISHERS, INC.
NEW YORK
1968

Originally Published and Copyright © 1941
by The Macmillan Company, New York
Published by Cooper Square Publishers, Inc.
59 Fourth Avenue, New York, N. Y. 10003
Library of Congress Catalog Card No. 68-29659

Printed in the United States of America
by Noble Offset Printers, Inc., New York, N. Y. 10003

To

G. L. C.

Foreword

IDEODYNAMICS

FOR MORE THAN TWENTY YEARS intellectuals have been occupied with the place of *ideologies* in human affairs. Attempts to evaluate these agglutinated and powerful collections of ideas have led to reinterpretations of literature, history, and philosophy. Recognition of their existence as something distinct from individual, orderly systems of thought, or *philosophies,* has been one of the triumphs of modern criticism, a discovery comparable, in the realm of thought, to smashing the atom in physics.

The discovery or recognition of the ideology opens up spacious new fields for intellectual endeavor and analysis. Ideologies are comparable to cosmic storms of force; sweeping the universe of thought, they determine much of human action, particularly on the grand scale, for few men act outside the influence of some ideology. A study of their impact on any past or present culture, a description of their tendencies and strength, is a new study— it is not criticism properly, nor history, nor philosophy, though it may make use of all of these. Such a study deserves a new name, and for it I propose a new word—IDEODYNAMICS: *the descriptive study of ideologies and of the results of the forces which they exert.* What extensions ideodynamics is capable of, I have no notion: theoretically we may some day be able to state the laws and write the equations of this science. Practically, however, they may prove as elusive as those of sociology and psychology. Today I am content with merely the descriptive potentialities of ideodynamics.

A descriptive science of ideas has an advantage over history which is commonly claimed for sociology: in current affairs its applicability is immediate. On the vulgar side, for example, it reveals the intentions of all propaganda. Yet even in the study of past cultures it has possibly some suggestions to offer to history. For want of a prior study in ideodynamics, perhaps, the thrilling new history of ideas which Robinson and Schlesinger crusaded for, and Parrington practised, is still somewhat short of full development. Important and stimulating as is Parrington's *Main Currents in American Thought,* it has nevertheless its amateurish aspect: the judgment of all things from within the tired swirl of the worn-out ideology of Jeffersonian agrarianism! Had its author worked backwards from a study of contemporary intellectual forces (the contemporary field is obviously the ideal field for ideodynamics), his perceptions were such that he himself would have been irked by the simplifications of *Main Currents*. Even a history of Jeffersonian idealism should show more torque and twist than Mr. Parrington's pages reveal, for one familiar with the behavior of contemporary forces could hardly plot the action of a previous force (as he did) in a straight line. This does not go beyond Newton's now discredited first law. Possibly ideodynamics provides the student of the history of ideas with a clearer understanding of the transmissibility and friction of ideologies than he can get in any other way.

If philosophy be the science of *what is possible,* then ideodynamics is the science of *what is:* a statement of the world's confusions from which philosophy, like poetry, may beguile us, but to which we must return for sanity and health. Aesthetics, the charmed domain of criticism, is not impervious to good received from ideodynamics: through it, forms are understood as shaped by the pressures of the ideology which creates them. Though panderers to the popular taste may still come trailing clouds of glory, the genuine critic will abjure "atmosphere" for the sake of truth. Ideodynamics is at once maid-servant and disciplinarian to criticism.

Wonderfully possessed by all the possibilities extending from an examination of contemporary ideologies, and especially eager to discover the relationship of the individual intellect to the ideology, yet possessed also by a lively sense of my own limitations, I began hesitantly some nine years ago the study of our contemporary culture. At long last I am prepared to be delivered of a volume, which, like a new-born babe, may be fair only in its creator's eyes. Yet, whatever its faults, I swear the thing is alive.

Intellectual America will be presented to the reader in two volumes: *Ideas on the March* and *Ideas in Conflict*. Under the first title I have rendered an account of the European ideologies which have swept into this country in modern times, forces alien in origin, but not necessarily without justification in the circumstances of our society once they found expression here. I admit they were destructive when they appeared—they were surely destructive of the old complacencies, but was not this *demolition preparatory to change?* I would not lodge against those obsessed by them any such wholesale condemnation as is contained in Mr. MacLeish's *The Irresponsibles*. I can still recall with quickening pulse the ecstasy produced among those of us who were young when our intellectual renaissance began and when it seemed natural to exclaim—

> Lord, what are we,
> That our eyes this glory see,
> That our ears have heard the sound!

I refuse to believe we were wholly mistaken in assuming that the deluge of strange new writing which swept out of memory the bracken, stagnant, flaccid stuff (then respected as literature) constituted a surge ahead for the life of the spirit in this country. The antique morals and provincial ways of thought, the ideologies of the Gilded Age (1865–1890), had to go, and those who assisted in their passing, whatever *their* ideologies, were the saviours of mankind. Yet even then we occasionally detected something histrionic in the conduct of the heroes—a kind of Kit Marlowish swagger, a John Lylyish simper, and even a Kydish caper, which led no procession into the future. We did not seriously take these young men and women as shapers: we took them for iconoclasts.

Time flows ceaselessly on, and perhaps too few of our illustrious ones have perished in brawls, which in this day fall into a ritual in publishers' offices and are useful for publicity. What was once an attitude or pose has become a habit of thought or a cult; there may be even a disposition to make permanent a point of view which was once a useful iconoclasm: the ideology has swallowed the carrier-atom. Weak spirits in challenging times turn their faces to the wall and for comfort's sake ask others to line up with them. Against this tendency I am as willing to inveigh as is Mr. MacLeish. One of the purposes of *Intellectual America* is to immortalize the heroes before they too far forget themselves. No one is much concerned about the morals of Kit Marlowe, but if Kit Marlowe had lived to preach Tamburlaine-worship to the Elizabethans, some one would have had to point out that England was not Scythia. Nor is the United States a European nation—either France or England or Germany or Russia. To point out this has been the only conscious exercise I have allowed my piety. Any discoverable excess must be attributed to a Scotch-Presbyterian, Yankee-Puritan ancestry. It is grandpapa speaking from beneath his stone and yew, and not the present writer.

History has many uses, and the comparison I have here invoked suggests, *though it does not insure,* the course of man's action in America. As I see it, the struggle for *political democracy* had two periods: first, a struggle for *political stability,* signalized by the creation of strong states under great princes: Henry VIII, Louis XIV, Frederick the Great; and secondly, the struggle for *political mobility*—indicated in the risings of the people against their monarchs. A practical harmony, the neutralizing of conflicting ideologies, was at last achieved between the urges for political stability and mobility in our Constitution and its Amendments.

I now assume the world to be painfully seeking *social democracy,* and I believe at just this point in time men appear to desire more than anything else *social stability;* hence everywhere their tolerance of the "strong man" (Hitler, Mussolini, Stalin, Konoye, Churchill—to come no nearer home), just as, at a similar period in the long war for political democracy, they tolerated the great prince. I judge ill of the spirit of man and of his compulsions, so it seems to me, if I assume his ultimate satisfaction with mere social stability. I anticipate an effort also to achieve true *social mobility,* but I foresee no rest for the laboring spirit of man until these urges are, somewhere in the world, harmonized for practical purposes in an institution or compact like our political Constitution.

Because a favored America led the world in a struggle for
political democracy, it is my fond hope that she will lead it in
that impending struggle which I foresee. Already the lines are
drawn, with the "stabilizers" on one side and the "mobilizers"
on the other: the Leftists who hope to achieve a stable state
through the dictatorship of the proletariat, and the Liberals
who hope to establish a classless society so mobile that a man
may move from bottom to top at a rate proportional to his
usefulness to mankind. Discussion of these ideologies and their
forces I have reserved for the second volume of *Intellectual
America,* where they are treated as *Ideas in Conflict.* Look there
for studies of Upton Sinclair and Sinclair Lewis, Thorstein
Veblen and John Dewey, John Steinbeck and Willa Cather, Earl
Browder and Thurman Arnold, and hundreds of other intellectuals. I am not unmindful that this indicated division of my
work is happily chronological, the economic collapse of 1929
shifting the interest from the iconoclasts to the shapers, just as
events of 1606 redirected English thought. But I do not want
too much made of this division: nothing precisely ceased or
began on October 29, 1929.

Again let me insist that I am not writing history: I am studying critically contemporary American culture with history as
one tool to shape history. Consequently the pattern of *Intellectual America* is not the pattern of any previous book. A history is a cone with a broad base of "fact" supporting the author's
"point" (which is usually something painful enough for mankind) : this study has the shape of a cornucopia, with its greatest
dimension at the top, where the years 1890–1940 in our thought
(the *present* for the generations of men now living) are given
the fullest representation. I am as anxious to produce the *effect*
of our intellectual life today as a novelist is to make one feel
the presence of his characters. Living intellectuals, atoms in the
currents of thought, are my actors. No attempt at all is made
to treat any *historical* figure completely, though many are cited
as *symptomatic* figures. Thus Whitman is introduced in my study
of the Freudians merely as a way of enforcing certain statistics.
No one should take him as an actor on the stage, and no one
should complain that he hasn't three or four dimensions.

I am not attempting to attach labels to any of the intellectuals here studied. Never conceivably would I allude to "Pound, *that Decadent*"; when I speak of Ezra Pound, I speak of "Pound, the Poet"—which is reverential enough for any man. And if I were to consider Pound by himself (that is, if I were writing mere criticism and were interested only incidentally in ideologies), I should adduce sufficient material to confound any label paster. But here I consider him in a very complex pattern where he bears a certain relationship to others and to ourselves. In this pattern it is convenient to distinguish him and his ilk by some epithet. If it were anywhere near as convenient to use symbols, I should do so, though I fancy that less would be gained in this way than some people have assumed.

In an intellectual survey, particularly in a survey with scientific pretensions, it may seem paradoxical to give very little attention to science; but I hold with Aristotle that science has not much significance for man until it is translated for him. Some scientists are born translators, and these I have honored as they deserved. There will be time enough for the others.

I am more concerned about my own translations from the French poets. This was a foolhardy thing to undertake, but I wanted my reader to have the substance of these poets and still have the illusion of reading verse. I am now fearful that the illusion is very transparent.

I want to thank Dorothy Alyea and Eda Lou Walton for suggesting improvements in these translations; I cannot thank Granville Hicks adequately for his help and encouragement—I still do not understand how a man who does not see eye to eye with me could aid me as much as he has. My obligation to others has been great and various. I name here in gratitude Nelson F. Adkins, Harold C. Bohn, Warren Bower, Carleton Brown, E. B. Burgum, William Charvat, Henry Steele Commager, Saxe Commins, Lawrence H. Conrad, Miriam L. Colston, Edward Dahlberg, Howard Dunbar, Frédéric Ernst, Eric Estorick, Waldo Frank, Emil Greenberg, Paul Haines, Sidney Hook, Joseph Kling, Donald S. Klopfer, Renée Kusselman, Daniel Lerner, Sidney Lind, Percy Long, Frank McCloskey, Bruce McCullough, J. D. Magee, Andrew Meyer, John Herbert Nelson,

James Putnam, A. H. Quinn, Meyer Schapiro, Margaret Schlauch, Samuel Sillen, John Terry, Charles C. Thach, William Troy, George C. Vincent, Donald O. Wagner, Homer A. Watt, Edmund Wilson, and Wesley D. Zinnecker. Especially do I want to thank the librarians of the Columbia University Library, of the Montclair Public Library, of the New Jersey State Teachers College Library, of the New York Public Library, of the New York University Libraries, and of the University of Minnesota Library. In a bibliography attached to the second volume I hope to indicate something of the very heavy debt I am under to other authors through the printed page.

Oscar Cargill
August 1, 1941.

Acknowledgments

The author gratefully acknowledges the kindness of publishers and individuals in granting permission to make extended quotation from their books in this work, as follows:

Conrad Aiken, for a passage from *Scepticisms,* published by Alfred A. Knopf, 1925.

D. Appleton-Century Company, for a passage from G. Stanley Hall's *Adolescence,* copyright, 1904.

Brandt and Brandt, for permission to quote (1) from E. E. Cummings' *Collected Poems,* published by Harcourt, Brace and Company, copyright, 1938; and (2) from the poetry of Edna St. Vincent Millay, published by Harper and Brothers and in copyright.

Dodd, Mead and Company, for a selection from *Last Songs from Vagabondia* by Bliss Carman. Used by permission of Dodd, Mead and Company, Inc.

Doubleday, Doran and Company, for (1) a passage from *The Octopus,* by Frank Norris, copyright, 1901, by Doubleday, Doran and Company, Inc.; (2) for a passage from *Life in Letters of William Dean Howells,* by Mildred Howells, copyright, 1928, by Doubleday, Doran and Company, Inc.

Duell, Sloan and Pearce, for a passage from Erskine Caldwell's *Tobacco Road,* copyright, 1932.

Farrar and Rinehart, for passages from *The Selected Poems of John Gould Fletcher,* copyright, 1938, and reprinted by permission of Farrar and Rinehart, Inc., publishers.

William Faulkner, for a passage from *As I Lay Dying.*

John Gould Fletcher, for a passage from *Preludes and Symphonies,* copyright, 1930.

Waldo Frank, as literary editor and executor of Hart Crane, for a passage from one of Crane's letters.

Harcourt, Brace and Company, for passages from (1) William Faulkner's *Sartoris,* copyright, 1929; and (2) *The European Caravan,* edited by Samuel Putnam, copyright, 1931.

Harvard University Press, for a passage from Clifton Joseph Furness' *Walt Whitman's Workshop,* 1928. Reprinted by permission of the President and Fellows of Harvard College.

Houghton Mifflin Company. The selections from (1) Henry Adams' *The Education of Henry Adams,* (2) Amy Lowell's *Can Grande's Castle,* (3) Amy Lowell's *Men, Women and Ghosts,* and (4) Archibald MacLeish's *Poems, 1924–1933,* are used by permission of, and by arrangement with, the publishers, Houghton Mifflin Company.

Mildred Howells, for a passage from *Life in Letters of William Dean Howells,* copyright, 1928, Doubleday, Doran and Company, Inc.

Liveright Publishing Corporation, for selections from *The Collected Poems of Hart Crane* and from *Collected Poems of H. D.,* published by Liveright Publishing Corporation.

Longmans, Green and Company, for a passage from Houston Peterson's *The Melody of Chaos,* copyright, 1931.

The Macmillan Company, for selections from (1) Henri Bergson's *Matter and Memory,* and (2) Marianne Moore's *Selected Poems.* By permission of The Macmillan Company, publishers.

New Directions, for passages from Ezra Pound's *A Draft of XXX Cantos.*

Random House, for passages from (1) Eugene O'Neill's *All God's Chillun Got Wings,* copyright, 1924; (2) Eugene O'Neill's *Moon of the Caribbees and Six Other Plays,* copyright, 1919; and (3) William Faulkner's *As I Lay Dying,* copyright, 1930.

Charles Scribner's Sons, for passages from (1) Conrad Aiken's *Selected Poems,* (2) F. Scott Fitzgerald's *The Beautiful and the Damned,* (3) Ernest Hemingway's *In Our Time,* (4) Ernest Hemingway's *The Sun Also Rises,* (5) Ernest Hemingway's *Death in the Afternoon,* (6) *Little Essays Drawn from the Writings of George Santayana,* edited by Logan Pearsall Smith, (7) George Santayana's *Soliloquies in England and Later Soliloquies,* and (8) Edmund Wilson's *Axel's Castle.*

Simon and Schuster, for passages from Thomas Craven's *Modern Art* and Theodore Dreiser's *The Financier.*

Gertrude Stein, for "Red Stamp," "Mildred's Umbrella," "Susie Asado," "Patriotic Leading," and a passage from *Three Lives.*

William Troy and *The Nation,* for a passage from "T. S. Eliot, Grand Inquisitor."

The Vanguard Press, for passages from James T. Farrell's *Studs Lonigan,* copyrights, 1932, 1933, 1934, 1935.

The Viking Press, Inc., for selections from (1) *Winesburg, Ohio,* by Sherwood Anderson, copyright, 1919, by B. W. Huebsch. By permission of The Viking Press, Inc., New York; (2) *Finnegans Wake,* by James Joyce, copyright, 1939, by James Joyce. By permission of The Viking Press, Inc., New York; and (3) *Portrait of the Artist as a Young Man,* by James Joyce, copyright, 1916, by B. W. Huebsch. By permission of The Viking Press, Inc., New York.

Contents

INTELLECTUAL AMERICA

IDEAS ON THE MARCH

"The covers of a book are responsible for
much error. They set a limit round certain
convenient groups of ideas, when there are
really no limits."
—T. E. Hulme, *Speculations*.

I

THE INVADING FORCES

"We are the Romans of the modern world,
—the great assimilating people."—Oliver
Wendell Holmes, *The Autocrat of the
Breakfast Table*

I

FRENCH NATURALISM AND DECADENCE

MEN ARE FEW who can read history to any advantage. "We
learn from history," wrote Hegel, "that we never learn anything
from history." A study in contemporary culture—particularly in
contemporary American culture—would seem to possess none of
the disadvantages of an historical study. Yet let not the reader
rejoice too soon. Let him plunge into the stream of contemporary
thought, and through all its rips and races, through all its shal-
lows and eddies, through its slime, ooze, entangling weeds, and
wet phantasmagoria, through its swells, whirlpools, plunging
tides, and restless gulfs he will detect either the slow, subtle pull
of separate currents or the stinging contact of their arrowing
clear particles. Here is *direction* if he will heed, here is something
proceeding from a source—here is history involved. All else is
battering confusion or puzzling stagnation. In the downstream of
Dark and Doubt the water is yet deeper, more roiled, and less
decipherable. What is gained by going in that direction whither
all willess, buffeted bodies are swept by the resistless force of
time? Let the few bold swimmers face against the descending
sweep of the flood, however strong, buoyed up by the certain
knowledge that, as Nature is our guide, the stream will divide
into tributaries, and the tributaries into sources and origins. It is
the way of the few, but it is the only way of simplification and

clarification. Where the rills come out of the swampy land of popular emotion, where they spring from the hard rock of economic and political fact, they tear away silt or sediment to color for ever their currents, so that to the fearless explorer are revealed the whole constituency and significance of the full stream of modern thought. It is his reward that the watershed of history is less broad than the timorous imagine and the sources less remote and fewer than they thought. By taking the clearest marked courses, and by occasionally referring to some elementary guide to the chief geological strata of past thought, we need go no further back than the generation of our grandfathers, nor survey no broader intellectual terrain than that of Western Europe and America.

Despite its scientific achievement, the world has made little intellectual progress since the two eventful decades which lie between 1850 and 1870. By then were formed the kinds of mind which are manifest in the world today. These minds are the product of two great events: the failure of democratic nationalism on the continent of Europe and the promulgation of the doctrine of evolution.

Democratic nationalism was the far swing of the pendulum from that internationalism, that infinitely complex totalitarianism, which was Roman Catholicism in the Middle Ages. As such, it carried the hopes of man for liberty of person, of thought and utterance, and of action, all of which had been restricted in one way or another by the papal dictatorship. When the power of the Church Universal began to wane, men turned naturally to their princes with the expectation that they would establish that better social order which is the eternal dream and despair of the race. Possibly as Niccolò Macchiavelli penned his epoch-making *Il Principe* in the year 1513 he had a vision of a fairer Italy than men had ever seen, achieved through the strong will and bold action of a prince who cared little whether or not he was a fit subject of Heaven. At least, so apt a scholar of politics as Jean Jacques Rousseau thought this was Macchiavelli's intention, and later students have done no more than to affirm Rousseau's view. In time men learned bitterly that, though an autocratic ruler might establish a powerful state, he might also patch up a truce with the

Church which would be more oppressive than the old, sometimes harmonious, dichotomy of Holy Roman Empire and Roman Church. Nowhere was this lesson learned better than in France during the regimes of the Bourbon kings and their ecclesiastical ministers. And so men began to dream a dream of a democratic nation in which the sovereign should be responsible to the people or to a supposedly immutable law established by the people.

In the brain of the most influential of all the public dreamers, in that of Jean Jacques Rousseau, this dream became extraordinarily prescriptive. It is well enough to say that when Rousseau opined that "the larger the state, the less the liberty" he had the city-state of Geneva in mind, for this he certainly did; but it is also true that in limiting the achievement of democracy to a nation in which there is a high degree of intimacy in all affairs he was defining something removed as far as possible from the internationalism of feudal times. Rousseau did indicate, however, his intention to show in a sequel to *Le Contrat Social* "how the external strength of a great people may be combined with the convenient polity and good order of the small state." Yet his implication is the extension of nationalism through federation or its like, not through totalitarianism. Indeed, the last chapter in his political treatise is a charge of hot shot directed at Romanism. Whoever speaks of a "Christian Republic" (he avers) is using mutually exclusive terms.

The democratic nation, then, becomes the vehicle of man's hope. When, in the early stages of the French Revolution, the Assembly issued its "Declaration of the Rights of Man and of the Citizen" it was following Rousseau and the other eighteenth century philosophers in the direction of realizing this ideal. Those who charge Rousseau with inciting the Revolution should, if they want to damage him for all time, demonstrate that his thinking, dominant in the early liberal stages of that great upheaval, was responsible for the failure of the Revolution. His counsel that democracy could be realized only in small political units led the Assembly to "pulverize" France, to give emphasis to the very factionalism which made that mighty effort abortive. Indeed, it might be contended that Rousseau gave to French politics its tendency towards ionization (so puzzling to an Anglo-Saxon) that has ever since made political action in that country relatively ineffective. Yet something should be allowed for the French temperament; tremendous as was the influence of Rousseau, it is doubtful if it extends this far.

Democratic nationalism as an ideal survived the conflict between the Girondists and the Jacobins, survived Danton and Robespierre, and dominated even the alternating policies of the Directory. We cannot understand the enthusiasm with which the French people turned to Napoleon until we realize that his advent meant a new emphasis upon this ideal. In fact, to some minds he seemed mystically summoned forth for the achievement of democracy, for had not Rousseau written in regard to his birthplace, "I have a feeling that some day that little island [Corsica] will astonish Europe"? It was in the spirit of the decree of the National Convention of November 19, 1792, extending the protection of France to all oppressed peoples, that Bonaparte marched into Italy as the representative of the sovereign French people, proclaiming—

Peoples of Italy, the French army comes to break your chains; the French people is the friend of all peoples; meet us with confidence. Your property, your religion, and your usages will be respected. We make war as generous enemies, and we have no quarrel save with the tyrants who enslave you.

This early rôle of liberator helped to fix Napoleon's character as "the incarnate democrat," and he always had a great following who saw him in no other light, even after he had accepted the hereditary principle for the succession of his title of Emperor. Consequently, when his unlimited personal ambitions led to disaster for his people, the cause of democratic nationalism appeared humiliated in his abdication.

With the support of hated foreign states, and by repressive laws, puppet monarchs kept the French people in check until the July Revolution of 1830, when the Royalists were overcome at the barricades by a furious mob. Factionalism split the victors and Louis Philippe was thrust forward as a constitutional monarch. In vain did his supporters cite the fact that he had fought in the Revolutionary armies and had endured poverty and hardship; in vain did Lafayette embrace him before the crowd at the Hôtel de Ville; there was no idealism attached to this sentimental umbrella-toter, and the French people saw him for what he was —a weak symbol of hereditary monarchy. The poet Lamartine summed up the verdict in the deadly phrase, *"La France s'ennuie,"* while Béranger and Victor Hugo drew invidious comparisons between the French king and the First Emperor.

The accumulated resentment of the people overbore the government of Louis Philippe in the "Red" rising of 1848, but the unexpected result of the first election in which Frenchmen enjoyed universal direct suffrage, as decreed by the revolutionists, was an Assembly moderate in tone and character. The people blundered, however, in their second experience at the polls when they were persuaded by the magic name of Napoleon to elect the miserable nephew of the great Emperor to the Presidency of France. In his three years as President, Louis Napoleon, properly styled "The Judas of the Nineteenth Century," subtly undermined the democracy which he headed by reducing the electorate, by turning the schools back to the Catholics, and by spreading throughout France the fear of monarchy. Consequently his *coup d'état* of the night of December 2, 1851, was endorsed by an enormous majority in a national plebiscite, and he became Napoleon III. To angry intellectuals this was, perhaps, merely an afterclap to the treachery Louis Napoleon had displayed towards Republicanism in Italy. The army he had sent there gave no succor to the defenders of Venice but expelled the followers of Garibaldi and Mazzini from the Holy City and reestablished the Pope.

Napoleon III as Emperor tried, after the Crimean War, to redeem his standing in Italy and to placate liberals at home by proclaiming his intention, on May 3, 1859, of making that country "free from the Alps to the Adriatic." After winning the battles of Magenta and Solferino, however, he patched up a sorry truce with Franz Joseph, the ultimate result of which was Italian unity without democracy, the practical Cavour settling upon monarchy as the only expedient for his country. Yet Cavour was certainly not an absolutist ("There is no great man who is not a liberal," he had proclaimed; "the degree of love of liberty is proportionate in every man to the moral education attained by him") ; hence even Italian unity was a disappointment to Cavour and to all liberals.

The half-victory in Italy was, however, the beginning of the end of Napoleon III. Before descending into the Italian plains this Bonaparte had been an autocrat at home: he had emasculated universal suffrage with official candidates, he had muzzled the press with *autorization préalable* and censorship, he had choked Republican opposition with the law of public safety. France had become, in a famous phrase, a sick room in which people spoke in lowered voices. On his return from Italy he no longer had the assured support of the clergy and the wealthy classes his earlier policies had won him. The former were dissatisfied with the outcome in Italy, possibly because they had been promised more; while the latter were angry because of a reciprocal trade agreement with England, engineered by Cobden. Consequently Napoleon *le Petit* had to make concessions to the opposition at home in the parliamentary reforms of 1860. These permitted, however, the formation of a coalition of anti-Napoleonic elements, known as the Liberal Union, led by Thiers. Circumvented in an effort to secure a backing from the middle-class liberals, Napoleon III turned to the workers, granting them the right to form unions and cooperative societies.

The Emperor now felt himself safe at home and embarked on a program of solving his foreign difficulties through intrigue. Taking advantage of the American Civil War, he sent troops to Mexico to win the crown of that country for Maximilian, brother of Franz Joseph, apparently hoping that in return Austria would yield Venetia to the Italians and thus silence criticism. On the other hand, he entered into a secret agreement with Prussia not to interfere should that power attack Austria. After the Germans were triumphant at Sadowa, in 1866, Napoleon was humiliated when he tried to secure his "reward"—an "innkeeper's account" which was whittled down from Mainz to Belgium, to Luxembourg, to nothing. An ultimatum from the United States forced him to withdraw from Mexico, leaving Maximilian to his fate. Meanwhile French liberals saw the final step in Italian unity taken with the aid of Prussia and not with that of France. In the midst of this exasperating confusion, Thiers declared, "There are no blunders left for us to make." Yet one did remain, but it was made by Parliament, rather than by the Emperor, when it defeated the efforts of Marshal Niel to strengthen the army.

Ridiculed by Gambetta and Victor Hugo, overwhelmed at the polls in 1869, Napoleon III was forced to concede reformation of the state to Ollivier, leader of the Third Party, and in May, 1870, a genuine parliamentary empire was established. But in this very hour of the promise of the triumph of French democracy came overwhelming defeat. Bismarck, fully comprehending the weakness of France, utilized the case of the Spanish succession as a cause for war and tricked Napoleon III and the French Parliament into taking the foolish part of the aggressor. He guarded against interference from England by publishing Bonaparte's absurd demand for Belgium and struck before France could effect a coalition with Austria. Sedan was succeeded by Metz, but when Paris capitulated, a people was defeated and not merely an Empire fell. This was the very climax of the misfortunes of the Republican cause in Europe, and was so felt, as we shall soon see, by intellectuals throughout the world.

Closing our ears to the heavy tread of history, we may detect the lighter, less certain steps of thought trailing the march of events here briefly outlined. Intellectuals never lived in more difficult times than those of nineteenth century France. Chateaubriand, true successor to Rousseau, affords ample evidence of the difficulties besetting the liberal during the Revolution, the Empire, the Hundred Days, and the Restoration. His nature was a wishful one,—he hoped for the betterment of mankind, but he dreadfully misread again and again the signs of the times. His first published work, *Essai Historique, Politique, et Moral sur les Revolutions* (1797), was an effort to reconcile the nobility to the Revolution; the immensely popular *Atala* (1801) suggests the control of natural passions (recently so freely displayed), while the *Génie du Christianisme,* opportunely published just prior to Napoleon's reestablishment of Catholicism in France, in 1802, is an effort to prove the Christian religion, and especially the primitive form of that religion, the most poetic, the most humane, the most favorable to liberty, to literature, and to the arts.

Chateaubriand's desire for order out of revolution is patent in all this early work. Following the murder of the Duc d'Enghien, he turned against Napoleon and referred to him as Nero, and later, from exile, penned his pamphlet, "On Bonaparte, the Bourbons, and the Need for Rallying to Our Legitimate Princes." Yet, though this pamphlet aided materially in the Restoration, Chateaubriand soon became disgusted with his Bourbon king, and, in 1817, issued another pamphlet attacking the monarchy, for which he was heavily penalized. He rallied yet again to the cause of order when Louis Philippe came to power, but soon relapsed into complete despair from which he did not emerge during the remainder of his life.

Ambitious and at times unscrupulous, Chateaubriand nevertheless was the gilded weathercock of hope in the France of clouded discouragement. The story of the wishful thinker might be pursued through the turbulent career of Victor Hugo, Chateaubriand's great disciple, were it profitable to do so, and such conflicting things as the *Ode à la Colonne* (in which he champions the first Napoleon's marshals) and *Napoléon le Petit* (an assault from the safety of Guernsey upon the Second Empire) might be placed in juxtaposition and commented on. But is it necessary to prove that French intellectuals generally were fervidly interested in the Republican cause and in French nationalism when there is evidence everywhere of this? Honoré de Balzac, for example, cannot be suspected of diverting too much of his abundant energy from artistic to political causes, yet even he subscribed to the delusion that Napoleon I was a liberator and England the friend of tyrants. Thus, in "The Atheist's Mass," appears a wholly gratuitous defense of the First Emperor as a Nationalist:

> ... In our own day, for instance, Napoleon was condemned by our contemporaries when he spread his eagle's wings to alight in England: only 1822 could explain 1804 and the flat boats at Boulogne. ...

Or is it necessary to cite the fiery poets of the Italian Risorgimento to show how sanguine and widespread among intellectuals were the twin hopes of Liberty and Nationality? In distant America, William Cullen Bryant championed the cause of the Greeks, the Spanish, and the Italians, while Walt Whitman, all aflame, wrote of the events of 1848—

> . . . the frighten'd monarchs come back,
> Each comes in state with his train, hangman, priest, tax-gath-
> erer . . .
> Yet behind all lowering stealing, lo, a shape,
> Vague as the night, draped interminably, head, front, and form
> in scarlet folds. . . .
> Liberty, let others despair of you—I never despair of you!

The struggle for democratic freedom—for Liberty of the individual and the Nationality of peoples—aroused irrepressible emotions in the breasts of all intellectuals, and the defeat of these twin hopes engendered a corresponding despair. Yet the expression of that despair took unexpected forms, hence we must look further than the mere defeat of Continental Republicanism for an explanation of the character of European and American thinking since 1870. We must look also to the philosophies engendered by the promulgation of the doctrine of evolution.

Rousseau's conception of a sovereign people made possible a whole new science of human behavior whereas the sciences of ethics, politics, and civil law had been seemingly adequate before. The fact that *The Social Contract* sets forth the exercise of the general will as moral and healthful implies the existence of a natural law which this will, unless subverted, regularly obeys. It was only a matter of time before a science of sociology should follow Rousseau's book, or, if the thinker were inspired, his statement of the social "laws" might even be evolutionary.

The connections of Auguste Comte, father of sociology, with Hume, Condorcet, and Saint-Simon are less fundamental to an understanding of his teaching than is his connection with his times. Positivism is inconceivable in the epoch of the absolute state. Although Comte declared flatly, "Positivism rejects the metaphysical doctrine of the Sovereignty of the People," he looked upon his teaching not merely as "a philosophical system," but also as "an instrument of social renovation" to be applied to "the work of moral and mental reorganization which constitutes the second phase of the great Western revolution." Comte very

sensibly extended the conception of a people to include all Western European humanity. Neither Germany nor Italy was then
unified, and Comte believed that his broad polity might be
achieved through the spread of social awareness over the Continent. "Affection must be the central point of the synthesis." We
need not dwell upon the elaborate Religion of Humanity, with its
calendar of lay saints, through which Comte hoped to achieve the
all-necessary "Public Opinion strongly organized" to support his
polity. It is of the utmost consequence, however, that Comte did
not conceive an ideal or static polity as possible. "Society is an
organism." The motto of Positivism is, *Order and Progress:*

Order is the condition of all Progress; Progress is always the object of
Order. Or, to penetrate the question still more deeply, Progress may be regarded simply as the development of Order; for the order of nature necessarily contains within itself the germ of all possible progress. The rational
view of human affairs is to look on all their changes, not as new Creations,
but as *new Evolutions.*

Though in the scientific researches of Buffon and Lamarck is
suggested a progression of forms and an evolution, here for the
first time, in the writing of Comte, is set forth a theory of the
evolution of human institutions. Comte's "Occidental polity" is
likewise an evolution from an improvement in his way of thinking
over that of Rousseau and the *philosophes.* For the first gift of
Comte to the world, made before he conceived his polity or the
Religion of Humanity, was a theory of "the general development
of the human intellect" according to "a fundamental Law to
which its progress is necessarily and invariably subjected. This
Law consists in the fact that the intellectual system of man . . .
passes through three successive phases, the Theological, the
Metaphysical, and the Positive or Scientific." In this view of
human intelligence, which glorifies the scientific attitude as the
highest development of the mind, there are implied other stages at
which supernatural or abstract reasons alone were possible as
explanations of phenomena in our thinking. That is, the scientific
phase is the product of an evolution from two earlier, and less
competent, phases of the mind. Thus the growth of the mind is
determined, not by individual effort—as had been conceived in

the past,—but by natural law. The intelligence becomes an organism. With both man's intelligence and his society reduced to phenomena, Comte could propose a new science for their study. In this way, as a capstone to all the sciences, "social physics," later more conveniently called "sociology," was born.

Comte's followers had very little interest in his broad polity and his Religion of Humanity, but his scientific theories influenced them profoundly. These followers included some of the most celebrated names of the mid-century in France. There was Émile Littré, the philologist who, as early as 1855, incensed all conservatives with his definition of the human animal in his *Dictionary of Medicine:* "HOMME. *Animal mammifère de l'ordre primates, famille des bimanes, etc.*" Littré, an extraordinarily homely man, was possibly the first human being in the world to be represented by the caricaturists as a monkey because of his evolutionary views. There was Louis Pasteur, the great scientist, and his less celebrated peer, Claude Bernard, whose *Introduction to the Study of Experimental Medicine* (1865) inspired Zola's *Experimental Novel.* There was Ernest Renan who not only approached the study of religion from a scientific point of view, but who, about 1848, wrote a mighty tome on *The Future of Science,* not published until years afterward. And there was Charles Augustin Sainte-Beuve who dug for biographical and critical facts with all the patience of a laboratory expert. Criticism for him was "the science of souls." He declared himself to be "a disciple of Bacon." So continuous was his labor that on one occasion he groaned, "My life is like a mill, a perpetual grinding." Yet, with the exception of Sainte-Beuve, these men were all Republicans in spirit, suffering for their liberal views, called to political duty, like Littré, when there seemed to be hope, all sharers in the desire for National safety and human liberty. Sainte-Beuve, a senator from 1865 to 1869, found himself, despite his convictions, in the Opposition to Napoleon III, a champion of freedom of the press and of education. He died a liberal.

Yet the greatest and most influential of Comte's disciples is still to be named: this was Hippolyte Taine, known to English readers, if known at all, as the author of a spirited and iconoclastic *History of English Literature* (1864) which closes with,

"The people who have listened to Tennyson are better than our aristocracy of townsfolk and bohemians; but I prefer Alfred de Musset to Tennyson." Britons have been much annoyed by "impertinent" comparisons, such as this one; they have never considered, however, what *The History of English Literature* meant to a Frenchman. Certainly it is not this, and similar all-too-candid statements of preference, which raised *The History* into one of the most important books of the nineteenth century for a native of France. There are more than two elements even in this comparison: if the incensed Briton will read again, he will discover that, while Alfred de Musset is held a better poet than Alfred, Lord Tennyson, *the English people are better stuff than the French Empire bohemians and bourgeois aristocracy*. The famous introduction to this great literary history declares that the factors which produce the temper of an age and determine the character of its literature are *"La race, le milieu, le moment."* The whole volume is an exposition of the thesis that the English race, hardly the intellectual equals of the French, have other qualities which make them superior—and better fortune, better circumstances, as well. "An Englishman entering on life, finds to all great questions an answer ready made. A Frenchman entering on life finds to all great questions simply suggested doubts."

While *The History of English Literature* may have been annoying to the Briton, this first comparative study of the intellectual fortunes of the two races was devastating to a Frenchman. Though the very success of the English, according to Taine, may be accounted for as the result of an early infusion of Norman-French blood, lifting them above other "German" peoples, the very race which has contributed most to this superior stock is incapable of doing anything for itself. Who can doubt that the pessimism of *The History of English Literature* comes directly from a comparison of the political fortunes of France and England?

... England is made; she knows it, and they know it. Such as this country is, based on the whole national history and on all the national instincts, it is more capable than any other people in Europe of transforming itself without recasting, and of devoting itself to its future without renouncing its past.

In Taine the warm hopes of Republicanism receive a cold douche of "scientific" fact. He was the first Frenchman to take stock: to observe that the sacrifice of various revolutions had brought his country less than a succession of niggardly Tory ministers had granted the British lower classes. Yet he knew how heroically his people had aspired. What, then, was the fault? Is it not forces over which they have no control? He answered his question partially in *The Origins of Contemporary France* in which he showed that the French people took the wrong step in 1789, that they transferred absolutism without destroying it, and that the later difficulties followed as a consequence. Taine was a determinist, whose belief in an unbreakable sequence of events was as much fixed by his view of the course of French history as by science, but he gave contemporary French literature and thought its prevailingly pessimistic tone.

Meanwhile the German invasion had startlingly enforced upon the Frenchman the feeling of racial inferiority which Taine had engendered with his history of literature. In that book Taine had poked fun at "the phlegmatic and grave" Germans, so docile and domestic; now what the French were assured was the finest army in Europe was overwhelmed by these poltroons and burghers in Prussian uniforms. The numbers, the stature, the military skill of the blonde invaders quickly destroyed all preconceptions about them, and they suddenly, in French eyes, took on the character of the vigorous, youthful Teuton tribes that in earlier times had poured down on senile Rome.

Decadence had gone further than Taine had intimated; the French stock itself was degenerate. This completely national reaction determined two types of literature which have prevailed, not merely in France, but throughout the world, since 1870. *Naturalism,* of which Zola was the first comprehensive exponent, is pessimistic determinism—the conviction that we are hurried towards evil and ignominious ends whether we will or not, that degeneracy is the common history of man. Those other thinkers who were influenced precisely as Zola was (yet despising him) by the doctrines of evolution to believe man a beast and, as an aftermath of the débâcle, to see life a chaos, fled from the contemplation of a world too much to bear to the ivory tower of pure art. The glory had departed from France during half a century of the mad pursuit of the chimera of Republicanism; France illustrated only decadence, and those Petroniuses who cherished an aristocratic taste for the old manners and forms ("bohemians," Taine called them) wilfully styled themselves *Decadents,* a very satisfactory epithet from a number of points of view. They produced a characteristic literature which has found its imitators and extenuators down into the present time.

Naturalism and Decadence—both philosophies of despair—were capable of many ramifications. The Naturalistic conception of man as a trapped animal licensed the idea that if he lived as one he was fully justified. Hence the enthusiasm for the animalistic exhibitions in life and literature which many Naturalistic writers display; hence the cult of *Primitivism,* which is no more than the worship of animalism for its own sake. Primitivism may take the form of "an innocent athleticism" as in the work of Jean Prevost and of Jean-Richard Bloch; or the form of a violent eroticism, as in Zola's *La Terre;* or yet again, the form of sadism, as in writers so seemingly antithetical as Maupassant and Huysmans. In any case it is as much a flight from the serious business of creating a rational world as is taking refuge in an ivory tower. It is nothing to excite wonder that Primitivists and Decadents often discover an affection for each other, if not for each other's ideas. They are all stragglers away from the fierce encounters of the modern world of thought.

Intellectualizing primitivistic tendencies is an obvious exercise for some of the adherents of Naturalism. No animal passion has been so thoroughly intellectualized, since 1870, as that of sex. *Freudianism,* a name by which it is convenient to designate the most conspicuous form of the rationalization of sex-primitivism, is the very antithesis of the romantic idealization of love before that date. Ever since Rousseau remarked that the health and prosperity of a society may be gauged by its fecundity, Frenchmen have been preternaturally absorbed in vital statistics, an absorption which was increased to anxiety after 1870 when their birthrate fell below that of Germany. The more anxious ones—the rich, neurotic and decadent, habitually vacationing in Vienna, formed a *corpus delicti* upon which the leading genius of that place, Dr. Sigmund Freud, made a matter-of-fact enough report. So palatable, however, was that report to decadent intelligences that the scientist was raised into a philosopher, and Freudianism as a patent, more than a therapy, spread over the world, its reception being humorously in inverse proportion to the birthrate, wherever it went.

Thus culminated, from causes we have ascertained, after the War of 1870 the growth of four of the kinds of mind that dominate contemporary thought: Naturalism, Decadence, Primitivism, and Freudianism, all interrelated and nourished on the substance of defeat. Yet the question may be asked, Why was the downfall of the French Empire and the triumph of Prussia an event of so much larger importance than the First World War? The answer must be that the conflict of 1914–1918 was entirely inconclusive in its results. France gained no victory to set the Gallic mind afire; when she contemplated her ruined towns and her million dead, she settled again into the despair which has typified the French mind since 1870. True, Aristide Briand labored heroically for a "United States of Europe" and Léon Blum attempted to break the venal control of the private bankers over the Banque de France and to nationalize the munitions industry, but neither leader won the support he deserved. The world depression, intensified in France by the failure of her diplomacy and the need for augmenting constantly her army, hardly proved a stimulus to new thought. French writers dealt more and more with the past (Proust is the great symptomatic figure) as though the present were a charnel house of which no decent word could be spoken. When the country moved into a new and disastrous struggle with Germany, its intellectual life appeared sluggish and drugged. Intellectual degeneracy, more than the stable military policy of the Maginot line and more than treachery, defeated France in 1940. This can be discerned even in such books as André Simone's *J'Accuse* and André Maurois' *Tragedy in France* which offer other reasons for the humiliation of the French. Now only a great event, and that unanticipated by any Frenchman, will set free again the mind of France. Wine of the vintage of 1789 will never be replaced by Vichy water.

GERMAN ABSOLUTISM

There is a sense in which much of modern European thought is a rationalization of Nordic triumph and Latin defeat in 1870. To appreciate this fact we must turn away from defeated France to victorious Prussia. Certain important trends in modern thinking can be traced back to Germany of the crucial period 1850–1870. In Germany only one first rate intellectual has ever espoused democracy. Indeed, as Croce points out, even "the unifying force of liberal character was always, in this nation, somewhat rare and intermittent." Balzac, commenting on the skill of the Germans with musical instruments, adds, "but they do not know how to play the great instruments of Liberty." Yet the tocsin of Liberty and Nationality had been sounded in Germany by Schiller during the Napoleonic wars. The apolitical Goethe can write warmly of his friend, "Through all Schiller's works runs the idea of liberty and this idea assumed different form as Schiller progressed in culture and himself became different. In his youth it was physical liberty that motivated him and passed over into his writings; in his later life it was ideal liberty." The range of Schiller is the distance between *The Robbers* (1781), a tragedy of the individual in conflict with the law, and *Wilhelm Tell* (1804), a drama incorporating the Rousseauistic ideals of individual liberty and nationalism. In the latter, the men of the cantons of Schwyz, Uri, and Unterwalden meet on the Rütli Rock to swear resistance against the Hapsburg usurpation:

> We swear to be a nation of true brothers,
> Never to part in danger or in death.
>> (*They swear, with three fingers raised.*)
> We swear we will be free as were our sires,
> And sooner die than live in slavery.
>> (*They swear, as before.*)

This has well been called "a Social Contract in a poetical setting." Yet there were reasons why the German people could not easily share the ideas of individual liberty of Rousseau or of any of the eighteenth century French philosophers.

Whoever does not appreciate the fact that most conceptions of national grandeur are associated in the German mind with a leadership of absolute right and of force has little knowledge either of German history or character. The German of Schiller's day who hoped for some polity more inspiring than that presented by the confusion of petty states and principalities of Middle Europe inevitably harked back to the Holy Roman Empire in the days of Charlemagne for his inspiration. Thus Fichte, first of the goose-stepping intellectuals, lecturing to much applause in Berlin in 1804 on "The Characteristics of the Present Age," again and again cites this Christian Empire with its "Politico-Spiritual Central Power" as his model state. He dreams, indeed, of the time when "the one True Religion, or Christianity, must and ought to become the creative and governing principle of a new State." Yet it is the unchallengeable authority that Fichte sought in the Christian Empire, the absolute and unimpeachable power of that polity:

Finally, Virtue can be no object of the State. Virtue is the constant and all-directing Good-will which strives to promote with all its power the purposes of the Human Race; and in the State particularly to promote these purposes in the way prescribed by it;—the desire and love to do this, and an unconquerable aversion to any other course of action. But that State, *in its essential character of a compulsive power,* calculates upon the *absence* of Good-will, and therefore upon the absence of Virtue, and upon the *presence* of Evil-will;—it supplies the want of the former and represses the outbreak of the latter by fear of punishment. Strictly confining itself to this sphere, it has no need to calculate upon Virtue, nor to take it into account for the accomplishment of its purposes. . . .

The sense of duty, of fealty, characteristic of the Christian Empire, appealed powerfully to Fichte, as it does to most Germans. "Religion discloses to Man the significance of the one Eternal Law which, as the Law of Duty, guides the free and noble, and, as the Law of Nature, governs ignoble instruments." "True freedom can be obtained only by means of the highest obedience to Law." Indeed, Fichte holds that in the Absolute or Perfect State, "no individual can propose any purpose to him-

self, and devote himself to its furtherance, which is his own
merely and not at the same time the purpose of the whole Community."

Thinking undoubtedly of the orthodoxy of thought and the
spread of Frankish customs under Charlemagne, Fichte gave
the German people a lasting conception of *Kultur:* "we may regard the State, particularly in the most perfect form which it has
assumed in any given Age, as at the same time the seat of highest
Culture of that Age. Barbarism stands directly opposed to the
purposes of this Culture wherever it comes in contact with them,
and constantly threatens the existence of the State; which thus
finds itself, even by the necessity of its own preservation, placed
in natural war with the surrounding Barbarism, and is compelled
to use every effort for its overthrow,—which latter, indeed, can
only be thoroughly accomplished by bringing the Barbarians
themselves under the dominion of law and order, and, in so far,
cultivating them. Thus, while thinking only of itself, the State
promotes the great purpose of the Human Race." In this fashion was born the idea of compulsive *Kultur* as the highest purpose
of the State.

Now while it is profitable to point out the connections of
Fichte's philosophy with the teachings of Macchiavelli (whom he
early translated into German), it is more worth while to observe
that his conception of the State as an absolute polity, essentially
non-ethical, yet demanding the complete energies of every citizen,
has been the prevailing conception of German thinkers since his
day and the idea apparently most acceptable to the German
people.

Hegel, who succeeded Fichte in the chair of philosophy at the
University of Berlin in 1818, sought to correct Fichte's vaguely
evolutionary "idea of universal history" but ended by adopting
a view painfully similar. According to Fichte—

    . . . the whole Life of Man is divided into *five* principal Epochs: that in
which Reason governs in the form of blind Instinct; that in which this
Instinct is changed into an external ruling Authority; that in which the
dominion of this Authority, and with it that of Reason itself, is overthrown; that in which Reason and its laws are understood with clear consciousness; and finally, that in which all the relations of the Race shall be

directed and ordered by perfect Art and perfect Freedom according to Reason. . . .

Fichte believed that two of the Epochs he had delineated had transpired and that now the Race was living in the Third Era, "the age of absolute indifference to all truth, and of entire and unrestrained licentiousness: the state of completed Sinfulness"! This is the age of Rousseau.

Now Hegel saw three main periods in history, the Oriental, the Classical, and the Germanic, which represented, for him, three distinct but evolutionary stages in the development of human freedom. The Oriental World first recognized "the *substantiality* of the ethical," that is, the existence of law proceeding from one source or one person who himself alone is free. In politics this is the monarch who is the substance of the State, of which his subjects are the accidents. In the Greek and Roman world, however, the idea of freedom is more extended: "individualities are developed" and the admission of certain "personal" rights to legal status is the step in the direction of general freedom. Finally, it was given to the Germanic nations to receive and to develop in the world the notion of true freedom, which was contained in Christianity as its central principle and ideal. Charlemagne gave mankind a systematically ordered State, but inasmuch as it was wholly dependent upon his genius and was not concurred in as an idea by the people (who were behind it in development), the State created by Charlemagne quickly disintegrated. No comparable State was born again until Frederick the Great created modern Prussia, in whose capital Hegel was lecturing. Frederick thought out and comprehended the universal aim or "reason" of the State, and was the first ruler who made this his supreme guide, ruthlessly suppressing all particularistic or individualistic pretensions opposed thereto.

But in the interim between Charlemagne and Frederick had occurred the all-necessary Protestant Reformation bringing "the free-spirit" to man. "Hereby was the new and final standard raised . . . the banner of the free spirit, master of itself *in the truth,* and only so. . . . The period from then till now has had, and still has, no other work to do than to mould the world according to this principle. . . . This is the essential meaning of the Reformation: namely, that the very nature of man defines him as free." Blessed with this inner spiritual and "complete" freedom, Germany, Hegel pointed out, has not suffered from the excesses of the Illumination which brought on the Revolution in France. The Prussian State, to him, is the highest political achievement of man; moreover, it is "in an essential sense the work of God himself." It would appear that the only difference between Fichte's conception of the perfect State and Hegel's conception is that Hegel contends that his is realized while Fichte places the realization of his State in a future epoch. In his *Philosophy of Law,* Hegel writes almost nonsensically:

> The State is the rational in itself and for itself. Its substantial unity is an absolute end in itself. To it belongs supreme right in respect to individuals whose first duty is—just to be members of the State. . . . [The State] is the absolute reality, and the individual himself has objective existence, truth, and morality only in his capacity as a member of the State.

Thus the two most important and influential writers on politics in early nineteenth-century Germany find a fanciful inner and spiritual liberty adequate reason for supporting an absolute State and for opposing the "anarchistic" ideas of the Republican thinkers of France.

Without leadership from the chief intellectuals, Republicanism in Germany was feebly upheld by a few university professors, with a result that strict supervision was established over the schools, and the liberal professors, Gneisenau, Jahn, Arndt, Humboldt, and others, either were forbidden to lecture, forced to resign, or imprisoned for their ideas. The struggle for Grecian independence and the news of the Revolution of 1830 in Paris raised a new crop of democrats, this time men definitely of the bourgeois class with which the cause of liberty became identified. Liberal deputies from this class met in secret assemblies in the South of Germany and excitement prevailed throughout the land. The "United Republics of Germany" was the theme of a great mass meeting at Hambach, in 1832, and thousands of citizens decked themselves in the black, red, and gold of the Republican movement. The poets of Young Germany took up the theme

of liberty and German unity, and, despite prohibitions and persecutions, succeeded in being heard. Distinguished in the names of
this poetic army in the 'forties were those of Fallersleben, Din-
gelstedt, Herwegh, and Freiligrath, the friend of Longfellow.
Herwegh wrote:

> Germans! trust the men who see,
> Iron will our present be,
> Clashing steel our future part:
> Now Black Death is all our earning,
> Fairy Gold to dust returning;
> And our Red, a bleeding heart.

Still, no first rate intelligence was born to lead the liberals and
this misfortune was the root of all others, for events opened up
in 1848 the only fair opportunity for democratic nationalism in
Germany. In South Germany Basserman moved in the Baden
Chamber for the establishment of the All-German Parliament
to supersede the Diet of the Confederation, even against the
will of the Princes, and Heinrich von Gagern seconded him in the
Chamber of Hesse. Then came the news of the overthrow of the
government of Louis Philippe in Paris. Immediately riots broke
out all over Germany and Austria. The red, black, and gold flag
of Republicanism was raised over the palace of the Confederation
Diet at Frankfort, and three days later, on March 13, 1848,
Metternich fled from Vienna.

Middle-class Germany could not consummate the victory it had
won with the aid of the workers over the German Princes. A
defection soon occurred in the ranks of the victors, and the Socialists split off to urge their own demands. In May, the Parliament
of All-Germany, which had been demanded, met in Frankfort.
Among the delegates was not a single able political thinker; instead of proceeding to the important task of preparing a constitution, they strove first to establish an authority and elected
Archduke John of Austria as Imperial Regent. The Princes,
moreover, were not immediately compelled to acknowledge the
authority of the Archduke, and as months of parliamentary inac-
tion and confusion flowed by, they slowly awoke to the fact that
they would not be forced to. Frederick William IV, of Prussia,

pledged in the name of the German Confederation to support the people of Schleswig in their struggle with the Danes, suddenly withdrew his support without consulting the Frankfort Parliament, and that body, fearing to lose its Prussian delegates, officially endorsed his action. Wild rioting took place in the city of Frankfort as a result, for the Leftists felt that the moderate liberals and conservatives in the parliament had betrayed them.

Meanwhile, after a summer of intrigue, in which Croat was turned against Magyar, Jellacić reconquered Hungary for the Hapsburgs and Count Felix Schwarzenberg re-formed the territories once again into a centralized empire, thus putting an end to the hope for a Greater Germany. With steadily diminishing numbers the Frankfort Parliament continued to deliberate, while deserters from its ranks, led by von Gagern, brought together the more important states into a federation with the king of Prussia at its head. Thus the supreme Republican effort in Germany resulted in a complete fiasco, and raised among the intellectuals in that nation a lasting suspicion of bourgeois or middle-class management which has colored much of modern German thinking.

Among the inheritors of this anti-bourgeois bias, himself a member of the middle class and in his youth an active participant in the struggle for democratic nationalism in Germany, was Karl Marx, father of the Communist philosophy of the State. Finding his early associates too tame and liberal leadership in Germany equivocal, Marx, after a study of the French Socialists, pitched upon the workers in Germany as the only possible source of successful revolution. Yet because industry was so backward in Germany, there was, when Marx became disgusted with Republicanism, no genuine proletariat in that country. The problem was to create this class; in his criticism of Hegel's *Philosophy of Law,* in 1843, he first affirmed that German liberation was to be sought in "the formation of a class in chains, a class which develops in bourgeois society, but which is not of it, of an order which shall break up all orders. The product of this dissolution of society reduced to a special order is the proletariat. The proletariat arises in Germany only with the beginning of the industrial movement. . . ." That is, Marx recognized Germany must develop industrially and produce a dominant bourgeois society before a

class-conscious proletariat could exist.   Yet "the impotence of
the German middle classes is the political impotence of Germany"; hence the workers are counselled to "fight with the
bourgeoisie whenever it acts in a revolutionary way, against the
absolute monarchy, the feudal squirearchy, and the petty bourgeoisie." By strengthening the great bourgeoisie, the proletariat
would be created in Germany.

Marx hoped, however, to short-cut on this lengthy procedure
when the revolt of 1848 occurred. From Belgium he hurried to
Cologne to edit the *Neue Rheinische Zeitung* in which he urged
the non-existent proletariat and its fictive armies to shorten,
simplify, and concentrate "the torturing death agonies of society"
by the only means, "revolutionary terrorism." When a sufficient
number of fanatics failed to arise and the revolution of 1848
collapsed in Germany, Marx reverted to his early theory that an
evolution was first necessary. "After the defeats of 1849 we in
no way shared the illusions of vulgar democracy . . . [which]
reckoned on a speedy and finally decisive victory of the 'people'
over the 'usurpers'," confessed Engels; "we looked to a long
struggle, after the removal of the 'usurpers,' between the an-
tagonistic elements concealed within this 'people' itself." The
growth of Germany, politically and economically, was to Marx's
liking. On July 20, 1870, when the Franco-Prussian War was
imminent, he wrote to Engels that he hoped the French would
be soundly thrashed, for then the center of the *Internationale*
would be in Germany.

The nearest Marx came to a realization of his purely communistic aims in his life-time, however, was in the Paris Commune of 1871. When Thiers suppressed the Commune, which was
as much weakened by its anarchistic allies as by the intrigues of
Bismarck and the desertion of the liberals, Marx drew from this
failure and the triumph of Bismarck his final convictions as to
successful tactics in revolution and the final character of Communism. In *The Communist Manifesto,* in 1848, Marx had set
forth that "the first step in the revolution by the working class is
to raise the proletariat to the ruling class, *to establish democracy."* In his *Critique of the Gotha Programme* (1875) he mocks
at "the old familiar democratic litany: universal suffrage, direct

legislation, plebiscite, and a citizen army, etc.," which the German Labor Party had adopted as its political demands. In a letter to August Bebel, one of the leaders of the party at this time, Engels wrote, "The conception of socialist society as the realm of equality is a superficial French conception resting on the old slogan of 'Liberty, Equality, and Fraternity'. . . ." To which he added that democracy, such as exists in Switzerland, is not to be aimed at, but rather *"Administration by the people . . .* [in which] all the functionaries will be responsible for all their official acts to every citizen before the ordinary courts and according to common law."

This is the Communist Society, conceived by Marx as the final political evolution. In *The Communist Manifesto* he had held that, after the proletariat has raised itself to the ruling class, the State will dissolve of itself (*sich auflöst*) and disappear. In his *Critique of the Gotha Programme,* Marx is much more specific about the steps in this momentous change: "Between capitalist and Communist society lies the period of revolutionary transformation of the former into the latter. To this also corresponds a political transitional period, in which the State can be no other than *the revolutionary dictatorship of the proletariat."* Engels makes clear the nature of this dictatorship in the letter to Bebel already referred to: "As long as the proletariat still *needs* the State, it needs it, not in the interests of freedom, but for the purpose of crushing its antagonists. . . ." Once absolutism is established, and all opponents are exterminated, no further political steps are necessary: Communist Society is itself confirmed.

Freedom, for both Marx and Engels, does not mean political freedom; indeed, politics goes out of existence in the Communist Society, since no opposition is conceivable. Freedom in such a society means only freedom from this opposition. There is an amazing similarity, when the verbiage of Fichte, Hegel, and Marx is analyzed, in their essentially German conception of the word "freedom." *Practically, it amounts to a spiritual inward delight in an outward powerful order which is completely repressive.* Communism is absolutism made palatable by the pleasant fiction that the people "own" the administration.

While Marx was evolving his program, between 1847 and 1875, great changes were occurring in Germany. With the establishment of the Federation of North Germany a new discipline was evoked, which made its first appearance in the schools, where the troubles of 1848 had been fomented. Ten years later an American visitor, Henry Adams, was "struck with horror" at the high school and university education in Germany:

> The arbitrary training given to the memory was stupefying; the strain that memory endured was a form of torture; and the feats that the boys performed without complaint were pitiable. No other faculty than the memory seemed to be recognized. Least of all was any use made of reason, either analytic, synthetic, or dogmatic. The German government did not encourage reasoning. All State education is a sort of dynamo for polarizing the popular mind; for turning and holding its lines of force in the direction supposed to be most effective for State purposes. The German machine was terribly efficient. Its effect on the children was pathetic. . . . As objects of education they were proofs of nearly all the evils that a bad system could give.

No opposition to Bismarck, who came to power in Prussia in 1862, could possibly be bred in these school children. This unscrupulous and extraordinarily able statesman the next year reached an "understanding" with Lasalle, head of the Workers' League, so that obstructionist tactics could hardly originate from that source. In King William, who had succeeded his insane brother in 1858, Bismarck had a "reasonable" monarch and one who very much needed him. Entirely devoid of any feeling for humanity and a firm believer in Prussia and the State, Bismarck bent every effort to unite Germany under Prussian leadership. He achieved success by bold intrigue and foreknowledge of the weaknesses of his opponents. First, a pacific union with Austria was avoided—for that would have meant Hapsburg leadership, then Denmark was defeated in war, after which Austria was borne down in the single important battle of Königgrätz, and finally, France was overwhelmed in the War of 1870. The German Empire, the dream of all patriots, was proclaimed in the Hall of Mirrors, at Versailles, on January 18, 1871. The fact that German unity was achieved, not through middle-class liberalism, but through the bold strategy of a ruthless absolutist, further discredited Republicanism in Germany.

The effect of this success was immediately discernible in German thought. The tedious rationalization to justify force in Fichte and Hegel is dropped for the forthright avowal of the virtues of the policy of "blood and iron." Heinrich von Treitschke, whose origins can be traced in Macchiavelli, Fichte, Hegel, and in the reactionary Rouchau, championed in the intellectual world the methods of Bismarck. With such ardor did he urge that Prussia should annex his native Saxony, in 1866, that his own father called him "a political Jesuit." Enemy of the old Federation, he advocated an *Einheitsstaat*—a unified State. In the Federation "the individual German States have lost their sovereignty," while "Prussia alone has remained the true State." Since there cannot exist in the newly formed Empire a conflict between the will of the Empire and the will of Prussia, he prophesies that Prussia will triumph—a prophecy borne out by events. The State can do no wrong, and the tactics which precipitated the War of 1870 only when Prussia was fully prepared receive Herr Treitschke's approval:

> We owe it to the clear-sighted audacity of Count Bismarck that this war was begun at the right time—that the Court of the Tuileries was not allowed the welcome respite which would have permitted it to complete the web of its treacherous devices. . . . The war began as a work of clear and statesman-like calculation.

In an address on "Luther and the German Nation," at Darmstadt, in 1883, Treitschke applauded the great Protestant for overthrowing the dictum that "spiritual power is higher than temporal power" and for teaching "that the State is itself ordained by God." In yet another address on the Empire he declared, "The Emperor rules by God's will, in virtue of inherent right; he is not a delegate of the Federal Council, nor yet a responsible official." The Reichstag is made up of "carpetbaggers." Thus did Treitschke fan the vanity of the Kaiser and lull the analytical faculties of the German people. Thus was 1914 made possible.

Heinrich von Treitschke without genius could convince a State and people already convinced; it took a greater man to transmute current German convictions into a philosophy that should at least have its fascination for the world. Nietzscheanism, like Marxism, is a rationalization of middle-class failure in Germany and of the victory of non-ethical, absolute power. Nietzsche hated mediocrity, but his talk about power, harshness, and immorality is a reflection definitely of the days in which he lived. As Santayana points out, this harmless young scholar and constitutional invalid did not personally crave either wealth or empire. He loved solitude, music, and books. Yet his intellect insisted that he order in some fashion the world of Naumburg, Bonn, Leipzig, Bâle, Bayreuth, and Berlin. Consequently he evolved his definition that life is power and the practice of power. The world, however, is filled with middle-class mediocrity ("Philistinism") which has created the fictions of Democracy and Morality for its own protection. Nietzsche's favorite men, "predestined for conquering and circumventing others," are Alcibiades, Caesar, and Frederick the Great. The Germans are a "slave-souled people" whom Bismarck will save. Such a master as the Iron Chancellor opened a glorious vista of the future, and Nietzsche's ecstasy got the better of him: "The time for petty politics is past; the next century will bring the struggle for the dominion of the world—the *compulsion* to great politics." Consequently his Zarathustra counsels:

> Ye shall love peace as a means to new wars, and the short peace more than the long.
> I do not counsel you to work, but to fight. I do not counsel peace, but victory. Let your work be a fight; let your peace be victory.
> A good cause, ye say, sanctifies even war; but I say unto you that a good war sanctifies every cause.

Friedrich Nietzsche's definition of the State is the most Prussian of all definitions, the most contemporary:

> ... I used the word "State"; my meaning is self-evident, namely, a herd of blonde beasts of prey, a race of conquerors and masters, which with all its war-like organization and all its organizing power pounces with its terrible claws on a population, in numbers possibly tremendously superior, but as yet formless, as yet nomad. Such is the origin of the "State." That fantastic theory that makes it begin with a contract is, I think, disposed of.

He who can command, he who is master by "nature," he who comes on the scene forceful in deed and gesture—what has he to do with contracts? Such beings defy calculation, they come like fate without cause. . . . Their work is an instinctive creating and impressing of forms, they are the most involuntary, unconscious artists that there are:—their appearance produces instantaneously a scheme of sovereignty which is *alive*. . . . They are ignorant of the meaning of guilt, responsibility, consideration, are these born organizers; in them predominates that terrible artist-egoism, that gleams like brass, and that knows itself justified to all eternity, in its work, even as a mother in her child. . . .

Of course, in such a State, the free man is a warrior. "The man who is truly free tramples under foot the contemptible species of well-being dreamt of by shopkeepers, Christians, cows, women, Englishmen, and other democrats." ". . . The future of German culture rests with the sons of the Prussian officers."

Yet this same Friedrich Nietzsche, in another mood, could declare that "Everything connected with the State is false; it bites with stolen teeth, and its very bowels are false." For the German philosopher was guided by Dr. Paul Rée to read the English positivists, Darwin, Spencer, and John Stuart Mill, and, while rejecting the Darwinian theory that life is essentially adaptation, to affirm the evolution of a Superman who should not need the State to cover his weaknesses. "There, where the State ceases to be, there begins the man who is not superfluous. There where the State ceases to exist—behold, my brethren! Do you not see the rainbow and bridge of the Superman?"

In this faith, which he shares with Karl Marx, that the State will "wither away" when his perfect man is evolved, Nietzsche reveals the secret, predictable repugnance of the sensitive man of genius to the dominance of the State. He, like Marx, failed to see that to replace power by another form of power was to continue hateful absolutism for ever and ever. With equal fervor he urges man to forget all present idealisms and to contemplate the man-who-is-to-be: "Higher than love to your neighbor is love to the highest man that is to come in the future. . . . Propagate yourself upward!" And again, "Let your highest thought be: Man is something to be surpassed." While Nietzsche's power to put more vividly than any other person the current aspirations of Germany made him the favorite philosopher of his countrymen, his Messianic delusion and eloquence captured for him a world audience. None caught so splendid a vision of the physical future of the Race.

The German reader of Nietzsche, ignoring the vital contradictions in his work, might convict him of insincerity, for he preached action and did not act. In Germany those who scoff at the teachings of Christianity and at democratic theory (thereby demonstrating their intellectual emancipation) yet who are inhibited from action, possibly by their very skepticism, are termed the *Intelligentsia*. In *Mein Kampf* Hitler applies the epithet to all intellectuals and in particular to university men. Whether it was ever applied to Nietzsche himself is immaterial—it will serve us as a term to use for the heritors of his teachings who are not men of action, but who idolize the ruthless strong man. These cynics, everywhere engaged in ridiculing ethics and morality, prepare the way for political absolutism, as did Nietzsche.

Undeniably the young Germans who fervently thought, in 1914, that the day of the Superman had arrived were largely followers, even if mistaken followers, of Nietzsche. Certain it is that Germany went into the World War I without ever having heard the absolutist ideas of her philosophers properly refuted or even seriously challenged. In a century Fichte, Hegel, Treitschke and Nietzsche, disseminated in turn by a horde of disciples and popularizers, had prepared Germany to put implicit trust in the *Machtvollkommenheit* of the Kaiser and his War Lords. Radiant young officers, nourished upon Clausewitz and Bernhardi, teachers of the virtues of militarism, confidently led their commands across the neutral Belgium border, having assured their sweethearts that they would be in Paris in two weeks and the War would be over.

The two weeks turned into four soul-searing years which completely exhausted Germany; her munitions-workers struck, her allies fell away from her, the sailors of her Grand Fleet mutinied, revolution spread from city to city, the Kaiser abdicated and fled, the Republic was proclaimed, the Armistice signed—was not Germany ready for new ways of thought? Yes, assuredly yes. Could the mouths of her dead young men have spoken, they would have denounced the idiocy of the absolutist dogma. Yet new ideas were not allowed to succeed in Germany. Democracy was discredited at the start by the treatment which the young German Republic received at the hands of the other democracies. The Versailles Treaty was hardly written in the spirit of President Wilson's fourteen points. Stripped of her territories and burdened down by war indemnities, the Republic struggled against impossible odds, made heavier by the deliberate, though understandable, policy of France to keep her weak. Within an iron ring of enemies, created by French diplomacy, Germany seethed with discontent and shuddered at the prospect of utter anarchy. An appeal for a moratorium on her war indemnity, favored by England, was refused by Poincaré and the Ruhr was occupied by French troops to assure collection of the debt. France herself was punished by the prodigious inflation which followed in Germany, and alarmed at the prospect of revolution, not merely in Germany, but in some of the "ring" countries about her, acceded to stabilizing agreement. For five years after acceptance of the Dawes plan, Germany enjoyed a respite—even a specious prosperity—financed in part by loans from Great Britain and the United States. A world depression, however, swept away all her gains, and at the beginning of the 'thirties, with a decade of democratic experimentation and failure behind her, Germany was ready to consider other expedients for the solution of her difficulties.

Only two courses were open to her—Communism or a reversion to the old philosophy of Absolutism. Of these alternatives, the first was not merely repugnant because of its confiscation of private property and probable submission to Moscow, but also because of its "international" character. Every German understood that the Republic had been managed in the interests of the international bankers and every German was heartily sick of anything that smacked of "internationalism." What the intellectual leaders of Germany were thinking, how they lumped the international pretensions of Communism and the international practices of capitalism as alike inimical to the survival of the State, is clearly enough indicated by the writings of the Munich philosopher-historian, Oswald Spengler. Evaluated in England and America as a gloomy and pedantic prophet of decadence because of the predictions of his major work, *The Decline of the West*, Spengler could have been read to more general advantage as the champion of "Prussianism" (the State dominated by the army) and the hostile critic of "Parliamentarism" (democracy). To Spengler, the former is representative of the "master-will," while the latter is the servant and tool of the "plunderer-will." Conflict between the two is inevitable, but in the end the "political creative-force" will triumph over the "international city-economy," the sword over money. "Ever in history it is life and life only—race quality, the triumph of the will-to-power—and not the victory of truths, discoveries, or money that signifies." Spengler rejected the literature of the nineteenth and twentieth centuries because of its predominant trend towards economic equality; in his conception of the State there is no room for equalitarianism of any sort. The State "in good condition" (in the athletic sense) is one which has a contented and reverent peasantry on the land, an army officered by the aristocracy, and the whole unified under a strong leader with definite political objectives in mind. All talk about "the mass," "the nation," and "democracy" is evil; to emphasize "economics" over "politics" is evil—wherefore both Communism and democratic nationalism are alike repugnant to the author. Spengler had no conviction, moreover, that Communism in Russia would ever achieve the ideals of Marx. Under the cover of this superficial "Western" philosophy, Spengler charged, the Asiatic hordes are stirring to overrun Europe again—to bring on another Dark Ages, another night. A strong Germany is the only hope of Europe.

Study of Spengler would have prepared the Western democracies for the triumph of Hitler in Germany and the end of the Republic in 1933. Not merely the Nazi laws forbidding the expropriation of the peasants' lands and the Nazi decrees appropriating the profits of industry and banking for the use of the State are forecast in *The Decline of the West* and in *The Hour of Decision*, but also the plan to make completely mobile the German army. That tanks and airplanes had outmoded the battleship and the fortress was an opinion delivered by Spengler seven years before the second great European war.

But the Western democracies were little interested in Hitler's

purposes; they revelled instead in journalistic accounts of how he
came to power—as if one convinced of his destiny and sure that
the end justified the means would not use some of the devices that
were commonplace in the Austria of his youth. Even *Mein Kampf*
was read more for Hitler's expressions of animosity towards the
Jews (whom he identified with Communism and with international banking) than for its political and economic philosophy.
This philosophy was the typically German one that we have
familiarized ourselves with by our casual examination of Fichte,
Hegel, Bismarck, Treitschke, Nietzsche, and Spengler. The Na-
tional-Socialist Party, led by Hitler, had as its primary object
the re-creation of the German State. This it achieved by subordinating the whole economy to the erection of a powerful war
machine—for its leaders were firmly convinced that victories in
the international field were more important than reforms at
home. Yet the employment of all in the interests of the State and
the taking of Germany out of the world economy of debts and
their settlement made a far happier nation than had ever existed
under the Republic. Working for the unified and absolute State,
the people recovered their health and optimism. Then, with its
war-machine perfected, German absolutism received its vindica-
tion in a series of astounding events—the reoccupation of the
Rhineland, the Austrian Anschluss, the knuckling-under of the
British at Munich and the absorption of Czecho-Slovakia, and
finally the lightning conquests of Poland, Norway, Holland, Belgium, France, Yugoslavia, and Greece, in sum, the greatest military victory in history.

Meanwhile Italy, with its successful Fascist State, born out of
the popularity of Nietzsche in that country at the onset of the
Great War, demonstrated that the will-to-power is a competent
driving force in a world of confusion. Alfredo Rocco, representative intellect in Italian politics, utters the same ideas that have
had the greatest currency in Germany: "Democracy vests sovereignty in the people, that is to say, in the mass of human beings.
Fascism discovers sovereignty to be inherent in society when it is
juridically organized as a State . . . Fascism proclaims that the
great mass of citizens is not a suitable advocate of social interests

for the reason that the capacity to ignore individual private interests in favor of the higher demands of society is a very rare gift and the privilege of the chosen few." Mussolini has put it much more succinctly: "All in the State, nothing outside the State, nothing against the State." The victories of the Fascist armies in Ethiopia, Spain, and Albania, and the invitation to Mussolini to share in "the banquet of France" probably weaned the last Italian away from the philosophy of Democratic Nationalism.

In Russia the failure of the Kerensky government and the blundering of the liberal middle class Mensheviki not only paved the way for Bolshevik triumph, but further demonstrated bourgeois incapability and the practical wisdom of Marx. Many Western liberals endeavored to see in the Russian experiment something other than an adventure in political absolutism, and the adoption of a constitution and the friendly overtures of Litvinoff to the democracies lent support to this view. The skeptics pointed out, however, that the constitution entrenched the Communist Party as the "Vanguard of Revolution" in power, and that through the Party and the Committees Stalin ruled with a power hardly rivalled in the world. Then the announcement of non-aggression and trade pacts with Hitler's government stunned those who had defended the Russian regime, and the sequence of events which included the establishment of "protectorates" over Latvia, Estonia, and Lithuania, the movement of the army into Poland to a boundary predetermined with Hitler, the attack upon Finland, its too prosperous democratic neighbor, and the annexation of Bessarabia gave Russia a character not visibly different from that of Germany. Supplementing the notable achievement of the "five-year" plans for the economic improvement of the country, these political victories gave totalitarianism in Russia the same sanction and approval it had received elsewhere. Possibly Marx and Nietzsche had not been synthesized in Russia, but the experiment had produced nothing by 1940 that could not have been forecast from German thinking at the end of the Franco-Prussian War. To intellectuals the collision of the U.S.S.R. with Germany had no particular clarifying significance, though it may have revived sympathy for the Russian people: it merely meant a trial of strength between totalitarian leaders and machines. Indeed, to the expense of the inconclusive Great War of 1914–1918 and of the rotten interlude of specious peace which followed it must be added the incalculable cost of having set world thought back to 1870.

3

ENGLISH LIBERALISM

When the critical period (1848–1870) in European history opened, England was not merely the first power in the world but she had more nearly achieved democratic nationalism than had any of her important neighbors. This was the fruit of more than three hundred years' growth of the spirit of liberalism, which took root nowhere in Europe so successfully as on her soil.

Liberalism was, first of all, the dissolvent of Roman Catholic totalitarianism and of feudal internationalism. The Primitive Church was communistic, even to the extent of permitting those who would not share their property to suffer death, and over the centuries the Church discouraged business enterprise and perpetuated and glorified poverty to keep the masses subservient to its will. Secular and regular clergy were organized in the interests of the poor, but as time passed, they found it ever easier to serve themselves. Before the invention of printing their almost complete control of the means of expression stifled criticism, and charges of heresy, tried in the ecclesiastical courts, eliminated the critics. When the corruption of the clergy became flagrant and the industrious could no longer bear the clamor of the multitudes of mendicants, men began to realize the sophistry of the sermons against greed. The Reformation taught the value of a realistic materialism as opposed to a specious renunciation of the world and a life of asceticism. St. Paul's dictum, "If a man will not work, neither shall he eat," became a fulcrum for upsetting an economy which exalted need and for thrusting in an economy which rewarded merit. Whether capitalism dates from John Calvin's famous letter defending interest, or whether the beginnings of capitalism prompted the writing of that letter is more or less an academic issue; but to Max Weber, who originated the former

theory, we at least owe our conception of the rise of Protestantism as something broader than a nationalistic and theological
revolt. It began in England, possibly with William of Occam and
certainly with Wycliffe, who sent a shudder through the whole
totalitarian fabric by affirming that the Church has no concern
with temporal matters, that for the clergy to hold property is
sinful, and that statesmen are justified in confiscating the goods
of clergymen who do not live up to their vows and serve the
poor.

Sacking of the Church occurred, as everyone knows, under
Henry VIII, who has been described as the perfect embodiment
of Macchiavelli's conception of the Prince. Yet Englishmen were
unwilling that an opulent Church should be displaced by a wealthy
and powerful aristocracy. "Above all things," wrote Lord Bacon,
"good policy is to be used, that the treasures and monies in a state
be not gathered into a few hands, for otherwise, a state may have
a great stock, and yet starve; and money is like muck, not good
except it be spread." And again, "Let states, that aim at greatness, take heed how their nobility and gentlemen do multiply too
fast; for that maketh the common subject grow to be a peasant
and base swain, driven out of heart, and, in effect, but a gentleman's laborer."

Invasion of what were regarded as ancient rights led to the
quarrel between Crown and Parliament, but the Civil War served
as an excuse to reduce the property and power of the feudal
aristocracy. An army-middleclass dictatorship under Cromwell,
with its attendant mercantile monopolies, proved forcefully to
the very class which established it the inestimable value of a just
distribution of power and property. "The wisdom of the few,"
wrote James Harrington in *Oceana*, "may be the light of mankind, but the interest of the few is not the profit of mankind
nor of a commonwealth. . . . Equality of estates causes equality
of power, and equality of power is the liberty, not only of the
commonwealth, but of every man." A firm believer in rotation
in government and an uncompromising liberal whose agrarianism was influenced not alone by the Roman historians of the
agrarian laws but also by the struggle with the feudal proprietors,
Harrington helped his contemporaries to realize what a protec-

tion was the possession of a little property, whatever its form, against the encroachments of absolutism.

Unchanged, however, from the days when the churches were dispossessed down into the nineteenth century was the liberal conception that property belongs primarily to those who create it by their industry. "Whatsoever a man removes out of the state that Nature hath provided and left it in," argued John Locke in 1690, "he hath mixed his labor with it, and joined it to something that is his own, and thereby makes it his property." Yet like his predecessors, Locke realized the desirability of fixing limits to a man's possessions. These he made surprisingly drastic: "As much as anyone can make use of to advantage of life before it spoils, so much he may by his labor fix a property in. Whatever is beyond this is more than his share, and belongs to others." Adam Smith in *The Wealth of Nations* did but elaborate upon Locke's conception that labor is primarily the source of property and the first claim to it, in defending the right of man to dispose freely of either his labor or his property:

The property which every man has in his own labor, *as it is the original foundation of all other property,* so it is the most sacred and inviolable. The patrimony of the poor man lies in the strength and dexterity of his hands; and to hinder him from employing this strength or dexterity in what manner he thinks proper *without injury to his neighbor* is a plain violation of this most sacred property.

More than freedom of speech and press, more than freedom in religious and scientific inquiry, which, however priceless, are concomitant blessings, the essence of liberalism is the equitable distribution of property—a distribution based upon desert. Towards such a distribution liberalism persistently aspired, and if the gripe of democratic idealism was strong upon Englishmen in 1850, it was because this aspiration still led men forward, whatever were the facts of their actual existence—and these were far from ideal, as anyone knows who has read *Das Kapital,* the illustrations for which are drawn almost exclusively from official reports upon British industry. The prospects of Englishmen were better in 1850, with the Reform movement in full flood, it is safe to say, than were those of any other Europeans. It did not seem impossi-

ble to hope for a broad achievement of economic democracy in
the island and in the empire as the second half of the century
began.

Without reflection one might assume that England, kept from
rushing to the aid of France in 1870 by Bismarck's "timely"
revelation of the designs of Napoleon III upon Belgium, was affected in no important way by the forces which made the two
vital decades in European history. Yet such actually was not the
case. Patently England profited when Germany, a nation not yet
industrialized, knocked out her potential rival, France, and aided
her in extending her markets throughout the world. In the same
period she saw the elimination of a powerful competitor for the
world's sea traffic when the Yankee merchant fleet was wrecked
by our Civil War. Those fast clipper ships, which could make the
run from Sydney to Liverpool in less time than anything that
flew the Union Jack, were transferred to her registry, were sunk
or crippled by Confederate privateersmen, or were commandeered
by the Federal Navy for the blockade of Southern ports and
for the transportation of troops and supplies. Whenever allusion
is made to the fact that Englishmen hold uncollectable paper to
the extent of millions of dollars in the "war indebtedness" of our
Southern States, the proper retort is that they paid a very small
price, all things considered, for assured domination of the seas.
Gambler and spectator at two ringsides, England enjoyed in the
decades 1850–1870 unexampled prosperity—prosperity which
lulled the minds of her intellectuals and convinced a majority of
all the people that England's destiny was a sure progress through
the coming centuries.

The popular philosophy of Herbert Spencer and his disciples
gave an evolutionary and scientific justification for the British
faith in inevitable progress, though Spencer had wit enough to
censure the common satisfaction in mid-century affluence as a sign
of progress. The quality of Spencer's mind is readily determined
from his early essay, "Progress: Its Law and Cause," in the
Westminster Review for April, 1857. Spencer first rebuked those
who held that progress is simply growth, material expansion, or
material improvement. Progress, for Spencer, is *organic*. Inasmuch as he had just been reading the Germans, Wolff, Goethe,

and Von Baer, he pronounced pompously that "organic progress consists in a change from the homogeneous to the heterogeneous. ... Whether it be in the development of the Earth, in the development of Life upon its surface, in the development of Government, of Manufactures, of Commerce, of Language, Literature, Science, Art, this same *evolution* of the simple into the complex, through successive differentiations, holds throughout."

The steps in this evolution are unimportant; what is important is that Spencer sold to the English-speaking world the idea of *necessary progress*. The theory of necessary progress is that we are better than our grandsires and our grandchildren are inevitably better than we, merely because the passage of time guarantees this unsought improvement in the race. "Progress is not an accident but a necessity. What we call evil and immorality must disappear. It is certain that man must become perfect." Every institution which England possessed, or with which she was experimenting, could be justified by this philosophy, and all apparent evil could be blinked on the ground that it was merely transitional phenomena. It is doubtful if a nation were ever offered a more congenial philosophy.

Though Spencer was officially denounced by the clergy, it is safe to assume that most Englishmen came around to his point of view through their own lucubrations, if not from reading him or one of his disciples. The prevalence of the belief in necessary progress can only explain the uncritical acceptance of certain vital changes in England's economy which occurred at this time. If one were asked to put a finger on the most momentous event in British history in the nineteenth century, one would probably not indicate the passage of the Companies Act of 1862 as that event, yet the choice of it could be defended possibly better than that of any other. The Act of 1862 forced into the pattern of the limited liability joint-stock company all English companies issuing securities for self-promotion. It created a kind of paper enterprise better calculated to survive in the tense struggles of the financial world than any of the forms out of which it had been evolved.

As a result of this act those who in the past had been termed "adventurers" and "speculators" became "subscribers" and "holders," and what had been termed "risks" became "invest-

ments." From the days of the South Sea Bubble the thousands
who annually put their savings in paper in the hope of increase
had been derided—

> Wrecks appear each day
> And yet fresh fools are cast away.

Adam Smith had given it as his considered opinion that the joint-
stock company would never develop into anything very useful to
mankind. Now, however, that the "security" was born, men could
be urged to invest in the offerings of these limited companies on
the grounds of expediency and wisdom. The Companies Act did
even more than was expected of it—it not only guaranteed
reasonable protection to investors, but it tremendously accelerated the development of industry, particularly the heavy industries which require vast outlays for establishment and expansion.
Especially useful was the creation of a stable paper empire for
the consolidation of enterprises, as the evolution of the "Big
Five" out of the multitudinous banking houses of the early nineteenth century bears witness. Crowned by the Bank of England,
which, under the influence of George Goschen's *The Theory of
Foreign Exchanges* (1861) and Walter Bagehot's *Lombard
Street* (1873), gradually gave up competing with the other
houses and assumed the all-important function of controlling
credit, this colossal financial empire can be described in no better
phrase than the evolutionary one of which Herbert Spencer was
so fond—"an economic organism."

Yet sustaining this great organism is a philosophy completely
at variance with the liberal assumptions of most Englishmen.
The possession of property was looked upon, prior to 1862, as
a guarantee of individual independence and liberty: the purchase
of stock, however, commits the individual to the support of a
conglomerate outside himself—is a surrender of a part of his
liberty. Only a few, the masters, gain freedom in a corporate
organization, and when all companies are practically integrated
into one great financial structure, the percentage of those possessing actual economic freedom is very, very small. Further, as
free enterprise is diminished, other freedoms disappear with it.
Press and Court and Parliament all serve the organism, and in-

dividual liberty is drained away. This is what happened in England, as one meaningless government succeeded another, culminating in the eclipse of true democracy in the "coalition" governments of War and post-War years. It is vain to point to the "reforms" achieved as different Parties rotated or joined in power; these reforms were all palliatives that the organism might endure. They are certainly not a sign that liberalism is still a creative spirit in England.

To describe the evolution of finance capitalism in England as "insidious" is almost to indulge in understatement. Practically all Englishmen—even those on the dole—are pledged to its perpetuation, for the whole economic life of the country is now absorbed in the organism. Yet with the nation dependent upon its proper functioning, finance capitalism serves relatively few people. Though the share- and debenture-holders of the five great brewing companies may be as many as 30,000 and Lipton's huge business may have 74,000 "owners," only 500,000 people altogether—out of England's 48,500,000—are owners of joint-stock properties. Since the greatest possessions are concentrated in the hands of a few, the disparity between the average and the large incomes of the years 1862–1940 must have been the greatest in England's history. Such a result is alleged, however, by critics like Harold J. Laski, of the University of London, to do no violence to the ideals of the founders of liberalism. Widespread belief that liberalism has inevitably led to this result, coupled with anxiety lest the general security be affected by any drastic change, has palsied English thought and destroyed the hope of constructive criticism. The development, first, of the cartel system in Germany (the challenge of which to British finance capitalism led to the Great War of 1914–18), and then of Russian Communism and the German Corporate state made Englishmen fearful of tampering with their economic system, since they might have to encounter external aggression while the process of alteration was going on. Their leaders chose the stock-jobber's way of solving their difficulties, buying off the poor with the dole and higgling with rival powers for international security. In the "appeasement program" of Prime Minister Neville Chamberlain the foreign policy of England reached an all-time "low." To offset the Franco-Russian understanding which the Tories feared might place Communism on England's doorstep or at any rate make France too powerful upon the Continent, the Tory government sold out the Czechs and encouraged Hitlerism, probably hoping ultimately to involve Russia and Germany in conflict. Discovery of the British designs threw Russia and Germany together in non-aggression pacts which made it possible for Hitler to fight in the West. And England and France were betrayed into challenging the thoroughly modern German war-machine and the integrated economy behind it with antiquated weapons and a clumsy financial machine. Only the lightning-keen weapon of the love of independence, sharpened through centuries of use, parried the heavy, brutal thrusts of England's foes.

Quite significant as the powers of Western Europe joined battle was the lack of any British idealism. Though Tory statesmen could denounce German aggression and swear to defend London "street by street," they could offer Englishmen nothing better to fight for than the preservation of the existing order with its millions of unemployed. And as the student of ideas scans British intellectual history since the mid-century, he is struck with the total lack there of a positive liberal program for a better life. True, writers like Sir William Ashley speak of "a working compromise" between "complete socialism" and "complete individualism" to be achieved in some future time, but they are sufficiently vague as to the *when* and the *how,* leaving the reader to feel that they hold it an inevitable evolutionary gift.

Unwilling to face their desperately difficult major problem, that of subduing finance capitalism without destroying all its benefits (a problem which calls for nationalizing the banks, distributing shareholding, limiting consolidation of enterprises, increasing specialization in industry, reducing taxes, and creating more real wealth), English intellectuals sought to prove their liberalism by adopting a philosophy of beneficent determinism or by being cordially receptive to foreign ideologies and "isms." The Fabian Socialists, thought to be the sharpest critics of the existing order in England at the turn of the century, showed a tendency to believe in an *inevitably* better social order as the re-

sult of forces already acting in human affairs. Perhaps this in
part was a result of their rejection of the Marxian theory that
revolution is the only way to a new economy, but it is a result
also of too much reading of Herbert Spencer. Thus Sidney Webb
wrote in 1889, "Owing mainly to the efforts of Comte, Darwin,
and Herbert Spencer, we can no longer think of the ideal society
as an unchanging State. The necessity of the constant growth and
development of the social organism has become axiomatic. No
philosopher now looks for anything *but the gradual evolution of
the new order from the old*. . . . The new itself becomes old, often
before it is consciously recognized as new." H. G. Wells, whose
Love and Mr. Lewisham, Kipps, Tono-Bungay, and *The History
of Mr. Polly* reveal better than any other books the bewildered
helplessness of the lower middleclass, is likewise inclined to in-
trust the improvement of things to the happy determination of
time, particularly when he writes about his conception of the inevitable World State.

Melancholy is the imitative character of modern English literature as compared with the abundance of thoroughly original
writing at the beginning of the nineteenth century. French Naturalism found its devotees in Hardy, Moore, Butler, Gissing,
Bennett, Galsworthy, and others. Conrad's primitivism had an
original quality, but the habit of reticence, formed from long
years as a ship's master, robs him of significance in an intellectual
history. Swinburne introduced Decadence into English literature
by imitating Baudelaire and by tantalizing the bourgeoisie. The
"weariest river" of hyperæstheticism, which he started flowing,
wound through the prose of Walter Pater and fell into the motionless sea of Oscar Wilde's criticism, fiction, and poetry. A
later generation of Decadents—Symonds, Flint, Joyce, the Sit-
wells, Aldous Huxley, and others—is still more Gallic, and while
immensely clever and subtle, is still impertinent and pointless.
Havelock Ellis, Bertrand Russell, and D. H. Lawrence have
made the preoccupations of Viennese sophisticates the daily concern not merely of Soho, but also of Tooting, without really
touching the reasons why birth control is imperative in England.
Auden, Spender, Lewis, and MacNeice have loudly protested
their enthusiasm for Marx—in the curiously decadent verse of

T. S. Eliot. Most Englishmen would insist, however, that Shaw
was a vital force, even if they could not answer the question, *For
what?* Indeed, in a daily paper George Bernard Shaw was voted
England's greatest nuisance—a sign at least of general familiarity with his work. Yet Shaw has never been taken seriously by
the British public; its annoyance is that of a stout, warm person
with a gadfly. Had England taken Shaw seriously enough to
analyze him, it would have found the greatest contradictions in
him: the professing Fabian Socialist who has drawn much of his
philosophy and wit from Friedrich Nietzsche: "Our only hope,
then, is in evolution. We must replace Man by the Superman."
"Democracy substitutes election by the incompetent many for appointment by the corrupt few." "Self-sacrifice enables us to sacrifice other people without blushing." Et cetera. Shaw, a considerably "lesser Voltaire," could not reasonably be expected to
produce a single effect, save irritation—he has hit out in too
many directions. Pound Dobbin over both head and tail and he
hasn't much notion whither you would have him go. Indeed, England has had no first-rate man in half a century to give her direction. Intellectually, she is a stagnant fen, and her luster is that
of phosphorescent wood. This is the upshot of her acquiescence
to the philosophy of *necessary progress,* the result of her past
complacence with her place in the sun, and the consequence of her
choice of a static, rather than a dynamic, economy.

4

THE PURVEYORS

In the midst of the two crucial decades in European intellectual history, 1850–1870, occurred the American Civil War, an
event of such importance that Charles Beard has called it "the
Second American Revolution." One neglected consequence of
that bloody fraternal struggle, which saw the influence of the
Southern planters over the national government superseded by
that of the capitalists and industrialists of the North, was the
disintegration of our maritime commerce. Although the former
fleet owners in the United States made a determined effort to

capture again their share of the world's shipping, they neither got this nor the support of American capital in their venture. American investors, as everybody knows, put their money into railroads and manufactures—into the interior development of the country, and cheerfully yielded up to England the dominance of the seas.

This shift of interest from distant ports to prairie towns is, of course, one of the most important factors in American intellectual history. Whereas Americans heretofore had followed with lively attention European thinking, their concern now was largely with things native. What is called the Gilded Age (1865–1888) was undoubtedly the most provincial period in our history. The early colonists who called London "The Town" were in closer touch with trans-Atlantic affairs than were the contemporaries of General Grant, Daniel Drew, P. T. Barnum, and Anthony Comstock. Literature was generally mediocre, Americans preening themselves on a "local color" variety which was totally innocent of any of the blandishments which lure a man of cultivated taste. Only a few intellectuals—among whom Whistler, Howells, and Henry James were most conspicuous—displayed anything which might be termed cosmopolitanism. In *The Innocents Abroad* Mark Twain used all the authority of his raucous wit to assure Americans that they sustained no particular loss in severing their cultural ties to Europe. After all, a man could get a better shave in Keokuk and Virginia City than he could in Genoa, Milan, Como, or Venice.

Yet the self-concentrated energies of the Gilded Age ultimately produced new connections with Europe. Our capitalists and industrialists came to need an ever-increasing supply of immigrant labor, their demands swelling the stream of prospective citizens from 247,453 in 1865 to 1,285,349 in 1907. Though this immigrant tide might be assumed the chief source of the infiltration of European ideas, it does not appear to have been so in point of fact. The evidence is overwhelming that the immigrant was more indoctrinated with "Americanisms" by our astute entrepreneurs than he was saturated with the latest European ideologies. His children—second generation Americans who sometimes neither accepted our morals nor took much interest

in the ancient traditions of their elders—may have proved eager
receptacles for alien ideas, but it would not appear that they received them chiefly from their parents. Indeed, America's great
immigrant throng seems to have influenced her intellectual history considerably less than did those relatively few Byzantium
scholars who fled from the Turks in 1453 affect the culture of
Europe.

Just as the glorious renaissance of English letters under Elizabeth was brought about by wealthy and talented young men journeying down into Italy, so our intellectual revival in the twentieth
century, our renaissance, was brought about by wealthy and
talented young men journeying to Europe. Our Wyatts and How-
ards and Sidneys were the sons of men grown prosperous in the
Gilded Age, or better still, impecunious but talented boys who
were liberally financed abroad by grants from funds first accumulated in that reckless era. The released largesse of America, so
much greater than that of Elizabethan England, since it came
from a raw, rich country and not from the pillage of Church and
galleon, kept a great host of Americans in Europe. After 1892
the Customs Service could report more than 90,000 American
citizens returning each year from Europe, and in 1913, just before the First World War, the number had risen to 286,604.
The War itself, an unmixed disaster for Europe, could not be
regarded wholly as such by Americans, for it took abroad at the
national expense more than two million young men in the expeditionary forces. To at least half this number the venture was a
holiday, for they saw no serious fighting. Some even attended the
Sorbonne as part of their training, but they absorbed no more
of the contemporary thought of Europe than did their fellows
on the front. If all the young Americans who were volunteer
ambulance drivers in France or Italy between 1914 and 1919 had
been killed, it has been said with some exaggeration, we should
have had no rebirth of letters in this country. Tourist travel to
Europe, resumed after the War, increased over one hundred per
cent during the years of ebullient prosperity in the United States,
1924–1930, according to August Maffry, of the Department of
Commerce. The creation of "tourist-third" class in 1923 and the
reduction of fares resulted in "the marked broadening of the

class of overseas tourists to include, among others, students and teachers in large numbers"—a consequence which could but lead to the further absorption of European ideas. With the beginning of the depression, departures for Europe rapidly declined, the decrease between 1930 and 1934 amounting to fifty per cent. The outbreak of a new European war in 1939 and the general exodus of Americans from that continent probably marked the end of the period of infusion of Old World philosophies in the bloodstream of American thought.

The mementoes which the American tourist brought back from his travels very likely will strike his contemptuous grandchildren as curious indeed, but future generations will probably be less puzzled by these mementoes than were the tourist's elders by the strange freight of ideas consigned to these shores between the years 1888 and 1940. Most of these ideas came from France and Germany, for our young intellectuals were not especially attracted to British thought. The reasons for this are clear enough: In the years prior to 1913, in the years which determined the trends, Americans felt themselves to be more liberal than Englishmen, for American life seemingly possessed more "social mobility" than did English life. Entail and primogeniture, which existed in England down to 1925, had been abolished in America for more than a century; our school system was not maintained chiefly for the education of the ruling caste, as was theirs, but for all youths of ability, whatever their station; and finally, finance capitalism, though well advanced in America as the Pujo Report revealed, had not as yet achieved the absolute dominance it had in England. Secondly, American youths, after sampling the British intellectuals, discovered inevitably their tame and imitative character, and just as inevitably pressed on to the French and German minds from which the British were derivative. Comparative figures on what American tourists spent in European countries—a pretty good index, after all, as to where their interests lay—clearly indicate the preference for the Continental countries over England. In 1929, for example, American travellers spent in France $137,143,000 and in Germany $44,676,000, as contrasted with the $40,590,000 which they spent in the United Kingdom, where the ties of blood and language were stronger.

So alien to the American tradition were the intellectual forces of France and Germany that it would seem that young Americans should have been repelled by them. Yet did Renaissance Italy repel the golden lads who journeyed thither? Despite the warning of Schoolmaster Ascham, *"Inglese Italianato è un diabolo incarnato,"* young English tourists to decadent Italy in the sixteenth century greedily sampled Bandello, Mercuriale, Castiglione, Macchiavelli, Almanni, Serafino, and other "degenerate" Italian authors; so, too, American youths, despite the scoldings of Schoolmasters Babbitt and More, sampled the writers of contemporary decadent Europe, and affected Naturalism, Primitivism, Marxism, and the other "isms"—so long as they were new and different. For like the young gentlemen of the English Renaissance, our youths were famished for intellectual provender —the genteel writers of the Gilded Age provided them with no more nourishment than Shakespeare or Bacon could have got out of the early Tudor dullards. Yet out of the muck in which each delved came a literary flowering and an intellectual revival which is the glory of the two nations.

The American Renaissance is so close to us that we have not as yet fully appreciated it; one thing, however, is certain—we cannot avoid its consequences. Minds excited to the degree attained by the Elizabethans could not easily return to somnolence —they played over all their problems, economic and political, as well as philosophical; and when men and institutions stood in the way of the solution of these problems, men and institutions fell. Whether our history will parallel theirs, whether we shall have our revolution and Cromwellian dictatorship, remains to be seen; but one can prophesy that we shall as certainly undertake the solution of our problems as did our predecessors. The American temper is for it, the American mind is awake. Hence the value of any essay to determine the tendency of the intellectual forces unleashed.

II

THE NATURALISTS

> "Heredity, like gravity, has its laws."—
> Émile Zola, Preface, *La Fortune des Rougons*.

I

THE GENESIS OF DESPAIR

ALTHOUGH NATURALISM, the first of the European schools of thought to make itself felt in America, has been described as one result of interpretation of the doctrines of Evolution, it must not be forgotten that there was a long preparation for it in France in the early part of the nineteenth century. One cannot ignore the fact that Auguste Comte's development of a science of society and his tremendous concern for the renovation of the family must have had an influence upon Émile Zola even if the latter did not read a book of Comte's, any more than one can forget the fact that Charles-Augustin Sainte-Beuve, thinking of his almost scientific examination of the minutiae of biography, described himself in the preface to his *Port-Royal* as "a kind of naturalist of souls (*un espèce de naturaliste des esprits*)." And Taine, too, might well be considered a naturalist in literary history, before Zola became *the* naturalist in literature. Indeed, the sottishness of the Angles and Saxons and Jutes, the influence of their environment upon them, as it appears in the irritating, but highly diverting, early pages of Taine's *History of English Literature,* must have been very suggestive to the novelist. Zola later corresponded with both Taine and Sainte-Beuve in an effort to find their origins. Naturalism, then, has a background in Positivism, a more comprehensive evolutionary science than Darwinism.

48

The truth is, Zola aroused so much hostility in France in his lifetime that his thought, his Naturalism, has never been properly studied, nor has it received the consideration due it there. The sum of French criticism upon Zola can very nearly be found in the none-too-profound observations that his Rougon-Macquart cycle owes something to Balzac's "Comédie Humaine," and that the writings of the physiologist Claude Bernard influenced him —though Bernard's influence appears to lie wholly in buttressing quotation in *The Experimental Novel*. Matthew Josephson, an American, has done more to set Zola fairly before the world than have all his countrymen. Havelock Ellis in *The New Spirit* and Henry James in his *Notes on Novelists* both broke lances for Zola, but the Frenchman's greatest servant, aside from Josephson, was his English publisher, translator, and biographer, Ernest Vizetelly, who went to jail in 1889 for printing his books.

Émile Zola, the son of an engineer who was part Greek and part Italian, was born in Paris, on April 2, 1840, but passed his boyhood and youth in Aix, in Southern France, which figures in his novels as the town of Plassans. His only heritage on his father's death was a lawsuit against this town for the latter's services in constructing a canal. A final settlement of this suit, after the litigation of years, gave Zola his education at the Collège Bourbon, in Aix, where he had for a schoolfellow the future Post-Impressionist painter, Paul Cézanne. At eighteen he went up to Paris to live in hunger in the Latin Quarter, possibly setting traps, like Maupassant, on the roof for sparrows, until eventually he was glad to take a position in the firm of Hachette and Company as clerk. While hitherto he had written poetry, he now turned to fiction, shifting his allegiance from Alfred de Musset to Honoré de Balzac. His early work in this field is relatively unimportant, even for an understanding of Zola himself. *Contes à Ninon,* a book of short stories, published in 1864, attracted some attention; in 1865 *Les Confessions de Claude,* a novel depicting life in Bohemia, was roundly and justly abused in the press; while *Thérèse Raquin,* given the public in 1867, shocked with its gruesomeness. More important, however, were the articles he contributed to various newspapers and to the *Figaro,* the staff of which he joined in 1866. His fervid, though

mistaken, articles on the Impressionists who were then undergoing attack, his ironical review of Louis Napoleon's *History of
Julius Caesar,* and his defense of the Goncourts' *Germinie Lacerteux* won him recognition as a fair and fearless controversialist
who could hit with either hand. When he predicted, in 1867, that
Manet would one day be in the Louvre, he was deemed insane
by the conservative critics.

At twenty-eight, with six books behind him, Zola seems to
have done his first serious thinking about his profession. He saw
that his talent was not for carefully wrought, psychological portraits like *Madame Bovary* and *Germinie Lacerteux.* He could
never be *précieux.* Yet though long rhythms, broad panoramas,
and great masses affected him most powerfully, he would not,
like Balzac, indulge in mere portraiture or try to paint the whole
of contemporary society. Balzac, like life itself, seemed to him
to need an interpreter. Taine had taught him that, above everything else, the novelist must have a philosophy. Convinced that
this was his own great lack, Zola deliberately started reading in
the Imperial Library with a view to finding a philosophy (not
forming one!) which should fit his work. He seems, in the elaborate notes which he took up to the summer of 1869, to have
been chiefly influenced by Doctor Prosper Lucas, a minor disciple
of Darwin. Lucas' *Treatise on Natural Heredity* is hardly a scientific work, for while it asserts the existence of laws of trans-
mission and the possibility that traits might lie dormant for a
generation, it also maintains the possibility of "atavism," a complete return to an earlier ancestor, and the "crossing" of the
characteristics of the mother and father, so that the son resembles the mother and the daughter the father, and like nonsense.
Though Zola utilized later most of the scientific "facts" of this
treatise, the greatest impression that it, and other similar volumes, made upon him was that one absolutely cannot escape his
origins, but is completely the creature of heredity. Thus Naturalism, which we have defined as pessimistic determinism, was born.

In his Preface to *The Fortune of the Rougons,* printed in book
form in 1871, Zola boldly announced his intention to study the
history of a single family in a series of novels that should com-
pass the events between Napoleon's seizure of the government in

1852 and his fall in 1870, an event which he needed artistically, "and which, as if by fate, I ever found at the end of the drama, without daring to hope that it would prove so near at hand . . . the terrible, but necessary, *dénouement* for my work." Although in his notes for his great cycle of twenty novels he had affirmed, *"If I accept an historical frame, it is solely to have a milieu which reacts . . . ,"* history has a larger significance in his books. A Republican, in spite of himself and his confrères, he believed that the Second Empire pandered to men's appetites, corrupted and seduced the people, and betrayed France for ambition. Such a conviction led him to begin his cycle with "the ambuscade of the *Coup d'État"* and to conclude it with "the treachery of Sedan." Thus, while each novel in his cycle deals with the individual lives of members of the Rougon-Macquart family, through these "dramas" is seen the greater tragedy of the country. In *The Fortune of the Rougons* a bewildered peasantry swarm over the countryside, into Plassans and out again to their doom. In *His Excellency, Eugène Rougon* (1876) the stupid herd is shown contentedly grazing while one of the favorites of the Empire rises to fame at their cost. In *Nana* (1880), the study of a courtesan who is symbolic of all those who enervated the court of Louis Napoleon and also of the extreme degeneracy of the Rougon-Macquarts, this same herd, with bands playing and with frenzied shouts *"À Berlin! à Berlin! à Berlin,"* passes beneath the open window of the room in which her pustular body lies deserted, dead from small pox. And finally, in the "terrible *dénouement"* which he needed for his work, in *La Débâcle* (1892), Zola describes the marching and confused countermarching of the French armies before they were bottled up in Sedan, that terrible defeat, and then the bloody fighting in Paris between the Communists and the Republicans—really but an episode, as he sees it, in the death of the nation when, like a great beast mortally stricken, it claws frantically at the wound in its own bowels. It is useless to insist that Zola's history is nothing; the shadow which moves behind the "dramas" of the Rougon-Macquart series is the greatest actor of all, the solid shadow of a nation tottering to destruction. One is never unaware of it; it illustrates destiny better than the puppets on the proscenium.

There is no God or Fate in the matter; the French people are themselves decadent, responsible (but not in a moral sense) for their own disaster.

Yet despite all their faults, of which the chief is their waning strength, the French people are betrayed. Zola's Republicanism gets the better of his philosophy. Nowhere does this receive clearer illustration than in the initial volume, *The Fortune of the Rougons*. Miette and Silvère, lovers as well as young Republican revolutionaries, are led to death, while the scheming Pierre Rougon and his wife Félicité through the plots hatched in their yellow drawing room lay the basis for the family fortune. On them, Zola lavishes a hatred of the bourgeoisie, which, while it may have been derived from the author of *Madame Bovary,* is personal and bitter. In no other book of his does Republicanism seem so much a chimera for the destruction of youth and the profit of the selfish middle class as in this. *The Fortune of the Rougons* is not a great book—aside from Félicité (who is out of Balzac), its people are cardboard people—but it illuminates the whole series. Zola's bitterness towards Republicanism is the bitterness of disillusioned youth (he was only thirty), the bitterness of a Republican who has hoped for too much. He is never again, no, not even towards the Emperor and his consort, who are Pierre Rougon and Félicité all over, quite so apparent and personal as here. *The Fortune of the Rougons* aids us in seeing that cupidity, rather than blind force, as Zola would have us believe (but cannot believe himself), is responsible for the downfall of France.

It is remarkable in Zola's notes to discover that he did not wish to be "political, philosophical, or moral," but "purely naturalistic, purely physiological." In only one of his novels did he succeed in being "purely physiological." That is in *Le Ventre de Paris* (1873), an astonishing novel with its setting in Les Halles, the great public market of Paris. Here all men are classed as Thin or Fat, and the Fat live off the Thin, which, for the time being, Zola noisily insists is the law of life. In no other book of his is the *milieu* more important; yet the tale is not an ideal illustration of the influence of environment upon the human animal—it is too bizarre, Rabelaisian, fantastic. The observa-

tions are not those of a photographer, but those of a caricatur-
ist. In this book, however, Zola exploited for the first time successfully the reportorial method of assembling all the minutiae
of his background for a studied effect, a method which to many
minds is Naturalism itself. Yet the one thing the Naturalists
have in common is not this technique, as we shall see, but the
philosophy of determinism.

L'Assommoir, which created a sensation when run serially in
the *Bien Public* in 1876, is all things that *Le Ventre de Paris* is
not. One of the half-dozen great novels of the nineteenth century, it is the most plausible exposition of the dogma that heredity and environment make completely a man or a woman. It tells
how Gervaise Macquart, a country girl of easy disposition, is
abandoned in Paris by her lover Lantier, how she later weds a
roofer by the name of Coupeau, and how they prosper together,
even running a little laundry with success, until Coupeau has a
bad fall, during the convalescence from which he becomes lazy
and takes to drink, gradually losing all ambition and eventually
reducing his wife to his own lax habits. Lantier, the former lover,
returns, and the two men become boon companions, sharing Gervaise and living off her until the shop is gone. Lantier again
deserts Gervaise, Coupeau dies a lunatic from drink in an asylum,
and Gervaise perishes of starvation beneath the stairs of the
very apartment in which she had first known prosperity. One cannot resist the argument of the book: Gervaise's pliant nature led
her into the very circumstances which destroyed her; even her
willingness to work encourages her husband's laziness; the return of Lantier is prepared for in the softening of Coupeau; and
debauchery and death are sequels as inevitable as the going down
of the sun. *L'Assommoir* may be counted the one perfectly plausible exposition of the philosophy of Naturalism.

The book is written with great gusto, Zola employing the
slang of the shops and gutters, a sludge of words, even in his
descriptions. The result is that there is no good translation of
L'Assommoir in English, and no just appreciation of the raciness
of the style. Yet the French themselves were not prepared to
admire the book on this score. A people of no conspicuous chastity, they rarely forgive an author who is not chaste in his style,

and many a writer, like Jacques Anatole Thibault, who has had little else but style, has gained enormous success in France. Zola was the first Frenchman after Rabelais to employ the living speech and was denounced for his pains. The coarseness of his expression, from the moral point of view, led to inane and emasculated English translations, with the result that Zola in translation has been a license for slack writing by British and American Naturalists.

More offensive even than the style was the fact that Zola intended *L'Assommoir* as a picture of the French working class. A vulgar, vain, foolish, and sottish people is revealed, and with a malice which was at once resented. Zola's delight in his mockery is patent to all who read the book, and the easy life with husband and lover which he pressed upon Gervaise (who is meant to represent the lax morals of her class) roused no more indignation than her comic wedding to Coupeau earlier in the book, or her famous fight with Virginie, another laundress, before her marriage. To Frenchmen the loose woman is less offensive than the hussy. Paris and the provinces shook with indignation, and Zola was made.

Yet Vizetelly assures us that, following the siege of Paris, the workingman was as degraded as Zola represented him, while the novelist himself insists that the book is a tract:

When *L'Assommoir* appeared in a newspaper, it was attacked with unexampled brutality, denounced, accused of every crime. Is it really necessary to explain here in a few lines my intentions as a writer? I have sought to picture the fatal downfall of a family of work people in the pestilential atmosphere of our faubourgs. After drunkenness and sloth come the loosening of family ties, filth engendered by promiscuity, progressive forgetfulness of all upright sentiments, and then, as a finish, shame and death. The book is simply a lesson in morality.

How, we may fairly ask, can the book be at once a moral tract and a piece of naturalistic reporting? The answer is, it cannot. In theory, Gervaise is responsible neither for her nature nor for what happens to her; and in fact, the novelist has made this altogether reasonable. If, then, she and her husband, and all those around her, are symbolical of the French working people, how

is any tract going to save them? Right here we are at the crux
of the whole matter: the truth is, Gervaise is representative of
no one but herself; the story is convincing because she is an individual, possessed of certain characteristics which bring about her
wholly plausible doom. Zola is revealed as a moralist eager to
generalize from a particular case which for once his art has
clearly set before us. Paradoxically, he is less of a Naturalist at
heart than some of his followers, although *L'Assommoir* tri-
umphantly illustrates the workings of determinism in the life of
a single person, for the Naturalist would see the absurdity of
reproaching the pliant woman for her forgetfulness of upright
sentiments, just as he would realize the weakness of selecting
such a character to demonstrate his philosophy.

The moralist and Puritan is even more visible in *Nana*. Bunyan's Mrs. Love-the-flesh, Mrs. Filth, and Madam Wanton are
all rolled into this one daughter of Gervaise and Coupeau, whom,
as Ernest Boyd points out, Zola produced to show the prostitute
as she really is, stripped of the romantic glamour in which she
had been enveloped by Dumas *fils,* Hugo, and Augier. The novelist knew nothing about the woman whom he sought to describe,
and had to rely upon the reminiscences of his friends, who were
not above deceiving him, and upon what information he could
gather from the ladies of the high-class *demi-monde* of the Second Empire to whom he was given introductions. Edmond de
Goncourt was probably responsible for Zola's meetings with the
infamous La Païva from whose own narrative he drew some of
the most startling episodes of the book, among them notably the
suicide of young Georges and the imprisonment of his brother
and rival, Philippe, who stole twelve thousand francs from the
chest of his regiment to buy baubles for Nana. Yet one courtesan
did not suffice Zola: through the saintly Ludovic Halévy, author
of *L'Abbé Constantin* and connoisseur in the field of Zola's interest, he gained information about the tastes and habits of such
creatures as Cora Pearl, Zulma Bouffar, Hortense Schneider, La
Castiglione, and La Bellanger. Nana represents them all, and in
consequence, is an allegorical, rather than a human, figure. While
the novelist accomplished much by showing the depraved woman
as an utterly selfish and calculating animal, he is not convincing

on the score of Nana's charms. This is what Anatole France
meant when he remarked that "Zola is never voluptuous enough
when he paints human degradation." Here the method of the
compiler was fatal. The appeal of this courtesan to men of taste
and good breeding (even gentlemen of the Second Empire) is a
stated fact rather than a seductive force in the book. Zola is too
much repelled by an object which he should somehow make attractive to be convincing, and the novel is another polemic directed against the immorality of the last days of Louis Napoleon.
Yet the book has elements of greatness: the scene at the race
track is a memorable one, the police raid upon the low hotel
where Nana took refuge is real enough, Count Muffat is palpably
well drawn, and Satin, whose amorous fondness for her own sex
distinguishes her, is perhaps one of the novelist's most original
figures. Nevertheless *Nana* is the novel one should cite as most
fulfilling Zola's requirements in fiction: as little imagination as
possible and no plot whatsoever. Driven by his strong moral
nature to punish Nana, yet unwilling to make her punishment the
result of her actions and the culminating episode in a plot, Zola
has her stricken by small pox, an altogether loathsome thing, at
the end of the tale. Robert Henryson, the Scotchman, punished
Criseyde for infidelity in a like manner and improved not at all
on Chaucer, but rather revealed the incensed moralist. A similar
revelation lies at the end of *Nana*.

The effect of heredity or of environment may be studied in the
case history of a single individual, as in *Nana,* or in the story
of a whole society, as in *Germinal* (1885), Zola's next important
novel. In the bulk of his books Zola is interested in biological
determinism; in *Germinal* he is for once fairly absorbed by economic determinism. The book is a study of the revolt of the coal
miners of Montsou, ground down by the operatives, brutalized
by long hours, small pay, unsanitary and dangerous working and
living conditions. They are led by Étienne Lantier, child of Gervaise and her lover, who is slowly won over to Communist doctrine
which has filtered in from the North. Of course, the workers
are defeated, but there are some magnificent scenes in the book
where, when they are completely out of hand, they smash and
burn and destroy as only an outraged mob can. The terrible abuse

they visited upon the body of the dead bread-dealer, Maigrat, a filthy animal who had cheated and robbed them all and seduced their daughters, is not soon forgotten. *Germinal* ends, however, in the sheerest melodrama. When the mines are flooded in an effort to destroy them, Étienne is caught below ground with Catherine, his loved one, and with Chaval, his rival; the three wall themselves up against the water, Étienne destroys his rival, but cannot keep Catherine alive till help comes. Troops restore order, the miners return to the mines, and Étienne leaves the coal fields on foot as he had come. Although the workers have turned from him as a leader, he is aware that this first revolt of the miners is but the beginning of a strife which will continue until something more like justice is realized. It is spring and the fields around are germinating; beneath the ground sprout also the seeds of other revolts.

Étienne saw, too, that failure had come out of cross purposes, out of inadequate preparation, and out of jealous leadership:

... Thus, this famous International which would have revived the world, had failed for lack of power, after having seen its formidable army divide and crumble with interior quarrels. Was Darwin then right, was the world only a battlefield where the strong devoured the weak, for the beauty and the continuity of the race? This question troubled him although he decided it as a man content with his own knowledge. But one idea scattered his doubts and enchanted him, that of taking up again his old explanation of the theory, the first time that he should speak. If it was necessary that one class should be devoured, was it not the common people, long-lived and still new, who would devour the bourgeoisie, weakened by enjoyments? The new society would be of new blood. And in this expectation of an invasion of the barbarians regenerating the old decrepit nations, reappeared his absolute faith in the next revolution, the true one, that of the workers, the flames of which would set on fire the end of the century with that purple of the rising sun that he saw bleeding even to the heavens.

He still walked along, dreaming, striking with his cane of cornelian the pebbles on the road, and as he cast his eyes around him, he recognized parts of the country. Just there, at the Fourche-aux-Boeufs, he remembered that he had taken command of the band the morning of the sacking of the pits. To-day the brutish work, killing and badly paid, was recommencing. Under the ground, down there, at seven hundred mètres, he seemed to hear deadened blows, regular and continuous; these were the comrades that he had just seen go down, the black comrades, who were striking in their silent rage. Without doubt they were vanquished, they had left there their money and their dead; but Paris would not forget the fiery blows of Voreux, the blood of the empire too would flow from that unquenchable wound; and if the industrial crisis was drawing to its close, if the manufactories were opening again, one by one, the state of war was not any less declared for peace was not hereafter possible. The coal workers had counted their men, they had tried their strength, they had aided the workers of all France by their cry for justice. Thus did their defeat reassure no one, the bourgeoisie of Montsou, troubled in their victory by the ill sound of the strike of the morrow, were looking behind them to see whether their end was not inevitably there at the end of this great silence. They understood that the revolution would be born again without ceasing, perhaps tomorrow, with a general strike, the union of all workers having funds and so being able to hold on for months, eating their own bread. This time, still, it was only a shoulder blow given to a society in ruins, but they had heard in it the cracking under their own feet, and they felt rising up other shocks and still others, even to that which would destroy the old edifice, already shaken, and would engulf it as the Voreux, going down to the abyss.

Étienne's ideas for the moment seem to be Zola's: the novel is not a "scientific" study, but rather a proletarian manifesto, and its popularity in the coal fields about Mons is readily understood. Zola has affected to believe that his naturalism has something in common with Marxism, and the general decadence of the upper classes is to be offset by the inherent strength of the proletariat. Yet he has forgotten the proletariat of Paris whom he pictured in *L'Assommoir;* indeed, he has even forgotten the proletariat of the earlier pages of *Germinal* who were debauched and sodden and hopeless before Étienne inspired them. He has proved the fire there is in the Marxian doctrine, but he has not shown that the workers, either of Montsou or Paris, are of the splendid barbarian physical stuff to regenerate the world. The evidence he offers and the conclusion he draws conflict with each other.

After having discovered economic determinism in *Germinal,* Zola deliberately thrust it aside as a theme in his later books. In *La Terre* (1887) he had an unusual opportunity to employ it effectively and to his disadvantage refrained from doing so. Although this story is written around the miserable fortunes of the peasant Fouan's two sons and daughter, and has only an incidental connection with the Rougon-Macquart cycle through the presence of Jean Macquart, the novelist had a chance to draw a comparison between the sensible scientific program of the

landed agriculturalist, Hourdequin, and the ignorant ways of
the peasants who are ever dividing their land into smaller and
smaller parcels, none of which can be cultivated advantageously.
Instead, equal disaster overtakes both, and Hourdequin, anticipating the common catastrophe of small landowner and large,
can only exclaim, "Let everything go to smash and all of us
perish, and the whole soil be covered with weeds and brambles,
since our race is decayed and the land exhausted!" Had Zola
possessed strong convictions in economics, he should have made
some distinction in the lots of peasant and large landowner. Had
he been more of an artist, the exhaustion of the soil of France
(very largely hypothecated, one thinks after a visit to Les
Halles) might have been made to chime with the melancholy
note of his whole great cycle, but it does not. Had he been a
political doctrinaire and not a professional pessimist, he would
not have repudiated equally, as he does, Hyacinthe with his
" '89" and his humanitarian motto of "Liberty, Equality, and
Fraternity," and Canon, the Communist, "with his schemes for
the compulsory and scientific reorganization of society." Instead,
all is ground into the earth in *La Terre*: both types of agricultural program and all schemes of social salvation as well. *La
Terre* is proof that the author of *Germinal* was a man possessed
by a mood and not by a conviction.

La Terre is the most dismal of all Zola's dark books, perhaps
because it is the most animalistic. The reader's sympathies are
soon attached to the girl Françoise Mouche in her heroic efforts
to resist the brutal physical attacks of her sister's husband,
Butteau, which she is successful in doing, even though the sister's
aid is invoked against her, until she is married to Jean Macquart,
when, with child, she is at last overcome—only to realize, during
the attack, that she is in love with Butteau. Him she protects
after a fatal quarrel in which she is thrown upon a scythe, closing
her lips to her devoted husband as she lies for hours dying.
Françoise's extraordinary realization of her love seems intended
to convey the theme of the book—the bestial quality of all
affection—symbolized by the notorious and over-discussed fecun-
dating of a cow at the beginning of the book. Yet Françoise's
defection—and it may fairly be called that—is beyond the cre-

dulity of the reader. All the people in the novel live like swine
save she; she seems, up to the last thousand words, to be the
exception necessary for the proof of the rule and for artistic
contrast in the story; when, therefore, she is shown to be like
the others, the reader has had a surfeit of proof. His mind rebels.
Zola has ridden the theme too hard. A countryside as lascivious
as that in *La Terre* (no other examples of repression are noted)
simply has no counterpart in life, neither in Africa, New England,
nor France. Perhaps through hyperbole the book accomplished
something in leading to franker discussions of the sexual basis
of affection, though a good many other books had to be written
before this was in any degree accomplished.

While *La Terre* adds nothing to the Rougon-Macquart cycle,
La Débâcle, completed five years later, brings the story of
defeated France to the climax Zola wished for it. In this novel
Jean Macquart, outsider in *La Terre,* is spectator to one of the
greatest pageants ambition has unrolled. Yet the fact that he is
the selected witness is of no consequence so far as his degenerate
family is concerned, any more than that he was a minor actor
in *La Terre.* His low station, however, gives the novelist an
opportunity to comment on the folly of his superiors, responsible
for the disaster at Sedan and the fighting in Paris. The American
reader has little interest in the precise share of the Emperor,
Marshal MacMahon, General Ducrot, General Douay, General
de Wimpffen, and others in these fatal events, nor in the politics
of the book, which together have made it the best selling novel
of Zola's in France; indeed, they make the book difficult for him,
yet he may enjoy as much as any Frenchman the spectacle of the
whole French army as tragic hero, the subordination of individuals to the mass, the fidelity of drawing in all the war scenes—
specifically the massacre of the civilian defenders of Bazeilles,
the horrors of the inadequate factory-hospital of Delaherche in
Sedan, and the vileness of the prison-concentration camp on the
island in the Meuse. Yet he must not mistakenly assume, from
the effect of these scenes on him, that *La Débâcle,* like so many
recent war novels, is a pacifist tract. Through the educated
Maurice, Corporal Macquart's friend, Zola spikes that assumption. To his sister, who cannot see why nations do not adjust

their differences without shedding blood, Maurice replies that war is itself existence, the universal law. "Would not the end of war be the end of humanity?" While *La Débâcle* may be as effective anti-war propaganda as Barbusse's *Under Fire,* this was not the author's intention. That a degenerate race must expect pain and punishment in conflict with a "newer and more vigorous strain" is his whole theme. Had France not been debauched by the Empire, the tone of the story might have been quite different, for Zola was altogether capable of writing a romance on war.

Zola concluded the Rougon-Macquart cycle with one of his poorest novels, *Le Docteur Pascal,* in 1893, a book worthy of brief examination, however, since certain deductions may be made from it in regard to Zola. For narrative interest it has the aged Doctor Pascal's love for his niece Clotilde—a pretty piece of sentimentalism based, it is said, upon an illicit autumnal affair which the novelist himself had. To Pascal, however, is attached more than an amatory interest, for this elderly scientist has kept complete records of the whole Rougon-Macquart family and from these has formulated a science of heredity. The story develops into a contest between Pascal and Madame Félicité Rougon for the possession of these documents: he, to give them to the world; she, to destroy them for the sake of family pride. Clotilde shifts her allegiance from one to the other as the arguments of love and religion have force with her. In the end, however, the old lady triumphs and the documents are burned. Thus the novelist dodges the responsibility of summing up his "science" and his philosophy, which is plainly the task he should have set himself in the book that was to be the capstone of the series. While fatigue may be pled in his behalf—he had been occupied by the cycle for twenty-three years, it is not a valid excuse, since the novelist possessed sufficient energy to complete six more books and plan a seventh, which he doubtless would have finished, had not accidental death intervened.

The reason why *Le Docteur Pascal* is no summary of the Rougon-Macquart cycle, no statement of the laws of heredity, no final exposition of a philosophy, is that such a summary, statement, or exposition was for Zola impossible. In *Le Roman*

Expérimental he had recognized the need of the scientist for caution, especially in regard to his conclusions:

> One studies nature and man, one classifies his documents, one advances step by step in employing the experimental and analytic method, but one must beware of settling things.

Yet this pronouncement is not typical of Zola. The man who proclaimed that heredity has its laws like gravity and accepted the notion that "vice and virtue are products like vitriol and sugar" had none of the instinctive caution of a Renan who would accompany every phrase by a "perhaps." Indeed, all Zola's creative work prior to this was preparation for a grand generalization. The whole purpose in writing novels, he frequently averred, was that these investigations should lead to developing the best elements and to exterminating the worst in man. Why, then, did he not summarize the best and the worst in *Le Docteur Pascal,* save that he was no longer so sure about the "laws" as he once had been? Had his going up and down the earth, had his investigations of workingmen (*L'Assommoir*), of domestics (*Pot-Bouille*), of peasants (*La Terre*), of miners (*Germinal*), of railwaymen (*La Bête Humaine*), of shopkeepers (*Au Bonheur des Dames*), of financiers (*L'Argent*), of politicians (*Son Excellence, Eugène Rougon*), of artists (*L'Oeuvre*), of soldiers (*La Débâcle*), of priests (*La Faute de l'Abbé Mouret*), had his unrivaled experience and observation shaken his faith in absolute determinism?

The answer perhaps is suggested in those novels which were written after the cycle was done, the trilogy called "The Three Cities": *Lourdes, Rome, Paris* (1894–1898) and the series called "The Four Gospels": *Fécondité, Travail, Vérité,* and *Justice,* of which he completed only the first three (1899–1903). *Lourdes,* the most important book in the trilogy, tells how the young Abbé Pierre, a skeptic in love with the crippled Marie de Guersaint, goes with her up to Lourdes in the hope that she may be cured through the miracles wrought there by Our Lady and that his faith may perhaps be restored to him. Since he had suspected her invalidism to be the product of nerves, he does not regard her cure as a miracle and is not himself converted. Further, he loses Marie for ever because she has taken a vow that she will never marry if cured. Instead of railing at the trick fate has played upon him (as Hardy would have had him do), Pierre contents himself with the hope for a new religion which shall make larger concessions to natural life. We are at once reminded of Comte's non-metaphysical, non-theological religion of humanity, his international association functioning under the aegis of science. Unable to make the anti-ethical, non-moral deductions implicit in Naturalism, Zola turned back to Comte for support. He shares Comte's respect for Catholicism ("the chief political masterpiece of human wisdom") without avowing it. Although it is common to assert that the trilogy is anti-clerical, it is so to a far less degree than one would have anticipated it to be— particularly when one reflects that Zola had thrown science and his own writing repeatedly against religion and that the Boulangist crisis was just passed.

In "The Four Gospels" series Zola at last generalizes about those elements which are best in human life and which are the positive virtues apparently in his new "natural" religion—fecundity, work, truth, and justice. Yet as virtues these are partially debatable even in a "natural" religion. For example, epicurean idleness has as much to commend it as work, and mere fruitfulness is under most conditions (one writes as a critic) a curse. Zola failed to summarize his thinking in *Le Docteur Pascal* and botched it in the novels which followed, for the system there produced has no consequential relationship to the Rougon-Macquart cycle. Though Naturalism owes something to Comte, there is a gulf between it and Comte's philosophy which Zola could not fill with seven books. It is doubtful, however, if Zola ever perceived this gulf, for he was, after all, not a thinker, but an ideologist, like Rousseau. This, perhaps, is why he has to be reckoned with in the modern world.

One cannot quit the man without paying tribute to his courage, so conspicuously manifested in the Dreyfus case. After the establishment of the Third Republic many German-Jews came to France, driven out of the Central European countries by anti-Semitism, and attracted by the bourgeois prosperity there. On these Jews Edouard Drumont opened fire in 1886 in a book

entitled *La France Juive,* which made a point of the evil influence
of Jewish financiers on the national life. Having aroused a good
deal of race hatred with his book, Drumont continued his campaign in *La Libre Parole,* a newspaper which he founded for this
purpose. He asserted that the anti-clerical policies of the government were of Jewish origin and that Jews in the French army
were German spies. This probably suggested to a group really
guilty of espionage the possibility of fixing their crime upon
Captain Dreyfus, a General Staff officer of Alsatian-Jewish
origins. Dreyfus was given a secret military trial, convicted, and
sent to Devil's Island, the whole affair being played up by
La Libre Parole. New evidence and confession led to a demand
to reopen the case, which Zola phrased most strongly in an article
headed "J'accuse." Zola had no other motive in entering the
case than to see justice done. Indeed, his long hatred of the
bourgeoisie, to which class the Jews generally belonged, might
have silenced him had it not influenced him to take the other side
in the matter. The result of his charges against the War Office
officials was his own indictment and forced flight to England.
Dreyfus, however, through the efforts of Zola and other French
liberals was eventually vindicated. The Dreyfus case would be
for Zola what Missolonghi was for Byron except that Zola
throughout his career had shown a moral earnestness, never perceived by the public, which not only functioned in this episode
but is the motivating force in all his writing. The question we
are left with is, whether a Naturalist can be a moralist or, at
least, the kind of moralist that Zola was?

The detachment, the philosophical firmness lacking in Zola are
found in Flaubert who, however, because of his intellectual and
artistic superiority, had faults which are harder to condone than
Zola's. Because only one of his books has had any influence in
America, and because at best he is a very dubious Naturalist, he
will receive but brief consideration here. Flaubert, son of a Normandy surgeon, planned novels as a child and turned to the writing
of them after the death of his father made it possible for him to
give up the legal studies which he detested. After seven years of
unremitting labor, he permitted his masterpiece, *Madame Bovary,*
to be published serially in the *Revue de Paris* in 1857. On this

book, on *L'Éducation Sentimental,* and on the unfinished *Bouvard et Pécuchet* rests whatever claim he has to be considered as a Naturalist, for Flaubert in his other work was a Romantic of the character of a Delacroix. He recognized a conflict within himself, though as he phrased that conflict the forces are somewhat obscured. "There are two distinct men in me," he wrote, "one who is in love with bellowing, with lyricism, with great eagle flights, with all the sonorities of the phrase and with the summits of the idea; another who digs and delves into the true as deeply as he can, who loves to bring out the little fact as powerfully as the big, who would like to make you feel almost materially the things he reproduces." Had he stated instead that there was in him a gross sensualist, fond of color, music, Orientalism, over whom the artist with torture kept a semblance of control, he would have been more nearly correct. This sensualist was the author of *Salammbô,* of *Herodias,* of the *Temptation of St. Anthony,* and of *St. Julian the Hospitaler.* Just two elements have kept these books from being ranked where they belong—on a plane with the work of Pierre Louys. The first of these is style—the most meticulous prose in any language, and the second is emphasis. A fault has here preserved the artist's rank. So obsessed is Flaubert with detail in these stories that by overwhelming them with detail he has buried their grossness. One has only to compare the verbose *Herodias* with Anatole France's "The Procurator of Judea" (which, in a sense, it doubtless inspired) to understand how lacking in economy it is. Yet Flaubert's passion for archeological detail diverts attention from some of his palpable faults, for example the sadistic pleasure the author derived from the slaughter of humans in *Salammbô* and of animals in *St. Julian.* Who can deny that the death of Salammbô, when realization comes to her of the love of Matho, is the sheerest melodrama?

On the other hand, how few nineteenth century novels measure up to *Madame Bovary, L'Éducation,* or even the unfinished *Bouvard et Pécuchet* for style, minute observation, and cumulative effect! The unfamiliarity of most Americans forty years ago with the French language kept them from appreciating what is best in Flaubert with the result that only *Madame Bovary* of all his work has exerted any considerable influence here, and its in-

fluence has been chiefly thematic. The heroine, convent-reared,
is through her reading a hopeless romantic, and when she becomes
the wife of a provincial physician, without really loving him although he adores her, she is shortly bored with him and plays
him false with one lover, then another, growing all the while
more self-indulgent, until through extravagance she has involved
him in financial ruin. When she has prepared for him inextricable
difficulty and for herself exposure, when she has reached the peri-
gee of her moral declension, she takes poison as a way out. The
tragedy of Emma lies not wholly in the fact that her surroundings and acquaintance are bourgeois, but also in the further fact
that her head was filled with romantic nonsense for which tem-
peramentally she had an insatiable taste—that her end was
predetermined. All this, however, is implicit rather than explicit
in the book, for Flaubert, although he was firmly convinced of
the evil in the constitution of things, was equally sure that the
novelist should not fill the rôle of interlocutor. "In the ideal I
have of art," he wrote George Sand, ". . . the artist ought not
to appear in his work any more than God in nature." And he insists that one should make even "an effort of the soul" to get
inside his characters and not draw them from himself. In this
regard, it is important to remember that *Madame Bovary* was
based on a real incident and that the function of the novelist
was, as he described it, to enter "into skins which are antipathetic
to me." For Flaubert hated every character in *Madame Bovary*,
as he did the vast majority of his fellow men, for their mediocrity. It should be noted, however, that this was not class-hatred
(as it is generally understood in America), for Flaubert says
flatly, "I call bourgeois whoever thinks meanly." Yet with a contempt for his characters which amounted almost to obsession,
Flaubert entered into them so perfectly that they all live—Emma,
Charles, Homais, Rodolphe, and Bournisien. And so, too, do the
scenes against which he sets them: the brief glimpses of the
French countryside strike one as better, or at least more convincing, than the whole of *La Terre*. Yet out of all this Americans
have got, as we shall see, in the main, only the theme of the
oppression of a spirit in uncongenial surroundings. Flaubert's

conviction of the essential meanness in that spirit they have missed altogether.

Besides Zola and Flaubert, these several other novelists contributed to the rise of French Naturalism in an important way: Edmond and Jules de Goncourt, Alphonse Daudet, Guy de Maupassant, and Joris-Karl Huysmans. Of these writers, the Goncourts and Huysmans as Naturalists were practically unread in America before the 'twenties and certainly were not directly influential here; Daudet was popular in translation (even Theodore Roosevelt quoted from him!), but his two best known books in this country—*Le Petit Chose* in the schools and *Sappho* in the boudoirs—appear to have provoked absolutely no reflection; and Guy de Maupassant, sold in complete sets and spread broadcast in anthologies of the short story, was yet far less influential than Zola, who was read, in the main, surreptitiously.

The Goncourt brothers endure in French literature primarily because of their famous *Journal,* rich in anecdotes of the literary and artistic world of the second half of the century (1851–1892), and an astonishing piece of self-dissection and revelation, deliberately planned as a work of art. Many years before Zola defined the experimental novel, the two brothers had approached the novel from the standpoint of science. Thus, in 1865, they observed, "The novel of to-day is made with documents narrated or copied from nature, just as history is made with written documents." Unfortunately, while the Goncourts gathered facts with great industry, they never evaluated properly their facts, so that anything approximating perfect synthesis is lacking in their novels. Describing themselves as "unhealthy impressionables," they had so great a flair for the abnormal that their books are all pathological. Although *Manette Salomon* (1867), with its picture of studio life, is probably the most authentic of their works, it is *Germinie Lacerteux* (1865), which, in a roundabout way, through George Moore, has exerted some slight influence in this country. This is the story of a serving girl, seduced and preyed upon by a rogue, who nevertheless satisfies her craving for love, a craving which drives her into utter degradation, since she is a nymphomaniac, when he deserts her. The authors describe their book as a clinical study of love, and indeed it is, since Germinie was drawn from a serving girl in the employ of their aunt who was unaware of the girl's dual life (as is the mistress to whom Germinie is devoted in the book) until after her death. Done with a pity lacking in their other works, *Germinie Lacerteux* had force enough to move George Moore to do something infinitely superior.

Besides their pathological Naturalism, the Goncourts are the originators of a flamboyant style, totally out of keeping with their professed "scientific" approach, yet well adapted to their morbid subject matter, to which they gave the name "impressionism." It is this style which Maupassant cursed as "the weird, complicated, overloaded, and Chinese vocabulary imposed upon us nowadays under the name of artistic writing." Impressionism came to America in the 'nineties, yet those who introduced it were probably completely unaware of any debt to the Goncourts.

Daudet, notebook-keeper, impressionist, follower of the Goncourts, brought to French Naturalism the gift of a warm nature which won him a popular success. The best elements in him are not easily copied (the pathos and humor of *Le Petit Chose* and the two collections of short stories, *Lettres de mon Moulin* and *Contes du Lundi*) or if copied, are more easily imitated from Dickens, hence his influence in America is, as has been remarked, undetectable. The "religious Naturalism" of Huysmans, an important departure from the work of Zola, decadent in character, probably owes its little appeal in America to its Catholic subject matter and its lack of constructive imagination.

To Guy de Maupassant, however, must be conceded the largest American reading public over the years of any French Naturalist: yet it has been an uncritical audience which has confined itself to the short story and merely noted the Norman's great economy of means, his faultless plotting, his studied objectivity, in a word, his *virtuosity*, rather than his meaning or significance. He meant to most of his readers what Hemingway means to most of his today. The anthologists apologized for his "melancholy tone," little realizing apparently how complete a materialist and pessimist he was. "The mediocrity of the universe astonishes and disgusts me, the littleness of everything nauseates me, and the poverty of human beings crushes me," he declared. His conviction of the smallness of humans made him content when he had found one salient trait in his character's soul: his people are all animated vices, and the fact that we cannot remember one of them explains adequately why his influence has been less than that of Zola and Flaubert. We remember an old woman who burned alive the Prussian soldiers billeted with her out of vengeance for her son's death ("La Mère Sauvage"), we remember a fiend possessed, but that is all we do remember. We draw nothing new about life from such a story as this. Maupassant's failure where psychological penetration is needed, as in the novel *Fort comme la Mort,* is the failure of a man who was by temperament impatient with the world. There is more than melodrama in that utterance to a friend in November, 1891, when it was apparent that he would die insane: "I entered literary life like a meteor, I will leave it like a thunderbolt."

2

BRITISH PESSIMISM

It was important for the development of American Naturalism that this philosophy was but little strained through the coarse, yet choked, mesh of British intelligence before reaching this country. The Victorian Englishman had so many concessions to make to propriety that his mind more nearly resembled a valve than a sieve. Fortunately American Naturalists were in the main directly influenced by the French. Nevertheless one Englishman and one Irishman materially modified French Naturalism in individual ways which have left their mark on American writing. Thomas Hardy and George Moore were converts to the philosophy of pessimistic determinism at a time when public disapprobation was a foregone conclusion for one who espoused unconventionality in anything, let alone thinking.

For many Americans Thomas Hardy stands for Naturalism, one book of his, either *The Native* or *Tess,* being perhaps the only Naturalistic book they have ever read. Yet Thomas Hardy, though by temperament fatalistic, did not settle into the Naturalistic way of expression until comparatively late in his career. A native of Higher Bockhampton, early apprenticed to an architect, and attracted to the writing of fiction only by the uncertainty of his profession, Thomas Hardy lived outwardly the conventionally good, average, quiet British life, which, if it is artistic, must produce extravaganzas of action and event by way of compensation, for your superior Englishman is by heredity an adventurer, ill at ease in contemplative rôles. And there is much that is primitive British in Thomas Hardy despite his Norman name, much that reminds us of Taine's comments on his forebears—an interest in drink, a fascination in sudden death, and a profound reverence for *weird* or fate. Hardy's first book, *Desperate Remedies* (1871), which his publisher called "a blood-curdling story," was written under the influence of the sensational Wilkie Collins, another average Englishman who did his swashbuckling in the imagination. A heavily overplotted story, with a murder, a suicide, a criminal impersonation, and an incredible tangle of relationships, *Desperate Remedies* is sadly typical of much that Hardy wrote. Mr. Joseph Warren Beach, devoted admirer and apologist for the novelist, has this to say about his work:

The most remarkable thing about Mr. Hardy's novels, for anyone who takes them in sequence, is their extreme unevenness of quality. It is everywhere agreed to rank the author of *Tess of the D'Urbervilles* as the most serious English novelist of his time. No one doubts that he has produced works of noble beauty, has made illuminating representation of life, has ranged his facts in the light of a significant philosophy. And yet this artist, this philosopher, this scientist in human nature, is the author of works that by their crudeness positively put his lovers to the blush.

Ten novels out of fifteen which Hardy published are in various ways wretched, and the high position assigned the author is maintained not only by the merits of five books but also by lack of serious challenge or rivalry. The solitariness of Hardy has been used as an argument for his apotheosis, and indeed his persistence almost alone in an adverse time speaks for his courage, yet it cannot be denied there is a degree of luck for the man who did not believe in good fortune in the very fact of his lonely circumstance. Monadnock, rising solitary from the plain, looks more like a mountain than it would if it were set among the White Hills to the north of it.

If Thomas Hardy is placed against the French Naturalists, it will at once be seen that his work had no meaning and little artistic significance before *The Return of the Native* was published in 1878. To be sure, *A Pair of Blue Eyes* (1872) dangles the daughter of a country vicar on a line in a fashion which some are pleased to call "ironical," and *Far from the Madding Crowd* (1874) keeps three male puppets in motion about a country doll with a dexterity which is amazing, considering the shortness of the strings. The author, who is never to achieve the Flaubertian ideal of self-effacement in his writing, notes "many miserable incongruities" in these earlier tales, but when all is said and done, justly rewards competence and merit where he finds it in his characters. Thus Smith and Knight who are hardly worthy of Elfride lose her to Lord Luxellian, and Gabriel Oak by devoted service wins his Bathsheba in the end, though it must be admitted she is a somewhat soiled article. The animadversions of the novelist, his vague fumblings for meaning, do not count against the argument of events in his tales.

With *The Return of the Native* (1878), however, all is different. The situation of *Madame Bovary,* of a woman ill content with her surroundings, is here repeated, with this exception, that Eustacia Vye is tied to Egdon Heath through marriage, not to a dull fellow, but to an idealist, Clym Yeobright, who has returned from Paris to the Heath with the fixed purpose of passing his life there as a teacher to the natives. When she married him, she hoped to win him over to her views, but it is he who prevails. Eustacia, moreover, is a woman with a past—*à la* Wilkie Collins, —for before Clym's return she had experimented with love with Mr. Wildeve, the gentlemanly innkeeper, who, now coming to fortune, offers her a way of escape when she quarrels and separates from her husband. In the end, however, she cannot go through with it and jumps into the millrace to be followed by Wildeve and Clym. When their bodies are dragged out, only Clym lives, a broken spirit, to preach his resignation to the world. The subplot of Thomasin Yeobright's marriage to Diggory Venn, after she had been wronged by Wildeve, is of small consequence, for the fortunes of Eustacia and Clym are, by the novelist's ordering, all with which we are concerned. They are defeated, not so much by their cross purposes—Eustacia's desire to reach the bright world of Paris and Clym's to stay on the Heath—as by "some indistinct, colossal Prince of the World" who has framed their situation and rules their lot. The Heath for them is His prison yard, a symbol of His ever perverse Presence, filling even the devoted Clym with foreboding. Hardy, through the pathetic fallacy, has elevated the *milieu* of Flaubert into an actor, the villain of the piece. As art, this is suspect, but it is enormously effective, like tilting the camera in photographing the cinema-melodramas so that the floor rocks dizzily under the characters. The "untameable, Ishmaelitish thing" is opposed not to one, but to both of them, nay, is the "enemy of civilization" itself, and the novelist in pity sees the victims of Egdon Heath far fairer than they could ever have been in life—Clym's face only a Pheidias of the future may cut, while "Eustacia Vye was the raw material of a divinity . . . The new moon behind her head, an old helmet upon it, a diadem of accidental dewdrops round her brow, would have been adjuncts to strike the note of Artemis, Athena, or Hera respectively!" Of course, this is nonsense, but it is nonsense which forces exaggeration throughout the tale, so that men cannot even throw dice without some unusual stage effect, in this case, absurdity of absurdities, the light of glow-worms! The heightening of the narrative in all its parts leads to the greater plausibility of the tragedy of Shadwater Weir, yet set that scene beside a similar one in Hawthorne's *Blithedale Romance* and the terrific exaggeration of Hardy bursts with overwhelming force. Had Flaubert been blind to the faults of Charles and Emma, had he lifted them into gods, then piled the Pelion and Ossa of the countryside upon them, *Madame Bovary* would perfectly resemble *The Return of the Native,* but we should have exchanged a work of art for something less—a polemic on the injustice of God to man. Yet Hardy has convinced legions of the uncritical of the actual hostility of Nature, of its sentient malice, through the power of his prose, one of the most magnificent pieces of over-writing, of passionate argument, in British literature.

The writing of *The Native* so exhausted its author that he had not the strength to lift his next six books (whose stuff is not radically dissimilar to that of *The Native*) into significance, although some of the author's great passion is responsible for the convincing delineation of Henchard in *The Mayor of Casterbridge* (1886), who, breaking through a web of incredibility, stands erect among Hardy's finest characters. *The Woodlanders* (1887), curiously suggestive of Henry James, has some moving situations, but its snarled and improbable plot deprives it of effectiveness. It is with *Tess of the D'Urbervilles* (1891), the simplest of his novels, that Hardy, after the longest hiatus in his creative career, an interval of four years, recovers the full strength of the earlier book. Again passion sweeps the reader off his feet, but in this case it is suppressed passion, felt under the deadly calm of what, for the author, are calculated statements of fact. Tess Durbeyfield, or D'Urberville, a beautiful girl, is ravished by Alec D'Urberville, an unprincipled gentleman of whom she had obtained employment in the hope of helping her wretchedly impoverished family. After her child dies, she is reëmployed in a great dairy where she meets Angel Clare, a young man of fine character, who in season declares his love for her. Tess has a fixed conviction of her unworthiness, but is persuaded by her mother to keep her past a secret from Angel Clare, which she does until circumstances convince her of the dire need of revelation. She does not discover, however, until the morning of her wedding day that the letter which she had prepared, telling all, and thrust under the door of Angel Clare's room had gone under the carpet, too, so that her fatal secret is still preserved. In the evening after the wedding she thinks she has a favorable opportunity when Angel Clare reveals an indiscretion of his own, and she confesses to her husband. Yet Clare is shocked, cannot overcome his repugnance for her, and leaves her for South America. Tess goes back to her family; together they suffer great misfortune; then literally to save the others from starvation, when she feels that Angel Clare will never return, Tess becomes the mistress of Alec. But Clare does come back, all contrition, to discover her living with Alec. In her desperation she kills her seducer, flees with her husband, but is taken at Stonehenge and hanged for the murder. When he sees her body swing at the end of its tether against the sky, Hardy's full passion bursts out: "Justice was done, and the President of the Immortals (in the Aeschylean phrase) had ended his sport with Tess."

Tess of the D'Urbervilles is a very deceptive book: blow on it anywhere as you would on iron and you will discover the hot passion of Hardy beneath—what was visibly dangerous in *The Return of the Native* has here been allowed to cool to blue and gray, but you take it only at great hazard. The flaw in Hardy's reasoning is that, the universe being what he makes it out to be, the raising of Tess to the stature of a figure set in opposition to it, a milkmaid deserving the pity of all mankind, is patently absurd. Hardy demands a Christian evaluation of the single life in a system which he represents as wholly without Christian ethics. His book would be a total failure if he did not depend upon readers with values that are ridiculous in the natural world of his vision. How many phrases in the novel serve only the purpose of arousing pity for Tess! Yet there is no deliberate chicanery in this; Thomas Hardy was a man who preferred a God who marked the sparrow's fall, and the fact that his suspicions have been aroused that the President of the Immortals is indifferent to such an accident stirs his deepest resentment; he is determined to charge Him with moral responsibility, which is another matter, since the devout may argue that the circumstances leading to the fall in reality are not the same as those of Mr. Hardy's contriving. It is a little difficult to hold God responsible for Mr. Hardy's plots—or for Victorian morality which determined Angel Clare's course of action following his wife's revelations. The French Naturalists more logically eliminated all metaphysical considerations: Zola was "satisfied to be a scientist"; he scoffed at Fate as "an old tool, absurd. . . ." Flaubert, a more genuine skeptic than Hardy, never allows Fate or God to appear as a cause in his books. The Victorian handicap under which Hardy labored in his scientific approach was such that he could not wash his thought of God, or of Fate, which he at times identifies with God. *Tess* is a tract thrown in the direction of a heavenly footstool which Mr. Hardy is not absolutely sure does not exist.

Tess of the D'Urbervilles was followed, in 1892, by a fantastic book called *The Well-Beloved,* in which the sex-instinct is symbolized in the passion of a sculptor, a worshipper of Aphrodite, for various feminine objects all of whom are for the moment the Well-Beloved. Despite the slight merit of the tale, it is the prototype of many similar things in America of even less worth. It would seem that there is an almost fatal stipulation that one kind of thinker, much preoccupied with the hostility of the universe and the remoteness of God, should write some time in his career a fevered book with the eternal pursuit of a nymph for its theme. The Freudians probably have an explanation for this.

Jude the Obscure, begun in *Harper's* in December, 1894, under the title *The Simpletons,* brought the career of the novelist to a close. So great was the outcry against this book that Hardy determined to write no more fiction. In this last novel Jude Fawley, who has aspired to study divinity at the university city of Christminster, is trapped by a coarse girl into marriage—a tie which makes it impossible, even when she has deserted him, for him to pay court to his cousin Sue Bridehead, whom he later meets and loves. Meanwhile, on his application at the university, he has been told to practice his trade of stone mason and not to aspire beyond his position. Seeing him drunk, without appreciating the causes, Sue becomes engaged to Jude's former teacher and inspirer, the aged Phillotson. During her engagement the two cousins are thrown much together, and Jude for the first time tells Sue of his marriage to Arabella, only to precipitate her wedding to Phillotson. Sue, however, cannot endure the schoolteacher, and the latter generously releases her from her bonds, whereupon she goes to live with Jude. Yet she will not be his mistress, and Jude lives with her in peculiar torment until the return of Arabella from Australia arouses Sue's fear that she will lose him, and so she yields herself to him. Sue is divorced by Phillotson; Arabella has an opportunity to make a good match if Jude will legally release her and take their child, who has been born without his knowledge. Jude agrees to both these stipulations, and he and Sue are now free to wed, yet the pair cannot bring themselves to the ceremony, because each has had such a bitter experience with legal wedlock. Thus they drift along in natural union, Jude finding it increasingly difficult to support Sue and the children born to them. Some vague comprehension of the burden these children are creeps into the queer little mind of Arabella's child, who, while Jude and Sue are away, takes his own life and the lives of the others. This grim tragedy powerfully affects Sue, the hitherto flippant skeptic, who now conceives it her religious duty to return to Phillotson. The schoolteacher welcomes her back and again is formally married to her. Jude, deserted, is once more game for Arabella, whose husband is dead. Drunk again, he marries her, but the will to live in him is gone. The novel closes with Jude's death after a painful illness.

Summing up, before she becomes converted, her bitter experiences with Jude, Sue declares, "There is something external to us which says, 'You shan't!' First it said, 'You shan't learn!' Then it said, 'You shan't labor!' Now it says, 'You shan't love!'" Jude, on his part, quotes from a chorus of *Agamemnon:* "Nothing can be done. Things are as they are, and will be brought to their destined issue." It is clear that the author has a firmer conviction than his characters that they are deliberately plotted against. We again ask the question, Who is it that has arranged this plot? The daily paper is filled with incomprehensible events, yet we can recall no such Lappet weave of relationships in the most sensational journalistic story as appears in *Jude.* While disaster is inherent in a marriage based wholly upon sexual attraction or in a marriage where one member is as strongly impelled towards the sexual act as the other is repelled by it, is it likely, in the first place, that Jude would exercise an appeal for women of such different temperaments as Arabella and Sue? Is it probable that Sue, book-wise and not unacquainted with men (having lived in London with an Oxford student before the story opens), would have ever become engaged, much less legally wed, to Phillotson, who, by way of what is called "irony," was originally Jude's inspirer? Is it possible that Jude and Sue in the course of the novel would each suffer such a neat reversal of attitude— the pious, hymn-singing Jude becoming a complete skeptic, while the frivolous Sue is little short of a religious fanatic at the end of the tale, submitting her quivering flesh to the torture of Phillotson's embraces like a martyr? Is not Phillotson's first release of Sue a little breath-taking? Argue that he was glad to see her go (this is not Hardy's explanation) and his magnanimity in receiving her back is difficult to explain. In the first event, he is too enlightened for his experience; in the second, too blind and selfish for his earlier enlightenment.

There is also a little too much poetic justice in the fact that Arabella, who led Jude into marrying her by a deliberately false claim that she was pregnant, bears him a child eight months after separating from him. Would the sexually irresistible Arabella normally steer a course among all other males straight back to another marriage with Jude? Were none of the characters in the book capable of learning anything? Perhaps Jude, Sue, and Phillotson were not, but surely Arabella was. *Jude the Obscure* is challengeable on so many scores in regard to verisimilitude, that, powerful though the total effect of the prose is, the thesis of the author is flatly not demonstrated for anyone with any intelligence. On the other hand, it is very gratifying to meet in Hardy characters who are not god-like in beauty (as were the principals in *The Native*) or bucolically "pure," like Tess. *Jude the Obscure* has the further great merit of discussing the impulsions of sex with a frankness no other British author achieved for two decades, yet with a dignity which (since it has not been said before) is one of the salient characteristics of Hardy's best work. Indeed, the chief merit of Thomas Hardy is that he compelled serious reflection in the most evasive decade in British and American history—the last ten years of Victoria and at the end of the Gilded Age. A man who could do this, whatever his artistic faults, is worthy of lasting respect.

More influential upon the rise of Naturalism in America than Thomas Hardy's *Native, Tess,* or *Jude* were two books by George Moore, *Confessions of a Young Man* (1888) and *Esther Waters* (1894). "Zola was the beginning of me," Moore wrote very truthfully, but before he encountered Zola, Moore had stored up a good deal of experience which was later exploited in his books. Son of a member of Parliament with a claim to distant relationship to Sir Thomas More, he was born at Moore Hall, County Mayo, Ireland, in 1852. An extraordinarily introspective youth, according to his own account, he early fell in love with Shelley who sustained him through the monotony of his school days at Oscott. When home, his father's racing stable was the focal point of his interest, and there he picked up all the curious lore about horses and jockeys and betting which he later used so admirably. The death of his father and a small talent in painting gave him the excuse at twenty to go to Paris which was his residence for the next ten years.

George Moore gravitated in the French city into what was then the most creative group of artists in the world, Monet, Renoir, Degas, Pissarro, and Manet, the last named becoming an especial friend. In this company he quickly learned that he was no painter, and turned to decadent verse for expression, Gautier and Baudelaire furnishing him models. Two volumes of poetry of "the fleshly school," *Flowers of Passion* (1878) and *Pagan Poems* (1881), attest to the fact that Moore might have easily become a minor Swinburne. Before these books were published, however, he had read with astonishment an article by Zola on the novel and immediately had become a convert to that man's theories. He returned to London, probably with the intention of reforming the English novel as a critic, but his style was "so rotten with French idiom" that the better journals would not tolerate his essays, and he was forced into fiction.

Moore's first novels are unimportant. *A Modern Lover,* in 1883, is a story of three women who sacrifice themselves for a shallow youth; while *A Mummer's Wife* (1885) studies the effect of sensual appetite on two quite different characters, good-natured Dick Lennox and his more temperamental wife Kate. They are perhaps not beneath the aims of a man who described art as a "sublime excrement." *A Drama in Muslin* (1886) is a slight book, but the drawing is better and firmer. None of these novels attracted any attention in America nor, singularly, did they find many readers here after George Moore became better known.

In 1888 George Moore published *Confessions of a Young Man,* an account of his early youth and days in Paris, with much incidental criticism and explanation of Decadence and Naturalism. The visit of Oscar Wilde to America had awakened considerable interest in the former, and the *Confessions* were widely read by those who wanted to inform themselves on topics that his advent brought into popular discussion. Moreover, the hero of the *Confessions,* "Edward Dayne," furnished young American aesthetes with a model for a sophisticate, sufficiently different to seem original. There are some bright quips in the book, like that on Hugo's poetry—"the structure of the verse was too much in the style of public buildings to please me," but the criticism is none too sound and the explanations are altogether too facile for the *Confessions* to serve as a manual. Nevertheless countless Americans learned all they know about Impressionism, Decadence, and Naturalism from this book, and some few were stimulated by it to inquire further into the subjects there scanned and to acquire a sounder knowledge of them.

The popularity of the *Confessions* in America prepared the way for a more serious consideration, at least by creative writers, of Moore's best novel, *Esther Waters,* issued in 1894, than was accorded the book in England. We had perhaps not the class prejudices to overcome which made the story unattractive to the average British reader. For Esther is a serving girl who, to the end of her tale, never even dreams of becoming a princess: she is seduced and has a child, but not by one of the gentry, rather by one of her own class, a servitor in the house in which she was then employed. Driven from Barfields because of her condition, she endures every hardship in order to rear her child (at the end of the book she has the pleasure of seeing him, a stalwart young man, in a soldier's uniform!), endures without bitterness or complaining, clinging to her purpose as she clings to her narrow religious faith, blindly, stubbornly, yet heroically. When at last she may make an advantageous marriage to a book clerk, the lover reappears, and it is to him, in recognition of the power of animal attraction, that she is wed. William Latch, her husband, is a bookie who cannot give up betting once he has acquired a bar, and the ultimate forfeiting of his license ruins him. After William's death Esther returns to the service of her first mistress following a painful interlude as a drudge in a cheap lodging house.

The merits of *Esther Waters* are great: it may bluntly be said that the author has more nearly achieved verisimilitude in this one book than has Hardy in all his novels. And curiously, this is one of the most English books ever written: where else is there a better study of the betting fraternity, of the whole serving class, of the British "pub" than here? In the decay of British genius it took an Irishman to do it, but that has in no way affected the authenticity or accuracy of the work. The characterization of Esther herself is the prime achievement of the novel, yet the minor people are sharply limned and live beyond the story's duration. Stack and Journeyman who have different systems for the horses, Mrs. Spires who "cares" for the unwanted children of serving girls until they conveniently expire, Sarah who steals her mistress' silver for a lover who deserts her, Fred Parsons who becomes a captain in the Salvation Army after Esther chooses William Latch in his stead—all these may be seen in any East End tavern. Without challenging credulity, Moore has given Esther an amazingly rich experience in order to reveal the great variety of ways in which the serving girl is victimized by those who employ her. As wet nurse, she is expected to allow her own child to die in order that the infant of higher birth may be properly suckled; she must, when receiving a mere pittance as housemaid, resist the temptation to pick up the small coin which has been deliberately "planted" merely to test her; and her duty is to report the foolish attentions of a son to her mistress though it means the forfeiture of her job. Esther displays a fine fortitude in the most trying situations, yet all that her pluck does for her is to land her precisely where she was at the beginning of the story, back at Barfields as a servant. Moore succeeds in convincing us, however, that without her strength of character Esther would have been forced down and down into prostitution and early death. She is the exception which really does prove the rule, and the thesis that the odds are against human beings, like herself, creatures of the lower class, is as well illustrated here as in any novel. Yet determinism is a generally conceded fact at the instinct level of intelligence, and what, after all, Moore has illustrated best is the blind nobility of maternal sacrifice in Esther Waters. It is a flawless character study.

Moore followed *Esther Waters* with *Evelyn Innes* (1898)

and *Sister Teresa* (1901), ordinarily considered among his better novels. They are, however, of less consequence to us, since they are really inferior to *Esther Waters* and since they exerted but a slight influence in America. They are more definitely "written" and indicate the passing of Moore as an important Naturalist writer. Moore discovered the "last temple of my soul" in Pater's *Marius the Epicurean* in the late 'eighties, and the magic style of that book completely captivated him. Even when he penned the *Confessions* he acknowledged that Zola had no style—one could find anything in him from Chateaubriand to the reporting in the *Figaro*. The late suddenness with which the importance of style burst upon Moore reminds us of Wilde's remark to the effect that Moore had to write for seven years before he knew there was such a thing as grammar and for another seven before he realized that a paragraph had structure. Yet from 1888 onward Moore was more occupied with form than with substance. Style, however, he never achieved and frequent revisions of his books have not eliminated their stylistic defects. *Esther Waters* is rather a neatly planned book, and there are vivid bits of writing in it (one remembers Parson's blonde moustache, receding chin, and "the red sealing-wax lips"), yet there remain in the novel innumerable head-and-tailless sentences, like the following:

On week days he wore a short jacket, and every day a ring of discoloured hair, neither brown nor red, but the neutral tint that hair which does not turn grey acquires under his chin.

Moore, after all, was more definitely Decadent than Naturalistic in his tastes, and it is not surprising to find him who had loved Gautier, Baudelaire, and Mallarmé swinging to Pater. *Marius the Epicurean,* with its aesthetic Christianity and its fake classicism, is responsible for *The Brook Kerith* (1916) and *Heloïse and Abelard* (1921) which Moore chose to regard as his most finished work. These novels must have been an enormous labor for their author with his little equipment, for they are more than passably well written, but they are as meaningless as the later work of Huysmans to Moore's contemporaries or to posterity. The Irishman's best is in *Esther Waters.*

Thomas Hardy and George Moore are the chief English sources of influence upon American Naturalism. Discovery and appreciation of George Gissing and Samuel Butler came too late to have any pronounced effect in this country. Naturalism was an established trend and Decadence had full momentum before we made thumbed classics out of *The Private Papers of Henry Ryecroft* and *The Way of All Flesh* in cheap American editions (1927). Americans had nothing to learn from the adulterated Naturalism of Arnold Bennett, and in the work of Rudyard Kipling and Joseph Conrad it was the Primitivistic rather than the Naturalistic (though they are related, as we shall see) that caught American attention. Although the British influence upon creative artists was thus confined, there must be conceded to it the tremendous importance of loosening up the popular mind in America for our own Naturalists. Moore and Hardy in the 'eighties and 'nineties won the first considerable American reading public that Naturalism had, and whoever blinks this fact does the British authors a great injustice. How fortunate it is that crusaders in thought recognize no international law and respect no national boundaries.

3

AMERICAN NATURALISM

The first important American to show in his writing any influence of Naturalism was Hamlin Garland, who, however, was by no means a Naturalist. Sanguine by temperament, inoculated against pessimistic determinism by his reading of Henry George and Herbert Spencer, Garland adopted from Naturalism a technical novelty or two, and a hint for the treatment of a scene and the handling of an episode. This sturdy son of the Middle Border belongs to another school and will be treated more adequately later. In passing, however, it is important here to note the several things which he introduced that were employed more fully by other writers. Of most consequence, probably, was Garland's use of impressionism. There had been conscious and unconscious users of impressionism in our literature before Garland, of whom

Lafcadio Hearn is the most conspicuous, but Garland's talk about his writing, his insistence on its originality, called especial attention to it and won for it an imitation none other received. Garland did not call his writing "impressionistic," but coined the word "veritism" to describe it, according to his account, after reading Eugene Vernon's *Esthetics* and Max Nordau's *Conventional Lies*. There is no reason to doubt him on this score, yet it is worth noting, to illustrate Garland's superficial acquaintance with things European, that Maupassant had used the word *"véritalistes"* in a eulogy of *Manon Lescaut* to describe the writers of his own school—and to distinguish their styles from that of the impressionists! The conspicuous thing about Garland's writing is its subjectivism, the true mark of impressionism. When he writes, ". . . the wild geese, honking wildly, as they sprawled sidewise down the wind . . . ," he is giving us his personal reaction to the flight of the geese, for if there is anything that geese do not do, it is to *sprawl sidewise;* however, they may *seem* to do this, and the touch is effective, like many others in the author's work. The *verity* he touched, however, lay within himself and not in the object he sought to describe.

As one thumbs over the stories collected in the volume, *Main Travelled Roads* (1891), one is aware of many other debts, besides that of style, which Garland owes to the Naturalists. The sketches are never quite "sordid," the passions are never quite "animalistic," yet one feels, as in the case of Farmer Haskins whom the sight of his youngster restrains from the murder of a gouging usurer, that, but for the rigid government of the author, they could at any moment become so. "The Return of a Private," a short story revealing how wholly without glamor was the return of the average Civil War soldier to his western home, owes more than the recollection of a title to Hardy's *Return of the Native*. The rare touches of sour humor, "I bet I've chawed hardtack enough to shingle every house in the coolly," remind us of the maunderings of the minor characters in *The Native,* while Smith, trudging alone up the valley, brings back to us the single figure set against the Heath with which Hardy's novel very effectively opens. On the other hand, the gloom of Garland is the depression of a mood and not a settled way of looking at life. Let a shower lay the dust, a stroke of luck raise the mortgage, and God's back in His Heaven and all's right with the world.

Garland came very close, however, to writing a Naturalistic novel, close enough for Sinclair Lewis to twit him about it in his speech accepting the Nobel award. In 1895, Garland published a piece of fiction called *The Rose of Dutcher's Coolly* which is a narrative of the early career of a woman journalist, up to the time when she enters into a marital contract, much freer in its terms than the conventions of the day allowed. These latter chapters of the book are a sort of cheery, answering cry to the doubts Hardy had raised about marriage in *Jude the Obscure,* serialized a few months earlier. The chief merit of the book, however, lies in its earlier chapters, describing the motherless girlhood of Rose, her discovery of the fascinations of sex with one of the neighboring country boys, and her departure for Chicago. Interspersed with scenes of bucolic charm, which remind us of the descriptive passages in Hardy's minor novels, are short bits of authentic reporting, reporting which took courage in 1895. The book as a whole, however, is amateurish and disappointing, perhaps because it promises more than it fulfills. The condemnation of Hardy was so bitter and so general that the American author had no desire to risk a like fate.

Stephen Crane, Garland's young friend, deliberately courted notoriety and was rewarded by slander more vicious than that accorded any contemporary. His beginnings were innocuous enough: the fourteenth child of a presiding elder of the Methodist church, Stephen Crane was born in Newark, New Jersey, on November 1, 1871. Twenty-nine years later, on June 5, 1900, he died of tuberculosis at Badenweiler, in the Black Forest. Between these two dates, he managed to pack a career as an amateur athlete, another as a correspondent in two wars and a skirmish, and a third as an author, with two books of poetry and ten of fiction to his credit. In addition, he married (the woman shared the abuse visited on him) and made lasting friendships with such people as Huneker, Wells, and Conrad. Henry James probably used him as a model for his elongated but brilliant journalist in *The Wings of the Dove.* Yet he stimulated the imaginations of the vicious most successfully: they charged him and his wife, Cora Taylor, with every kind of dissipation and wickedness, with a consequence that Crane's last years were spent in England, to escape abuse.

In 1892, Crane wrote and published, on money borrowed from his brother, a novelette, *Maggie: a Girl of the Streets,* under the pseudonym of "Johnson Smith." This book has the distinction, not only of being the first piece of undisguised Naturalism produced in this country, but it is also one of the first books distinctly modern in temper to be issued here. Maggie Johnson, a daughter of Rum Alley, in whose "dream gardens there had always walked a lover" is victimized by Pete, "a very elegant bar-tender." When she returns home after three weeks with Pete, her tough brother and drunken mother revile her, precipitating her into street-walking. Maggie's career terminates with suicide in the East River.

There is no question whatsoever about Crane's inspiration for the book: it is wholly the product of reading Zola's *L'Assommoir.* Yet we ought not to have mentioned them in the same breath, for in comparison with Zola's great document *Maggie* reads like a burlesque. To be sure, Zola despised the characters of *L'Assommoir,* yet he could not help entering into Gervaise and making her live for us. Crane does not know his characters, and, emboldened by the satire of Zola, the latter's merciless ridicule, draws only caricatures for us. He is wholly devoid of any sympathy for Maggie, but this comes not from a scientific detachment, rather from ignorance. The novelette is smartly overwritten in an impressionistic manner which was to become Crane's hall-mark: "The girl, Maggie, blossomed in a mud puddle"; "His [Pete's] blue, double-breasted coat, edged with black braid, was buttoned close to a red puff tie, and his patent leather shoes looked like weapons." The slang of *L'Assommoir* has stimulated Crane to set down some Bowery coinages: one of Pete's mistresses, after a return from Buffalo, whither she had gone with another man, declares, "Well, he didn't have as many stamps as he tried to make out, so I shook him, that's all." Yet the dialogue is of the variety-show order, and if read aloud, always provokes a laugh. It is painful to estimate this little book fairly, for Crane was roundly abused for writing it, and our sympathies are wholly with him. Yet to rank *Maggie* with any of the genuine masterpieces of Naturalism is ridiculous.

After the failure of *Maggie* Stephen Crane devoted his energies to the writing of a novelette of the Civil War, which became *The Red Badge of Courage.* The author being impoverished at the time, Hamlin Garland paid for the typing of the manuscript and arranged for its serialization. So great was the success of the tale in the Philadelphia *Free Press* that book publication in New York and London followed without difficulty, in 1895. Crane suddenly found himself famous. *Maggie* was republished in 1896, was scored for its subject matter and "immorality," and failed a second time. It had faults. but not those which were assigned it in the reviews.

As for *The Red Badge,* the author, though doubtless inspired by Zola's *La Débâcle,* which he denied reading, constructed his story out of materials which lay nearer to hand. In Ambrose Bierce's short story, "One Officer, One Man," Crane got suggestions for a psychological study of a soldier in his first battle and some hints for humor and style; he appears to owe most, however, to a series of articles in *Century Magazine* entitled "The Recollections of a Private," by Warren Lee Goss. Goss' articles have a cynical attitude towards war and many vivid descriptions of "unheroic" private soldiers. Out of *La Débâcle* Crane got only the episode of the soldier who announces before the battle that he is going to die, the fight in the woods, and the characterization of his lieutenant who bears a rememblance to Zola's Lieutenant Rochas. Contrary to what has been asserted, *The Red Badge of Courage* probably owes nothing to Tolstoi's *War and Peace* or to his *Sevastopol.*

The Red Badge is an amazing *tour de force,* recording as it does the thoughts, impressions, and experiences of a youth during his first battle—a fight which lasted for three days, and which, though it is here unnamed, we know from the circumstances and from a later story, called "The Veteran," to have been the battle of Chancellorsville. The youth, as was to be expected, runs away, but later receives a wound from a musket brought down on his cranium by a more terrified comrade, so that, with this red badge of his courage, he is taken for a hero and proceeds to act like one. Bravery had not hitherto been so enthusiastically dissected. Better documented stories of war exist today, but Crane's accomplishment deserves more praise, since the pattern of his work is wholly original. Perhaps nothing is more convincing than the way in which, without the author remarking on it, the youth Henry Fleming loses all identity in the story. Those who have had army experience can testify that nothing makes a more lasting impression on the spirit than this.

The Red Badge of Courage in its thesis and on its main points is psychologically true. Yet this is not to deny that the book is badly overwritten at times. Take the death of the "tall soldier" at what Crane describes euphemistically as his "rendez-vous." First his chest heaves "with a strained motion"; this increases in violence "until it was as if an animal was within kicking and tumbling furiously to be free"; then he is shaken "by a prolonged ague" while there is "a curious and profound dignity in the *firm* lines of his awful face"; the tremor of his legs causes him "to dance a sort of hideous hornpipe" while "his arms beat wildly about his head in expression of imp-like enthusiasm"; finally, after "a slight rending sound" he falls only "to bounce a little way from the earth." This is the writing of an amateur, but a gifted amateur, a man whose presence, both Conrad and Wells aver, had more of genius in it than that of anyone else they knew.

It must be admitted, however, that only two pieces of writing from the pen of Stephen Crane possess that finish which marks the maturity of a writer, and these are both short stories, "The Open Boat" and "The Blue Hotel." What has here been said about *Maggie* fits equally well Crane's novelette, *George's Mother* (1896), but his other long fiction falls beneath this in merit. *Active Service* (1899), apparently designed as a "best seller," is incontestably cheap. The short stories which use the Civil War as material, for example, "The Grey Sleeve," are deserving of the epithet "well-made," yet they lack true distinction. There is authentic reporting in the book Crane made out of his Spanish War experiences, *Wounds in the Rain* (1900), and his discernment in child psychology, as revealed in *Whilomville*

Stories (1925), is enough to cause enthusiastic exclamation, yet none of the separate pieces in these volumes has the roundness and fulness of great art.

Crane's poetry is fascinating for its crisp statement of the author's ideas. Almost any sophomore can quote verbatim the dialogue between the self-important man and the universe or the lines ridiculing the seeker after truth who found the path strewn with weeds, so graphic are these squibs; but whether these pieces are poetry is debatable. Crane, we are told, produced his two volumes of verse, *The Black Riders* (1895) and *War Is Kind* (1899), after hearing the poems of Emily Dickinson read by William Dean Howells; but we also know that he had been introduced to the free verse of Walt Whitman by Hamlin Garland, who had imitated the Master of Camden. In cutting the long primitive rhythms of Whitman to achieve the cryptic quality of Miss Dickinson, whose best verses were rimed, Crane did an unreflecting thing which has since been widely imitated. It would seem that one of the chief excellences of Whitman's poetry lies in the fact that his long primitive lines are adapted to the expression of elemental emotion. Free verse is not free if cut into the bits which Crane and others have chopped it; the tidal energy is channeled, cribbed, and confined. Crane's verses as poetry have the fault that Poe stigmatized as "epigrammatism."

To revert to the two selected short stories, one has for these only praise. "The Open Boat," based on an ill-fated filibustering expedition to Cuba during which the steamer *Commodore* sank off the Florida coast and Crane with three others struggled more than fifty hours to return to the shore in a small boat, is as graphic a piece of reporting as one will ever read. In the selection of his details, in the chalking up of them, Crane is superb; there is none of the showmanship which marred his early work. The result is an almost Flaubertian detachment and objectivity, admirable for the tense situation. "The Blue Hotel" is the story of a Swede who, feeling that he has already been marked for death, through his fear brings about his own destruction at the hands of a gambler in a Nebraska saloon. This story is handled a good deal in the manner of Hemingway and suggests to us that Primitivism, as we shall observe again, is but one development of Naturalism. Hemingway could have done no better than to prop the dead Swede up so that his "eyes fixed upon a dreadful legend that dwelt atop of the cash-machine: 'This registers the amount of your purchase.'" One feels that Crane might have telescoped two decades of writing in the short story had he been permitted to live.

Frank Norris, who succeeded Crane as Naturalistic standard-bearer in this country, had almost as short a life, dying of complications following an appendicitis operation at thirty-two. Norris was born in Chicago, on March 5, 1870, the year in which Zola began the serial publication of *La Fortune des Rougons*. He was named Franklin for his father, a wealthy wholesale jeweler, with business in Chicago and New York. His mother, Gertrude G. Doggett, had some reputation as an actress. In 1884, Franklin Norris, Sr., moved his family to Oakland, California, and the next year the future novelist was enrolled at Belmont Seminary, a fashionable boys' school. He immediately broke an arm at football, and developing a latent ability to sketch during his convalescence, he was taken abroad to study at the famous Atélier Julien in Paris. After a year the others returned to America, and the unguided seventeen-year-old boy began to neglect his art for reading. Froissart, his first passion in French literature, was cast aside for Flaubert, Maupassant, Daudet, and Zola. Because his father saw one of the installments of a romance, entitled *Gaston le Fox,* which he was writing for his younger brother Charles, and was angry at the waste of time, Norris was ordered home to prepare for college. The discipline does not appear to have affected him greatly, for he wrote a three-canto poem in the manner of Sir Walter Scott, called *Yvernelle* (1892), and contributed an article on "Ancient Armour" to the San Francisco *Chronicle* during the course of his preparatory studies. He entered the University of California with the class of '94, dallied away four years there, but, while failing to impress his teachers, completed and sold short stories to the *Argonaut* and the *Overland Monthly*.

Norris left the University of California without a degree for Harvard, where he spent the school year 1894–95 and where he came under the intelligent guidance of Lewis E. Gates in English 22. With Gates' encouragement and direction, *Vandover and the Brute* was drafted and completed, and some work was apparently begun upon *McTeague*. Returning to San Francisco, Norris was sent by the *Chronicle* in October, 1895, to report on a trip to be made—nobody knows how—through the jungle from Cape Town to Cairo. At the outbreak of the Boer War, he enlisted in the British service at Johannesburg, was captured by the Boers and thrown into prison, where he contracted African fever. Shipped home, Norris spent months in regaining his health in San Francisco in 1896. *McTeague* was completed at the end of this recuperation period, at the "Big Dipper" mine in Placer County, in the summer of 1897. Having joined the staff of a little local magazine, *The Wave*, he ran there a weekly column called "Little Stories of the Pavement." *Moran of the Lady Letty*, serialized in *The Wave*, attracted the attention of John S. Phillips, of the firm of Doubleday, McClure & Co., and Norris was summoned East as a reader for the publishing house and *McClure's Magazine*. This led to the publication of his novels, to further writing, and to his marriage to Jeanette Black. In 1902 he returned to California intending to cruise in the Pacific in his own yacht, but was stricken by appendicitis, and died.

The development of Frank Norris as a writer may be described as a progress up from Robert Louis Stevenson and Romance. If one turns back to the short stories of '92 and '93, printed in *The Wave* and the *Overland Monthly*, one discovers that the major enthusiasm of the budding writer was for R.L.S. and his confections. "The Jongleur of Taillebois," in *The Wave* for July 16, 1892, was written by an impressionable youngster upon whom the picture of the lawless Villon of "A Lodging for the Night" and the lesson of the power of conscience contained in "Markheim" had exercised an equal effect. Amelot, having murdered Yéres, conceals his body in a pit prepared for the roots of one of the great pines which William the Conqueror has ordered transplanted to New Forest. Fifteen years later, caught in this same forest in a hurricane, Amelot is crippled by the fall of this great pine and is forced to give up his career as a professional soldier to become a minstrel. In one of the tournaments of music in Provence, Amelot is handed an instrument containing the wood of the tree, but he can control neither the music which issues from it nor his own lips, with the result that his crime becomes known. When he is about to be hanged, he bursts from his warders and would have made good his escape but for the fact that the portcullis, also made of the wood of the tree, gathers vengeful momentum at the last instant, as he speeds under it, and crushes him. Dying, he is hanged from a gibbet built of wood from the Black Pine. No comment, of course, is necessary upon such a concoction, yet in the youth's defense it should be pointed out that his faults are derived from his model where they are subtly overlaid with the rich paste of a studied style. "Lauth," in the *Overland* the next year, is a more ambitious development of the stuff of "The Jongleur."

There was enough talent displayed in Norris' early work to have assured him a great popular success had he stuck to historical romance for the next ten years, when that kind of writing found unrivaled public favor. Something in the youth rebelled at the thought—perhaps Gates helped him to see how shallow it was, for he took himself off to South Africa, Charles Norris tells us, in a deliberate effort to find himself. The trip, however, marks a shift of literary deities for him; he who had kissed the toe of R.L.S. now knelt on one knee before Rudyard Kipling. The author of *Plain Tales from the Hills* had brought Western readers a world they thought was India; might not he, Norris reasoned, exploit South Africa with equal success? Here, too, were savage tribes, bold adventurers, great riches and greater poverty—the very stuff of Kipling. The excellence of the *Chronicle* articles of '96 speaks of the thoroughness with which young Norris went about his self-imposed task of absorbing South Africa. One short story, "A Salvation Boom in Matabeleland," describing what happened to Otto, a Salvation Army sergeant from Toledo, Ohio, when he stopped playing an organ to a thousand drunken Zulus, is all that is left to show what the fever did to wreck Norris' hopes in South Africa. Kipling would not have been ashamed of the story, unless he renounced all his early work, for here are employed those lively incongruities, those whimsical exaggerations which he learned from Bret Harte, and Harte learned from Dickens. "A Salvation Boom in Matabeleland" is in tradition, and compares favorably with other pieces in its tradition.

Forgotten in a San Francisco warehouse when Norris went off to South Africa was the manuscript of a novel, also done largely under the influence of Kipling. This was *Vandover and the Brute,* a story of a young man who yields more and more to his baser nature, the "brute" in him, until, having seduced a girl who commits suicide, he is socially ostracized, and gradually deteriorates into an animal, in the end suffering from a kind of insanity known as lycanthropy, in which the victim fancies he is a wolf and crawls on all fours, imitating the beast. *Vandover* is a lurid tale, partly the product of the author's fears of the results of youthful and harmless dissipations and partly the result of reading Kipling's *The Mark of the Beast*—the story of a man likewise transformed for having stolen a sacred gem from an Indian temple. Incredible as *Vandover* is as a complete story, portions of it reveal the latent abilities of Norris as no previous work had done. The best passage in the novel depicts a shipwreck off the coast of California; the hero in an overloaded small boat sees a sailor pound to pulp the fingers of a Jew in the water who has caught the gunwale, and applauds the action though he is troubled afterwards by his recollection of it. The first example of the "survival of the fittest" theme, this passage remains one of the most memorable in Norris' work. Then, too, the relations of father and son are well studied, particularly the father's grief over Vandover's conduct. The final scenes of the novel, in which Vandover is reduced to serving as handy man to a friend who had previously defrauded him, have the the sordidness of the French Naturalistic school and are fairly effective. Most disappointing in the book, considering the fact that Norris knew better, is the representation of Vandover as an artist. That Norris was willing to sacrifice the painter and whatever ideals he himself had to the popular notion that the artist is necessarily a dissolute fellow is beyond comprehension. And what conceptions of painting he had!

For a time during the late 'nineties Norris paid lip service to Richard Harding Davis. The latter had scored a whacking success with his pictures of aggressive East Side Irish boys and young-men-about-town whose papas and mamas were in the Four Hundred. Norris wrote considerable short fiction with characters patterned on both types. "The Heroism of Jonesee," in *The Wave,* May 16, 1896, is the best managed story dealing with young San Francisco toughs; while "Thoroughbred" in the *Overland,* for February, 1895, most successfully evokes the Davis hero of the other type. The "Buldy" Jones stories of art students' pranks in Paris are of the same genre, but more original. The Davis influence extends, however, over to the drawing of the males in *Moran of the Lady Letty* (1898) and *Blix* (1899). Mr. H. L. Mencken can think of only one book to compare favorably with the latter in its sympathetic display of the "mooniness of youth"—and that is George Ade's *Artie!* Mencken has forgotten, among other things, not only *The Sorrows of Young Werther* but also Tarkington's *Seventeen,* which, though false to youthful psychology, compares favorably with *Blix* and surely with *Artie.* The chief interest in *Blix* is autobiographical. Condy Rivers is Frank Norris of *The Wave* and *Overland Monthly* period, hack writer for the Sunday Supplement to the *Chronicle,* a youth with a tremendous zest for life and a wholly uncritical attitude towards it and himself. If the book has any merit, it is its complete *naïveté,* but surely it ought not to be praised for this.

Moran of the Lady Letty, the story which attracted the attention of Phillips, deserves a more thorough analysis than *Blix,* even though it carries no more conviction of authenticity with it, for it is one of the sources of Jack London and the first vogue of the primitive in America. Ross Wilbur, a member of the social set of San Francisco, is shanghaied aboard the *Bertha Millner,* a shark-fishing vessel commanded by the unscrupulous and brutal Captain Kitchell, who undertakes to give Wilbur, in the words of Norris, "a nautical education." At sea, they encounter the disabled *Lady Letty* which, despite the presence of its owner, Moran Sternerson, a young lady with the muscles of a Titaness, Kitchell proceeds to take as a prize. A sudden tempest sinks the *Lady Letty* and Captain Kitchell with it, leaving Wilbur and Moran in charge of the *Bertha Millner* and its coolies. After fishing shark off Magdalena Bay, they enter into an arrangement with some Chinese beach-combers to share the plunder from a beached whale, in which, however, a fortune in ambergris is discovered. The beach-combers seize this by force, but lose it when Moran captures their leader, Hoang, files his teeth until he confesses where it is *cached,* and defeats them in pitched battle. At the end of this struggle Moran goes completely berserk, and Wilbur himself is forced to subdue her. From that moment Moran acknowledges him her master: " 'You've beaten, mate—I admit it; you've conquered me, and' she continued, smiling again and shaking him by the shoulder—'and mate, do you know, I love you for it.' " With Wilbur in command, and Moran assisting him, they make for Coronado Beach where, as one risen from the dead, Wilbur is hailed by his old "crowd." He now finds them and their interests disgusting to him; he hopes to re-outfit the *Bertha Millner* and with Moran run arms into Cuba. While he is ashore arranging to sell the ambergris, Moran is knifed to death by Hoang who escapes with the prize after cutting the ship adrift. At the end of the tale Wilbur stands watching Moran and the *Bertha Millner* "melt away into the gray of the horizon."

Moran of the Lady Letty is the kind of story of which mere synopsis is completely destructive, for the worst aspects of the "thriller," the cinema-melodrama, are thereby revealed. Yet the book contains one element which we may ticket as permanent in the work of Frank Norris and new in American fiction. This is the presence of the superman or, in this case, of a superwoman of the "blonde beast" type. Moran has a "fine animal strength of bone and muscle," "pale blue eyes" under "sandy, heavy eyebrows," and an "enormous mane of rye colored hair . . . braided into long strands near to the thickness of a man's arm." She eats with her knife, drinks half a tumbler of whiskey and water with each meal, and when angry, swears like a buccaneer; when Ross Wilbur (who was formerly on the Yale crew) thumps her solidly between the eyes with his fist, she is totally unaffected by the blow. She lapses easily back to the tenth century in a fight, and is, in the words of the author, "Brünhilde again, a shield-maiden, a Valkyrie, a Berserker, and the daughter of Berserkers."

This young lady comes indirectly from Nietzsche, probably through some expositor of the German, like Max Nordau. She is a fictional embodiment of some of his fantastic dreams, and her fictional offspring have spread like immigrant children through our literature. Her witless, heavy-handed progeny in the further work of Norris, in that of Jack London, Upton Sinclair, Theodore Dreiser, and others, mark off American Naturalism from British and European. One cannot regard her introduction, however, with much enthusiasm. What avails it to paint the victims large when the whole thesis of the Naturalist is the superior strength of blind force to the *wills* of men? Is not the defeat of an intellect by fate or chance more persuasive, from a deterministic standpoint, than the crushing of saurians? Does not the introduction of the superman throw the emphasis unduly upon fate or chance, as in British Naturalism, rather than upon heredity, the inferior biological seeds, as in the original Naturalism of the French writers? Has Norris' most distinct contribution to Naturalism made the thesis more plausible?

The principal figure of *McTeague* (1899) is another "blonde beast," a sleepy-witted superman, whose fatal origins, however, are rather carefully sketched in by the author. McTeague's father was a shift-boss in the Big Dipper Mine, in Placer County, where McTeague himself had been employed as a car-boy and where he developed the musculature which makes his tremendous figure so formidable. The father was given to periodic sprees, and this "alcoholism" becomes a latent tendency in his son. When drunk, Old Man McTeague was an "irresponsible animal, a beast, a brute," liable to commit great violence. Eventually the mine boss, "corroded with alcohol," collapsed and died in a few hours.

McTeague's mother ran the camp bunkhouse and dining hall; she was "an overworked drudge, fiery and energetic for all that, filled with the one idea of having her son rise in life and enter a profession." Her chance to realize this ambition came when the camp was visited by a travelling quack, a "practical" dentist, to whom, when he left, young McTeague was apprenticed. His mother's death and the small legacy which she left him made it possible for McTeague to "set up" for himself on Polk Street, in San Francisco, in the days before dental inspection pretended to be rigid. Here we meet him for the first time on a Sunday afternoon, asleep in his dental chair, his belly full of a heavy meal, washed down with beer—an indolent, gross, and stupid animal, grotesquely adorning the dental profession. A mother's blind ambition for her son has raised these many pounds of beef and bone to a position from which "a fall" is possible; no other force could have done it. Yet the mother's will cannot overcome McTeague's heritage from his sire, the dangerous great physique and the craving for alcohol which leads him to murder and his own destruction. For this passive brute when provoked is as dangerous as a wounded elephant—the jungle beast whom McTeague's screaming when infuriated calls to mind.

The action which lays bare the animal in McTeague is vigorous by ordinary standards, but restrained when compared with that of *Moran of the Lady Letty*. All goes well with McTeague until his friend, Marcus Schouler, brings his cousin, Trina Sieppe, for dental work. McTeague falls in love with his patient, but realizing that she is "Marcus' girl," he confesses his helpless passion to his friend, who, fond of heroics, impulsively decides to "pull out." With a clear path, McTeague makes blundering progress in his suit and eventually becomes engaged to Trina. Then, quite unexpectedly, Trina wins a lottery prize of five thousand dollars, and Marcus Schouler regrets his altruism. In Frenna's saloon Marcus quarrels with McTeague, but later makes up with him when McTeague and Trina are married. At a picnic three years later, however, the repressed anger of Schouler flares up in a friendly wrestling match; furious at being bested by the doctor, he bites McTeague's ear, and the latter promptly breaks Schouler's arm, with a result that they are now out-and-out foes. Trina, meanwhile, has changed; the possession of more money than she has ever had before has had the effect of making her miserly, and she scolds McTeague for the smallest unnecessary expenditure. McTeague receives a legal notice— doubtless Marcus who has been prominent in a civic improvement association has something to do with it—that, because he has never obtained a diploma from a dental college, he is forbidden to practice his profession any longer. He falls back to living upon Trina's investment, and she, more niggardly than ever, goes to work as a scrub-woman. McTeague sinks lower and lower, strong drink becoming an accelerating factor in his decline. He steals from Trina, and finally kills her, fleeing to the very mine where he had worked as car-boy. He is easily traced, however, not only because of his huge figure, but also because he persists in carrying his canary in a cage with him. Forewarned that the sheriff is almost upon him, McTeague flees, this time heading straight into Death Valley. Of the posse, only Marcus Schouler follows him and eventually overtakes him. When they come to grips, McTeague succeeds in killing his enemy, but not until the latter has shackled them together with the handcuffs which he carries, so that his body moors McTeague to certain death in leagues of blazing sand.

McTeague is the first American novel to employ *in extenso* the technique of Naturalism; so far as Norris had a master at all it was Zola, as a comparison of the picnic, vaudeville, and nuptial feasting scenes with similar episodes in *L'Assommoir* will reveal. The niggardliness of the Lorilleux family in Zola's book probably suggested the minor plot of Maria Macapa's gold plate and its share in the seduction of the Jew, old Zerkow. And the bold handling of sex—bold then for an American novel—may be traced directly to the French novelist's influence. Yet the book is distinctly Norris' own, the product of five years' labor with the theme. More than anything else he wrote, *McTeague* exemplifies his theories of fiction. Naturalism for Norris is not an outgrowth of Realism—"the kind of fiction that confines itself to the type of normal life,"—but of Romance—"the kind of fiction which takes cognizance of variations from the type of normal life." Norris grants the existence of law with Zola, but is pleased to note, not the exceptions, but rather the expression of the law in unusual cases. Hence the whole background of McTeague is sketched in: that he might, under the burden of defeat and stimulated by alcohol, commit a brutal murder seems the normal working of the law. Hence the thrifty Sieppes and the sheltered life of Trina are brought us to make it clear that she might marry the relatively prosperous McTeague, the first man to arouse the sex instinct within her, and that she might become miserly. Her conduct is in response to law. Now what constitutes the "variation" from the normal type of life in their case? Is it not the chance circumstance of Trina's winning the lottery prize? Brutes find their way into the dental profession, any patient will testify, and wives with small fortunes become miserly without much provocation, but into the lives of how few such characters suddenly falls a sizable lottery prize? Is not the effect of this "variation" worth studying, Norris asks us.

Our answer depends upon what we choose to regard as the consequences of the award. Are they important enough themselves to warrant a special study? Would McTeague and Trina have lived out a life of animal content together had there been no prize? Norris, though never a profound psychologist, has fortunately been so explicit about the emotions of Trina and McTeague that an answer is not difficult. Brute lust and sadism, which made the object less desirable to him even with the first kiss, impelled McTeague; Trina, frightened of him at the outset, can endure him only when his passion awakes an echo in her which helps her to forget him. Indeed, it is a question whether the prize does not afford a distraction that makes life with McTeague at all possible for her. It would appear that disaster was the obvious outcome of this marriage, prize or no prize. Again, McTeague was surely destined eventually to be driven out of the dental profession whether Marcus Schouler, impelled by jealous envy, informed on him or not. Did the prize really affect Marcus Schouler as the novelist argues that it did? Schouler is plausibly drawn as given to heroics and his withdrawal in behalf of his friend is altogether possible, yet he is also portrayed as capricious, vain, and selfish. That he should eventually repent of his altruism is not so much determined by the prize as by his character. And we have already seen that McTeague's fondness for drink and Trina's predeliction to thrift are a part of their early endowment. Just what, then, does the prize add to the story? It appears merely to accelerate the action, to hasten consequences otherwise prepared for. It saves the novelist the pain of minute preparation for his end, spares him the labor of Zola in *L'Assommoir* and of Flaubert in *Madame Bovary*. To pretend that it adds special interest to the study is absurd, since the obvious effect of its introduction is to obscure the functioning of the true forces in the tale. Norris, it must be remembered, was not writing a moral treatise upon the vicious effects of success in gambling. Yet this is the implication of the introduction of the lottery prize in his book. With Hardy's *Tess* we know that the author intended to demonstrate that chance or Fate is a major force in human affairs; with *McTeague* we are not certain that the author had any such intention. Yet if this were his purpose, we have shown that his demonstration is a complete failure. When an author customarily represents life as meaningless, he does so with very definite convictions. Norris would seem to lack these very convictions, to shift his ground, and to want philosophy. Not life, but his book, is meaningless. One questions whether any study of "variation" would not lead to this sort of confusion.

A different kind of criticism of *McTeague* is implicit in *A Man's Woman* (1900), Norris' next book. We have already noted the folly of employing supermen in novels which merely record their destruction. The inconsistency of this Norris apparently felt after writing *McTeague*. In a world of brute force it would have been more significant if only the brute had survived. *A Man's Woman* is dominated by a hero who recognizes that "he, the strongest, the fittest, would survive." This is Bennett, the Arctic explorer, "an enormous man" with "the look more of a prize fighter than a scientist." After incredible hardships in the Arctic, he comes back to civilization long enough to rescue the heroine when her horse runs away, by beating the animal to death with a hammer, to contract typhoid fever and to conquer that with the heroine's aid, and, having married her, to learn the tedium of normal life. Lloyd Seabright understands her man, however, and packs him off again to the Arctic, where he may match his violence with that of Nature and know definitely that he is "a man, and not a professor." *A Man's Woman* is more Nietzschean than Naturalistic, for Norris has discovered the importance of the will. Bennett's triumphs are in part a result of his willing their accomplishment, of his conviction of superiority. The novel is too extravagant to be taken seriously itself, yet it indicates that the author was at the time not quite fixed in his ultimate belief that men are wholly the pawns of their circumstances and constitutions. He is temporarily persuaded that the will is factor enough to offset the other forces, even if he has not convinced his readers of this. Bennett has only to thrust out his ugly lower jaw to conquer infinity itself.

Moran Sternerson, McTeague, and Bennett, however, are far less philosophical, than impulsive, creations. There was in Frank Norris a gusto for conflict that was typical of most Americans of the era of Theodore Roosevelt. The man loved a fair contest. "One good fight," he is quoted as saying, "will do more for a boy than a year of schooling." Yet it is Naturalistic dogma that the contestants are very badly matched; Nature can crack the bones of her victims without effort. In endowing his heroes with Homeric brawn Norris was unconsciously trying to equalize the contestants, to make a good fight of it. It is spectacle, however, rather than justice, which he has in mind. While Hardy was of a disposition to taunt the gods with cowardice and to enlarge the weaknesses of men to make the bitter inequality the more apparent, Norris could abandon without feeling this or that particular figure to seek out a new champion with better sinews and a tougher heart for another trial with the gods. Bennett was inevitable after the defeats of Moran and McTeague. Yet because each merely provides spectacle, neither in victory nor in defeat do the supermen and superwomen of Norris move us. Like our pugilistic heroes, they are over-touted. We do not believe in their muscles, their jaws, their hearts. Never very real to us, they carry little conviction about life itself. Because we can attach no more feeling to them than we can to Odin or Frigga, they being quite outside the animal kingdom, we cannot generalize from their careers. Where Norris has employed supermen and superwomen, he has undeniably destroyed the illusion of life so essential to credence in determinism.

The love of mere spectacle was responsible for the conception of Frank Norris' next work, though in its actual development he subordinated for the first time that passion to others of more consequence. In a letter to William Dean Howells, thanking him for his review of *McTeague,* Norris wrote:

> . . . I have the idea of another novel or rather series of novels buzzing in my head these days. I think there is a chance for somebody to do a great work with the West and California as a background, and which will be at the same time thoroughly American. My idea is to write three novels

around the one subject of *Wheat*. First, a story of California (the producer), second, a story of Chicago (the distributor), third, a story of Europe (the consumer) and in each to keep to the idea of this huge Niagara of wheat rolling from West to East. I think a big epic trilogy *could* be made out of such a subject, that at the same time would be modern and strictly American. The idea is so big that it frightens me at times but I have about made up my mind to have a try at it.*

The central idea for this trilogy probably came from a careful reading of Zola's *La Terre* where large and small agriculturalists are represented as threatened with extinction from the flood of cheap grain being poured in from America, but the expansion of this idea so that the grain inundates and smothers its producers and distributors, as well as the French farmers, is Norris' own. Incidentally, it is an idea peculiarly American, the first suggestion in literature that the very abundance of Nature could prove destructive. The overproduction of wheat in 1898–99, and the consequent glutting of the market, with its attendant fall in prices, show the pertinence of Norris' theme at the time when he wrote. Yet this abundance, unlike the forces dealt with by Zola, was man-made, and not inherited. Norris glossed this fact altogether. The two novels which he completed of his trilogy treat Wheat lyrically as an incomprehensible force, a force which impels the producer and distributor, and is not created, governed, or manipulated by either. This is patently absurd, but it is an idea that many dull wits humbly yield to. Crop surveys, crop-control, intelligent agriculture are beyond their ken. It is not to Norris' credit that he made a popular superstition the dominating conception of his last and most mature novels.

The Octopus (1901) is Frank Norris at his best. Aside from the passages of self-pity in the semi-autobiographical *Vandover and the Brute,* this novel is conspicuous among his writings for its show of feeling, here an elevating compassion for the victims of the blind forces he unleashes. Contrary to the general rule, his coming to New York broadened and mellowed Frank Norris. It may have been the pervasive influence of Howells, felt at that time by the best of the city's *literati,* the Dean of Letters to whom Norris confessed that *McTeague* "was not the whole

* Copyright 1928 by Doubleday, Doran & Co., Inc.

truth, and that the novel that is true to life cannot afford to ignore the finer things." Shortly after this he was to classify the novel into three types: the novel of adventure, such as *The Three Musketeers;* the novel of character, such as *Romola;* and the novel with a purpose, such as *Les Miserables*. Of this third type he wrote, "The third, and what we hold to be the best class, proves something, draws conclusions from whole congeries of forces, social tendencies, race impulses, devotes itself not to a study of men but of man." While this definition is shot through with Zolaism, it demands a broader type of novel than any book Zola produced save *Germinal*. That this study of the French miners exercised an influence upon Norris nobody would deny, but beyond Zola and beyond Howells was another writer, Leo Tolstoy, whom Norris was reading at this time. Mr. Hartwick has shown that Tolstoy's critical theories are diffused through *The Responsibilities of the Novelist,* Norris' essays on fiction craft, published in 1903. The great Russian has also quickened the social sympathies of the American author in *The Octopus*.

The story is based upon an episode in California history, the Mussel Slough Affair of 1878. It arrays the farmers of the San Joaquin Valley against their traditional foe, the P. & S.W. Railroad, the Octopus whose tentacles of steel are wrapped around every farm, from the hop fields of Dykes to the great ranches of Broderson and Magnus Derrick. Through the merciless application of rate-schedule changes the railroad can bleed the farmers while they are submissive; but when they resist, it can destroy them by calling mortgages and by dispossessing them. The farmers organize to control the state rate-fixing commission, but, although they succeed in putting Magnus Derrick's son Lyman upon the commission, it does them small good, for Lyman sells them out to the railroad. Finally, when they have been harassed beyond endurance and are threatened with eviction, they resort to arms, but the railroad, calling upon the law as it had all but a moral right to do, triumphs over them, and their best men are slain, while the helpless survivors—men, women, and children— are left destitute. It is an involved tale of bribery, corruption, violence, and bloodshed, told with visibly restrained emotion.

Yet while Norris' sympathies are plainly with the farmers, he does not hold the railroad officials responsible for their suffering. Presley, an Eastern poet in the San Joaquin in search of health and an epic, becomes a "Red" after witnessing the fate of his farmer friends and visits old Shelgrim, President of the P. & S.W., with some vague notion of reforming him, but instead is made to see that the Railroad, like the Wheat, is merely a force which men serve.

"Believe this, young man," exclaimed Shelgrim, laying a thick, powerful forefinger on the table to emphasise his words, "try to believe this—to begin with—*that Railroads build themselves.* Where there is a demand sooner or later there will be a supply. Mr. Derrick, does he grow his wheat? The Wheat grows itself. What does he count for? Does he supply the force? What do I count for? Do I build the Railroad? You are dealing with forces, young man, when you speak of Wheat and Railroads, not with men. There is the Wheat, the supply. It must be carried to feed the People. There is the demand. The Wheat is one force, the Railroad, another, and there is the law that governs them—supply and demand. Men have only little to do in the whole business. Complications may arise, conditions that bear hard on the individual—crush him, maybe—*but the Wheat will be carried to feed the people* as inevitably as it will grow. If you want to fasten the blame of the affair at Los Muertos on any one person, you will make a mistake. Blame conditions, not men."

"But—but," faltered Presley, "you are the head, you control the road."

"You are a very young man. Control the road! Can I stop it? I can go into bankruptcy if you like. But otherwise if I run my road, as a business proposition, I can do nothing. I can *not* control it. It is a force born out of certain conditions, and I—no man—can stop it or control it. Can your Mr. Derrick stop the Wheat growing? He can burn his crop, or give it away, or sell it for a cent a bushel—just as I could go into bankruptcy—but otherwise his Wheat must grow. Can any one stop the Wheat? Well, then no more can I stop the Road."

Presley regained the street stupefied, his brain in a whirl. This new idea, this new conception dumfounded him. Somehow, he could not deny it. It rang with the clear reverberation of truth. Was no one, then, to blame for the horror at the irrigation ditch? Forces, conditions, laws of supply and demand—were these then the enemies after all? Not enemies; there was no malevolence in Nature. Colossal indifference only, a vast trend toward appointed goals. Nature was, then, a gigantic engine, a vast cyclopean power, huge, terrible, a leviathan with a heart of steel, knowing no compunction, no forgiveness, no tolerance; crushing out the human atom standing in its way, with nirvanic calm, the agony of destruction sending never a jar, never the faintest tremour through all that prodigious mechanism of wheels and cogs.

Poor Presley! he was a young man, a consumptive, and a poet, after all, and not a sophist. One is to suppose that thereafter he never ate a meal without considering his mashed potato as a force and his fork as a force, both of which he merely served. Another and greater poet once wrote in scorn——

> The horseman serves the horse,
> The neatherd serves the neat,
> The merchant serves the purse,
> The eater serves his meat;
> 'Tis the day of the chattel,
> Web to weave, and corn to grind;
> Things are in the saddle,
> And ride mankind.

And added—

> There are two laws discrete,
> Not reconciled,—
> Law for man, and law for thing;
> The last builds town and fleet,
> But it runs wild
> And doth the man unking.

In Emerson's view man is king of his destiny so long as he governs and controls things, crops, railroads, capital, forces, so long as he admits obligations to other men; he becomes an atom governed by things when he yields to the type of argument advanced by Shelgrim here. Presley and Norris, typical of vast hordes of Americans, ought perhaps to be described as Animists, rather than Naturalists, since they endow things thus with superior life and force to men.

The Octopus puts the case of the farmer with such feeling that, despite the philosophy of the book, it might almost have become a tract against the capitalists who own the railroad but for one thing: Norris astutely interposes between these capitalists and the public wrath an appropriate villain to receive their due. This is S. Behrman, agent for the Pacific & South Western Railroad in the San Joaquin Valley. The reader is made to feel that it is Behrman who has raised the rates, who has planned the road's tactics in the political manoeuvres, who directs the road's

revenge. Consequently, when he accidentally trips over a coil of
rope and falls into an open hatch of a vessel being loaded with
wheat, to be buried alive by the grain in the ship's hold—one of
the most powerful episodes in American fiction—the reader experiences what is pleasantly called "katharsis," emotional relief,
as in the highest tragedy, for poetic justice done. Analysis later,
however, may fill him with misgivings. Why did Norris select as
agent one who obviously is a member of a hated race? One recalls Zerkow of *McTeague* and the Jew in *Vandover*. At its best,
this is a cheap trick; at its worst, a contemptible thing. Beside it,
the courage of Zola in the Dreyfus case seems godlike. It is not
only the fact of bias which offends us, but the use of bias to deflect attention from where, in all conscience, it should be centered.
Repulsive in himself, Behrman is made to shoulder Shelgrim's
sins, too. We no longer look upon the method of our introduction
to the latter as innocuous, but question the author's motives.
Presley, sitting in Shelgrim's outer office before his audience,
hears the railroad president propose to double the salary of a
worthless subordinate as an untried means to cure him of his
periodic sprees. At this Presley marvels (as well he might), but
then he notices the great executive's shoulders "humped and
rounded, as if to bear great responsibilities, and great abuse."
This humanitarian, this patient sufferer, is not the Shelgrim we
had expected, and with Presley we are impressed, then overcome. Later, however, we wonder why the novelist chose to present Shelgrim in quite this way. We speculate as to whether he
ever wrote Howells again that he had not been quite truthful.
There is more to *The Octopus* than the presentation of a deterministic philosophy.

There is, for example (to drop an altogether distasteful
topic), a careful synthesis of much reading. We have mentioned
Tolstoy and Zola's *Germinal*. Passages in the book suggest as
well *La Bête Humaine* (for the slaughter caused by the "wild"
engine), *Fécondité* and *La Terre* (for the descriptions of the fertility of Nature), Stevenson (for the romantic treatment of the
shepherd Venamee and for much symbolism), and D'Annunzio
(for the characterization of the heroine, Hilma Tree). Such a
list does not pretend to be all inclusive. There is in the book—if

we ignore the falsely characterized Presley, Behrman, and Shelgrim—much fine character drawing: Hooven, the comical Dutchman with his fine courage; Annixter, the intemperate; Harran, the four-square; Dykes, with his touching passion for his "little tyke"; and Magnus Derrick, the "governor," tortured into shameful rôles, a native dignity humiliated. Finally, there is a sensuousness, an epic surge to the prose, a storm of verbal music, that marks the book off from most other Naturalistic narratives written in America.

The Pit: A Story of Chicago, serialized in the *Saturday Evening Post* in 1903, was, according to Norris' plan, a study of the distribution of American wheat, but in actuality it is the story of vast speculation in the Board of Trade Building, of the efforts of a financial superman and plunger to corner the market, and of his (and others') ruin beneath a deluge of wheat when the market breaks. It is also the story of this man's conquest of a woman's heart, his neglect of her for gambling once he has possession, but of his repossession in defeat and illness. The novel belongs to what Norris himself had described as the simplest kind of fiction —the story of adventure. While the scene is Chicago and chiefly the grain pit, and not the reeling deck of the *Bertha Millner,* this tale in fundamental design is not greatly different from *Moran of the Lady Letty.* The chief fictional interest is the rise and fall of the superman, Curtis Jadwin, the most plausible superman of Norris, yet inferior to Dreiser's Cowperwood as a realistic study of the American financier. If we surrender our ethics to Jadwin's code, his story has absorbing interest. It is every bit as good as the story Zola tells in *L'Argent*—that story of the Bourse which inspired Norris. Both authors are equally ignorant of economics, a fact which in no way affects the purely narrative interest. On the other hand, the romantic and sentimental side of *The Pit*— the story of Laura's relations with Jadwin—is incredibly commonplace and stupid. Laura is not realized at all (the intelligent Boston girl who repeatedly says, "he don't"), the pretty face which unquestioningly accepts her husband's explanation, "The wheat cornered itself. I simply stood between two sets of circumstances. The wheat cornered me, not I the wheat." Though she knows his failure has ruined thousands and precipitated hard times, she will not admit he is in any way to blame ("He had suffered, too"). This may be natural now that she has him back, but where is her New England heritage of which the Naturalist is supposed to make much—where are her traditional moral scruples? Norris has deceived us as to her origins; she has never set her dainty little foot within the town limits of Barrington, where Norris alleges she was born; she was got by Gog out of Magog in a Chicago hotel.

The best writing in *The Pit* is found in those passages describing the insane clamor on the floor of the Board of Trade Building; Norris nowhere uses detail to better advantage. The worst passages in the book employ the same detail to convince us of the cultural advantages of Chicago, which are, from Norris' account, somewhat less than those of Ogiet Uhl Yakub. Perhaps the chief interest attached to *The Pit* is an announcement that the third book in the Trilogy of the Wheat will be *The Wolf, a Story of Europe,* which "will probably have for its pivotal episode the relieving of a famine in an Old World community." We assume from this that Norris has extended his plan of showing the effect of cheaper American grain upon the French peasantry (his original idea, derived from Zola) to a display of American munificence in relieving the famine we have created. Thus, while the Wheat has passed "resistless, along its ordered and predetermined courses from West to East, like a vast Titanic flood . . . leaving Death and Ruin in its wake," it will in "the larger view" have worked for "good," bringing "Life and Prosperity [?]" to Europe. We cannot regret that Frank Norris did not live to write such a book.

Over Frank Norris, over Stephen Crane, over all other American Naturalists towers Theodore Dreiser, in Mencken's phrase, "the Hindenburg of the novel." In him, rather than in Hardy or Zola, is found the very quintessence of Naturalism. Hardy believed in a Fate which might capriciously become good again; Zola worked for a better moral order; but Dreiser believes in nothing and works for nothing. "All we know," he declares, "is that we cannot know." And again, "I can make no comment on my work or my life that holds either interest or import for me. Nor can I imagine any explanation or interpretation of any life, my own included, that would be either true—or important, if true. Life is to me too much of a welter and play of inscrutable forces to permit, in my case at least, any significant comment. One may paint for one's own entertainment, and that of others— perhaps. As I see him the utterly infinitesimal individual weaves among the mysteries a floss-like and wholly meaningless course— if course it be. In short I catch no meaning from all I have seen, and pass quite as I came, confused and dismayed." And in summary, "Life cannot be put into any mold, and the attempt might as well be abandoned at once."

The complete nihilism of Theodore Dreiser, which marks him off from the Naturalists of the old school, is a product of his unconditional surrender to the philosophers, generalizers, and pseudo-scientists who have made up his painful reading, for contrary to a wide misconception, Dreiser is literate and has read and brooded over many books. He has read them eagerly, it would appear, for years trying to find an authority who would illumine life for him by giving it meaning or significance. "I am one of those curious persons [he groans] who cannot make up their minds about anything. I read and read. . . . But I find that one history contradicts another, one philosopher drives out another. Essayists, in the main, point out flaws and paradoxes in the current conception of things; novelists, dramatists, and biographers spread tales of endless disasters, or silly illusions concerning life, duty, opportunity, and the like. And I sit here and read and read, when I have time, wondering." The first and most potent influence upon his mind came in the chance discovery of Spencer and Huxley at twenty-three. He confesses that the reading of the former's *First Principles* quite blew him, intellectually, to bits, while Huxley's two studies, *Science and Hebrew Tradition* and *Science and Christian Tradition,* divested him of his last shred of Catholicism, in which he had been reared. But his reading did not stop here, and he acknowledges freely a debt to other books more or less of one character: Carl Snyder's *The World Machine* (1907), Jacques Loeb's *The Mechanistic Conception of Life* (1912), and John B. Watson's *Behaviorism* (1925). Containing more dogmatic vinegar than anything Zola read, they turned the litmus of the reader's mind to a deeper hue than that possessed by any of his predecessors.

It was a mind peculiarly susceptible to negations, a mind easily influenced to doubt, a provincial, cheated, hesitant mind which Dreiser possessed at the beginning of his career. Unlike most Hoosier minds which rub up pretty easily, it was one which would never take a polish, and true to promise, has kept its clayey, dull, rustic, sincere character to the present. Its qualities were undeniably determined by the poverty and hardship of Theodore Dreiser's youth. Dreiser admits as much in *Dawn: An Autobiography of Early Youth* (1931), where in a memorable allegory he compares his mental growth to that of a lily with its head trapped in a bowl of stones, the bent stem forming a whitish-green, powerful hoop which eventually dragged out the head to bloom, though there was no sunlight where it stood. Some mysterious natural force, one feels, besides his super-abundant ego, raised Dreiser from poverty, social inferiority, and ignorance.

Dreiser was born in Terre Haute, Indiana, on August 27, 1871, into a family of ten children. His father, a Catholic by faith, Dreiser has described as a "bigot" and "a narrow hide-bound religionist." As a weaver, due to injury and bad luck, the father was never regularly employed and was frequently sepa-rated from his wandering family, whose sole guide was a "happy . . . pagan mother" who had resigned her Moravian faith at marriage. An older brother, Paul, made some success as a writer of popular songs, and the mother and three children lived with him in Warsaw, Indiana, where Theodore had the conventional schooling. At sixteen he went up to Chicago to gain employment, and after slaving as a dishwasher, scene painter, and hardware clerk, he was glad to accept a loan from a former high school teacher, who perceived his buried worth, to attend the University of Indiana, where, however, he remained only a year. Back in Chicago, he drove a laundry wagon, then collected installment payments for a real estate office. Because he withheld twenty-five dollars to buy himself a hat and an overcoat, he was "fired" from this last position. He caught on in a newspaper office, that of the Chicago *Daily Globe,* in June, 1892, and began a varied reporting career, with the St. Louis *Globe-Democrat* and *Republic,* the Cleveland *Leader,* and the Pittsburgh *Dispatch.* For three years he was editor of *Every Month,* a musical review published in New York. In 1898 he ventured into marriage with "a religious, thoughtful, well-read" St. Louis girl, but discovered it was "a binding state." He begged her to set him free and she did. At about the same time, yielding to the persuasion of his friend Arthur Henry, the novelist, Dreiser turned to writing fiction. When it was proved that this would not support him, he returned to editorial work, first laboring for Street, Smith & Company, publishers of "wood pulp" magazines, then for the *Broadway Journal,* and finally for the Butterick publications. Success as a novelist released him from this kind of servitude. As he tells his own story, he adds to these details the frank record of many sexual encounters which have helped him to reach his conclusion that, in the "chemical scheme of life," sex desires come first.

Theodore Dreiser's career as a novelist is, in one sense, a history of the struggle for freedom of discussion in America. His first novel, *Sister Carrie,* did not even reach the censor. Doubleday, Page & Company, which had accepted the book on the enthusiastic recommendation of Frank Norris, suddenly had scruples about bringing it out, and when forced to do so by the author, who insisted on his contract, actually published it but did not market it, storing all but a few unstamped copies, which Norris smuggled out, in the basement of their plant. Though the book was favorably reviewed in England, the episode gave Dreiser a poor reputation with publishers here, which accounts for the fact that seven years elapsed before another house (B. W. Dodge Company) was willing to reissue the book, and a full decade before anyone would undertake another Dreiser novel. In 1911, Harper issued *Jennie Gerhardt,* and *The Financier* the following year. With *The Titan* in type in 1914 this publishing house was seized with qualms and suppressed the book. Dreiser transferred his rights to the British firm of John Lane which brought out *The Titan* and *The Genius* here. After the latter book had been out a year, the New York Society for the Suppression of Vice notified the publisher that it violated the state laws against

obscene literature. Upon the threat of prosecution, John Lane
withdrew *The Genius* in July, 1916. Inspired by a group of English novelists, including Arnold Bennett, W. L. George, Hugh
Walpole, and H. G. Wells, who cabled a denunciation of the
Society's attack, the Authors' League of America took up arms
in defense of the book. The row raised an obscure, plodding
author into a prominent one, and Dreiser was able to publish
profitably through Boni & Liveright a number of minor books—
A Hoosier Holiday (1916), *Plays of the Natural and Supernatural* (1916), *Free and Other Stories* (1918), *Twelve Men*
(1919), *Hey Rub-a-Dub-Dub* (1920), *A Book About Myself*
(1922), and *The Color of a Great City* (1923), while awaiting
the outcome. When all restraints were removed from *The Genius,*
it was reissued in 1923 and went through a dozen printings—
despite its 736 dull pages—in three years. Since that episode
Dreiser has had no difficulty publishing his books, but he himself
became the petitioner for an injunction in 1931 against the Paramount Corporation for altering his original story of *An American Tragedy* in cinema production. No other American author
has ever had so much trouble in getting his early work before
the public, and his persistence speaks for the tough fibre of his
heart.

The novels of Theodore Dreiser before the public, freed of all
legal charges of salaciousness, still present unusual problems for
the critic. He may not praise Dreiser for this or that with any
surety that Dreiser deserves the praise. Avowedly indifferent to
ethics, Dreiser has taken his material wherever he has found it,
so that some of his books are more definitely compilations than
anything issued under a man's own name since the Renaissance.
A case in point is *An American Tragedy* where the book is based
upon the easily available records of the Chester Gilette-Grace
Brown murder in the files of the New York *World*. At times
Dreiser has expanded a tiny suggestion into a dramatic episode,
but at other times he has reproduced his original—word for
word, comma for comma, period for period. Thus Judge Deven-
dorf's charge to the jury, as reported in the *World*, December 5,
1907, is lifted verbatim. A less complete reliance is illustrated in
the letters which Clyde Griffiths and Roberta Allen exchange in

the novel. Dreiser has expanded these somewhat from the original. In the following specimen the italicized words represent the text of a letter from Grace Brown to her seducer, printed in the *World* on April 11, while Dreiser's additions are in Roman:

Clyde, *I have done nothing but cry since I got here. If you were only here I wouldn't feel so badly. I do try to be brave, dear, but how can I help thinking* at times that *you will never come for me* when you haven't written me one single note and have only talked to me three times since I've been up here. *But then I say to myself you couldn't be so mean as that,* and especially since you have promised. Oh, you will come, won't you? *Everything worries me* so now, Clyde, for some reason *and I'm so frightened, dear.* . . .

It is hard to see wherein Dreiser's expansions have given this letter the quality of literature; and it is more difficult still to discern wherein he has improved upon the *World* story for dramatic interest in telling his tale. The odd proportions of the novel, so frequently remarked upon, are the practical proportions of the newspaper account, where more space is naturally devoted to reporting the trial than in delving into the facts of Chester Gilette's youth. For punctuation, phraseology, subject matter, episode, and form, then, Dreiser is indebted in this one novel to an original; what he has created lies largely outside these categories and is the critic's chief concern. But *An American Tragedy* is not an isolated case of "borrowing" among Dreiser's books. *The Financier* and *The Titan* are known to be based upon newspaper accounts of the notorious Charles Yerkes, and it may be that Dreiser has employed the daily journals, though admittedly less extensively, for episodes in his other books. This is a dependence which would seem to have grown upon him, resulting in the charges of plagiarism over *Dreiser Looks at Russia* in 1928.

The earlier Dreiser, author of *Sister Carrie* and *Jennie Gerhardt,* is a creative artist who derives legitimately from Zola, Hardy, and George Moore. Especially do these books show the influence of Moore's *Esther Waters.* Yet when the critic has noted the large degree of direct and indirect dependence in Dreiser, he has not settled all of the extra-critical problems connected with the man. One more exists—how much do the better novels of Dreiser owe to anonymous people who have put them in shape? The best-made of them all is *Sister Carrie,* written practically under the direction of Arthur Henry. Yet we are told that Dreiser's manuscript was twice the size of the finished book. Henry cut forty thousand words out of the manuscript, perhaps more, and there must have been further excision before the novel went to press. When his books have form (not many of them have), how much credit does Dreiser deserve?

One could become quite exercised over Dreiser's indebtedness to others were it not for the fact that what Dreiser has borrowed is of relatively small consequence. Clyde Griffiths, after all, isn't Chester Gilette, and the *World* story isn't *An American Tragedy.* The details are all there, but in the *World* these details indict and condemn Chester Gilette, while a great compassion in *An American Tragedy* makes Clyde Griffiths a stumbling, bewildered human and raises a reasonable doubt as to his responsibility in the affair. Dreiser has brought to stuff already organized prejudicially (from his point of view) an attitude to undermine the whole organization, not as narrative, but as logic. In this sense he is not so much the Hindenburg, as the Clarence Darrow of the novel, the defender in all his works of both the strong and the weak whom society has condemned. Lacking the wit of the great criminal lawyer, he has nevertheless the same approach to the sentiments and understanding, and the same attitude towards the criminal as had Darrow. Both deflect the charges against their clients towards things which no ordinary jury or reading public can defend—the imperfect mechanism called man and the mechanical perfection called society. Each sets about and succeeds in the arduous task of identifying the juror, or reader, with the client; each asks, What would you do with these handicaps in this situation? Because the transference is a long and delicate process, Darrow's trials are long and Dreiser's books are extraordinarily bulky. The client whom Darrow acquits has been tried before and found guilty a million times by his fellows; there is nothing novel to the case until Darrow takes it over. And so it is, not with one, but all of Dreiser's books of fiction: his materials are everybody's and nobody's—they are old and prejudiced—till he takes possession of them by revitalizing them. This the plagiarist has never done.

With *Sister Carrie* (1900), his first novel, Dreiser set out to show that any country girl, fond of fine clothes and the bustle and excitement of the city, might, if placed where she had no alternative but to give up both, yield almost unwittingly—so gradual the process—to the seducer. Caroline Meeber, affectionately called "Sister Carrie" in her family, meets on the train on her first trip to Chicago—whither she is proceeding to live with an older sister and to seek work for her own support that the family burden may be lessened—this girl of inadequate background meets an experienced victimizer of girls of her type in Drouet, a clothing salesman. To him she foolishly grants a later rendezvous. In Chicago, she immediately goes to work in a shoe factory for four dollars and a half a week, the position having been found for her by her cautious and calculating brother-in-law. She soon discovers, when she has paid her board, that there is little left to buy the pretty things she needs. From the despair of pointless drudgery, fully as much as from the lack of a cloak, she succumbs to a cold, is ill for several days, and loses her position.

New work is hard to find, and the brother-in-law will not have her in his house as an extra burden and hints that she should return to Columbia City. Meanwhile Drouet has bobbed up again. He takes her to luncheon and presses money upon her which she does not know how to refuse. In yet another encounter he outfits her in fine clothes, for which her vain heart yearns yet which she does not dare wear back to her sister's. This leads to Drouet's hiring a room for her, where she may conceal her new finery, and to her decision to take refuge there from her sister's insistence that she return to their native place. With every tie to her past broken, with no position to take refuge in, Carrie is an easy victim for Drouet and shortly is living in an apartment which he has provided. These early chapters of *Sister Carrie* successfully challenge comparison with Hardy's *Tess* and George Moore's *Esther Waters*. The element of violence in the seduction of both Tess and Esther saves the creator of each the pains Dreiser lavishes in making Carrie's fall psychologically plausible, with a consequence that they are somewhat less convincing than the American here. On the other hand, Tess suffers implausibly, Esther plausibly, and Carrie not at all from conscience, once each is victimized. Here the Irishman is more convincing than Hardy or Dreiser, but Dreiser is on better ground than Hardy, for Carrie's selfishness, her new interest in clothing herself properly and in improving her manners, provide an absorption which crowds out qualms that the novelist might have represented. It is this side of her nature, and not mere lasciviousness, which makes her enjoy the freedom and means to cultivate her natural beauty and grace. And it is this side of her nature which develops in the book. Hardy fails to note how new opportunities with either Alec or Angel affect Tess at all. Esther's seducer brought no advantages.

Thus far the story is Carrie's and thus far, save in its psychology, it is a story with many nineteenth century parallels. Now, however, a new figure is introduced—George Hurstwood, manager of a fashionable Chicago bar and friend of Drouet. The drummer is flattered by the friendship of this able man, and desiring to appear well in his eyes, decides to exhibit his "prize" to his friend. It is a fatal choice, for Hurstwood, unhappy with his wife, is drawn to Carrie and shortly is infatuated with her. On her part she responds to the flattery of this well-poised, confident man whose abilities she recognizes as superior to those of Drouet. Hurstwood not only is attentive and generous, but gives her her first theatrical experience, procuring a rôle for her in *Under the Gaslights* in an Elks' benefit. Meeting her with reckless freedom while Drouet is away on a trip, he is betrayed both to his wife and to the travelling man. Mrs. Hurstwood takes legal steps leading to a divorce; Drouet quarrels with Carrie, but realizes that she means so much more to him now he cannot part with her, though he makes a show of doing so by going to live in a hotel. The girl herself, learning for the first time of Hurstwood's marriage, closes her mind towards him. The latter, however, slightly under the influence of drink, and made rash by his passion, steals ten thousand dollars from his employers, persuades Carrie that Drouet has been injured in order to get her to go with him, and entrains for Detroit on his way to Canada. Carrie is indignant when he confesses his ruse, and remains distant and angry until he agrees to marriage and the ceremony is performed. They are located in Montreal by a detective, and Hurstwood is forced to make partial restitution. Continuing on to New York, they live humbly while Hurstwood attempts to start again in business. Only moderately successful at first, Hurstwood, his confidence in himself gone, ashamed of his defalcation, is defeated before defeat comes to him. The loss of his little capital in a poor venture forces him to hunt for work, at which he is not successful, and in dullness and poverty he and his wife, sitting and waiting in their little flat, drift apart. Provoked at Hurstwood's lethargy and despair, Carrie herself seeks employment and is lucky enough to get a position in a chorus. For a time she supports him, but when over months he gets only one job—that of "scab" in a Brooklyn street-car strike,—she leaves her husband to share a room with one of the girls. Success attends her efforts on the stage, and suddenly she bounds into popular favor; meanwhile Hurstwood, after doing menial tasks in a hotel, becomes ill with penumonia, and is so weak, following his recovery, that nothing but beggary is left. When Broadway lights burn with his former wife's name, Hurstwood turns on the unlit gas in a cheap room to end the story in which he has usurped the chief interest.

In the enthusiasm of unexpected discovery Theodore Watts-Dunton wrote long ago of *Sister Carrie* that "between its covers no single note of unreality is struck." It, indeed, among Naturalistic novels is one of the most convincing on the score of verisimilitude. To be sure, one can quibble over a few very minor details, like that of the safe door clicking shut, thus abetting Hurstwood in his theft. But there is nothing implausible in the book. H. L. Mencken speaks of the story as "broken-backed" merely because the reader's interest shifts from Carrie to Hurstwood. We are far from feeling this an important structural defect. It is as if the very momentum of Hurstwood's precipitous plunge carried the lighter Carrie aloft; one's meteoric rise is certainly a comment on the other's headlong fall. And how much deeper did his abyss appear to Hurstwood when he viewed his selfish, pretty wife upon the heights! What better way of suggesting despair than this? If anyone but the clumsy Theodore Dreiser had worked out this contrast, we should have had volumes on its aesthetic excellence. Whether the effect was planned or not in no way touches its potency. It is more vital to note that *Sister Carrie* is a better novel than a tract—perhaps the only one of Dreiser's books about which this might be said—and that, like life itself, it is deterministic to a determinist and moral to a moralist. The former sees Carrie, Drouet, and Hurstwood caught in the webs of their desires; the latter, Hurstwood self-punished for his evil choice, and Carrie developing only the evil and selfish strain in herself from the first. It is an unusual Naturalistic novel which leaves the reader as free to draw his conclusions from the facts as does *Sister Carrie*.

One half suspects that Dreiser thought *Sister Carrie* a failure because it turned out differently from his plans for it, and that he wrote *Jennie Gerhardt* to improve upon it. Dreiser's second novel is more imitative than his first. No Hurstwood enters the ninth chapter and runs away with the story. It is the tale of a hotel scrub woman's daughter who is left pregnant by wealthy Senator Brander on his death, though he was apparently honest in his intention to marry her. When her fanatical German father discovers her affair, he hustles her out of his house. A younger brother hires a room for her, and after her baby is born, she joins him in Cleveland. As a household servant she attempts to support her child, but circumstances make it easy instead for her to become the mistress of rich young Lester Kane. Upon his bounty she lives comfortably and is even able to aid her relatives, including Old Gerhardt, who blesses her before he dies. Lester's family objects to his complaisance in his affair, desiring him properly wed to a person of his own station. Unwilling that he should sacrifice himself for her, Jennie gives him up. Dying, with his wife in Europe, Lester Kane summons Jennie to his bedside, and the two understand that, in the face of all convention, they are really man and wife.

It is a pretty story wherein the heroine exhibits all those Christian virtues in which Dreiser can see so little merit. If it is truly written that the meek shall inherit the earth, Jennie is entitled to at least a continent. Her devotion to her paramour is excessive; certainly very un-American, it suggests the deference for the male that is European and is a more likely attitude for one of Jennie's mother's generation than for one of her own. In his effort to show that there might be greater affection in an illicit relationship than in the conventional marriage, Dreiser has over-reached himself: Jennie belongs in the company of angels or in some old legendary. More than Tess, she might be described as "a pure woman." That there was carnal pleasure in her relations with either the senator or the rich young heir we would have no reason to believe, since the novel is silent on this score. Sentimentality and an hereditary Teuton attitude are responsible for this; we are told that Jennie is Dreiser's favorite among his characters. She is his ideal: the submissive woman created for masculine delight, without brains and with conveniently few emotions. How false she is, a comparison of her story with that of Esther Waters instantly reveals: ignorant, but intelligent, Esther has character and force—she lives for us; Jennie is so much dough. It was folly for Dreiser to study again the fallen servant-girl after Moore had done so good a job of it; even in the little details of a maid's life Dreiser is weak beside the Irishman. Dreiser did not really know Jennie.

A greater weakness in the novel is his portrayal of the Kanes— a "socially prominent" family of wealthy carriage makers. Here Dreiser missed a splendid opportunity for satire that neither Moore nor Zola would have passed up. There is a certain awe of the Kanes' position and wealth in Dreiser's attitude, while it is patent that they are *nouveaux riches,* vulgarians with a thin veneer of manners. It does not strike Dreiser that Lester's continued content over the years with his placid mistress is essentially bourgeois. Miss Dorothy Dudley admits the inadequacy of Dreiser's treatment of the Kanes and makes a point that American aristocracy have never, like British and European society, welcomed novelists in their drawing rooms. She holds them responsible for Dreiser's feeble representation of their kind. Of course, the answer to this is that the novelist was under no compulsion to draw that with which he was unfamiliar and that his intuitions might have served him better than they did. *Jennie Gerhardt* is weak and unconvincing because the character drawing is bad, that is, bad with one exception—Old Gerhardt, the Lutheran bigot, is convincingly done, one of Dreiser's best portraits. Some reviser failed the novelist, it should be pointed out, when he let the last chapter stand in the manuscript. This picture

of the funeral of the sulky-maker's son is one of the most sentimental passages in fiction.

In method *The Financier*, published in 1912, owes more to
David Graham Phillips than to Frank Norris' *The Pit*, to which
it seems to be related through its study of the speculator. Phillips,
like Dreiser a reporter, based his fiction so closely upon newspaper stories that frequently his characters were identified and on
occasion libel was threatened. Dreiser avoided this danger by selecting an historical, rather than a living figure, but his dependence upon newspaper files was great. As has been pointed out in
relation to *An American Tragedy*, Dreiser possessed himself of
his material by reinterpreting it. Charles T. Yerkes, whose career
in Philadelphia, Chicago, and New York is represented in the
newspapers as highly reprehensible, becomes the product of his
origins, environment, and reflection, as Frank Algernon Cowperwood in *The Financier*, and in *The Titan*, its sequel. At the outset of his story Dreiser quotes from *Richard III*:

> I came into the world feet first and was born with teeth.
> The nurse did prophesy that I should snarl and bite.

Cowperwood early conceives that life is a struggle in which the
fittest survive and have their desires. Witnessing in a store window day by day the efforts of a lobster to catch a squid which has
been placed in its glass tank, and one day finding the squid cut in
two and being devoured, young Frank Cowperwood perceives the
law for his governance in life. Son of a bank clerk, who is himself
to rise to a vice-presidency and to become questionably involved
in his boy's schemes, Cowperwood gets his early training in the
commission market but soon graduates into the manipulation of
the securities of Philadelphia street-car companies, through public loans arranged by political friends. With the city treasurer's
office in his control, he might easily have achieved his desire to
become the wealthiest man in America had he been more discreet
in love. Married to a woman who cannot satisfy him, Cowperwood becomes infatuated with Aileen Butler and makes her his
mistress. She is the daughter of one of the most unscrupulous
and powerful men of Cowperwood's acquaintance. Old Butler,

terribly and justly incensed when he learns of the affair, bides his
time until the Chicago fire, with its general depressing effect upon
the market, has Cowperwood hard pressed, and then he pushes
him to the wall. Exposed and convicted, Cowperwood is sent to
jail, but has influence enough to conduct his affairs from his cell
and to recoup his fortunes in the panic of 1873. Influence also
shortens his term, and not much the worse for his experience, he
plans to begin life anew when released from prison.

The Titan (1914) presents Cowperwood's later career in Chicago where, divorced and married to Aileen, he is excluded from
society. This does not prevent him from philandering, and he has
a long procession of mistresses, including the wives of acquaintances and stenographers in his employ. At the end of the trail he
is rewarded for his perseverance by the generous novelist with
the free gift of a young lady of great charm from Louisville,
Kentucky, who proposes to take him away to Paris or London
where he will be understood. As in Philadelphia, these affairs
multiply his enemies and contribute to his final defeat in the
traction business. It was with the publication of The Titan that
Dreiser announced that it and The Financier constituted the first
two volumes of "A Trilogy of Desire." Perhaps because there is
nothing further desirable after The Titan, the trilogy was never
completed. Two decades ago Stuart Sherman described The
Titan as a "huge club sandwich composed of slices of business
alternating with erotic episodes," and there is no reason to
change that adequate description today.

Our condemnation of The Titan is on the score of tedium and
not of morals. Perhaps had The Financier never been written, we
should care more for The Titan, but facts that can be discerned
on the face of a penny gain nothing at all by being magnified a
thousand times. The Titan is merely The Financier written in
capital letters. Cowperwood, furthermore, in possession of a
fixed view of life, is a far less dramatic figure than the boy and
young man arriving at that view, and being punished for the first
time for holding it. There is in The Titan, moreover, no characterization to compare with that of the abject Stener and the
outraged Butler of the earlier book. Whatever drama there is in
nefarious political and financial chicanery is quite worked out in

The Financier. While Cowperwood is thwarted in *The Titan,* he is never actually defeated—his biggest set-back in finance is accompanied by his greatest fortune in love, an altogether adequate compensation for his nature; in *The Titan* he never knows complete despair. These feelings are his after his trial and sentence in *The Financier,* before he knows that it is possible to salvage something of his fortune. It is possible for us to attach ourselves sympathetically to Cowperwood in *The Financier;* he is wholly revolting in *The Titan.* The trial itself, given in extraordinary detail, for Dreiser is interested in the emotional reactions of all connected with it—judge, jurors, witnesses, and spectators—is on the whole better managed than the account of the aldermanic vote on the franchise in the closing chapters of *The Titan.* Finally, *The Titan* is possible only by changing the character of Aileen Butler of *The Financier.* Nothing is more preposterous than Dreiser's sympathy with Cowperwood's social aspirations and his pretense that Aileen is the chief barrier to their realization. This outrage to the character of Aileen, however, is apparent only to those who have read both books.

The Financier is the best picture of the non-ethical, amoral superman of business in American literature. The Philadelphia of art, architecture, literature, and Quaker manners does not exist in the book, but the Philadelphia of the Gas Ring, of the Boodlers and Butlers, of the Republican political machine, is in the book— complete. A greater aesthetic talent would have found ironies in a contrast of the two; knowing Dreiser's limitations, we are glad that he did not attempt it. The most amusing thing about *The Financier* is the author's occasional display of complete naïveté. When he pompously declares, "Finance is an art. And it presents the operations of the subtlest intellectuals . . . ," we gasp a bit, but we soon learn to take this pontificating none too seriously. Similarly, when Dreiser tells us, as he does after bringing Cowperwood and Old Butler together following the latter's discovery of his daughter's seduction, that "It was a wonderful situation," we learn not to let this kind of indiscretion mar the story for us. Yet when his emotion gets the better of him and sweeps him into a tirade against the world as it is, we have to give ear to him whether we want to or not, or whether aesthetics justifies it or not. There is a notable outburst when Stener's wife learns that he has been a tool in the hands of others:

> ... The damnable scheme of things which we call existence brings about conditions whereby whole masses suffer who have no cause to suffer, and, on the other hand, whole masses joy who have no cause to joy. It rains on the just and the unjust impartially. We suffer for our temperaments, which we did not make, and for our weaknesses and lacks, which are no part of our willing or doing. Who by taking thought can add one cubit to his stature? Who can make his brain better? His thoughts swifter? His courage greater? Who is it that can do anything it was not given him to do? All good things are gifts. There are no creations of the mind alone. Creations, achievements, distinguished results always sink back into so many other things. They have their roots in inherited ability, in environment, in fortune, in a lucky star. There is no possible contradiction of this. It is so. So was it ever. So will it be from everlasting to everlasting.

It is Dreiser's pity—his compassion for the sorriest scoundrels—which more than anything else elevates and sustains *The Financier*. Pity is an element in *The Titan*, but it is lavished wholly upon Cowperwood, who, though he is represented as anything but a free agent, is no more pitiable than a Bengal tiger, loose in what he helps to make a jungle. Pity has degenerated in *The Titan* to the most mawkish, maudlin, and stupid sentimentality.

The 736 pages of *The Genius*, which followed *The Titan* within a year, are the dreariest reading imaginable. Though the book possibly owes something to Mary Austin's *An American Genius*, and to the reminiscences of one or two erotic young illustrators whom Dreiser knew as an editor, it is largely autobiographical. Replete with amours, *The Genius* is the story of a talented boy's struggle for success, first in Chicago, then in New York. Eugene Witla is a painter, but behind him one discerns Theodore Dreiser, the novelist. Indeed, the letter which Ruby sends Eugene in the novel is reproduced as from "Alice" to "Theo" in *A Book About Myself*. Yet *The Genius* is duller than all the autobiographical narratives rolled together. If we ask why this is, we discover that it is because Eugene has so few interests—sex and erotic art being about his limits. The autobiographer is a livelier fellow, objective to a greater degree, and a keen, if puzzled, observer. Eugene, oversexed, and wholly preoccupied with his difficulty, is a very tedious person. It is not

wholly because Angela Blue, his wife, is older than he and inhibited that they are unhappy together. Eugene would have been
unhappy and tedious could he have possessed himself immediately of Suzanne Dale, the nineteen-year-old society girl whom
he seeks in vain at the end of the story. Granting that there are
good episodes in the book, and some excellent characterization
(Angela Blue, for example, is handled with more tenderness and
comprehension than one would expect from Dreiser), *The Genius* is undeniably dull, ponderous, and heavy. Events in the
book cast so long a shadow before them that there is no light
when they arrive. The elephantine, lumbering style, fascinating
because of its awkward progress elsewhere, here sits down in
deadly earnest on the reader. Unlike *Sister Carrie* and *The Financier, The Genius* plainly is not bigger than its faults. Floyd
Dell who worked on the manuscript for the author was not insistent enough on alterations and excisions.

An American Tragedy (1925) takes an undisputed rank beside *Sister Carrie* and *The Financier* among Dreiser's books.
Clyde Griffiths, the bewildered hero of the tragedy, is the son of
Old Praise-the-Lord (Asa) Griffiths, a street evangelist, and of
an ignorant farm girl whose hymn-singing abilities have made
her a desirable wife for Asa. While the family is connected with
a mission in Kansas City, Clyde gets his first steady employment
as a drug clerk. Next, as a bell-hop in a hotel, he steals a car for
a good time with a group of cheap companions, but they kill a
child and wreck the car. In terror, Clyde flees to Chicago, where,
again working in a hotel, he is discovered by a forgotten wealthy
uncle who owns a collar factory in Lycurgus, New York. At the
uncle's insistence Clyde is given a minor position in the fabric-
shrinking basement by his cousin Gilbert, a boy somewhat older
than Clyde, now acting-manager of the collar factory. Clyde
makes so good an impression on his uncle that he is placed in
charge of the stamping room and becomes the over-lord of
twenty-five girls. With one of these young women, Roberta
Allen, Clyde falls in love. She is a country girl of warm passions
and really is much more drawn to Clyde than he to her. They
have frequent clandestine meetings, and Roberta even changes
her room to give him unrestricted privileges.

Meanwhile the young social set of Lycurgus, led by Sondra Finchley (who hates Clyde's cousin, Gilbert, and acts partly from spite) take up the boy and set his head awhirl. He cools towards Roberta who correctly suspects that Sondra is her rival. At this juncture she finds she is pregnant, and Clyde and she try in vain to bring about an abortion. Roberta begs him to marry her, and in desperation, Clyde prevails upon her to go to her people for a month. Meanwhile on motor trips to the lake country and at parties in Lycurgus he has made an almost complete conquest of Sondra: she promises to run away with him in the fall. Roberta now writes that, if he does not come to her rescue, she will return and denounce him. With an ill-defined plan (but not a complete resolve) to put an end to her, Clyde agrees to meet her and they go to Big Bittern Lake as a preliminary to marriage. In the boat Roberta suddenly senses something strange and rises to protest to Clyde; angrily he pushes her away, striking her with a camera, then impulsively reaches "half to assist or recapture her and half to apologize for the unintended blow—yet in so doing completely capsizing the boat." As they go over, the boat wale strikes Roberta's head, leaving a mark to tell against Clyde, who now for the first time really acts at the suggestion of the evil voices which have all along been prompting him—and swims away from the drowning girl. Clyde is arrested and brought to trial by a man, Orville Mason, the district attorney and his nemesis, whose thwarted sex life makes him avid to punish this boy who has had such easy success with women. Though Clyde is sympathetically and ably defended, Mason plays to the papers and the crowds, with the result that there is a popular demand—voiced in outbreaks in the courtroom—for Clyde's conviction. Found guilty, he is sentenced to death, and is executed when the Court of Appeals refuses to intercede and after a religious fanatic, who has become interested in him, literally reconvicts him before the governor.

In *An American Tragedy,* after years of fumbling with his theme, Dreiser at last has found the ideal vehicle for it. From the first of his writing he has tried to show that a sex-impelled human being, whose desires drive him to break the moral code, is not responsible for his actions. He has hitherto been only partially successful in demonstrating his theme: in order to involve Hurstwood in precisely the circumstances which would lead to his destruction Dreiser had to get him partially drunk on wine; Jennie Gerhardt is so much like soft wax that when she is pushed over the line it has little significance; Cowperwood may be impelled by forces over which he has little control, yet his actions are so close to what they would be could he exercise deliberate choice that the demonstration is not very convincing; while with Witla and the poor pervert of *The Hand of the Potter* the theme is so obvious that demonstration is *de trop*. Clyde Griffiths, however, is neither drunk nor an imbecile, is neither superman nor subman, but a type of thousands of poor boys to whom temptation opens vistas which compel more powerfully than any restraints they have learned. Had the circumstances of Roberta's death been less complex than Dreiser made them, had Clyde strangled the girl with his hands in a field, the question of his moral responsibility would still be an open one. A society which surrounds some of its youth with every luxury while denying to others everything but "opportunity" must share the blame whenever a crime of violence occurs. A society which pays no more regard to children than was paid to Clyde in his early youth has a dubious right to punish them when they go astray. Clyde is more plausibly a victim than any of the other victims that Dreiser presents to us. He is more deserving of pity than any other character his author has created.

Paradoxically, Dreiser is an effective novelist and *An American Tragedy* is a moving book because he is only a third-rate thinker. He is not at heart a Naturalist at all. His Clydes and his Cowperwoods, his Jennies and his Carries, are impelled to action by forces surging through them: but if society acts as blindly or as culpably, Dreiser is much exercised by it. He frankly plays at favorites, demanding that his chosen few be held irresponsible, but that the sex-stirred mass (made up of much the same individuals) be judged for crying out in the court room and for being swayed by the papers. For him, as for Hardy, society must remain Christian. A genuine Naturalist, like Maupassant, has no illusions about society. His utter cynicism frees both individuals and the masses from all morals. Yet the emotional Dreiser, with

his confused logic, is more appealing, for it seems a fairer thing
to be merciful with the lone individual and severe with the mass
than it does to be equally merciless towards both. Sportsmanship,
however, is a poor argument in a world where it is claimed the
dice are all loaded, and one is faced with the simple choice of con-
demning Dreiser as a "double-standard" Naturalist or, ignoring
his pretensions of system altogether, to praise him for humane
values that lie quite outside his system.

Besides his five novels, Dreiser has written and printed many another hundred thousand words. These are of interest, but if he
survives it will be on the merits of the novels primarily. Of the
minor work, the repetitious autobiographical narratives have
their value for analyzing Dreiser and as source books for the
novels. The collection of essays, *Hey Rub-a-Dub-Dub* (1920),
repeats, without added clarity, ideas which may be garnered in
the fiction. Of the four volumes of short stories and character
studies, *Free and Other Stories* (1918), *Twelve Men* (1919),
Chains (1927), and *A Gallery of Women* (1929), the first is
the most important. The much reworked short story "Old
Rogaum and his Theresa" is the only piece of writing of Dreiser's
that one can say is absolutely finished, and it is the only bit of his
creative work which exhibits any humor. Of the plays he has
written—*Plays of the Natural and Supernatural* (1916) and
The Hand of the Potter (1918)—the latter has the casual interest of being about the only thoroughgoing Naturalistic
American play. It is the study of a sexual pervert whose adequate
defense is, "Can you blame a man when he ain't right?" It failed
in presentation, and Mencken is correct in describing it as clumsy
and banal. Dreiser hasn't the skill with dialogue necessary for
the theatre. Nor has he the sense of rhythm essential for verse.
The plays are no worse than his one volume of short prose lines,
Moods Cadenced and Declaimed (1926), which altogether lacks
"the breath and finer spirit" of poetry.

Tragic America (1931), a sociological study, sheds more light
on Dreiser, possibly, than any work we have examined. After a
demonstration that America is "owned" by a very few multi-
millionaires, and that their influence extends to other countries,
Dreiser declares himself for a new constitution and a centralized

authority acknowledging the rights of the masses. This is an astonishing shift of position for the man who formerly believed that all progress comes through the selfishness of the "titans" whom he now attacks. Yet we should not be surprised by it: the surprising thing, after all, about Dreiser is that a man of his temperament should ever have adopted the Naturalistic way of looking at things. Impressionable, not sure of his intellectual processes, and put to it to justify a predatory sexual bent, he was swept into Naturalism not because he desired it as an explanation of life, but because he could not resist it as an explanation. Always he contemplates it with a kind of horror; never does he achieve the objectivity of the true Naturalist, of a Flaubert at his best. It is probably with relief that he has put it all behind him— quite illogically, of course—and turned to his own brand of communism. The real Dreiser is a sentimentalist, and it was inevitable that he should one day drop the cloak of his Naturalism. *Tragic America,* his activities in Kentucky, and his recent antiwar tract, *America Is Worth Saving* (1941), reveal a man who has existed all the while but has preferred not to be seen. Now he has merely stopped arguing against his heart.

With Dreiser's conviction of human irresponsibility profitable comparisons and contrasts may be drawn from the views of Clarence Seward Darrow, the most famous criminal lawyer of his day, and from those of Earnest Albert Hooton, the Harvard anthropologist. Darrow's background, so far as it included poverty, inferior schooling, and the small town experience, closely resembled that of Dreiser, as *The Story of My Life* (1932) reveals. There is, however, in his origins one notable difference— his father was the village agnostic, steeped in Jefferson, Voltaire, and Paine. Though the children were forced to attend the Presbyterian Sunday-school, the family stood as a unit in opposition to the generally accepted views on religious and social matters in the town of Kinsman, Ohio, where Darrow passed his juvenile years. Kinsman and Meadville, Pennsylvania, where Darrow had one year of preparatory college work, were later synthesized for the sketch of *Farmington* (1904) in Darrow's first venture into fiction. Not intrinsically valuable as a novel, though an early item in "the revolt from the village," *Farmington* nevertheless suggests how deeply rooted was Darrow's "instinct to doubt the majority view." The chapter satirizing the school readers, for example, shows Darrow as a child skeptical of the traditional virtues, while Dreiser was a confused stumbler after light.

Supported chiefly by his sisters, Darrow had, like Dreiser, but a year of higher education—in the law school at the University of Michigan. He completed his reading for the bar in a Youngstown office, and after private practice in Andover and Ashtabula, moved to Chicago in 1888. In the absence of clients, he became a volunteer worker for Cleveland's reelection and thus made his first influential friends in Chicago. It was, however, his espousal of the Single Tax idea that gave Darrow his first leg up towards fame. Mayor DeWitt Cregier, who heard him speak with Henry George, offered him the job of special assessment attorney; three months later he was assistant corporation counsel, and ten months after that he found himself acting corporation counsel— and head of the law department of the city of Chicago. Needless to say, about this time he began to doubt the Henry George philosophy. The talk about natural rights disgusted him—"Nature admits no rights."

Darrow resigned from the employ of the city to become attorney for the Chicago & North Western Railway Company. In his autobiography he confesses that he found his position irksome, for his sympathies were frequently with the small claimants rather than with the corporation. Certain animadversions on the railroads in *An Eye for an Eye* (1905), a novel in which one of the leading characters is a switchman, bear out his contention that he felt unhappy pressing the cases of the powerful company against its weaker opponents. In 1894 he found himself in an intolerable position—placed on an all-railroad committee to fight the Debs strike, Darrow not only was in opposition to the idea of using the injunction against the men, but he was also in sympathy with the strikers. The president of his road let Darrow sever direct relations in order that he might defend Debs after the latter was enjoined and indicted by Federal Grand Jury. Thus began Darrow's forty-odd years of championing unpopular causes—years that made him one of the best known of non-political personages.

When one tries to find the element of consistency in Darrow's defense of Debs for conspiracy, of Bill Haywood and his associates for the murder of ex-Governor Steunenberg, of the McNamaras for dynamiting the Los Angeles *Times* building, of wealthy Loeb and Leopold for their savage sex crime, of Scopes for teaching evolution in Tennessee, and of Lieutenant Masson for avenging the assault on his wife, one is apt at first to be nonplussed. Yet there is a consistency perceivable in this sensational record beyond mere opposition to the prevailing opinion in the communities where these men were tried, which had already convicted them. Darrow believed, as both his autobiography and *Crime: Its Cause and Treatment* (1922) show, that all men are capable of crime if pushed into a position where they cannot gratify their desires in any legitimate way. "Punishment as punishment," he wrote, "is not admissible unless the offender has had the free will to select his course." Darrow gravitated into this position after reading Judge John P. Altgeld's *Our Penal Code and Its Victims* during his Ashtabula days. In his famous trials, then, so far as Darrow was concerned, there was no question as to the technical guilt of the defendants; his concern was whether or not they were free agents. It is obvious that his conclusion was that his clients in every case *had* to break the law—the dynamiters in order to hold up the end of labor against the ruthlessness of capital in the West, the sex perverts to satisfy their irresponsible natures, and Scopes to preserve his cherished intellectual integrity. The range of defendants is great enough to suggest that Darrow was completely skeptical in regard to the freedom of will of any law-breaker. He defended men with the most varied motives with as clear a conscience as Dreiser showed in defending such disparate creatures as Cowperwood and Clyde Griffiths.

How willing to exonerate every law-breaker Darrow was, is best shown by his fictional tract, *An Eye for an Eye* (1905). In the Naturalistic tradition, this novel relates how a Chicago potato peddler murdered his wife with a stove poker at the end of one of their frequent rows and is hanged for his crime. The author tries to show Jim Jackson a completely irresponsible person. He had impulsively proposed to a waitress because a red blouse had set him off and they had begun their marital life with a deposit on their furniture. When their poverty led to violent quarrels and they desired to separate, the legal fees, the Roman Church, and a child stood in the way. On the day of the murder Jim impulsively bought a steak instead of a glass of whiskey—if he had bought the whiskey, they would not have fought over the way in which the steak was cooked; and if the coal-hod had been in the kitchen where it ordinarily was, instead of in the living room, Jim would not have laid hold of the poker. Finally, the co-incidence of a wave of civic virtue—a crusade against crime— led to popular pressure for Jim's execution, a fate the inex- perienced lawyer assigned him could not forfend.

Here, surely, is presented one of the major issues of our times. Has society failed with Jim and ought society to be punished, or is Jim a failure and well enough eliminated? That we are ter- ribly confused about this issue not merely the frequent miscar- riage of justice but the mounting costs of our penal institutions— society's crude way of punishing itself—demonstrate. Do we solve nothing by hanging Jim? (We waive the question whether his crime was second degree murder since Darrow makes this in- cidental.) Why not let Jim go free? Yet will not another red blouse lead to another bashed head, if Jim is the irresponsible person Darrow makes him out to be? Jim is a cipher well enough cancelled on either side of the ledger by any showing of Darrow's —it is only when the dogma of human irresponsibility is dis- missed and Jim is considered as a potential social liability or asset on his own showing that we get anywhere at all. If Jim did not learn self-control as a boy and the prospect is as forbidding as Darrow makes it out to be that he will learn self-restraint through an expensive course of higher education in a modern penitentiary, hanging him was pure social economy—nothing less.

Darrow's attempt to excuse Jim has the same motivation that led Dreiser to pardon his amoralists—befuddled human sym- pathy. But this befuddlement, carried over to the courtroom and expanded in newspaper headlines, added to the confusion of an already confused age. It was not merely the dogma of human ir- responsibility that was persuasive; it was that dogma enforced by the respect engendered for the man who had bravely fought for Debs, had appeared for the miners during the anthracite coal arbitration, and had energetically worked for the repeal of the Volstead Act—to enumerate some of the unambiguous deeds in Darrow's career. Fairly won prestige was used, perhaps unconsciously, in ways that bred disrespect for law and condoned antisocial acts of impulse. You can "beat" the law, no matter how culpable, if you have a smart attorney—was undeniably one popular conclusion that might be drawn from the legal career of Clarence Darrow.

No such sentimentalism as betrayed Dreiser and Darrow is exhibited by Professor Earnest Hooton, author of *Apes, Men, and Morons* (1937), *Crime and the Man* (1939), and *Twilight of Man* (1939). However, Hooton is only a ninety-nine per cent Naturalist—he believes that if man will take certain steps, which it does not seem likely that he will take, man may deflect his feet from the certain disastrous course in which they were set. But for the Jim Jacksons and Clyde Griffiths, Hooton has no hope whatsoever.

In Hooton's background are the same small-time elements that are found in Dreiser's—religious zeal, small means, and village experience. Son of an immigrant English clergyman, who was himself the son of a harness-making Methodist exhorter, Earnest Hooton was born to a Scotch-Canadian mother in Clemensville, Wisconsin, in 1887. After dividing his youth between this town and Manitowoc, where he went to high school, Hooton attended Lawrence College and the University of Wisconsin. He became an instructor in Latin and Greek while working for his doctorate, but attendance at Oxford, whither a Rhodes scholarship carried him, influenced him to turn his attention from "dead languages to dead men." A potent force in making an anthropologist out of Hooton was Professor R. R. Marett, who wangled an appointment at Harvard for his protégé. Today Dr. Hooton is head of the Department of Anthropology in Harvard University and reputedly one of the best showmen in American education.

Most pertinent of Hooton's books in regard to issues raised by *An American Tragedy* and *An Eye for an Eye* is, of course, *Crime and the Man*. This book is a popular presentation of the findings of a staff of workers, directed by Hooton and richly en-

dowed by the Rockefeller Foundation, which spent a dozen years
gathering, classifying, and generalizing data on criminals. Hooton's thesis is that crime is not the result of an unhappy environment but solely the result of heredity. In fact, Hooton might be
looked upon as a revisionist of Cesare Lombroso, Italian crimi-
nologist, who held that there is a specific criminal type, an atavistic and degenerate being distinct from other humans. Instead of
designating a criminal type, Hooton has indicated that certain
features occur more frequently in criminals than in law-abiding
persons, and that certain specific features are more characteristic of one class of criminals than another. Further, criminals with
different racial backgrounds tend to commit different crimes. To
illustrate : robbers tend to be tall and thin, and to have such other
characteristics as attached ear lobes, heavy beards, and diffused
pigment in the iris. Robbers are least apt to be "pure Nordics".
Sex offenders tend to be "shriveled runts, perverted in mind and
body," distinguished frequently by round heads and narrow
noses, among other things. They are most often Dinarics. The
only way, according to Hooton, to eliminate crime is to improve
the human organism by the practice of eugenics. Reduction of
poverty, regular employment, slum clearance, and character
building are relatively futile efforts to decrease crime, for they
aim at the "inconsequential" factors in the production of criminals.

More objections can be brought against the Hooton thesis
than there are room for here. After Lombroso's studies were
published they were upset by Charles Goring who found the features then designated as criminal to be typical of comparable
non-criminal groups. If a group of non-offenders of the same
racial constituents as Hooton studied could be assembled, would
his generalizations hold? Particularly suspect are his allocations
of different features to different criminal classes, and of different
crimes to various racial types. Criminal records on which such
allocations must have been based are notoriously untrustworthy.
As everyone knows, a man may be arrested, indicted, or convicted for only one of several crimes he may have committed.
The determination of racial types, furthermore, in a study of
some 17,000 offenders, must have been very frequently an arbi-

trary matter. How often, for example, does one see a "Pure Nordic"? Accepting Hooton's data, for the sake of argument, as reliable, can one infer general criminal tendencies from them? In a society where short men are admired (as they are in Italy at the present), are they as frequent sexual offenders as Hooton makes them out to be in prevailing tall, Nordic-American society? Is not environment, then, a possible factor in crime? Can much credence be given *Crime and the Man?*

Hooton's two other books, *Apes, Men, and Morons* and *Twilight of Man,* are collections of essays pitched to one tune: Man is allowing himself to degenerate after his aeons of painful struggle upwards from the ape—only compulsory sterilization of the unfit can stay the swift decline of man into moronism. Hooton offers little convincing evidence of the present degeneracy of man. His favorite line is something like this: the ape-mother needed no help in giving birth to her young, whereas the human mother is well-nigh helpless; therefore the biological competence of the latter is less and this is equivalent to degeneracy. However, for rhetorical purposes any sort of evidence serves Hooton: democracy is government by the suffrage of morons, while Hitlerism is the rule of the pathological. All institutions are thus indiscriminately laid under tax for the proof of his thesis. Not even science escapes—it is not the blessing we think, for although the triumphs of the few may have created "delusions of grandeur in the otiose brains of countless morons," science has done as much to perpetuate the unfit as it has to keep alive the intelligent. Hooton conveniently ignores or discounts things like the lengthening of the life span, the increase in this country in the average height in a generation, and the Iowa experiments in improving low intelligence by improving the environment. His dire predictions probably should not be taken too seriously. But this counsel does not mean that his work should be thrust aside. Despite his jocosity—and he is an exceptionally quizzical writer—Hooton is the best antidote in the world for sentimentalism—especially that sentimentalism which asks us to place a higher value on the anti-social, than on the useful, human being. In particular Hooton should be read for the brave things he says in behalf of the Negro and the Jew.

It seems like one of those caprices of fortune which the Naturalists celebrate in their books that the gauming Theodore Dreiser and the fastidious George Santayana should belong to the same school. It is Santayana, however, who is in strange company, rather than the Indiana German, for the Naturalists have been in the main men to whom university education has been denied, and who, powerfully affected by their own reading in the popular expositors of science, have accepted the dismal view because it blotted out all others. So Zola, so Hardy, so Dreiser. Not so, however, George Santayana, whose life has been passed in university cloisters and who knows surely all the dodges from determinism provided in the labyrinth of idealistic philosophy. Son of Augustin Ruiz de Santayana and Josefina Barrás, he was born in Madrid, Spain, on December 16, 1863, but when only nine years of age, he was brought to the United States by his mother to be educated. He attended Harvard College during the years 1882–86, then after two years in Berlin, returned to Harvard to take his Ph. D. In 1889 he was appointed an instructor in Philosophy at Harvard, and except for two interruptions, he served the University for twenty-two years. He spent 1896–97 in study at King's College, Cambridge, England, and during the winter of 1905–06, he was Hyde lecturer at the Sorbonne, in Paris. His professional advancement was surprisingly slow: he did not become an assistant professor until 1898, and not until both Royce and Münsterberg advocated his promotion. A professorship was not given him until 1907. In part this was due to the neglect of those in authority at Harvard, and in part to Santayana's retiring and modest disposition. He had a preference for solitude; during his early years he had adopted solipsism— the belief that he was the only soul alive. Resigning from Harvard in 1911, he went abroad, to live, however, chiefly in university towns, as if his spirit craved academic and humanistic surroundings—if no more than the silent spires of Oxford, the meadows of Cambridge, or the ruins of Rome.

With all his reading over the years in philosophy and literature, it is remarkable that Santayana has not taken refuge, after the fashion of most academic humanists who instinctively hate science because they fear it, in some traditional evasion of the world of fact. Perhaps the consciousness that the American university teacher of arts and letters is conspicuously an escapist has determined for Santayana his position, for he has deliberately and notoriously avoided most of the marks of his profession. The popular lecturer to Radcliffe girls has had somehow to be more virile than the average academician, and how better than in his philosophy? Consequently there is a masculine gusto in his acceptance of the teachings of science.

"In natural philosophy I am a decided materialist—apparently the only one living," he declares. "I believe there is nothing immortal. . . . No doubt the spirit and energy of the world is acting in us, as the sea is what rises in every little wave; but it passes through us; and cry out as we may, it will move on. Our privilege is to have perceived it as it moved."

And again:

A thorough materialist, one born to the faith, and not half plunged into it by an unexpected christening in cold water, would be like the superb Democritus, a laughing philosopher. His delight in a mechanism that can fall into so many marvellous and beautiful shapes, and can generate so many exciting passions, should be of the same intellectual quality as that which the visitor feels in a museum of natural history, where he views the myriad butterflies in their cases, the flamingoes and shell-fish, the mammoths and gorillas. Doubtless there were pangs in that incalculable life, but they were soon over; and how splendid meantime was the pageant, how infinitely interesting the universal play, and how foolish and inevitable those absolute little passions. Somewhat of that sort might be the sentiment that materialism would arouse in a vigorous mind, active, joyful, impersonal, and in respect to private illusions not without a touch of scorn.

Yet is not here revealed an essentially academic attitude towards life? The adjectives are "vigorous" and "active," but the materialist whom Santayana presents is not in any sense a participant in life—he is merely a passive observer who makes no real connection between the fauna of the museum and his own life. The problem of what is "real" is the crux of Santayana's philosophy. Yet he is explicit enough: ". . . I am a follower of Plato in his doctrine that only knowledge of ideas (if we call it knowledge) can be literal and exact, whilst practical knowledge is necessarily mythical in form, precisely because its object exists and is external from us." Thus while he describes himself as an "ignoramus trusting what he hears from the men of science," it is clear that Santayana looks upon science as a kind of mythology or poetry, the use of which is pure entertainment.

I am quite happy in this human ignorance mitigated by pictures, for it yields practical security and poetic beauty: what more can a sane man want? In this respect I think sometimes I am the only philosopher living: I am resigned to being a mind. I have put my hand into the hand of nature, and a thrill of sympathy has passed from her into my very heart, so that I can instinctively see all things, and see myself from her point of view: a sympathy which emboldens me often to say to her, "Mother, tell me a story." Not the fair Scheherazade herself knew half the marvellous tales that nature spins in the brains of her children. But I must not let go her hand in my wonder, or I might be bewitched and lost in the maze of her inventions.

It is difficult for the critic of Santayana to see what "practical security" is contained either in "ignorance" or in "pictures," and he unfairly suggests that Santayana's resignation in being "a mind" has been practically secured by institutions bent on destroying both ignorance and illusion. Has Santayana clung to the hand of nature, or is his acceptance of science mere pretense, involving no more, for example, than a public declaration that one believes in the *ideas* of Wordsworth's ode, "Intimations of Immortality"? Is Santayana's joyfulness in the cosmic museum genuine or merely affected?

Scattered through his writing are inadvertent glimpses of the world which Santayana privately acknowledges as real but which has no reality in the "dreaming mind" of the philosopher. Thus, though the spectacle of the starry heavens, "the incomprehensible multiplicity of worlds," is immensely impressive to Santayana, he admits it may even be "intensely disagreeable." Contrasting literature, music, and science, he incautiously affirms that science discloses "the bleak anatomy of existence." The materialist who accepts mechanism as a complete explanation of the universe will not worship the universe, he tells us, "but his delight will be rather in the clear things of the imagination, in the humanities, by which the rude forces of nature are at once expressed and *eluded*." And whoever embodies his ideals in part or for a season has transfigured, for Santayana, the "fatal process" of life into "a liberal art." "A free mind," he asserts (at the same time defining anything but a free mind), "like a creative imagination, rejoices at the harmonies it can find *or make* between man and nature; and where it finds none, it solves the conflict so far as it may and *then notes and endures it with a shudder.*" Where, in these utterances, is the disciple of Democritus, the happy spectator of flamingoes and shell-fish, the contented mind absorbed in the poetic beauty of the universe? Santayana is not an exception among the Naturalists: his pessimism is as fundamental as Flaubert's despite his farraginous "symbols" and "essences," despite his verbal raptures, despite his vigorous whistling in the dark.

If Santayana were not a pessimistic determinist, he would allow for some freedom of the will—his dreaming mind might choose (as it does in fact) the spectacles for its delight. But the will, he says, is a peculiarly American delusion: in his famous attack on August 25, 1911, before the Philosophical Union, at the University of California, "The Genteel Tradition in American Philosophy," Santayana lashed out at the doctrine of self-reliance in Emerson and at the pragmatism of William James, both equally dependent on the will. Above the will Santayana places the intellect, which, on his analysis, would appear to be little more than a perpetually open shutter to a capriciously focused camera. "I am resigned to being a mind." If the sole reason for existence is cinema-attendance, one can see little virtue in Santayana's insistence on clinging to reality. Why not be completely bewitched in the maze of Mother Nature's inventions?

The inconsistency at the very core of Santayana's philosophy deprives it of much value as a system, but it does not rob his writings of the things for which they are chiefly prized—gifts of phrase which open vistas and glamorously distract attention from the argument, and flashes of intuition which make us forget even the exquisite character of the prose. If one is content to disregard the vain effort at systematization and will browse, either in the five volume *Life of Reason* or in the completed volumes of the *Realms of Being,* he will discover some of the most profitable and entertaining reading in the language—or better yet, if he i incapable of picking bright diamonds out of mica, let him turn to Logan Pearsall Smith's *Little Essays Drawn from the Writings of George Santayana,* and be similarly rewarded. Misled long ago by his doctoral study of the moral idealist, Lotze, into making a somewhat similar attempt to reconcile science and imagination by crediting them both with validity in the life of nature, Santayana is essentially a humanist with a Renaissance passion for beauty, music, art, and poetry. Had he lived in Italy before Bacon or Galileo, he would never have given nature a thought, save as an ornament to man, and today it most frequently appears in his writing in the brilliant emblazonry of that servitude. Not really at home in our era, he has done his best work in criticism, thus profiting by his detachment. He has the early Renaissance affection for the Greeks; one can understand why Homer, Lucretius, and Dante are his idols, and why Goethe, Whitman, and Browning are offensive to him. His best criticism is found in his destructive analyses of various German thinkers, cf British Idealism, of the "New Physics," and in his appreciation of Democritus, Dante, and Spinoza. His least palatable work is found in *Character and Opinion in the United States* (1920) where his patronizing of Royce and James—even if they deserve it—reflects as much upon the author as upon his victims. His book on aesthetics, *The Sense of Beauty* (1896), extravagantly puffed by his friend Münsterberg, has its good passages, like all his writing, yet it is very much itself in the genteel tradition.

Holding poetry one of the highest manifestations of the life of reason and himself much occupied with poetic theory and the poetry of others, Santayana is the author of four volumes of verse: *Sonnets and Other Verses* (1894), *Lucifer; a Theological Tragedy* (1899), *A Hermit of Carmel and Other Poems* (1901), and *Poems (Selected)* (1922). The early poet was about equally interested in Lucretius, Petrarch, and the medieval Tennyson. All trace of this third influence is obliterated in the selected poems. Santayana's verse is lucid and musical without being distinguished. Its best quality is its paganism. One prefers, however, Petronius and Lucretius to most of their modern imitators. Although his verses do not embody his philosophy, there is no point of inconsistency here. The Renaissance man—warrior, sculptor, architect—invariably wrote verses with borrowed or traditional ideology. And some of them—Bandello, Sidney, Lyly —wrote both poetry and novels in this manner.

The publication of a novel by a distinguished philosopher is so rare an event that when Scribner issued Santayana's *The Last Puritan: A Memoir in the Form of a Novel,* in 1936, the book was eagerly snatched up and read. Many to whom the philosophy had proved difficult perhaps hoped for a short cut in the novel to the ideas of the thinker. And, to be sure, there is a modicum of Santayana in *The Last Puritan,* yet the book is less philosophical than *The Magic Mountain* or the *Buddenbrooks* of Thomas Mann. The author's chief model probably was Samuel Butler's naturalistic novel, *The Way of All Flesh,* itself a more thoughtful book than *The Last Puritan.*

The story is an attempt to explain, on the basis of inheritance, the unhappy career of wealthy, virtuous Oliver Alden, who went to an early death in the First World War, after having exhausted apparently all that life held for him. In the words of the author, his hero "was the child of an elderly and weary man, and of a thin spun race; from his mother he got only his bigness and athleticism, which notoriously doesn't wear well. A moral nature burdened and over-strung, and a critical faculty fearless but helplessly subjective—isn't that the true tragedy of your ultimate Puritan?" The author begins his tale by paying deference, after the manner of Zola, to a biological superstition—that one's son resembles one's brother more than he does one's self; consequently we are introduced to Nathaniel Alden, Oliver's desiccated uncle, before we meet his father, Peter, who has no discernible Puritan traits. Nathaniel (whom we do not meet again, the author's point having been made) is guardian of Peter and trustee of his fortune till he 'comes of age. The fortune had been made by the grandfather in Boston tenement rents, uncertain and miserable payments wrung from the poor. Peter is more of a character out of Barrie—"bad in a nice way": sent eventually to Harvard, he breaks into the chapel to purloin the College Bible as an initiation "stunt" commanded by a secret society; caught by the night watchman, he brings the heavy book down on the latter's head, killing him instantly. Wealth and influence free Peter from all legal charges, yet he is at once sent abroad in the care of a tutor, thus beginning his life-long wanderings. At thirty-five, fancying himself neurasthenic, he entrusts himself to the care of Dr. Bumstead, of Great Falls, Connecticut, whose bouncing daughter Harriet snares him for a husband. Peter refashions the Bumstead mansion, but after his only son Oliver is born, returns to his yacht, his far journeyings, and his opium dreams. In thus presenting Oliver Alden's forebears, Santayana awakens our first doubt as to his accuracy: Is the complacent Harriet of so little account in determining the character of her son? The author is flagrantly in error about Oliver's intelligence; that he has any critical faculty is pure assertion. Did not the real Oliver possess some of his mother's self-esteem until events shook him up? The truth is, Oliver is a perfect neuter—the result of combining in equal parts the acid of the Alden and the alkali of the Bumsteads.

Oliver's career is adumbrated in Santayana's explanation. A born athlete, the boy goes in for football, track, and rowing wholly out of a sense of duty to the schools which he attends. After making the lone touchdown for Williams in the game with Harvard, Oliver is less moved by victory than is Alonzo Stagg with his forty years of football; he explains (and there is no pretense of modesty) that circumstances merely connived for his triumph. And he is equally unaffected, when, having transferred to Harvard, he is defeated as a member of the crew on the Thames by Yale. The Puritan man of action—Prynne, Cromwell, Endicott—was a man of powerful emotion, and if Oliver is an unnatural American youth, he at least is no Puritan. When the United States entered the Great War, Oliver quite properly enlists but is wholly miserable as a soldier. Santayana is vague as to the reasons for this, though he does indicate Oliver's ill health as a contributing factor. Now the effort to make the World Safe for Democracy was perhaps the last expression of American Puritanism, from one point of view; and if Oliver had been a thorough-going Puritan, he would have embarked on this enterprise with the sanguinism of a Wilson, or as a pacifist, would have as violently opposed our participation in the conflict. Such a repre-

sentation would have given especial significance to Santayana's
title, yet he, drawing from a model whom he does not understand, represents Oliver as merely bewildered and unhappy. One
concludes that the real Oliver presented psychological problems
that Santayana does not appreciate.

The "true tragedy" of Oliver is his inability to make anyone
love him for himself. Neither father nor mother cares very much
for him. On his part, he forms a great admiration for two other
young men, Jim Darnley, the dashing captain of his father's yacht,
a fellow wholly without moral scruples, and Mario Van de
Weyer, a younger cousin who, through the grace of an Italian
mother and an education abroad, is a true Latin and a natural
man—witty, seductive, and charming. To Santayana Oliver is
something of a fool for his worship of "Lord Jim" Darnley
who flatters him for the millions he can dispense, but Mario is
all that Oliver should, yet cannot, be. Why Oliver is less of a fool
for admiring Mario is not clear, for beneath his polish Mario is
as predatory an animal as "Lord Jim." He is no more scrupulous
in his use of Oliver than is the sailor man, and at the end of the
book professes an utter contempt for him. Mario, in contrast to
Oliver, is splendidly drawn, but we do not fancy Santayana's
beau idéal. He puts his own philosophy in a sentence at the outbreak of the Great War: "If you're a man you must be ready to
fight every other man and to make love to every pretty woman."
We do not wonder later that Mario suggests to Santayana the
spirit of the new Italy (where Santayana has recently resided)
any more than we do that he has become a Knight of Malta, having progressed from gallantry to chivalry, and from chivalry to
religion—when it proved convenient. The charming Mario tells
us as much about Santayana as any of his books of philosophy.

There are two women in Oliver's life as well as two men: his
cousin Edith, really much more of a humbug than Oliver, who,
catching a vision of what life with him would be, refuses him for
a handsome rector; and Rose Darnley, Jim's sister, who, with the
same clairvoyance, also turns him down. That they could not love
Oliver is plausible, but that they should have resisted his millions,
his good looks, and his athletic renown a little taxes the credulity,
since both girls, not altogether plausibly, are represented as being

equally materialistic and sophisticated. The one person in the world who probably entertained some affection for Oliver was his tutoress, Fräulein Irma Schlote, whom Santayana introduces primarily (as we know from his criticism) to emphasize the Nordic element in Oliver's training. Yet in Santayana's analysis, a love of Goethe is about all that Oliver and Fräulein Schlote have in common. He forgets, however, the importance of this inculcation of Teuton Romantic Idealism in his later handling of Oliver. Emphasis on this element would have changed the portrait to a closer approximation of the real Oliver, but *that* Oliver was not wholly a Puritan.

Despite the fact that the drawing of Oliver is a complete failure, *The Last Puritan* has, besides the portrait of Mario, points of excellence. The more minor the character, with this exception, the better is he drawn. Oliver's uncle, Nathaniel, is superbly done, and the crab-like mystic Caleb Wetherbee is at least memorable. Harriet Bumstead, representative of thousands of uninteresting women, emerges from the thousands as interesting. And there are felicities of phrasing in the book which are a delight to the reader. The best thing in *The Last Puritan,* however, is the remarkable letters which Fräulein Schlote writes home—letters thoroughly in character and so delightful that we wish the epistolary method of narration, the invention of Richardson, were not wholly out of fashion. A *novella,* even an imperfect one, or a formidably bulky one (contradiction of terms!), is not an altogether unhappy addition to the work of the most conspicuous modern humanist.

Possessed, like Santayana, of that refinement that borders on pure aestheticism (a rare quality among Naturalists), Gamaliel Bradford was the most devoted follower of Sainte-Beuve whom that great Frenchman has had among the users of English. It is a mistake, as Gertrude Richards pointed out, to compare Gamaliel Bradford with Lytton Strachey—there is "no connection between their aims, method, or finished work." In Bradford's intimate journal the entry which records his reading of Strachey's *Queen Victoria* records also his despair: "Nothing that I can possibly do can ever come near it." And nothing that Bradford ever did approaches the brilliant performance of that subtle, sophisticated, and intellectually dissolute Englishman. For Bradford aimed at sympathetic penetration into the souls of his subjects—not at objective analyses of their foibles and limitations. He was appreciative—too much so—even compassionate towards the persons whom he sought to portray. Benedict Arnold, Aaron Burr, *et al.* are not "damned souls," he mildly insisted, but "damaged souls." "I can't help hoping that every one of them has just a wee chance of heaven." By his willingness to appear as devil's advocate for those characters who had been condemned by past standards, Bradford gained a position for himself in the "new" literary movement, but not in the "new biography."

One limitation Bradford never overcame—he knew nothing of active life. A frail child, he was able, because of the affluence of his father, a Boston banker, to indulge himself in ill-health, and that indulgence became a habit in which real and fancied pain vied in tormenting the neurotic. His mother, a daughter of Henry W. Kinsman, of Newburyport, Daniel Webster's partner, died of tuberculosis when her small son was only three, and the haunting fear which Gamaliel's father had that the disease would claim his boy was responsible for sending the child to Washington in the winter to escape the inclement weather and to the Adirondacks and Wellesley Hills in the summer. A persistent cough rewarded the lad with a trip to Southern Europe. Some sort of nervous breakdown forced abandonment of the plan to secure a Harvard degree, and Bradford withdrew from the college in his freshman year. If allowed to follow his own inclination, he would have written poetry, but the father, insisting on a more practical preparation for life, tried to teach him the "ins" of banking. This program was given over in 1882, and Gamaliel Bradford was allowed to pursue his heart's desire—a career in letters, the father having lost hope that his son had long to live. But half a century sped away before death claimed its long-intended victim, on April 11, 1932, in a home where he had been safeguarded and tenderly watched during his intermittent illnesses by his wife, the former Miss Helen Ford, whom he married in 1886.

It was not until 1914 that Bradford employed the literary form—the "psychograph"—which gave him contemporary fame.

Between the time he quit his father's office and the latter date, however, he wrote voluminously, but published comparatively little and that inconsequential in a final estimate of the man. He found himself in neither prose nor verse, in neither the novel nor the drama. Many critics have pitched upon his *Lee the American* (1912), the volume which brought him from obscurity, as the thing marking the beginning of his typical work, but *Confederate Portraits* two years later seems more worthy of that designation. *Lee the American* is a chronological biography, more suggestive of the performance of William Roscoe Thayer, popular biographer with whom he was intimate and whose success may have influenced Bradford to try the field of biography. Certain it is that Bradford's forte was not the full-length portrait; *Lee the American* was easily superseded by Douglas Freeman's *R. E. Lee, a Biography* (1935) and Bradford's four other long studies, *A Portrait of General George Gordon Meade* (1915), *The Soul of Samuel Pepys* (1924), *Darwin* (1926), and *D. L. Moody, a Worker in Souls* (1927), though marked by his later manner, are not indispensable, so far as their subjects are concerned.

Confederate Portraits is the beginning of an effort to do something different from the conventional, chronological study of a man. It is an attempt to produce the "bare soul" (Sainte-Beuve's phrase) of the person selected for study. This unriddling of the self Bradford achieved by a process of distillation, gathering the revelatory sentences or phrases by going through "an enormous waste of material." He prided himself, with much justice, on his ability to select the precise thing which should send a beam of light out of his man as one would catch the right angle for the highest iridescence of a gem. "I remember how impressed Thayer was, when he was working on *Cavour*," Bradford confided to his *Journal*, "with my picking out with an hour's casual reading that magnificent phrase, *Je suis fils de la liberté, et c'est à elle que je dois tout ce que je suis.* Thayer put it into his book, and I believe he got it from me." Out of many hours of reading, Bradford distilled the "magnificent" phrases which he carefully fused together to form what, in an essay in *The Literary Review* for April 28, 1923, he designated as a "psychograph." How meticulously the selection and joining were done the annotations clearly show.

Yet, with all Bradford's conscientiousness there is a deep gulf between his "psychographs" and the studies on which he frankly admitted they were modeled—the *Causeries du Lundi* of Sainte-Beuve. No doubt whatever that Sainte-Beuve also pored over enormous wastes of material in his search for the precious, revealing phrase—both men were prodigious readers, but Sainte-Beuve was a man of the world as well as a scholar—he brought a knowledge of life to the handling of the phrases which he culled. The great weakness of Bradford is that he produces his men and women without relation to time and space; the "psychographs" glow, to be sure, but the rays they emit are as frosty as the wink of an ether-hung star. Fancy treating St. Francis of Assisi without any knowledge of the Middle Ages, Casanova without displaying the decadence of Italy, and Lenin without embroiling him in the Revolution. Yet this is what Bradford did. He ranged far —from Pericles to Henry Ford—but he could do this because he did not work up the background for his characters. Contemplating them as timeless phenomena, he fixed no responsibilities upon them—he never judged them. Turn to that famous stricture in the *Causeries* upon Voltaire—"Voltaire was pleased to regard men as fools or children, and had not humor enough to laugh at them; he put loaded fire-arms into their hands without troubling himself as to the use they might make of them"—and you have a precise illustration of the element most wanting in Bradford's "psychographs." His characters are all essences, "souls," not *philosophes,* revolutionaries, mystics, enthusiasts, traitors. The aoristic tendency of Bradford's mind is further illustrated by the fact that, when he chose to experiment with the dialogued sketch in *The Haunted Biographer* (1927), the *Imaginary Conversations* of Landor satisfied him as models though the lively *Heavenly Discourses* of C.E.S. Wood would have shown him the way to make his chatter relevant to contemporary life.

If there is in the roll of Bradford's volumes of psychography and about psychography (sixteen books in all, of which *Damaged Souls,* 1923, is the best) no one title which positively assures him of immortality, *The Journal* (1933) edited by Van Wyck Brooks accomplishes the highest reach of his ambition. It is a truly great book. "My pursuit of psychography," he noted down on July 29, 1916, ". . . gives me a feeling that I should like to leave documents which would be of service to a succeeding psychographer." Though *The Letters* (1934) solicit the attention of the future analyst of this man, it is doubtful if they supply any such incentive as *The Journal*—only a small portion of which has been published. Through it is perceived the highly sensitive, complex organism and the questioning intelligence which were Gamaliel Bradford. Here, on the one hand, is the troubled invalid and neurotic—the victim of terrifying attacks of vertigo and of new disorders, like "chromophobia," that were the product of his imagination. And here, on the other, is displayed the critic who is so conspicuously absent in the vignettes that he drew of other men. For example, as he read he noted that Dreiser's *An American Tragedy* gives a greater sense of reality than any novel by Edith Wharton, that Henry Adams was a playboy, that the Goncourts were limited in temperament. . . . The pungency of his comments indicates that, could he have broadened his experience, he should have followed Sainte-Beuve into the field of criticism, going beyond the men to their works, in order to employ to best advantage his genius. As it is, one can heartily endorse Burton Rascoe's recommendation of *The Journal* to the young as an "education in taste," and to the old, who believe their lives difficult, as "a record or perseverance and fortitude and accomplishment in spite of the most terrific handicaps."

Of all the American intellectuals who have espoused Naturalism, Pearl Buck is the one writer whose literary origins can with least certainty be traced back to France. In her Nobel lecture, *The Chinese Novel,* delivered before the Swedish academy at Stockholm, on December 12, 1938, without denying the influence of other literatures upon her, she affirmed that she was born and reared in the tradition of the Chinese novel, a tradition which teaches that the paramount object of the novelist is the entertainment of the common people. So simple a purpose might seem to exclude the possibility of any shading of pessimism, save that the folk have always been fond of the lugubrious, as witness many an

English ballad. Examination of *All Men Are Brothers* (1933), Mrs. Buck's translation of *Shui Hu Chuan,* reveals many similarities between Mrs. Buck's work and at least one Chinese novel, particularly on the score of simplicity and affected artlessness, qualities given to that book not merely because it was intended for the people but because one of its makers, Shih Nai-an, pretends that life is too short for a novelist to care whether a work is done well or ill. There is, then, in the tradition which Mrs. Buck cites a note of defeatism perhaps adequate to cover all that exists in Mrs. Buck's writings, and we might choose to regard her work as an accidental contribution to the main stream of Naturalism. To accept this explanation for the naturalistic elements in the author's novels, however, is to assume her too oblivious to the European tradition with which she has some affinity, too oblivious for credence when the lady's awareness of other things in the contemporary world is taken into account. Shall we posit, then, that at some formative period in her career she was attracted to the French Naturalists or their disciples?

Yet when? Though she was born Pearl Sydenstricker, of Dutch and Huguenot French extraction, in Hillsboro, Tennessee, on June 26, 1892, practically her whole life, before she became well known, was passed in China, where her parents were missionaries. In 1917, she was married to another American missionary, John Lossing Buck, and had five harrowing years in North China, undergoing famine, pestilence, and bandit raids, before her husband accepted a position as head of the farm management department of Nanking University. Later, after she and her family had escaped the Communist terror in Nanking, Mrs. Buck, who had taught English literature prior to the rising, became a teacher in the same subject in the National South-eastern University. She continued to reside in Nanking until after *The Good Earth* (1931) had made her famous. Coming to the United States, she divorced her missionary husband and married Richard J. Walsh, president of the John Day Company, her publishers, in 1935. But long before this there was an important interlude in her Chinese experience—when she was seventeen, she came to America to attend Randolph-Macon College, where she not only was popular with her fellows, being elected president of her class, but also was distinguished for her literary accomplishment. Is it not possible that a knowledge of Zola dates from that interlude?

Certainly there are aspects of Mrs. Buck's trilogy—*The Good Earth* (1931), *Sons* (1932), and *A House Divided* (1935)—which strongly suggest Zola. Here is a complete history of the Wang family for several generations, a family as typical of contemporary China, we judge, as was the Rougon-Macquart family of France of 1848–1870. It is a sensual history, too, of loving, of breeding, and of death. Behind the rise of the Wangs is one man's greed for the earth, just as, behind the rise of Zola's family was the greed of Madame Félicité Rougon. Of course Mrs. Buck displays her family against a feudal-contemporary background, while Zola selected the Second Empire as his backdrop, but one has only to compare her treatment of Wang the Merchant and Wang the Landlord with her portraits of Wang the Farmer and Wang the Tiger to realize that for the nonce Mrs. Buck is nearly as hostile towards the trader class as was Zola. Bickering relatives and their quarrels, a throbbing passion for the soil, and other elements, as well as similarity in titles unite *The Good Earth* and *La Terre*. The thickness of the world between does not so much separate Zola and Mrs. Buck as does temperament; one is excitable and voluble, the other, dispassionate and controlled. The difference shows up most in style, however; not in their convictions about life. Mrs. Buck's writing is simple and unaffected—Zola's is, as we have seen, something different with every mood.

The Good Earth is not only the best book in the trilogy; it is also the best book that Pearl Buck has written. In Wang Lung, Mrs. Buck created a character more meaningful, probably, to Asiatics, who place farmers second only to officials and before artisans and traders, than to Americans. She looks upon his struggle upwards from a meagre beginning and against flood, drouth, and the invasions of robbers and insects with Oriental approval. It is only after the Wangs quit the land that confusion, degeneracy, and decay begin. In *A House Divided,* which might be regarded as Mrs. Buck's *La Débâcle,* this theme is deliberately pointed up by a quotation allegedly from Ch'ao Tso, an early Chinese essayist on agriculture, to the effect that tilling the soil leads to all the virtues, whilst leaving the land leads to crime. The seeds for the downfall of the Wangs, however, are sown by Wang Lung as surely as are the acorns of their prosperity. *The Good Earth* is not merely a study of Wang Lung's rise into a landed proprietor, but it is also his amatory history. For after Wang Lung became prosperous, he tired of his soil-wife, O-lan, who had been through every adversity with him, and he took him first a painted lady, named Lotus, out of a tea-house, and then, in his old age, a little serving girl, called Pear Blossom. But Lung's third son, Wang the Tiger, whom he had always intended for the soil, so that the family fortunes should be rooted in the land, had secretly worshipped Pear Blossom, and his father's conquest of her provoked him to break away and join the army of a war-lord. Thus no one of the Wangs truly clove to the sod, though Pear Blossom and Wang Lung's half-witted daughter take residence, after his death, in the earth house where he began, to symbolize ironically the barrenness of that dwelling. Indeed, Mrs. Buck misses none of the possible connections of things in pointing her moral. The great merit of *The Good Earth,* however, is the conviction it carries of verisimilitude to all the vicissitudes of Chinese life— nothing changes or passes which does not seem probable. And particularly well done is the portrait of O-lan whose loyalty to her lord never wavered. Earth of the earth-earthy, she triumphs in the end over her rivals, though her ugliness goes clear to the bone.

The excellence of *The Good Earth* prejudiced the probable success of its sequels. *Sons* is, of course, a study of three lesser men than lusty Wang Lung: a merchant, a rent collector, and a war-lord—the last, the scowling black son of the founder of the family who ran away. Focalized on this brother, Wang the Tiger, whom the other two finance to their advantage, the book is probably accurate enough so far as it is a history of a mercenary chieftain, but it is only moderately interesting as fiction. *A House Divided* follows the youthful career of Wang Yuan, son of the Tiger, who rebelled against the rule of his father, as the Tiger had rebelled before him. Yuan belongs to the new generation in China: he is the student his father wished to be, but he is also a revolutionary and a partial imitator of things European. Yet all of this is a veneer. Fundamentally he has the same pull towards the soil as had his grandfather. When he and his cousin Sheng are arrested as Communists and rescued by his step-mother (who pays an enormous sum for his release), they are sent off to America to be out of harm's way. But there Yuan studies scientific agriculture to be of use to his country after the revolution. He returns to China to fall in love with a modern Chinese girl, to become disillusioned with political revolution, to reach an understanding pity for the senile war-lord, and to contemplate a new attachment to the earth. Mrs. Buck, however, is not satisfied with this straightaway development of her theme. She is also interested in convincing Americans that the Chinese are susceptible to culture; consequently we are given more than an adequate view of the modern home of Yuan's foster-mother and half-sister, are shown all the Wang relatives who move with ease in the cosmopolitan society of a large Chinese city, and we are allowed to follow Yuan to America, not merely that we may suffer a deserved rebuke for the racial hostility displayed towards him, but also to get a comparative estimate of his worth, for he leads his class in college and an American girl throws herself at him. We may praise the author for her crusading liberalism, but we must acknowledge that it makes her novel diffuse and chaotic.

Communism, which deluded Wang Yuan, makes the wheels go round in a novelette, *The Young Revolutionist* (1932), which Pearl Buck published immediately after *The Good Earth*. Ko-sen, the only child of a farmer, is promised to the Temple by his father, if he is cured of a dreadful fever. Becoming a temple-boy, Ko-sen hates religion as his prison-house, and when he makes his escape with another boy, naturally joins the revolutionary army after he hears a Communist orator denounce religion. He and Fah-li, his comrade, are used as shock troops with numberless other young men. Following a battle attended by great carnage among these boys, Ko-sen hunts for his lost and sorely wounded Fah-li, waits for him during the torturous hours of his lingering death in a Christian hospital, feels his antipathy towards all religions melt away in his respect for this foreign faith, and returns to the farm from which he came. Admirable as is Mrs. Buck's attempt to attribute the conversion of Chinese youth to Communism to their ignorance (and thus forgive them for the hardship they had caused her and her family), her plea probably will not do for the rank and file who (as she recognizes elsewhere) have a genuine grievance against foreign missionaries as well as against their own priests. The inherent sentimentalism in *The Young Revolutionist* flaunts its colors boldly in *The Mother* (1934), story of a nameless peasant woman, meant to be typical of all Chinese women of her class, who, unfortunately for her, challenges comparison with O-lan of *The Good Earth,* beside whom she seems a literary abstraction. Mrs. Buck's pity for her sex, present in all her books (despite the denial seemingly afforded by the controversial article, "America's Medieval Women"), here approaches the mawkish. Two volumes of short stories, *The First Wife and Other Stories* (1933) and *Today and Forever* (1941), repeat with new emphasis themes found in her longer works, while an effort to employ an American setting for a novel, in *This Proud Heart* (1938), resulted in the most unhappy production of Pearl Buck's career.

The Patriot (1939), however, kept Mrs. Buck in favor with the novel-reading critics. This again is the story of a Chinese youth, I-wan, son of a leading banker of Shanghai and grandson of a general under the Emperor, who is persuaded to become a revolutionist. In danger of arrest and execution when Chiang Kai-shek, contrary to the expectations of the Party, purges the city, I-wan is packed off to Japan to take refuge with Mr. Muraki, a merchant friend of his father. Despite the prospect of a war between the two countries, I-wan, having fallen in love with the daughter of his host, Tama, gains the consent of her parents to their marriage. In the perfect felicity of his married life I-wan forgets the plight of his country and almost forgets that he is Chinese. Then a clear call comes to him to go back to the homeland to defend it against the Japanese invader. Leaving behind his wife, who understands that he is only doing his duty and who will teach his small sons to respect him, I-wan returns to China to serve under Chiang Kai-shek and to become the latter's instrument in augmenting his armies by securing cooperation from the Communist forces in the North.

The Patriot is admirable for at least two things: it treats with perfect impartiality both the Japanese and the Chinese, and it handles Communism more plausibly than Mrs. Buck had been able to do in her earlier books. I-wan lives long enough in Japan to appreciate all the admirable traits of the island people—their gentleness, gaiety, love of order, and obedience to the Emperor. Through the transformation effected in the lovable Bunji, once he is drafted into the army and gradually accepts the German philosophy of the military caste, I-wan sees who are the true enemies of his people, and over one of these enemies, General Seki, he secures a personal victory in the contest for Tama's hand. But the Japanese are no more susceptible to the poison of the power philosophy as individuals than are the Chinese. After I-wan returns to China, Chiang Kai-shek executes as a proved traitor I-wan's older brother, I-ko, who, educated in Germany, admired too much the efficiency of the Japanese machine and sold out his comrades to it. That some of the Japanese totally disapprove of the policies of the military clique is shown in the suicide of Aiko and his wife after the former had been called for service in China.

I-wan became a Communist in a strange fashion. Arrested with other students in a round-up merely because he was reading Karl Marx, he was released from jail as soon as it was known whose son he was; but he insisted on the release also of a cellmate who had captivated his fancy—one En-lan, a University student and peasant doctrinaire. Having decided to attend the University, I-wan is introduced into a secret group of revolutionists by En-lan and soon becomes one of the most enthusiastic workers. His particular assignment is to prepare certain factory laborers for a general strike in anticipation of the arrival of Chiang Kai-shek who will surely overturn the government. En-lan, from his better acquaintance with life, tries to persuade his friend not to expect a millennium, but I-wan is too much the impetuous idealist. When Chiang "betrays" the revolution, I-wan is disillusioned. He also fears that, through a blunder of his, En-lan has been caught and slain. After his hegira, however, when he has been convinced that through Chiang Kai-shek the Japanese will be expelled and China set free, he is rejoiced to find En-lan still alive and commander in the North of an important contingent of Communist soldiery

En-lan's decision to aid the Chinese generalissimo is made too much the result of I-wan's persuasion, perhaps, and not enough of Marxist opportunism; otherwise the treatment of the whole revolutionary issue is mature and realistic. There is memorable writing in the book, scenes in which national and racial differences are treated with proper comprehension of the hidden hurts beneath the surface gloss and suavity, earthquake and tidal wave in Japan are described without melodrama, but the one thing most likely to haunt the reader is the silent, accusing face of the Communist girl student who loved I-wan, turned towards him as she was dragged from the classroom to the execution which he escaped.

To the field of biography Pearl Buck has contributed two volumes, *The Exile* (1936) and *Fighting Angel* (1936), adumbrated portraits of her missionary parents. Carie, the wife, is a genius of resourcefulness and "spunk." Her American garden under an equatorial sun in a Chinese town far up the Yangtze River is a miracle of the kind commonplace to Carie: When a daughter had diphtheria she went into a brothel to capture a dissolute doctor, pushed a strumpet off his knee, and rushed him off to administer anti-toxin. The author is harsher towards the father, Andrew, native of West Virginia, scion of "the preachingest family in Greenbrier County, with dissenting blood as strong as lye." But Andrew plainly was a rather formidable person, utterly, if not fanatically, devoted to his cause, as blind to the small results his work produced as he was oblivious to the discomfort and pain he caused his family. Joined, the books suggest that the missionary movement has hardly stimulated in the Chinese great enthusiasm for either Americans or Christianity. Mrs. Buck, critic of the movement in *Is There a Case for Foreign Missions?* (1932) for its effort at rigid indoctrination and its lack of appreciation of native needs or culture, broke with her church on this issue. Aside from their relation to the controversy over foreign missions, Mrs. Buck's biographies reveal that her Naturalism, like that of many another Naturalist, is possibly a product of a revolt against the dogmatic discipline of her youth.

When Mrs. Buck became the third American to receive the Nobel Prize for literature, the whole literary fraternity raised its eyebrows. The award was a "political" award, and Mrs. Buck did well to disclaim that she deserved it—it should have gone to Theodore Dreiser. But to reflective Americans outside the fraternity, to the "barbs" at least, the prize seemed well given as a reminder that pure aestheticism is not everything in letters. If the standard of her work was not so uniformly high as that of a few other craftsmen, what she wrote had universal appeal and a comprehensibility not too frequently matched. How many other books about Asia, not sensational like Ossendowski, are as readable as is *The Good Earth?*

Naturalism started in France with the affirmation that man could be studied as an animal is studied, that he is entirely the product of forces which work upon him. Naturalism in America has been much strengthened by the very positive reassertion of these views by the Behaviorist, Professor John B. Watson. A native of Greenville, South Carolina, and educated at Furman University and Chicago, Watson made important experimental studies with animals in the laboratories of the latter school, publishing his results in *Animal Education* (1903). He has served as professor of experimental and comparative psychology at Johns Hopkins University (1908–1920) and since as lecturer in the New School of Social Research, in New York City. More than any other man, save William James, he has given psychology the tremendous prestige it enjoys in this country.

When Watson began his experiments with animals, he worked under the influence of the British psychologist, C. Lloyd Morgan, whose books, *An Introduction to Comparative Psychology* (1894) and *Animal Behavior* (1900), insisted on the importance of knowing every step in any act before interpreting it, and on the importance of the trial and error method in animal learning. E. L. Thorndike, an American animal psychologist, was the first person in this country to take up and to continue Morgan's experiments. Others followed, and the studies in the learning of animals were soon supplemented by studies in the learning of humans. Yet there was no generalization of all this laboratory work before the publication of Professor Watson's three highly important studies, "Psychology as a Behaviorist Views It" (1913), "Image and Affection in Behavior" (1913), and *Be-*

haviorism—An Introduction to Comparative Psychology (1914). What stands at the present as a final statement of his views, and those of his school, may be found in the volume called *Behaviorism,* published in 1925, although *The Ways of Behaviorism* (1927) is later in date.

In his early papers Professor Watson has all the exuberance of a Taine making his first statement of the effect of natural forces upon literary criticism and history. This exuberance persists, however, in *Behaviorism,* written more than a decade later, which may properly be described as one of the most sanguinary volumes ever produced in this country. Behaviorism, Watson tells us, closes the gap between the physical, chemical, and psychological worlds. It has driven all the philosophers to cover, so that philosophy is "gradually disappearing and becoming the history of science." It is replacing religion with "experimental ethics." It has punctured such absurd notions as "consciousness," "soul," "will," and so on. The conquest of the whole universe apparently lies ahead of it. Professor Watson's boundless enthusiasm for his subject was infectious: shortly after his first papers appeared those busy lecturers, the professional educators, took up his ideas and spread them broadcast over the country. In 1925, George A. Dorsey's book, *Why We Behave Like Human Beings,* one of the best-selling, and incidentally one of the liveliest books of nonfiction, carried the ideas of the school to the widest possible popular audience.

Behaviorism was launched in 1912 as an attack upon the claim that "consciousness" is the subject matter of psychology; it asserted that the subject matter of human psychology is "the behavior or activities of the human being." After deriding the notion of "consciousness" as merely a substitute for the old religious concept "soul," Watson pointed out that psychologies which started out with this approach were not strictly "scientific," but introspective. That is, "consciousness" cannot be observed, according to his claim, while human activity or behavior can be. If psychology is to be a science, it must abandon introspection for observation, just as the physical and chemical sciences have done. The first step in this direction is to eliminate from the scientific vocabulary all such mediaeval and subjective terms as sensation, perception, image, desire, purpose, thinking, and emotion—a rather clean sweep, the startled elder psychologists had to admit. In the behaviorist vocabulary at the outset only two terms are permissible, "stimulus" and "response," since these cover completely what may be observed. For example, if a rod (the stimulus) is placed in a baby's hand, all that the psychologist can properly report is the closure of the baby's hand on the rod (the response). In this view of things man is an organism constantly assailed by stimuli and responding to these stimuli. Stimuli themselves are not only external but internal, like the presence of food in the stomach, or the quantity of fluid in a gland. Responses are also stimuli, for a muscle tensed is stimulus for another response. The goal of the Behaviorist is to predict absolutely the response to any given stimulus, or from the response to state what the stimulus was which caused the reaction.

In order to achieve his goal the Behaviorist must know a great deal about the human organism. This is a machine as "efficient as a steam engine," which incorporates three kinds of apparatus: the sense organs, the reacting organs, and the nervous system. The sense organs are those containing epithelial cells in which some kind of physical and chemical change takes place when the appropriate stimulus strikes or impinges upon them. This change sets up a neural impulse in the nervous system (in the peripheral nerves, the spinal cord, the brain) which over this internal telegraph is carried to the organs of response, the muscles and the glands. In their laboratories the Behaviorists have done a highly commendable job, apparently, in studying the human machine, particularly the organs of response, for much had been done with the nervous system before they undertook their studies. Perhaps the most startling aspect of the Behaviorist conception of the organism was the reduction of the brain, from the seat of "consciousness," to a sort of automatic central switchboard in the communication system. Thinking, like talking, is muscular response: *"thought is in short nothing but talking to ourselves."* It develops because the child is told, "Don't talk aloud—daddy and mother are not always talking to themselves," and then, "Quit whispering to yourself," and finally, "Can't you even read without moving your lips?" Thus overt speech becomes whispered speech, and whispered speech in turn is reduced into the faintest bodily substitutes for words.

Now, while the Behaviorists have abased man to a mere "reaction mass," to a body without a soul and without a mind, or rather a mind "snared in an unbroken circuit of stimulus and response," their Naturalism appears to have certain aspects which may be regarded with somewhat less pessimism than was the old Naturalism. For example, while the Behaviorists admit there are heritable differences in form and structure, they do not believe that "mental" traits are inherited. Watson throws out the "present conclusions" of the geneticists as based upon "the 'old' and faulty psychology." Thus, if the Behaviorists are right, the whole Rougon-Macquart cycle of Zola is laid upon a false premise. On the other hand, the Behaviorists, relying upon the work of the scientists Pavlov and Bechterew, have asserted that both glandular and muscular responses may be "conditioned," and that stimuli may be "conditioned." By this they mean that a new response to a given stimulus may be learned, or that a substituted stimulus may produce the response which once only a given stimulus would produce. For example, if every time one were given an electric shock, a red light were flashed, one would soon withdraw his hand on the appearance of the red light without the electric shock. Such a response is clearly a "learned response" and the existence of this sort of thing suggests that human behavior may be greatly modified. Particularly have the Behaviorists stressed the early training of the child as a mighty factor in determining his later activity. Thus, while the Behaviorists believe that "man's emotional life is built up bit by bit by the wear and tear of environment upon him," man is not an abject slave to his environment. By choosing the responses he desires, and by substituting stimuli, or *vice versa,* he may make of his child, of himself, of society, what he chooses. The old Naturalism admitted no such freedom.

Yet on reflection (which we are denied, save as a verbal habit) there seems no justification for Professor Watson's optimism. If thought, like talk, is response to stimuli, whence will come the thought to "break" with the stimulus that is harmful? Can either a nightmare dispel itself or a thought exorcise itself by its own power? Behaviorism in this light is determinism with the whole emphasis upon environment, the term "environment" here being extended to include the stimuli-aspects of the automaton itself. When Professor Watson, for example, asserts as a fact that the Russian revolution "has thrown back the intellectual and scientific progress of the Russian people possibly hundreds of years," we may properly inquire if he is not rather helplessly responding to old stimuli, and we may ask how he is ever going to free himself of these stimuli. He cannot *will* to free himself of them since he has no will. Indeed, prejudice would seem to be easier in his conception of thinking than in the old conceptions of reason, judgment, and mind. Only the accident of substituted stimuli can disabuse his "thought" of its prejudices. In this view of man there is little cause for rejoicing.

Perhaps philosophy is not quite so dead as Professor Watson has thought it. It may survive still, not as "the history of science," but rather as *the science of what is possible.* As such it still remains the critic of the systems men build, whether they are poets, novelists,—or Behaviorists. It is *possible* that consciousness or soul (to use the more opprobrious term) still exists, despite an examination of the human mechanism which has not revealed it. Taking a radio apart tells us little about the ether waves which animate it or the broadcasting station from which they emanate. The waves still exist after the box has been pulled to pieces, and it is *possible* that consciousness has somewhat the same intangible relationship to the anatomical and physiological structure as this. Certainly the studies of Watson neither credit nor discredit such an idea. It is one of the oldest superstitions that the soul may be laid bare with a scalpel, and when Watson cuts away the viscera from the muscles of the thorax and exclaims, "See, here is the brain," there is something quaintly mediaeval about him. The ancients were convinced that the soul resided in the breast. When the layman turns from the volume *Behaviorism* with its handsome generalizations to so frankly a popular book of exposition as Alexis Carrel's *Man, the Unknown* (1935), in which the body is described more or less as a floating world, and discovers therein a profound conviction of all that Watson has discarded, the layman may be in no position to decide as to the correctness of either of these gentlemen's views, but he has received a wholesome lesson in caution. He knows that he knows too little about himself to generalize about man as these learned doctors have, and in sustained suspended judgment he is more "scientific" than either of them.

The creative Naturalist who, until very recently, has placed, like Watson, a preponderant emphasis in his fiction upon environment in shaping character and destiny is James T. Farrell, author of the "notorious" trilogy, *Studs Lonigan* (1935), and other books. Farrell, a product of Chicago's South Side, having been born there, September 27, 1904, first drew a portrait of himself as Danny O'Neill, one of the smaller boys in Studs Lonigan's "Fifty-eighth Street gang" in *Young Lonigan* (1932). Though he rubbed out this portrait with his thumb, so to speak, when he began his still unfinished fictional autobiography, the sketch still satisfactorily supplies the essential facts of his early life. Danny is a "punk", an undersized "goofy" lad who wears glasses, yet is tolerated by the gang because of his willingness to "shag" flies and because of his hero-worship of Studs. In this novel, however, there is no indication of private reservations on Danny's part in regard to the activities of his hero or the adolescent brutalities of the gang. The critical faculty in Danny is awakened after he is graduated from St. Cyril High School and has matriculated at the University of Chicago. We meet him then, in *The Young Manhood of Studs Lonigan* (1934), as a youth cleansed by courses in sociology and philosophy, in his educated purity smelling a little "soapy" from the lingering idealism of John Dewey and other saints of the lakeside school.

. . . He remembered himself as a boy, one of the neighborhood goofs. Around the corner he was now more of a goof than ever. His nostalgias for past experiences in the neighborhood seemed to have died too. He hated it all. It was all a part of a dead world; it was filthy; it was rotten; it was stupefying. It, all the world he had known, was mirrored in it. He had been told things, told that the world was good and just, and that the good and just were rewarded, lies completely irrelevant to what he had really experienced; lies covering a world of misery, neuroticism, frustration, impecuniousness, hypocrisy, disease, clap, syphilis, poverty, injustice. . . . He envisioned a better world, a world of ideals such as that the Russians were attempting to achieve. He had to study to prepare himself to create that world. . . . He wanted to be a writer. . . . Some day, he would drive this neighborhood and all his memories of it out of his consciousness with a book. . . .

Some such katharsis of his own consciousness Farrell first attempted with the three volumes of *Studs Lonigan,* but in attempting it, he fixed the grim import of this terrifying case history permanently in the memory of each and every one of his readers. To accomplish this Farrell drew not only upon a fuller knowledge of hoodlum life than that found in *Youth and the City Streets, The Bitter Cry of the Children, The Gang,* or *The Gang Age,* and as easy familiarity with the argot of poolrooms as ever Ring Lardner possessed, but also upon a thorough understanding of what other craftsmen in the realistic field have accomplished in the last three decades, for his trilogy profits from the impressionistic Naturalism of Frank Norris (compare the picture of Old Man Lonigan contentedly smoking his stogy early in *Young Lonigan* with that of McTeague with his pitcher of steam beer), from the brutal directness of speech and action of Erskine Caldwell and Robert Cantwell, from the technical experimentation of John Dos Passos, and from the anti-Catholic revolt of James Joyce. Though Mr. Farrell never quite equalled each of the others in the field of their specialty, his synthesis of their teaching and his experience makes *Studs Lonigan* the ripest example of Naturalism in American literature, or as it has been called, "the most impressive study of degeneration since Zola's *L'Assommoir.*"

Studs, whose real name is William, is the son of a fairly prosperous Irish house-painter and contractor and a narrow, bigoted, devoted, "good" woman whose dearest wish is that he shall enter the priesthood. There is nothing abnormally vicious, however, as with the tainted ancestry of Zola's characters, about Studs' parents, even if they are not intellectual giants. The girl Frances, the delightful nagging sister of Studs whose life runs in a small stream through the pages parallel to his, establishes the fact that a normal lower middle class career was possible for Studs, that environment, rather than heredity, is the determining force in shaping him. We meet him first in the bathroom surreptitiously finishing a cigarette before his graduation from St. Patrick's

grammar school while his sister clamors outside—a meeting symbolical of the trivial violations of school and parental authority
which constitute the beginnings of the downfall of Studs. We
follow him and his parents and sister to the exercises, attend
more carefully than he to the nauseous platitudes of Father Gil-
hooley, and *debouch,* after him, into the long, idle summer vacation which determines his whole future. In this fatal interval he
dons his first long trousers, becomes conscious of the proximity
of girls as girls, gives more attentive ear to the filthy wisdom of
his elders on the street-corners, proves his prowess in battle with
a bigger boy and his right to bully the smaller ones, enjoys the
thrill of having his "wisecracks" laughed at for the first time by
the poolroom gang, chews his first tobacco, masturbates, and
begins a predatory sexual life by being drawn into a "gang shag"
offered by a vicious little female named Iris. Yet this is not the
"story of a bad boy"; it is the story of a normal boy, proud of
his biceps and his chest expansion, diffident and inarticulate before Lucy Scanlon whom he loves, and unperceptive before the
hoydenish, sagacious Helen Shires who loves him and warns him
in vain against the very company he is keeping. Studs Lonigan is
a healthy adolescent whom unemployment and free association
with varying degrees of viciousness corrupt without much volition on his part. *Young Lonigan* may be "clinical," but it is surely
not offensive by being as factual as Professors Allport and
Thrasher, while its defense as fiction is that it lives. Studs Lonigan, whether you like it or not, is in this book as real a character
as Huck Finn—and more portentous.

The Young Manhood of Studs Lonigan, which traces the next
twelve years in Studs' life, is perhaps the most terrifying book
which has been written in America. Yet it merely follows out
logically the path of Studs' spiritual degeneration as indicated in
Young Lonigan. The idle summer grows into an idle year, the
adolescent finding it easy to play truant while his parents presume that he is in high school. When it is discovered that he has
deceived them, the Lonigans force Studs, who is absolutely recalcitrant about school, to go to work for his father at house-
painting—at which he dallies, "killing time" waiting for the evening release to join the poolroom gang. With his gang he is in

the Seventh Heaven—a heaven in which the angels are all
"broads" who are easily "made," in which the harmonies are
vulgarity, profanity, and filth, and in which the virtues are sexual
virility and intemperance. Studs is soon a member of the "Alcohol Squad," led by "Slug" Mason, a returned soldier. Perpetually "soused," Studs reaches a point where "most things are
just plain crap to me." His minds runs continually on sex; while
entertaining the most chivalrous notions regarding womanhood
in the abstract, his conduct towards her in the flesh becomes increasingly depraved. In a vain effort to appear as a man of the
world at his sister's sorority party, he wrecks for ever his long-
entertained hopes of a future with Lucy Scanlon by attempting to
force her while taking her home in a cab. In his better moments,
he hunts "shines" to frighten them from the Fifty-eighth Street
area towards which they are slowly rolling in a black wave, boy-
cotts effectively with the gang a restaurant which employs a
Greek socialist waiter incautious in his speech, and as one of the
"Fifty-eighth Street Cardinals" cripples permanently and deliberately "Jewboy" Schwartz, the star of an opposing team, in
a game of "prairie" football.

In brief interludes of fear he attempts reform; but at com-
munion his mind wanders to the body of the young woman in
the pew beside him, while his efforts to repair the damage done
his body successively by alcohol, influenza, gonorrhea, and more
alcohol are equally distracted. At the curtainfall at the end of
The Young Manhood of Studs Lonigan, he is an abhorrent,
vomit-stinking, insensate, battered thing lying at the base of a
fireplug on Fifty-eighth Street, following a New Year's "reunion" party of the gang in a disreputable hotel in the Black
Belt, a debauch which rivals all the loathsome scenes in literature, including even the famous Walpurgis Night episode in
Ulysses, by which, as William Troy indicates, it was doubtless
suggested. This wreck, the author comments, was the boy who
stood before Charley Bathcellar's poolroom thinking that some
day he would grow up to be "strong, and tough, and the real
stuff."

The Young Manhood of Studs Lonigan is as veracious as its
predecessor, yet it is less dramatic, because it is foreseen. Farrell

remedied, as best he could, this inevitable defect by supplying episodes of lurid melodrama—melodrama as unhappily "real" as the multiple rapes and murders in the daily tabloid. In these melo-dramatic episodes, however, Studs usually plays a secondary rôle —the artist realizing that, if the sensational episode is thus slightly "off center", credibility is more easily achieved. This is both in-genious and effective, and indicates the thought that Farrell ex-pended upon the structure, as well as upon the substance, of his tale. Yet this clarity of intention does not prevail throughout the volume. The most ambiguous aspect of *The Young Manhood* lies in its vigorous satire of the Catholic clergy of Chicago. Far-rell has made it clear enough that he has no metaphysics, that he has no credence in supernatural powers. Of what importance then is it to him that these representatives of God on earth are false, vain, bigoted, and corrupt? To be sure, Studs vaguely fears the hell of their theology and is sometimes held by their rant, but Farrell nowhere shows that this does his hero any positive harm. The attack, then, whatever its justification in clerical hypocrisy, is pointless so far as the development of the story is concerned.

The author is at his best in producing, by a series of vignettes, the atmosphere of depravity in which Studs moves. No one has so convincingly proved the numbing effect of low company as has James T. Farrell.

"Quarter after one!" said Slug, standing with Mike at the window.

They heard the click of the cue balls from the back where Stan Simonsky was practicing. An elevated train rumbled. An automobile whizzed by. A heavy-footed, well-formed girl passed.

"How you like it?"

"Push-Push!" mumbled Mike.

Although Mr. Farrell does not believe in the hell of the theo-logians, he prepared for his hero in *Judgment Day* (1935) so satisfactory a substitute that hell itself should hold no fears for the culprit afterwards. Studs beholds comrade after comrade of the old Fifty-eighth Street gang rot to death, destroyed by dis-ease and dissipation, until he is haunted by the fear of death, which severe illness and a bad heart make very near and real to him. The depression brings idleness, but not an idleness he may enjoy. Both he and his father plunge in "Imbray" stock, and when each is pushed and looks to the other for aid, he finds the other in his own predicament. Studs loses his small savings and Mr. Lonigan ultimately all his property. The force of this catastrophe, long impending, is not felt fully until other events have produced a crisis in Studs' career. Meanwhile he has had an affair with a girl named Catherine, a short, plump girl, with a stubby nose, black eyes, and a round, full-cheeked face. Though she is very common clay compared with the vision of Lucy which still haunts Studs, he realizes not only that he cannot do without her, but also, in his franker moments, that she is much too good for him. Together they visit movie houses, dance marathons, and in season the beaches and parks; alone Studs desperately hunts in vain for work. Constant contact with Catherine, with no prospect of marriage, is too much for him, and she becomes pregnant. The vista of married life with this devoted Irish girl is disclosed to Studs only over a wall, the wall of economic impossibility. Then pneumonia, contracted while sitting in a burlesque show in wet clothing after tramping about in the rain for work, blots out the vista for ever,—Mrs. Lonigan refusing Catherine even the consolation of a death bed marriage to Studs so that the girl's child may have a name, though she does procure the last rites of the Church for her son. When Studs dies, Mrs. Lonigan is prostrate and his father and younger brother Martin are both befuddled by drink.

Judgment Day is a better piece of writing than *The Young Manhood of Studs Lonigan,* though it is a sort of appendage to that book. Illness, the doctor's orders that he must not drink, and the intercession of Catherine free Studs from the Fifty-eighth Street gang, and for the first time in his career he perceives values which have no origin in the poolroom. While he is sadly mixed in his attitude towards Catherine, carnal desire ever triumphing over wistful Celtic yearnings for domestic bliss, he no longer gets pleasure out of sexual adventure even if he is unable to resist the temptation of these adventures. The "urinal smell" of his last ten-cent burlesque show makes Studs feel that he will become "diseased or contaminated just by sitting in it." Studs' futile and feeble struggle against the fearful odds of his own nature, against the haunting thoughts of illness and death, against bad luck and the business depression raises the book in interest over its predecessor where he was merely washed along with the gang. He is not a tragic figure in any sense, but he is a pathetic one. The author's firm grip on reality, however, keeps pathos from turning into sentimentality. While the lechery and abandon of *The Young Manhood* is doubtless typical of boom days in Chicago, Farrell there has not succeeded in making those lush times real to the extent that he has made the depression real in this book. Studs moves here like a figure against a stagnant fen; a dead city towers over him and menaces him. Yet there is no anger in him—he never realizes that he is the victim of forces beyond his control, like some of the silly characters in the work of the earlier Naturalists. Old Lonigan, robbed of his property and with his son dying, looks uncomprehendingly at a Communist parade and wonders why the police permit it. Studs and his father "take it sitting down"; their whole world is decaying and they are unaware of it. Up to the end they expect to land on their feet. Yet here at last, while maintaining their individuality, they are more than individuals: they are types of a free, careless race into whose *laissez-faire* morals, the subject of jest a decade or two ago, the author reads dreadful significance. The world is getting too complex for the wild Irishman, or any other man, for that matter, to solve his problems with his fists. The world is through with these roisterers, tolerated as the strong backs and rough hands which built our cities and railroads. And the world, ready to dispense even with their masters, shoves them first over the precipice.

The abilities exhibited in *Studs Lonigan* do not show to as great advantage in Farrell's three volumes of short stories, *Calico Shoes* (1935), *Guillotine Party* (1935), and *Can All This Grandeur Perish?* (1937), for the cumulative effect of the trilogy is lacking. Farrell, like Zola and Dreiser, is instinctively a Naturalist in method; such a writer is never completely successful in an abridged form, and this chiefly accounts for the fact that Farrell is relatively unimpressive in the short story. One tale alone, "Big Jeff," in *Guillotine Party,* is so original that, had the author but perfected it, it would be a landmark in the history of the short story. Farrell's tales of Parisian and Bohemian art life are especially unconvincing. He is not a sophisticate. Yet these books do not positively discredit him as does *A Note on Literary Criticism* (1936). With all the precipitate energy of Zola he flings himself in this volume into the petty wars the "leftist" critics have engendered. Though his position that literature is at once "a branch of the fine arts" and "an instrument of social influence" is defensible, and though he has plainly taken up arms in the worthy cause of defending Joyce, Proust, and himself from the real and fancied charges that their pictures of decadent bourgeois life do not advance the Marxist cause, he makes of his book such an omnibus of condemnation that he robs his strictures of all force. To condemn Michael Gold and Granville Hicks with the same breath that he dismisses Plato, Aquinas, and Spinoza might be taken by the former gentlemen to be a kind of flattery. Yet Farrell in a few sentences or with a syllogism decapitates critic after critic in a kind of "mass slaughter" or "purge" of criticism. Not only do Gold, Hicks, Plato, Aquinas, and Spinoza fall, but also Pater, Spingarn, More, Babbitt, Foerster, Clark, Rahv, Seaver, Sinclair, Dell, Strachey, Calverton, Schneider, Morrow, Mirsky, Radek, Phillips, Waldo Frank, Freeman, Conroy, Burgum, Briffault, Cowley, and Tolstoi. The only critic whom Farrell endorses is the Russian, Chernishevski, of whose writings he has read apparently but a single essay in translation in *International Literature*. His total incapacity for criticism is indicated in his casual treatment of Plato's concept of absolute justice. This is a "static ideal . . . beyond the process of change" to which real problems cannot be referred. Therefore, the concept is "fantastic." One wonders what Mr. Farrell thinks of Euclid's static ideal of a straight line: can nothing be referred to such an ideal merely because the fairest line the best draughtsman can draw looks like the edge of an old razor under a microscope? Mr. Farrell has listened uncritically to John Dewey whose *Experience and Nature* and *Art as Experience* have had too great an effect upon him. *A Note on Literary Criticism* is further marred by the kind of jargon for which the former Chicago ideologist is notorious; Farrell writes of "the end result," of a "universalized moral order," of "ex-

tremism," of the "refreshment value" of literature, of "abso-
lutized" criteria, of "generalized conclusions," of "organismal"
impossibilities, etc. The pity is that Mr. Farrell is much more
intelligent than he appears to be in this volume. Zola has survived his indiscretions, and Farrell will his.

In 1933 Farrell issued what might be called an "exploratory"
novel, *Gas House McGinty,* in light of the later use he has made
of the same material. Though there is a sense in which Professor
Beach's phrase, "unplotted pandemonium," is a completely adequate summary of the book, *Gas House McGinty* aims at revealing the effect of constant nagging and persistent sadistic torture
of a gang of Irish workingmen, the drivers of the "Continental
Express Company," upon the object of their ridicule, Ambrose
J. McGinty, boss of the call office, later reduced in rank because
of a "shindy." Every kind of crude joke is perpetrated upon Mc-
Ginty, from stealing the pillow which he brings to the office because he is tormented by hemorrhoids to getting a "fairy" to
make up to him. Even at home McGinty does not command the
respect necessary to compensate him for the abuse of the office;
his wife Mame, a bigoted, suspicious creature, is frankly contemptuous of him and breaks up the covert friendliness between
himself and his little stepdaughter, Josephine. To escape from
life which frustrates and baffles him, Gas House indulges in self-
glorifying dreams—reveries at work and phantasmagoria at
night. One chapter, devoted to the epic adventures of McGinty
in sleep, reveals the unfortunate Irishman dreaming of his personal conquest of God. Sound enough psychologically, perhaps,
from an artistic point of view *Gas House McGinty* is a mélange
in which the dream technique and the photographic technique
yaw apart. But Farrell was vastly to improve upon the book.

Jim O'Neill, a sick truck driver for the Continental, and
Danny O'Neill, his son, are minor characters in *Gas House Mc-
Ginty.* In a new series of novels, *A World I Never Made* (1936),
No Star Is Lost (1938), and *Father and Son* (1940), Farrell
has apparently embarked upon a venture in autobiographical fiction, with Danny and Jim as complementary characters, which
threatens to outdo and overreach Thomas Wolfe's notorious and
prodigious revelation of the intimate life of himself, his father,

his family, and all his acquaintance. In the first two volumes of
this new work it appeared that Farrell was hopelessly mired in
his material, for the story carried Danny forward to only his
fourteenth year, having picked him up on a Sunday, in 1911,
when he was a snivelling baby of five. Danny lives with his grandmother, Mrs. O'Flaherty, a coarse-grained, pipe-smoking, vigorous old Irishwoman, because his father Jim, a poorly paid teamster, cannot afford to feed all of his numerous brood of children.
In the O'Flaherty household are Danny's uncles, Al and Ned,
quondam shoe salesmen, his Aunt Margaret, a hotel employee,
and two of his little sisters. Narrative interest in the first two
volumes of the series is greatly diversified: it springs from such
varied things as Danny's expanding dreams and ambitions with
childhood growth, Aunt Margaret's prodigious sprees and amorous adventures, Uncle Al's worries over his self-assumed responsibility to bring up Danny properly, friction between the
O'Neills and the O'Flahertys, desperate illness with improper
medical attendance in the family of Jim O'Neill, and the slut-
tishness and religious fanaticism of Lizz O'Neill, mother of the
unequal brood. Among all the wild Celts in the two novels, Chicago riff-raff and barbarians if there ever were any, the incompetent teamster father, Jim O'Neill, is especially invested with lovable qualities—a tenacious tenderness for his children, even for
those separated from him and taught to hate him, and an unflag-
ging spirit in the face of abuse. If Farrell had never written
Father and Son, Jim O'Neill would still remain a refutation for
the central thesis of the author in his works—that people can do
nothing for themselves: are wholly shaped by their environment,
for Jim achieves dignity in defeat. Aeschylus, whose view of the
world is possibly as dark as that of the modern Naturalists,
thinks that this is so signal a victory over life that he grants it
only to noble personages. It is *lèse-majesté* in Jim, perhaps, but
more convincing because the odds are greater.

In *Father and Son* Farrell suddenly achieved a mighty harmony out of what had hitherto threatened to be the "melody of
chaos." The unification of the express companies brought about
by Woodrow Wilson during the World War produced a period
of brief prosperity in that business, and Jim O'Neill, elevated to

night wagon dispatcher, began to dream of a home of his own and savings in the bank. A spree and brawl on Armistice Day, however, are the last important episodes in which Jim O'Neill appears as a whole and healthy man. Fighting and dissipation, anxiety and hard work have taken their secret toll; a paralytic stroke, followed by another and another, reduces this once proud slugger to an old man, half-blind in one eye, defective in his hearing, who must clumsily drag the right side of his body along the sidewalk, while the street gamins follow after, mocking him and tormenting him. For a while Jim persists in working, tortured at night in the dispatcher's coop by the presence of death at his hand, but eventually he is forced to give up. Then come the hours of increasing invalidism, shock, coma, and drooling death. Graphically real is every moment of that suffering—the perpetual anxiety of the paralytic increased by the regret that his manly boy Bill must go to work, by annoyance that his wife Lizz has time for religious observances and wakes but none for housework and their children, and by worry over Danny.

Most of all, worry over Danny. Without the father's close care and discipline, in an environment where there is no wise check upon his inclinations, Danny is developing in a way that alarms his father. He is ashamed of the old man, of the harridan Lizz, and at times of his whole connection. Danny lives chiefly in his reveries, in which he fancies himself a priest (the dream quickest abandoned), a super-athlete, a charmer with the women, a "frat" man and a college hero. His career in Saint Stanislaus high school, where he neglects or cribs his school work, and is cynically indifferent to the counsel of the priests, but shines as an individual star in athletics (while wrecking team play), provides Danny with a narrow ground for his delusions of grandeur. He is at times pained by the derision of his fellows and by his ill-success with the girls, but mostly he is obtuse to these things. His father sees him as a lazy wastrel, unable to keep the after-school or Saturday employment which comes his way, with warped ideas about what society owes him. When Danny ends up in a hospital for a night as the result of a spree, Jim makes the last determined effort of his life to change the direction of his son's career. The boy must account to him for his time after school. must work, and must contribute to the care and support of his sisters. Though Danny lies to Jim, *Father and Son* closes with Danny employed in the call-office (where he is subject to constant harassment from the other men), determined for once in his life to make good. Jim's career ends in utter misery and humiliation, but not in defeat—he has deflected his son perceptibly from a course which might have ended in a ruin comparable to that of Studs Lonigan. It is from the play of personality upon personality, father upon son, and son upon father, when neither perfectly understands the other, that Farrell secures the harmony and unity of his novel. *Father and Son* is a great novel and a solid commentary upon the handling of a theme that in a measure evaded both Joyce and Wolfe. In Jim O'Neill, Farrell searched out a father who is the peer of all. Furthermore, if we are to infer that Jim has given to Danny's life new direction, we realize that, for the first time in his fiction, Farrell has admitted the possibility of altering an environment-determined destiny by the force of the human will. His Naturalism is no longer the lionnet it first was.

From the python-like coils of his struggle with his autobiography (which, with *Father and Son,* carries Danny O'Neill only through high school) Farrell emerged, in 1939, to issue a timely novelette, *Tommy Gallagher's Crusade,* which seems to provide yet another exception to the author's early thesis that environment determines all. The protagonist of this story is apparently unable to shape his destiny in spite of all the reformatory influences in his surroundings. Farrell's novelette is a mercilessly accurate limning of an American Fascist—a young Irish loafer, follower of "Father Moylan," the radio-priest, and a member of the latter's "Association for Christian Freedom." Tommy's "crusade" is against the Jews and the Communists. He conducts it by hawking *Christian Justice,* an incendiary weekly edited by Father Moylan, on New York street corners; by picketing noisily the broadcasting studios which have shut the radio priest off the air; by pushing solitary Jewish pedestrians into the gutter when he himself is with his cohorts; and by attempting with other ruffians to break up outdoor meetings. In vain his whole family —father, mother, and two brothers—cajole, reason, threaten, and denounce him. He will not give up his delusion that he is making America safe for "Christian democracy," or what would be equally salutary, so far as he is concerned, go to work. The bad egg in a sober, industrious Celtic family, Tommy discredits the others, flouts his father's philosophy of live and let live, and makes a general nuisance of himself. Even when he is soundly thumped, he will not learn, but salves his wounds in self-pity. Farrell implies that there is no hope for the Tommy Gallaghers —they are the inexplicable riff-raff of civilization, the dirt of corners in which is bred the insidious political diseases of our time, the brute element which gives the rabble-rousers their power. Perhaps the novelette is as valuable, however, for the brief glimpses it gives us of the other members of the Gallagher family as it is for its abstersion of Tommy. We need to remember, when notorious city boss and demagogic priest are perchance Irish, that they are not necessarily representative of their race, and that their hatreds and vices are not shared by their less conspicuous but more worthy countrymen.

Very popular once with the young intellectuals were the erstwhile Naturalistic views of Joseph Wood Krutch, expressed most succinctly in his volume, *The Modern Temper* (1929). Mr. Krutch is a native of Knoxville, Tennessee, where he was born on November 25, 1893. Though he entered the University of Tennessee with the intention of becoming an engineer, he was deflected into literature by reading George Bernard Shaw's *Man and Superman*. After serving in the Psychological Corps of the United States Army, he resumed graduate work, which the War had interrupted, at Columbia University. A Cutting Traveling Fellowship took him abroad in 1919–1920, and in 1923 he became a Doctor of Philosophy. He has taught at Brooklyn Polytechnic Institute, at Vassar College, and in the Columbia School of Journalism. In 1924 he joined the staff of *The Nation* as dramatic critic and associate editor. His reviews in that journal have commanded a respect accorded to but few American critics. Besides *The Modern Temper*, Krutch's most important books are *Edgar Allan Poe: A Study in Genius* (1926), *Five Masters: A Study in the Mutations of the Novel* (1930), *Was Europe a Success?* (1934) and *The American Drama Since 1918* (1939).

The Modern Temper is a study of the grounds for pessimism in the intellectual convictions current just before the depression though Mr. Krutch freely acknowledges that it is presumptuous to maintain that only one mood existed then. Despair is generated primarily by the ripening of civilization, in the author's view, which is also the view of Oswald Spengler. Freud has pointed out that the child is completely happy in his mother's womb, is coddled by his parents in infancy, and is allowed to discover the moral discord of the world only by degrees as he matures. Similarly, races have their infancy, adolescence, and maturity. As civilization grows older it is compelled to abandon one after another of its illusions for the bitter world of fact. To the adolescence of the race belongs the world of illusion—of poetry, mythology, and religion; to the mature race science presents a world which has none of its purposes—happiness, order, and reason. All human values have collapsed in the last sixty years, Krutch maintains, before the iconoclastic march of the united sciences.

By destroying all his illusions, man's intellect has devised a painful dilemma for him: he can neither go back to a state of relative ignorance nor can he cling to his faiths and repress his doubts merely because it would be desirable to do so. "The world of modern science is one in which the intellect alone can rejoice." Yet the intellect is not man's salvation, for the intellect teaches acceptance of the universe, which is the way of animals. Man's body may become more healthy and his machines more wonderful, but every reason for living will be gone. "Ours is a lost cause and there is no place for us in the natural universe, but we are not, for all that, sorry to be human. We should rather die as men than live as animals."

Such is the tenor of *The Modern Temper,* yet the book is made up, in the main, of witty, discursive essays refuting other views of the universe. "The Paradox of Humanism," for example, is an essay revealing how fallacious is the so-called Humanistic disapprobation of the natural man and of sexual indulgence. Krutch points out that man is the only animal that does not rigidly subordinate sex to the function of reproduction, the only one who loves the whole year around. "Debauchery rather

than abstinence is 'humanistic' " and "the Don Juan is characteristically human, because he has seized upon something which
Nature has instituted for her purposes and tried to utilize it for
his own." The ant, who has perfectly adjusted himself to Nature,
makes man realize what it is to be human, to "live dangerously."
The stability and discipline of the ants do not commend themselves
to man: they are illustrations of the social virtues which are all
animal. Does the Humanist want us to be disciplined and animal
or licentious and human?

In the essay, "Life, Art, and Peace," Krutch attacks the view,
held by Ernest Renan, Henry James, and others, that life is an
art. In such a view it makes no difference whether a man is good
or bad so long as he plays his rôle well. Krutch compares this
position with that of the Gnostic to show that it at least is not
a practical one. Nature will not tolerate individuals to exist upon
principles so antithetical to those necessary for animal survival.
Art furnishes a means by which life may be contemplated, but
not a means by which it may be lived.

Russian Communism is Mr. Krutch's topic in his concluding
essay. He points out that the decadent nations have never been
saved by their philosophers but by influxes of simpler peoples
who have not been "ripe" enough to despair. Such a simple people are the Russians who have adopted a well-nigh primitivistic
philosophy of life—that nothing is really important save those
things upon which the welfare of the race depends. These young
barbarians may overrun Europe, destroying many things only to
build them up again, thus illustrating Nature's right to recapture
her own world. But in the end, even the Russians will discover
the quarrel between the individual spirit and Nature, and they,
too, will despair. Even if communistic society should never ripen,
if it should develop into some changeless, efficient routine, like
that of an ant hill, we should have no cause to rejoice since we
would be alien to such a society and could not forget what science
has taught us.

To some intelligences despair is a perfectly logical reaction to
the world, and Mr. Krutch is more logical in *The Modern
Temper* than are most of his brethren of the Naturalistic school.
Indeed, his is a syllogistic pessimism. For consistent, reasoned

despair, it may as well be understood, there is no absolute refutation. There are considerations, however, of equal, but no greater validity than Mr. Krutch's, that might incline a person of different temperament to take an opposite view of the world and of the significance of scientific studies than his. The inference that science will prove *progressively* destructive of human values seems gratuitous, particularly in view of the fact that modern physics—even if it is seeking what it wants to find—has set itself in opposition to the revelations of other sciences with its picture of a limited and symbolical universe. Prophesying from the trends in science for the last sixty years as to what future science will bring forth is risky business, no matter what the conclusion. That science has or will destroy ethics, as Krutch contends, for example, depends entirely upon one's definition of ethics. If ethical conduct is ideal or perfect conduct, as conceived by any race at any given time, it is difficult to see how science much affects it. For example, while science may alter our notions of adultery, it cannot in the least affect the existence of a *positive* conception of perfect love. For the pair in wedlock, and for the future pair living happily in what today we describe as an adulterous state, there is still the vision of an ideal or perfect relationship, not to be achieved by them, yet still a lure for conduct. That science can affect absolute values is to some minds still a very debatable issue. The modern man's conception of the good, like his conception of the beautiful, is less different from that of the Greeks than many a skeptic would have us believe. Yet this, of course, does not touch at all upon the question of whether or not it is a gloomy spectacle that man should thus be eternally pledged to the pursuit of ideals when the stage floor he struts upon seems so without them. Mr. Krutch is properly distressed by the fact that man is different from his environment.

For the purposes of this study the validity of pessimistic determinism is of small importance beside the consequences of wide credence in such a philosophy. Nietzsche's sound diagnosis of Naturalism as leading to debility of the will makes clear the gravity of the national situation if Mr. Krutch's assumption— though Krutch himself (we understand) no longer assumes this —that the prevailing temper in America at the present time is pessimistic. That a large number of Americans should believe that men are powerless in regard to their destinies means that masses are as indifferent to all proposals for human betterment as they are apathetic towards the injustices which, to their way of thinking, lie in the very nature of things. Mass insensibility is the gravest menace to political health, for it delivers the body politic up to any small faction with fixed purpose and a will to power. The only possibility of Fascism in this country lies, not in the popularity of the doctrines of Fascism, but rather in the debility of the public will through wide acceptance of the philosophy of Naturalism. While a "will-not-to-believe" in Naturalism becomes a civic duty, one can never have any security in a weal based on a deliberately false choice, so that the only possible hope for America is that this temper is less prevalent than has been asserted. It is important to note that the leaders in the American Naturalistic school are by no means *convinced* Naturalists—they betray themselves by pet schemes for human betterment, schemes in which no genuine and thorough-going pessimist has any legitimate interest. The volition to clutch at a straw is yet a manifestation of the spirit and a sign of hope. Since no accurate census is possible, we can merely affirm our belief on this evidence that Naturalism has by no means settled down as a dark cloud on this land and that any brisk wind of controversy might quickly dissipate its vapors.

III

THE DECADENTS

"... I wish Edgar Poe, who is nobody in America, to become a great man for France."—Charles Baudelaire, *Lettres,* p. 91.

I

ART AS A REFUGE

"IN PASSING let us spit upon Edgar Poe," urges André Breton in a manifesto addressed to his brother *surréalistes*. Other modern French poets have shouted, "Down with Poe!" Yet, despite this evidence of their desire to escape his chains, most French poets, and all save a few modern American poets, are completely under the dominance of ideas which he first promulgated and have been influenced by an aesthetic which he first formulated. Notwithstanding the amusing charges against his virility, Edgar Allan Poe is the father of much contemporary poetry.

Poe belonged, of course, to the Romantic school and, like other Romantics, was interested in the apotheosis of his own ego.

"I dwelt alone
In a world of moan
And my soul was a stagnant tide. . . ."

It may be argued that stuff of this sort is worth only the query, "Who cares?"; yet the Romantics won the favor of the world by their amazing assumption that everyone was peculiarly and completely absorbed in the poet's agonies and raptures. Poe, however, disdained this victory and pressed on to another which made him unique among the poets of his time. He held that for the poet the mere *expression* of his feeling is enough whether it is communicated or is communicable to another or not. With him began what Max Eastman, in reviewing the work of Hart Crane, E. E. Cummings, Gertrude Stein, and Edith Sitwell, termed "the cult of unintelligibility."

"Poetry," declared Poe, "is the rhythmical creation of Beauty. . . . With the intellect or with the conscience it has only collateral relations. . . ." The poem, to his mind, differed from the short story "by having for its object an *indefinite* instead of a *definite* pleasure. . . ." Music is the prime essential of verse, "since the comprehension of sweet sound is our most *indefinite* conception."

Hardly content with implying that the best poetry is unintelligible sweet sound, Poe rather prided himself on the general obscurity of some of his work. In a letter to P. P. Cooke, touching on his tales "Morella" and "Ligeia," he writes, "As for the mob . . . I should be grieved if I thought they comprehended me here." In days when the public was almost as naïve as it is today and persisted in identifying the narrator "I" with the author, Poe contemptuously tossed his readers such bits of illusory explanation as, "I am come of a race noted for vigour of fancy and ardour of passion. Men have called me mad; but the question is not settled whether madness is not the loftiest intelligence. . . . We will say, then, I am mad." In verse he emphasized the difference between himself and the commonality of men:

> "From childhood's hour I have not been
> As others were; I have not seen
> As others saw; I could not bring
> My passions from a common spring.
> From the same source I have not taken
> My sorrow; I could not awaken
> My heart to joy at the same tone;
> And all I loved, *I* loved alone. . . ."

Yet he probably did not anticipate that his poetry should be as completely misunderstood as it was (the *Edinburgh Review* charged that Poe caused the death of his wife that he might have a fitting theme for "The Raven"!), or that certain pieces, such as

"Al Aaraaf" and "Ulalume," should never find a satisfactory interpreter.

Without anticipating precisely these results, Poe nevertheless invited a misapprehension of his purposes by throwing dust in the eyes of his readers. Yet, after due allowance is made for his pleasant deceptions and for his deliberate cultivation of the "gothic" (the tale of horror in vogue when he wrote), one must admit that there was something fundamentally wrong about the man. His declaration, in "The Poetic Principle," that the tendency of passion is "to degrade, rather than to elevate the soul" and his avowal that a dead woman is a more proper subject for a poem than a live one should disturb the thoughtful critic. Mr. Krutch, despite all the scholars, is right in regarding Poe as a neurotic, though he is probably mistaken in assuming that the poet's inhibitions sprang "from the death of some woman upon whom his desire had irrevocably fixed itself." Had Krutch access to the documents which Mr. Hervey Allen employed in his biography, *Israfel,* he might have conjectured a more plausible cause for all Poe's difficulties. We now know that the poet's foster-father, Mr. John Allan, was most irregular in his conduct, maintaining several mistresses in Richmond, and that Poe, self-constituted defender of Mrs. Allan, upbraided the man for this. Thus, as a mere lad, the poet became the champion of a purity which his intense mind—revolting from the revelations of Allan's promiscuity—carried to an abnormal chastity.

Poe was able to conduct himself with enough consistency to convince some of his acquaintance of his virtue. Wilmer, who knew Poe well, declared he was "of all the men I ever knew—the most *passionless.*" Yet there is plain evidence that the poet was highly sexed. Nearly every poem that he wrote either celebrated some woman for whom he professed an ideal regard or was dictated by the wish of some woman. Besides there is the undeniable record of his attempted assault, when drink had sufficiently removed his restraints, upon Mary Devereaux in Baltimore in the summer of 1832. The miracle is that, when the intensity of Poe's nature is considered, there were no more episodes of this sort. The reason must lie in the probability that the poet unconsciously employed this very energy in maintaining an ideal chastity.

After death took his sexless child-wife Virginia (with whom his life must have been a horror) and he contemplated union with the Providence poetess, Mrs. Whitman, he wrote one of the most revealing letters of his life, confessing that the merest whisper in the past concerning her "awoke in me a shuddering sixth sense, vaguely compounded of fear, ecstatic happiness, *and a wild inexplicable sentiment that resembled nothing so nearly as a consciousness of guilt.*" At the same time he was writing another lady to whom he was devoted, Annie Richmond, ". . . I CANNOT live, unless I feel your sweet, gentle, loving hand pressed upon my forehead—oh, my *pure virtuous, generous, beautiful sister* Annie!"

Now, though the world may not accept the simple explanation of Poe's inhibitions here offered, his neurotic attitude toward love is a fact that cannot be denied. Out of his renunciation of normal passion came his compensatory conception of a supernal or ideal beauty to be worshipped, which made him aver that the death of a beautiful woman is the ideal subject for poetry. And from this proceeds his theory that music best expresses this yearning for which there can be no return. Bluntly, Poe's entire aesthetic can be traced to a motivation not greatly different from that which inspires necrophilia—the lust for the bodies of the dead. It is revelatory of the pretension of modern poetry and its supporting criticism that so much of both may be traced directly to this one poor, warped mind. Yet such is the case.

If one ignores the plagiarism of his work and the abortive efforts of Fitz-James O'Brien to reproduce the effects of his short stories, Poe found no immediate imitators in America. He did not at once become the head of a cult. A chain of circumstances, however, won him almost immediate attention in France. On three successive days in June, 1846, the Parisian newspaper, *La Quotidienne,* published in instalments a paraphrase of the tale, "The Murders in the Rue Morgue." On October 12 of that year E. D. Forgues printed in his journal, *Le Commerce,* an abridgment of the same tale under the title, "A Bloody Mystery." Not long before this Forgues had had a run-in with the newspaper, *La Presse,* upon which he had rightfully proved charges of plagiarism in so absurd a case that all Paris had rocked with laughter. *La Presse* naturally swore vengeance. In a two-column article it now accused Forgues of stealing from *La Quotidienne*, which had issued the first French version of Poe's story. Forgues replied that he had not copied from *La Quotidienne*, but from *The Tales of Edgar Poe, a littérateur américain.* He demanded that *La Presse* print his reply, which it could not very well do since the reply contained language which was obnoxious. Forgues went to law, lost his libel suit, but gave Poe great notoriety. Monsieur Langlois, lawyer for *La Presse,* declared, "Thanks to Forgues everybody is going to know that Monsieur Edgar Poe made these stories in America. . . ." In the next half century in France thirty-four translations in book form of the American writer were offered the public.

Whether or not Charles Baudelaire became interested in Poe before the Forgues suit, whether or not he began *Les Fleurs du Mal* under the influence of Poe or later redacted his poems to suit Poe's theories, is of minor consequence: Baudelaire became Poe's champion and interpreter in France, and no author has ever had a more sympathetic defender and *entrepreneur.* Writing of his first discovery of the American, Baudelaire confesses to a spiritual kinship startling in its completeness: "In 1846 or 1847 I became acquainted with a few fragments of Edgar Poe. I experienced a peculiar emotion. . . . I found—believe me or not—poems and tales of which I had already a vague, confused, and ill-ordered idea, and which Poe had known how to compose and bring to perfection." And again, in a letter to a friend, "The first time I opened a book written by him, I saw with fear and delight, not only themes dreamt by me, but sentences, thought by me, written by him, twenty years before."

To appreciate why a feeling of *fear,* as well as of delight, was a part of Baudelaire's first reaction to Poe, one has to know something of the life of the great French lyric poet. When Charles Baudelaire was born in Paris, on April 9, 1821, his father was sixty-one years old. Madame Baudelaire married again, in 1828, following the death of her husband. Colonel Aupick, the step-father, never captured the confidence of the boy, though he did what he defined to be his duty by sending Charles to the College of Lyons and to the Lycée Louis-le-Grand.

Continual bickerings grew into a violent quarrel, in 1841, over Baudelaire's determination to follow a literary career. His mother and the Colonel apparently felt that a long sea voyage might cure the youth of his distemper and they arranged that he be shipped to the East Indies. Baudelaire went no farther on this forced cruise, however, than the Island of Réunion; he was back in Paris in February, 1842, still determined to be a man of letters. Now of age, he dissipated a begrudged patrimony while he struggled, amid the dubious surroundings of literary Bohemia, to succeed in his chosen profession. Probably when he was most impoverished and when success seemed most distant, he came upon the work of Edgar Allan Poe. His delight in the perfect expression of that which he had dreamed was succeeded by the awful knowledge that the very thing he had aspired to do was already accomplished by another. Across the floor of whatever little chamber he occupied floated the shadow of a great despair. He had been anticipated and his struggles were in vain!

There was, however, in the soul of Charles Baudelaire an incalculable something which rallied him against despair. He himself has written of the natural perversity of man, but no man ever illustrated his thesis better than himself. Yet out of Poe he took the doctrine for his own regeneration. Of the spirit of *Perverseness,* wrote Poe, "philosophy takes no account. Yet I am not more sure that my soul lives, than I am that perverseness is one of the primitive impulses of the human heart—one of the indivisible primary faculties, or sentiments, which give direction to the character of man. Who has not, a hundred times, found himself committing a vile or silly action, for no reason than because he knows he should *not* . . . ?" In his tale, "The Black Cat," Poe records hanging the cat *"because* I knew that in so doing I was committing a sin—a deadly sin that would so jeopardize my immortal soul as to place it—if such a thing were possible—even beyond the reach of the infinite mercy of the Most Merciful and the Most Terrible God." No one but Baudelaire would have turned to the works of his predecessor and made from them "one of the most accurate and brilliant translations in literature." No one but him would have devoted so large a share of his life to the mere exposition of the American's theories and to the jealous improvement of his reputation.

Yet from this same perversity proceeded the pustular flow of *Les Fleurs du Mal*—a volume which is highly original in that it gives an extension to the ideas of Poe never conceived of by the latter. A gruesome poem, now thought to come from another pen than Baudelaire's, is generally held to epitomize *The Flowers of Evil*. It is entitled "A Carrion" (*Une Charogne*):

1.

Recall the object that we saw, my soul,
That mild, soft morning of a summer day:
Beside the unused path a body foul
Upon a seamy bed of pebbly clay,

2.

With legs extended like a pliant whore,
Discharged its nauseating odors in the air;
Its belly, putrid as a running sore,
Insulting every passing eye, lay bare. . . .

5.

And flies buzzed happily above this rot,
Whence issued, like a syrup, slow and thick,
A rout of crawling things—have you forgot?—
Whose writhing made the very rags seem quick. . . .

10.

And even you shall come to this sad end—
Descend to ordure and to loathsome rot,
My angel, lustrous star towards whom I tend,
O Beauty! even this shall be your lot!

11.

Yes, such you shall become, O graceful queen,
When after the last sacrament, you mold
With other bones that nourish grasses green
And feel the fevered flesh grow truly cold.

12.

Then, love, speak fairly of me to the worms
Who shall consume your beauty soon with kisses;

Report how I immortalize the forms
And essences of all my pretty misses.

What are these verses but a powerful resetting of those which Poe's deranged Ligeia made her lover recite as she lay dying?

4. . . . But see, amid the mimic rout
    A crawling shape intrude!
A blood-red thing that writhes from out
    The scenic solitude!
It writhes!—it writhes!—with mortal pangs
    The mimes become its food,
And the seraphs sob at vermin fangs
    In human gore imbued.

5. Out—out are the lights—out all!
    And over each quivering form,
The curtain, a funeral pall,
    Comes down with the rush of a storm—
And the angels, all pallid and wan,
    Uprising, unveiling, affirm
That the play is the tragedy, "Man,"
    And its hero, the conqueror Worm.

Ultimately Poe published this piece under the title, "The Conqueror Worm." When this "worm" emerged from the new cocoon Baudelaire wove about it, it was ready to wing its way through French poetry. "A more or less successful imitation of Baudelaire's awful verses entitled 'The Corpse'," says F. P. Sturm, "has been the beginning of more than one French poet's corrupt flight across the sky of literature."

In melodious "Annabel Lee" Poe sang of the sufferings of his child wife and himself from cold and hunger and disease in New York—"the kingdom by the sea." From this monody it is instructive to turn to the companion pieces of Baudelaire which set forth the social diseases of Paris, "Crépuscule du soir" and "Crépuscule du matin." In the one, vice invades the entire city in the night; in the other, all the wretches of the metropolis—the *femmes de plaisir,* the beggars, the sots, and the sick—move in stupid sleep or arouse themselves wearily to their accruing misery. The poet, however, is not repelled by this spectacle (there is no moral purport in the Baudelairian pictures) but is exalted by it! Indeed, he tells us in his "Epilogue" to the *Petite Poèmes en Prose* that this is the source of his inspiration:

1. Montmartre I climbed with heart that did not quail
   To contemplate the city sprawled below,
   The hells of cathouse, hospital, and jail—

2. Where evils rampant as the flowers grow.
   Thou knowest, Satan, lord of my distress,
   I climbed to voice no adolescent woe.

3. But with an ancient lecher's greediness
   I wished to try again that monstrous trull
   Whose melting love restores my youthfulness. . . .

Poe made a descent into the infernal regions in "Ulalume" and played facetiously with the devil in a goodly number of his short stories, but it is rather to his doctrine of perversity and to the influence of Byron that the "Satanism" of Baudelaire must be traced—the wild "Litany to Satan," the symbolic "Don Juan in Hell" and the little prose poems, "The Temptations," "The Glass Vendor," and "Let Us Flay the Poor." Anatole France, commenting on Baudelaire's purpose, with his "Satanism" in mind, remarked that "he aimed to offend God and make the angels weep." Baudelaire, however, had the pit more definitely in mind than the heavens, and it was *épater le bourgeois* that his most offensive verse was written. No author ever had a more cynical opinion of his countrymen than he. "The Frenchman," wrote Baudelaire, "is a backyard animal. . . . He is an animal of the Latin race; filth does not displease him; in his home, and in literature, he is scatophagous. He dotes on excrement. . . ." The chief difference between Poe and Baudelaire is the amount of "Gallic salt" the latter added to his confections.

To assert, however, that Baudelaire is wholly a poseur is to miss the essential sincerity of the man—his intense hatred of boredom, which he would dissipate at all costs. To maintain that he is no artist is to be blind to some of the most striking tone and colour contrasts in literature and deaf to some of the most haunting melodies. Yet to contend that his aesthetic is entirely anti-social is to be on very secure ground. He made no pretence of his hatred for the commonality, and while he pandered to the bourgeois appetite, in the very dishes he offered he maintained there were pleasures which the mob could not enjoy. "I love thee, infamous capital"; he wrote of his sordid Paris,

> ". . . Courtesans and thieves
> Enjoy your subtle pleasures often when
> There's naught in them the stupid crowd perceives."

He believed it possible to associate joy with beauty, but objected to doing it, because "joy is a most vulgar ornament"—something demanded by the herd. Innocence, genuine passion, the idealisms of man did not interest him. "All love is prostitution," he asserted. "The one and the supreme bliss of love rests in the certainty of doing *evil*. Both man and woman know, from birth, that in evil lies all bliss." "What is annoying in love, is that it is a crime in which one cannot do without an accomplice." "Glorious empires can be founded on crime, and noble religions on imposture." "God is a scandal, a scandal that rebounds." He carried Poe's idea that poetry has nothing to do with morals so far that he was fined three hundred francs (at the intercession of the Empress reduced to fifty) for outraging public decency. His verses are peopled with whores, hoodlums, and eccentrics. Théophile Gautier termed him a *"poète de décadence"* and compared him with the Latin poets of the decline of Rome. One cannot condemn him, like a French or American court, for his subject matter, yet one can observe the preoccupation which made him oblivious to what the public thought and the mechanism he set up to justify that preoccupation. "No poem," he declared, "is so great, so noble, so truly worthy of the name of poem as that which is written solely for the pleasure of writing a poem." Music rather than thought is the essential of verse. "Music deepens the sky." Baudelaire gave to France the fully matured fruit of Poe's thought, yet so mature was the fruit that there were in its yellow skin already visible the signs of decay.

In describing Baudelaire as a "Decadent," Gautier used the epithet in a very special way. Decadence, he said, is "art arrived

at that point of extreme maturity yielded by the slanting suns
of aged civilizations . . . struggling to render what is most
inexpressible in thought, what is vague and most elusive in the
outlines of form, listening to translate the subtle confidences of
neurosis, the dying confessions of passion grown depraved, and
the strange hallucinations of the obsession, which is turning to
madness. . . . The style of Decadence is the ultimate utterance of
the Word, summoned to final expression and driven to its last
hiding place. . . ."

Théophile Gautier's "aged civilization" was the French Empire—already tottering toward a fall. The Franco-German War
of 1870 seemed to enforce the prevailing notion that the Nordic
races, so plausibly represented by the youthful German nation,
were to displace in the sun the Latin, now become senile and
barren. To the bleary eyes of Paul Verlaine, *perhaps* "the purest
lyrical singer France has known" and unquestionably the country's most debauched poet since François Villon, the blonde stal-
warts of the Prussian army had seemed like gods. He wrote:

> I am the Empire at the end of the Decadence
> And I see the tall and white Barbarians go by . . .

"Decadence"—the word gripped the stunned imagination of
defeated France; it became an explanation for the despair of the
people; hence it was only natural that it should find some attachment to literature. As an adjective, *Décadent,* it was hurled
against a new generation of poets, a generation in revolt against
the Parnassians, members of the French Academy and pension-
ers of the Emperor, only two of whom assuredly possessed
genius, Leconte de Lisle and José Maria de Heredia. The
"Decadents" were the followers of Baudelaire, enthusiastic young
talkers who met at the Chat Noir (named by Rudolph Salis after
Poe's tale) and at other places on Montmartre to discuss literature and art. For them Anatole Baju founded the little review,
Le Décadent. The publication was so named to take all the sting
out of the epithet which had been flung at the founders and
contributors. "To avoid the suspicion which this ill-favored word
would throw on us," declared Baju, "we have preferred, in order
to kill it off, to adopt it as a flag."

Paul Verlaine and Arthur Rimbaud are the only Decadents who survived the death of their review. Aside from the music of his verse, Verlaine does not appear to be an important poet. His subject matter is extraordinarily trite—Pierrot as a shadow disturbs the heart of Columbine, Scaramouche and Pulcinella stand dark blots against the moon, the perfume of a loved one mingling with that of the roses starts a "dainty" fever in the veins of the lover. Or, "why so sad, my soul?" It is all very pretty, a little febrile, a good deal affected, and essentially false. Melancholy and sentiment, sentiment and melancholy, but the kind of a plaintive tune which will always make the tender heart palpitate. However, one poem of Verlaine's, "Art Poétique," sets forth again the idea that poetry is essentially music and not sense:

I.

Though a note may melt in the thinnest air
    And even a tune be quickly lost,
    Put music first whatever the cost
To riming and counting and taking care.

2.

When the choice of words for a verse is made,
    Do not your search unduly prolong,
    For what's more dear than a tipsy song
Where sense in nonsense is boldly displayed?

8.

... For ever music and music still!
    Your verses should be an innocent glance
    A lover steals in Love's vigilance,
A treachery sensed though his act is nil!

9.

Like the wind of morning, crisp and pure,
    Which scatters the scent of mint and thyme,
    Thus free and careless should be your rime—
And all the rest is literature!

Life to Verlaine, as to Poe, was a dream within a dream, and out of the intangible stuff of dreams he made his poetry.

> . . . Nuance only marries firmly
> Dream to dream and flute to horn. . . .

Wit, or sense, was "cruel", and as for "eloquence"—wring its neck! Sense, eloquence, and logic belong to mere *literature*. Verlaine probably had the Parnassians in mind, but ultimately his scorn of "literature" was to inspire Dada and the Revolt against Literature.

In 1871, Paul Verlaine invited to the small apartment which his wife's people permitted the couple to occupy in their home, the insolent and mad poet, Jean-Nicholas-Arthur Rimbaud. This most "cursed" of all the *poètes maudits* was the son of an active army captain and of a peasant woman with strong but narrow religious convictions. Born at Charleville, in the Ardennes, on October 28, 1854, Arthur Rimbaud as a boy was amazingly precocious, an inveterate prize-winner, yet headstrong and entirely uncompromising. At sixteen he ran away to Paris to read to the Parnassians his poem, "The Drunken Boat." Arrested and sent home at the request of his mother, he ran away again and again. He is reputed to have enlisted in the Commune of 1871, and this is not entirely improbable, for from his radical teacher, Georges Izambard, he had drawn a great love for the terrorist leaders of the French Revolution, Robespierre and Marat. Between his sixteenth and his nineteenth year, he composed his *Illuminations,* poems in verse and prose, like Baudelaire's, which made him famous, although they were not published until after his death. These and other verses he showed to Verlaine, who was quick to perceive their merit.

Yet Verlaine's wife and her parents did not like the older poet's companion. He had a playful way of smashing furniture which he never replaced and of leading Verlaine, who was something of a moral weakling, into viciousness. Moreover, he was without visible means of support. Their attempts to evict him and separate him from Verlaine had unexpected results,—Verlaine went off with the young madman. The two wandered through Belgium on foot and went to London where they found some irregular employment as teachers. Verlaine wrote, "We are studying English hard, Rimbaud and I, from the works of Edgar Poe, from the collections of popular songs, from Robert-

son, etc. Our faulty pronunciation makes us tell fibs to the trades-
people, at the public houses, and book-shops."

Meanwhile Verlaine's wife had entered a suit for separation,
alleging an "abominable relationship" existed between the
truants. If anything of the sort did exist, Rimbaud was anxious
to terminate it; he had already left Verlaine when the latter fell
dangerously ill and he returned to nurse him back to life. Recovered from his illness, Verlaine quarreled with Rimbaud, deserted
him, leaving him penniless. The older poet hoped to effect a
reconciliation with his wife and went to Brussels to accomplish
that. When he failed, however, Verlaine sent money to Rimbaud
to join him. Their reunion led to Verlaine's getting very, very
drunk, and twice attempting to take Rimbaud's life with a pistol.
He succeeded in wounding Rimbaud in the hand, and the latter
caused him to be arrested. As a result, Verlaine passed two sober
years in jail at Mons and became a convert to a prosy Catholicism.

> "O my God, You have wounded me with love.
> Behold the wound which is still vibrating.
> O my God, You have wounded me with love."

Rimbaud then printed *A Season in Hell* on which he had
labored for months, and, dissatisfied with his work fully as much
as with the criticisms it had received, foreswore poetry for ever.
During the next few years he wandered over most of Western
Europe; in 1876 he enlisted in the Dutch colonial army, was sent
to Java, where he deserted, and, making his way home, again
indulged in another period of wanderings. In 1879 he managed
a stone quarry in Cyprus; and in 1880 he became a trader in
Southern Ethiopia, after a twenty-day trip on horseback across
the Somali desert. As agent, he purchased for a French company
gold, ivory, skins, perfumes, and coffee; on trading expeditions
he crossed the Bubassa and penetrated into Ogaden, and wrote
of what he saw to the *Société de Géographie*. For a while he had
an Abyssinian mistress whom he left for a dangerous trip to
Menelik. She was as dark as unsweetened chocolate. He then
created a private business trading in firearms and gold, attempting to amass the fortune which had been his dream for a decade.

In the very prospect of prosperity, he was suddenly stricken with a "cancer" of the bone, which affected his right knee. After an incredible trip back to civilization and a shockingly painful voyage to Marseilles, he underwent an amputation which failed to save his life. At the end he was attended by his sister, Isabelle Berrichon, a devout Catholic, who affirmed that he embraced Christianity. If the impulsiveness of the man is taken into account, this act does not seem incredible. Yet he died chanting, "Allah Kerim! Allah Kerim!"

For Arthur Rimbaud, more than for all his predecessors, poetry lay in those regions traversed by an unhinged reason. "I accustomed myself to simple hallucinations," he declared, ". . . I ended by finding sacred the disorder of my soul." The poet, he felt, manifests himself only by a "studied disorder of all sense." He becomes the supreme *savant* through recourse to folly, to crime, to illness induced by drugs or alcohol. Through sadism he may find the Unknown—which Rimbaud promptly equated with God. He despaired, however, of recording his findings. He was confounded by the elusiveness of words—the hallucination of words. He cried out for a "language, a tongue which shall be a refinement of all essences, which shall sum up all: perfumes, sounds, colours. A tongue which shall define the unknown quantities and qualities it awakens. . . . Oh, for a language!" Rimbaud wanted to translate the untranslatable, that which he could not apprehend.

His work perhaps more clearly indicates what he tried to do than does his comment on that work. Here are a few verses from his "Le Bateau Ivre," which is, in a sense, one of the most original poems of the nineteenth century. Despite the originality of the poem, however, the reader will probably be struck by a vague resemblance between the descriptions of the subaqueous regions in it and those in Poe's "City in the Sea":

The Drunken Boat

I.

As I descended through unnavigable straits
I was no longer steered by sunburned guides—

Wild Indians had sent them to their fates,
All nude they hung with arrows through their sides.

2.

And I was wholly innocent of equipage,
Nor was my hold with corn or cotton filled;
When guideless I dropped downward stage by stage,
The pliant currents sped me where I willed.

3.

Into the furious churning of the tides
I ran, last winter, like a silly child,
Unmoored peninsulas on their strange rides
Never enjoyed a chaos half so wild.

4.

The floods have blessed the watches I have stood
When lighter than a cork I danced the wave;
As those eternal prowlers searched for food,
I scoffed the beacon lights that others save. . . .

6.

And afterwards I bathed in poetry,
That green ethereal ocean where floats past,
Through stars and milky way occasionally
A drowned man, rapt and brooding to the last. . . .

10.

I dreamed the night tinged green with dazzling snows,
And sleepy lovers struggling without words,
(Warm icebergs slowly circling on strange flows)
The blue and yellow cries of phosphorous birds. . . .

14.

Soft ice, pale suns, spent waves, and hot, charred skies,
And hideous wreckage in the sea's deep rooms,
Where giant serpents half devoured by flies
Fall from the twisted trees with black perfumes. . . .

16.

Sometimes, a martyr tired of zones and poles,
The sea, whose sobbing made my buffets sweet,

Showed me its orchids in unfathomable holes,
And charmed me as a woman at my feet. . . .

23.

But I have wept too much. Dawns break the heart,
Moonlight is vile and bitter sweet the sun;
Strong love has brought an enervating smart,
Smashed be my keel! To sea I now would run!

24.

If I desire a stream in Europe, 'tis
That shrouded water 'neath the midnight sky
Where squats a child in sadness, loosening his
Play boat as frail as a May butterfly.

25.

I can no longer in your surges bathe,
Nor lift their troughs for carriers of trade,
Nor swell the navies that the buntings swathe,
Nor swim past eyes of barges on parade!

In this extraordinary poem Rimbaud has made a virtue out of what Ruskin described as the pathetic fallacy. He asks that his reader fancy himself a water-logged craft and that he enjoy the sensual experiences of disintegration. He asks further that, as the disembodied spirit *of a boat,* the reader visit the scenes which he once loved and thought magnificent (the towers and battlements of Europe) and that he condemn these scenes as lustreless compared with those in the bowels of the ocean where he has churned. A rare poetic touch is that in which the spirit is permitted to take local habitation, if it desires, in the play boat of a child, for the imaginative world alone can rival the subaqueous regions. Throughout are found the accents of great poetry, which translation inevitably muffles:

> *L'âcre amour m'gonflé de torpeurs enivrantes*
> (Sharp love stuffs me full of languid ecstasies)

And—

> *La mer, dont le sanglot faisait mon roulis doux*
> (The sea whose sobbing made my buffets sweet).

Rimbaud's most startling effects, however, are achieved by carrying sense impressions of one category over into another, as in—

> The *blue* and *yellow cries* of phosphorous birds

And in—

> Where giant serpents half devoured by flies
> Fall from the twisted trees with *black perfumes.*

This deliberate confusion of sense impressions, a controlled disease for producing the fever of poetry, technically *synesthesia,* is one of the few ways in which fresh imagery may be born. Many Romantics had indifferently experimented with its possibilities, notably the German Hoffman and our own Edgar Allan Poe. In the mystical "Al Aaraaf" Poe had written—

> Sound loves to revel in the summer night
> Witness the murmur of the grey twilight . . .
> That stealeth ever on the ear of him
> Who, musing, gazeth on the distance dim,
> And sees the darkness coming as a cloud—
> Is not its form—its voice—most palpable and loud.

To this Poe appended the note, "I have often thought I could distinctly hear the sound of the darkness as it stole over the horizon." Elsewhere Poe wrote, "The orange ray of the spectrum and the buzz of the gnat . . . affect me with nearly similar sensations. In hearing the gnat, I perceive the color, in perceiving the color, I seem to hear the gnat." And in his *Marginalia,* he remarks that Tennyson appears "to see with his ear." Perhaps the happiest use Poe ever made of his experiment is found in the lines ideally confusing thought and sound—

> "Ligeia! Ligeia!
> My beautiful one!
> Whose harshest idea
> Will to melody run. . . ."

To Poe's interest in synesthesia and to his declaration, "I believe that *odors* have an altogether peculiar force . . ." may be traced Baudelaire's sonnet,

Correspondences

All Nature is a temple opulent
In which each pillar murmurs words confused
To man, who knows but sense and is unused
To probe for feeling or a kind intent.

Like echoes from an infinite Beyond
That mix and mingle in the starry dark
Or from some cavern cause our awed remark,
So perfumes, sounds, and colors correspond.

Perfumes as sweet as childhood's tender flesh
As soft as music, like green prairies fresh,
Or rotten-ripe, triumphant, over-rich,
Fill pores, and nerves and taste and touch bewitch,
As amber, musk, benzine sometimes condense
To titillate the spirit and the sense.

Doubtless encouraged by Verlaine and his Bohemian friends, Arthur Rimbaud, purely as a bit of mystification, pushed the experiment further:

The Vowels

A black, E white, I red, U green, O blue!
Some day I shall your origins impart.
A, black, thick hair about the vilest part
Of man, the smell of pits, and things taboo.

E, purity of vapors and pale sky,
The sun on glaciers or on parasols.
I, purple, spit blood, lips of cruel dolls
Drawn thin with drunk intent to crucify.

U, cycles, undulations of turning tides,
Deep peace in copulation, peace besides
That study prints on brows of aged men.
O, bugle ringing clear in field and fen,
Bold clamors calms of men and gods surprise,
O, stern Omega, ray from her violet eyes!

In bidding farewell to his muse in *A Season in Hell,* Rimbaud especially railed at his synesthetic accomplishments, his "magical sophistries," closing with the quiet remark, "That is over. To-day I know how to honour beauty"; yet these remain his most solid results.

Second Frenzy

Alchemy of the Word

As for myself, the story of one of my follies:

For a long time I had bragged of possessing all possible landscapes, and had been derisive about the vogue of painting and modern poetry.

I was in love with idiotic paintings, storm doors, decorations, the back drops used by vaudeville artists, signs, popular colored cartoons, out-of-date literature, Church Latin, lewd books without spelling, medieval romances, fairy tales, primers, old librettos, simple refrains, and native rhythms.

I dreamed of crusades, voyages of discovery of which there are no accounts, republics without histories, suppressed religious wars, revolutions in manners, the migrations of races and the submerging of continents: I trusted completely in magic.

I invented the color of vowels!—*A* black, *E* white, *I* red, *O* blue, *U* green.—I regulated the form and the use of each consonant, and, with the aid of natural rhythms, I flattered myself that I had invented a poetical language capable of being apprehended, one day or another, by all the senses. I reserved the rights of translation.

It was, at the outset, a kind of research. I wrote of silences, of nights; I set down the inexpressible. I fixated vertigoes. . . .

As original in his own way as Arthur Rimbaud and accounted as great a force so far as modern poetry is concerned was another Decadent, Stéphane Mallarmé, who became the chief—"prince of poets," he was called—of the Symbolist group. Mallarmé was born in Paris, on March 18, 1842. His family, long in minor government circles, sent him for his education to a rich boarding school in Auteuil, where he consorted with the children of nobles and affected a compensatory title of his own invention, "le Marquis de Boulainvilliers." To a notebook he committed his earliest verse, written in imitation of the ephemera of Théodore de Banville. In the words of a French critic, Mallarmé was "seduced by the fairy evocations of Banville and impregnated by the dolorous lyricism of Baudelaire." Perhaps through the latter he, too, came to the work of Edgar Allan Poe. In his *Poésies* a sonnet, "The Tomb of Edgar Poe," is followed by a sonnet, "The Tomb of Charles Baudelaire." The better to understand Poe, he made a serious study of English, with the result that he determined to become a teacher in this subject to his countrymen. After completing his studies at Sens, at twenty, he made a trip to England where he resided for some time. His first teaching was done in the South of France, but about 1873 he returned to Paris and shortly afterwards received an appointment as professor in the Lycée Condorcet.

Meanwhile he had associated with the Parnassians and had contributed to *Le Parnasse satirique* (1864), *Le Parnasse contemporain* (1866), and *Le second Parnasse contemporain* (1869). The Parnassians refused, in 1875, to include Mallarmé's masterpiece, *L'Après-midi d'un Faune* in their third anthology and forced the poet, who had quietly developed beyond them, out of their group. That same year he published a prose translation of Poe's *Raven,* a translation which may have affected, because of its prose lines, the rise of *vers libre* in France. This book was illustrated by his great and good friend, Edouard Manet, as was the separate edition of *L'Après-midi d'un Faune,* issued in 1876. The next year witnessed the publication of his *Complete Poems,* but it created little stir.

In 1885, an unforeseen event brought Mallarmé out of obscurity. In that year Joris-Karl Huysmans, the Naturalist novelist, published his satire of the Decadents, *Against the Grain (À Rebours).* This book, called the "Breviary of the Esthete," was for a long time supposed to be a sympathetic photograph of the "Decadent," but Professor G. L. Van Roosbroeck has put it in its true light. It is a subtle caricature of the New Esthetes, the Decadents, of the Eighties. "With it Huysmans has derided their phantastic over-refinement, their mingling of sense impressions with music, color, perfumes, and with the luxuriousness of soft silks and velvets. All through the book runs, like a red thread, a constant vein of parody—the parody of the Undreamed Dream of the Exquisite Sensation."

The hero of the book, the Marquis des Esseintes, whose name suggests a combination of *Essences* and of *Saints,* is "the last frail representative of an aristocratic family, undermined for generations by stubborn anemia, a number of strange maladies and secret vices. An orphan since early childhood, he grew up in seclusion, tortured by obstinate fevers and a whole series of wasting diseases. He has become a maniac—the maniac of hyperaestheticism. . . ." *Against the Grain* is a record of his diseased taste, his posturing, and his subterfuges for dodging raw life.

Des Esseintes has drawn meagre intellectual pap from the flat breasts of the Latin writers of the Decadence. Already Baudelaire in a note to "Franciscae meae Laudes" had remarked how fit the language of the Latin decadent poets was to express the passions of modern French poetry. Although Lucan is tolerated, the hyperaesthete has contempt for Virgil and Horace, but only adoration for Petronius and Apuleius. Among the moderns, Edgar Allan Poe, Charles Baudelaire, Paul Verlaine, Villiers de l'Isle Adam, Tristan Corbière, Theodore Hannon—all Decadents—receive his approval.

Yet it is the unknown Stéphane Mallarmé who is unstintingly praised by Des Esseintes. ". . . He loved the works of this poet who, in a century of universal suffrage, in a time when trade was triumphant, lived only for Letters, protected from his sordid environment by his contempt for it, consoling himself, far from the world, to intellectual delights, to visions conjured by his brain, refining upon the already specious thoughts with scribblings of Byzantine delicateness. . . . " Stéphane Mallarmé is the incarnation of "the decadence of a literature irreparably affected in its organism, weakened in its ideas by age, exhausted by the excess of syntax, sensitive only to the curiosity which fevers sick people, yet hastening to say everything, now at the end, torn by the wish to atone for all its omissions of enjoyment, to bequeath its subtlest memories of sorrow on its death bed."

Huysmans' satire had just the opposite of its calculated effect: it heightened the interest in Decadence and it fixed attention upon Mallarmé for the first time in his career. Everyone inquired about this little-known and recondite poet. A group of young writers who had been frozen out of the review, *Le Décadent,* and who had been further alienated by abusive attacks, now proclaimed Mallarmé their master and adopted for their special kind of Decadence the epithet, Symbolism. Gustave Kahn edited the official weekly organ of this group, called *Le Symboliste.*

Symbolism moved poetry a step further from the comprehension of the average reader than the synesthetic effects, the unusual subjects, and the hallucinations of Arthur Rimbaud had done. In place of *description* the Symbolists substituted and defended *suggestion*. "Do you know what Symbolism is?" inquired Jules Tellier: "The word is rather pompous, but the thing is very simple. To symbolize consists plainly, after one has found an image expressive of a state of the soul, in expressing not this state of the soul, but only the image that materializes it." Such a poem as Mallarmé's "Sigh" (*Soupir*) fulfills the requirements of this definition, but frequently Symbolism was pushed further than this. At times it affected the very language which the poet used. Thus the poet writes of "the wandering sky of thine angelic eyes" and of "the forest of your hair." "Evening bleeds upon the curbs" for him when the sun is setting. For more extreme examples an interpreter is required. Mallarmé wrote on one occasion, "I bring to you the child of an Idumean night," meaning "an Edomite baby," but more definitely, "a poem I have written in the night." This poet avowed that "To name an object is to suppress three-quarters of the enjoyment of the poem which consists in the pleasure of guessing little by little." The Symbolists substituted the rhymed rebus for poetry.

Symbolism had another characteristic often overlooked by the critics. It stressed the importance, above everything else, of the *unreal* experience, of the dream. In this sense Symbolism was the open enemy of the new Naturalism. Poe had written in "Dreams":

> ". . . Yes! tho' that long dream were of hopeless sorrow
> 'T were better than the cold reality
> Of waking life. . . ."

For the Symbolists, as for Poe's Egaeus, "the wild ideas of the land of dreams became, in turn, not the material of every-day existence, but in very deed that existence utterly and solely in itself."

Suddenly emerging from obscurity as the prophet of a new cult, Mallarmé assumed gracefully the robes of his office. Not many months after the publication of *Against the Grain*, Mallarmé began to hold the famous Tuesday night sessions in his apartment in the Rue de Rome. Here foregathered not only all the Symbolists, but ultimately most of the young men who were to make modern French literature. To name but a few: Paul Claudel, Edouard Dujardin, Théodore Duret, Félix Fénéon, André Fortainas, Réné Ghil, André Gide, Gustave Kahn, Jules Laforgue, Pierre Louys, Camille Mauclair, Stuart Merril, Albert Mockel, Charles Morice, Henri de Regnier, Adolphe Retté, Marcel Schwob, Laurent Tailhade, Paul Valéry, Francis Vielé-Griffin, Charles Vignière, and Teodore de Wyzewa.

Mallarmé, leaning gracefully against the mantel, his shoulders covered by a grey shawl, spoke the piece which André Gide has accused him of carefully preparing and rehearsing. Was the text usually out of Poe? No record of these famous conversations exists, yet what the master stood for is clear enough. The guests, sent home at eleven with a glass of wine poured by Mademoiselle Geneviève, had to reflect on the divinity of Poetry; on observations that it has nothing to do with morality or truth, but its sole province is Beauty, that it is above everything else music and harmony, and that the reality of words is as great as that of life. Or they resolved to learn more about Wagner, or Whistler, or Gauguin, or Swinburne, whom Mallarmé praised. How Poe, leaning by that same mantel, would have enjoyed such an audience!

The French call Mallarmé *"un fumiste"* for which there is no better equivalent in English than "a joker." With much talk he magnified the differences between himself and the Decadents, but save for being a better mystifier and more erudite, he is as much of a Decadent as Baudelaire, or Verlaine, or Rimbaud. In the prose poem, called "Autumn Lament," he writes: ". . . . Thus, in the year, my favorite season is during those last languid summer days which come just before the autumn; and, in the day, the hour when the sun lingers before fading, with rays of copper-yellow on the grey walls, and of copper-red on the window-panes. And, just so, the literature from which my soul demands delight must be the poetry, dying out, of the last moments of Rome, provided, nevertheless, that it breathes nothing of the rejuvenating approach of the Barbarians and does not stammer the infantile Latin of the first Christian prose. . . ." He acknowledged the dubious compliment of Huysmans with a "Prose pour des Esseintes" published in *La Revue Indépendante.*

Nowhere does Mallarmé's contempt for the race at large receive more emphatic statement than in his experimental piece, "The Windows." Greedy of "azure" as any bed-ridden invalid, and disgusted with the realistic writers whose appetites "root in the dung of happiness," the sick poet would flee to the empyrean if he could, but doubts assail him—

7.

I flee, but stop myself against the sash;
For though I turn my back on life, I'm blessed
And bathed by the eternal dews which flash
Their gold on each celestial morn. So rest.

8.

Yet I, adoring my reflection, fade;
O that the glass were Art and permanent
My dream! Immortal then what now is shade,
Raised high in Beauty's lovely firmament.

9.

The "Real" is master here below, alas!
Which drives me to the hospice of pure art;
This dirty vomit from the human ass
Assails a nose held tight as I depart.

10.

Are you demeaned who know the bitterness,
O Soul, if I with you revolt and flee
From filth on my two wings so featherless
And risk our falling through eternity?

Yet how sincere is Mallarmé's misanthropy? Is it a deep-rooted disgust with mankind or an affectation to attract attention? All Mallarmé's acquaintance speak of his lack of passion and enthusiasm. He was an intellectual who teased feeling into his poetry, who simulated even disgust. His verse in the main is synthetic, but the borrowings from which he made his amalgam are less recondite than is generally supposed. Poe supplied him

with his aesthetic, Banville with his nymphs and fauns and fairies
—this we have seen. But his themes are chosen in the main from
one aspect of Browning's work—the poet who had the reputation that Mallarmé most coveted, for *obscurity*—when Mallarmé was in England. Much of Mallarmé's writing has been
done to conceal this simple, and it must be confessed, rather
bourgeois source. That is why the poet attacks so vigorously
mundane happiness (Mallarmé made this a vogue), for with
this element introduced few would suspect his relationship to the
optimistic son of the British green grocer. It was a kind of smoke
screen between himself and his origins. Mallarmé truly was a
fumiste.

L'*Après-midi d'un Faune*, Stéphane Mallarmé's masterpiece, is
a most ingenious synthesis of all his sources. A Faun, seated alone
at noon on a mountain, recalls some nymphs whom he had raped.
Yet he is not certain that he did not dream the episode, and with
his flute seeks to define more sharply his vision. He feels again
a kiss and a bite and is assured the event was real. But when he
ceases to play, doubt comes again. In music is his only reality.
Against the sky red Etna glows, and on its side he sees the goddess Venus. He is about to possess the delightful phantom of all
his dreams when drowsiness overtakes him. It is said that this
poem was inspired by a painting by Boucher in the National Gallery in London, though the Faun cavorts in Banville, Victor
Hugo, and even Mrs. Browning. More interesting to us is the
fact that Mallarmé planned to have *The Afternoon of a Faun*
produced on the stage with music and dances, for the great virtue
of the poem is its melodies. The piece is literally the summation
of all Poe's teaching: it is written primarily for its musical
effect, and the action is a witty adaptation of his theme—

> *All* that we see or seem
> Is but a dream within a dream.

Studied more coldly, however, L'*Après-midi d'un Faune* is
the monologue of an unsure artist and lover who, despite his
hooves, his horns, and his flute, bears a startling resemblance to
Browning's Andrea del Sarto. The latter, "the perfect painter,"
tries to hold to him his cold mistress, Lucrezia del Fede, by call-

ing up to her recollection past pleasures together when he was the sure master of his art. Failing, he yields her with a sigh to the "cousin's" whistle outside their window. The changes instituted by Mallarmé are trivial, but the substitution of the languorous Faun for the cuckold painter makes the subject seem immensely more remote from human experience. The frustration and futility are, however, in "Andrea del Sarto".

L' Après-midi d'un Faune

These nymphs I would immortalize—
What fair
Chimeras waver in the drowsy air
Above my tufted sleep.
Was love a dream?
My doubts, piled high in hoary darkness, seem
To harden as a tendril does to wood.
Which only proves, alas, how I delude
Myself who take a blushing rose for nude . . .
Let us reflect . . .
Suppose these creatures bright
A product of your sensuous appetite,
O Faun! That most chaste nymph whose liquid eyes
Are cold and blue as any spring denies
Such nonsense; while the other's warm, moist mouth
Breathes sighs like wind at noon from out the south
Upon your fleece. But no! Humidity,
Like this which choked the dawn perfidiously,
Admits no cooling whisper anywhere
Of water, save the mellow notes that flare
From out my flute. For only one wind blows
And, ushering my measured music, goes
To vent itself in heaven from my reed;
Nor is that azure marred by my notes' speed
More than the calm of gracious space is stirred
In the return of some immortal word.

You shores of that Sicilian swamp where I,
Pushing aside the starry blooms, espy
My image wrinkling in the sun's, O, say
How I cut here the hollow reeds I play,
And how I tamed them; how a prelude soft
Upon these pipes did wing its way aloft
To where, beside a fountain ivy-clad

On sward of gold,'a pallid sleeper had
Repose, to frighten swans or nymphs to flight,
Who plunged . . .

               Fallow, that hour which, hot and white,
Marked not false Hymen's flight-achieving ruse
While I debated still the note I'd choose.
Then let me rouse to passion's early flame,
Which ravaged me like lightning when it came,
With, lilies, one of you for innocence.

Besides the kiss, surpassing continence,
Which rumor lightly gives to everyone,
My virgin breast, in passion bared to none,
Displays the print of an immortal tooth.

But hush! Such alchemy one tells, forsooth,
To one's reed only, which translates the dream
Into a mournful solo with a theme
Refined; and thus false beauty is created
To which this loveliness is unrelated;
Thus love is purged, and fancy bled all white
Of breasts and flanks to captivate the sight,
In one's sonorous, vain, and empty line.

Strive, then, evasive instrument, malign
Panpipe, to bloom beside your native lake
Again! To sing of goddesses I take
My way alone and lightly feign rebirth
In dreams of them flung prostrate on the earth:
Thus, having long since sucked the grape's clear juice,
I laugh to banish doubt at this abuse,
And raise to heaven's zenith my new grape
(The breath I blew within preserves its shape),
And drunk, I lie till night regarding it.

O nymphs, let's multiply the scenes that flit:—
My roving glance, which pierced the reeds' thick mesh,
Fell burning on these lovely creatures' flesh,
Who, shrieking, in the water tried to cool
The smart; their waving hair disturbed the pool
With gold, and then the gold in waves was lost:
I scattered pebbles running to accost
Some laggard, when in my very path I found
Two darlings locked in sleep upon the ground.
(Destroyers of the thought of being two!)

To ravish both I did not need undo
Their chaste embrace; and then I stole away
To where the roses drain their scent; our play
As shadows told, consumed the ebbing day.

I love that virginal anger; what intense
Delight to bear down naked innocence
Protesting my devouring lips! How fear
Pounds in the heart, like hooves in mad career,
Of timid maidens soon deflowered! The thought
Starts foolish tears—a tribute cheaply bought.
Too jubilant at having stilled these fears,
I erred in trying to divide the dears
Whom heaven's self had thus securely tied;
For when I bent my wrinkled face to hide
My mirthful triumph in the elder's hair
(With single finger the younger of the pair
Repelling, lest she kindle with the flame
That burned her mate, and she, the sweet, to shame
A naïve stranger), that ungrateful prey
In my embrace unconquered, got away,
And shrilly laughed at my complete dismay.

Enough! With each horn bound by golden curls
They'll drag me soon to watch these lily girls
Enjoyed by others. I, the ripe fruit see
With musky odor lure the incestuous bee;
So, too, my blood with its tumultuous fire
Should quickly call whole legions of desire.
When on dried leaves in the declining day
Red Etna is reflected in washed gray
And gold, I see proud Venus venture forth,
Her cool heel spurning lava as if earth,
While all about the growling thunders die.
I seize the queen.
　　　　　　O bliss!
　　　　　　　　　　But no, I lie!
Now gorged with words this soul and body swoon,
Succumbing to the silence of the noon.
I must in sleep forget my blasphemy
And contemplate no more obliquity
Than that my gaping mouth some grape receive.

Fond pair! I seek the shade which you perceive.

No one will deny that Mallarmé's verse gives some of the pleasures of chamber music or assert that we should value his word-pictures less than the pink things of Boucher and Frago-nard. Yet this is not the greatest art, and it is strange that it should have had so pronounced an effect upon modern poetry. Mallarmé himself was afflicted with a sense of failure. *"Ma poésie,"* he declared, *"est une impasse."* His effort to refine Poe, Baudelaire, Banville, and Browning—in a word, to refine that already refined—led inevitably to frustration. The moderns who have used Mallarmé have really turned from him back towards life (with a few exceptions), and their poetry is stronger than his, though no more musical, for this reason. The most notable example of his failure is his "Herodiade" where he cannot suc-cessfully maintain a dialogue between the glamorous lady, now imagined as faded, and her nurse. Intimates of years and placed in a boudoir where there need be no reserve, they are undeniably dull because their author is not "up" to them:

> HERODIADE.—Nurse, am I beautiful?
> NURSE.   A star in truth,
>   But that lock hangs. . . .

Browning struggled all his life to be understood; Mallarmé, to be misunderstood; yet today it is the latter who seems banal and the former who has freshness and strength, despite the more or less bourgeois obviousness of his themes. The certain headi-ness one feels in an ivory tower—undeniably one of the keenest pleasures a superior mind may enjoy—is in a degree communica-ble and Mallarmé has communicated it; however, it is not the sum of human experience nor all that a man of sensibility may enjoy, and when Mallarmé tries to secure the same effect of aloofness in all his poems, particularly in those poems, like the "Herodiade," where the situation calls for a warm and intimate touch, we grow bored and turn away. Mallarmé is a musician who has drawn a note of rare beauty from his instrument, but has so protracted the note that he has pained, where he might have ravished, his auditors.

Half way between Arthur Rimbaud and Stéphane Mallarmé stands Jules Laforgue, of whom Arthur Symons says, "He has invented a new manner of being René or Werther: an inflexible politeness towards man, woman, and destiny." This studied reserve of Laforgue was probably his only security; he was a dying man all his life long. Born at Montevideo, Uruguay, August 16, 1860, of Breton parents, he was taken at four to Paris for his schooling, where he suffered the tortures of the damned from loneliness. At six he began to write verses and at nineteen he joined the Hydropathes, a fantastic literary circle of which the most prominent member was Gustave Kahn. He did some research at the Bibliothèque Nationale for a pittance, and then, in 1881, he was hired as a reader to the Empress Augusta, grandmother to the German Kaiser. In Berlin, he met and became infatuated with an English girl who bore a name curiously like one of Poe's heroines, Leah Lee; their insipid love letters, which have found their way into print, reflect awkwardly on the blasé tone assumed in the *Moralités Légendaires*. Laforgue's acquaintance with the world was very largely through books. Despite the fact that the young reader had already showed signs of tuberculosis, the two were married in London, on December 31, 1886. The marriage consumed what little fire Laforgue had left—he died in Paris on August 20, 1887, four days after his twenty-seventh birthday; and his bride, who had contracted his disease, followed him to the grave eight months later.

No contemporary writer so completely assimilated the spirit of Decadence as Jules Laforgue. Life is boredom and love a three minute ecstasy. Laforgue has been compared to Heine, and indeed in their sophisticated attitude towards the emotions there is a resemblance; yet where there is resiliency in Heine, there is defeat in Laforgue. The German Jew did not have to read by the hour to the grandmother of his country's conqueror. Yet never does Laforgue rise to grandeur; never does he rail against Almighty God, as does Heine, for the world's illusion:

> Also fragen wir beständig,
> Bis man uns mit einer Handvoll
> Erde endlich stopft die Mäuler,
> Aber is das eine Antwort?

> (Thus we ask incessantly
> Until someone with a handful

Of earth finally stops our mouths.
But is that an answer?)

Instead, Laforgue whines phthisically of the world's ills, but ends
by always giving them a personal application:

... Sing and Dance for Life is short
And all is vain—while there on high the moon dreams
As cold as in the time when man was not ...
... And I, how many days have I to live?

Yet Laforgue comes very close to epitomizing Decadent
thought, or lack of thought. When on a carnival night he
searches the heartless void for an answer, but receives as a reply
only the melancholy echo of the bestial song of some strayed
reveller, we are in the presence of as profound an intuition as
any Decadent ever had. We are to be fundamentally moved by
such lines as—

Oh! la vie est trop triste, incurablement triste
Aux fêtes d'ici-bas j'ai toujours sangloté
"Vanité, vanité, tout n'est que vanité!"
—Puis je songeais: ou sont les cendres du Psalmiste?

(Oh! life is overmuch sad, incurably sad,
At fêtes here below I am always sobbing,
"Vanity, vanity, all is but vanity!"
Then I think, Where are the ashes of the Psalmist?)

Particularly do Laforgue's various poetic complaints, such
as the "Complaint of Forgetting the Dead," and "Complaint of
the Lad with Heart's Disease," reveal him as innocuous, unripe,
and immature. In "Albums" Laforgue tries to follow the fancies
of a healthy boy and sees himself, "freed from literature, scalped
of his European brain, a big, bad man and desperado" in the
Far West and on the Prairie. The effect is at once ludicrous and
pathetic—poor Laforgue never had a normal boyhood and this
is perhaps the sorriest effort to find the Eternal Fountain in
literature.

Laforgue is at his best in the "Hamlet" of *Moralités Légendaires*. Here he conceived the then novel idea of bringing "Ham-

let" up to date by mixing historical and modern styles, by introducing nineteenth century manners and episodes, and by taking the leading rôle himself. Émile Laforgue, the poet's brother, has written, "If you wish to know Jules Laforgue, you have only to read his *Hamlet*. He is entirely there. It is himself whom he has painted—the resemblance is striking." Maeterlinck declared the piece truer than Shakespeare's, and there is no denying the ending is superior—it could hardly be otherwise. The substitution of an adolescent, sentimental Dane for a melancholy one, however, deprives Laforgue's effort of dignity. Much of the interest of his creation derives from the fact that it is a variant from a powerful and familiar legend. We are attracted to it as we would be to a dancer who capriciously left a waltz, executed a fantastic step or two, and then returned to his partner. Moreover, the piece in itself quaintly resembles a motion picture scenario:

. . . Hamlet [eloping with an actress] perceives that just then they are about to pass close to the cemetery.

(The cemetery . . .)

And there he, bitten by some strange tarantula, gets down from his horse that he hitches to a tree, an indifferent and melancholy tree.

"Kate, wait for me a minute. I must visit the tomb of my father who was assassinated, the unfortunate man! I will tell you about it. I will return immediately as soon as I can gather a flower, a simple paper flower to serve us as a bookmark when we shall read again my drama and find it necessary to stop to kiss each other."

He strides on by moonlight among the shadows of the stones, made darker by the cypress trees. He goes directly to the tomb of Ophelia, of *the* Ophelia, already so mysterious and legendary. And there, arms crossed, he waits.

(Decidedly.)

> "The dead—
> So discreetly
> They sleep
> Very late."

"Who goes there? Is it you, wretched Hamlet? Why do you come here?"

"It is you, my dear Laertes? What good wind? . . ."

"Yes, it is I; and if you were not a poor, demented soul, not responsible according to the latest findings of science, you would be paying, there on their tombs, for the death of my honourable father and that of my young and talented sister."

"O Laertes, it makes no difference to me. But I shall consider your viewpoint."

"Just Heaven! what absence of moral sense!"

"Then you know what has happened?"

"Come! Away from here, fool, or I will forget myself. When one ends in madness, it is because he began by pretending it."

"And your sister?"

"Oh!"

At that moment there is heard in the ghostly clear night the howl of a farmer's hound, so excruciatingly alone that the heart of that excellent Laertes (who might well have been the hero of this story—alas, I think of it too late) overflows with the inexplicable anonymity of his destiny at thirty years. This is too much. And seizing Hamlet's throat with one hand, with the other he stabbed him through the heart with a real dagger.

Our hero sinks to his knees in the grass, and vomits mouthfuls of blood. He acts like an animal closely pursued by certain death. He tries to speak. . . . he succeeds in uttering:

"Oh, oh! *Qualis . . . artifex . . . pereo!*"

And the soul of Hamlet returned to adamantine nature.

Laertes, typical human idiot, leans over and kisses the poor slain man on the forehead. He squeezes his dead fingers, and then, running blindly, he flees across the enclosure to become a monk for always.

Silence and the moon. . . . Cemetery and nature. . . .

"Hamlet! Hamlet!" called Kate, who was shivering with cold, "Hamlet!"

The moon sheds over all an icy silence.

Kate decides to come and see for herself.

She sees. She is stunned by that livid and cold body in the moonlight.

"He has stabbed himself. O, Heaven!"

She leans over the tomb and reads:

OPHELIA
DAUGHTER OF LORD POLONIUS
& LADY ANNE
SHE DIED WHEN SHE WAS EIGHTEEN

And the date, to-day.

"It was she whom he loved! Then why did he ravish me with love? Poor hero. . . . What shall I do?"

She leans over, kisses him, and calls him:

"Hamlet, *my little Hamlet!*"

But death is death, as has been known since life began.

"I am going to return to the Castle with the horses, and hunt up again the equerry who witnessed our departure, and I will tell him all about it."

She hurries off, turning her back towards the full moon which streams way off there across the plains, the plains towards Paris and the brilliant Valois who are holding high court.

Thus was all made known, the reprehensible dramatic blow against personality, the elopement, etc. Someone was sent with candlesticks of the highest quality to look for the body. . . . Oh, historic evening, after all!

But Kate was William's mistress.

"Ah, Ha!" said this man, "So you wished to run away from Bibi, did you?"

(Bibi is an abbreviation of Billy, which is a diminutive for William.)

And Kate receives a beautiful hard blow, which is neither the first, nor shall it be the last, alas. Even so Kate is so fair that in another age Greece would have raised fanes to her.

And all returned to order.

One Hamlet less. The race is not lost, whatever one may say.

In the works of Verlaine, Rimbaud, Mallarmé, and Laforgue are found practically all of the elements which contribute substance, form, and mood to one school of modern American poetry. With Baudelaire, these four men gave France a new birth of lyric poetry, the first genuine singing in that land since the Middle Ages. They broke the fetters of the hexameter, dissociated classical imagery, and established the relationship of music and verse. Yet they could not transcend their times; the melancholy, the frustration, the despair of their defeated country, fully as much as their own abnormality, either determined the tone of all their verse or forced them away from life into pure art, as surely as his uncultured countrymen drove Poe into similar realms of aesthetic nonsense. On this score we may find some excuse for them; but what apology can we make for twentieth century Americans who, while they have improved the forms of the French poets—this is excellent—yet have imitated their despair and assumed their decadence? One fault of American writers has been their servility, and the very poets who, in 1920, seemed so original, today appear as feeble and as imitative as any we have produced, not excluding the young Longfellow and the young Lowell.

Before turning to our own poetry, we may sketch in lightly the development of poetry and poetic theory in France to the present, for not only have modern Americans imitated the Decadent masters, but they have also copied from their contemporary French imitators. The two greatest poets of the North, however, Maurice Maeterlinck and Emile Verhaeren—both affected by the Symbolist movement, though in quite different ways,— have found no important disciples in this country although there has been ample appreciation of their work. It is with lesser figures that we must deal.

One of these is Edouard-Joachim Corbière, who called himself Tristan. Born in 1845, he was fifteen years Laforgue's senior. Many effects usually assigned to the latter are found first in Tristan Corbière. Those poems of painful puberty, the complaints of Laforgue, are somewhat forecast in the other's work. Thus the "Complaint of the Lad with Heart's Disease" should be compared with Corbière's "Rhapsody of the Deaf Mute." Corbière's most distinctive contribution to verse was an irreverent, an untranslatable, an epigrammatic slang, so cacophonous in effect, however, that Corbière has but a dubious place as a singer. He died at twenty-nine, after appending to a neurotic childhood a full index of dissipations in Bohemia. Tuberculosis flung back in his face his last blasphemy. Huysmans wiped the poor soiled countenance with a soiled cloth and declared Corbière a poet to the world.

Jean Papadiamantopoulos, who conveniently wrote under the name of Moréas, promised to do great things in the early days of Symbolism. He reverted to classicism—a classicism tinged with Byronism, however. At the same time an interest in Renaissance vocabulary lent his verse a certain metrical freedom and obscurity. He will probably be remembered chiefly for his efforts to revive certain philological archaisms. Moréas was not ill; he was merely eccentric. Gustave Kahn pretends to have invented *vers libre,* but is himself more bizarre than important. René Ghil, Belgian by birth, has tried to elaborate the famous "Vowel Sonnet" of Rimbaud into a theory of verse which he calls "verbal instrumentation." His long poems, arranged under chapter heads, rather than under titles, have been more influential than meritorious. Paul Fort, without any great talent—one can count all the pebbles in the bottom of his stream—won fame as long ago as 1896 with his *French Ballads,* a volume which was mainly remarkable for the fact that it contained three distinguishable forms: prose, rhythmical prose, and verse. The rhythmical prose was most interesting, for, besides its irregular beat, it contained the figurative language, the alliterative adornment, and even the rimes of verse.

The one poet most definitely linking the great Decadents with the French moderns is Paul Valéry, who emerged from almost complete obscurity, so far as the general public was concerned, in 1921, when his literary contemporaries, in a referendum in the review *La Connaissance,* voted him the best poet in France. Four years later Valéry was elected a member of the French Academy to fill the vacancy left by the death of Anatole France. Born, in 1871, in the little town of Cette on the Mediterranean, he met the poet Pierre Louys while attending the University of Montpellier and became his devoted friend. The latter encouraged him to write and published his first verses in *The Conch,* of which Louys was the editor, in 1889. When he became twenty, Valéry went up to Paris and entered into the Symbolist discussions led by Mallarmé. He published a few poems in the reviews and won the approval and friendship of the chief of the Symbolists. Listening to Mallarmé, Valéry was astonished that "through the exhaustive study of his art and with no scientific education, he should have arrived at a conception so abstract and so close to the most abstruse speculations of certain of the sciences." Stimulated by this "divine" talker, Valéry arrived at his theory that literature is primarily valuable to the artist as a mental exercise. "The completed work of art," he avers, "I consider as without interest. The only thing that arouses my curiosity is its actual creation." It is gratuitous to point out that this is a perfectly logical development of Poe's original thesis that literature is primarily expression.

Conceiving the functioning intellect—functioning in art—as the most important thing in the world, Valéry embodied, in 1891, his ideas in a study which excited much comment among the erudite, *Introduction à la Methode de Leonardo da Vinci.* In the extraordinarily versatile Italian, Valéry saw a genius who was "a complete system in himself," greater than all his accomplishments. Finding as much interest in da Vinci's projects as in his performances, Valéry questioned that, if once a principle is grasped, it is not "quite useless to waste one's time applying it." Valéry's next book, *La Soirée avec Monsieur Teste,* gives us a Hamlet (M. Teste) entirely occupied with his own mental processes. He has erased the living—"il raturait le vif"—and indulges purely in speculation, becoming a rather hideous Frankenstein, a thought machine.

Mallarmé died in 1898, so that Valéry never had with him that discussion of ultimates for which he yearned. It is doubtful, however, if Mallarmé could have dissuaded him from the course he now chose to follow, for the arguments of M. Teste were enforced emotionally by a disappointment in love. Valéry gave up literature and devoted his leisure, when not employed in the Ministry of War or the Agence Havas, to mathematics and philosophy. Twenty years passed with the publication of but a single lyric. Then, in 1917, he married Mallarmé's daughter, and André Gide, who had known him since his Montpellier days, persuaded him to print again. *La Jeune Parque,* published in 1917, and acclaimed by the erudite, was followed by *Odes* and *L'Album de Vers Anciens* in 1920, *Charmes* and *Fragments du Narcisse* in 1922, *Poésies* in 1923, *Variété* in 1924, and numerous other small volumes. By shrewdly limiting his editions and by expensive printing, Valéry has made his books collectors' items and has subtly disseminated the idea that their intrinsic worth is very great. Actually, so far as the race is concerned, their value is not infinitely greater than that of the manuscript verses of some jolly balladeer who is willing to exchange them for bread.

Valéry is the only poet who has refined on Mallarmé with any success. His connection with the great Symbolist is obvious and has been stressed by every critic. Writing of Valéry's early verse, Edmund Wilson observes, "What we find in these poems today is chiefly the chaste-celestial, the blue-and-white mood of such poems as Mallarmé's 'Apparition' in what seems a thinner diluted form. Paul Valéry, like his master, is 'haunted' by the 'azure'; but that azure is less a pure blue realm and more a rarefied upper air. . . ." The later poetry shows the same refinement in epithet, is more definitely cerebral, and has progressed further in the direction of Decadence in subject matter. That is, instead of the lusts and dreams of a sensuous old faun, we are given in the celebrated poem, "Narcissus," the self-admiration of a sad pervert as he stands in a forest pool—a pool as near to Nature as Watteau. Valéry is what Mallarmé might have been had he had his own example and the studies of Freud to work from. Feeble in one sense as Mallarmé is, he is undeniably the more original of the two men; his transformation of Browning is more complete than is Valéry's "refinement" of L'Après-midi d'un Faune in the "Narcissus."

Books like Radclyffe Hall's novel, *The Well of Loneliness,* have established the presumption that sexual inversion is not the fault of the person who suffers from it and have won for the sufferer the sympathy of all understanding people. Valéry's "Narcissus," however, does not aim at this sort of illumination. Among its several purposes, it strives to make vice as attractive as it really is—here the influence of the erotic Pierre Louys is seen—and succeeds beyond applause. Aesthetic enjoyment of "Narcissus" is really limited to a kind of attenuated Narcissism, so great is the fidelity of the piece. Yet this is not the most vicious aspect—it may even be questioned if it is a vicious aspect at all— of the poem. The peculiarly noxious thing about this poem is its thesis—derived ultimately from Bergson—that in seclusion and the night, and in a deranged, frustrate, and heated state, the immutable self may be found. The distraught sufferer knows not whether the image in the pool is his slave, or he its, until the climax of the poem, which is the climax of the orgasm, when he discovers it is his "illimitable soul"! Daylight, here symbolical of what Valéry might term "bourgeois" or "willful" reason, breaks the illusion repeatedly. It is in the seductive suggestion of the superior value of the neurotic experience that Valéry is preëminently a Decadent.

Self-auscultation is the thesis of Valéry's best-known poems— *La Jeune Parque, Le Cimetière Marin*—but this listening for the soul is best done under abnormal conditions. We are constantly reminded of Bergson's *Matter and Memory,* containing that able study of aphasia from which is deduced that memory is the one thing which makes existence continuous. Memory fades altogether in Valéry's poems—where is it in "Narcissus"?—but there emerges instead a phantasmagorical thing which Valéry insists is the true self. "Cease willing," counsels Bergson, "detach yourself from life, disinterest yourself: by that effort you pass from the self of yesterday to the self of dreams, a self less strained but further-reaching than the other." Valéry's process for achieving this ultra-self is not by detachment but by self-concentration—inevitably morbid and unhealthy. "The important thing," he says, "is not so much to know oneself as an immutable being always identical with itself." The "immutable being" of Paul Valéry gives one a cold shudder.

Though again and again Valéry affirms his preoccupation with the intellectual life, the body itself looms so large in his "thought" that there is place for nothing else. "I love thought," he declares in the introduction to the *Cimetière Marin*, "just as other men love the nude which they spend their lives in painting." The figure has its significance. In his own "detachment" and that of Leonardo da Vinci, who provoked a famous essay by the poet, there is the same absorption in the flesh which is a denial of the "perfect mastery over their natures" that they assume they have achieved. As one studies Valéry's lucubrations in the first and second series of *Variété* the conviction comes that his writing is a sort of pathetic *apologia pro vita sua*—a revelation of the years that he has subdued his flesh with the philosopher's stone of abstraction in the desert of fantastic desires. The horror of that long silence of his and what it covered! Then the merciful deliverance suggested by Freud. The world may well turn with a shudder from his erotic poetry where vice purrs like a sleek cat, but there is no doubt whatever that those poems have been for him an escape and an expression. The real reason why Valéry is not interested in his completed poems, *but in their composition,* is a psychical one—finished, they have served him all they can. Creation for Valéry has been a process of sublimation—even though the product is not sublime.

Aside from the appearance of the writings of Freud, the world has not moved for Valéry since the 'nineties. His decadence is Mallarmé's grown a little Viennese. His "Crisis of the Spirit" could as well have been written after the Franco-Prussian War as after the great cataclysm of 1914–1918. All the younger poets of France were profoundly affected by the Great War. A poetic melancholy inherited from the Symbolists was not a completely adequate expression for that experience. Neither were they able to retire from a world which insisted on military service, which rained bombs on their ivory towers, or exploded mines beneath their fragile underpinnings. As a result, their verse recorded a kind of shell shock: the ordered intelligence gave away to a consciousness pervaded by a kaleidoscopic jumble of impressions—the chatter of fear-stricken idiots punctuated by the cheerful staccato of machine gun fire, fragments of camouflaged latrines plunked against the enamelled azure of the Symbolists in lewd geometric patterns—and all flickering, flickering, like the last several pictures in a broken cinema film.

In 1916, in the darkest moment of the War, Dadaism and "the revolt against literature" were born. In that year in Zurich, Switzerland, a small group of refugee intellectuals banded together under the leadership of the dark little Roumanian mystifier, Tristan Tzara, to start the "mouvement Dada," to publish a *Bulletin,* and to issue manifestoes. Meanwhile, the poet André Breton, serving as an interne in the neurological hospital in Nantes, had encountered there a most extraordinary wounded soldier, a former Beaux Arts student with flaming red hair, by the name of Jacques Vaché. This man gave to Dadaism a program and a manner. It is probably wrong to suppose that he was completely mad; his mild insanity drew shrewd suggestions from Jules Laforgue's "Pierrot Fumiste" or from the monkey tricks of Tristan Corbière, who on one occasion paraded in Rome with a pig, a dress suit, and a mitre. The conduct of Jacques Vaché was, nevertheless, most extraordinary. For a time after his discharge from the hospital he labored on the docks as a stevedore, sallying forth at night in the most outlandish attire—a combination of the uniforms of several nations—to make a round of the motion picture houses and cafés. He took to himself titles and bestowed on his friends the names of famous personages in history or literature. He kept his mistress, a rather striking young woman, sitting stiffly motionless in a corner while he regaled his guests with tales of adventures of the most improbable sort.

When his act was played out, shortly before the Armistice, he committed suicide by taking, and forcing two of his friends to take, a large overdose of opium. When found, their bodies were said to be contorted with mirth.

Jacques Vaché was a complete Nihilist, one for whom the "stars were unhooked" and life was very "tiresome." Homicide he looked upon as "an amusing experience" and art as "a stupidity." Art ought to be "something funny and a trifle boring." Genuine humor he defined as "a sense of the theatric, joyless futility of everything, when one is enlightened." He cursed all modern writers, with whose works he showed an astounding familiarity, poked fun at the satanic lyricism of "dear old rotten Baudelaire," condescended to the ghost of Mallarmé, and admitted that he had surpassed Rimbaud, for whom, however, he had an intense admiration. After Vaché's death, André Breton carried his ideas up to Paris, where he joined Tristan Tzara and his group, lately come from Zurich. Whereupon Dadaism took on significance. Other names emerged from the group and famous converts were made. Guillaume Apollinaire, André Salmon, and Max Jacob—former cubists—became interested, Gide and Valéry supported the movement, but the real leaders were Tzara and Breton, with a number of younger men, Louis Aragon, Paul Éluard, Francis Picabia, and Philippe Soupault. The group issued a review, which bore the flamboyantly satiric title of *Littérature*.

In 1920 Dada held a series of public manifesto readings and demonstrations which created so much excitement in Paris (as they were calculated to do) that thousands of people attended. The first several meetings, here accurately enough described by Tzara, were typical of all:

. . . The début of Dadaism in Paris took place on the twenty-third of January, at the matinée organized by the Dadaist review *Littérature*. Louis Aragon, a slender young man with feminine features, A. Breton, whose behavior displays the stigmata of the religious sectarians, G. Ribemont-Dessaignes, a man whose simple appearance conceals the fiery temper of the great accusers of humanity, and Philippe Soupault, whose facility of expression flows forth in bizarre images, gave readings from their works. Picabia who has undergone so many influences, particularly those of the clear and powerful mind of Marcel Duchamp, exhibited a number of pictures, one of which was a drawing done in chalk on a blackboard and erased on the stage; that is to say, the picture was valid for only two hours. As for me, announced as "Dada," I read aloud a newspaper article while an electric bell kept ringing so that no one could hear what I said. This was very badly received by the public, who became exasperated and shouted: "Enough! Enough!" An attempt was made to give a futuristic interpretation to this act, but all that I wanted to convey was simply that my presence on the stage, the sight of my face and my movements, ought to satisfy people's curiosity, and that anything I might have said really had no importance.

At the Grand Palais des Champs Elysées, thousands of persons of all classes manifested very uproariously—it is impossible to say what—their joy or their disapproval, by unexpected cries and general laughter, which constituted a very pretty accompaniment to the manifestoes read by six people at once. The newspapers said that an old man in the audience gave himself up to behaviour of a character more or less intimate, that somebody set off some flashlight powder and that a pregnant woman had to be taken out. It is true that the papers had also announced that Charlie Chaplin was going to deliver a lecture on Dada. Although we denied the rumor, there was one reporter who followed me everywhere. He thought that the celebrated actor was up to some new stunt and was planning a surprise entrance. I remember with tenderness that Picabia, who was to have taken part in the demonstration, disappeared as soon as it began. For five hours it was impossible to find him. The séance ended with a speech by "The King of the Fakirs," M. Buisson, who has a curious occupation: he predicts the future every day to those who wish to listen to him on the Boulevard de la Madeleine. In the evening he sells papers at the Métro exits.

Several days afterwards, there took place in a church which had been transformed into a cinema—premises belonging to the Club du Faubourg—at the invitation of that association, which includes more than three thousand workers and intellectuals, an explanation of the Dadaist Movement. There were four of us on the stage: Ribemont-Dessaignes, Aragon, and Breton; and I. M. Léo Poldès presided. On this occasion the audience were more serious: they listened to us. Their disapproval was expressed in shrill cries. Raymond Duncan, the philosopher who walks about Paris in the costume of Socrates, was there with all his school. He came to our defense and quieted the audience. A debate followed. The very best Socialist orators took sides and spoke for or against us. We replied to the attacks and the audience boiled in unison. Aragon wrote a moving article on that memorable matinée in *Les Écrits Nouveaux*.

A week later, a public debate on Dada took place at the Université Populaire. Éluard, Fraenkel, Dermée, Breton, Ribemont-Dessaignes, Soupault and I participated with all the force of our temperaments in a séance torn by political passions. All the manifestoes of the presidents appeared in the Dadaist review, *Littérature*—it is well known that the Dadaist movement has three hundred and ninety-one presidents and that anyone can become a president without the slightest trouble.

391 was also the name of a review which several of us started; it expanded and became a periodical of world-wide reputation. People finally became afraid of it, because it described things as they really were without any attempt to soften them. How many critics came to regret having uttered so many imbecilities!

A scandal provoked by the hypocrisy of certain Cubists in the bosom of a modern art society brought on the complete schism between the Cubists and the Dadas—an event which gave great force of cohesion to the nineteen dissenting Dadaists.

Paul Éluard, whom we call the inventor of a new metal of darkness, began to publish his review, *Proverbe,* in which all the Dadaists collaborated and which contributed a vein of its own. It was chiefly a matter of contradicting logic and language. This is how Soupault characterizes the collaborators of *Proverbe:*

> Louis Aragon, the Glass Syringe.
> Arp, Clean Wrinkles.
> André Breton, the Glass of Water in a Storm.
> Paul Éluard, the Nurse of the Stars.
> Th. Fraenkel, the Great Earth Serpent.
> Benjamin Péret, the Lemon Mandarin.
> G. Ribemont-Dessaignes, the Steam Man.
> Jacques Rigaut, the Hollow Plate.
> Philippe Soupault, the Musical Urinal.
> Tristan Tzara, the Man with the Pearl Head.

Dadaist hand-bills and boo˙s were spreading the agitation through Paris and the whole world. . . .

(tr. Edmund Wilson)

With Dada, Decadence in France reached its terminal moraine. Here all the rubbish was deposited in a heap. "The day the word 'Dada' was invented," affirms André Gide, "there was nothing more to do. Everything written since has come too late. These two syllables reached the goal of sonorous inanity, of a meaningless absolute." Dada was, first of all, an assertion that literature has no significance as communication. "Is it believed that the psychic base common to all humanity has been found?" asked Tristan Tzara, scornfully. "A work of art is never beautiful, by decree, objectively, for all. Criticism is therefore useless, it exists only subjectively for each one, and without the slightest character of generality." This is an old affirmation, implicit in Poe, that art is wholly subjective, that it is self-expression. Hence the assault, in all the manifestoes, upon intelligence. Not reason, but intuition, inspiration is important. Dada is the "absolute undebatable belief in every good immediate product of the spontaneity":

Logic is a complication. Logic is always false. It draws out the thread of notions, words, in their formal exterior towards the ends of illusory centers. Its chains slay, myriapod awful asphyxiant independence. Married to logic, art would live in incest, engulfing, swallowing its own tail always its body, fornicating with itself, and temperament would become a nightmare tarred with Protestantism, a monument, a lot of lumpish grizzly intestines.

(tr. Samuel Putnam)

The Dadaists, however, ultimately divorced the creative act entirely from the intellectual life. Creation became for them mere novelty, "vibrant to crucify boredom," produced in any manner whatever. "Dada is the chameleon of rapid and interesting change." Tristan Tzara is probably the first person in literary history to make no pretence whatever of employing even the imagination in composition:

How to compose a dadaist poem

Take a newspaper.
Take shears.
Select in the newspaper an article of the length which it is your intention that your poem should be.
Clip the article.
Then cut out carefully each of the words which compose this article and put them in a bag.
Shake gently.
Then lay each clipping down in the order in which it comes out of the bag.
Copy conscientiously.
The poem will be like you.
And there you are a highly original and charming sensitive writer, not yet appreciated by the mob.*

(tr. Samuel Putnam)

* Example: When the dogs cross the air in a diamond like ideas and the appendix of (M. Tzara's Note.)

Taking the Dadaists no more seriously than they took themselves, it is impossible to see how Decadence could find anything beyond them, how any novelty *which could not be generally appreciated* was left. In his search for new sensation and for new effect André Breton was literally forced to make his way back to Rimbaud along the path which the aesthetic avalanche had left. Surrealism was born. Feeling, like Vaché, that "all is contradiction," Breton turned from logic and outward reality to the stuff of the subconscious and of dreams. Breton himself is a neurological specialist and most of the super-realist group which he gathered about him have some acquaintance with Freud. In place of the scissors and newspaper of Tzara, these mystifiers (influenced by Gertrude Stein) have substituted automatic writing. In his original manifesto for super-realism, in 1924, Breton defined it as "Pure psychic automatism, by means of which one proposes to express, either verbally or by means of writing, the real functioning of thought. Dictated by thought, *in the absence of any control exerted by reason,* and without regard to any aesthetic or moral preoccupations." The justification for this kind of writing Breton found in the fact that "the marvelous is always beautiful, anything that is marvelous is beautiful, and only the marvelous is beautiful." Super-realism, despite Breton's assertion that Poe and Baudelaire are "bourgeois," takes us back to Baudelaire's notes upon his dreams and to Poe's assertion that Life is but "a dream within a dream." Indeed, when the first number of the review, *La Révolution Surréaliste,* appeared in December, 1924, with its sensational discussion of "Suicide, is it a Way out?" any critic familiar with literary history must have been forcibly reminded of Poe and his morbid speculations. Decadence in France ceased to be creative and turned back upon itself like a dog to his vomit.

Now that the course and consequences of Decadence in poetry have been surveyed in France, it is possible to call attention to the work of two men, one primarily a critic and the other a philosopher, who by their writings have abetted the course of Decadence in France and who have had a sturdy following of Americans, especially of American expatriates. The first is Rémy de Gourmont, minor Symbolist poet, minor novelist, but critic of the first order. Gourmont was born on April 4, 1858, in a château in Normandy. He was educated at the Lycée de Coustance, and then studied law at the University of Caen. In 1883, Gourmont went to Paris where he secured a position in the Bibliothèque Nationale and began the extensive reading which was to make him one of the most learned men in Europe. He met the leading Symbolists, after reading Mallarmé's *Vogue,* and became one of the few intimates of J. K. Huysmans, author of *À Rebours.* The latter's sour wit sharpened Gourmont's critical faculties and prejudiced him in favor of the Decadents—Mallarmé, Verlaine, Maeterlinck, and Huysmans himself. About this time, too, he fell hopelessly in love. The object of his attentions, Madame de Courrière, inspired his much abused novel, *Sixtine,* and the *Lettres à Sixtine,* published only after his death. In 1890 Gourmont was chiefly instrumental in founding *Le Mercure de France* in the pages of which thereafter was to be found all the significant work of the Symbolists.

Rémy de Gourmont incurred public disapproval and sacrificed his position in the National Library by writing an article for *The Mercury,* in 1891, entitled "Le Joujou Patriotisme," in which he poked fun at militarism in general and at the idea of a revenge *putsch* against Prussia in particular. Unfortunately just at this time an unsightly growth appeared upon his face, so that all public scrutiny became for him an anguish. He took himself completely out of the world, retiring to an upper floor in the Rue des Saints Pères, where he read indefatigably and wrote prodigiously, publishing much under the pseudonym of Richard le Bury. With perhaps more excuse than the average Symbolist could offer, Gourmont analyzed and dissected himself; aided by a Nietzschean skepticism and a genuine interest in psychology, he brought to his extreme subjectivism the tone of scientific aloofness and detachment. In 1902, he was responsible for the appearance of *La Révue des Idées* which aimed to popularize recent scientific discoveries and the more difficult literary theories. An American poetess, Nathalie Barney, became for a time his mistress and persuaded him to make his appearance among men again. To her he wrote the *Letters to the Amazon* and the

Intimate Letters to the Amazon which were printed posthumously.

Gourmont could be dismissed out of hand if one had merely to consider his verse, such things as the "Litanies of the Rose" with its imitative lines:

> Hypocrite flower,
> Flower of silence, etc.

Or, if one had merely to deal with his novels, of which the Huysmans-like *A Night in the Luxembourg,* is perhaps typical. "Gourmont, who entitled his poems *Divertissements,* was too perspicacious," says René Lalou, "not to know the same title would suit all his imaginative works." But it is for a body of meaty and provocative criticism that the man is distinguished. It is hardly necessary to add, after the *Dial* devoted a decade to Rémy de Gourmont, that this body of criticism is, in one sense, a fleshly body, a sensuous body. At its worst, it is eroticism or the expression of a man forced into unwilling chastity. *La Physique de l'Amour* may, of course, be defended on the score that it was ostensibly an effort to popularize more or less scientific treatments of the sex instinct and machinery in man and animal, yet when this book is thought of in relation to *A Virginal Heart, Letters to the Amazon,* the erotic poetry, and the repressions of Gourmont's creative life, it seems infinitely more subjective than scientific. With so definite a bias, it is possible for Gourmont to declare, "We write as we feel, as we think, with our whole body. Intelligence is but a form of sensibility. . . ." And from that to proceed to "The reasons of idealism plunge deep down into matter. Idealism means materialism, and conversely, materialism means idealism." In this kind of definition there is no distinction. Gourmont delighted in paradox, however, and adroitly evaded the charge of cultivating contrariness for its own sake, declaring, "A mind of some boldness will always seem paradoxical to timid minds."

A keenly functioning anti-intellectualist ("In our ignorance of all finality is not a pleasant sensation more important to our happiness than an exact piece of reasoning?"), Rémy de Gourmont's most obvious connection with the Decadent School in literature, aside from that afforded by his creative work and his critical defenses of Mallarmé, Villiers-de-l'Isle-Adam, Huysmans, and Verlaine, is in his conviction that the best creative activity is subconscious. "Inspiration, during the waking state, seems the clearest manifestation of the subconscious in the domain of intellectual creation. In its most pronounced form, it would seem to approximate somnambulism." Yet he has not thought his way out of the dilemma, imposed by a theory that demands the utmost freedom of creation, the dreaming mind, and the utmost finish in the created work, perfection of form, for which he stood: "The process of thinking is a sport, although this sport must be free and harmonious. The more it is looked upon as useless, the more one feels the need of making it beautiful. Beauty—that is perhaps its only possible value." No wonder that he places highest *a pure art which is concerned exclusively with self-realization.* No definition of it even should be given; for such a definition could not be made without connecting the idea of art with ideas which are foreign to it, and which would tend to obscure and sully it."

An art such as Gourmont conceived, but would not define, an art which is *wholly subjective,* lies, of course, beyond criticism. If art is self-realization, its beauty has a connection with the degree of realization, and who but the artist may compute that coefficient? One of the penalties attached to evaluating Decadent Art is to be told its excellencies are beyond the comprehension of the critic who only "obscures" or "sullies" these excellencies in his attempts at evaluation. Gourmont evoked for Decadence that freedom from judgment which is license.

As licenser of Decadence and coiner of paradoxes (the counterfeit of wit) Rémy de Gourmont attracted wide attention, but his greatest critical achievement was his assault upon the validity of truisms. The very vigor of a single essay, "The Dissociation of Ideas," makes *La Culture des Idées* an outstanding book of our times. Observing that "man associates ideas, not at all logically or in accordance with verifiable exactitude, but with his pleasure and his interest," Gourmont was led to the conclusion that "most truths are merely prejudices." He then furnished future generations with a criterion for detecting established falsehoods: *"A truth is dead when it has been shown that the relations between the elements are habitual and not necessary."* The great task of the critic is to break down or dissociate truisms, as Gourmont saw it. "The only fruitful quest," he says elsewhere, "is the quest of the non-true." The modern assault upon habit and custom was largely initiated by this man, particularly in America, as we shall see.

Gourmont accurately describes Dissociation as a "method of deliverance"; it is for that method, rather than for his own accomplishment in dissociating ideas, that Gourmont deserves the gratitude of posterity. He himself dissociated the truisms that beauty and woman are synonymous, that all great literature is necessarily some form of mariolatry—thus effectively destroying the theory of Poe (though he did not have the American in mind) that "the death of a beautiful woman is, unquestionably, the most poetic topic in the world." Yet he concluded, as we have seen, precisely as Poe did, that the purest art is self-expression, self-realization. He broke down the truism that education pursued for its own sake has any value. "Without being as widespread as it might be, and as it will be, education is very much in vogue. We live less and less, and we learn more and more. Sensibility surrenders to intelligence. I have seen a man laughed at because he examined a dead leaf attentively and with pleasure. No one would have laughed to hear a string of botanical terms muttered with regard to it. . . ." Yet why isn't education pursued for its own sake (which always means the satisfaction it gives to the pursuer) as legitimate as poetry pursued for its own sake? "It is painfully absurd," cries Rémy de Gourmont, "to learn for learning's sake, to burn for the sake of burning." Why isn't it just as absurd to write poetry for the sake of self-realization? Gourmont pursued both vices with much personal satisfaction, if we read the record correctly.

Gourmont's calm assertion, "The state of dissociation reached by moral commonplaces seems to bear a rather close relation to the degree of intellectual civilization," has itself become one of the most widely accepted truisms of the last twenty years. It will bear a little dissociation. Moral laxity appears to be one of the products of a "ripe" civilization, but all our past "ripe" civilizations have been those in which the wealth has been largely sequestered by the few who have demanded of the writers they have endowed justification of their licentiousness. Because economic factors have made loose morality and great literature synchronous in the past, it does not follow that loose morality is responsible for great literature. When one considers the supple and wily Voltaire, who, after all, lived well—on the beneficence of several degenerates—as an example of intellectual achievement, Gourmont appears to be correct. When one reflects, however, on the amount of sexual repression there must have been among the mass of people in Voltaire's time because of impossible economic conditions and heavy taxes (a repression of which the sexual orgies of the Revolution give ample evidence), one is distressed by the superficiality of Gourmont's observation. So far as history may be offered in witness, the state of dissociation reached by moral commonplaces bears a closer relation to economic injustice than it does to the degree of intellectual civilization. To whatever extent Gourmont's dissociation affects prudery and hypocrisy, it is excellent; so far, however, as it condones the licentiousness of the few, it is a decadent and vicious sophism. A genuine morality, which means an adequate life for all, based on a general economic security, should be the aim of every great writer. Gourmont, who dabbled in a wide variety of subjects, particularly in *erotica,* let economics strictly alone, with the result that his generalizations, so far as they affect conduct, are suspect. Ten thousand enthusiastic young dissociators have followed his lead in breaking down moral concepts, but they have buried ever and ever deeper beneath the ruins of the systems they have destroyed the real cause of the hypocrisy they have learned to hate. The immediate results of dissociation have been disappointing.

The philosophical system of Henri Bergson has lent Decadence as much support as has the criticism of Rémy de Gourmont. Bergson, the child of Anglo-Jewish parents, was born in Paris, on October 18, 1859. While a youth he became a naturalized Frenchman. During the course of his brilliant school career he often reflected on literature as a life occupation, but it was philosophy which he ultimately chose. For twenty-one years, from 1900 to 1921, he was Professor of Philosophy at the Collège de France, where his lectures were probably the most popular of any given since the time of Abelard. All fashionable and intellectual Paris attended them; printed and translated, they won champions and critics in Germany, England, and America. The furore his work created exasperated Bergson while it deprived him of the peace he needed for reflection. So frequently did he change his residence in Paris to escape his admirers that he was locally dubbed "the wandering Jew." Following the First World War and his resignation from the Collège de France, his popularity waned somewhat; later it was completely restored by the acceptance of his ideas by the mathematical physicists, Alexander, Eddington, Einstein, and others.

Bergson's *Creative Evolution* is an attempt to explain the entire universe, rock and tree, bird and bush, poet's song and mathematician's formula, as different manifestations of one elemental force or stream. This purposive stream, which he calls the *élan vital,* is conceived as consciousness at the instinctive, rather than the intellectual, level. Of this consciousness the intellect is but a specially developed function, which has made distinctions and divisions in the eternal flux for its own purposes; hence to the intellect alone solid objects and space are realities—in a word, matter is intellectually constituted, matter is an illusion. The only reality is the *élan vital* which may be realized by intuition.

By delegating to the subconscious life so great an importance, and by challenging the validity of the constructions of the intellect, literally *by incriminating the reason,* Bergson has reinforced the Decadents. Communication is largely established on an intellectual level; but if no truth can be communicated, the literature which aims at this is not only mistaken but subversive, for it perpetuates the pleasant fictions of the intellect. On the other hand, writing that is wholly subjective has worth, for it may record or suggest the all-important intuition. The purpose of art, says Bergson, "is to send to sleep the active or rather the recalcitrant forces of our personality, and thereby to induce in us a condition of perfect docility, in which we realize the idea suggested to us, in which we sympathize with the sentiment expressed." Thus by reducing the reader to a comatose condition (Bergson's own phrase is "a spiritualized hypnotic trance") intuitions may be conveyed. Art, then, is a medium only at an emotional or instinctive level. Yet even here as a medium its possibilities are limited, for the actual sentiment is not apparently communicated; instead sympathy (a half-appreciation) for the sentiment is aroused. Bergson places the ideational content of words below their emotional content for this reason. "The word which is sharply outlined, the brutal word, which is the receptacle of all that is stable, and all that is common, and consequently impersonal, in human experience, crushes or at all events covers over the more delicate and fugitive impressions of our individual consciousnesses."

Particularly in his various statements about the character of intuition and of the subconscious mind has Bergson been influential in the development of more recent Decadent literature. If the intellect has "spatialized" the universe, setting boundaries to things, giving to the sea of endless change a shore, so too it has established a kind of mental time, a clock and a calendar— a past, a present, and a future. Yet in reality, were there no intellect, there could be only the present—the instant of the intuition. This instant, aside from its perception, however, this infinite duration—is Time. The intellect has so tyrannized over the subconscious mind that this precious instant hardly exists:

We assert then, at the outset, that if there be memory, that is, the survival of past images, these images must constantly mingle with our perception of the present, and may even take its place. For if they have survived, it is with view to utility; at every moment they complete our present experience, enriching it with experience already acquired; and as the latter is ever increasing, it must end by covering up and submerging the former. It is indisputable that the basis of the real, and so to speak instantaneous, intuition, on which our perception of the external world is developed, is a small matter compared with all that memory adds to it. Just because the recollection of earlier analogous intuitions is more useful than the intuition itself, being bound up in memory with a whole series of subsequent events, and capable thereby of throwing a better light on our decision, it supplants the real intuition of which the office is then merely—we shall prove it later—to call up recollection, to give it body, to render it active and thereby actual. . . .

In innumerable passages of this sort, Bergson has pictured consciousness, save for its rare intuitions, as a cinematographic review of a flux of past events in a sequential, rather than a consequential, order. His insistence that memory and perception are the same in practice has legitimatized the so-called "stream-of-consciousness" method, all "cerebral fiction," all Superconscious, Subconscious, and Unconscious poetry. Whatever his meaning may be for philosophy—his glorification of the present realized at a non-intellectual level would seem to make him a Romanticist —for literature he has destroyed meaning and enthroned chaos. Bergson is the impeccable champion of the literature of self-realization.

2

AMERICAN DECADENCE

"The poems distilled from other poems will probably pass away," wrote Walt Whitman in 1855. French Decadent poetry has debatable faults, but the modern American poetry which has imitated it has a weakness criticism cannot ignore—it too frequently records an unfelt passion in a derivative, non-essential form. In a word, it is a *literary* poetry. Its bookishness, its artificiality, are not completely redeemed by the fact that it is less erotic (this may be assigned to timidity) and broader in its themes and implications than the French. It has not the virtue of genuine novelty which won it its first applause in America. Nor has it any particular meaning or significance for America or for the world, since its emotion has no tangible relation to any real experience, since its whimsicalities are those of Laforgue and Corbière and its despair is simulated from the defeatism of the 'seventies and 'eighties in France. Of the three adjectives which utterly damn—"feeble, imitative, tame"—much modern American poetry deserves the second beyond all challenge.

The first important contemporary American poet to find the French Decadents was undeniably Ezra Pound, but in the main he found them for others and not for himself. Yet there persists enough of the French influence upon him to ruin or to mar some of his best effects. Why Hailey, Idaho, should have produced this earnest searcher after foreign culture is one of the mysteries of literary history, yet Pound was born in that remote place on

October 30, 1885. He was only fifteen years old when he entered the University of Pennsylvania where he spent two years before transferring to Hamilton College to take his degree in 1905. His undergraduate work in the Romance languages was so brilliant that he received an appointment as instructor at the University of Pennsylvania. Here, and at Wabash College, he served until 1907, meanwhile taking his M.A. degree. It is worth noting that Master Pound's attachment to books and learning began when he was very young, for it seems to have precluded a wide acquaintance with life itself. Pound is probably aware of this deficiency (he repeatedly praises Chaucer for his rich experience), yet he is not conscious enough of it to correct the effect it has had upon his verse. The bluster, the brusqueness and false virility, of his poetry are an attempt to compensate for the lack of real substance, of experience in his life. After all, the most glorious library adventure can hardly atone for lack of encounters in the street.

To gather materials for a doctoral dissertation on Lope de Vega, Pound went abroad; there he remained more than a third of a century, and the dissertation has become one in the prosody of many literatures. His first year in Europe he travelled in Spain, Provence, and Italy, then settled for a brief time in Venice, where his first book of poems, *A Lume Spento,* was published. Late in 1908 he went to London, issued two volumes of poetry within a year (*Personae* and *Exultations*), and became an eager participant in the literary discussions of the town. His early volumes of verse show him an admirer of Browning and the troubadours. He came to the French either through a young Englishman, T. E. Hulme whom Pound has occasionally praised, or through another friend, Ford Madox Hueffer who calmly puts himself down as "doyen of living writers of Vers Libre in English." Pound at once initiated a campaign for the "new poetry" —writing and lecturing for it. Because the word "Symbolism" had certain old associations in English, he invented the word "Imagisme" to replace it. In 1914 he edited the first anthology of the "new poetry" under the French name, *Des Imagistes.* The collection contained work from the pens of Richard Aldington, Skipworth Cannéll, John Cournos, Hilda Doolittle, F. S. Flint,

James Joyce, Ford Madox Hueffer, Amy Lowell, Allen Upward, William Carlos Williams, and Pound. *Des Imagistes* was still being fought over by the critics, when disaffection occurred in the ranks of the poets—Miss Lowell, "the Brookline empress" (as Kreymborg so appropriately calls her), a woman who had reached robust maturity of years without much robustness or maturity of verse, and one of the latest come of all the Imagists, quarreled with Pound and usurped his empire. She arranged for the next three appearances of the Imagist anthology in Boston and herself became the fugleman of the movement. Pound and his friends were "squeezed out"; John Gould Fletcher and D. H. Lawrence, however, became contributors in the new volumes. Pound's statement of what the Imagists aimed at, contained in *Pavannes and Divisions* (1918), is more illuminating than all Miss Lowell's pronunciamentos. What in the Imagist credo, issued by Miss Lowell, is as clarifying, when the connections of the movement are remembered, as Pound's version of the principle of rhythm: "to compose in the sequence of the musical phrase, not in sequence of a metronome"? Incidentally, *Pavannes and Divisions* is today the best possible book for the neophyte in poetry to read before he begins serious composition.

Meanwhile Pound, Wyndham Lewis, and Gaudier-Brzeska had started another movement, Vorticism, and had founded the radical *Blast* in an effort to overturn academical conservatism in art and poetry. Only two numbers of *Blast* appeared before it became defunct, but it excited more comment, possibly, than has the entire run of the *Atlantic Monthly* since Howells left it. The cautiousness of Pound's own creative experiments at this time should be noted; his primary service seems to have been the inspiration of others. "What struck [the *Blast* group] about Pound," Wyndham Lewis recollects, "was that his fire eating propagandist utterances were not accompanied by any very experimentalist efforts in his particular medium. His poetry, to the mind of the more fanatical of the group, was a series of pastiches of old french and old italian poetry. . . ." Pound rounded out a decade of propaganda in London; moved to Paris, where he resided in a garden studio in the Rue Notre Dame des Champs and became "more Parisian than the Parisians"; after four years, he tired of this, and transferred his *ménage* to Rapallo, on the Italian Riviera, where he continued to reside, working on his *Cantos* and translations (it is said that he could not tell always which he had at hand), experimenting with music, issuing broadsides on the teaching of literature—for the buried pedagogue in him would out, despite himself, whence *How to Read* (1931), *The ABC of Reading* (1934), *Make It New* (1934), and *Culture* (1939). Recently he was forced to visit the United States to learn what was happening here. But according to interviewers, he not only visited us, but visited us with imprecations. The herd is still the herd, according to Ezra.

Novelty has been for Ezra Pound (as it was for the French Decadents) too heady a wine; he has proclaimed every new thing with great vehemence and he has dug up the forgotten strange from dead literatures and exhibited it with the frenetic volubility of a merchant of the *Marche des Puces*. Pound has wasted more creative energy in vain pursuits than any other man of his generation. The two years thrown away on *The Exile,* for example, the poet could hardly spare even out of a profligate literary existence. Yet history will have to reckon with his "divagations," for, like the Spanish captains, he has brought back from them strange treasures. It may be one of the conclusions of the historians, for instance, that what Pound has done in a third of a century for other men equals the worth of his own work. He was the first to recognize the genius of James Joyce and Rabindranath Tagore, to announce the revolutionary art of Wyndham Lewis and Gaudier-Brzeska, to champion the music of George Antheil. Pound's *Cathay,* in 1916, inspired by the manuscripts of his friend Fenollosa (as well as by the *chinoiseries* of Decadent France) prepared the way for the almost excessive interest in Japanese and Chinese poetry; his edition of Cavalcanti is reputably the best; Americans know Rémy de Gourmont's *Philosophy of Love* through Pound's translation; he has discovered and proclaimed the merit of certain forgotten gems of English poetry—like the exquisite pastoral bewailing the death of the Earl of Rochester. As a composer he has " 'set to music' a great deal of the best poetry of Villon and Cavalcanti"—an accomplishment of which he is intensely proud; his opera, *Le Testa-*

ment, was given in Paris in 1926. Few literary wastrels can produce so good a record.

Pound has divided writers into six classes: the inventors, the masters, the diluters, good writers without salient qualities, the writers of belles lettres, and the starters of crazes. The first two of these classes he has defined with an eye towards his own immortality; the inventors are the "men who found a new process, or whose extant work gives us the first known example of a process," while the masters are "men who have combined a number of such processes, and who used them as well or better than the inventors." One might object that a master does more than to combine and to employ skillfully other men's inventions: he brings transcendent or divine significance to what was before merely fact; he subordinates or conceals his process with great adroitness while charging his form with feeling. A master excels in other ways, Mr. Pound should understand, than in the art of appropriation.

Like Walter Savage Landor whom he greatly admires, Ezra Pound is an amazing virtuoso. To one who has sampled in the original some of the verse of the trouvères and troubadours, from Guy, chatelain de Coucy, to Guillaume de Ferrière, the execution in our barbarous tongue of such things as "Pierre Vidal Old," "Provincia Deserta," and "Sestina: Altaforte" is nothing short of astonishing. Passably well done are "The River-Merchant's Wife: a Letter" and "Exile's Letter"—both "from the Chinese of Li Po." The "Ballad for Gloom" and the "Ballad of the Goodly Fere" could have been written by any first-rate Pre-Raphaelite, but only by a first-rater. No one acquainted with the Anglo-Saxon original will deny to his translation of "The Seafarer" the preservation of the spirit of his original. And who in English has produced the *effect* of the classical hexameter, has caught the "tremulous cadence slow" with its eternal note of sadness which blind Homer and Sophocles heard long ago by the Ægean, so well as Ezra Pound? Here is the melodious close of the second of the *Cantos:*

> Olive grey in the near,
>   far, smoke grey of the rock-slide,

Salmon-pink wings of the fish-hawk
cast grey shadows in water,
The tower like a one-eyed great goose
cranes up out of the olive-grove,

And we have heard the fauns chiding Proteus
in the smell of hay under the olive trees,
And the frogs singing against the fauns
in the half light.
And. . . .

Yet Pound's virtuosity, his skill in imitating Li Po, Homer, Ovid, Catullus, Propertius, Bion, Jaufré Rudel, Bernard de Ventadour, Peire Vidal, Arnaut Daniel, Dante, Cavalcanti, Villon, Browning (what a list!) will not disguise the fact that he owes most of all to the French Decadents with whom he always associates Gautier. Rimbaud, Laforgue, Corbière, by his own admission, have influenced him—as has Mallarmé. His "Portrait d'une Femme" is a perfect companion piece for Mallarmé's "L'Aprèsmidi d'un Faune," and one can see how other pieces, like "The Garden," for example, are derivative. Such a poem as "Les Millwin" connects the language of Rimbaud and the rickety children of Laforgue with the poetry of Thomas Stearns Eliot:

Les Millwin

The little Millwins attend the Russian Ballet.
The mauve and greenish souls of the little Millwins
Were seen lying along the upper seats
Like so many unused boas.

The poem "La Fraisne" with its gaunt, grave, and quite mad old councillor, whose bride is "a pool of the wood," is related in a generic way to Paul Valéry's "Narcissus"; and Pound's study in white, called "Albatre," has been influenced by Gautier and Whistler's "Symphony in White." The innumerable poems in which Pound rails against respectability owe as much to Corbière as to Villon.

Pound has long looked upon the *Cantos* as his masterpiece, yet in the *Cantos,* most of all, he is a Decadent. Long ago, in one of his rare explanations, Pound told a friend that the key to the *Cantos* was "the presentness of the past." The phrase is Bergson's and the purpose of the poem is to represent the rich mind of an intellectual, an avid poetry lover, thoroughly saturated with memories. Inasmuch as Pound has set for himself the prodigious task of reproducing the effects of all past poetry and prose for which his savant cares, broken by rare intermittent flashes of intuition, he has mapped out a rival performance for James Joyce's *Finnegans Wake*. Though the structure will suggest that of a Bach Fugue (See W. B. Yeats, *A Packet for Ezra Pound*, 1924) "with no plot, no chronicle of events, no logic of discourse," one of the two dominant themes, "the descent into Hades from Homer and a metamorphosis from Ovid," will again put the reader in mind of Joyce. Yet it is still a poem primarily for bibliophiles and scholiasts. The average reader is not going to pick much that is intelligible out of such a pot-pourri as that at the beginning of Canto II, which, however, is an almost perfect setting forth of Bergson's conception of memory:

> Hang it all, Robert Browning,
> There can be but one "Sordello."
> But Sordello, and my Sordello?
> Lo Sordels si fo di Mantovana.
> So-shu churned in the sea.
> Seal sports in the spray-whitened circles of cliff-wash,
> Sleek head, daughter of Lir,
>   eyes of Picasso
> Under the black fur-hood, lithe daughter of Ocean;
> And the wave runs in the beach groove:
> "Eleanor, ἑλέναυς and ἑλέπτολις!"
>   And poor old Homer blind, blind as a bat,
> Ear, ear for the sea-surge, murmur of old men's voices:
> "Let her go back to the ships,
> Back among Grecian faces, lest evil come on our own,
> Evil and further evil, and a curse cursed on our children,
> Moves, yes she moves like a goddess
> And has the face of a god
>   and the voice of Schoeney's daughters,
> And doom goes with her in walking,
> Let her go back to the ships,
>   back among Grecian voices." . . .

Yet he who is saturated in literature, particularly the literature of Ezra Pound's masters, doubtless can enjoy all the pleasures of reminiscence in this verse—and who has said that this is not a special province for poetry? The *Cantos* promise to be the greatest piece of echolalia ever written. However, do not over-look the fact that, for all this joinery, there are no "contours" or "edges", no uncalculated pauses or awkward changes of rhythm in the *Cantos*. They are one musical composition.

Pound, however, with all his passion for music—"Poetry atrophies when it gets too far from music"—has never professed a desire to be wholly unintelligible, wholly Decadent. "Great literature," he says, "is simply language charged with meaning to the utmost possible degree." Again, "Literature is news that STAYS news." And yet again, "Language is obviously created, and is, obviously, USED for communication." In one of his in-nocent, early poems, called "Commission," he instructed his songs to go "to the lonely and unsatisfied . . . to the nerve wracked . . . to the enslaved by convention . . . to the bourgeoisie" . . . and ". . . to them whose failure is concealed." Ezra Pound *wanted* an audience. It was after he failed to find an immediate audience that he adopted the typical Decadent attitude:

> . . . This our reward for our works,
>   sic crescit gloria mundi:
> Some circle of not more than three
>   that we prefer to play up to,
> Some few whom we'd rather please
>   than hear the whole aegrum vulgus
> Splitting its beery jowl
>   a-meowling our praises. . . .

Perhaps the best in Pound, and the only thing which can be called in an intimate sense his own, is contained in the few poems like "Villanelle: the Psychological Hour" and "Hugh Selwyn Mauberley," which touch his long, and at times bitter, struggle for personal success. In these alone we find something besides the man of sensibility; here is the student who has pursued his love until the flesh rebelled, here is the lover swingeing the lout who has not his apperceptions, and here is the nervous, self-conscious human being unhappily revealed to his fellows. All the weariness, not of one night of study, but of a life-time devoted to the poetry of other men, is concentrated in the Rimbaud-like novelty called "The Eyes," with its Provencal music and its unlooked-for ending. All the bitterness of his fight for recognition is packed into "Salutation the Third" in which he bares his teeth with a snarl at the "smugness" of the London *Times* and guffaws at the "gagged" reviewers. All his poignant loneliness is poured softly into the "Villanelle." For Ezra Pound, who led the American procession into Decadence, has been the first to feel the penalty for what is essentially a pose—the inevitable desertion of the "not more than three" who are weary of maintaining the attitude of comprehension for what, in the main, they do not understand. Fuming in his beard, mumbling to himself, Pound is our own Grangousier, deserted in Rapallo.

Yet if Americans were generally acquainted with Pound's *Jefferson and/ or Mussolini* (1935), they would consign him to a place more distant and warmer than Rapallo. Pound frankly admires the Italian dictator, and his strangely-titled book attempts to persuade us that Mussolini has so much in common with the Virginia statesman that we should venerate, rather than censure, him. Each man was mastered, not by the "will to power," but by the "will to order." Yet argues Pound, rather naïvely, Jefferson willed the accession of Louisiana in an act typical of Mussolini. Thus the exceptional thing in Jefferson's career is cited to excuse the habitual thing in Mussolini's. Though the resemblance between the two leaders is specious, Pound advances a rather plausible justification for the advent of the Fascisti. When the rival parties in a democracy have both been corrupted by the bankers, the rise of one-party government, he feels, is inevitable. Actuated by a Flaubertian hatred of the bourgeoisie, Pound appears almost liberal in his attack upon the bankers—a theme he has interwoven of late also into the *Cantos*. His true motivation is aesthetic, however, rather than humanitarian—the banker merely symbolizes a class indifferent to order, whether in poetry or politics, and the reader is left with more than a faint suspicion that the Fascist order is very congenial to Ezra Pound. As has been remarked earlier, the primitive strong man has a peculiar appeal to the Decadent, and to find any Decadent paying obeisance to a dictator should astonish no reflective person.

It is an easy transition from Pound to Miss Amy Lowell whose sublime bulk has blotted out his sun so long. To many Americans she is still the *vers libre* movement. And just sixteen years ago, when she died, on May 12, 1925, the New York *Herald Tribune* described her with the resounding phrase "a Principality and a Power." As a Bostonian (she was born in Brookline, Feb. 9, 1874), as a grandniece of James Russell Lowell and sister of A. Lawrence Lowell, then president of Harvard University, as a person of wealth and social consequence, Amy Lowell was bound to attract attention by whatever she did; but she set gentle Victorian America agog when she came back from a poaching expedition in England with a totally new kind of poetry, with an enthusiasm peculiarly Bull Moose in quality, and with a black cigar the smoke of which she blew in the reporters' faces. Americans have always been especially susceptible to lady evangelists, and they took Imagism from her as they had taken phrenology from Victoria Woodhull, temperance from Carrie Nation, Christian Science from Mary Baker Eddy, and the gospel of Jesus from Aimee Semple Macpherson. Miss Lowell was probably the most successful propagandist that poetry has ever had in this country (and this does not fail to recognize the claims of Harriet Monroe and Margaret Anderson); it is a fact that the interest of the American public in poetry has steadily declined since Miss Lowell's death.

Yet to be worth a column of newsprint any day in behalf of poetry does not make one a poet. There is no blinking the fact that Amy Lowell, even at her best, was both imitative and mediocre. Any one who has the curiosity can easily enough trace the sources of her verse; after a third-rate volume of sentimental rimes, *A Dome of Many Coloured Glass* (1912), published when she was no longer young, she was led to the French poets by John Gould Fletcher and by Ezra Pound, and in 1915 printed her findings in *Six French Poets,* a book eulogizing Paul Fort, Albert Samain, Rémy de Gourmont, and others—mostly second-raters. Though she derived much from various sources, the chief influence upon her work was that of the minor French Decadent experimentalist, Paul Fort. All the best effects of Amy Lowell are discoverable in this versifier. Miss Lowell was as Decadent as the inhibitions of a mind that was at once puritanical and provincial would let her be. Like Fort, she went in, mainly, for the pretty-pretty. Her once much-touted polyphonic prose yearns for the "azure" of the Decadents even when the subject of her verse is a description of Constantinople, as in this passage from *Can Grande's Castle* (1918):

> Empire of the East! Byzantium! Constantinople! The Golden City of the world. A crystal fixed in aquamarines; a jewel-box set down in a seaside garden. All the seas are as blue as spring lupins, and there are so many seas . . . The Bosphorous winds North to the Black Sea. The Golden Horn curves into the Sweet Waters. The edge of the city swerves away from the Sea of Marmora. Aquamarines, did I say? Sapphires, beryls, lapis-lazuli, amethysts and felspar. Whatever stones there are, bluer than gentians, bluer than cornflowers, bluer than periwinkles. So blue that the city must be golden to complement the water. . . .

This is what Miss Lowell in her enthusiasm described as "an orchestral form. Its tone is not merely single and melodic as in that of *vers libre,* for instance, but contrapuntal and various." And *this,* by the way, is typical of the slovenliness of Miss Lowell's writing. What is a "various tone" or a "contrapuntal tone"?

Like Fort, too, Amy Lowell was impressionistic; painting for her seemed more important than music, despite all that she wrote upon the relations of melody and verse. Hers is a weaker Decadence than Mallarmé's—in no sense so keenly intellectual. Her untutored admiration for Keats' sensuousness is partially responsible for this (as it was with James Russell Lowell), and occasionally in her writing there is an impressionistic bit which is amazingly suggestive. It is a pity, for example, she did not pursue further and develop with a more rigorous art such a piece as "Bath" with its suggestion of Cubism, rather than making it a trivial *jeu d'esprit:*

Bath

The day is fresh-washed and fair, and there is a smell of tulips and narcissus in the air.

The sunshine pours in at the bath-room window and bores through the water in the bath-tub in lathes and planes of greenish white. It cleaves the water into flaws like a jewel, and cracks it to bright light.

Little spots of sunshine lie on the surface of the water and dance, dance, and their reflections wobble deliciously over the ceiling; a stir of my finger sets them whirring, reeling. I move a foot, and the planes of light in the water jar. I lie back and laugh, and let the green-white water, the sun-flawed, beryl water, flow over me. The day is almost too bright to bear, the green water covers me from the too bright day. I will lie here a while and play with the water and the sun spots.

The sky is blue and high. A crow flaps by the window, and there is a whiff of tulips and narcissus in the air.

The lack of critical sense responsible for the failure to understand the possibilities of this piece is also responsible for the careless use of "lathes" and "deliciously" (a vulgarism mistaken for a synesthetic effect) and the incongruous suggestion of "in the water jar." Despite its flaws, this prose-poem, with its emphasis upon sensation and its climax in the high blue sky, would have delighted the Decadents—this is what they all longed for, from Mallarmé down,—a bath in azure! Miracle of miracles, that only the plump Boston poetess should have succeeded in taking it.

Such distant cousins that their common Gallic blood is forgotten, Miss Lowell's "Patterns" and Mallarmé's "L'Après-midi d'un Faune" are nevertheless related to each other. Miss Lowell wished to study frustration and disillusionment, too, but it had to be adequately explained in her poem. Yet perhaps the very woman spoke out against the conventions she accepted; at any rate, this is the most effective poem in all her verse, thumb the pages however earnestly one will for its equal. Impressionism again triumphs, there are certain gaucheries of rime, and the piece just escapes sentimentalism, but it does escape. One should note, though, how deeply buried is the satyr-figure in the poem, half suppressed by the author's early puritanism:

> Underneath my stiffened gown
> Is the softness of a woman bathing in a marble basin,
> A basin in the midst of hedges grown
> So thick, she cannot see her lover hiding.
> But she guesses he is near,
> And the sliding of the water

Seems the stroking of a dear
Hand upon her. . . .

I would be the pink and silver as I ran along the paths,
And he would stumble after,
Bewildered by my laughter. . . .

Good as "Patterns" is, it must be observed that no great poet
would have added the stanza beginning, "In a month he would
have been my husband"; the tendency to elucidate is possibly a
family fault—at least James Russell and A. Lawrence Lowell
had it. The purpose of the stanza is to explain that the intense
passion earlier revealed in the poem would have eventually been
legalized, that—quaint American notion!—it was all right, since
these people were to be married anyway. Miss Lowell did not
quite succeed in breaking the "pattern" herself.

American reviews of a decade ago speak warmly of Amy
Lowell as a critic. Yet there is very little merit in her three
volumes of prose—*Six French Poets* (1915), *Tendencies in
Modern American Poetry* (1917), and the *John Keats* (1925).
Caustic British reviews of the last work were said at the time to
have caused her death. This is not altogether probable, but they
certainly made her suffer greatly, for no author ever emotional-
ized a subject more completely than Amy Lowell did Keats, and
her pain must have been in some measure proportional, yet one
cannot say the strictures were undeserved. With tremendous
energy she had pursued, and with ample means she had gathered,
Keats material for years, repeatedly and arrogantly denying
others any use of it until her work was done; those who resented
her monopoly not without reason were critical of her results.
She invited the treatment she received, yet she could not fairly
complain that her critics were unjust.

She herself possessed no critical acumen. The credo of the
Imagist poets, which she is generally given the credit for phrasing (who would have dared to issue a manifesto without her
sanction?), touches only the trivial in an aesthetic system: "the exact word," "new rhythms," "concentration," etc. Her judgments,
seen equally well in *Tendencies in Modern American Poetry*
and in the labored *A Critical Fable* (1922), done in imitation of

a far greater *Fable for Critics,* are a vain woman's judgments:
warm praise for her friends and for those whom she has been told
to admire and petty carking against those towards whom for
private reasons she is ill-disposed. A good example of her hatchet
work is "Astigmatism" in *Sword Blades and Poppy Seed.* Her
blows are aimed at Ezra Pound who offended by protesting that
the Imagists, particularly Amy Lowell, Fletcher, and "H.D.",
were too fond of the pretty-pretty, of irises, poppies, gillyflowers,
et cetera.——

> The Poet came to a stream.
> Purple and blue flags waded in the water . . .
> The Poet lifted his cane,
> And the iris heads fell into the water.
> They floated away, torn and drowning.
> "Wretched flowers," said the Poet,
> "They are not roses."

In no other country on earth would Amy Lowell have achieved
the reputation that she did here, but once having achieved that
reputation, in no other country would she have been forgotten so
soon and so completely. Who can name a poem of merit of hers
today beyond "Purple Grackles," "Patterns," or "Number 3 on
the Docket"?

More willing to acknowledge the influence of Ezra Pound than
Miss Lowell ever was, John Gould Fletcher, a poet whom Miss
Lowell recruited for her anthologies, links Pound and the Sym-
bolists in describing his own poetic origins:

"It all happened in the spring of 1913, in Paris. Except for two or three
minor pieces, the whole of the first forty pages of this book [*Preludes and
Symphonies*] was written then. At that time, I was just over twenty-six
years of age and had spent the last five years of my life in London. 'The
New Poetry' had just begun to be talked about, on the other side of the
Atlantic, and its first heralds, Lindsay, Masters, Sandburg, had scarcely
made a stir. The Imagists, with whom later I was to affiliate myself, had
not yet attained to the dignity of a collected anthology. I had only read the
work of one of them, the pioneer Ezra Pound. During the course of the
month in which I was to finish *Irradiations,* I was to make his acquaintance.
My gods proved to be different from his: I depended on Whitman, Blake,
Shelley, and the French Symbolists, while he preferred the remoter and
perhaps purer sources of Anglo-Saxon, Provençal, and ancient Chinese in-

spiration. In *Irradiations* my dependence on the Symbolists is particularly marked. If the reader will turn to the pages of an almost forgotten book of Symbolist verse, *Les Fêtes Quotidiennes* by Guy Charles Cros, published by the *Mercure de France* in 1912, he will find such phrases as "les écharpes violettes de nuit tombent à plis legérs sur les epaules de la terre" and "les petits trilles polychromes des étoiles" which I imitated faithfully in *Irradiations*. There are also echoes of Verhaeren strewn up and down these pages. I can only say in extenuation that every poet necessarily borrows something from other poets, just as every man is necessarily influenced in his life by his surroundings; and it is not the fact of such borrowings, but what is made out of them, that is important. In any case, *Irradiations* owes much to the Symbolist school. And the *Symphonies* owe still more."

No other writer of his school is so frank as John Gould Fletcher. He neglects to mention by name, however, Arthur Rimbaud, to whom he is greatly indebted, but he may not at first have been directly influenced by Rimbaud—he may have worked his way back to him. The relationship of the two is shown by Fletcher's attempt to rewrite Rimbaud's famous sonnet, "Les Voyelles,"—an attempt which led Miss Amy Lowell to declare, when she was trumpeting for the Imagists, that "Mr. Fletcher is a more original poet than Arthur Rimbaud, and has a finer ear"! Had Miss Lowell chosen a poem to illustrate Fletcher's inferiority to Rimbaud, she could not have done better than to choose the one she did. Fletcher bears the same relation to Rimbaud that Thomas Holley Chivers does to Poe. Chivers, who went so far as to change his birthdate in order to be taken for Poe's predecessor, reduced the latter's technique to an absurdity in imitating him. The reader is asked to compare such lines as Mr. Fletcher's—

> Chryselephantine image, Athena violet crowned . . .

> Tears that drip on the wires, Aeolian melody . . .

> Butterflies, bumblebees, buzzing about a hot rose . . .

with Chivers'—

> Many mellow Cydonian Suckets,
> Sweet apples, anthosmial divine,

> From the Ruby-rimmed Beryline buckets,
>   Star-gemmed, lily shaped, hyaline . . .
> Like that sweet, golden goblet found growing
>   On the wild emerald Cucumber tree,
> Rich, brilliant, like Chrysopraze blowing,
>   I then brought to my Rosalie Lee . . .

and draw his own conclusions.

Although Fletcher cites Galton's *Inquiry Concerning Human Faculty* in support of the "colour vision" on which his *Symphonies* are based, the true source of these *Symphonies* is the Decadent experiment with synesthetic effects. The Symbolist longing for "azure" prompted the writing of the "Blue Symphony," the "Violet Symphony," and "Midsummer Dreams: Symphony in White and Blue," and the other symphonies naturally followed. Despite an occasional exquisitely melodious line, and a happy choice of image, there is much that is maudlin in these concoctions:

> . . . The vast dark trees
> Flow like blue veils
> Of tears
> Into the water.

Fletcher, Arkansas-born, descendant of pioneers, the son of a hero of the battles of Chickamauga and Murfreesboro, came to see the ridiculousness of his early diaphanous Imagist verse, its colors no more natural than tinted fingernails, and in his later poetry has tried more earnestly to find reality. In pictures of skyscrapers, of modern suspension bridges, of night landings on the Mississippi, and of Mexican quarters, there are some satisfying vignettes. For example,

> By an alley lined with tumble-down shacks,
> And street lamps askew, half sputtering,
> Feebly glimmering on gutters choked with filth, and dogs
> Scratching their mangy backs:
> Half-naked children are running about
> Women puff cigarettes in black doorways,
> Crickets are crying
> Men slouch sullenly

Into the shadows:
Behind a hedge of cactus,
The smell of a dead horse
Mingles with the smell of tortillas frying. . . .

This is the way to regeneration, but Mr. Fletcher is still greatly
occupied with color, color for its own sake; and there have crept
into his poems imitations of people less worthy in this day to be
imitated than are the Decadents:

. . . Babylon and Samarkand
Are mud walls in a waste of sand.

Indeed, in the romantic phraseology, in the personal disillusionment and bitterness, and in the Nietzschean raillery at Christianity which are found in the more recent pieces in *Selected Poems*
(1938), even the friendly reader will see the decay of Mr.
Fletcher's genius. Future poetry lovers, if they turn to his work
at all, will most likely choose his autobiography, *Life Is My Song*
(1937), for its reminiscence of the days when it did not seem
likely that the poet's promise would be so much more than his
accomplishment.

Hilda Doolittle, daughter of an astronomer, sometime student
at Bryn Mawr, acquaintance of Pound in his Philadelphia days,
became a member of his group of insurgent poets in London in
1912. Pound, as London agent for *Poetry*, sent her first imagistic
verse to that magazine, where it was published in January, 1913,
under the initials "H.D.", followed by the word "Imagist." In
this early group of insurgents was an English poet, Richard Aldington, who, like Hilda Doolittle, had a passion for Hellenic
verse. In October, 1913, "H.D." married Richard Aldington.
That winter they translated Greek and Latin poems together.
The marriage did not last a decade, but the influence of the poems
the couple read together appears to be permanent in "H.D.'s"
poetry.

Miss Doolittle formerly was extravagantly praised. Laudation
began with Professor Mackail's appreciation of the "Choruses
from Iphigeneia in Aulis" in the London *Times*. Miss Lowell,
thinking of her own fame, was more cautious: " 'H.D.' is not a

great poet, but she is a rarely perfect poet." Whoever called her "a frozen Lesbian" committed so great an indiscretion that he is completely forgotten. The average estimate of "H.D." a decade ago is Mr. Alfred Kreymborg's: "She is indeed the perfect Imagist; and one is tempted to call her the most perfect or nearly perfect of all American poets. . . . In her steady development, she still adheres to 'the exact word,' to poetry 'that is hard and clear, never blurred nor indefinite.' Hard and clear though her poems are, they are also profoundly musical. Cadences echo the meaning as faithfully as in the fragmentary relics of her great idol Sappho. More than any other descendant of the immortal Lesbian, this American deserves the proverbial laurel. . . ."

It is comparatively safe to mention the Tenth Muse of Greece and an American poetess in the same breath. Those who have read Sappho do not know the poetess and those who know the poetess have never read Sappho. The epithets most frequently applied to Hilda Doolittle's poetry are "restrained," "chaste," and "hellenic." With the possible exception of the last—since there is no agreement as to what the adjective "hellenic" means— these epithets do not adequately describe Lesbian poetry. And the "restrained," "chaste," and "hellenic" quality of "H.D.'s" verse is frequently nothing more than prosiness. Consider, for example, not only the dullness but the lameness of the first stanzas of "At Ithaca" from *Heliodora* (1924), which is surely meant to be "Grecian":

> Over and back
> the long waves crawl
> and track the sand with foam;
> night darkens and the sea
> takes on that desperate tone
> of dark that wives put on
> when all their love is done. . . .

Besides aspiring to imitate Sappho, "H.D." has translated some of her verses, but it remains a fact that even in translation of the ancient poet "H.D." has been surpassed not only by Byron and Rossetti, but also by William Ellery Leonard and Allen Tate. The truth is that "H.D." has taken so devious a road back to

Greece—that followed by the Symbolist Jean Papadiamantopoulos, through the Latin Decadents admired by Des Esseintes, with a glance even at Ovid—that she has rarely arrived there, perhaps only in translations of certain choruses. Indeed, despite the "classical" tunic of prose style which she forces her verses to wear, they are as often Decadent as anything else. The reader who makes the test will be surprised to discover how many times the "frustrated satyr" theme of Mallarmé appears in Miss Doolittle's work. Sometimes the theme is obvious and is advertised, as in "Pursuit" in *Sea Garden* (1916) and in "Holy Satyr" in *Heliodora*. But more frequently the theme is elusive, as in "The Cliff Temple," also in *Sea Garden*. In this poem, the poetess fancies herself following the "mysterious, beautiful, white myrtle flesh" of her god up endless reaches of loose rock, where "no hill-goat tramples—no mountain sheep has set foot," only to fall, when she clutches at him, on the hard shards, hoping then only for pity, but hoping in vain. The poem appears to describe accurately enough what should be the fate of any American poetess who, in the sandals of Mallarmé, takes up the futile pursuit of the faun of Greek poetry.

Though never classed as an Imagist himself, Conrad Aiken owes much to the Imagist John Gould Fletcher. This is a singular indebtedness, for of all the American Decadents Aiken has the most natural justification for his position in the circumstances of his life and intellectual development. A man who, as a boy of eleven, had discovered that his father had slain his mother and taken his own life after a quarrel, might be pardoned a little yellow melancholy, or even a flight to an ivory tower. A man who, as a child, had fed on Edgar Allan Poe and was first inspired to versify by the latter's poems might be held to have arrived at Decadence somewhat logically. A man who "drank considerably more than the average undergraduate" at Harvard might be expected to have a blue hang-over which conceivably would affect the tone of his verse. Yet Conrad Aiken's first mature poetry was largely imitative of Browning and Masefield. Indeed, so pronounced was the influence of Masefield on Aiken's first volume of verse, *Earth Triumphant and Other Tales* (1915), that the poet himself attempted to forestall censure by declaring that he had experimented with narrative verse of the type before he had ever heard of the British poet, yet, says Houston Peterson, "the influence of *The Everlasting Mercy* and *The Widow in the Bye Street* is painfully obvious." It was direct contact with Fletcher which freed Aiken from this influence yet established another perhaps ultimately more ruinous to the poet's lasting fame. Fletcher, after publishing *Irradiations,* had returned to Boston from England, and in the spring of 1915 Aiken moved from Cambridge to Walnut Street to be near him. That *Irradiations* represented for Aiken a very high, though not the highest, accomplishment in verse is seen by his carefully considered praise of the book in *Scepticisms* (1919):

... It is a sort of absolute poetry, a poetry of detached waver and brilliance, a beautiful flowering of language alone, a parthenogenesis, as if language were fertilized by itself rather than by thought or feeling. Remove the magic of phrase and sound, and there is nothing left: no thread of continuity, no relation between one page and the next, no thought, no story, no emotion. But the magic of phrase and sound is powerful, and it takes one into a fantastic world where one is etherealized, where one has deep emotions indeed, but emotions star-powdered, and blown to flame by speed and intensity rather than by thought or human warmth.

Conrad Aiken felt that the symphonies of Fletcher, perfect in their way, might be more effective music if reset to suggest a theme. The problem, however, was to avoid destroying the sense of detachment which the absolute poetry of Fletcher produced in him. Thought, story, emotion, which ordinarily supply continuity in verse, for this reason would not do—that is, in their common forms. Aiken was forced to adopt the dream, the freed consciousness, to supply the themes for his symphonies. Deeply read in psychological theory, particularly in the sex psychology of Havelock Ellis and Sigmund Freud, well acquainted with the conceptions of consciousness held by Freud, James, and Bergson, and from childhood filled with a reverence for dreams derived from Edgar Allan Poe, Aiken's choice was a wholly natural one. The result of that choice, however, is astounding. Since turning to the dream for the themes of his symphonies, Conrad Aiken has written in excess of fourteen thousand lines of verse representing the vagaries of the errant consciousness. This amazing production entitles him to the distinction of being America's most considerable Decadent poet.

Not only the quantity but the character of Conrad Aiken's work makes him our leading Decadent. The theme of the first of his symphonies, *The Charnel Rose* (1918), might, according to the poet, "be called nympholepsy—nympholepsy in a broad sense as that impulse which sends us from one dream, or ideal, to another, always disillusioned, always creating for adoration some new and subtler fiction. . . . It has been my intention merely to use this idea as a theme upon which one might build wilfully a kind of absolute music. . . . Thus, beginning with the lowest order of love, the merely carnal, the theme leads irregularly, with returns and anticipations as in music, through various phases of romantic or idealistic love, to several variants of sexual mysticism; finally ending . . . in a mysticism apparently pure."

The dream-pursuit imagined by the poet begins with a nymph who walks in moonlight and disappears, it shifts to the woman of the lamplit town who despite her beauty is a harlot, it veers from the lustful contemplation of the bodies of young men to the temptation offered by the corpses of the graveyard, it introduces the sad company of hermaphrodites, sadists, and masochists, it ends, after the nympholept has imagined himself Christ, with the discovery that "It is our own death we seek in seeking love." No Decadent ever imagined or executed a more lugubrious theme. If the author aimed to produce pure music, *The Charnel Rose* is a failure because its symbols are so vivid and definite that they linger long after the suggestions of genuine musical phrase would be lost in the suggestions of the following musical phrase or in the echoes and silences of the chamber in which the music is played. *The Charnel Rose* is a content poem, and must be judged for its subject matter, or condemned because it does not, like absolute music, produce the detachment necessary for delight.

The high point of Aiken's second symphony, *The Jig of Forslin* (1916), in which he follows the sleepless dreams of a tailor in a gaslit room, is an adventure with a vampire:

> . . . Her white brow flushed, and by my side
> Laughing, with little ecstatic cries,

She kissed my mouth, she stroked my hair,
And fed upon me with fevered stare.
'One little drop!' she murmured then—
'One little drop from this red vein,
And safe I await the sun again—.'
I heard my heart hiss loud and slow;
A gust of wind through the curtains came;
It flapped the upright candle flame.
Her famished eyes began to glow,
She bared my arm; with a golden pin,
Leaned, and tenderly pricked the skin.
And as the small red bubble rose,
Her eyes grew bright with an evil light,
She fawned upon me; and my heart froze
Seeing her teeth so sharp and white. . . .

'Vampire!' I cried. The flame puffed out.
Two blazing eyes withdrew from me.
The music tore discordantly.
The darkness swarmed with a goblin rout.

Yet even this horror (or is it mere romantic nonsense?) is surpassed by certain cerebral adventures described in *The Pilgrimage of Festus* (1923). Festus, according to Aiken, is "anybody or nobody"—in a word, everybody, and "the motive is a
desire for knowledge." In *The Pilgrimage* Festus fancies himself
an old man, a planter of beans and a dreamer of dreams, who at
last realizes that only in pursuit of these aberrant visions may
he grow into the "universe" which is himself. Many are the
rôles that he now assumes in his dreams, but the most remarkable
of all is that of a Roman emperor in the day when such a potentate could satisfy every sadistic desire. Festus craves the
pleasure of seeing a beautiful girl dissected:

*** But bloodshed bores me . . .
Let the gross mind love elephants in torchlight
Trampling the plashy flesh, or tossing entrails
Under the moon! For me, more subtle pleasures. . . .
Here for example on a marble table
You have a princess from an eastern province,
Most delicately reared; and here are surgeons.
We bind her down with silken thongs, well-coloured,
Lest, moved too much by the flattery of knives,

Too modest under the shrewdness of such tongues,
She'll writhe and spoil our play . . . For what's our purpose
But to explore this passion men call life
To the red and smoky end? to tear aside
Curtain on steamy curtain of red fibre
In hot pursuit of—what but life or death?

'Well—then—the first incision. . . . Have it slow.". . .

*** Princess, is there a lover awaits you somewhere—
Comes in the moonlight, putting up his hands
Against a small-leaved bough to press it backward
Or break its fragrance? Stands in the blue-dark shadow
Close to the fountain, watching how it huddles
Its amethysts in the moonlight on wet marble,—
Repeating to himself in a foolish wonder
Your trifling vast eternal world-swung name?
You've heard him praise you, maybe, heard the music
Incredible with which his voice embalms you,
Saying his rituals of eyes and eyebrows,
Lips, hair, and tortured hands, the throat like honey,
The voice like—what? . . . But where's his praise to ours,—
His voice to our love? Pale and faint externals!
While we, with steel-blue tongues, in sweet persistence
Press in from outwards, make our slow incision,
Dissect, as it were, the cry of pain itself. . . .
We have our rituals no less than he.
Is this the golden eyebrow we have loved?
Let us discover if its roots are gold,
That they be also praised; and this sweet pulse
Shaking its music through its world of flesh,
The whole white tingling length, in bells of crimson,—
Making the soft wrist so sweetly tremble,
Carrying into the brain's enchanted forest
Its elfin far-off murmur of horns and cymbals,
Sweet hint, amid that jungle dark and savage,
Of laughing girls and youths forever singing,—
Shall we explore it to its secret source,
To some black and smoking pool? . . .

"This scene," says Mr. Houston Peterson, who has written on
Conrad Aiken with more sympathy than has any one else, but is
here nevertheless repulsed, "is a masterpiece of decadent horror,
carefully conceived and almost perfectly developed. As Poe de-

cided that the death of a beautiful young woman was the ideal subject for serious poetry, Aiken seems to have decided that the vivisection of a beautiful young woman would be the last presumption of the dreaming male, freed from all human fetters. Thus would Festus compensate himself, once and for all, for the abasements and humiliations he had experienced under the feet of the eternal feminine. Thus would Festus epitomize in a single act that incorrigible sadism which colors almost half the acts of human beings. Why we should find pleasure in inflicting suffering, mental and physical, even on those we love, has never been sufficiently explained. Fundamentally it may be an expression of our resentment at living itself, or at the existence of another sex, or at the existence of other people besides ourselves. Whatever the explanation, it seems probable that Festus has discovered the ultimate sadistic satisfaction."

Decadence, which shrieks and sings in *The Pilgrimage of Festus,* finds more subdued expression in the other poems of Aiken. The well-read reader will discern that the ghostly atmosphere of *The House of Dust* (1920) is that of Poe's "City in the Sea"; that the conquests of *Punch: The Immortal Liar* (1921) are not dissimilar to those of the Faun of Mallarmé; and that *Priapus and the Pool* (1922–25) has some relationship to Paul Valéry's *Narcissus.* It is further clear that, while T. S. Eliot owes something to *The Jig of Forslin* and *The House of Dust,* Aiken's debt to Eliot in the morning song of *Senlin* (1925) —one of the finest things that Aiken has written—is so great as to affect one's pleasure in the piece. Aiken undeniably has music— a thin, entrancing wail which beguiles one into mazes from which there is no return. Unreason was never made more seductive and degeneracy never more alluring than in his verses. What an eerie triumph for an American! Yet make no mistake— triumph it genuinely is, whatever its non-aesthetic implications.

Some time prior to the publication of his *Selected Poems,* which won the Pulitzer Prize in 1929, Aiken, for reasons best known to himself, decided to abandon sadistic themes and symphonic composition. *John Deth,* contributed to *The Second American Caravan* (1928) but excluded from the *Selected Poems,* marks a transition to experimentation in form and to fixity in theme, the poet becoming entranced with the sway of death over life. In *Time in the Rock* (1936), after deploring our inability to think and the chaos of our wills, Aiken prays that we may, in our daily death, "learn unconsciousness alone," as a substitute for our grovelling between faith and doubt. One sees in this utter negation the same sort of spiritual defeat and personal frustration that has overtaken the poet's friend, John Fletcher, so that the two are united in the decline of their genius as in their origin. *John Deth* is the lightest expression of this theme, an allegorical ballad in which Deth learns that he cannot die. Certain aspects of this poem are of peculiar interest to students of American literature, for there are curious parallels between it and Freneau's "The House of Night," on the one hand, and Drake's *The Culprit Fay*, on the other. Aiken may not have known either, but the resemblance once observed helps to fix his mood as that of mixed sentimentality and gothicism. The most novel treatment of the theme is found in that strangely named volume, *The Coming Forth by Day of Osiris Jones* (1931). In the manner of a medical student performing an autopsy on the body of a vagrant, Aiken catalogues in their dreadful paucity the "big moments" in the life of average Mr. Jones, on whom, at birth, death set his mark. But Jones, alas, makes a blurred impression as a result of the disjunctive technique employed, and since we cannot sympathize with a blur, the poem fails to arouse the pity and terror which it should. More impressive is the century and a half of "preludes" to death with which Mr. Aiken has filled the volumes, *Preludes to Memnon* (1931) and *Time in the Rock*. The purest distillation of hypochondria, these preludes contain some very impressive lines, though in the main they are wooden, stony and prosaic. Aiken's want of metaphysics handicaps him in this department; after all, he is not a philosopher, but the poet of unnatural heats and haunting melodies.

Like Edgar Allan Poe, Aiken has written fiction as well as poetry, and fiction which displays the same taste for the macabre. One novel, *King Coffin* (1935), deals with a megalomaniac, who, like Festus, has homicidal tendencies, while two other novels, *Blue Voyage* (1927) and *Great Circle* (1933), relate how their heroes, William Demarest and Andrew Cather, respectively, review their whole lives, after they have been spurned by the women they love, to discover that their personal inadequacies spring from psychoses formed in youth. Only one novel, *Conversation* (1940), deals with people anywhere near normal or average, and this has its fantastic passages, for example, the Freudian dream of the mistress with its symbolic allusions to the wife. Three volumes of short stories (*Bring! Bring! and Other Stories*, 1925; *Costumes by Eros*, 1928; and *Among the Lost People*, 1934) produce glimpses of people hovering, almost indistinguishable, on the edge of the shadow world. The bulk of the fiction is done in the stream-of-consciousness method, but the author is possibly more interested in the harmony of the words than in Joycean technique and Freudian science. Each prose piece is a musical composition, attending which, however, the listener is nervously aware of the composer's effort to produce vibrations too rapid and ethereal for the human ear. Non-utilitarian and imagistic, the prose can also be catalogued, without too much strain, as Decadent poetry, and Aiken's reputation will suffer less if it is treated so.

Although Imagism was a prettified form of Decadence, and although all its practitioners save Pound were distinctly minor poets, there is no gainsaying the stimulating effect it had upon the production of literature in this country. Yet a new poetry movement was in the making without it, for Robinson, Lindsay, and Sara Teasdale had already quickened interest in verse. Imagism, or better, Amy Lowell, accelerated the movement tremendously. What a Boadicea was she! If a New York reviewer in those days wrote an unfavorable review of one of her protégés, she promptly entrained for the city and had it out with him with the result that he was more cautious in the future. Through the ample breach she opened in the wall of public indifference a band of literary "isms" poured: Vorticism, Vocalism, Pointillism, Futurism, Cubism, and Dadaism. This rage for poetic novelty was happily burlesqued by the "Spectrist" movement which Arthur Davidson Ficke and Witter Bynner originated; their "Spectra" were widely lauded before the critics discovered they had been gulled. Of the experimental work done between 1915 and 1918 the publication *Others* contains the best. Here some interesting, though not important, Decadent verse may be found from the pens of Alfred Kreymborg, Conrad Arensberg, and a few other inspired Greenwich Villagers.

One of the contributors to *Others* was Wallace Stevens, who, however, has never identified himself with any group and owes nothing to the puffery of a clique. A Hartford lawyer, who got his training at Harvard, he is the one American of whom it may most accurately be said that he has written poetry primarily for his own entertainment. After ten years of printing in magazines, Stevens allowed a few of his poems to be collected, in 1923, in a volume called *Harmonium*. The verses bear perhaps the most extraordinary and mirth-provoking titles ever concocted for poetry by an Anglo-Saxon: "The Paltry Nude Starts on a Spring Voyage," "Tea at the Palaz of Hoon," "Le Monocle de Mon Oncle," "Hibiscus on the Sleeping Shores," "The Emperor of Ice-Cream," "To the One of Fictive Music," etc. These are, of course, an open publication of Wallace Stevens' debt to Jules Laforgue, whom he was the first of all Americans thoroughly to appreciate.

Beside the Imagists Wallace Stevens is a towering intellect. But the company of French Decadents, where he rightfully belongs, somewhat dwarfs him. His eccentricities are parodies of their inventiveness; his verbalism, an effort to mimic their curious juxtaposition of words. The miasmatical striving of Mallarmé for azure becomes "The Indigo Glass in the Grass," or receives fantastic expression in the "Banal Sojourn":

Two wooden tubs of blue hydrangeas stand at the foot of the stone steps.
The sky is blue gum streaked with rose. . . .
. . . And who does not seek the sky unfuzzed, soaring to the princox?
One has a malady, here, a malady. One feels a malady.

This is pure Laforgue. If the reader will compare Stevens' "The Weeping Burgher" with the lines which Jules Laforgue has his Hamlet compose (and which he intends to ridicule), he will be astonished at their similarity. Indeed, Stevens' lines are more fitting to that homicidal maniac than are those which Laforgue assigns to him.

Adopting the attitude of futility peculiar to Laforgue, Wallace

Stevens has also adopted the aesthetic of the Symbolists, with its chief tenets that poetry is music, and that music in its effects more nearly approaches supernal loveliness than does any other art. Out of this aesthetic he has wrought many an obscure and lovely poem, but none other quite so perfect as "Peter Quince at the Clavier." Here, blended with a rich Orientalism, is the music of Poe and Mallarmé, and a charming reassertion of the immortality of beauty slain. Unable to phrase in any other way adequately his love for his mistress, Peter Quince evokes with his music a vision of the red-eyed elders peeping at Susanna in her bath. The plied keys tell how Susanna's "music," the beauty of her nude body, touched the "bawdy strings of those white elders," overmastering them. Clashing chords report the discovery of Susanna's shame and the flight of the simpering Byzantines who had attended her. Yet Susanna lives—

> The body dies; the body's beauty lives. . . .
> Now in its immortality, it plays
> On the clear viol of her memory,
> And makes a constant sacrament of praise.

So, by corollary, Peter's music will preserve immortal his mistress. Stevens has done the very thing that Conrad Aiken tried to do in his poetry. Though "Peter Quince at the Clavier" is nearer the fugue in character, rather than the symphony, it suggests a musical composition better than do Aiken's more ambitious pieces, because of its *indefiniteness,* an indefiniteness so subtle that this attempt at mere description destroys it. Most remarkable is the *felt* presence of Peter Quince's lady auditor, felt in the last line of the poem and after the notes of the clavier have died away. There are few better executed poems in modern English than this.

In "The Paltry Nude Starts on a Spring Voyage" Stevens uses the figurehead of a whaling ship more or less as Rimbaud had used the "drunken boat" in his most famous poem. But Stevens does not find the cruise through splintered imagery as inviting as had Rimbaud; consequently his poem, aside from its opening allusion to Botticelli's *The Birth of Venus,* does not come off well. Such a line as, "She scuds the glitters," one would be more likely to attribute to the barker of an aquatic girlie show than to a leading poet. The hunger of the wooden nude for "purple stuff upon her arms," that is, seawash, is assignable however, only to a versifier of the Decadent school.

Yet Stevens does more than to continue, sometimes unhappily, the Decadent tradition. In his work a great circle is completed and the serpent swallows its own tail. Not content with imitating Laforgue and his contemporaries, Stevens goes back to Baudelaire and Poe. "A Carrion" and "The Conqueror Worm" revive in such a piece as "The Worms at Heaven's Gate" in which a famous pagan beauty, Badroulbadour, is reassembled, so to speak, from the bellies of the worms—an eye, an eyelash, a white lid, and the cheek on which the lid declined—a piece at a time. A true grotesque (despite its probable satire of the realistic method), the poem is also a kind of sigil impressed mysteriously by Poe on one of his distant progeny.

Aroused by the swift concatenation of events in the middle 'thirties, Stevens again permitted book issue of his poetry—in *Ideas of Order* (1935), *Owl's Clover* (1936), and *The Man with the Blue Guitar* (1937). These books do not add to his reputation, for in a new seriousness the bravura of *Harmonium* is gone. Stevens has spoken of "the essential gaudiness of poetry," a quality undeniable in his early verse and probably achieved because poetry was for him so definitely divorced from life—so much a pastime. Now that he is aware that this is an "age of concentric mobs" and "Marx has ruined Nature, for the moment," he is not able to impart either lilt or whimsicality to his verse. His own "essential gaudiness" is gone. Yet he is not interested in any political reconstruction or new ordering of the world. The only "order" he is sure of is that which the imagination imposes. Consequently his advice to the poet is to continue to "practice arpeggios" though "they throw stones on the roof." One remembers unhappily that the French Symbolists took refuge in pure art when the political scene became too complicated for their comprehension.

It would be a piece of pedantry to indicate the whole debt of Wallace Stevens to French Decadence; it is sufficient to show that his work is narrowly confined within the Decadent tradition and has limited originality. Yet within the limitations he has accepted, he has functioned intelligently and well. The Imagists never clearly knew what they were about; their definitions were vague, and their purposes confused. Stevens' superior gifts of intelligence and humor have made him a better poet, but not a great one. There are more breadth and music in Pound who still isn't one of the world's great poets. It may be said, perhaps, that Pound's work, though imitative, is superior to Stevens' because his imitation is of a wider range of poetry. Homer, Dante, and Villon are greater poets than any in the Decadent tradition. Had Pound, with all his mimicry, confined himself to a tighter aesthetic, to imitating a more deliberately limited group of masters, Stevens would have surpassed him, for Stevens constructs his poems from Decadent formulas, while Pound apes the produced effects of other poets. All theory should make Stevens the greater poet, for notwithstanding Pound's much talk, he is not a thinker; all fact, however, and by that poetic results are meant, establishes Pound securely above Stevens. Line by line examination of the work of the two does not favor a theory that one possesses greater sensibility than the other; both at times show a rare felicity for the right word; both can be inept. One must conclude that the sole point of Pound's superiority is in his imitative scope. The choice of what he will do is far more important to a poet's success than is generally admitted (particularly in these days when it is popular to deny choice in these matters), and Stevens, aiming wholly at Decadent effects, has produced good verse with these effects, but nothing more.

Decadence in France, we have seen, is a product of the Prussian triumph of 1870 and the feeling that the Gallic race was degenerate. The fear of national sterility begot all this poetry. Verlaine and Rimbaud hint at the theme of racial degeneracy but do not give it full poetic statement. Nor could they very well do so. Those who flee from life to art invariably profess—and, being what we are, this is a false profession—to be attracted to art wholly for its own sake. The deliberate consistency with which some poets have maintained an exclusive absorption in art is a denial of their intelligence and a proof of their awareness of life itself. To write a thousand lines without a contemporary allusion is a triumph of perversity, but if it indicates anything, it indicates that the author is unusually sensible of that which he has avoided. Even Mallarmé did not wholly succeed at this game, though he came nearer doing so than any other poet in the record. Yet the major theme, defeated and sterile France, the least adroit of the poetasters could avoid, and did successfully. So, too, when the World War I had wrecked Western Europe and had reinforced the philosophies of despair, the Dadaists, who had their origins in this chaos, with singular pertinacity avoided all direct reference to it. It remained for an American, for one not tremendously involved, to state the obvious. "The Waste Land" has been implicit and imminent in the Decadent movement from its inception, yet no Frenchman could write it for the privy fear that he would be charged with inconsistency. Friends would say that for a popular effect he had deserted the Creed; art for art's sake had lost a practitioner. A reputation for intelligence (which always means consistency) is prized higher in France than the production of literature. That is why modern France has never produced an indispensable poet. Paul Valéry had the disposition to write "The Waste Land," as his "Crisis of the Spirit" shows. There is no indication, however, that he would have done as good a job as has Mr. Eliot.

"The Waste Land," coming at the culmination of Decadence, is the greatest poem thus far produced in the twentieth century. Born of the years of chaos following the War, its major theme is the spiritual sterility of contemporary life. "I will show you fear," declares the poet, "in a handful of dust." First, however, he must reveal the mysterious life which breeds in that dust, all the mighty power which lies in it. Out of it are engendered the lilac and the hyacinth girl, the tree and the son of man. The fructifying of the seasons and the thing called love are identified as the same under symbolism borrowed from pagan ritual, from magic, and from poetic legend. "I will show you fear in a handful of dust"—to what end is all this engendering? The poet's answer is death: eternal recurrence is for death.

> He who was living is now dead
> We who were living are now dying

"The Waste Land" is a graveyard poem, and to find its parallel one must turn to the eighteenth century where Gray's "Elegy" with much the same melancholy enforces the same theme. No soldier storming the new Heights of Abraham will repeat—

> Datta. Dayadhvam. Damata.
> Shantih shantih shantih—

yet Eliot has shown the paths of glory lead inevitably to the grave. Only, for Eliot, the Present is the tomb. About this tomb are scattered the fragments of past cultures (hence the strewn verses of the poets he admires, all deliberately chosen, like those from Webster who "was much possessed by death and saw the skull beneath the skin," to enforce the theme), mixed with snatches from vaudeville and the chatter of morons. In this present death the soul is now securely locked:

> . . . I have heard the key
> Turn in the door once and turn once only . . .

Like the "Elegy," Eliot's poem is the product of scholarship, of meticulous selection of elements, of much polishing; like the "Elegy," it stands far above its author's other work and above the other work of the time—a highly original, important poem.

In its philosophical content—perhaps one should say *theological* content, since Eliot appears to trace modern spiritual sterility back to Henry VIII ("the barbarous king") and to Puritanism (Tiresias)—the poem has been less immediately important than in some of its effects. The spring-ritual, sex-drive theme is worked out with extraordinary ingenuity—the range of illustration running from the April freshet on the Thames (with its veiled relation to the Osiris legend through the nuptial song of Spenser) to the Fisher King of the Grail story, from the man whose "vanity requires no response" in the woman whom he assaults to Tereus the ravisher of Philomel. The tale of Albert's Lil in "A Game of Chess" (the second section of the poem), who has borne him five children, who has wrecked her health and her looks ("and her only thirty-one") in producing a miscarriage, and who now faces the loss of her Albert hot from the

War to the very dissembler who advises her to make herself "a bit smart"—this tale of Lil is something which will stand by itself without any shoring as a dramatic monologue. It would be difficult to surpass the irony of the drooling "Goonights" of the young bucks and girls of Lil's class which Eliot adds as a "flashback" to this piece.

Faced with the problem of subordinating description to music in a poem which is largely descriptive, Eliot solved it in a way which will be the despair of future technicians. Not only are the narrative and descriptive passages of the poem marvelously varied in their melodic effects, but Eliot has managed to introduce and to suggest an astonishing variety of fragmentary music or musical sound without injury to the unity of the poem. The patter of the rain, the ironic chirp of the cricket in the dead land, a sentimental-melancholy theme from *Tristan and Isolde* (which at the same time has its relation to the vegetation ceremonies)—

> Frisch weht der Wind
> Der Heimat Zu
> Mein Irisch Kind,
> Wo weilest du?—

the sough of the desolate and empty sea, the eternal wail of Philomel, the shuffle of footsteps on the stair and the wind under the door, the scamper of rats and the rattle of dice, the throbbing of the taxi-motor and the scratch of the gramophone needle, the caught fragments of foreign speech—all these mingle into a great harmony which is perhaps the most satisfying effect of the poem.

In giving the particular universal significance, too, Eliot is peculiarly happy. The selection of Stetson out of the procession of dead down King William Street, and the eager query if the body buried in the garden has begun to sprout, is an illustration of this. To the reader of sensibility the poem offers the widest variety of pleasure of any poem of our day. There is no more compact piece in all literature.

Yet the reader who has a fair knowledge of contemporary literature can see the glue in the joints of "The Waste Land" no matter how cunningly Eliot has joined the whole. The "woman who drew her long black hair out tight" while the towers of Alexandria, Jerusalem, Athens, Vienna and London are falling reminds one instantly of Carl Sandburg's "Four Preludes on Playthings of the Wind" and suggests how generic this poem is to Mr. Eliot's conception. The very rats which run among the ruins of Sandburg's "greatest city" have migrated to the desolate places of Eliot's poem. Even poor Lil and her Albert come from the French Decadents by way of Mr. Stevens and Mr. Pound. The latter's *Cantos* undeniably have influenced the structure of "The Waste Land" though this is better than anything Pound has written. Miss Millay, closely following the Coleridge tradition, had used the rain as a symbol of spiritual rebirth after death in "Renascence," a poem starred with pseudo-Decadent imagery, as early as 1912; that section entitled "Cinders" in T. E. Hulme's Bergsonian *Speculations* (1924) is so much in the temper of "The Waste Land" that the author seemingly could not have been ignorant of it. The necessity that this philosophical-descriptive poem should be a musical composition is derived from the Decadent aesthetic. The theory that escape is only through dreams—after the discovery that life is a prison—certainly has a familiar quality. And finally, the line from Kyd's *Spanish Tragedy* at the end of the piece, "Hieronymo's mad again,"—a line entirely uncalled for save as it reflects on the personal bitterness of the poet—suggests that Mr. Eliot, like Mallarmé, is not above hoodwinking the general public. Eliot is enough of a craftsman, however, so that his joinery is never offensive to the taste. Synthesis, which all poets have practised more or less covertly, is here brilliantly and openly shown to be an important part of literary composition.

The emotion of "The Waste Land" is not that of experience recollected in tranquillity, but rather the outpouring of a spirit at the very crisis of experience. Yet that experience was not outward and manifest, but inward, and perhaps even partially subconscious in its nature. The outward life of the poet has been smooth enough. Born, in 1888, into the family of a brick manufacturer who had married a schoolteacher, Eliot was educated at Smith Academy in his native St. Louis. A paternal grandfather had established the first free school west of the Mississippi, obtained the first public school tax levy in the West, founded Washington University, and started a Unitarian Church still in existence. Though the Eliots may be traced back to Massachusetts, they came from Old England to escape Cromwell's persecutions, hence the glib representation of Eliot as a Puritan on the basis of his ancestry has little foundation in fact. After reading a commencement poem to his Academy class, Eliot came East to Harvard where he finished his undergraduate work in three years and struck out for an M.A. in his fourth. At the University he shed his early Byronism and became absorbed in philosophy. The year before taking his bachelor's degree he found the French Decadent poets commended in Arthur Symons' *Symbolist Movement in Literature*. "I myself owe Mr. Symons a great debt," he confesses in a review of Quennell's *Baudelaire and the Symbolists*. "But for having read his book I should not, in the year 1908, have heard of Laforgue and Rimbaud; I should probably not have begun to read Verlaine; and but for reading Verlaine, I should not have heard of Corbière. So the Symons book is one of those which have affected the course of my life." Poems contributed to the Harvard *Advocate* in 1909–10 show only the influence of Laforgue, yet he was ready to discuss the work of Fort and Jammes and the *vers libre* movement before leaving Cambridge. It was natural, then, after taking his M.A. degree, that he should go on to the Sorbonne for further study, though his ultimate object was to do a dissertation on the philosophy of F. H. Bradley. Eventually, after still more reading at Harvard and at Merton College, Oxford, Eliot in 1914 settled in London, where he has been variously occupied as a bank clerk and editor. In 1927, he became a British citizen, and a short time later, a communicant in the Anglo-Catholic Church. He returned to America to lecture to much applause in 1932–33.

The imprint of Pound is clearly marked on Eliot's earliest volume of verse, *Prufrock and Other Observations* (1917). "The Portrait of a Lady," "Aunt Helen," and "Cousin Nancy" are reworkings of Pound's "Portrait d'une Femme" and "The Garden." "The Love Song of J. Alfred Prufrock" stems from the same poems, yet its remarkable figures suggest a close study of the French Decadents—

The yellow fog that rubs its muzzle on the window panes—

while Prufrock's observation that he is not Hamlet, but "an attendant lord" (there is no reason for introducing this observation) shows a specific absorption in Laforgue. Still, Pound gave the grand design. "The *Boston Evening Transcript*" is an assault which gets all its courage from a similar attack by Pound on the London *Times*. Particularly imitative, though here Laforgue also intrudes, is "Conversation Galante" and "La Figlia Che Piange." Muffled echoes of Mallarmé, Rimbaud, and Corbière can be heard in "Mr. Appollinax" which is, however, written with as much zest as anything Mr. Eliot has penned. The reader can decide whether a certain British philosopher with rather liberal views towards marriage is appropriately the "faun" of this poem. Yet while the *Prufrock* volume is derivative, it was, because of its singular unity of tone, a more effective propellant in the direction of Decadence than were all its predecessors. A major figure had arrived in American poetry.

Of the pieces added to the *Poems* of 1920, "Burbank with a Baedeker: Bleistein with a Cigar," "Sweeney Erect," "A Cooking Egg," and "Sweeney Among the Nightingales" all suggest a deepening of the Laforgue-Corbière influence, a tendency towards gathering fantastic collocations of words, such as we have seen in Wallace Stevens. Furthermore, in addition to Anglicizing French materials and modernizing his references, Eliot has possessed himself completely of the Decadent loathing for the bourgeois and of the Romantic idea of the glory of the past—an idea which Edmund Wilson has correctly traced to Flaubert. In "Gerontion," instead of the flat implication of the "Sweeney" poems, bourgeois sterility is symbolized:

> Here I am, an old man in a dry month,
> Being read to by a boy, waiting for rain. . . .
> My house is a decayed house,
> And the jew squats on the window sill, the owner. . . .

The old man stands for what was called "gentility" and "good breeding" in the quaint days before the First World War; now he and his kind are driven into a sleepy corner by the Trades—and the Jews. The rain that should bring rejuvenation will never fall, despite the myths; inspiring adventure will never come to these sorry times and dull places he inhabits. In dreams and in the boy's reading only will he escape the dreadful present.

Here, *in posse,* is "The Waste Land." "Gerontion" marks the mature poet, and it is for this and for "The Waste Land" that Eliot has been revered by the younger generation. Mr. Wilson has tried to count the cost of that reverence to this generation, and his estimate reminds us again forcibly of Gray and the "graveyard school" the latter's influence created:

". . . As for 'The Waste Land,' it enchanted and devastated a whole generation. Attempts have been made to reproduce it—by Aldington, Nancy Cunard, etc.—at least a dozen times. And as Eliot, lately out of Harvard, assumed the rôle of the middle-aged Prufrock and to-day, at forty, in one of his latest poems, 'The Song of Simeon,' speaks in the character of an old man 'with eighty years and no tomorrow'—so 'Gerontion' and 'The Waste Land' have made the young poets old before their time. In London, as in New York, and in the universities both here and in England, they for a time took to inhabiting barren beaches, cactus-grown deserts, and dusty attics over-run with rats—the only properties they allowed themselves to work with were a few fragments of old shattered glass or a sparse sprinkling of broken bones. They had purged themselves of Masefield as of Shelley for dry tongues and rheumatic joints. The dry breath of 'The Waste Land' now blighted the most amiable country landscapes; and the sound of jazz, which had formerly seemed jolly, now inspired only horror and despair. . . ."

In *The Sacred Wood* (1920) Eliot has insisted that poetry is an escape from emotion, but no poet of the whole Decadent school has been more driven by emotion than he. This is perhaps what raises his poetry above that of his predecessors. The others put the sterility of their times out of their lives and occupy themselves wholly with their art; Eliot cannot contain his horror and aversion. The very existence of "Apeneck" Sweeney, of Bleistein, of Albert and his Lil, is almost too much for him. Repulsion is succeeded by fascination, and, like Flaubert, Eliot finds himself against his will occupied with that which he detests. Originally committed to despising all that is mean or bourgeois (in the Flaubertian sense) Eliot has shown a tendency of late to identify this with all that is human or natural. Thus *Sweeney*

Agonistes (1932), that "Aristophanic melodrama" of the demi-monde of London, is prefaced by two highly significant quotations, one from *St. John of the Cross,* ". . . the soul cannot be possessed of the divine union, until it divests itself of the love of created beings" (quoted with the wrong emphasis, by the way) ; and the other from the *Choephoroi* in which Orestes (here Eliot) exclaims, "You don't see them, you don't—but *I* see them : they are hunting me down, I must move on." Fear of his fellow creatures, horribly symbolized in Doris, Dusty, Wauchope, Horsfall, Klipstein, Krumpacker, and Sweeney of the melodrama, has driven Eliot into classicism in literature, royalism in politics, and Anglo-Catholicism in religion. The crisis in realization came at about the time of the creation of "The Waste Land."

That he was gathering his luggage, that he was about to take flight, is evident as early as the 1920 *Poems*. To be sure, "The Hippopotamus," an attack upon the Roman Church (suggested by similar things done by Rimbaud and Corbière), would not seem to indicate that Eliot had, at that time, considered religion as a haven. On the other hand, in "Mr. Eliot's Sunday Morning Service" the poet reflects seriously on the fact that a painting of the baptism of the Lord by an artist of the Umbrian school, though cracked and brown, still fills the bosom with piety while all the empty exercises of "the sapient sutlers of the Lord" do not. It is in contrast to "the unoffending feet" of Jesus which still shine "through the water pale and thin" that the animal Sweeney is set in his Sunday morning bath comfortably shifting "from ham to ham." The disgust of the poet is apparent enough ; so, too, is the drift of his thought. This is no new pre-Raphaelite interest in the subject matter of religion as colorful material for poetry, but hesitant consideration of the values of religion itself. All doubt is resolved in "The Waste Land" which, despite its picture of desolation, ends with a note of spiritual hope. "The Hollow Men" (1925) pronounces an anathema upon this soulless generation which too late will stop its mad dance to whimper meaningless fragments of prayer.

It is a short step, not a stride, from "The Hollow Men" to *Ash Wednesday,* published five years later. This is the prayer of a Missourian who, only forty, fancies himself an "aged eagle" taught "to sit still" to await the resurrection of spiritual things. As a poem, *Ash Wednesday* is a failure for two reasons: the poet has closed his mind, and the metrical form of the piece is not suited to the religious mood. Eliot has not considered the full literary possibilities of his subject, there is no effective aposiopetic allusion as in "The Waste Land," no genuine liturgical and historical richness, but a mere dull repetition of phrase,—as if exemplifying the superstition of intrinsic value in the word. Commination, not foreign to the mind which wrote "The Hollow Men," would at least have given the poem force. Offensive, particularly in the fifth section, are the mumbled repetitions and the ill-begotten internal rimes, like "rejoice-noise-voice" and "word-world-whirled."

If *Ash Wednesday* fails altogether to soar, so, too, does the religious pageant *The Rock* (1934) with its absurd picture of the labor agitator, its ardent defense of "Montagoo Norman," of the Bank of England, and its presentation of Henri Bergson as mid-wife at the birth of Christ. The choruses are the best poetry in *The Rock,* and of them, that which introduces Part II is as effective as any. The intelligent reader is amused, rather than shocked, by the astonishing mumbo-jumbo of Bergson's time theories in this chorus:

... Then came, at a predetermined moment, a moment in time and out of time,
A moment not out of time, but in time, in what we call history; transecting the world of time, a moment in time but not like a moment of time, etc. . . .

In so meticulous a writer, the phrase "advances progressively backwards" used to describe the age, in this chorus, is a very unhappy choice, for *backwards* to his age of faith Mr. Eliot wishes us progressively to go. This ambiguity is typical of the whole play; Eliot is "sitting" rather than thinking. The contention of *The Rock* that the economic difficulties of the World are caused by a lack of spirituality is, in this case, the conclusion of a sectarian propagandist. Mr. Eliot, with his business training, knows better. His attitude, moreover, takes religion back to the age of magic. Compassion and charity, thought of in the broadest sense, may help us to solve our difficulties, but the difficulties lie in a system which Mr. Eliot defends—and which he identifies with the Church of God. The grand climax of *The Rock* is an effort on Eliot's part to make substantial the myth of the founding of the Abbey at Westminster by St. Peter. How convincing that effort is depends largely on the prejudices of the spectator; what it establishes, however, is the narrow sectarian ground Eliot has chosen for his religion.

There is nothing mystical about the new Eliot; there is instead in him a resuscitation of the old harsh dogmatism of Archbishop Laud. In attempting to produce an effect in England and America such as the Neo-Thomists have produced in France, Eliot has revived merely Church politics and fiercely partisan denomina-tionalism. This is best seen in the warm commendation of the stout Churchman Lancelot Andrewes—whom no one else surely would put above the liberal Dr. John Donne. Donne is con-demned for having sought refuge in religion from the tumults of a strong emotional temperament. Has Mr. Eliot forgotten Saint Augustine? We do not understand what he means by saying that Donne is much less the traditional spiritual man than Andrewes. Nor can Andrewes be made to appeal to us because he occupies a place "second to none" in the "history" of the English Church. In passing, however, we must praise the essay, *For Lancelot Andrewes* (1929), as the most finished example of Eliot's stud-ied prose.

After Strange Gods (1934) is apparently the examination of the principles of heresy that Eliot promised in 1929. This book is, beyond all challenge, one of the narrowest and most bigoted critical books of modern times. After innocently observing that modern writers have hardly been criticized at all for their morals, Eliot assails some first rate men for their heterodox, rather than orthodox, beliefs. While he defines orthodoxy in literature as a conviction of the presence of good and evil as active principles in the world, his treatment of writers and of issues is purely on sectarian grounds. To the good Anglo-Catholic, which Eliot has become, John Milton is full of intellectual and moral aberrations and *Paradise Lost* might be a better poem if its author had held more "normal" doctrines. In the traditional society, which he hopes the Southern Agrarians will fertilize into burgeoning again, Eliot sees no place for any large number of skeptical Jews. (We think at once of his already revealed anti-Semitism in his portraits of Bleistein, Klipstein, and Krumpacker, and we begin to wonder if his attitude towards Sweeney is not a good British High Churchman's or a good Bostonian's hostility towards Ireland and the Irish.) But this is not the worst. Irving Babbitt is assailed for having become fascinated in Confucius (which, says Eliot seriously, is a sin if one is not an Oriental) and Ezra Pound for having created a literary Hell "altogether without dignity." D. H. Lawrence, Thomas Hardy, and William Butler Yeats are immoral because certain of their works do not recognize evil as an active force and because Mr. Eliot suspects they do not believe in the Doctrine of Original Sin. In reviewing *After Strange Gods* in *The Nation,* Mr. William Troy is forced to consider the relative morality of T. S. Eliot and of those whom he condemns, as follows:

. . . It is possible to discover . . . in Mr. Eliot's persistent refusal to see the modern world as it is, a wilfulness that is at least as morally reprehensible as any of the sins of the several heretic modern writers whom he singles out for rebuke. D. H. Lawrence undoubtedly suffered from being cut off from a settled religious and social tradition; his work is tainted to a marked degree with the modern vices of "sincerity" and "personality." It is even possible to agree that in many cases his influence has been more harmful than good. But what still gives to his work a moral justification, what cancels whatever incidental unmoral or "diabolic" elements may be found in it, is his effort, the essentially *moral* effort, to include all of the truth as he perceived it in the vision of the modern world that he left at his death. There was in him no sacrifice of honest perception for the sake of intellectual structure which, however appealing it may be to the dialectic faculties, no longer has sufficient feasibility for our time. A distinction that may be made, therefore, is between the morality of the writer conceived as effort—the unrelenting effort to integrate his perceptions with his beliefs, to reconcile the actual with the ideal—and the morality of the artist conceived as conformity to a systematized body of beliefs deriving from the conditions of an earlier religion and culture. Of these two views of morality Mr. Eliot has chosen the second; and the unfortunate consequences of his choice are revealed not only in his verse, in the progressive weakness of everything that he has written since "The Waste Land," but in his prose, in such a frank admission as this of the separation in the same personality between the artist and the critic: "I should say that in one's prose reflections one may be legitimately occupied with ideals, whereas in the writing of verse one can only deal with actuality." In psychological terms, this amounts to nothing less than a "schizoid" state of the personality; and since one of the objects of morality is the unification of the personality, one can only conclude. that there is something profoundly wrong with Mr. Eliot's view of morality. For the poet nothing could be more useless or infertile than a system of beliefs which cannot stand up under the pressure of the actuality with which he has to deal. And in the critic who, like Mr. Eliot, is also a poet nothing could be more indefensible than this blithe acceptance of the divorce between "ideals" and "actuality." Do we not have here an example of that *unregenerate* self-deception which, as everyone knows, is one of the ways in which Mr. Eliot's favorite antagonist, the devil, works in the modern world?

To avoid the anomaly of judging contemporary things by past standards, Eliot has retreated completely into the past in *Murder in the Cathedral* (1935), a pageant play on the murder of Thomas, Archbishop of Canterbury, in 1170. Of all his recent work, this is the one piece into which the religious spirit is deeply and thoughtfully infused. Thomas Becket's struggle with the Tempters, his decision that to do a right deed for the wrong reason is not permissible, his steadfastness in his purpose, his gentle dignity in the face of his own immolation, raise him on the stage to a position comparable to what he once held in the imaginations of the devout. The chorus has probably not been more effectively employed in modern times than in this play, and the two chants immediately preceding the murder of Becket contain the only verse of Eliot which may be described as emotionally powerful. In the anticipatory horror of the scene toward which his play is swiftly moving ("I have eaten smooth creatures still living . . .") Eliot forgets the cunning restraints he has always exercised over his poetry and allows it to swing out in its own strong rhythm. As for the murder itself, we had expected the play, before reading or seeing it, to fail completely at this point, but as it was done in the Federal Theatre, in New York, it was electrically effective. The weaknesses of *Murder in the Cathedral* are, first, the imperfect distinction between the Tempters at the beginning of the play (here the equivalent of lack of characterization), and, secondly, the employment of too ob-

vious Shavian technique in stopping the play for the murderers
to step to the proscenium to discuss the affair with the audience.
We instantly think of Shaw's Epilogue to *Saint Joan,* and while
realizing that this is written to offset that, we wish the Christian
champion did not have to rely upon the scoffer's tricks to answer
the scoffer. The result is that we leave the theatre with a sense
(in the main, unjustified) of the play's amateurishness. *Murder
in the Cathedral* is, however, some sort of a triumph for the man
who had announced, just a few years previously, that his only
dramatic satisfaction was in the High Mass well performed.

Yet conventional morality is more important in Mr. Eliot's
scale of values than is dramatic achievement. Instead of learning
from the presentation of *Murder in the Cathedral* that implicit
ideas do not encounter from an audience the resistance received
by preachments, Eliot took the success of his play as encouragement to further moralizing. His modernization of Aeschylus'
story of the house of Atreus in *The Family Reunion* (1939) is
no study of crime and expiation, like the *Choephoroe,* but rather
an account of how the Furies avenge themselves on a North
English household because both father and son had wished to be
rid of their wives. With as much actual crime as there is in the
world, Mr. Eliot's absorption with the sin of merely wishing
seems like absorption with the very trivial indeed. And what a
trimming down of Aeschylus! Eliot appears bent on turning the
theatre into a theological seminary. Prithee, brother, is it a sin
to wish as well as to act?

It is a relief to find the author abandoning the drama for the
tract. In *The Idea of a Christian Society* (1940) Eliot pleads
with those intellectuals who believe in the "dogmatisms" of
Christianity to form a select body, a "clerisy," whose influence,
radiating outward, would correct the morals of the mass and
create a Christian State by impelling the politicos (who are not
necessarily reverent men) to respect the ethics of Christianity in
their actions. Because it takes proper account of the separation
of Church and State, the idea is a pretty one; but behind the
critic's doubt that intellectuals would agree sufficiently on the
dogmas of Christianity to secure united action is the memory of
all the explosions of Protestant sectarianism. Whatever there is

of cohesiveness in Christianity appears to lie below the intellectual levels where dogmas are established. Still, the idea, tentatively and even timidly advanced by the author, seems worth a try, particularly if the initiators were willing to stick to the sphere that Eliot assigned to them.

In the 'twenties, following the publication of *The Sacred Wood* (1920), Mr. Eliot was regarded as the champion of a "pure criticism" to match the "pure art" of the writers of the Decadent school. The essays, "The Perfect Critic" and "The Imperfect Critic," in *The Sacred Wood* attack with commendable vigor "impressionistic" criticism and "abstract" criticism, while setting forth the virtues of "intellectual" criticism as practiced by a writer of fine "sensibility"—a word which Mr. Eliot re-endowed with meaning. Eliot points out that impressionistic criticism is a creative, and not a critical, activity; that abstract criticism—the criticism by established law—fails because the words of the canon change in value; but that the effort to evaluate a work of art by a "free" or disinterested intelligence is the only possible critical activity. One has no quarrel with Eliot for picking flaws in the "impressionistic" and "abstract" methods of criticism, especially in the extremes which he uses for illustration, but one is a little skeptical of his or any other man's ability to achieve the detachment which he so warmly advocates. "A literary critic should have no emotions except those immediately provoked by a work of art." Splendid. But what is "emotion"? Does Mr. Eliot's method liberate us from the necessity of definition? Once we have defined, will our terms never change in value? On the other hand, how is the critic really to perceive a work of art without re-creating it in his own mind? Are his image and the work of art the same? Can he avoid impressionism if he would? There is little psychological reality, and much ascetic nonsense, in such a fine austere statement as, "the end of the enjoyment of poetry is a pure contemplation from which all the accidents of personal emotion are removed." Such a criticism would be better termed "mechanical" than "intellectual" since only a machine could achieve the "purity" which Eliot desires.

Pursuing his "impersonal" theories, Eliot avows that "honest criticism and sensitive appreciation is directed not upon the poet but upon the poetry." Fair enough, but Eliot as a critic has rarely practiced this austere criticism, and never at all with controversial subjects. Commenting recently upon Professor Irving Babbitt, who had the bad taste to point out some inconsistencies in Eliot's writing, he states, ". . . yet to my mind the very width of his culture, his intelligent eclecticism, are themselves symptoms of a narrowness of tradition, in their extreme reaction against that narrowness. . . . It would be an exaggeration to say that he wore his cosmopolitanism like a man who had lost his *complet bourgeois* and had to go about in fancy dress. But he seemed to be trying to compensate for the lack of living tradition by a herculean, but purely intellectual and individual effort. . . ." Again, in an ardent piece of writing, the purpose of which is rather transparent, Eliot insists that "the important fact about Baudelaire is that he is essentially a Christian born out of his due time, and a classicist born out of his due time. . . ." Granted that these contentions were true (and they are not), what have they to do with an "honest criticism" of the poet according to Eliot's standards? And in passing, let us remark that there is nothing more artificial and false in criticism than the tediously enforced paradox. In yet another essay, commenting on Shakespeare's *Hamlet,* Eliot writes, "Why he attempted it at all is an insoluble puzzle; under compulsion of what experience he attempted to express the inexpressibly horrible, we cannot ever know. We need a great many facts in his biography. . . ." Why do we need facts in Shakespeare's biography if our concern is with his work? How does Mr. Eliot know that *Hamlet* is based upon a personal tragedy? Is not this a kind of "impressionistic" criticism? Rémy de Gourmont, who supplied Eliot with many a neat phrase, including the definition, "Poetry is a superior kind of amusement," is dismissed by Mr. Eliot, in a rather top-lofty manner, as "an amateur." Is this a wholly dispassionate judgment?

As late as November, 1929, when his essay "Experiment in Criticism" appeared in *The Bookman,* Eliot was struggling to maintain a pure criticism. In this particular essay Sainte-Beuve is censured for regarding literature as a part of history. The critic should see that "literature is primarily literature" and not submerge it in larger interests in his criticism. This caution is well uttered, but it comes from a man who had, a few months previously, in a prefatory note, qualified his definition of poetry to this extent: "On the other hand, poetry has something to do with morals, and with religion, and even with politics perhaps, though we cannot say what." Pure criticism is then impossible, for the degree to which a poet or a dramatist has admitted morals, religion, and politics, determines the degree to which these contaminations will have to be admitted by the critic. Mr. Eliot has apparently seen this for himself, for he has written less and less on the theory of criticism and has indulged more and more in the practice of criticism. And perhaps it is as a functioning critic that Eliot's limitations in the field have been revealed. His *Homage to John Dryden,* his essays on the Elizabethans, his study of Dante are all cautious and scholarly. Yet Swinburne and Pater, whose criticism Eliot deplores, are more incandescent and more stimulating. A single essay of Sainte-Beuve is more informative than all that Eliot has written. Eliot's supreme contribution to modern criticism is the dubious counsel to examine literature primarily as literature, which counsel, however, has had the effect of elevating the tone of literary criticism both here and in England; yet it must be conceded that, for example, William Troy in the novel and Babette Deutsch in poetry, whom Eliot has greatly influenced, have made far better practical use of his counsel than he. On the whole, one regrets these essays of Eliot, especially when one reflects that with the same expenditure of energy he might have produced a memorable poem or two. The cost is too much for the little we have gained.

A poet of less emotional depth than Eliot, Hart Crane gave freer play to his feelings in his verse, with the result that he seems much more spontaneous, more intense, and more impassioned. Yet his work is not the product of creative frenzy in the ordinary understanding of the phrase. *The Bridge,* for example, was months and years in the making. Crane's total product is small; a handful of verse represents twenty years of composition. Son of a father who did not care, and of a mother who cared too much, Crane began to write poetry at thirteen, published in *Bruno's Bohemian* at fifteen, received high encouragement before he was twenty, and had two volumes acclaimed before he committed suicide in his thirty-second year by leaping into the ocean from the stern of the *Orizaba* at noon on April 27, 1932. His life was chaotic, but his manuscripts were not. He was constantly paring down his product, scrutinizing and revising it, destroying what did not satisfy. The impression of fervor and haste one gains from his verse is really got from the protestations and vocabulary of the poet and not from his method. Poetry was never composed more deliberately than Hart Crane composed it—in deliberate imitation of Arthur Rimbaud. Had the author of "The Drunken Boat" ever seen Brooklyn Bridge, "harp and altar, of the fury fused," he would have described it in the language and fashion chosen by the American poet.

Instead of directing his admirers to Rimbaud, or to the unknown poet whose sheaf of poems was found among his papers after his death (the troublesome "Greenberg MS"), Crane, naturally enough, sought to rationalize his borrowed technique. Charged with writing incoherent and meaningless lines, he replied that he was "more interested in the so-called illogical impingements of the connotations of words on the consciousness (and their combinations and interplay in metaphor on this basis) than . . . in the preservation of their logically rigid significations at the cost of limiting subject matter and perceptions involved in the poem." Rimbaud would be delighted with this, though he would scorn the poet who offered an explanation of his work. In actually composing such lines as—

> Outspoken buttocks in pink beads
> Invite the necessary cloudy clinch
> Of baudy eyes . . .

Crane was much more interested in imitating as closely as he could Rimbaud than in the "illogical impingements of the connotations of words on the consciousness." Never was a plausible explanation stuffed with so much sawdust.

Through roots pushed far down into Decadent muck, Hart Crane drew the nourishment which produced the exotic blooms gathered and pressed in *White Buildings* (1926), *The Bridge* (1930), and *The Collected Poems* (1933). One moniliform tracer even reaches back to Edgar Allan Poe, as the "bleeding eidolon" of "Legend" indicates. Reading the opening lines of "Lachrymae Christi" which describe the "benzine rinsings from the moon," one is reminded instantly of Poe's—

> ... An opiate vapour, dewey dim
> Exhales from out her golden rim. ...

And there are other echoes of the "Bostonian." The now rather hackneyed "On the window licks the night" of "Fear" comes from Mallarmé, while Laforgue supplies the inspiration for "The Idiot" and for "the syphilitic selling violets calmly" in "Moment Fugue." The latter also, through Eliot, is responsible for the portrait of the young woman in "Modern Craft" whose "flesh of moons" the poet has touched:

> ... She hazards jet; wears tiger lilies;—
> And bolts herself within a jewelled belt.
> Too many palms have grazed her shoulders:
> Surely she must have felt.

The nephew who contemptuously guesses at the "confusions" which reign beneath the "merciless tidy hair" in "The Fernery" has consorted too much with Eliot's aunt's nephew. "Chaplinesque" is not so much an effort to be American as it is to imitate the Dadaists who affected to admire greatly the Hollywood comedian when they were revolting against "literature" and against sense. Finally, "The Mango Tree" is at once Dada, Gertrude Stein, and E. E. Cummings. Yet all these ramifications of Decadent influence are less important than the single effect of Rimbaud. Arthur Rimbaud taught Hart Crane to love the sea and to capture the fleeting changes of expression on that vast, mobile countenance in fantastic, yet accurate, combinations of word and metaphor. Name any sea poem of Crane's, and there you have Rimbaud. Particularly is this true of the second section of "Voyages" and of "At Melville's Tomb." Particularly is this true of *The Bridge*.

If *Key West* is any indication of the preoccupations of Hart Crane's last months, there is no sign that he was losing his interest in the Decadents, for the poems of this sheaf show wider reading in the school than do the earlier poems. Yet there is, at the same time, more effort here to capture reality than anywhere else save in *The Bridge*. "O Carib Isle," "The Hurricane," "Bacardi Spreads the Eagle's Wings," and "Eternity" (in the Uncollected Poems) have the merit of catching the phantasmagorical reality which is peculiar to the Caribbean and Gulf, despite their occasional absurdities of phraseology. The triumph of them all is "The Air Plant: Grand Cayman." "This tuft that thrives on saline nothingness" is also to Hart Crane an "angelic dynamo" and "ventriloquist of the blue." One wonders how this tropical plant could be more effectively described, and it is a good guess that it could not. Something of the imponderable mystery which takes such curious forms in life is suggested by the poem, and this effect is not dissipated by the pretentiousness of the closing lines.

In an essay on "Modern Poetry," written in 1929, Crane took the view that revolution in verse, though it still flourished, no longer existed as an all-engrossing program; he saw the poet's concern now as "self-discipline toward a formal integration of experience." With approval he quoted Coleridge to the effect that "no work of true genius dares want its appropriate form." Crane conceived a poem architecturally, and it was with design, with structure, that he was most concerned in *The Bridge,* as his letters to Otto Kahn, his sponsor, show. He chooses to describe *The Bridge* as "an epic of the modern consciousness," but while he includes enough of our political and literary history to satisfy the Bergsonian's insistence upon the presentness of the past, there is too much of the present in *The Bridge* for it to have been written by an immediate disciple of Bergson. The Bergsonian theory of consciousness came to Hart Crane only as a literary technique which he found in *The Waste Land* and other poetry. Consequently *The Bridge* possesses more reality and more strength than many other pieces of its school.

There are undeniably some modern experiences better represented by the fragmentary-consciousness method than in any other way. One of these, surely, is a ride in an underground train. Emerson first advocated the exploitation of railway materials in

verse, and Whitman's "To a Locomotive in Winter" is an obedi-
ent response to his master's suggestion, but the later poets who
have tried to go further and to describe the underground train,
or their impressions while riding in one—Jules Romains, Chester
Firkins, and Amy Lowell—have found the subject too much for
them. Hart Crane has succeeded where they have failed. In one
section of *The Bridge,* "The Tunnel," he has not only given the
effect of this engulfing experience on a mind of unusual sensitivity, but he has made the experience symbolical of the soul's
encounters with the Frankenstein of modern machinery. Walled
in by sound with elbow companions one would never voluntarily
choose, one naturally permits the mind to wander in fields fan-
tastically remote from anything suggested by the situation. Yet
the need to establish equilibrium, to fend off jostling, to close
one's ears to confidences uttered within inches of them, makes
one receptive to suggestions from the situation even while maintaining interest in the remote field of voluntary choice. Thus a
poet, recoiling inwardly from the sense impressions a ride in the
subway thrusts upon him, may elect to think about literature, yet
his situation determines that he shall reflect upon Poe and all of
the lugubrious chaos down by the dank tarn of Auber. This association, which occurs in *The Bridge,* constitutes one of the superb
effects of modern literature, while it makes clear also Hart
Crane's relationship to the whole Decadent tradition:

> Whose head is swinging from the swollen strap?
> Whose body smokes along the bitten rails,
> Bursts from a smoldering bundle far behind
> In back forks of the chasms of the brain,—
> Puffs from a riven stump far out behind
> In interborough fissures of the mind . . .?
>
> And why do I often meet your visage here,
> Your eyes like agate lanterns—on and on
> Below the toothpaste and the dandruff ads?
> —And did their riding eyes right through your side,
> And did their eyes like unwashed platters ride?
> And Death, aloft,—gigantically down
> Probing through you—toward me, O evermore!
> And when they dragged your retching flesh

Your trembling hands that night through Baltimore—
That last night on the ballot rounds, did you
Shaking, did you deny the ticket, Poe?

For Gravesend Manor change at Chambers Street.
The platform hurries along to a dead stop.

How can a moment's reverie, all that is permitted one, be
better caught than in this passage? An almost scientific verisimilitude lifts *The Bridge* into one of the important literary creations of our time, but symbolism, structure, imagery, music—
the "melody of chaos," if you will,—and philosophical depth
make it one of the great poems in contemporary American literature. Beside it, Rimbaud's greatest work pales into a romantic
and sentimental dream.

Brooklyn Bridge is a symbol of all the strands of experience
that are woven into the native consciousness. The idea is magnificently conceived. Instead of following Eliot into medieval lore
and magic, into the *esoterica* of scholarship, Crane, taking a
hint from Whitman, built up his poem partially out of popular
fable. Columbus facing vast uncertitude, Pizarro, Cortes, Captain Smith, Priscilla—the heroes and heroines of the average
schoolboy's history book are here. No Fisher King confounds
the simple with a hidden relationship to the fertility myths, but
here Powhatan's daughter and an Indiana half-breed mother tell
of the teeming richness of the land.

The very luxuriance and abundance of America are further suggested by the imagery of the poem. The rapidly varying matter,
the rush of one experience into another, the cinema-like shift of
scene—all these evidences of unexampled richness make the
Rimbaud-like collocations of words more plausible. Synesthesia
for once is amply justified: the reader feels that in this instance
hostile words must adhere—it is part of the essential compres-
sion of the poem. Whence the justification for the "inviolate
curve" of the Bridge cables, the yawn of the "subway scuttle,"
the "swift unfractioned idiom" of significance in the structure,
the "dreaming sod" of the prairie, the "jellied weeds" along the
Atlantic shore, the "delirium of jewels" sought by Columbus
in Cathay, the "nervous shark tooth" on the sailor's chain, and

the rum which "was Plato in our heads" (this last filched from Herman Melville).

Although so many elements are compressed and fused into *The Bridge,* the sound effects of the poem are not all crash and thunder. The too swift movement of the apostrophe to the Bridge with which the poem opens—a movement chosen, of course, to suggest the pace of our life—is immediately decelerated by the slow iambs of Columbus' meditation. "O Thou who sleepest on Thyself apart" yields, in turn, to the simple measure of the popular song—

> *And Rip forgot the office hours*
> *And he forgot the pay;*
> *Van Winkle sweeps a tenement*
> *way down on Avenue A.*

Yet no one time or tune predominates; the poet handles equally well jazz, the primitive rhythm of Whitman, pentametre, and short lines. Perhaps the most successful medley—really an astonishing visual and melodic experiment—is found in the section called "Cutty Sark," which attempts to give the effect upon the consciousness of a waterfront dive. Suggestions of the mad prose of Melville's *Mardi,* the chantey and the ballad, the fragmentary line of E. E. Cummings, the mechanical wail of the nickelodeon, and the boastings of the sailors are all worked together without any straining on the part of the poet. Crane has analyzed the section himself as well as anyone can:

". . . Cutty Sark is a phantasy on the period of whalers and clipper ships. It also starts in the present and 'progresses backward.' The form of the poem may seem erratic, but it is meant to present the hallucinations incident to rum drinking in a South Street dive, as well as the lurch of a boat in heavy seas, etc. So I allow myself something of the same freedom which E. E. Cummings often uses.

"Cutty Sark is built on the plan of a fugue. Two 'voices'—that of the world of Time and that of the world of Eternity—are interwoven in the action. The Atlantis theme (that of Eternity) is the transmuted voice of the nickel-slot pianola, and this voice alternates with that of the derelict sailor and the description of the action. The airy regatta of the phantom clipper ships seen from Brooklyn Bridge on the way home is quite effective,

I think. It was a pleasure to use historical names for these lovely ghosts. Music still haunts their names long after the wind has left their sails. . . ."

Finally, *The Bridge* asserts the unity and design of the cosmos. If, in *The Waste Land,* are epitomized all the flux, the futility, and the negation of our day, here in this poem are hope and affirmation. Just as the mind of the poet has fused all the chaotic elements of his matter into an artistic whole, so a greater Consciousness has fused the very stuff of the universe into one great pattern. In *The Bridge* Bergsonian optimism has combined with a deeply submerged faith to produce the first Decadent poem to turn definitely away from Decadence:

> . . . Atlantis!—hold thy floating singer late!

> So to thine Everpresence, beyond time,
> Like spears ensanguined of one tolling star
> That bleeds infinity—the orphic strings,
> Sidereal phalanxes, leap and converge:
> —One Song, one Bridge of Fire! . . .

Like Hart Crane, Archibald MacLeish has tried to break with the Decadent tradition after becoming a convert to it. His protracted struggles and defeats, however, suggest classic Laocoön loaded with the Python, with a more agonized, single, central figure and a livelier and more supple serpent. World War II appears to have provoked, at long last, a really effective spasm, and the captive has divested himself of the last loathsome loop and coil, but whether MacLeish has actually crushed the head of his fond reptile under his heel is not so certain. Though he may write no more consciously Decadent poetry, we have no assurance that he can avoid its tone and mood. Had Laocoön at last shed the crushing burden of his Python, would he have been able to stand erect ever again?

The poet did not begin his career as a Decadent. The early verse of MacLeish (which he himself rigorously excluded from *Poems: 1924–1933*), contained in the volumes *Tower of Ivory* (1917), *The Happy Marriage* (1924), and *Nobodaddy* (1926), is the verse of a poet who had not reflected enough and who had accepted all too readily the academic standards of

verse. Prominent in athletics and preeminent in his studies at the
Hotchkiss School and at Yale, and then, after grinding at law
at Harvard, rushed into the war, MacLeish might well complain
that he had had but little life of his own, little time for reflection.
One can understand the romantic quality of the *Tower of Ivory,*
the echoes of William Vaughn Moody in *Nobodaddy* (a dramatic reworking of the Adam, Eve, and Cain story, with a title
from Blake), and of William Ellery Leonard in *The Happy
Marriage.* Yet one should detect also in the last volume Mac-
Leish's first resentment against the traditions which he had
accepted on faith:

> Take Helen,—all you hear of her
> In lectures is a learned slur
> Of couplets solemnly undressed
> To indicate the female chest,
> Till Helen's lost and nothing's sure
> But that she had, praise God, a breast.

The poetry of Eliot and of Pound suggested new techniques and
new subject matter, wherefore MacLeish gave up the practice
of law (he confesses he could "never believe in the law," though
he was successful at it) to go to Paris in the winter of 1923 to
study the French Decadents. His first important poem, *The Pot
of Earth* (1925), treats in Decadent technique one of the magic
symbols of the fertility myth, as explained by Sir James Fraser.
This subject, of course, was suggested by Eliot. MacLeish had
at last arrived at a stage where he could declare, "A poem should
not mean but be."

The Hamlet of A. MacLeish, in 1928, first compelled the
serious attention of critics. The poem was undeniably the result
of reflecting upon Jules Laforgue's "Hamlet." Like it, *The
Hamlet of A. MacLeish* is a wholly subjective piece in which
the author fancies himself in the major rôle. The light raillery
and the perfectly imagined adolescence of the French piece are
lacking, but their loss is more than compensated for by the depth
of tone, the genuine dramatic quality, and the imaginative grasp
of the new treatment. Ever conscious that he has challenged
comparison with one of the world's great poets, MacLeish has

depended upon general familiarity with that other poet's legend to carry the fable and has devoted all his energy to realizing psychological states that the other has neglected. He has surpassed Shakespeare in rebuking the Queen's lechery, in representing the hypersensitivity of Hamlet, and in passages has equalled him in versification. Particularly admirable is the treatment of the scene at Ophelia's burial which Shakespeare so badly botched. The raw gash in the earth for the drowned young woman's body suddenly precipitates the protagonist out of his theatrical posing into a ditch in Flanders:

> I'll tell you how I loved too, all my loves,
> My bed quilts, bolsters, blankets, my hot hands,
> My limbs, my rumps; my wretchedness: my lust,
> My weakness later and lascivious dreams.
> I'll tell you. Oh, I'll tell you. Lean your ear.
> By God, I'll match them at it. I'll be stripped
> Naked as eels are, gutted, laid on salt,
> Sold in the fish stalls. I'll be ox-chine nude,
> Quartered to cold bare bone. Look, behold me
> Bearing my dead son's body to the grave.
> See how I weep. How many of them all
> Have lost a son as I have? Or see here:
> The Marne side. Raining. I am cold with fear.
> My bowels tremble. I go on. McHenry
> Hands me his overcoat and dies. We dig the
> Guns out sweating. I am very brave:
> Magnificent. I vomit in my mask.
> Or here. In Belgium. Spreading on my young,
> My three times buried brother's stony grave
> The bone-pale scented violets and feeling
> Yield at my knees the earth: and crying out
> Two words. In agony . . .
> > > > I'll tell it. Oh
> I'll tell it. Louder! Shriek!
> > > > The sky's there!

Yet the poem closes with a melancholy passage on age that has been purged of heat, of feuds, and of bitterness. Life is a delusion, and the real encounters are in dreams "where none will praise our art." "The eloquent Osrick," whose invitation to a "playful bout" is here commented on, seems suddenly to have discovered a kinship to J. Alfred Prufrock. Thus *The Hamlet of A. MacLeish* ends on the proper Decadent note.

There are restiveness and dissatisfaction with Decadence, how-ever, in MacLeish's next volume, *New Found Land* (1930). Lack of punctuation, abrupt transitions, and fragmentary thought—even the rhythms of *The Waste Land* and the *Cantos* —will not disguise the fact that the poet desires to get back to American themes. Over against such lines as—

> Our history is grave noble and tragic
> Many of us have died and are not remembered
> Many cities are gone and their channels broken
> We have lived a long time in this land and with honor

put even such a banal utterance as this—

> ... Be proud New York of your prize domes
> and your docks & the size of your doors & your dancing

—and the poet's inclination is apparent. One is startled to dis-cover not only nostalgia but sentimentalism in "Memory Green." The American expatriate, strolling along the Friedrichstrasse at dusk or shuffling through the fallen leaves upon a Paris quay, feels suddenly the "June warm wind" and tears start to his eyes and his lips murmur, "Ah, where?" Thus the American Indian Summer calls beyond the Atlantic and even beyond his recol-lection. "Not Marble Not the Gilded Monuments," strangely imitative of Edna Millay, suggests MacLeish's earliest verse. Yet the best piece in *New Found Land,* "You, Andrew Marvell," pictures a Decadent night creeping on over Western Europe. The beauty of the language of this poem is unrivaled in Mac-Leish's verse and is touched only once or twice in all modern American poetry:

> And here face down beneath the sun,
> And here upon the earth's noonward height,
> To feel the always coming on,
> The always rising of the night.
>
> To feel creep up the curving east
> The earthly chill of dusk and slow

Upon those under lands the vast
And ever-climbing shadow grow,

And strange at Ecbatan the trees
Take leaf by leaf the evening, strange,
The flooding dark about their knees,
The mountains over Persia change. . . .

Hart Crane had contemplated doing a long poem on the conquest of Mexico, but even though he went so far as to go to that country for materials, his dissipations hindered him altogether from getting anything done on his epic. "The Circumstance" survives, however, as mute evidence of his interest. MacLeish, noting the tonic effect of Spain on his friend Hemingway, had begun work on the identical material four years before Crane, and as early as 1929 had made a sober trip on foot and mule back from the Coast to the Valley of Mexico. Out of this trip and out of diligent study he worked up *Conquistador* (1932).

In the main *Conquistador* is not a successful narrative poem; too much of the cerebral technique still survives with the author, and the poem is rather an echo in the skull of the narrator than a forthright tale of adventure. The admirable "Bernal Diaz' Preface to his Book" is more successful than the body of the poem because of its reminiscent quality and static subject matter —to which the technique appears to be better suited. It has been pointed out that, in assuming the rôle of Diaz in the body of *Conquistador,* MacLeish has made the soldier-narrator somewhat ambiguous—now he is the blunt, unreflective, unresponsive veteran; now the aesthete "sensitive to landscapes, nightfalls, colors, water sounds, the flutter of wings and other delicacies of sensation." Always the poem has something of the effect of a dream; always there is something a little Decadent about it. We must not forget that the poet's conclusion is that "the dead are more living than the living dead"—a conclusion we might agree with if we knew how inclusive is the term, "the living dead." The best passages, however, are those in which the bluff soldier comes through. Violent language and a *terza-rima* stanza without rime, but closely knit by alliteration, give the poem a marching stride in these passages that all of the material so

much demands. How much MacLeish owes to Pound is apparent
to anyone who studies the verse and the oaths of *Conquistador,*
yet the poet himself has contributed enough to cancel most of
the obligation. Verse and action conspire to make the rebuke of
Cortes to his rebellious followers at the end of the Fifth Book
the most vigorous passage in the poem, and an example of the
health which the whole might display if the author were willing.

Archibald MacLeish passed beyond *Conquistador* before his
book was published. He reached the conclusion that the poet
should write of and for his time, without regard at all for posterity. Although he first asked for the approval of a few friends
only, men of his own generation, like Ernest Hemingway and
John Dos Passos, he soon sought a larger audience. In "Invoca-
tion to the Social Muse" he asserted that there was nothing
worse for his trade than to be in style, to bear arms, or to take
part in maneuvers, that the true vocation of the poet was not to
lead, but to follow, the armies. Yet the bitterness of the "Invo-
cation" ("We are whores, Fräulein") plainly indicated that, if
this were really the poet's lot, MacLeish wanted none of it.
He had reacted completely from the pure aestheticism, the anti-
didacticism of the Decadents. There was even danger in the
violence of his return out of exile that he would take an extreme
position to offset his earlier defection. "Frescoes for Mr. Rockefeller's City" at once suggested the possibilities of the emergence
of a new MacLeish who would sing of the hope and promise of
America and of a MacLeish who might become the poet of the
American Legion. The menace of the latter appeared very imminent. The former soldier, the ardent patriot, the hater of Marx,
Lenin, and Stalin, of Comrades Edward Remington Ridge and
Grenadine Grilt, of "d'Wops and d'Chinks" and of the New
York *Daily Worker* dominated the poem and alarmed the lib-
erals. Immediately the cry went up that MacLeish was a Fascist.

The emotional violence of the "Frescoes for Mr. Rockefeller's
City" certainly discredits the poet, but later events have shown
that it was wrong to take it too seriously. It should have been
understood as the surplus of feeling of an intellectual expatriate
who had rediscovered his native land. There is no new brew of
any quality without a "head." In the "Frescoes" there is reas-

serted a faith in America's destiny which is inspiring. It cannot
be a blind patriotism which sees that after Harriman, Vander-
bilt, Morgan, and Mellon have plundered the country, that after
Bruce Barton has robbed it spiritually, its great riches are in no
sense depleted, its future is still secure:

> *She's a tough land under the corn mister:*
> *She has changed the bone in the cheeks of many races;*
> *She has winced the eyes of the soft Slavs with her sun on them:*
>
> *She has tried the fat from the round rumps of Italians:*
> *Even the voice of the English has gone dry*
> *And hard on the tongue and alive in the throat speaking:*
>
> *She's a tough land under the oak-trees mister:*
> *It may be she can change the word in the book*
> *As she changes the bone of a man's head in his children:*
> *It may be that the earth and the men remain. . . .*

If the country and the people are not more important than our
systems and forms, Emerson and Whitman are as easily condemned as Archibald MacLeish. This has been the faith of
America since its founding.

"Landscape as a Nude," the first section of the poem, may
draw its title from Gertrude Stein, but its inspiration is from
Hart Crane and Carl Sandburg. This picture of the country as a
brown girl, lying on her left side, her flank golden, inviting all
lovers, is born of the Pocahontas conceived by the other two
poets. The passion for the soil and the sunlight is not patriotism
in any ordinary sense, but something deeper and finer, something
to inspire another hundred years, something to be sought for
even beyond internationalism. The fourth section of the poem,
"Oil Painting of the Artist as Artist," is a fierce attack on all
American expatriates, on all those little poetasters ardently cultivating the arts abroad. "The plump Mr. Pl'f" who has washed
his hands of America, who prefers a tidy stream with a terrace,
and "cypresses mentioned in Horace or Henry James" to "your
flowing Mississippi" represents all that upon which Mr. Mac-
Leish has turned his back. Not only is he done with simulated
affection for foreign strands, but he is done with subjectivism,

with the Past as the only appropriate subject matter, and with
Decadence as a philosophy as well.

A brave announcement, surely. Yet the books which Mac-
Leish published immediately after the "Frescoes"—*Panic: A
Play in Verse* (1935) and *Public Speech* (1936)—represent a
sort of retreat, a retreat, however, which led the poet to what
he may have regarded as a more tenable position. *Panic* really
is a play on Decadence—on the moribund capitalism which
produced the depression of 1929. In an open letter "To the
Young Men of Wall Street" in the *Saturday Review* of January,
1932, MacLeish had warned these young men that ". . . Only
the credulous hope anything further from the generation now
in control (more or less) of American capitalism . . ."; at the
same time he assured them of his faith in Democracy: ". . . We
prefer the toleration we know to the lesser toleration of change."
It must not be assumed, then, as has been done, that *Panic* is a
"proletarian" play. The tycoon McGafferty belongs to a banking
generation which believed in its luck or its star, was sure that
you could not be a "bear" on America. When McGafferty discovers that Time is his foe, he is as bewildered as Prufrock.
Even the assurances of his mistress Ione are in vain; he feels
his grasp gone; he is suddenly old; but for the providence of
suggestion he would become a trembling, mumbling dotard—
when a friend commits suicide, he realizes that here is a way
out and he ends his own whimper with a bang. Yet while the
Unemployed rejoice in McGafferty's fall, MacLeish nowise rejoices as do they. Fate is a drum pounding out a march to a
new order—yes, but the play contains no assertion of what this
order shall be. It is significant, however, that when in the play
the Unemployed are boldest and bait McGafferty, they are led
by a blind man. Is this a hint that the proletariat today are led
by the blind? So it would seem. MacLeish would appear to look
merely for a more liberal leadership in Wall Street to assure
him of the toleration that he wants.

As a play, *Panic* is not especially effective, and the reasons
for its failure in presentation in New York are clear enough.
McGafferty is hardly individualized, and Ione has but one good
speech, in which she bursts out against "the pretty pink room"

where for years in pink she has waited for five-thirty. Here, for
a moment, *Panic* has some of the Aristophanic quality of Eliot's
fragment. It is soon lost, however, in the general maundering
about fate, in which the Bankers and the Unemployed bear an
equal burden. The verse is the chief interest of the play, and
MacLeish called particular attention to it in press interviews
and in a Preface to the printed version. His contentions that the
rhythm of American speech is not that of Elizabethan England
and that the blank verse of Shakespeare has too long dominated
the stage are sound, but the verse he employs in *Panic* is less
melodious and less natural, we think, than that of some of the
passages of *Conquistador*. We found lines ending in "and to"
and "of the" weak in that poem, but lines ending in articles and
prepositions are much more frequent in the play. The result is
to force the breath in reading in a manner that is wholly unnatural to American speech. The verse of *Panic* is still too
"literary."

In *Public Speech* MacLeish warned the Leftists that neither
blood nor mere talking makes men "brothers," but that men are
brothers for having participated in the same actions, for having
suffered the same hurts and indignities. In "Speech to a crowd"
he urged that the world is theirs who will take it. To "the detractors" he asserts his right to praise excellence wherever he
finds it. Yet in what is by all odds the best poem in the book,
"The German girls! The German girls!" he again satisfied
liberals that he is not a Fascist by assailing the Nazi regime in
Germany in scurrilously beautiful, masculine language. Mac-
Leish's denunciation voices a fundamental truth: that the Nazi
regime could not exist without the endorsement of the German
women: but it comes badly from an American: for who forced
the German girls to their knees? What was our share in the
failure of the chaotic German republic? Our little interest then
in democracy has now endangered our own democracy: and it
may be a bloody justice that we shall lose our own for lassitude
and selfishness and stupidity between 1919 and 1933 when the
feeble German republic might have been saved. If we do, the
German girls will not be wholly responsible.

The bold Anglo-Saxon strength of language in this poem, as

exhilarating as the wind off the North Sea, is reinforced by a
meter that unconsciously reaches back more than a thousand
years for some of its effects. Anglo-Saxon scholars would tell us
that such a line as—

> Bring you blood to the breasts and the bride's look on you—

is an almost perfect example of what is called the "A-type" of
alliterative line in *Beowulf,* the primitive Old English epic. Here
is vigor unrivalled in Decadent poetry.

Yet the net effect of the volume *Public Speech* was that Mac-
Leish had returned to quasi-Decadent aloofness towards the
world about him. Not only does the volume close with a typically
involuted, obscure poem, called "On the Stair," but in " 'Dover
Beach'—a Note to That Poem" MacLeish insists that a man's
a fool after forty to struggle to maintain a position. In resigned
expectation of obliteration he should wait for the rush of the
young men to go over him like a wave:

> Let them go over us all I say with the thunder of
> What's to be next in the world. It's we will be under it!

At only forty a man's part should be more than this.

On Sunday evening, May 11, 1937, at seven o'clock there
was broadcast over the Columbia network a radio-play by Mac-
Leish, entitled *The Fall of the City.* Produced under the direction of Irving Reis, with a cast which included Orson Welles
and Burgess Meredith, this radio-play had every advantage
that an entertainment of its sort might have. Yet the listener
got the impression that there were no actors in the piece: shadowy dreads and fears stalked the stage. This, perhaps, was what
Mr. MacLeish desired, for his object was to show that the populace of a city might surrender without a struggle to a tyrant or
dictator who is a hollow man, merely because it is too terrified
to resist. Effectively utilizing the rôle of the radio commentator,
the poet gave to a production that is without dramatic conflict
the illusion of swift action. In no sense an important literary
production, *The Fall of the City* is nevertheless an ingenious
creation. It hints at what might be done artistically with the

radio-play. A year and a half later, on October 27, 1938, Mac-
Leish offered the radio audience another verse play, entitled
Air Raid. This was simpler than its predecessor, yet it was still
a Decadent creation—MacLeish himself in an interview with
Orrin E. Dunlap, Jr., which appeared in *The New York Times,*
speaking of the production wholly in terms of sound, called it
a symphony rather than a drama. Again, the commentator has
the important rôle, but small individual parts stand out as they
do not in *The Fall of the City*. Both pieces inspire nervousness
in the auditor, but they do not arouse pity, for the author does
not quite appreciate the fact that the necessary identification of
the auditors with the people in the play is impossible while the
latter are so slightly developed.

To the *Land of the Free* (1938) MacLeish supplied what he
called a "Sound Track"—the term is from the "talkies"—to
photographic studies of poverty made largely for the Resettle-
ment Administration. The pictures provide what the radio-plays
lacked—real individuals whom we may pity. In a note, MacLeish
tells us that the pictures were meant to illustrate the poem, but
"so great was the power and stubborn inward livingness of these
vivid American documents that the result was a reversal of the
plan." Yet the indubitable excellence of the pictures should not
blind us to the fact that MacLeish's lines are admirably suited in
each instance to them. His performance is a most praiseworthy
thing, since the art form itself is so new—only Pere Lorenz
having tried anything of the sort before MacLeish. To those who
had long followed the poet, the experiment had another interest:
Did it indicate that Mr. MacLeish had abandoned Decadence
for positive political action? There was no doubt that it was
this particular composition which led Franklin Roosevelt to nomi-
nate the poet as head of the Library of Congress, but the reader
was hardly entitled to draw a very sanguine conclusion from
the poem itself. Like the tolling of a church bell, there echoes
through it the refrain of the disfranchised and ousted: "We
don't know; we can't say." The few oblique hints at action of
several sorts are inconclusive—like the radio-plays, *Land of the
Free* is essentially defeatist. Time, the weary Titan, struggled
on, but Mr. MacLeish didn't know and couldn't say. . . .

The outbreak of another great war in Europe galvanized MacLeish. Like vapors before dawn, his miasmas, doubts, hesitances, and fears all vanished, and he became a chooser-of-sides and a volitionist. Though the title of his contribution to the twenty-fifth anniversary number of *The New Republic* of November 8, 1939, might be defeatist in tense—*America Was Promises* —the poem itself has a clarion-clear note of optimism. "Never was green deeper, earth warmer: never were there promises as now," MacLeish assures us. The American people must not be misled by the querulousness of its aristocracy of wealth and talents—a Europeanized and purchasable aristocracy. Their country is as full of promises as ever, and every one of them will be realized provided we will remember that *"promises are theirs who take them."* With an eye on what happened in Spain and Austria, in Poland and China, MacLeish adds grimly that others will take them if we don't. Orotundish and rhetorical, *America Was Promises* may not be as satisfactory from an aesthetic point of view as some of the poet's earlier pieces, but it is exuberantly healthy.

The tonic eloquence of *America Was Promises* worked no miracles before MacLeish followed it up with a prodigious purgative in *The Irresponsibles* (1940), the final draft of a speech and essay directed againt those intellectuals whom he held accountable for the defeatist attitude of the American people towards a war being waged in the defense of democracy. Most commendable of all, he acknowledges himself not guiltless in this matter. That he should charge himself and his coevals with too pure an objectivity, however, proves him either a charitable critic or too facile a diagnostician. But that need not particularly concern us. *The Irresponsibles* has irrevocably committed MacLeish to the abandonment of Decadence—his future must lie in some other direction. The overthrow of France, brought about in part (as MacLeish must realize) by decadent intellectualism, was the event which evoked his renunciation, but he has been clearly restive and uncertain ever since the *Frescoes* were written. The momentous question now is, Can a writer, nurtured and matured wholly within a special tradition, retain any excellence after denying that tradition? Tolstoi did, and so, too, may MacLeish.

Reflection, which caused Archibald MacLeish to desert the ranks of the expatriates in 1928, may have been with Gertrude Stein anxiety which sent her scuttling home after more than thirty years abroad. If she was ever going to ring the bell, the event could not be postponed much longer. Not that Miss Stein was showing signs of age or debility, but that there were definite indications that the interest in Decadence was on the wane. Americans were tiring of the novelty of novelty and were showing a tendency to seek again genuine values in art and literature. Close always to the canvas daubers of Paris, the Derains and Picassos, she had seen American millionaires cool towards Cubism and Surrealism in oils and turn to the honest brushwork of Thomas Benton and Grant Wood, and more alarming still, to the propaganda in paint of Diego Rivera. What was the matter with bourgeois America that it should buy with genuine discernment of worth for the first time in its history? Useless for her friends to poke fun at these manifestations of sense, Gertrude Stein was anxious: she had her immortality to think of,—she must hurry home to see. That even in Paris she could not realize what had happened since the debacle of 1929 seems inconceivable, until one reads her impressions of the World War I in the *Autobiography of Alice B. Toklas* (1933) and realizes how little, aside from the personal inconvenience, that cataclysm meant to her. Accustomed for years to think entirely in terms of self, the supreme egocentric of the most perfect clique of egocentrics, she probably felt there was a lack of drum-pounding in America; the critics needed the stimulation which only her presence could give. Preceded by the *Autobiography* and by the most astonishing press-agenting, she arrived. Linotype machines beat out a lead pavement of welcome, college presidents introduced her with puns upon "pigeons on the grass alas," the radio amplified her mellifluent cadences until one could almost detect the drops of oil—but nothing happened. The drum was beaten but nobody marched. There was no new poetry movement out of Gertrude Stein's return from exile. It was rather noisy, but it was the kind of noise which attends one of those Pennsylvania Dutch funerals—with which Miss Stein is possibly not unfamiliar.

This was her second attempt to achieve immortality, and one must admit that it was better than the first. The former was made in 1914 when Miss Stein attempted to get aboard and ride in on the New Poetry wave. She had published in 1909 a highly important book of fiction, *Three Lives,* which had not been properly received, and had written a "monumental" novel, *The Making of Americans,* which she could get no publisher to accept. These experiments in fiction (which are of the utmost consequence, as will be shown later) were the result of previous laboratory work in psychology. Miss Stein, a Baltimore Jewess, had aspired once to be a doctor, and in her preparation for the study of nervous disorders, had labored under the direction of Professors Hugo Münsterberg and William James of Harvard. Her most conspicuous achievement in the laboratory was a study of automatic writing with Leon M. Solomons, reported in the *Psychological Review,* in September, 1896.

Miss Stein possibly bethought herself of this study of automatic writing when she was considering, back in 1912 and '13, how she could astonish the public out of its indifference. Viewed from her position, it would have been singular if anything except automatism had occurred to her. It must not be forgotten that Miss Stein's preoccupations, up to a short time before this, were primarily scientific rather than literary. Feeling as all poets did who had become acquainted with French verse that the only future for American poetry lay in that direction, Gertrude Stein was at once attracted to the psychological aspects of Decadence. Now the most novel effects of Decadent verse were, as we have seen, synesthetic effects. These effects were secured by arbitrarily associating sense impressions of different categories to produce fresh imagery. Beyond synesthesia lies only one possible kind of association—automatic association, where a word *of itself* suggests another word. *Tender Buttons* (1914) is a synesthetic title, but most, if not all, of the poems contained in the volume appear to be the product of pseudo-automatic writing, a pseudo-automatism practiced so diligently that it has affected Miss Stein's expository style.

To reinforce her experiment in automatic writing (verse, if

you will), Miss Stein had the arguments of the Cubist painters, two of whom, Derain and Picasso, were then very close to her in Paris. Coming at the end of a long reaction in art against story-telling in pictures, these men and Bracque had evolved a canvas made up of "abstractions"—unrelated geometric elements without meaning. Gertrude Stein, who had read James and Hegel on the meaning of meaning, sought, as did the Cubists, to remove all narrative elements from verse. Hence, her declaration that her purpose was "the destruction of associational emotion in poetry." *Tender Buttons* is really a series of Cubist pictures in words. In theory, they are poems in which the meaning of the word is entirely self-contained and does not depend upon external reference. It is an effort to discover intrinsic values in words —to disregard words as symbols or signs. As a scientific experiment *Tender Buttons* is an interesting failure; as art the book is a preposterous joke which, since it failed, its author has had to take seriously. If anything is clear, it is that Gertrude Stein hoped, in 1914, to astonish the American public as Picasso had astonished Paris—in order to attract attention to her serious work. *Tender Buttons* failed to attract much attention because a superior publicist, Miss Amy Lowell, happened along just then and attracted the entire attention of the public to herself and her group. There is no denying that Gertrude Stein had what, in common parlance, is known as a "bad break."

Tender Buttons is a failure as a scientific experiment because Miss Stein has no perfect criteria for distinguishing the automatic from the conscious creation; because, without separating them, she has printed the two together. Consider such a poem as "A Red Stamp." Here it would seem that the associations were largely conscious and deliberate. The piece appears to be an absurd diatribe against the noble and innocent science of philately. If the stamps are new (French stamps with the *fleur-des-lis*), they carry mail by train (exhaust noise, distance, and dust); this does not appeal to the poetess as sufficient reason for preserving them (when they are dirty and canceled) in a catalogue. The trouble with the poem is that the parts have too conscious a reference; the piece has too much meaning:

A Red Stamp

If lilies are lily white if they exhaust noise and distance and even dust, if they dusty will dirt a surface that has no extreme grace, if they do this and it is not necessary it is not at all necessary if they do this they need a catalogue.

It may seriously be doubted if any first rate psychologist would accept this piece as an example of automatic writing. In "Mildred's Umbrella" even the layman can get the "meaning," *i. e.,* the obvious associations, though he may have to be told that "Mildred" is Mildred Aldrich with whom Miss Stein became acquainted at this time.

Mildred's Umbrella

A cause and no curve, a cause and loud enough, a cause and extra loud clash and an extra wagon, a sign of extra, a sac a small sac and an established color and cunning, a slender grey and no ribbon, this means a loss a great loss a restitution.

Miss Stein, then, has not been able to distinguish automatic creation from conscious creation; at times she has even *edited* her allegedly automatic writings, which fact makes *Tender Buttons* of dubious scientific worth. It would seem as if the person of aesthetic sensibility ought to be as much affected by this mixture of genres as the scientist. One cannot but conclude that those who profess to derive an exquisite pleasure from *Tender Buttons* are really delighted with altogether dissimilar constructions in their own minds which have been started by the poems. In a word, they have deceived themselves about the intrinsic aesthetic values of the pieces in *Tender Buttons*.

One important fact should be noted about *Tender Buttons*—it reveals no profound knowledge of the subject matter, of the philosophy, or even of the vocabulary of Decadence—the literary movement on to which Miss Stein engrafted her work. This ignorance in her own tradition is characteristic of Gertrude Stein, though her casual reference to the death of Europe in *Everybody's Autobiography* (1937) indicates a dawning awareness of her lack. She but feebly grasped the significance of Cubism,

and when painting went over to Surrealism she was lost altogether. It is instructive to compare her surrealistic efforts with
those of the poets Robert Desnos and Paul Eluard. Or compare
the beginning of "Dan Rafael A Nephew" by Gertrude Stein—

"Arthur two our age chance will tree behaviour for finally left come to
such now their stability compress in union against made hence for the close
of establishment leak and forfeit a plenty of united practice of their popularity just now goes as made a piece of inclined to their fairly. . . ."

—with such a genuine and diverting surrealist squib as the following by "Theo Rutra":

Andre Masson

The loorabalboli glides through the algroves suddenly turning upon
itself. There is a spiral splatter of silver. A thunderbelt lies in white. The
rolls drum down the hidden malvines, where the gullinghales flap finwings
casually. The feathers of the salibri glint in the marlite. Then the loorabalboli sings: "O puppets of the eremites, the weedmaids fever love. Send
Octobus to shores of clay; thieve younglings out of sheaves of ice." And
troutroots dance. There is a blish. A wonderlope whirs through the floom.

—and it will be apparent that there are degrees of idiocy.
Despite the satirical intent of the "Andre Masson," it contains
the shrewder setting forth of the subconscious functions, is more
definitely aware of Freud and Dadaism, and hence is more
surrealistic.

Curiously, nothing in Miss Stein suggests that she has read
Freud, Jung, Lévy-Bruhl, or any recent psychologist. Apparently also without being aware of the aesthetic liberation attempted by Joyce, Murray Godwin, and the Surrealists who
wrote for Eugene Jolas in their "revolution of the word," Miss
Stein confesses complacently that "she tried a bit inventing words
but she soon gave that up. The english language was her medium
and with the english language the task was to be achieved, the
problem solved. The use of fabricated words offended her. . . ."
Of course, these experiments, fruitless as they seem, had more
purpose than merely to fabricate words. Small wonder that
since *The Autobiography* appeared all her French group have
denounced her. *Testimony Against Gertrude Stein* (1935) cor-

rectly charges her with ignorance, with "hollow, tinsel Bohemianism," and with never getting "beyond the stage of the tourist."

Perhaps among her later pieces, where she has employed slang, where her intention is satirical, where there is a good deal of the rogue, there is more worth. A convenient illustration is—

A Patrotic Leading

Verse I

> Indeed indeed
> Can you see
> The stars
> And regularly the precious treasure.
> What do we love without measure.
> We know.

Verse II

> We suspect the second man.

Verse III

> We are worthy of everything that happens.
> You mean weddings.
> Naturally I mean weddings.

Verse IV

> And then we are,
> Hail to the nation.

Verse V

> Do you think we believe it.

Verse VI

> It is that or bust.

Verse VII

> We cannot bust.

Verse VIII

> Thank you.

Verse IX

> Thank you very much.

And surely, *Four Saints in Three Acts* (1934) is the most amusing libretto ever written for the opera, as well as one of the most consummately harmonized. Its theme is relatively a simple one—the eternal attraction and repulsion of opposites. But it is the refinement of this theme that astonishes: Saint Ignatius stands for the analytical intellect; Saint Theresa (who appears in two phases) for non-intellectual creation; the marriage scene ("two and two") represents union, while the third scene, labelled *Saint Ignatius and one of two literally* represents separation again. After the death of Saint Ignatius, the whole cycle is repeated. The theme is no more emphasized by the characterization and the action than by the language. Here again, attraction and repulsion: "He came and said he was hurrying hurrying hurrying to remain he said. . . ." Yet aside from the harmony of sound, the detailed working out of the theme, it is the play on language, the puns, the exaggerations, the humorous juxtapositions which entertain the reader. Saint Ignatius (the intellect) could be "actually in porcelain standing," suggests an egg: ". . . An egg and add some. Some and sum. Add sum. Add Sum." To the sophisticate, could anything be more amusing? When the later work of Gertrude Stein can all be got together, she can be judged as a humorist, and certainly certainly most surely she will have some rank, though rank and then some. However.

A poetess whose work certainly does not suffer by contrast with that of Gertrude Stein is Marianne Moore. If Miss Stein has too little familiarity with her tradition, Miss Moore probably has too much. In her attitude towards poetry there is an ennui which suggests the pose that Stéphane Mallarmé affected to conspicuous advantage long ago in Paris, a reluctant admission of forced interest, of polite curiosity:

> I, too, dislike it: there are things that are important
> beyond all this fiddle.
> Reading it, however, with a perfect contempt for it,
> one discovers in
> it after all, a place for the genuine. . . .

Yet T. S. Eliot detects in one of her early poems the slight influence of "H.D.", while J. S. Watson, Jr., suspects that her "matter-of-fact constructions" and "critical rather than poetic phrases" are derived from Rimbaud. We would suggest a general resemblance of her poetry to some of the descriptive verses of Wallace Stevens, like "Exposition of the Contents of a Cab," "The Indigo Glass in the Grass," and "Anecdote of the Jar." Her poem "A Grave" belongs, however, to a Decadent sea-poetry which includes such items as Poe's "A City in the Sea" and Rimbaud's "Le bateau ivre." Miss Moore's editorial work on *The Dial* familiarized her with the whole range of Decadent verse, from Pound and Eliot, who were published there, to Valéry and Gourmont, who were translated. So great a familiarity with tradition has had a curious effect: Miss Moore, convinced that novelty for its own sake is a treasure, and more aware than the others of the difficulty of achieving anything new, or at least different, has yet sought the unusual with extraordinary perseverance. Not only has she read and reread Chaucer, Spenser, Browne, Defoe, Bunyan, Dr. Johnson, Burke, Leigh Hunt, Trollope, Hardy, James, Yeats, W. H. Hudson, and George Saintsbury, who are relatively unimportant so far as she is concerned, save as they have taught her "to exposit accurately," but she has also conned to more advantage articles and advertisements in *The Dial, The English Review,* the *Illustrated London News, Punch,* and *The Spectator,* and especially has she followed Henry T. McBride's page on art in *The New York Sun.* These things have led to other reading as the notes to *Observations* and to *The Selected Poems* show. Reading and conversation, she freely admits, have been the inspiration of her poetry.

Self-discipline, the anxious comparison of her phraseology for explicitness with that of those whom she has revered, was preceded by the most rigorous discipline that a young mind could endure in the America of three decades ago. For Miss Moore, a St. Louis girl (born there in 1887), was graduated from Bryn Mawr College in 1909, an institution presided over by such female martinets and pedants as Miss M. Carey Thomas, who taught *the* Chaucer course and was president of the college, and Mrs. Grace Frank, author of such juicy tid-bits as "Aoi in the *Chanson de Roland.*" Not the tendency to supply her poems with learned footnotes alone, but the scholarly pursuit of erudite subject matter as well, suggests the influence of the female seminary upon her. There is something vastly amusing in her naïve admission of her serious cultivation of athletics and sport—she has read John McGraw's *How to Play Baseball,* Christy Mathewson's *Pitching in a Pinch,* Harold Baynes' manual on dogs, etc., etc. Good girl! but how like a blue-stocking. After Bryn Mawr, Miss Moore taught stenography for three years, and then from 1919 to 1925 was an assistant in one of the branches of the New York Public Library. She had begun contributing poetry to *The Egoist* in 1915 and ten years later became one of the editorial staff of *The Dial,* serving with that magazine until it became defunct in 1929.

Miss Moore's poetry is contained in three volumes, *Poems* (1920) published without her knowledge by friends, *Observations* (1924), and *Selected Poems* (1935). The last-named volume contains a prefatory endorsement and benediction by T. S. Eliot who declares: "My conviction, for what it is worth, has remained unchanged for the last fourteen years: that Miss Moore's poems form part of the small body of durable poetry written in our time. . . ." Paul Rosenfeld, in 1925, expressed a hope that a small minority, desiring quality, would constitute a permanent public for the poetess. Marianne Moore has not lacked for able champions.

Like Eliot, the poet has shrewdly supplied the reviewers with summary phrases for her work. Of these, seemingly the most meticulous is "there is a great amount of poetry in unconscious fastidiousness." Yet this hint is most misleading, for while "unconscious fastidiousness" in another may provide a poet with a very charming theme, poetry itself is the product of the *most conscious* fastidiousness—certainly Miss Moore's is. The poetry of things does not exist, is a contradiction of terms, but once an awareness of things is raised into the passion of the connoisseur, then the language, though scientific in content, is poetic in its complexion. Feeling is absolutely essential to poetry, and the phrase "unconscious fastidiousness," in which the terms neutralize each other, suggests too slight an emotion for song. It is passion, however, though a cultivated passion, which elevates

Miss Moore's "explicit" statements into poetry. In the following poem it is with intense feeling that she satirizes a type of mind which any critic of sensitivity has a mortal dread that he may some time exemplify:

To a Steam Roller

The illustration
is nothing to you without the application.
   You lack half wit. You crush the particles **down**
    into close conformity, and then walk back and forth
           on them.

Sparkling chips of rock
are crushed down to the level of the parent block.
   Were not "impersonal judgment in aesthetic
    matters, a metaphysical impossibility," you

might fairly achieve
it. As for butterflies, I can hardly conceive
   of one's attending upon you, but to question
    the congruence of the compliment is vain,
        if it exists.

If emotion is one essential quality of verse, music is another. While Marianne Moore's verses are suffused with deep feeling, their singing qualities are less certain. Let us consider, as representative of her work, this selection:

An Egyptian Pulled Glass Bottle
in the Shape of a Fish

Here we have thirst
And patience, from the first,
   And art, as in a wave held up for us to see
   In its essential perpendicularity;

Not brittle but
Intense—the spectrum, that
   Spectacular and nimble animal the fish
   Whose scales turn aside the sun's sword with their polish.

Here is all the feeling necessary for verse, the collector's delight in the *objet d'art,* the bibelot—and how lightly trips off the first stanza! In the second, we apprehend the first difficulty, not in the pardonable assonance (rather than rime) of "but" and "that," but in the artificial emphasis upon "that." Still, if the stanza did not conclude with the monstrous and wholly unmetrical fourth line,

> whose scales turn aside the sun's sword with their pol*ish*,

we might overlook the earlier technical flaw, yet a poet who would leave in print a line like this has no ear at all and the mouth of a comedienne. Try reading it aloud.

While reviewers and critics have praised her "metrical originality" (and surely the patterns of "The Jerboa" and "The Fish" are entrancing), they have had much less to say about the execution of these patterns, which is frequently far from flawless. Capriciously divided words at the ends of lines to preserve the pattern and to secure the elusive rimes suggest the possibilities of expanding indefinitely the list of English rimes if the practice becomes general; on the other hand, one cannot desire the further spread of Miss Moore's habit of ending lines with weak words, like "a", "an", "the", "to", "in", "as", etc. For so fastidious a person to split an infinitive as she does in "Critics and Connoisseurs" ("proclivity to more fully appraise") distresses us almost as much as it did to read in Mr. Eliot's essay on Baudelaire that "Goethe . . . was interested in many subjects which Baudelaire *left* alone." Neither of these writers is quite the meticulous craftsman each is represented to be. Most but not all, of their effects are good. Particularly fanciful, the true stuff of verse, is the imagery of Miss Moore. Vivid and memorable are "the mouse's limp tail hanging like a shoelace from its mouth," "authors . . . that write the most are . . . the supertadpoles of expression," the waves "as the scales on a fish," and "England with its baby rivers and its little towns . . . ." Indeed, as with Logan Pearsall Smith, the captivating charm of phrase gives one an appetite for further reading in these "Trivia" in verse. We are beguiled into thinking the *impedimenta* of life of transcendent importance, and the camp worth more than the field, for it is in this view of things that Miss Moore has made her most original contribution to Decadence.

Is Your Town Nineveh?

Why so desolate?
In phantasmagoria about fishes,
what disgusts you? Could
not all personal upheaval in
the name of freedom, be tabooed?

Is it Nineveh
And are you Jonah
in the sweltering east wind of your wishes?
I myself have stood
there by the Aquarium, looking
at the Statue of Liberty.

For E. E. Cummings, as for Gertrude Stein, poetry has been a means of advertisement. He has been more conscious of this end, perhaps, than he has been of developing an aesthetic. Both the substance and the form of his verses appear to have been selected with the idea of producing a sensation, of attracting attention to himself. "It is with roses and locomotives (not to mention acrobats Spring electricity Coney Island the 4th of July the eyes of mice and Niagara Falls) that my 'poems' are competing," he declares in the foreword to *Is 5*. It is for this reason that this volume begins with pictures of five plump whores, Liz, Mame, Gert, Marj, and Fran, and not wholly because these dames are related to the ladies who fascinated Baudelaire.

Cummings has only an apron-string connection with Decadence,—he has merely swept over the movement, without being genuinely affected by its philosophy or the purposes of its experimentation, to gather ideas for exploitation. Cummings' typography really conceals how imitative he is. Amy Lowell, Conrad Aiken, Guillaume Appollinaire, Gertrude Stein, T. S. Eliot and perhaps Marianne Moore have been heavily drawn upon. Yet because Cummings has exaggerated all that he has imitated, some extremes of Decadence are found in his work.

Appollinaire, minor Decadent and friend of Gertrude Stein, composed before his death certain poems which he called "calligrams"; these were poems the lines of which, frequently broken, were so arranged on the page to produce familiar, simple forms, like that of the Eiffel Tower, for example. It seems probable that Appollinaire got the inspiration for his "calligrams" from the English metaphysical poets, who, from Donne onwards, have been considerably exploited by the later Decadents. Cummings has made no attempt to shape his "calligrams" into recognizable pictures, but some of the effects of Appollinaire are facilely imitated in many of Cummings' verses. The following poem, from *Is 5* (1926), represents certain aspects of the vertiginous Appollinairean technique, here ably adapted:

Three
ii

Among
    these
        red pieces of
day (against which and
quite silently hills
made of blueandgreen paper

   scorchbend ingthem
-selves-U
pcurv E, into:
           anguish (clim
b)ing
s-p-i-r-a-
l
and, disappear)
        Satanic and blasé

a black goat lookingly wanders

There is nothing left of the world but
into this noth
ing il treno per
Roma si-gnori?
jerk.
ilyr, ushes.

One who gets satisfaction from cubist pictures and the poetry of Gertrude Stein should derive some pleasure from this piece. No one poem is written throughout in Miss Stein's manner, but in nearly every one there is a phrase or line or two suggestive of

her work, as here in a "goat lookingly wanders." (The addition
of the adjective "black" does violence to Miss Stein's theories.)
Peculiarly Gertrudian is the beginning of "La Guerre" in *Tulips
and Chimneys* (1923):

> the bigness of cannon
> is skillful,

while many of Cummings' most successful satires are the results
of heightening effects Gertrude Stein has already obtained, as
in—

> "next to of course god america i
> love you land of the pilgrims and so forth oh . . .",

which most readers will recognize as another version of Miss
Stein's "A Patriotic Leading." Though hers is the predominant
influence, the poet is not wholly dependent upon Gertrude Stein,
as has been remarked. A special development in his work may
be followed through if one begins with the satire on "the Cambridge ladies" in his first volume, *Tulips and Chimneys,* and
proceeds to read through all the irreverent and mostly indecent
poems on "irreproachable ladies firmly lewd" in subsequent volumes, not failing to miss (as no one has) the immortal piece
dedicated to "my dear old etcetera" in *Is 5.* It is then plain that
Cummings' Hogarthian gallery of prostitutes is filled with the
fallen sisters of "Mr. Appollinax," who have solicited as Lil
and Doris in Mr. Eliot's less pleasant poems. It is the rare
wench among these who is healthy; more commonly she is a
"brittle whore" with a "corpse-coloured body" and an "improbably distinct face." The poet's parade of trulls in his work reminds
one of the Saturday evening performances on Montmartre in the
'twenties for goggle-eyed American tourists, preferably Harvard
boys; but it is to be presumed that Cummings himself exhibits
his women as part of a primitivistic program clearly discernible
in his work. His primitivism, however, is not atavistic—a return
to the aboriginal—but rather a masochistic display of extreme
Decadence. The genuine savage has no such complete absorption
in the other sex as Cummings' poetry exhibits. Furthermore,

these are not "camp women" but the dregs of Decadent society. It is a false sentimentalism to attempt, as Cummings does, to find vestiges of the virtues in them. After reading his ditty on Bill's chip who peached on him to the bulls, one concludes that she got what she deserved though she died "looking hunks of love."

Cummings' *Eimi* (1933) reveals the obtuseness, the egocentricity of the man. The book describes in battered and dissected idiom his sense impressions in an imaginary trip to Russia. There is neither the grandeur of folly nor the elevation of supreme effort in the description, only concentration on self. The very title, *Eimi,* means "I am." Cummings, despite a superficial objectivity, is as much motivated by vanity as the rest of the Decadents.

The naughty boy, the sophomore, the undeveloped mind in Cummings is very tedious, but an explanation for it is not hard to find. His psychology is similar to that of the great athlete who, after his graduation from college, finds life dull as compared with the triumphs of the stadia, and lives for ever in his past—his talk and his ideas those of the good fellow and idol of a former day. Cummings had an astonishing juvenile experience during World War I; for after driving an ambulance in France at twenty-three, he spent three months in a French prison for the indiscretions found by a censor in his letters, then served as a private in the American Infantry. In 1922 he gave an admirable account of his imprisonment in *The Enormous Room,* and the praise which this volume deservedly won, because of its speed, economy, and sophomoric irreverence, apparently turned the author's head. He has never advanced beyond *The Enormous Room* and it is unlikely now that he ever will.

As one surveys the whole of his work, one is convinced that Cummings is miscast as a poet. The Dunsany-like fantasy *HIM* (1927), published in part in *The Dial,* would indicate that he might have made a permanent reputation in the drama had he devoted himself to playwriting. The sprightliness of the dialogue, the excellence of some of the scenes as pure diversion (as, for example, that in which the plainclothesman faints after discovering the "Unconscious" of an Englishman in a trunk), and the author's success at "squeezing fourdimensional ideas into a twodimensional stage," all recommend his genius. "Him" of the play is a struggling dramatist who complains that playwriting is too hard. And it *is* too hard, which is the reason why Cummings has not persisted in it. The ballet, *Tom* (1935), represents a possible revival of interest in the theatre, but the piece in execution is far beneath the promise of the idea. Not enough work has been put upon it. Poetry, at least the kind he has written, is much easier, wherefore volume after volume, and even a *Collected Poems* (1938). It is gratifying that the public has lost interest.

As early as 1925, commenting on the United States, Cummings observed—

> . . . things are going rather kaka
> over there, over there.
> yet we scarcely fare much better—
>
> what's become of (if you please)
> all the glory that or which was Greece
> all the grandja
> that was dada? . . .

Dada was dead, and the American followers of Decadence, those Expeditionary Forces whose object was to make the world safe for hyperaestheticism, were slipping away. Cummings reestablished himself in the United States that year; MacLeish came home in 1928; and following the stock market crash in 1929, there was a general exodus from Paris of expatriates. Harry Crosby, sun-lover and versifier, committed suicide in the late afternoon of December 10, 1929. Eugene Jolas' magazine, *transition,* vehicle of so many of the expatriates, to the support of which Crosby had contributed liberally in his last year, brought out its final number in June, 1930. Before it was issued, however, Harry Salemsom had sold to an American newspaper syndicate a series of lurid articles purporting to describe the American Art and Literary Colony of Paris, a series which gave the glamour of drugs, drink, and debauchery to what in the main was prosaic enough an experience. In 1931, Malcolm Cowley issued a study of his compeers in exile, *The Lost Generation,* and by 1934, with the return of Eliot and Gertrude Stein, the American Decadent movement belonged to literary history. No important worker in the Decadent tradition, save possibly Frederic Prokosch—that strange German-American youth who has poured a necrophilitic passion for Oriental decadence into three well-written books, *The Asiatics* (1935), *The Assassins* (1936), and *The Seven Who Fled* (1937)—has made an appearance since *transition* went under, while many who were Decadent when that was the fashion have turned to a different philosophy and other themes. The task of evaluation is already left to the historian.

One thing is perfectly clear about American Decadence—it has given us four names, those of Ezra Pound, T. S. Eliot, Hart Crane, and Archibald MacLeish, as deserving of immortality as those of Baudelaire, Mallarmé, Rimbaud, and Valéry. Nor will many be found to controvert the fact that it is hard to find four other poets of equal importance with these in either recent English or American literature. Yet that is no answer to the charge that these men have spent a good deal of genius on derived themes and hackneyed ideas. Pound is tediously repetitious, Eliot has ended "not with a bang but a whimper," Crane dwelt largely "in possibility" rather than in accomplishment, and MacLeish, after deserting Decadence, has arrived only at chauvinism as yet. A charitable future, puzzled by the fact that when life shrieked around them, these were bookfellows, drawing a thin pap from the printed page (and it in French), may rank them with the metaphysical poets of England, or even above the pre-Raphaelites, but it cannot accord them many of the encomiums with which contemporary reviewers have showered them. Here are things which may compare favorably with *L'Après-midi d'un Faune* or even with Gray's *Elegy,* but there is no "Ode to the West Wind," no "Hymn to Intellectual Beauty," no "Adonais." Shelley is still secure, despite the attack of T. S. Eliot, and Milton may be permitted his admirers. It cannot be denied, however, that Decadence has weakened intellectual America by alienating literature and the people, by depriving them of the nourishment of poetic ideas, here obscurely symbolized and in-verted, while persuading those who could understand this symbolism and inversion, that life is futile and only art is worth while. Like Naturalism, Decadence has exerted an enfeebling influence on American character, and possibly has done the greater damage, since it has affected only superior minds.

IV

THE PRIMITIVISTS

"Your civilization is your disease; my
barbarism is my restoration to health."—
Paul Gauguin, *Letter to Strindberg.*

IF RUDYARD KIPLING had known Gertrude Stein, he would have
been astonished to learn that, as long ago as the 'nineties, he
himself prepared the way for her. To Englishmen bewildered
by the pre-Raphaelites, perturbed by Swinburne's admiration for
Baudelaire, annoyed by Oscar Wilde's eccentricities and finally
disgusted by the revelation of his perversity, the poetry and fiction of Rudyard Kipling came as a great relief. Here were
emotions they could share and actions they could understand.
Yet Kipling was no more popular in the British Isles than he was
in America, for he came at a time when there was evidence on
every hand that literature and art in this country might adopt
the hyper-aestheticism affected in England. The *Century Magazine* under Gilder had become "arty"; the publishing houses of
Copeland & Day, Stone & Kimball, and Thomas B. Mosher
throve on wide margins and élite type; imitations of the Kelm-
scott and Bodley Head presses crowded each other in the book-
shops; and Walter Pater, Arthur Symons, and Austin Dobson
were read with an avidity which presaged imitation. Kipling,
whose stories were Bret Harte and Dickens with a Punjab setting, seemed nevertheless an elemental Adam come to confound
the race. He pointed the way back to sanity and health. Without
a word of reproof, he stood a condemnation to powder-puff
aestheticism. Youths who rouged and spoke French suddenly
found themselves without an audience. Kipling's imperialism
also suited the temper of a nation looking forward to conquests
in the West Indies and the Philippines; his virility inspired

readers who were soon to hear expounded and to see illustrated the doctrine of "the strenuous life." Fortified spiritually by Kipling, Bliss Carman and Richard Hovey wrote *Songs from Vagabondia* (1894) and defied the aesthetes to their false teeth:

> ... I'm sick of all these Yellow Books,
> And all these Bodley Heads;
> I'm sick of all these freaks and spooks
> And frights in double leads.

> ... I'm sick of all this taking on
> Under a foreign name;
> For when you call it *decadent*,
> It's rotten just the same. ...

In San Francisco, where one out of every two persons was an ardent Kipling fan, Gelett Burgess published on wall-paper, in a pamphlet which was "neither rectangular nor rhombic" in shape, a burlesque chap-book, *Le Petit Journal des Refusées,* with the following dedication:

> 'Tis for Thomas B. Mosher of Maine,
> Whose dinkey toy prefaces give me a pain.

Kipling's Corporal Mulvaney forced Richard Harding Davis to realize the merit of his Irish lads, Gallegher and Burke; Kipling's *Mark of the Beast* furnished Frank Norris with a model for *Vandover and the Brute;* and then Norris' short stories, his *Moran of the Lady Letty* and *A Man's Woman* inspired Jack London. Thus a return to the "primitive" became a vogue in this country at the beginning of the century. Yet with all the talk about "primitiveness", there was small indication in the work of these romancers—from Kipling to London—that they knew what the genuine primitive was, or that they cared to know.

In all the world, in 1903, there was but one literary person who had anything approximating a scientific or realistic (for they are essentially the same thing) interest in primitive mentality. And that one person was Gertrude Stein. A student of William James and Hugo Münsterberg at Radcliffe, she had engaged in studies and experiments to determine the deeper currents in what

James had first called "the stream of consciousness." Attention has already been directed by B. F. Skinner, in the *Atlantic Monthly,* to an article which Miss Stein published with another advanced student, Leon M. Solomons, in the *Psychological Review,* in September, 1896, entitled, "Normal Motor Automatism." Mr. Skinner has brought out the surface fact that the skill which Miss Stein acquired in automatic writing in these experiments, she has employed in her later "creative" work, but by implying that Miss Stein is a fakir and has concealed this simple "secret" (isn't it obvious to anyone who has read her poems?), Mr. Skinner has postponed, rather than hastened, the general comprehension of Miss Stein's work. For automatism is after all a means and not an end; it is a technique and not a purpose; Mr. Skinner has shown us nothing at all about Gertrude Stein's intentions.

Now the study of automatic writing, or perhaps we should say (after reading *Everybody's Autobiography,* 1937) the study of the automatic writers, brought out the fact that beneath the consciousness lay another self—something which Freud was to label the subconscious—which directed the hand in automatic writing without interfering with the processes of the consciousness itself. The existence of this buried thing, this primal self, had been conjectured by Francis Galton, as long ago as 1883, in his *Inquiries into the Human Faculty and Its Development.* Galton wrote, "Out of this ante-chamber [of consciousness] the ideas most nearly allied to those in the presence-chamber appear to be summoned in a more or less mechanically logical way, to have their turn of audience. . . ." What Gertrude Stein perceived was not only the universality of this primitive mind (the "unconscious" is her name for it) but also the fact that, if the conscious mind could be eliminated, this subconscious mind would most clearly represent the instinctive or "mechanical" mental processes of the savage—the processes which governed him and were his "thought" before he had reason or "intelligence." She observed further, for she was a keen observer, that the consciousness does not necessarily suggest its occupations to the subconscious mind, but that the latter has its own preoccupations—literally simple ideas on which it ruminates. Hence the significance of her often uttered observation in *The Making of Americans* (1925), "There is always then in every one, repeating. . . ."

Yet the current literary vogue of 1903 and her psychological studies, while they may be used in explanation of Gertrude Stein's work, have less to do with its actual inception than had certain events in the world of art, events which Miss Stein witnessed as a sympathetic and intelligent observer after her arrival in France, for shortly, under her brother's expert tutelage, she became a discriminating critic and patron of the new art, and helped to "discover" Cézanne, Matisse, Derain, Picasso, and Juan Gris. Just at that time art, which had seemingly exhausted the possibilities of impressionism, received a new stimulus in the discovery of the high merit of negro sculpture, introduced from Northern Africa. Though Vlaminck is believed to be the first to apprehend the worth of the simplified emotional form of this sculpture, and Modigliani to make the most effective early use of it in painting, Pablo Picasso (who had contracted to paint Gertrude Stein's portrait) lived with the Spanish sculptor, Agero, designer of bas-reliefs on African models, and must have done some very acute thinking about this time on the subject. It was while she was sitting for her portrait for Picasso that Miss Stein began work on the "Melanctha" story in *Three Lives* (1909). To the prevalent enthusiasm in Paris among the artists whom Gertrude Stein knew well must be assigned the immediate origin of this first, and all-important, tale of Gertrude Stein.

"Melanctha" is the story of a negro girl, Melanctha Herbert, who was "pale yellow and mysterious and a little pleasant like her mother" but whose real strength "came through her robust and unpleasant and very unendurable black father"—a father whose insane suspicion branded the young girl as a "wanderer" (in a large, homely sense) before she actually became one. The bloody slashing that this man received from a coachman whom he drunkenly accused of seducing his daughter, though Miss Stein compresses the episode, is an important source for many a sanguinary scene in later primitivistic literature. Moreover, the dispatch with which the author plasters up "the good strong cut that went from James Herbert's right shoulder down across the front of his whole body" is responsible in part for the terseness with which injury and sudden death are treated by her followers. The men especially do not want to be outdone in coolness and concentration by the girl-who-failed-to-be-graduated from the Johns Hopkins Medical School.

Important as the episode is to later fiction, it was of absolutely no consequence to Melanctha Herbert. She continued to stray, hanging around docks and buildings where men worked, making advances to these men, drawing them on, learning from them, yet always escaping from them. Then, at sixteen, she formed an attachment for Jane Harden, a nearly white negress of twenty-three, who had had much experience and who completed Melanctha's education, teaching her how to be safe, "when she wanted to be safe in this wandering." Thus "Melanctha tried a great many men, in those days, before she was finally suited." Finally, however, she met a young mulatto, a doctor, Jefferson Campbell, who "was all the things that she had ever wanted. . . . A strong, well built, good looking, cheery, intelligent and good mulatto." His goodness, which was not religious but in which he took pride, was an annoyance to Melanctha. She protested that if he were so afraid of losing it, his goodness could not amount to much. The conversation they had about his virtue was the beginning of their interest in each other. This interest on Melanctha's part was passion which quickly prompted her to ask the doctor "to be friends with her"; on Jeff Campbell's part it was less clearly defined, perhaps only kindliness at first, or curiosity. His nature was not ardent, and the warmth which his goodness and gentle ways aroused in women invariably repulsed him. His phlegmatism and his native caution, his early scruples (for he saw clearly enough the faults of Melanctha) made him an indifferent lover. When finally there was no doubt in his mind that he loved Melanctha, passion for him was dead in the girl. She had taught him a love which, no matter how much she respected him, she no longer could reciprocate. She gave herself to Jem Richards, a betting negro, a reckless man who knew all about horses, whose success represented something she had always liked. After he left her, Melanctha worked a short time and then, stricken with consumption, died.

Here, in synopsis, is the first genuinely primitivistic study in

American literature. The author, with extraordinary penetration, has seen that it is not always the jarring of wills, the conflict of violent natures, which makes the course of love uncertain; she has discovered, with the help of her medical science, that the element of "timing" is an important one in passion. Doubtless there are earlier uses of this theme in world literature, but it is exceedingly difficult to recall them. Miss Stein, to enforce the theme and to show how easy love is when both natures are ripe for it, throws Jem Richards and Melanctha Herbert together at the end of the tale. Yet there is to be no happiness for the girl who had learned to be "safe" in love. Her faith shaken in herself since her affair with Jeff Campbell, she insists on marriage with Jem only to drive him from her by her very insistence. Consumption is a final irony, for Melanctha had burned herself out before disease destroyed her. "Melanctha Herbert always loved too hard and much too often." Thus the tale is a consistent study of a type, the analysis of an ardent, self-consuming nature.

In the telling of "Melanctha" Miss Stein was as original as in choosing her materials. She foresaw that she must make the tale as simple in statement as it was in its substance. There must be nothing in it which would not be naturally phrased in the mind of Melanctha herself had she dramatized her own story. It must contain the phrases she would repeat if she were thus constantly dramatizing it. This is accomplished by restricting the vocabulary (suggested perhaps by the simple phrasing of the first of Flaubert's *Trois Contes* which Gertrude Stein had been translating) and by repeating certain descriptive pnrases which characterize the types of people found in the tale. There is no automatic writing in "Melanctha"; there is, however, exploited what Miss Stein had learned in her experiment in Cambridge and by reading Galton:

. . . Rose Johnson and Melanctha Herbert had been friends now for some years. . . .

Rose Johnson was a real black, tall, well built, sullen stupid, childlike, good looking negress. She laughed when she was happy and grumbled and was sullen with everything that troubled.

Rose Johnson was a real black negress but she had been brought up quite like their own child by white folks.

Rose laughed when she was happy but she had not the wide abandoned laughter that makes the warm broad glow of negro sunshine. Rose was never joyous with the earth-born, boundless joy of negroes. Hers was just ordinary, any sort of woman laughter.

Rose Johnson was careless and was lazy, but she had been brought up by white folks and she needed decent comfort. Her white training had only made for habits, not for nature. Rose had the simple, promiscuous unmorality of the black people.

Rose Johnson and Melanctha Herbert like many of the twos with women were a curious pair to be such friends.

The student of literature, familiar with the now discarded theory of ballad origins, will say that the tale of "Melanctha" is built up by "incremental repetition," and just as this device heightens the effect of the ballad, so it improves this tale. When the originality of the material, the ingenuity of the telling, and the effect desired by the author are all taken into account, it is hard to see how this piece could be improved. Both for historical reasons and for intrinsic merit, "Melanctha" must be ranked as one of the three or four thoroughly original short stories which have been produced in this century.

The other two stories in *Three Lives* are of less consequence than "Melanctha." Like it, they are portraits aiming to set forth the generic or essential things in the characters studied. Like it, they owe a great deal to the new painting. Indeed, Gertrude Stein tells us that she did the actual writing of these stories facing Cézanne's *Portrait of a Lady* which she had recently acquired. How much her use of adjectives reminds us of the laying of heavy brush strokes of primary color on canvas! Melanctha is in one delineation "a graceful, pale, yellow, intelligent, attractive negress"; in another, "the subtle, intelligent, attractive, half white girl"; Rose Johnson is "this coarse, decent, sullen, ordinary, black childish Rose." In "The Gentle Lena" Miss Stein describes a "patient, gentle, sweet and german" servant girl who does always exactly as she is bidden, even marrying the man selected for her, though she does not feel like marrying. In "The Good Anna" is portrayed "a small spare, german woman" who is always fretting and saving for others, yet always lending all her savings to shiftless, unfortunate people.

It will be observed that these types of characters are partially delineated by the way in which they love. In *The Long Gay*

Book, begun in 1909, Miss Stein indicates that men and women can be distinguished, can be classified as to "how they love, how the women love and how they do not love, how men do not love, how men do love, how women and men do and do not love and so on to men and women in detail. . . ." Even in *Three Lives* there is a hint of this interest in the abstract consideration of types which ultimately dislocated Miss Stein's occupation with generic traits. This interest in abstraction came, of course, from the new painting. Mr. Thomas Craven, in *Modern Art,* has described admirably the various stages passed through by Miss Stein's great and good friend, Pablo Picasso, in his painting in the next few years:

> In 1907, influenced by the simplified carvings of the negroes, he [Picasso] made drawings in which the human head approximates an abstract design; and some three years later, pursuing his natural inclination, he went completely abstract. First, he blocked out an object in planes and angles—the head, for instance, though still recognizable, being reduced to an assemblage of geometrical fractions. In the next phase, the head was hacked into sections which were arbitrarily shuffled together so as to bring into a single focus aspects observed from several points of view. Or, as his satellites put it, "moving round an object, he seized several successive appearances which, when fused into a single image, reconstituted it in time." The head is now only an eye, a nose, and an ear scattered in splintered wreckage. In the last phase, Cubism paradoxically went flat. The three visible planes of the cube, by the process of extension were carried beyond the limits of vision—to the frame of the canvas—ceasing to function as indications of solidity and becoming automatically three flat tones. The head, needless to say, disappeared. Representation was annihilated. Art at last was pure, perfect, abstract, and absolute.

Now, just as Pablo Picasso arrived at "pure" art, by reducing painting from representation to solid geometry, to fragmentary solid geometry, and finally to plane geometry, so Gertrude Stein may be said to have tried to produce "pure" literature and to have progressed by comparable stages to this end. The first stage in this progress may be said to be an effort to formulate abstract conceptions of people. This effort is seen in *The Making of Americans,* Miss Stein's 900-page novel:

> There are then two kinds of women, those who have dependent independence in them, those who have in them independent dependence inside

them; the ones of the first of them always somehow own the ones they need to love them, the second kind have it in them to love only those who need them, such of them have it in them to have power in them over others only when these others have begun already a little to love them, others loving them give to such of them strength in domination. . . .

The Making of Americans is without dialogue and without action; Miss Stein calls it "a description"—which is accurate. "Events," asserts Miss Stein, ". . . should not be the materials of poetry or prose." Characters, however, are delineated in the book and are recognizable. In fact, in her account of the dressmakers and governesses employed by the Herslands, in her brief record of the relations of Mary Maxworthing and Mabel Linker, who run a dressmaking business together, Miss Stein is still very close to the method which she employed in *Three Lives*.

The next stage in Gertrude Stein's progress towards pure abstraction in type drawing may be said to be represented by "Ada" in *Geography and Plays* (1922). It was in order to do "portraits" of this sort that Gertrude Stein gave up the composition of *The Long Gay Book* and *Many Many Women*. She had discovered that it was impossible to eliminate the narrative interest from fiction (as *The Making of Americans* reveals) and have much of anything of value left. The word-portrait is much nearer the brush-portrait than is the novel; consequently in its favor Miss Stein abandoned fiction writing. "Ada," her first portrait, we now know to be a study of Alice B. Toklas, the companion for twenty-five years of Gertrude Stein. In form, "Ada" may be said to correspond to the "fragmentary solid geometry" stage of Picasso's painting. It is not the story of "Ada" precisely; yet by reading the fragmentary material about her brother's love affairs, about her letters to her father, and about her grandmother's way of smelling flowers and eating dates and sugar,—in a word, by *moving about* the character—we certainly gain some sort of notion of her.

The third and final stage of Miss Stein's progress towards the abstract, which means *the complete elimination of narrative,* might be represented by any number of "portraits" selected from Miss Stein's work. Because it contrasts sharply with "Ada" and Miss Stein prints it beside this piece in *Geography and Plays,*

"Susie Asado" might be taken as representative of the ultimate in portraiture, a stage comparable to the "plane geometry" period in Picasso's work. Not only narrative is eliminated, but the fragments of the portrait are related to each other only through an association suggested by the sounds of the words. Miss Stein has filled her picture as would Picasso by letting the form of one object suggest another. In a different medium the association is excusably aural.

Susie Asado

Sweet sweet sweet sweet sweet tea.
Susie Asado
Sweet sweet sweet sweet sweet tea.
Susie Asado.
Susie Asado which is a told tray sure.
A lean on the shoe this means slips slips hers.
When the ancient light grey is clean it is yellow, it is a silver seller.
This is a please this is a please there are the saids to jelly. These are the wets these say the sets to leave a crown to Incy.
Incy is short for incubus.
A pot. A pot is a beginning of a rare bit of trees. Trees tremble, the old vats are in bobbles, bobbles which shade and shove and render clean, render clean must.
Drink pups.
Drink pups drink pups lease a sash hold, see it shine and a bobolink has pins. It shows a nail.
What is a nail A nail is unison.
Sweet sweet sweet sweet sweet tea.

After achieving pure "abstraction" in portraiture, it was only natural that Gertrude Stein should try "still lifes" (her phrase) and "landscapes." Most of the material in *Tender Buttons* belongs to the "still life" category, while the things called "plays" are really "landscapes." By the time she had begun to make "landscapes" Miss Stein's thinking was very involved, indeed. Probably from Eddington (whom Alice B. Toklas ranks with Picasso and Gertrude Stein among the real geniuses whom she has known) she got confused notions of Bergson's time theories. Looking back upon her creations, she calmly asserts that in

Three Lives she has employed "a prolonged present" and in *The Making of Americans* "a continuous present," and adds, "Having naturally done this I was naturally a little troubled with it when I read it"! This is bosh. Of the "plays" she writes, "I felt that if a play was exactly like a landscape then there would be no difficulty about the emotion of the person looking on at the play because the landscape does not have to make acquaintance." This, however, makes sense. A purely scenic thing with words and music, but without representation or narration, might produce on the stage something of the effect of a cubist landscape in painting. And that is precisely what *Four Saints in Three Acts* (1934) did.

Although she has succeeded in writing something which may "revolutionize opera," the course which Gertrude Stein has followed since creating *Three Lives* cannot be said to have been a profitable one. It is true that the present has no comparative standards save in painting for the judgment of her later work, and the future must decide whether portrait painting, still life painting, and landscape painting of the sort that she has done with words have any usefulness. She herself has passed judgment on her fiction writing by abandoning it, yet the present, moved by her early studies and cold towards her painting, may fairly question whether she has not been unduly and unwisely influenced by Picasso, and whether, in transferring some of his ideas to literary composition, she has properly defined her medium. Definition for the cubist is easy: his dimensions are two; his materials, canvas and paint; and his "time" the everlasting present of his finished picture. Yet what are words? Mere type on page? Is a word the same in one font as in another? Or are words merely sounds? When does a word begin, when does it end, and how long does it last? What is its time? Has it a "prolonged present" or a "continuous present"? Isn't a word itself always a "narrative" or a "representation"? Is "abstraction" even possible with words? Miss Stein must once have seen this last difficulty, for she tells in *The Autobiography of Alice B. Toklas* (1933) of manufacturing words. Should not the present condemn her work to the degree that it appears constructed upon the analogy of experimentation in another medium rather than upon logical deductions in her own? Surely it is not what it pretends to be; and being pretentious, it is rococo; and being rococo, it is bad. And in this condemnation there is less frivolity than in the tricks which she and Picasso have perpetrated on the public. Yet *Three Lives* remains—an intrinsically important and tremendously influential book.

Gertrude Stein did not immediately find an appreciative reader of even *Three Lives*. Sherwood Anderson, whose brother Karl, the portrait painter, possessed the training and the wit to understand what Miss Stein had done and was trying to do, seems to be the first American definitely affected by her work. Sherwood tells how Karl, dissatisfied with the explanation of Miss Stein's writings then current in America, "bought *Tender Buttons* and brought it to me, and we sat for a time reading the strange sentences. 'It gives words an oddly new intimate flavor and at the same time makes familiar words seem almost like strangers, doesn't it,' he said. What my brother did, you see, has set my mind going on the book, and then, leaving it on the table, he went away." The novelist also adds, "I had already read a book of Miss Stein's called *Three Lives* and *had thought it contained some of the best writing done by an American.*"

Anderson probably had had nothing published, though he had written much, when he first read Gertrude Stein. Born in the little town of Camden, Ohio, on September 13, 1876, the third of a family of eight children, Sherwood Anderson had had little formal education, since the restless nature of his "loveable, improvident" father made impossible the fixed residence necessary for adequate schooling. At twelve, he was put to work to add to the family income; at seventeen, he went up to Chicago, where he drifted from job to job, finally enlisting in the Army and serving in the Spanish-American War. To his amusement, on his return to Ohio from Cuba, he was hailed as a hero; he married and became the manager of a paint factory in Elyria, Ohio. Like John Webster, the hero of his novel, *Many Marriages,* Sherwood Anderson, tired even of easy success and perplexed by the problems of modern life, put on his hat one day and walked out of the factory and out of the town, never to return. He was dictating a letter to his stenographer when the impulse came to him to do this, and he stopped short in the middle of a sentence and said to her:

"My dear young woman, it is all very silly but I have decided to no longer concern myself with this buying and selling. It may be all right for others but for me it is poison. There is the factory. You may have it if it pleases you. It is of little value I dare say. . . . Now at this moment, with the letter I have been dictating, with the very sentence you have been writing left unfinished, I am going out that door and never coming back. What am I to do? Well now, that I don't know. I am going to wander about. I am going to sit with people, listen to words, tell tales of people, what they are thinking, what they are feeling. The devil! It may be I am going forth in search of myself."

Stuart Sherman fancied that fifty years hence some literary antiquarian will point to the account of this episode in a *Story Teller's Story* and say: "There is one of the historic moments in American literature."

Anderson went up to Chicago to join his brother Karl, to live in a hall bedroom, and to struggle with composition while he earned his sustenance in an advertising agency. Through Karl Anderson, Sherwood met most of the important members of the old "Chicago group"—Theodore Dreiser, Floyd Dell, Ben Hecht, and Carl Sandburg. All these men were very helpful in the formative years of Anderson's work, but Dreiser and Dell were especially influential, as an examination of *Windy McPherson's Son* (1916), *Marching Men* (1917), and even *Poor White* (1920) shows. The influence of Gertrude Stein comes later.

Windy McPherson's Son, for which Floyd Dell found a publisher after a good deal of difficulty in 1916, is a sorry piece of patch work, yet of value to those who wish to study Anderson. The novel in the main describes how Sam McPherson, the son of a shiftless braggart, a typical war veteran, pulls himself up by his bootstraps to great commercial success. The backbone and much of the viscera of the book have been cut out of Dreiser's *The Financier*. Certain episodes in the early life of the boy and the characterization of his father are autobiographical and consequently fairly vivid. After Sam achieves success and marriage to Sue, the daughter of his employer whom he is obliged to smash (compare *The Financier*), life is only momentarily fair for him.

When Sue is in childbirth, Sam has a choice between his wife, and a child at great risk to his wife, whereupon he chooses his wife. There can be no children for the couple as a result. Sam and Sue drift apart, great success in the munitions business is without meaning for him, and, as Anderson himself had done and as so many of his heroes were tediously to do, Sam McPherson quits business, partners, and his wife. The remaining chapters of this disorderly book are devoted to his wanderings, and in particular, to his difficulties, as a common laborer, with the bosses. (It is here that the influence of Floyd Dell is seen.) On one occasion Sam takes over the direction of a strike by the girls in a shirtwaist factory. He might have brought this to a successful conclusion, had not an official organizer by the name of Harrington interfered. "Sick and disgusted," he again takes up his wandering. Eventually, having gone home with a woman of no character, he persuades her to give him her children, and with these he returns to Sue. The couple are reconciled, and Sam undertakes "to try to force himself back into the ranks of life."

Obviously, if the birth scene be excepted, there is little in this novel that is primitivistic. It is instead a piece of sentimental naturalism. To be sure, the vocabulary is limited and the sentences are simple. Yet these limitations are in part Anderson's own and in part those of the Chicago group, which was more or less dominated by Robert Herrick's theories of style. If *Windy McPherson's Son* adds little to the growth of primitivism, *Marching Men,* which followed it in 1917, adds still less. This rather addled novel repeats some of the plot structure of its predecessor, has some vague recollections of *Germinal,* and a good deal of sentimentalism about the working man. Beaut McGregor, son of a martyred Pennsylvania coal miner, envisions the day when laborers shall march by the hundred thousand, and as a result, a collective brain will grow. It would probably be better for the workers if the brain grew first and they marched to some purpose afterwards.

Winesburg, Ohio, published in 1919, is an altogether different thing. When the book appeared, reviewers characteristically began comparing Sherwood Anderson with Dostoevski and Chekhov, neither of whom he had read. A few years later, Mr. Carl

Van Doren pointed out that the book belonged to "the revolt from the village" school and averred that the chief influence upon it was Edgar Lee Master's *Spoon River Anthology*. It is clear today that the *Spoon River Anthology* contributed only the paste and the title which brought these tales together under one cover. It was not the generic force responsible for their conception. That was supplied by Gertrude Stein's *Three Lives*. If *Winesburg, Ohio* is reexamined, it will appear that the book is made up of studies of "how men do not love, how men do love, how women and men do and do not love and so on to men and women in detail. . . ."

The naïve simplicity of Anderson's first style is gone, and a studied, conscious simplicity of style is in its place, a style suggested by that of *Three Lives,* yet in a sense original and the author's own. Further, the broad, intelligent sympathy, the understanding of Gertrude Stein, always fenced off a little by attempted objectivity and by this very stylistic manner, is here, too. Consider this passage for these things, this passage taken from the poignant tale called "Hands":

. . . In his youth Wing Biddlebaum had been a school teacher in a town in Pennsylvania. He was not then known as Wing Biddlebaum, but went by the less euphonic name of Adolph Meyers. As Adolph Meyers he was much loved by the boys of his school.

Adolph Meyers was meant by nature to be a teacher of youth. He was one of those rare, little-understood men who rule by a power so gentle that it passes as a lovable weakness. In their feeling for the boys under their charge such men are not unlike the finer sort of women in their love of men.

And yet that is but crudely stated. It needs the poet there. With the boys of his school, Adolph Meyers had walked in the evening or had sat talking until dusk upon the schoolhouse steps lost in a kind of dream. Here and there went his hands, caressing the shoulders of the boys, playing about the tousled heads. As he talked his voice became soft and musical. There was a caress in that also. In a way the voice and the hands, the stroking of the shoulders and the touching of the hair was a part of the school-master's effort to carry a dream into the young minds. By the caress that was in his fingers he expressed himself. He was one of those men in whom the force that creates life is diffused, not centralized. Under the caress of his hands doubt and disbelief went out of the minds of the boys and they began also to dream.

And then the tragedy. A half-witted boy of the school became enamoured of the young master. In his bed at night he imagined unspeakable things and in the morning went forth to tell his dreams as facts. Strange, hideous accusations fell from his loose-hung lips. Through the Pennsylvania town went a shiver. Hidden, shadowy doubts that had been in men's minds concerning Adolph Meyers were galvanized into beliefs.

The tragedy did not linger. Trembling lads were jerked out of bed and questioned. "He put his arms about me," said one. "His fingers were always playing in my hair," said another.

One afternoon a man of the town, Henry Bradford, who kept a saloon, came to the schoolhouse door. Calling Adolph Meyers into the school yard he began to beat him with his fists. As his hard knuckles beat down into the face of the frightened school-master, his wrath became more and more terrible. Screaming with dismay, the children ran here and there like disturbed insects. "I'll teach you to put your hands on my boy, you beast," roared the saloon keeper, who, tired of beating the master, had begun to kick him about the yard.

Adolph Meyers was driven from the Pennsylvania town in the night. With lanterns in their hands a dozen men came to the door of the house where he lived alone and commanded that he dress and come forth. It was raining and one of the men had a rope in his hands. They had intended to hang the schoolmaster, but something in his figure, so small, white, and pitiful, touched their hearts and they let him escape. As he ran away into the darkness they repented of their weakness and ran after him, swearing and throwing sticks and great balls of soft mud at the figure that screamed and ran faster and faster into the darkness. . . .

Winesburg, Ohio has not the detached hatred which distinguishes the *Spoon River Anthology*. Dull and brutal men are in it, but it is not so much they who are held up to ridicule as it is their victims who are sympathetically examined and exonerated. The meek, the fearful, the bewildered yield up their secrets to an understanding interpreter who studies them primarily as their affections reveal them. Consider the story of Elmer Cowley, the son of a farmer who has opened a general store in Winesburg but who still is rustic in his ways and dress—to the son's great embarrassment, for he is lonesome and does not want to be thought "queer." Elmer Cowley finally runs away, but the last thing he does is to fall in a fury upon George Willard, town reporter, beating the latter because he personifies to him the sophistication of the town. George Willard had been amused one day—and Elmer had not forgotten the trivial incident—when he had seen the seedy shopkeeper's son putting new laces in his shoes. Yet at the time he received his beating, Anderson tells us, George Willard was considering ways of making a friend of Elmer Cowley. There are cruelty and brutality in *Winesburg, Ohio,* but the characters with whom Anderson wants us to sympathize are quite as apt to be the cruel and brutal ones as are their enemies. Had a lesser artist, say an Irvin Cobb, handled the tale "Queer," he would have made George Willard a perpetual "kidder", and we should have felt a bourgeois and poetic justice (they are the same thing) in his thrashing. The tales of Anderson are not meant to supply catharsis. They are meant, instead, to show what a sorry thing all around frustrated affections are. *Winesburg, Ohio* was Anderson's first book to attract a wide public, and with it he may be said to have come of age.

By comparison with *Winesburg, Ohio, Poor White,* published in 1920, is a step backward. Anderson reverts to the industrial problems that he had confusedly fumbled in *Windy McPherson's Son* and *Marching Men.* The book, meant to show what an inventive genius and a financial wizard in collaboration can do to a small town, abandons this theme to treat in detail Hugh McVey's difficult adjustment to marriage. Both themes are handled fairly well, though Anderson is plainly more absorbed by the second; it is the coupling of the themes which spoils the book. Dreiser had interested Anderson in D. H. Lawrence, and from Lawrence, Anderson had moved on to the more technical treatments of sex. Without other evidence as to when this occurred, one would say it took place when *Poor White* was partially written, so abrupt is the transition in that book. This is certain, *Poor White* is the first book of Anderson's to approach problems of the affections as technical sex problems. The knowledge of these things in *Winesburg, Ohio* is intuitive and artistic, rather than technical.

A working knowledge of psychoanalysis and a modified primitivism are responsible for the best work of Sherwood Anderson. This is found in the two collections of short stories, *The Triumph of the Egg,* published in 1921, and *Horses and Men,* which appeared two years later. Between these books lies *Many Marriages,* an effort to raise sex knowledge into a kind of religion, a novel in which symbolism and ritual vie with each other for attention. Because all three of these books belong to another tradition, they will be handled in detail elsewhere. Such short stories as "I'm a Fool" and "I Want to Know Why" are original contributions to primitivism, however, as well as fine psychological studies. Coming from the mouths of boys, the simple narrative style of these tales needs no such rationalization as does that of Gertrude Stein's "Melanctha." And the raw experience is not callously thrust at the reader, as in so many primitivistic works, but comes, as it comes to the characters, by the reader's stumbling upon it. One who desires illustration of this will find it in the admirable close of "I Want to Know Why." No other American, with the exception of Mark Twain, has achieved such complete rapport with youth as Anderson exhibits in this tale.

Paul Rosenfeld persuaded Anderson to take a trip abroad in 1921. It was a momentous, yet disastrous, adventure for the novelist. He sat in the little paved square before Chartres cathedral and meditated (i.e., had deep thoughts) as he imagined Henry Adams had done. Ever after, when a "feeling of being very small in the presence of something vast" took possession of him, he invariably asked himself, "Can it be Chartres, the Virgin, the woman, God's woman?" And he went to Paris and sat at the feet of Gertrude Stein. To read his account of the visit in his *Notebooks* (1926), one would think that all the pair did was to munch cookies. Yet in that meeting Sherwood Anderson learned for the first time he was a "primitive" and the leader of a school. He came away extremely self-conscious and impressed with his aesthetic importance.

It would be worth pointing out that the great difference between Miss Stein and Mr. Anderson is the difference between head and heart, if that were not to deny Miss Stein sentiment and Mr. Anderson intelligence. Yet essentially this is the difference between the two authors. Anderson, in *A Story Teller's Story*, tells us of being hurt when a speaker praised him as the author of the Winesburg tales, but spoke slightingly of the figures that lived in the tales. " 'It is a lie. He has missed the point,' I cried to myself. Could the man not understand that he was doing a quite unpermissible thing? As well go into the bedroom of a woman during her lying-in and say to her: 'You are no doubt a very nice woman, but the child to which you have just given birth is a little monster and will be hanged.' . . . As I sat listening certain figures, Wing Biddlebaum, Hugh McVey, Elizabeth Willard, Kate Swift, Jesse Bentley, marched across the field of my fancy. They had lived within me, and I had given a kind of life to them." There is a sense in which Sherwood Anderson may be said to have *felt* his characters and to have realized them in this way. After his talk with Gertrude Stein, Anderson felt (he was always to *feel*) that it was important for him *to think*. The results are seen in what he wrote after 1921.

Anderson's only thoroughly conscious primitivistic novel, *Dark Laughter,* published in 1925, is an ineffectual book. Yet in conception it was excellent. Anderson meant to contrast the easy love of the negroes with the thwarted and abortive loves of intellectual people. When the whites are frustrate in the drawing room, negro laughter mocks them from the kitchen. There is an element of incitement in this laughter even for the reader, and one cannot help thinking that Anderson's idea should have germinated a play rather than a novel. Yet had Anderson attempted it, the play would have been a more complete failure than the novel, for he cannot produce the talk of cultured people. His Bruce Dudley, his Aline Aldrich, and in particular his Rose Frank, are unconvincing characters. He does not raise them into intellectuals by asserting that Dudley had thrust into his hand a copy of Joyce's *Ulysses* before he left Chicago, that Rose Frank attended the "Quat'z Arts Ball," and that Aline listened to a man named Joe talk "suavely, kindly" about "Cézanne and Picasso and others." One is reminded of what Gertrude Stein said to Hemingway—"Remarks aren't literature." The jumble of prose and verse, and of fragments which are neither prose nor verse, which makes up the book adds nothing to the technique of the novel nor to Mr. Anderson's reputation, though conceivably it might have, had the novelist been able to bring it off. To discover him at his worst, turn to the passage where Bruce Dudley is improbably reminded of Paul Gauguin (Miss Stein had compared Anderson to Gauguin) when he watches a brown girl dressing in a bedroom opposite his in New Orleans.

Tar: A Midwest Childhood (1926) has aspects which suggest

comparisons with Wordsworth's "Goody Blake and Harry Gill" and "The Idiot Boy." Simplicity has been simplified until the reader aches for subtlety. The novel is vaguely autobiographical, though Anderson warns the reader that "Tar" Moorehead is not himself and the Moorehead family are not his father's family. The most objectionable part of the book (the first half of it) is an effort to produce the impressions of a child under five years, teary, thumb-sucking babyhood—possibly the most difficult subject in literature anyway. Anderson makes a prodigious botch of it. His account of becoming lost, eating grass, and getting stung by a bee, for example, is rivaled only by the inanities of Wordsworth. Study of Floyd Dell might have helped him render plausible the advent of a drunken father at the kitchen dinner table or a trip downtown with his mother, though one cannot be certain that with any aid the early chapters of *Tar* could be salvaged. Once he has got his hero out of skirts and curls, however, Anderson manages much better, and the latter portion of the novel is good reading, though one wishes the writer had carried the narrative beyond his mother's death and the boy's release in ballplaying.

After some seven years' experimentation with Freudian themes, Anderson issued another primitivistic book, a collection of short stories entitled *Death in the Woods,* in 1933. The initial story, which recounts the awe of a boy who was present when the beautiful nude body of an old woman was found in the snow after it had been stripped by dogs, is at once elemental and lyrical in the fashion of the Russians. It is nip-and-tuck between this tale and "A Jury Trial" as to which is the better in the volume. The latter, however, is quite unlike Anderson's earlier primitivistic tales —in the fashion of Hemingway it deals with a hill murder among moonshiners, the murderer being coerced by an unconscionable bully. All the stories in *Death in the Woods* are good, but one other may be singled out as especially interesting, "A Meeting South," for some will see in the pain-racked poet-aviator of New Orleans a portrait of Anderson's friend William Faulkner, here gathered like a brood-chick under the protective wing. The tenderness which was a personal characteristic of Anderson is nowhere better exhibited.

In a different way Anderson's novel, *Kit Brandon* (1936), suggests another protégé of his—Scott Fitzgerald, *the* Scott Fitzgerald of *The Great Gatsby*. It is the story of the daughter of a Virginia mountaineer who becomes a notorious rum-runner for her father-in-law out of a restless love for deviltry when her husband proves too weak to master her. Kit, for all her wild energy, is a puzzled and confused Gatsby, conscious that she has missed something in life, even though she enjoys all the luxury of the successful bootlegger of the prohibition era and though many men endeavor to "make" her. She is not particularly a soiled person, though she had yielded herself to a boy in the mill where she had worked after running away from her father. That, however, was an act of charity, such as she could give, for the lad was dying of tuberculosis. Never does she truly love, though she warms towards a college boy who is killed in an automobile crash. A bigger collision occurs, in a psychological sense, between herself and her father-in-law who kills his son and sends her into hiding in the hills. Kit gets nowhere with her reflecting, yet perhaps the millgirl Agnes who had had the idea "of people at last finding each other through universal participation" was on the right track. Still Agnes "wanted something wiped out," but Kit was not for that—she would restore something to American society, she knew not what, so that men and women would be kind and generous once more. Despite the bafflement of the heroine, despite brief excursions into pathology, *Kit Brandon* is one of the most readable of Anderson's books: living beings move through swift rounds of action, spiral to significance, or are hurled off centrifugally into the predestined void. Without offering a tenable conclusion as to a course of action, Anderson accomplished his purpose of revealing the social and psychological illness of America. And he did this literally without injury to his status of amateur—the one thing he seemed to hug as most precious. Yet perhaps he was right—amateurism is usually so briefly preserved in America that, if one can maintain his, he should make every effort to do so. That Anderson died, still a "gifted amateur" at sixty-four—at least in his public's notion of him—is not the least of his triumphs.

Primitivism scored its first great popular victory with the early plays of Eugene O'Neill. The dramatist owes little to Gertrude Stein or Sherwood Anderson, although it is said that he was an early and appreciative reader of *Three Lives*. O'Neill goes back for his origins to Kipling, Jack London, and Joseph Conrad, to an early and innocent primitivism. Yet he did not need to rely upon these gentlemen for materials, for few of our authors—even Jack London himself—have knocked around more than has Eugene O'Neill. Son of James O'Neill, the actor who "cleared fifty thousand" season after season in *Monte Cristo,* Eugene Gladstone O'Neill was born in the Barrett House, on Broadway at Forty-third Street, New York, on October 16, 1888. Since his mother accompanied his father on his road tours, O'Neill was put in a private school. Thus six years of his life were passed in various Catholic and non-sectarian boarding schools before he was matriculated at Princeton in the fall of 1906. In June of that school year he was suspended, according to legend, for having thrown a beer bottle through a window of President Wilson's house. His father having an interest in a mail-order jewelry business, O'Neill became secretary of the firm. In 1909, he married Kathleen Jenkins, but left for Honduras before his son was born the following year. The couple were divorced in 1912. Like Jack London in the Klondike, O'Neill found illness and not gold in Honduras. Invalided home, he managed a theatrical company on a tour, then shipped on a Norwegian barque to Buenos Aires, lured into this, so Oliver Sayler says, by reading Conrad's *The Nigger of the Narcissus*. In the South American city he worked for Westinghouse, Swift, and Singer in turn, but finally became "a bum on the docks." He shipped on a cattle steamer to South Africa and return, and then signed as ordinary seaman on a British tramp bound for New York. Back in the metropolis, O'Neill lived at "Jimmy the Priest's," a waterfront dive, picking up an occasional job—one a trip to Southampton on a mail boat.

For a while he had a brief rôle in his father's company; this was just before he did his first professional writing—as reporter for the New London *Telegraph*. Then, in December, 1912, the irregular life he had led took its toll—his health broke down and it was found that he had a touch of tuberculosis. In the five months he spent in the sanatorium at the Gaylord Farm, Wallingford, Connecticut, Eugene O'Neill did the first serious thinking of his life, and for the first time tried "to digest and evaluate the impressions of many past years in which one experience had crowded on another with never a second's reflection." After his discharge, he spent fifteen or sixteen months with an English family on Long Island Sound and did his first dramatic writing— eleven one-act and two long plays. He was told by those who read his scripts that he needed technical advice, and at the suggestion of Clayton Hamilton, he enrolled in Professor Baker's "47 Workshop" class at Harvard. It is generally believed that O'Neill got nothing from Baker, but such is not the case. Baker had already turned out a capable playwright in Edward Sheldon whose *The Nigger* and *The Boss,* in 1910 and 1911, pointed somewhat in the direction O'Neill was to go. Baker's insistence that the negro should be exploited in the theatre, for example, is only one of the things that O'Neill took away with him. Yet it is easily conceivable that O'Neill, who had more or less grown up in the theatre, was bored with some of the discussion of rudiments so necessary for the beginners in the class. Still, if he did not profit from class discussion, it is likely that he derived something from the critical methods of the "47 Club" (not to be confused with the workshop) about which little has been written. After spending the winter of 1915–16 in the congenial company of bohemians and anarchists in Greenwich Village, O'Neill went down to Provincetown, where he became acquainted with the Players, then organized and led by George Cram Cook. *Bound East for Cardiff* and *Thirst* were produced before the Company moved to New York; there the success of the Provincetown Players was O'Neill's success, too.

In 1914 James O'Neill had paid for the publication of his son's first book, *Thirst and Other One-act Plays,* since repudiated by the dramatist. The title play has interest for us, though it is admittedly poor. It represents three people dying of thirst on the life-raft of a wrecked steamer: a dancer, a gentleman, and a West Indian mulatto. The stage directions demand that the producer

duplicate Winslow Homer's "Castaway" with the two additional
figures, and also advise him that "on the still surface of the sea,
the fins of sharks may be seen slowly cutting the surface of the
water in lazy circles." The dancer feels that the mulatto sailor
(who is stoically indifferent to their plight) has drinking water
concealed somewhere and first offers him her necklace and then
herself for a drink before she dies. When the negro proposes to
the gentleman that they eat her body, the latter indignantly
pushes it into the sea. Angered by this folly, the negro buries his
knife in the other's back, but the wounded man locks with him,
and they both totter into the sea.

Here is a plot, as Barrett Clark has pointed out, which would
have delighted Jack London, and indeed is reminiscent of his
work. The reader will find parallels in such tales of London's as
"The *Francis Spaight*," "Just Meat," "To Build a Fire," and
others. The complete "wash-up" of the wreck survivors—rhetorical and melodramatic—is the type of episode which, to London's
way of thinking, "causes God to laugh." O'Neill from this source
brought wholesale butchery and violence to contemporary primitivism. Mr. Clark writes, "Of the thirty-six O'Neill plays I have
seen or read, there are only five in which there is no murder,
death, suicide, or insanity. In the others I find a total of eight
suicides and one unsuccessful attempt; twelve important murders
(not counting incidental episodes referred to in the text); twenty-
three deaths, nearly all due to violence; and seven cases of insanity." This is the severest criticism ever made of the dramatist.

In 1919 were collected the best of the one-act plays that
O'Neill had written in five years, under the title *The Moon of
the Caribbees and Six Other Plays of the Sea*. This collection
contains two excellent primitivistic pieces: "The Moon of the
Caribbees" and "The Long Voyage Home." The latter play reveals how Nick, a crimp, in Fat Joe's London waterfront dive
picks sober Olson as his victim among the four men of the
steamer *Glencairn* who have been paid off. Olson has saved his
pay in order to visit his old mother in Sweden. Olson's soft drink
is drugged, and he is carried off to the *Amindra,* bound round the
Horn, while his companions are absent. The dialogue is the rough-
est that had been read on the American stage up to that time,

JOE—[*Threateningly (to the whore who had helped to pluck* OLLIE).] Guv us what yer took!

FREDA—Took? I guv yer all 'e 'ad.

JOE—Yer a liar! I seen yer a-playin' yer sneakin' tricks, but yer can't fool Joe. I'm too old a 'and. [*Furiously.*] Guv it to me, yer bloody cow! [*He grabs her by the arm.*]

FREDA—Lemme alone! I ain't got no—

JOE—[*Hits her viciously on the side of the jaw. She crumples up on the floor.*] That'll learn yer! [*He stoops down and fumbles in her bosom and pulls out the banknote, which he stuffs in his pocket with a grunt of satisfaction.* KATE *opens the door on the left and looks in—then rushes to* FREDA *and lifts her head up in her arms.*]

KATE—[*Gently.*] Pore dearie! [*Looking at* JOE *angrily.*] Been 'ittin' 'er agen, 'ave yer, yer cowardly swine!

JOE—Yus; an' I'll 'it you, too, if yer don't keep yer marf shut. Tike 'er aht of 'ere! . . .

Nevertheless "The Moon of the Caribbees" is much the finer play—in fact, the finest of all O'Neill's one-acters. The episode is relatively simple: some West Indian negresses bring rum concealed beneath the fruit which they have arranged to sell aboard the British tramp *Glencairn*. The crew becomes quite drunk, takes its pleasure with the women, gets into a brawl during which one of its members is knifed, and tumbles into the forecastle when the mate descends upon them and orders the women ashore. The play gains its significance from two spectators whom O'Neill posts on deck—the Donkeyman who has "sworn off" because of his age and his health, and who can really view the scene with philosophic calm, and "Smitty," the butt of the crew, who has plainly gone to sea after an unhappy love affair. His disgust is obvious, and when Pearl, one of the negresses, tries to make up to him, he sends her below with Yank, and tries to drink himself into forgetfulness. Later, when Pearl slaps his face with all her might as she whirls by him in a drunken dance in the arms of Yank, he is powerless to do anything about it. O'Neill succeeds in a situation vaguely comparable to that in *Dark Laughter* where Anderson fails. We feel acutely the helplessness of "Smitty" in the primitive circumstances for which his experience has not prepared him. Of course, O'Neill's task is simpler than was Anderson's, for his approach is here wholly objective.

In 1920 *The Emperor Jones* was produced with Charles Gilpin, the colored actor, in the title rôle. O'Neill based the story, according to an interview, on an anecdote told him by a circus man about the "late" President Sam of Hayti who swore he would never die of a lead bullet, but would take his own life first with a silver one. The elaboration of this theme in the play, during which the half-civilized negro emperor wastes both five lead slugs and his silver bullet, and the gradual reversion to type of the man, are elements which suggest Jack London and *The Call of the Wild*, though a vague resemblance to Kipling's "The Man Who Would Be King" should be noted. Yet no one has ever thought that Eugene O'Neill's plots were his forte. The play has all the possibilities of caricature, yet escapes caricature completely. This is because of the fine workmanship of the dramatist, who demands no sudden transformation in the character of his principal, but reduces him by wholly plausible stages. With two murders on his conscience, those of a negro porter and a white prison guard back in the States, and with all the subtle stirrings of savage superstition aggravating his condition, Jones is a convincing victim of the hallucinations which terrify him in the island jungle. The emotional conviction is heightened by the use of a monotonous, rhythmic drumbeat, the tempo of which is accelerated as the negro's fear approaches hysteria. First and last, this is one of the most ingenious plays ever written—even if some of the "tricks" had been used before (for example, the drumbeat, which had been employed by Austin Strong in *The Drums of Oude*). Those who saw Charles Gilpin in the part of Emperor Jones saw one of the finest pieces of acting of modern times, in no way eclipsed by the performances, splendid in their turn, of Paul Robeson and of Lawrence Tibbett in Greenberg's musical version of the play.

Anna Christie (1921) is a reworking of an earlier play, entitled *Chris Christopherson,* unsuccessfully produced the year before. Here again is the sort of plot in which an author of the Kipling-London tradition would naturally take great delight. Chris Christopherson, a superstitious old barge captain, has kept his daughter Anna out on a farm in the West, away from "dat ole davil, sea," which he fears might ruin her as it has spoiled his life. But while he is taking liquor with a trull at "Johnny the Priest's," his daughter enters, has a colloquy with the woman in which she reveals that she, too, belongs to the "profession," but is properly counseled to conceal this from her father. Accepting Anna as the "pure" child of his hopes, Chris induces her to share his quarters on the barge. She is just beginning to feel this is a "home," such as she has never known, when, ten days later, while at anchor off Provincetown in a dense fog, they pick up three castaways, one of whom, a brawny Irishman named Mat Burke, tries to make love to her despite his weakened condition. When Anna knocks him down and out (true daughter of such an Amazon as London describes in "The Night Born"), Mat discovers that the attraction of the girl for him is no passing fancy, but the deepest seated passion of his life. He wants to marry Anna Christie, but her father will have none of it, since the old man has a proper notion of the character of a sailorman. As a result of their wrangling, Anna tells them how she was ruined by a cousin on the farm in the West, and how, after trying nursing, she had gone into a house of prostitution. Equally shocked, Mat and Chris desert her in Boston, each going ashore separately on a "bender." Two days later, however, her father returns, followed by Mat, and in a general love feast Mat pledges to marry Anna Christie when he learns that she has felt no emotion for men in the past and really loves him. Both sailors discover that independently they have engaged to ship to Africa on the same boat. Anna promises to wait for them "in a little house." One even fancies a rose-vine by the door.

Though *Anna Christie* won the Pulitzer Prize for 1922, it is not one of O'Neill's best plays, and he himself (with better judgment than the critics) appears to recognize this, for he does not include it among the dramas he selected for the representative volume of his work, *Nine Plays,* published in 1932. Not only is the action most obvious, but the whole play is washed in Irish sentimentalism, which appears to exude from Mat Burke. The speech of the characters, whether Swedish or Irish, suggests that O'Neill was affected by the marked rhythms of John Synge's *Playboy of the Western World.* Indeed, old Chris more resembles one of Synge's battered tinkers, with his melancholy prophesy-

ing, than he does a stupid Swede, and this impression grows with
the development of the play. Anna is girdled in the same sentimentalism and is far from convincing as a regenerate prostitute.
There is no little revealing touch to show her girlhood on the
farm, which in life would have left its mark in speech and action,
as well as upon character. On the other hand, O'Neill was under
no compulsion to defend the "happy ending" of the play from
The New York Times reviewer. Nothing in the situation called
for tragedy, while the character of Mat Burke was such, as
A. H. Quinn has pointed out, as to aid Anna in her regeneration
—a compound of two Irish qualities, "a worship of the purity of
woman, and a superlative self-conceit." Of course, we ought to
think of *Anna Christie,* not altogether from the immeasurable
distance that our times are from the early 'twenties, but also as
of the year of its presentation, when Francis Hackett wrote in
The New Republic, "after seeing Mr. Eugene O'Neill's *Anna
Christie,* I am so drunk with fantasy extracted from hard-boiled
human beings that I don't know how to become sober." Obvious
though it is, *Anna Christie* undeniably advanced the American
drama.

Caricature and melodrama triumph in *The Hairy Ape* (1922),
a play built, like the *Emperor Jones,* on the return-to-nature
theme, but with much pointless, and rather witless, radical talk,
of the type that London used to indulge in so handsomely. A
thrill-seeking public of the boom years, awed by the reputation
of O'Neill, convinced by the earlier more or less authentic scenes
of the play and the fine acting of Louis Wolheim, vigorously applauded the presentation. Apparently no one has had the courage
to say that the very conception of Yank shaking hands with the
gorilla, and then, crushed and dying from the animal's embrace,
addressing the audience as a circus barker, "Ladies and gents,
step forward and take a slant at de one and only—one and
original Hairy Ape," is hopelessly absurd. The curtain saves the
play from laughter. Yet the subduing of Yank with a fire-hose at
the end of Scene Six added a new "thriller" to primitivistic literature.

All God's Chillun Got Wings (1924) shows O'Neill tiring of
primitivism. In this play, Ella, a white girl, marries Jim, the col-

ored boy who has loved her from a child, after her white husband, a young tough, deserts her. Jim is ambitious to be a lawyer, but repeatedly fails his examinations because of his too great consciousness of his white examiners. Ella for a while is happy with Jim, but as time passes she becomes more and more aware of his blackness, until she is quite mad because of it. She plots against his success, then tries to kill him, and after the failure of her attack prays forgiveness. "Will God forgive me, Jim?" she asks. "Maybe He can forgive what you've done to me," Jim replies; "and maybe He can forgive what I've done to you; but I don't see how He's going to forgive Himself." At the end of the play neither Ella nor Jim has become actually primitive; her mind affected, Ella proposes a solution:

ELLA. (*brightly*) Well, it's all over, Jim. Everything'll be all right now. (*Chattering along*) I'll just be your little girl, Jim—and you'll be my little boy—just as we used to be, remember, when we were beaux; and I'll put shoe blacking on my face and pretend I'm black and you can put chalk on your face and pretend you're white just as we used to do—and we can play marbles—only you mustn't all the time be a boy. Sometimes you must be my old kind Uncle Jim who's been with us for years and years. Will you, Jim?

JIM. (*with utter resignation*) Yes, Honey.

ELLA. And you'll never, never, never leave me, Jim?

JIM. Never, Honey.

ELLA. 'Cause you're all I've got in the world—and I love you, Jim. (*She kisses his hand as a child might, tenderly and gratefully.*)

JIM. (*suddenly throws himself on his knees and raises his shining eyes, his transfigured face*) Forgive me, God—and make me worthy! Now I see Your Light again! Now I hear Your Voice! (*He begins to weep in an ecstasy of religious humility*) Forgive me, God, for blaspheming You! Let this fire of burning suffering purify me of selfishness and make me worthy of the child You send me for the woman You take away!

All God's Chillun Got Wings is the finest drama of O'Neill's first period. Despite the threatening toughs of the early scenes, despite the grinning African mask which Jim's sister has given him as a wedding gift, despite the raw joke at the end of the play on poor, faithful, religious Jim, the play is too poetic, however, to be thoroughly primitivistic. For the first time the psychology of his characters is not obvious, but subtle. One of the finest touches in the play is the portrayal of the hostile attitude of Jim's sister, Hattie, who is an educated negress, a school teacher. Hattie fancies that she is detached, objective, yet her reactions are innate, defensive. Then, too, O'Neill has made as good a use of symbolism in this play as in any that he has written. Not alone the African mask, nor the wedge of buildings in the opening scene which separates a street of blacks from a street of whites, nor Jim in black and Ella in white deserted on the sidewalk after their marriage, suggests the universal oppressiveness of race distinction; the play is filled with details capable of sudden importance and significance. The audience before it leaves the theatre reads meanings into all things, as Ella does, setting them without exception into the categories, black and white. It is a pity that racial hostility and bigotry make it difficult to cast and to present *All God's Chillun Got Wings*.

With the two-act play *Diff'rent* written in 1920, Eugene O'Neill turned to Freud for themes for his dramas. More and more psychoanalysis interested him and his later work was to be done largely in this field. Even *All God's Chillun Got Wings* shows, in Ella's choice, for Jim to play any rôle but that of husband (preferably, dear old *Uncle* Jim), a fine understanding of the ways a character might choose to escape an intolerable situation. O'Neill abandoned primitivism because he plainly saw its limitations. It takes only a certain amount of skill to prepare raw food, and primitivism did not extend his powers. The psychoanalytical play—even granting that its characters are made by formula—is more challenging. Fully aware of the larger demands—and also of the larger rewards—Eugene O'Neill turned to the analytical study of frustrate and abnormal lives.

Far removed from the work of Eugene O'Neill in pretentiousness, but rivalling it at times in verisimilitude, particularly in regard to the accuracy with which it reported the American idiom in speech (though O'Neill is sufficiently accurate here) is the writing of Ring Lardner. The latter was a seasoned newspaperman and syndicate writer, well intrenched with readers of the "You Know Me, Al" stories in the *Saturday Evening Post,* when the critics got around, in 1924, to accord serious recognition to a new volume of his, *How To Write Short Stories*. Even then,

Lardner had literally to bludgeon his way, beating the critics about the ears with a preface ridiculing their formulas. "How to begin—or, as we professionals would say, 'how to commence?' . . . Blasco Ibáñez usually starts his stories with a Spanish word, Jack Dempsey with an 'I' and Charley Peterson with a couple of simple declarative sentences about his leading character, such as 'Hazel Gooftree had just gone mah jong. She felt faint.' "

Magnificently equipped to "spoof" and willing to ladle out any amount of persiflage, Ring Lardner was partially responsible for his own delayed greatness. He not only kept the critics from taking him seriously; he does not appear to have taken himself very seriously until the last decade of his life, when illness and the premonition of death sounded in him greater depths. Corny athletes, the girl friend, problems of the pay check, and the crowding of the substitutes' end of the players' bench were as far as his interest travelled, from all that we know, in the first thirty-eight years of his life. That interest provided some luminous entertainment, but one was always ready for the next act as soon as the boards were clear.

The writing Lardner did between 1923 and 1933, when he died of tuberculosis at his East Hampton, Long Island, home, is much of it literature in its own right, however, and much of it is important because of its influence on other writing. The short stories gathered in *Round-Up* (1929) contain the cream of his work and provide the best basis for a just appreciation of his genius. Four or five stories in this volume are as good as any of their length that have been published in America: "I Can't Breathe," "Haircut," "Zone of Quiet," "Some Like Them Cold," and "Champion." Examination of the last-named tale provides the most satisfactory short answer to the query, Why regard Ring Lardner as a Primitivist? "Champion" is a summary debunking of the traditional "build-up" for the great athlete: Midge Kelly, welterweight champion of the world, is undressed more effectively than he ever got out of his street clothes, and what is disclosed is raw brute, unfit to be handled with gloves, properly approached only with a fence stake. Lardner has produced, without a quiver of emotion and without yielding the slightest to the temptation to accord poetic justice, a peeweebrained sadist, irresistible in achieving his desires because of the singleness of his purpose, everything concentrated on self. Such a portrait belongs conspicuously displayed in the new gallery of revolting supermen.

Yet Lardner is also primitivistic in his treatment of the shallow-pated female who preys upon the fellow "in velvet" and cheerfully drops him when he is broke: who can adjust her emotions to whatever circumstances and the telephone at eve may bring her. There are not wenches in literature much more worthless than those whose yawns display their silver teeth among the gold, as Lardner unpleasantly sketched them in *Round-Up*. Their lubricated talk flows easily on all subjects, revealing, as their creator intended that it should, a paucity of culture and understanding, but an unbounded confidence in their predatory skill. Many a wanton in the work of other writers is related to these slinking pusses in *Round-Up*.

The supreme effect of Ring Lardner, however, is secured by the revelation of drama through an actor or witness who understands less of the grim import of what he tells afterwards than does the reader. The perfect application of this formula is found in the tale, "Haircut," which has been widely acclaimed as Lardner's best short story and one of the best of modern times. Out of the aimless professional patter of a small-town barber Lardner constructs, and at the same time half conceals, the story of the deliberate, but justified, execution of a perpetual practical joker, a "card" who is really a cruel busy-body. Though the method chosen to narrate this tale would seem to one unacquainted with it wasteful, actually every word is probably more effective than the accompanying snips of the barber's scissors. Lardner had become marvelously adept at securing economy within garrulity, and at the height of his powers produced models that imitators have found spare enough when they tried to secure the same results with equal brevity. Though his total output of genuine artistic stories was small, Ring Lardner was one of the important early figures in the development of American Primitivism.

F. Scott Fitzgerald also made a major contribution to Primitivism and a minor one to literature, in 1925, with *The Great Gatsby*. Fitzgerald, a product of St. Paul, Minnesota, and of

Princeton University, had achieved enormous success with his first novel, *This Side of Paradise,* in 1920. It is a task to reread this book to-day, yet it started a vogue for novels of undergraduate life. Amory Blaine, its hero, was sentimentally conceived by Fitzgerald, who apparently held Princeton and the Universe to blame because there was no God in this boy's heart and only a riot of ideas in his head. *This Side of Paradise* has an historical permanence, not only because it was the first novel of the Jazz-Age, but also because it represents so perfectly what passed for thought in this country between 1919 and 1929. The pert, sophomoric wisdom of the book, in a self-conscious, aphoristic style, was retailed by "collegians" throughout the nation and by alumni throughout the world. The "flapper", whom perhaps Fitzgerald was the first to draw, appeared almost simultaneously in the Winter Garden show and in the Folies Bergère.

The Beautiful and Damned (1922), Fitzgerald's second novel, despite a wealth of episode, much untrammeled talk, and more alcohol, is duller even than its predecessor. Fitzgerald tried to wring the withers of his readers for his hero, Anthony Patch, who had two misfortunes, to wit: a multi-millionaire uncle who objected to debauchery, and a spoiled girl-wife who would not take care of her "laundry." (In one of the most touching and significant scenes in the book, poor, dear Anthony stuffs it into the laundry-bag himself.) Hopelessly handicapped by his misfortunes, Anthony tries to drink himself into continuous oblivion, yet is sober long enough (pp. 275-276) to realize that his uncle has cut him off. With only a few thousands a month to live on (from a previous legacy), Anthony suffers through scenes of incredible poverty while a lawyer tries to break the will. When the lawyer succeeds, Anthony has had to endure so much that his mind (*i.e.,* the sweetbreads in his head) is quite affected. In the last episode in the book ("Together with the Sparrows") Anthony Patch, the broken man, heir to millions, is shown tucked in his deck chair on the *Berengaria,* headed for Europe where he will recuperate.

The Beautiful and Damned is possibly the greatest piece of balderdash ever penned by a capable author, but the most shocking part of the whole business is that the author is patently sincere. Fitzgerald, to judge him by his best-known books, honestly felt that his duty was to make glamorous the life of the upper bourgeoisie, to give its frivolities an importance which they do not have. He was the ballad maker of the class that Barbara Hutton and Smith Reynolds have made sufficiently ridiculous, the writer of the new romances of chivalry. In his last novel, *Tender is the Night* (1934), we meet his disillusioned darlings and jaded neurasthenics on the Riviera (now somewhat older, but no more mature), longing apparently for the return of the Jazz-Age. The hero wants to give "a really *bad* party . . . where there are brawls and seductions and people going home with their feelings hurt, and women passed out in the *cabinet toilette.*" It is somehow fitting that the creator of the flapper should have expired of heart-failure in Hollywood (1940) while engaged in writing a novel on the motion-picture industry, tentatively called, it is said, *The Love of the Last Tycoon—A Western.*

The Great Gatsby is out of line, then, with Fitzgerald's other fiction, and it is important for the author's reputation to know that it was consciously different and not merely accidentally so. "I had recently been kidded half hay-wire," he confessed in explaining how he happened to write the novel, "by critics who felt that my material was such as to preclude all dealing with mature persons in a mature world." The story of *The Great Gatsby* is told by a minor character, Nick Carraway, the son of "well-to-do people in a Middle Western City" and a graduate from "New Haven" in 1915, who came to New York to sell bonds in the spring of '22. For no very clear reason he rented a house in West Egg, Long Island, and found himself a neighbor to a millionaire bootlegger by the name of Gatsby. Carraway serves as a half-reluctant go-between for this man and his own cousin, Daisy Buchanan, wife of the fabulously wealthy Tom Buchanan, when they desire to renew an acquaintance dating from before the First World War. Gatsby, then a young and penniless lieutenant stationed at Camp Taylor, had fallen in love with a Louisville girl, Daisy Fay, but her family had broken up this affair and she had married Tom Buchanan, scion of a Chicago family and nationally famous as a football player while at "New Haven." Carraway partly excuses himself for his share in bringing together the former lovers by his knowledge that Tom is having a cheap affair with the wife of a small garage owner, named Wilson. Furthermore, blue bruises on Daisy's wrists testify to the cruelty of her husband. After Tom discovers Daisy's rekindled affection for Gatsby, which discovery occurs at a hotel party in New York, he grandly asserts his mastership and bids the bootlegger drive Daisy home. The car they take runs down the garage owner's wife, Myrtle Wilson, whose unfaithfulness has been suspected by her husband, and proceeds eastward without stopping. Wilson, crazed with grief, hunts down Gatsby, shoots him, and commits suicide. Months later Carraway is accosted by Tom, who is shopping for a pearl necklace for someone, on Fifth Avenue. He learns that the frenzied Wilson had gone to Tom first, suspecting the latter as the hit-and-run driver, since he had stopped with the car on the way in town. Tom, however, had directed him to Gatsby. And Carraway knew that Daisy, who still lived with Tom, was the one who had driven the death-car. Yet he perceived that Tom felt entirely justified in what he had done. "It was all very careless and confused," Nick Carraway summed up. "They were careless people, Tom and Daisy—they smashed up things and creatures and then retreated back into their money or their vast carelessness, or whatever it was that kept them together, and let people clean up the mess they had made. . . ."

The Great Gatsby is one of the swiftest moving of modern novels. Its speed and its hard surface polish should have made it more popular with a generation which was fond of quick acceleration, high lacquers, and bright chromium. From the point of view of appeal to the class of readers who like these things, however, the book has two weaknesses: first, Buchanan's affair with Mrs. Wilson is too muddy; and secondly, the most brilliant writer who ever lived could not attack the popular conception of the ex-football hero, as Fitzgerald does, and expect a wide audience. The least read of all his novels (prior to its inclusion in the Modern Library), The Great Gatsby has proved, however, to be the one most influential upon other writers. The author aimed to present the rich, selfish athlete and his wife as less ethical than the bootlegger, Gatsby; and so far as Tom and Daisy are concerned the portraiture is hardly to be surpassed, but in sharpening the lines of their sterile and selfish natures, he softened and sentimentalized his drawing of the lawbreaker. It is but a step from *The Great Gatsby* to *Little Caesar* (1929) by Burnett, *To Have and Have Not* (1937) by Hemingway, and other attempts to lionize the gangster and bootlegger. *The Great Gatsby,* then, not only brought new materials to Primitivism, but it also vulgarized Primitivism. Fount of a kind of degeneracy, the novel is still better than many of the books it has influenced.

Fitzgerald was the first Primitivist to be influenced by James Joyce, the great Irish novelist, and later American Primitivism owes much to the Dubliner, yet Joyce was in no sense a Primitivist. One of the greatest literary figures of our time, he was so rich in materials that a dozen literary movements could plunder him and yet not impoverish him. Essentially he was a decadent Romantic, who, having found Naturalism insufficiently challenging, moved on towards extreme subjectivity and extreme provincialism, the one proving a perfect antidote for the other. Following Henry James, who introduced the edited "stream of consciousness" in *The Ambassadors* in 1903, and Edouard Dujardin, whose earlier experiments with an inedited "stream" had passed unnoticed until Joyce called attention to them, the novelist developed the interior monologue to an extent undreamed of by his precursors. In *A Portrait of the Artist as a Young Man,* first published in *The Egoist* in 1914–15, Joyce studied the conscious and subconscious life of a future poet, Stephen Dedalus, as he developed from a child to a young man with definite convictions as to his career. Overshadowed by *Ulysses, A Portrait of the Artist as a Young Man* has not been properly appreciated for its subtle study of the maturing sensitive mind. The adroitness with which Joyce associated the thoughts of the boy and youth with his development is so great that even the acute reader has no sense of "stage" or change in that development. He wakes to the realization in the midst of his reading that Stephen has left behind him the tearful, puzzled baby of the early chapters and that the movement of this riper mind is extraordinarily fascinating.

Complete as is the verisimilitude of *A Portrait,* it was unsatisfactory to Joyce who sought a greater subjective truth. His association with the Imagists (see his two collections of verse,

Chamber Music and *Pomes Penyeach*), particularly with Ezra Pound, led him to theories of the mind held by Bergson—especially to the theory of the importance of memory. Realizing, as Pound did, that precise truth as to the random associations of the mind of an individual is better symbolized than reproduced, Joyce sought in *Ulysses* (1922) to give the *effect* of free association by reproducing the flickering life of a few hours in Dublin as it impinges upon the consciousness of three characters amidst all their eternal dreams of past experience, which includes not only contacts in life but in their reading and dreams as well. The amplitude of the subconscious storehouse into which the actual experience of the duration of the novel is thrust as small tid-bits of reality is suggested by a symbolic pattern for the novel —that of the Homeric epic of the wanderings and homecoming of Ulysses, which, as Joyce realized, symbolizes the "Past" most clearly for the Western mind. Yet, lest this pattern for the action be identified as the pattern for the thought, the novel is saturated with other symbolism, symbolism, for example, of medieval Catholic theology—a device which admirably suggests the dominance, even in the subconscious mind of the Dublin Irishman (whether Catholic, Protestant, or Jew) of the great Roman Church. And a thousand, or better, ten thousand literary allusions in the novel make the three minds we coast upon representative of the heritage of the West in unconscious culture. *Ulysses* for Western Europe and Pound's *Cantos* in a lesser sense for America are ideal embodiments of the consciousness of man in our time—according to Bergson. Not only have developments in the theory of the subconscious mind led Joyce beyond *Ulysses,* but his own desire to achieve the universal in the subconsciousness led him to create for his new novel, *Finnegans Wake* (originally called *Work in Progress*), a hero who is Everyman—H. C. Earwicker whose initials stand for "Here Comes Everybody." Freud has been added, but has not supplanted Bergson, and the narrative is the substance of one night's dream of the hero. In its aural associations, in its philological constructions, the new book is not a novel at all (any more perhaps than *Ulysses* is) but a great prose poem. It is hard to conceive any further reach of aesthetic construction in this direction.

Out of all this imaginative munificence Americans have garnered as yet relatively little. Indeed, Joyce, in his most·interesting aspects, is still a closed book to them. First of all, and here he is especially influential upon the Primitivists, Joyce challenged Americans to rid themselves of the last vestiges of Victorian reticence in regard to language—to particularize in round Anglo-Saxon terms about the anterior and posterior parts of the body. His example has been a bad one, for his imitators have been foul for the sake of being foul; there is not always the natural occasion for the use of the terms which makes them more or less palatable with Joyce. One thinks of the little episode in *A Portrait of the Artist as a Young Man* in which the mathematics instructor tried to enliven his lecture by a reference to *The Mikado:*

—So we must distinguish between elliptical and ellipsoidal. Perhaps some of you gentlemen may be familiar with the works of Mr. W. S. Gilbert. In one of his songs he speaks of the billiard sharp who is condemned to play:

> *On a cloth untrue*
> *With a twisted cue*
> *And elliptical billiard balls.*

—He means a ball having the form of the ellipsoid of the principal axes of which I spoke a moment ago.—
Moynihan leaned towards Stephen's ear and murmured:—What price ellipsoidal balls! Chase me, ladies, I'm in the cavalry!—

Then Joyce exploited the wholly vulgar episode as no one else in literature before him, Casanova and Boccaccio not excepted. It is his example which has emboldened the later Primitivists. None of them has quite touched the animalism of Mollie Bloom, but several—Hemingway, Faulkner, Caldwell, and Henry Miller—have excelled all but the chamber episode. One feels that in *Ulysses* Joyce was deliberately baiting the censors; but in *Dubliners* and *A Portrait of the Artist as a Young Man* the repulsive episode is incidental and not forced. One recalls the vulgar badgering of devout Aunt Dante by Stephen's father and uncle, both rabid Parnellites, at the long Christmas dinner as a case in point.

A scattering both of outhouse terms and of mildly vulgar episode appears in Fitzgerald's work, but his chief point of contact with Joyce was in his effort to do school life as realistically as Joyce had done it in *A Portrait of the Artist as a Young Man.* One might not suspect this from reading *This Side of Paradise,* which seems more of a travesty than a serious effort, yet such is the case. Joyce's elevation of the Jew, Leopold Bloom, into the important rôle of Ulysses has begotten a regular tribe of Ben in American literature, beginning with Fitzgerald's Bloeckman (in *The Beautiful and Damned*) and including such diverse Semites as Hemingway's Robert Cohn (in *The Sun Also Rises*) and Faulkner's Julius Kauffman (in *Mosquitoes*). Even Fitzgerald's hatred of the great athlete was probably inspired by Joyce's dislike of the physically arrogant, as witness Nasty Roche and Blazes Boylan. The tendency towards structural experimentation, with rapid and abrupt shifts of scene, the writing of dialogue as in drama, the advancement of the story by the inclusion of passages from Gloria's diary in *The Beautiful and Damned,*—all are suggested by the work of Joyce. Fitzgerald adopted nothing else from the master, but others have. Dos Passos, Faulkner, Hilda Doolittle, Conrad Aiken, and many more have experimented with the interior monologue; Thomas Wolfe, as we shall see, has imitated Joyce's subjective approach to locale. And finally Wolfe, Caldwell, Dos Passos, and others have aped some of the effects of the Irishman's style, though none has quite touched the Nashean-Jabberwocky extremes of *Finnegans Wake:*

The Ondt was a welltall fellow, raumybult and abelboobied, by-near saw altitudinous wee a schelling in kopfers. He was sair sair sullemn and chairmanlooking when he was not making spaces in his psyche, but laus! when he wore making spaces on his ikey, he ware mouche mothst secred and muravyingly wisechairmanlooking. Now whim the sillybilly of a Gracehopper had jingled through a jungle of love and debts and jangled through a jumble of life in doubts afterworse, wetting with bimblebeaks, drikking with nautonects, bilking with durry dunglecks and horing after ladybirdies (*ichnehmon diagelegenaitoikon*) he fell joust as sieck as a sexton and tantoo pooveroo quant a churchprince, and wheer the midges to wend hemsylph or vosch to sirch for grub for his corapusse or to find a hospes, he wist quit.

Had any American imitated this (and hasn't Cummings?), he would not be writing prose but poetry—and Decadent poetry at that, for that is the tradition to which most of Joyce's work belongs. Americans, as we have seen (though perhaps it is too early for congratulations), seem to be on their way out of that tradition.

That some sort of boundary separates, even artificially, mature Primitivism from the Decadent tradition may be surmised from the attitude of such writers as Ernest Hemingway and William Faulkner towards the Decadent poets. Though Primitivism owes much to James Joyce and Gertrude Stein, who in most of their writings are genuine Decadents, and to Sherwood Anderson, whose free verse and experimental prose in *Dark Laughter* show that he was not quite hostile, and though the Sweeney poems of Eliot and the verse of both Cummings and MacLeish suggest the growth of Primitivism out of Decadence itself, the later Primitivists will hold no traffic with the Decadents. Hemingway's collection, *In Our Time,* contains a short story called "Mr. and Mrs. Elliot" based upon the sterility of a poet by the name of Hubert Elliot who has an income of nearly ten thousand a year, who has done work at Harvard, and who prefers to live abroad. Though Hemingway denies that any of his characters in this book are real people, the reader probably will not assume that resemblance between the "pure" Hubert and T. S. Eliot is wholly fortuitious. Again, in *Death in the Afternoon,* in one of those famous Shandyean passages that the author has with the Old Lady, the poet of *The Wasteland* is cited as a decorous authority on "lust" and its uses in poetry, after Hemingway has damned the whole sterile lot of New Humanists, with whom he seems to identify Eliot. Faulkner began his literary career as a Decadent poet; his first published work was a contribution to *The New Republic* (of August 6, 1919) entitled "L'Après-midi d'un-Faune." Yet despite the fact that his volume *A Green Bough* (1933) contains sweetish echoes of Eliot, Cummings, and Swinburne (the Victorian Baudelaire), he allows a favored character in *Mosquitoes* to conclude—

". . . all modern verse is a kind of perversion. Like the day for healthy poetry is over and done with, that modern people were not born to write poetry any more. Other things, I grant. But not poetry. Kind of like men nowadays are not masculine and lusty enough to tamper with something that borders so close to the unnatural. A kind of sterile race: women too masculine to conceive, men too feminine to beget. . . ."

Moreover, the chapter entitled "Lovesong of J. A. Prufrock" in *Pylon* seems a deliberate attempt to throw into contrast Mr. Faulkner's and Mr. Eliot's portraits of an ineffectual. The hostility of the later Primitivists towards the Decadents is undeniably an effort in part to emphasize their own importance. Then, of course, everyone prefers his own brand of sentimentality, and the attitude that "life may go by so long as I have art" is offensive to those who fancy that action, however raw and crude, is living. The fact that both Faulkner and Hemingway attack T. S. Eliot need not be interpreted as personal animosity: these gentlemen have guessed correctly that Eliot is the most important man of his school, and remembering that Shadwell gained immortality of a sort through his attack upon Dryden, they have thus insured their own fame. In the last analysis, however, these attacks are merely a sign of Primitivism kicking free of its Decadent origins.

Ernest Hemingway, whose beginnings may be traced not only in the work of Fitzgerald, but also in that of Stephen Crane, Sherwood Anderson, and Gertrude Stein, may be said to be the writer who first made the general public aware of Primitivism. He was also the first of the Primitivists to taste the dust and ashes of the War, and to bring a hard-boiled cynicism to his writing in place of the play-boy disillusionment found in the novels of Fitzgerald. Hemingway was born in Oak Park, Illinois, where his father was a practicing physician, on July 21, 1898. After a school career made locally memorable by his skill as a boxer and football player, he reported on the *Kansas City Star*. Before America entered the War he had gone to France with an ambulance unit and had been transferred to Italy, where his services were eventually rewarded by the two highest military decorations which that country confers. After the Armistice he returned to the United States, married, and reentered journalism. Brilliant work on the *Toronto Star* won him an appointment as foreign correspondent and, like Stephen Crane (whose work attracted him), he was sent to Greece to watch the revolution there. On his return to Paris he became a syndicate correspondent and settled into the serious study of literature.

Hemingway's first published volume, *Three Stories and Ten Poems,* was printed in Dijon, for the Contact Publishing Company, in 1923. Hemingway is no poet, and so far as is known, has abandoned verse entirely. His early rimes do suggest, however, an effort to imitate Crane and possibly Ambrose Bierce:

Ultimately

He tried to spit out the truth;
Dry-mouthed at first,
He drooled and slobbered in the end;
Truth dribbling his chin.

Though Hemingway is easily shown familiar with Crane's work ("The Blue Hotel" is written in a style peculiarly suggestive of his) it is Anderson, and to a lesser extent Fitzgerald, who appear to be his masters in his first book. "My Old Man," the best story in the volume, is an affectionate portrait of a none-too-honest jockey by his son, who grudgingly yields to the detractors after his father's death at the water-jump:

George and I went out to the gate and I was trying to stop bawling and George wiped off my face with his handkerchief and we were standing back a little ways while the crowd was going out of the gate and a couple of guys stopped near us while we were waiting for the crowd to get through the gate and one of them was counting a bunch of mutuel tickets and he said, "Well, Butler got his, all right."

The other guy said, "I don't give a good goddam if he did, the crook. He had it coming to him on the stuff he's pulled."

"I'll say he had," said the other guy, and tore the bunch of tickets in two.

And George Garner looked at me to see if I'd heard and I had all right and he said, "Don't listen to what those bums said, Joe. Your old man was one swell guy."

But I don't know. Seems like when they get started they don't leave a guy nothing.

In attaining the point of view of a boy and the atmosphere of the racing track Hemingway is every whit as successful as Anderson; had the former never written, this story could be properly acclaimed. As it is, it stands for the thoroughness with which Hemingway has studied his model and is a completely satisfactory explanation for his later success.

"Up in Michigan," another of the tales, is an account of a rural seduction, bordering upon rape; more violent than Anderson, it is not otherwise different from his work. "Out of Season," the third story in the volume, depicts a Fitzgerald young couple in Italy trying to fish without leads. Here Hemingway tries in vain to produce quite the effect of boredom typical of Fitzgerald's work.

In Our Time (1925), Hemingway's second volume, contains tales and sketches done both before and after *Three Stories and Ten Poems.* The only new influence detectable in his work is that of Gertrude Stein, as easily seen in the prologue to the first section as anywhere:

Everybody was drunk. The whole battery was drunk going along the road in the dark. We were going to the Champagne. The lieutenant kept riding his horse out into the fields and saying to him, "I'm drunk, I tell you, mon vieux. Oh, I am so soused." We went along the road all night in the dark and the adjutant kept riding up alongside my kitchen and saying, "You must put it out. It is dangerous. It will be observed." We were fifty kilometers from the front, but the adjutant worried about the fire in my kitchen. It was funny going along that road. That was when I was kitchen corporal.

At no time was Hemingway to go any further in his imitation of Miss Stein than here. She has merely been useful to him in attaining a naïve colloquial style, a style which countless young writers in turn were soon trying to imitate. The most vivid story in the book, "Indian Camp," records a boy's impressions during a trip taken with his father, a physician, who went to an Indian camp to assist in birth a woman who had been in labor three days. The father did a Caesarian operation with a jack-knife and sewed up the woman, while the son with head averted held a basin for him. When it is all over, they discover that the husband, an invalid in the bunk above the woman, unable to stand her pain, has cut his throat with a safety-razor. The story is an interesting comment on the passivity of the Indian, but it is not a great story. The two best tales in the book, artistically considered, are "The Three Day Blow" and "Soldier's Home." In one, two lads experiment cautiously with strong drink; in the other, Krebs is forced back into the social pattern after a month of idleness in the bosom of his family following his return from the War. "Cat in the Rain," a more subtle study than either of these, does not quite come off. All one can think of in reading it is Anthony and Gloria Patch bored with each other in a California hotel— though this is Italy. There is really no great thing in *In Our Time,* though the volume is strewn with material which Hemingway was to exploit successfully later on; moreover, there is some poor and melodramatic writing in it. "The Battler" may be based on an actual experience, but the deranged pugilist and his negro keeper suggest the caricatures of Faulkner rather than anything else. Some one has meanly said that "A Very Short Story"— which contains a plot outline later utilized in *A Farewell to Arms* —has a more appropriate ending for the hero than has the novel. The girl does not die, and the young lieutenant, who has gone off to America and forgotten her, contracts "gonorrhea from a sales girl in a loop department store while riding in a taxicab through Lincoln Park." *Chacun à son goût.*

In 1926 Hemingway published his first novel, *The Sun Also Rises,* with a quotation from Gertrude Stein as a salutation: "You are all a lost generation." The opening pages of the book remind one instantly of Fitzgerald. A rather luckless "collegian" is introduced—a Robert Cohn, former middleweight boxing champion at Princeton, who has got his nose flattened to its improvement, for Cohn is a Jew. He has been married, but his wife has run off with a miniature painter, leaving him to be appropriated by a forceful lady with whom he lives three years in Paris before getting a novel accepted by an American publisher. This success changes him so that he is not so pleasant to have around —at least, to the American press correspondent who is telling the story. Jake Barnes, the narrator, is further annoyed with Cohn when the latter, having broken with his Frances, takes a fancy to Lady Ashley, a young Englishwoman who is living very

easily and recklessly in Paris. Jake himself loves Brett Ashley—
has loved her ever since he was invalided to England from Italy
during the War. Cohn doesn't know this, and when he tries to
pump Jake about her, finds the latter almost belligerently evasive.

Nor does Cohn discover that Brett loves Jake—has loved
him hopelessly ever since she nursed him when he was suffering
from the war wound which had made him a eunuch. The life that
both lead—Jake's drinking and Brett's wantonness—is an effort
to laugh off the bad joke of Jake's sterility. Cohn does not see
that he is tolerated because of Jake's hunger for constant companionship, any more than he realizes, when Brett goes off with
him to San Sebastian, that he is but compensating for the lover
whom she may not have. Consequently he is perplexed when she
does not keep a rendezvous in Spain where he and Jake and an
amiable drunkard by the name of Bill have gone to fish. She is
compensating now in San Sebastian with Mike Campbell, her
fiancé.

When Jake and Bill return from their five days' fishing to
Pamplona, they find Campbell, Cohn, and Lady Ashley all in-
stalled in the Hotel Montoya. Cohn had gone up to San Sebastian to fetch the other two, and now, quite numb, follows them
everywhere. The entire party is remaining in Pamplona for the
fiesta and the bull fights. The fights bring another character into
the story—Romero, a handsome nineteen-year-old matador.
With this youth Brett, despising herself, falls hopelessly in love.
Cohn, who has borne the abuse of Mike and the sheathed contempt of Bill and Jake, now explodes. He knocks out both Mike
and Jake in a café, goes to the matador's room where he finds
Brett, and proceeds to pummel that youth. He floors the valiant
Romero so many times that he sickens of hitting him, begins to
weep when Brett berates him, and permits Romero to hit him,
which the matador does not hesitate to do—full in the face. Then
exit Cohn. The next day the others watch Romero, bruised and
sore, achieve a great triumph in the ring. When it is all over,
Brett and the matador go off together, and the party breaks up.

Jake lingers at San Sebastian after Mike and Bill are gone.
While there, intuitively foreseeing the event, he receives a tele-

gram from Brett in Madrid to come after her. Her passion partially satiated, she has realized that she will ruin the young matador if she stays with him, and she has sent him from her. She and Jake take a little ride "to see Madrid" before they start back to Paris, where, she says, she is going to marry Mike Campbell. As they bang about in the old cab, Brett for the only time in the novel drops her pose:

"Oh, Jake," Brett said, "we could have had such a damned good time together."

Ahead was a mounted policeman in khaki directing traffic. He raised his baton. The car slowed suddenly pressing Brett against me.

"Yes," I said. "Isn't it pretty to think so?"

The reader, remembering Lady Ashley's kaleidoscopic course through the novel, shares Jake's cynicism. He suspects, as Jake does, that Brett wants only what she cannot have, but neither he, Jake, nor Brett herself will ever be sure of this. Yet the reader is certain of one thing—he has read one of the best unified, most dramatic novels produced by an American since World War I. Hemingway has used great ingenuity in keeping his theme to the fore. For example, when the whole party goes down to watch the bulls being unloaded during the fiesta, only the reader is conscious of how that incident is made to grind salt into Jake's flesh. The best proof that Hemingway is an artist is that he does not comment at all. This is the way the episode is led up to:

"Have you got tickets?"

"Yes. I got them for all the unloadings."

"What's it like?" He was pulling his cheek before the glass, looking to see if there were any unshaven patches under the line of the jaw.

"It's pretty good," I said. "They let the bulls out of the cages one at a time, and they have steers in the corral to receive them and keep them from fighting, and the bulls tear in at the steers and the steers run around like old maids trying to quiet them down."

"Do they ever gore the steers?"

"Sure. Sometimes they go right after them and kill them."

"Can't the steers do anything?"

"No. They're trying to make friends."

"What do they have them in for?"

"To quiet down the bulls and keep them from breaking their horns against the stone walls, or goring each other."

"Must be swell being a steer."

One of the virtues of *The Sun Also Rises* is that the characters are contemporaries. Most of the figures in modern novels suggest people who have lived in print before; Hemingway's characters in this book have not. It may be that Fitzgerald and Joyce have suggested to him people to look for, and it is true that he has used Gertrude Stein's "type psychology" of classifying people by "the way in which they love" for distinguishing his characters; but he has found his people in life and studied them there. Bill is a relatively minor character in the novel, introduced for the sole purpose of demonstrating that Brett did not run with every man, yet Bill lives. A dialogue occurs when Jake and Bill are fishing which reminds the reader instantly of Cohn's earlier effort to pump Jake about Lady Ashley, but more important still (and Hemingway realizes this) it brings out the difference between Bill and Cohn in Jake's attitude towards them. To realize what a marvelous adept the man is at creating men through dialogue the passages really should be read against each other. The unremarked parallelism is one of the sweetest things in literature. And incidentally the latter passage contains some of the best clowning we know, too.

Characterization, naturalness of dialogue, and the manipulation of his materials to get the most out of them make Hemingway's novel outstanding. Yet it is the temper of the book which individualizes it. Not all nurses in the War saw their lovers die of dysentery, not all war wounds are so liable to provoke a nasty smirk as Jake's; the unmentioned disillusion of this couple, however, *is* typical of all whom the War touched, and they breed infection, spreading it throughout their generation. Cynicism as an habitual, non-intellectual response is a different thing from cynicism as a deliberate pose, or pessimism as a philosophy, yet Hemingway is the first to make us feel this, to realize the despair of it. *The Sun Also Rises* has no peer among American books that have attempted to take account of the cost of the War upon the morale of the War generation, and European books, such as Remarque's, with their greater documentation, are no better polemics against war than this, which was meant for no polemic at all.

It is more painful to contemplate Hemingway's descent from the significant to the trivial, in his next book, *Torrents of Spring* (1926), than it is to realize the full import of *The Sun Also Rises*. Whatever tempted Hemingway to write *Torrents of Spring,* probably only he knows, for the book is a satire of those to whom he owes most—Sherwood Anderson and Gertrude Stein —for the formation of his own style. Perhaps he thought in this way to demonstrate his independence or to prove his maturity. To be sure, there are aspects of *Dark Laughter* and of *The Making of Americans,* the books here burlesqued, that merit satire, but the thing could have been done adequately in a paragraph. Hemingway took ten days and 143 pages to do it, and the result is indescribably tedious. Some one told him to sharpen his wit before he perpetrated the Shandygaff of *Death in the Afternoon.* This is the stuff he once thought howlingly funny:

> Scripps had a daughter whom he playfully called Lousy O'Neil. Her real name was Lucy O'Neil. One night, after Scripps and his wife had been out drinking on the railroad line for three or four days, he lost his wife. He didn't know where she was. . . .

The most amusing thing about the book is that Yogi Johnson's adventures with the Indians are a better burlesque of certain things Hemingway has written, for example, "Ten Indians" (in *Men Without Women*), than they are of Anderson's writings.

By all the rules of sport and innuendo, Hemingway should never have published *Torrents of Spring,* for he was not prepared for the consequences. He is too thin-skinned for this kind of a game. Anderson did not flay him alive, but Gertrude Stein paid him off with a few lines in the *Autobiography of Alice B. Toklas*—lines well calculated to make Hemingway writhe. She admitted that she and Anderson had formed Hemingway, but that "they were both a little proud and a little ashamed of the work of their minds." She intimated that Hemingway was a little "yellow" and she regaled her readers with an anecdote describing how the fur-bearing novelist was accidentally knocked out by a young chap whom he was teaching to box. Hemingway let this ride for a long time, but he burned under it, and finally could no longer check his resentment. It comes out in the end in *The Green Hills of Africa* in a conversation between himself and P.O.M. (Poor Old Mamma), during which he implies that a "bitch" whom he has helped to get published has returned his kindness by calling him "yellow," and P.O.M. consoles him by insisting that the bitch is just "malicious." Hemingway seems to have forgotten that he began the row. It is a good thing for his reputation that nobody read *Torrents of Spring*.

The collection of short stories, *Men Without Women,* published in 1927, was widely read, and deserved to be, for it contains at least four capital narratives. "The Undefeated" and "Fifty Grand" are very much alike in plot, the former dealing with a particularly inept bullfighter, just out of the hospital, who receives a cogida in the lung in the "nocturnal", and the latter with a prize fighter who cashes in when he comes to the end of the trail. Both men exhibit the courage that is folly, and, because it is folly, very little written about. "The Killers" is an excellent short story because the author manages to maintain the threat of action without ever supplying it, yet at the same time not disappointing his reader. The best story in the book, however, is "Hills Like White Elephants," in which a man persuades a girl to have an abortion not for her sake, but for his own. His monstrous selfishness is so subtly buried by the author that the reader may be no more aware of it than the girl. The tale is ostensibly about a quarrel between the pair at a junction while they wait for the Barcelona express, a difference apparently induced by the heat so that they disagree about the appearance of the hills and the taste of the liquor, then as violently agree about everything. From a psychological point of view, the piece is wholly admirable: not a speech is made that has not its justification as the man and girl fence, avoiding the thing uppermost in their minds, both afraid, but with different kinds of fear. The other stories in the volume merely pad it out to give it book length. "A Canary for One," for example, is as apt an illustration as one could wish for, to show what Hemingway cannot do. It is a tale of an American couple bound back to Paris to set up separate residences who have to listen to a more elderly American lady expatiate on the virtues of their countrymen as husbands and wives. The tale is flatter than the country through which the train passes, because Hemingway has not made his elderly lady convincing. Dowdiness cannot be conveyed by his method, and speech which does not crackle he cannot reproduce. O, if the lady could have been profane!

Hemingway's second novel was awaited with extraordinary interest, and when the Boston police forbade the sale of the May, 1929, *Scribner's*, containing the first instalment of *A Farewell to Arms,* they aroused something like national resentment. As the story unfolded in succeeding issues of the magazine, it became apparent that it was the best piece of objective reporting, *Plumes* and *Three Soldiers* not excepted, that had appeared on the War up to that time by an American. It tells how Frederick Henry, an American lieutenant in an Italian ambulance unit, met Catherine Barkley, an English nurse, in Gorizia, and had desired her merely because "this was better than going every evening to the house for officers where the girls climbed all over you and put your cap on backwards as a sign of affection between their trips upstairs." Catherine, whose fiancé had been killed on the Somme, yielded after first rebuffing him. A few days later Henry was severely wounded and sent to a hospital in Milan where again he encountered Catherine, but this time realized that he was in love with her and offered to marry her. She refused his offer because she realized that marriage would separate them. Only when he was ordered back to his post in October, did she tell him that she was going to have a baby. She still refused to marry him, but he resolved to return to her as soon as he could. At the front Lieutenant Henry was caught in the Caporetto retreat and was forced to abandon his ambulances in the mud. Arrested at the long wooden bridge over the Tagliamento by the Italian military police and threatened with immediate execution, he escaped by jumping into the flooded river. With difficulty he made his way to Milan and then followed Catherine to Stresa where he found her. Warned that they will be arrested as deserters, they cross the Swiss frontier at night. They passed together an idyllic winter in the Alps, moved to Lausanne for

Catherine's lying-in, and parted there for ever when she died in childbirth.

There is no denying that parts of *A Farewell to Arms* are as great writing as Hemingway has done or ever will do, for they can hardly be surpassed. His description of the retreat of the Italian army after the Austrians had broken through at Caporetto challenges comparison with Stendhal's narrative of the retreat from Waterloo, and his study of how sensual appetite may grow into love is as carefully documented a record of the course of passion as any in the modern novel. The speech is more natural than a stenographic account; trite endearments, like "darling," miraculously give no offense. Yet *A Farewell to Arms* on certain points is not the perfect piece of workmanship that *The Sun Also Rises* is. The death of Catherine can better be justified on sadistic than aesthetic grounds. The author put his own need ahead of his reader's. Then, too, the character drawing is much more successful in *The Sun Also Rises*. Lieutenant Henry and Catherine Barkley typify any young man and woman caught in the World cataclysm—it should be noted in particular that Henry is a type character ("the War was a lieutenant's War") just as Henry Flemming (the private) is a type character in Crane's *The Red Badge of Courage*. Cohn, Jake Barnes, and Brett are individuals whom no catastrophe could obscure. Finally, the effect of the book is hardly unified, and certainly not what Hemingway wished. Indeed, while aiming at quite the opposite, Hemingway has glorified war; if one could be sure of winning a Catherine Barkley, even for a short time, war would have less terror than it does. In the last analysis, *A Farewell to Arms* is romantic and not altogether convincing.

The concealed sentimentalist of *A Farewell to Arms* is smoked out in *Death in the Afternoon* (1932). The effort that Hemingway makes in this book to exalt into an art the killing of an harassed and utterly fatigued animal is patently absurd. It has nothing in common with tragedy, as he insists it has. Nor is it even on the level with cock-fighting where at least the contestants are fairly matched. On the other hand, it is a spectacle which appeals to latent emotions in most men, but they are degrading, rather than elevating, emotions. If Hemingway were honest about the appeal of the spectacle, his book would be admirable, for it conveys to the reader sensations that he can get only if he will hang over the barrera and forget that he is civilized. Pretense spoils the writing, which is excellent. Unusually chary of figures of speech, Hemingway scatters a handful through *Death in the Afternoon* that are unforgettable—Villata, "awkward looking as a praying mantis," and Gintanillo, so badly wounded by a horn that the sciatic nerve had been pulled out "by the root as a worm may be pulled out of the damp lawn by a robin." Singularly, the best parts of the book—the conversations between the author and the Old Lady—have no necessary connection with bull-fighting. These are vastly amusing:

[Hemingway has just described his own efforts as an amateur bull-fighter.]

Old lady. Then I may take it you have abandoned the bull ring even as an amateur?

Madame, no decision is irrevocable, but as age comes on I feel I must devote myself more and more to the practice of letters. My operatives tell me that through the fine work of Mr. William Faulkner publishers now will publish anything rather than try to get you to delete the better portions of your works, and I look forward to writing of those days of my youth which were spent in the finest whorehouses in the land amid the most brilliant society there found. I had been saving this background to write of in my old age when with the aid of distance I could examine it most clearly.

Old lady. Has this Mr. Faulkner written well of these places?

Splendidly, Madame. Mr. Faulkner writes admirably of them. He writes the best of them of any writer I have read for many years.

Old lady. I must buy his works.

Madame, you can't go wrong on Faulkner. He's prolific, too. By the time you get them ordered there'll be new ones out.

Old lady. If they are as you say there cannot be too many.

Madame, you voice my own opinion.

Hemingway did not keep his promise, made in jest to the Old Lady, to devote himself more to the practice of letters. He went big-game hunting in Africa, then deep-sea trolling off Florida and Cuba, where he caught the largest marlin on record. He even got himself elected Vice-president of the Salt Water Anglers of America and had a species of rosefish named after him. Late in

1936 he became interested in the Loyalist cause in the Spanish revolution, gave money for the equipment of ambulances, and with Dos Passos and MacLeish formed Contemporary Historians, Inc., for filming *The Spanish Earth,* a motion picture which should give the Loyalist version of the origins of the civil war. Hemingway accompanied the photographer and director of the picture to the front before Madrid, helped to write the story, translated the Spanish dialogues, and was the speaking expositor between sequences in the picture. After addressing the Second National Congress of American Writers in New York in June, 1937, Hemingway returned to Spain as correspondent for the North American Newspaper Alliance, and remained there until the Loyalist cause was lost. Sporadic and uneven writing came out of these busy years, but writing which, if it had not the finish of Hemingway's earlier work, slowly gathered force and significance. A collection of short stories, entitled *Winner Take Nothing* (1933), heading the list, shows no advance in Hemingway's art nor radical shift in his subject matter. Label the book a grisly calendar of ills or "typical Hemingway," and it is sufficiently characterized. *The Green Hills of Africa* (1935) is Stewart Edward White's *Simla* done over again, but with the attention more especially fixed on the hunters than upon the hunted. Particularly well studied are the comradery of the camp and the jealousy of one sportsman for another. Yet the effect of the whole is rather slight. The reviewer who summed up the book by remarking that it is an account of how Hemingway thought he had bagged a rhino but it turned out to be Gertrude Stein can hardly be blamed for his innuendo. Still if the caustic remarks on other writers have no intrinsic merit (and it is not our contention they have none), Hemingway's insistence that New York spoils writers and fresh impetus can be got only from new and raw environments is worth noting, at least, as marking a particular stage in his development. It is only by a backward glance that we recognize it to have been the end also of an era.

The publication of *To Have and Have Not* in 1937 really reopened the issue of whether or not Hemingway was capable of further development as a writer and thinker. Although this is the most carelessly constructed of his novels, being in fact nothing more than three short stories with the third interminably pieced out to give proper bulk to the book, *To Have and Have Not* cannot be regarded as less important than *A Farewell to Arms* for an understanding of the author. It is a novel with moral and social implications which Hemingway believes that every American should understand. The hero, Harry Morgan, belongs technically to the *petite bourgeoisie,* those little fellows of the middle class who, according to Marx, in a time of economic crisis are pushed down to swell the ranks of the revolutionary proletariat. Less technically, he is anything but a little fellow—a great broad-shouldered, quick-thinking man, owner of a power boat which he rents to the tourist-fishermen of Key West at thirty-five dollars a day. A former soldier and policeman, he is proud of his independence, his home, his wife Marie, and his two daughters, though he would have preferred the latter to be boys. In fact, he is more American than the national anthem.

In the first act of his drama he is badly trimmed by a Mr. Johnson whom he has trusted for three weeks while trolling for black marlin off Havana. Johnson, an inept fisherman, loses Morgan's $360 reel, rod, and line, and then deciding that he wants no more fishing, flies secretly from Havana to the mainland, and out of the story, with his bill unpaid. Morgan, stuck in Cuba, agrees to run a dozen Chinamen into the United States at one hundred dollars a head. Having loaded his Chinamen and pocketed his money, Morgan strangles the agent, Mr. Sing, then unloads the hapless yellow men in a Cuban cove a few miles from Havana and heads for home, untroubled by any reflection that his ethics are no better than those of Mr. Johnson, his non-paying customer. Mr. Sing, he notes, "certainly wasn't much of a business man. . . ."

Twelve hundred dollars in a depression do not last very long, and in his second act Harry Morgan is reduced to rum-running with his boat. The audience (which perhaps spent too much time between acts drinking at the bar on the mezzanine) sees only the end of this act, when Harry, shot through one arm, tries in vain to dump his cargo in shallow water with the hope of retrieving it later. A wealthy snooper, however, reports its location to the Coast Guard and both boat and cargo are confiscated. But this is not Morgan's greatest misfortune, for the doctors are unable to save his arm.

The third act follows fast. Harry Morgan, in desperate straits, but still confident in his ability to win out, is persuaded by "Bee-lips" Simmons, a shady lawyer, to run three Cuban "revolutionaries" across to the island. The particular irony of this venture is that Morgan, at the outset of the story, had refused to carry other fugitive revolutionaries from Cuba to the States and had seen them machine-gunned. When he and his helper, Albert, are at the rendezvous in a hired boat, the revolutionaries prove to be bank-robbers and gunmen. "Bee-lips" and Albert are slain, and as they head to sea Morgan realizes that his passengers will dispose of him as soon as is convenient. He manoeuvres skillfully to throw the Cubans off guard and to obtain a machine gun which he has concealed for just such an emergency. When Harry Morgan rises from beside his engines with his gun spitting bullets, Hemingway means that we should see him as an heritor of a fighting past, the representative of Anglo-Saxon pluck and American resourcefulness. Of course he gets his men, but unfortunately one of them, whom the initial burst of his machine gun had merely wounded, shoots him in the belly first. Because the gunfire has punctured the gasoline tanks, Morgan has to cut off his motors and drift until picked up by the Coast Guard. Still alive, though he has lain in the tropical sun for hours, bleeding internally, he is rushed to Key West to die on an operating table. The only intelligible thing he says after being found is to the effect that "one man alone ain't got no . . . chance." "It had taken him a long time to get it out," comments Hemingway, "and it had taken him all of his life to learn it."

Collectivist, then, in intent, *To Have and Have Not* was nevertheless unsatisfactory to the Marxists. They did not object to the "candid camera" studies of the rich degenerates of the art and yachting colony at Key West which Hemingway ineptly thrust into the story with some ill-conceived notion of maintaining suspense while the Coast Guard ship is towing Morgan's boat to port. Nor did they object to the portrait of Mr. Johnson. But what troubled them chiefly was Harry Morgan. Now in all truth Harry Morgan is an admirable fellow—good in a boat, good in a bed, good in a fix, with no other ambition than to sustain his family and to hold his head up among his fellows. A little ruthless, perhaps, with the morals of Henry Morgan the pirate, or of Joseph Stalin, who is reputed to have been a robber before he became a dictator. Harry never discovers much "social consciousness"; in fact, about all that is beaten into his head at the end of the tale is that, given his circumstances, a man alone is licked before he starts. His reasons then for collective action are surprisingly selfish; he appears to give less thought to those with whom he might collaborate than he did to Mr. Sing. Joseph Stalin might understand this, but the leftist reviewers around New York were a little shocked. Nor did they like the portrait of "Richard Gordon," romantic egoist and author who has lately adjusted rather facilely to the Party "line" and is writing a novel on the Gastonia strike. Hemingway, they allowed, might be well intentioned, but he was really a bumbler—a sportsman turned Stalinist: they were unprepared either to admit that he was grossly realistic about the Harry Morgan type or that he was boldly evasive in regard to their dogmas.

The Spanish Civil War first had the effect, so it would seem, of pushing Hemingway still further left. Stalinist, apparently, in a heavy, plug-ugly, brutal way is the three-act drama which he placed first in the volume entitled *The Fifth Column and the First Forty-nine Stories* (1938). But the play is also a Richard Harding Davis melodrama, with a Vassar girl (who has to be sacrificed that the hero may better serve the Cause), and a spy plot, and a counter espionage movement, and all of that. It is a kind of International cocktail, to be drunk with the eyes shut, for the most impossible ingredients have been shaken into it and are liable to part company at any moment. Effervescent sentences, however, make their impression on the nostrils and tear ducts: one remembers that the Fascists shell Madrid just when the cinema closes and that an experienced executioner and torturer states it as his considered opinion that priests die best. The forty-nine stories really give the volume a muzzle velocity of two tons, like the guns Hemingway uses to hunt with. The full impact of these tales gathered in one volume is probably greater than that of the work of any other writer of short fiction since disease destroyed the brain of Maupassant. Yet only four of the tales are new. Two are experimental in technique, "The Capital of the World" and "The Snows of Kilimanjaro," and only one touches Spain of the Civil War, "Old Man at the Bridge"—a vignette of a refugee from the Fascist advance towards the Ebro. The four-star tale of the lot, "The Short Happy Life of Francis Macomber," tells how a wealthy but cowardly sportsman, after twice running from danger, discovers his manhood, and how his hitherto contemptuous mate, knowing that he will now throw her over, puts a bullet neatly in his head. Animadversions on the rich in these later tales and the *realpolitik* background of *The Fifth Column* do not quite convince one, however, that Hemingway is a good Communist. Charity, even sterile literary charity, to the Macombers is not in the Party line.

An article in the magazine *Ken* (for April 21, 1938) and the novel *For Whom the Bell Tolls* (1940) clear up much of the ambiguity created by the writing which immediately preceded them. The article, "Dying, Well or Badly," is written to convince Americans that Spain is a democratic country with a republican form of government, and that if Italy can be beaten in Spain, as Napoleon was beaten there, the war threatened by the Berlin-Rome-Tokyo axis may be averted. Hemingway is not a Communist; he is an anti-Fascist.

So, too, is Robert Jordan, hero of the great novel *For Whom the Bell Tolls*. Jordan, grandson of a Civil War officer and an Instructor in Spanish at the University of Montana, becomes a dynamiter for the Loyalist side in the Spanish Civil War, not merely because a leave of absence for study put him in that country during the hostilities and his experience as a road builder while going through college qualified him for the job, but because he is convinced that the Spanish affair is a prelude to a Fascist assault upon democracy everywhere. His death, symbolic of the Loyalist defeat, is not the accidental demise of an adventurer, then, but an event of consequence to every free man. In prefixing to his novel a magnificent sentence from Dr. John Donne, Hemingway insures the book against any misinterpretation on this score: "No man is an *Iland,* intire of it selfe; every man is a peece of the *Continent,* a part of the *maine;* if a *clod* bee washed away by the *Sea, Europe* is the lesse, as well as if a *Promontorie* were, as well as if a *Mannor* of thy *friends* or of *thine owne* were; any mans *death* diminishes *me,* because I am involved in *Mankinde; And* therefore never send to know for whom the *bell* tolls; It tolls for *thee."* Americans may not lightly dismiss the death of Robert Jordan, nor the overthrow of the Spanish Republic: by so many degrees American democracy is itself weaker and every free man's liberty so much less.

Yet there is no "pressing" (in the sense that athletes understand) of this theme in the book; Hemingway means that the reader should infer it as naturally as one intuits that an opponent is not "on" his game. Perhaps if the times were not these times and one were not anxious about so many things that the novel touches almost casually, one might assume that the theme of *For Whom the Bell Tolls* is that a man may live as much in seventy hours as he does in seventy years. And a passably good case could be made for this assumption. Robert Jordan, assigned to destroy the only bridge behind the Fascist lines to thwart the bringing up of reinforcements when General Golz hurls a surprise attack upon the enemy's front, has, in the three days he is with the guerilla band which is supposed to aid him, varied adventures enough to satisfy any normal man's hunger for excitement in a life time. He has to establish himself in a band where the leader is opposed to his enterprise, he has to "call" a cold-blooded murderer who has every reason to kill him, he has to wangle for his life and his mission with every faculty at his command. Jordan has but one cohort to begin with, old Anselmo, who guided him through the lines and helped him pack in his explosives and tools: Anselmo, however, is as staunch a friend as ever a man had—in the end, he is killed by a flying girder while helping the young American blow the bridge. Next, Robert Jordan converts to his cause the woman Pilar, mistress of the guerilla leader and a prodigious ally. This Pilar, indeed, though she is obscene as only a poet or prophet may be, is as grand a character as Hemingway has ever drawn, a truly great heart and spirit. Her allegiance brings others over to Robert Jordan—Primitivo the taciturn, Fernando the curious, Agustin the fiery, Sordo the courageous, and many more. But the best thing that Pilar does for him is to send to his bed Maria, a beautiful girl who had been raped by the Falangists when they had killed her father, the Socialist mayor of a little town—a girl whom Pilar had protected and nursed back to sanity since she had joined them following the dynamiting of a Fascist train. Pilar sees that the hard yet romantic young man is worthy and she knows the healing power which love will have for Maria; her reward, mixed with the gall and wormwood of her realization that if she were not forty-eight she herself might contest for the affection of Roberto, is that the affair of her making is a transcendent success. The analysis of Pilar, Maria, and Jordan in terms of their special relationship (in terms of the Steinian type psychology of love) is one of the most difficult problems that the novelist could set himself, and though he solves it admirably, his solution creates another problem—that of unifying their relationship with the tale. His failure to raise Maria into a clearly-recognized symbol for Spain itself, cruelly wronged and twice defeated, is the only failure in the novel. But this itself is a consequence of his method, for he elected, as he had done with Brett Ashley, to give us Maria by indirection. The reader has to infer all that she symbolizes.

The only convert not made to Jordan's cause is the tough and wily Pablo, demoralized leader of the guerillas, who, after nearly wrecking everything, returns in the last moment to aid in the destruction of the bridge and the elimination of its guards—still independent and hostile, but unable to be "alone". Dangerous from the outset, to Robert Jordan's way of thinking, and smelling of death to Pilar's occult nostrils, the blowing of the bridge brings disaster—most of the guerilla band is slain in the fighting at the bridge heads, and when the survivors attempt to make off, Jordan's horse, hit by a light shell, rolls upon him, mashing a leg. While Pablo and Pilar carry off the resisting Maria, Robert Jordan prepares, amid surges of pain, his sub-machine gun for a reception of the pursuing Fascist cavalry and his own permanent departure.

A great love story and a greater adventure story, *For Whom the Bell Tolls* adds immeasurably to the stature of its author. Admittedly a great narrator, Hemingway had no more laurels to win as such; all that he could now achieve was to show himself a more resonant personality than the metallic creator of Brett Ashley and a greater humanitarian than the ringside spectator at bull fights and boxing matches of his early books. This he has now done, and his fame is secure for a long time.

When Ernest Hemingway satirized William Faulkner's literary fertility, he may have been animated by jealousy, yet he indicated fairly Faulkner's greatest fault—he has been altogether too prolific. Eighteen books have fallen from his pen in sixteen years; count them: *The Marble Faun* (1924), *Soldier's Pay* (1926), *Mosquitoes* (1927), *Sartoris* (1929), *The Sound and the Fury* (1929), *As I Lay Dying* (1930), *Sanctuary* (1931), *These Thirteen* (1931), *Idyll in the Desert* (1931), *Salmagundi* (1932), *Light in August* (1932), *Doctor Martino and Other Stories* (1933), *A Green Bough* (1933), *Pylon* (1935), *Absalom, Absalom!* (1936), *The Unvanquished* (1938), *The Wild Palms* (1939), and *The Hamlet* (1940). This array contains some of the most fascinating experimentation in this country; yet it cannot be said to contain any masterly creation. It is work which promised more than any other, but work which has never fulfilled the very high expectations it first aroused. If Faulkner never succeeds in this regard, it will be one of the veritable tragedies of our time, for he has in his veins the regal blood, not merely of an F.F.M., but also of genius.

William Falkner (later, Faulkner) was born in New Albany, Mississippi, on September 25, 1897, but has spent most of his life in the college town of Oxford, where he was educated at the University of Mississippi. In 1918 he joined the Canadian Flying Corps, was sent to the Western Front, and suffered injury when his plane crashed. After the armistice he returned to Oxford, worked as a painter and carpenter, again went off to Europe for a tramping trip, and then spent a year in New Orleans, living and quarreling with Sherwood Anderson in an apartment on St. Peter Street in the Vieux Carré, while he worked at his first novel, *Soldier's Pay*. Since then he has taken what appears to be permanent residence in Oxford with his wife and two step-children. It is interesting to note that, as his material fortunes have improved, Faulkner has more consciously adopted the attitudes of the gentry among whom he has settled.

Faulkner's first book, *Soldier's Pay,* is undeniably one of his best though it is also one of his most conventional novels. It depicts the return of Lieutenant Mahon from the War to his father, an Episcopalian rector in the deep South. Mahon has crashed with his plane and is much the worse for it—face gone, mind emptied of reality, he lapses through oblivion into death in the course of the story. It is this creature of fragmentary body and dreams that Private Gilligan and Mrs. Powers, the latter widowed by the War, take compassion on and gouvernance over when they find him on a train in the care of a porter. For a time they are attended by a cadet of the Air Service, Julian Lowe, who fancies that he has made a conquest of Mrs. Powers; she, however, manages to pack him off to his mother and ultimate marriage in California. In Georgia, Dr. Mahon welcomes all three and insists that Mrs. Powers and Gilligan remain awhile with him. Donald Mahon's fiancée, Cecily Saunders, vacillates between horror of him and her selfish desire to martyr herself to him. To save him from Cecily, Mrs. Powers marries him, and Cecily gives herself to George Farr, a weak fellow with whom she has been playing. About this tangle of human passions cavorts Januarius Jones, a satyr who has absolute faith in his technique to seduce a woman, but through the caprice of fate fails with Cecily, and through unequal wit fails with Mrs. Saunders, yet succeeds with Emmy of the kitchen, a poor girl who had yielded to Lieutenant Mahon before the War. After the death of young Mahon, Mrs. Powers takes her departure, refusing regretfully marriage with sterling Joe Gilligan on the ground that, having twice failed as a wife, she is destined to make no man happy.

Soldier's Pay is very ingeniously constructed—so artfully that its pattern seems wholly artless and the many incidents but casually related to each other. The wantonness of fate is precisely what Faulkner has tried to suggest, but it is an inadvertent rather than a deliberate wantonness—not the planned caprice of Hardy but the undesigned malice of Conrad is what he has aimed at. From Conrad he has adopted, too, the rather simple device of a broken plot pattern and the trick of beginning with a seemingly unimportant incident. The influence of the Anglo-Polish novelist can be seen in the structure of many of Faulkner's novels. *Soldier's Pay* shows the further influence of F. Scott Fitzgerald on both style and incident (note especially that scene at the dance where Mr. Dough and Mr. Rivers vie for the favors of Miss Cecily Saunders, so reminiscent of "The Jelly Bean") and of Sherwood Anderson, particularly at the end where the rector and Joe Gilligan listen to a negro religious service. Despite the author's obvious debts—and even Mallarmé must not be forgotten—*Soldier's Pay* is a good book, though beneath *The Sun Also Rises* as a study of the after-War spirit.

Mosquitoes is, in a sense, a more imitative book than *Soldier's Pay*. Faulkner's model here seems to be Aldous Huxley, but Faulkner fails where Huxley sometimes succeeds, largely because he hasn't the latter's ability to portray intellectuals—even bored and drunken intellectuals. The novel revolves around a yachting party planned by a lady who is a patroness of the arts in New Orleans. The whole purpose of the novelist is to show the ennui of talented and sensitive people who are forced to accept not only the gifts but even the company selected by their benefactress—a theme first developed by Norman Douglas, but handled most effectively by Mr. Huxley. Faulkner's Mrs. Maurier lacks distinction in dullness, is merely agitated flesh rather than a great piece of caricature, and his Fairchild, Talliaferro, Mark Frost—supposedly the *intelligentsia* of New Orleans—outdistance her in dullness. From the standpoint of the reader the life of the party is Mrs. Maurier's brainless niece who has a really exciting adventure on a swamp road with a modest sailorman bent on protecting her from mosquitoes that are less considerate of her flesh than he. The presence of a thug and his gal, invited by the niece, fails to add much to the interest.

Sartoris, published in 1929, and dedicated to Sherwood Anderson, is the weakest of all Faulkner's novels, yet it is perhaps the most revealing. Pure romance, it glorifies the recklessness, the hare-brained valor of Bayard Sartoris—the last of a long line of Mississippi Sartorises—who, home from the War, tries to kill himself by driving a high-powered car off a bridge, and, failing at that, succeeds with an airplane which drops off its wings when banked too abruptly in the sky. Mr. Faulkner applauds everything that Bayard Sartoris stands for. He detects in his wanton self-destruction all the glory and chivalry of the South. To enforce the theme, there are frequent allusions to an earlier Bayard Sartoris who served under Jeb Stuart in the Civil War. And in order that this conception of manly conduct may not perish from the earth Bayard Sartoris has been permitted by the author to leave his seed in a wench by the name of Narcissa—so we discover in the last pages of the narrative. *Sartoris* is a peculiarly witless story about an especially witless hero, yet it reveals the essential sentimentalism of the author. More "Southern" here than Stark Young, Faulkner fears that the game is about played out, for God is losing his interest in these figures of His special creation:

> The music went on in the dusk softly; the dusk was peopled with ghosts of glamorous and old disastrous things. And if they were just glamorous enough, there was sure to be a Sartoris in them, and then they were sure to be disastrous. Pawns. But the Player and the game He plays. . . . He must have a name for His pawns, though. But perhaps Sartoris is the game itself—a game outmoded and played with pawns shaped too late and to an old dead pattern, and of which the Player Himself is a little wearied. For there is death in the sound of it, and a glamorous fatality, like silver pennons downrushing at sunset, or a dying fall of horns along the road to Roncevaux.

Faulkner was not completely betrayed into this kind of weakness again until he wrote *The Unvanquished*. It is latent in him, however, and some of his Primitivistic excesses may be best accounted for, possibly, by the resistance which he has always had to offer to it.

The Sound and the Fury, issued in the same year as *Sartoris*, is one of the few really important experimental works of fiction done in America. Inspired by Joyce, Faulkner has adopted the stream of consciousness technique in telling this story, but has made his own contribution with a unique time pattern and by selecting the mind of a thirty-three year old idiot for the first bed of his turbulent, disorderly stream. Then the current passes with a rush through the mind of a prospective suicide at Harvard and next is forced through the mean sieve of the cortex of a small-store clerk. Well aware that Benjy Compson's mind is full of snags and rips for the average reader, and that his successors' thought streams present difficulties, Faulkner has tried to clarify his story by producing, in the last section of the book, the events of "April Eighth 1928" from an objective point of view. The device reminds one of Henry James' use of Colonel and Mrs. Assingham as "reverberators", or commentators on the action, in *The Golden Bowl,* yet it is by no means so successful a device—Faulkner succeeds in making his theme clearer, but not the action of his story, which still must be dredged out of those earlier streams of consciousness.

The theme of the story is the decay of the Compson family, a genteel Mississippi family—just the sort of theme one would expect Faulkner to turn to after *Sartoris.* This is illustrated by the life of Quentin Compson, whose mind is exposed to us on "June Second 1910" (second section of the book) before he commits suicide in Cambridge, Massachusetts, where he is attending Harvard College. The reasons for his suicide may be gathered from his reflections which too frequently revert to his sister, Caddy, and the predicament she finds herself in. It is only when we listen years later to Quentin's brother Jason (who has become the sole support of the family) lamenting his inability to control the young girl, Quentin, and only when we have the reported flight of this girl, on the night of April 7, 1928, with a showman that we thoroughly understand the reasons for the decline of the Compson family—and it is only then that we appreciate why Benjy's mind has dwelt on *two* Quentins and understand his references to Candace, the Caddy of the story and mother of Quentin, the runaway girl. Far from being

> a tale
> Told by an idiot, full of sound and fury,
> Signifying nothing,

Faulkner's novel is the boldest planned study of incest and family degeneracy in American letters. Nor is there anything quite the equal of this tale for technical finesse. Always adroit in opening his narratives, Faulkner has excelled himself here. Benjy, the idiot, and his little colored body-guard, Luster, are hunting golf balls along what was once the Compson pasture fence when a remark addressed by a golfer to his caddie sets off a train of thought in the mind of the idiot, related first to Caddy, his sister, and then to scattered episodes in thirty years of Compson family history. Extraordinary ingenuity is exercised so that these episodes should recur in the mind of Benjy by no more than what would appear to be the most casual association.

Equally to be praised is the insertion of that little episode of Quentin Compson's last day in which a small stray girl attaches herself to him with the result that he is falsely accused of designs upon her. And certainly the way in which the author plays off the degenerate, helpless whites against the capable, unchanging negroes is one of the triumphs of the story. Yet the novel itself is a failure, despite the great skill which has been used in making it, for the simple reason that it is nobody's tragedy. If the central figure is Quentin the man, too much emphasis has been put on Quentin the daughter; if the story is hers, he figures altogether too largely in it—the author has exercised altogether too much ingenuity in revealing the incest without showing its effect on the girl. Further, though the author intends Quentin the man to suffer the tortures of the damned his last day on earth (and certainly he is plagued by conscience quantitatively as much as are the Macbeths), he lacks the textual fineness to be a tragic character. He is a sensitive soul only to the author—not as he is presented to us. So far as one can discover he hasn't a single intellectual interest; and while this deficiency may be typical of the Harvard undergraduate, it doesn't make a tragic figure. As for Quentin the girl, though she is more sinned against than sinning, it is pure sentimentality to attach much significance to her career. Supercharged emotionally, *The Sound and the Fury* is nevertheless all wrong emotionally. The Compsons are so lacking in intrinsic worth that we do not really care what happens to them.

Jason Compson, who must represent the mean average in the family, is Faulkner's best-drawn character and perhaps the best villain in American fiction. A bully and a coward, he whines about his sacrifices to his mother while he is pursuing one of the most selfish courses imaginable. Thought for him is a long process of self-commiseration. Virtuous to ostentation, he has one of the foulest minds in literature. The several pages following his profound reflection, "Once a bitch always a bitch, what I say," contain some of the best narrative writing done in America, even though they suggest the need of a purgative afterwards. Largely in reported dialogue, they reveal such a sure mastery of the rhythms of parried speech as to make one wish that their author would attempt the drama. Any critic who ignores this section of *The Sound and the Fury* is hardly entitled to pass judgment on the creative abilities of William Faulkner.

Most happily conceived, Faulkner's next book, *As I Lay Dying* (1930), is but poorly executed. In it there are signs of haste and of fatigue. ("I wrote *As I Lay Dying* in six weeks, without changing a word.") By brief episodes and a shifting point of view Faulkner tells of the death of Addie Bundren and the efforts of her family to take her body to Jefferson for burial. Their chief impediment is the flooding river, but second only to that is their own stupidity, for the author has chosen for this book a less sensational but more decadent family than the Compsons. Anse Bundren, sire of the family, is, in the fixity of his purpose to give his wife the burial he had promised her, the prototype of the simple elders of Caldwell's stories, and *As I Lay Dying* has suggested much to the latter writer. Caldwell, it will be seen, has done better with Faulkner's material than Faulkner himself. Vardaman, the idiot son, and Dewey Dell, the pregnant daughter, are characters either novelist could have drawn. Cash, the earnest carpenter, whose thoughts even occur to him in numerical order, is the most original creation in the book, but, like the others, he is more of a caricature than a man. The least satisfactory study is that of Darl whose thoughts run in peculiarly poetic periods. Faulkner has waded into Joyce beyond his depth with the result that this son of a Mississippi poor white thinks like a student of Bergson:

The river itself is not a hundred yards across, and pa and Vernon and Vardaman and Dewey Dell are the only things in sight not of that single monotony of desolation leaning with that terrific quality a little from right to left, as though we had reached the place where the motion of the wasted world accelerates just before the final precipice. Yet they appear dwarfed.

It is as though the space between us were time: an irrevocable quality. It is as though time, no longer running straight before us in a diminishing line, now runs parallel between us like a looping string, the distance being the doubling accretion of the thread and not the interval between. . . .

Sanctuary (1931) gave Faulkner an unholy reputation, but from his point of view it is not an insincere book. He may assert as boldly as he chooses that he wrote it to make money—all books in a sense are written with that in view,—but his true purpose was social satire. Thoroughly convinced of the decadent state of the South and as indignant as a Southerner could be about it, with some of the hot fury of a Randolph, Faulkner hit out against the hypocrisy and pretense which keeps the South from being self-critical. Only a man who loved his section too much could have written such a book. It is an attack upon a gentry who endorse prohibition because the nigger can't be trusted to drink, and thus license the bootlegger and gangster; a gentry who still conceive all women as languishing dependents to be defended even unto death, and who are convinced that the youth of Virginia are still the flower of chivalry. Only incidentally does it reveal the gunman as a degenerate and lynch law as a very dubious sort of justice. If the good people of Mississippi and Tennessee did any reading, or understood what they read, Mr. Faulkner himself would long ago have been martyred and perhaps immortalized.

Sanctuary relates how Temple Drake, a typical college "teaser," steals away from her university dormitory for a party with a callow youth from the University of Virginia, named Gowan Stevens. Both pride themselves on being hard and bad and, above everything else, sophisticated. Running out of liquor after he has already had too much, Gowan Stevens insists on visiting a lonely country bootlegger's. He wrecks his car and is stranded at the bootlegger's with the girl. Stevens thereupon gets insensibly drunk, and Temple Drake, terrified but unable to escape, passes through a night of horrors. The next day young Gowan comes to, is frightened himself, and without scruple deserts her. By that time, Popeye, a gunman at the bootlegger's, has decided he is going to have Temple at any cost, and he shoots one of the gang to get her. After a peculiarly revolting attack upon her, Popeye carries Temple off to a dive in Memphis. When the murder is discovered, Lee Goodwin, the head boot-legger who had taken some pains to protect Temple Drake, is arrested for the crime. His defense is undertaken by an honest but ineffectual lawyer, Horace Benbow (a minor character in *Sartoris*), who, having learned about Temple and valuing her as a witness to the murder, eventually traces her to the Memphis dive, where she has already been metamorphosed into an un-seeing, unthinking thing. When Benbow attempts to use her as a witness, she perjures herself—for an unscrupulous prosecutor has reached her, too, and he has been aided by her new reverence for Popeye. Lee Goodwin is at once convicted, and that night a Southern mob drags him from the jail and burns him alive. Temple's father takes her to Europe, and some months later Popeye is executed for a murder he did not commit.

Sanctuary is too much of a polemic to be a work of art In his desperate earnestness, the author has burlesqued his theme; he has written a five act tragedy with five fifth acts. The charac-ters violently posture and shriek throughout. Melodrama has been equipped with all the modern gadgets, but under the cowling it is still melodrama. Witless and shallow as Temple Drake is, the explanation for her testimony is yet artistically inadequate, particularly the implication that the prosecutor influenced it either one way or the other. Granting that Popeye could not perform the sexual act, granting that he might have induced another to do it for him in order that he might have a degenerate gratification in it, and altogether conceding that he might slay this substitute if he became jealous of him, it is still too much to ask the reader to put any credence in the resulting scene— a funeral that turns into a roughhouse in which the coffin is upset, the corpse tumbled out on the floor, and the painted wax plug in the small blue hole in the center of his forehead is jarred out and lost. This isn't horrifying—it is downright funny. *Sanctuary* can be read for amusement as soon as one realizes that it is a tract, and not a camera study. The most hilarious episode in the story deals with lascivious Senator Snopes, of the state legisla-ture, who, having come to Memphis to slake his sexual appetite, takes lodgings in a whorehouse without being aware of its character. This is cut from the same cloth as other incidents in the story. Faulkner's violent contempt for the average Southern legislator, the Huey Long supporter, has inspired it—but it is funny.

The evidence seems to indicate that Faulkner burned up a prodigious amount of creative energy on *The Sound and the Fury*, *As I Lay Dying*, and *Sanctuary*. Nothing of equal importance came from his pen until nearly a decade had flown, when *The Hamlet* was published. *Light in August*, issued in 1932, a year after *Sanctuary*, is Faulkner's longest novel, but it is not his most impressive. In it he tries to handle two stories: the search of Lena Grove for the father of her baby and the efforts of Joe Christmas, who believes himself a mulatto, to get himself lynched. Both stories had great possibilities, but haste has prevented the author from realizing upon them. Lena Grove, who, near the end of her pregnancy, serenely sets out to walk into Alabama to find her lover, with never a doubt as to her ability to overtake him, is, despite her simplicity, a noble figure, unlike any other in Faulkner's fiction. Had he been willing to tell only her story, to fasten his whole attention upon it, to develop more fully the character of Lucas Burch whom she seeks, and of Byron Bunch whom she finds through misdirection, *Light in August* might be a far more lasting piece of fiction than it is. Faulkner has the ability and even the bawdy humor to write a great picaresque story—and here was the stuff for it, a serio-comic situation of epic possibilities—but the author is so convinced that simplicity of structure and of incident has no merit in fiction that it is doubtful if he will ever do the great work of which he is capable. Joe Christmas' story, on the other hand, is so complex that violent incident alone will not do to set it forth. Faulkner realizes well enough that neither the reader nor Christmas must ever know certainly what his blood is—the handling is admirable in this regard, but Faulkner has not thought it important to build up carefully the slow growth of Christmas' hatred for the whites, which led him to the murder of Miss Burden. The few episodes he chooses to illustrate this are not convincing. In fact, the introduction of the grandfather who has always hated the bastard and hopes for the end which comes to him, defeats this very purpose, for it adds an aggravation which is not universal. The account of the final pursuit, mutilation, and death of Joe, however, is well handled. Nowhere else in fiction is so faithfully realized mob fury, the hubbub it causes, and the frozen terror of the victim. Yet whatever merits *Light in August* has, are still further obscured by the discontinuity of episode which here approaches the limits of the fantastic. It may be flatly asserted that Faulkner has gained not a single thing from his method of narrative in this tale, while he has lost much. The continuation of the narrative after Christmas' death, chiefly for expository purposes, is decidedly anti-climactic in effect.

Pylon, a product of the rushing presses in 1935, ought to have been a great book, for it touches material essentially fascinating which Faulkner is supposed to know well. It depicts the adventures and death of Roger Shumann, circus-flier, who, with his wife Laverne and his child, his mechanic Jiggs, and a parachute jumper, is the chief attraction for the reader at the air meet at Feinman Airport, during the Mardi Gras. To these five people and their destinies attaches himself a fantastic character by the name of Prufrock, a reporter whose admiration for the fliers in the end is hard to distinguish from his love for Laverne. He buys them drinks and food, pilots them about the city, and takes their abuse for praise. They are a hard lot: Laverne lies with Shumann and the jumper in turn, with the result that she does not know who is the father of her prospective child. When a group of newsmen comment unfavorably upon the relations of these three after Shumann's death, Faulkner promptly labels them scavengers, but it is an epithet which the general public has already applied elsewhere with about as much justification. Faulkner is not interested in these people because of their profession: they hardly get in the air at all, but flop around in bed or on the ground in alcoholic vomit. It is a cheap book.

In *Absalom, Absalom!* (1936) Faulkner gives a Southern recipe for avoiding incest, which is to set one of your sons to shoot his half-brother when the latter becomes engaged to his sister. For the man who has read all of Faulkner, or who reads this book in connection with *The Sound and the Fury, Absalom, Absalom!* has a dramatic import that is no part of the story itself,

for the events of the narrative are strained through the consciousness of Quentin Compson, a Harvard student in 1910,
who, shortly after this, is to commit suicide because he, too, has
been involved in incest with his sister. Quentin receives the story
through Rosa Coldfield, one of the actors, picks up details from
his father and grandfather, witnesses one final episode, and pieces
together the rest in a five-hour discussion with his roommate.
His own connection with the story at so critical a juncture in his
life is highly improbable and has the effect of weakening both
novels. That is, the suicide of Quentin in *The Sound and the
Fury* was explicable enough, but now with this added commentary seems extraordinarily dubious. Possessor of this staggering
tale and of the guilty knowledge of his own crime, Quentin
more probably would have laughed both off as a man who has
taken an overdose throws off poison. Some lack of artistic sensibility has permitted Faulkner to attach the monstrous cancerous
growth of *Absalom, Absalom!* on to his most artistic novel.
The relation of the two novels is better forgotten.

Absalom, Absalom! by itself is the story of Thomas Sutpen,
poor mountain white, who conceives the idea of founding a
family. He unfortunately forms a union with the daughter of a
Haitian sugar grower, whose tainted blood is kept a secret from
him. When he buys her off and starts again in Mississippi in
1833, she follows, watches, plans revenge. The engagement of
her son to Sutpen's daughter by his second wife precipitates an
involved series of tragedies, rehearsed and re-rehearsed from
every possible angle. The tedium of the telling in this tale is the
greatest in all of Faulkner's books. Further, there is no relief
of any sort from the snarled twine of his sentences—no humor,
no pathos, no dialogue; the knots of Quentin's "ratiocinations"
(Faulkner's word) simply have to be picked one after another.
It is a dull book, dull, dull, dull. The one moment in it is in the
last paragraph when honest Shreve asks Quentin (as one might
ask Faulkner), "Why do you hate the South?" and he reiterates,
"I don't. I don't! I don't hate it. I don't hate it!"

Faulkner's next book proved that he does not hate that collection of ideas which seems to be the South to most Southerners:
he merely hates the growing collection of facts in his section

which do not match that idea. *The Unvanquished* (1938) is that romance of the Civil War and Reconstruction which one would have predicted from *Sartoris* that William Faulkner must inevitably write. Though five of the seven episodes of the novel appeared originally in that fit repository, the *Saturday Evening Post,* the certainty that this kind of writing would be well rewarded was not the chief motive in its production; a weary author, nurtured on folklore, again surrendered to the pressures of sectionalism and the chivalric tradition. That Faulkner resisted with every instinct of his profession is obvious, but the very chemistry of his blood worked against him. In the end, the artistic conscience merely saved him from focalizing his tale upon a gallant Confederate cavalry officer (a combination of Lochinvar and General Forrest) whose sweetie rode in the saddle beside him, disguised as a man. Such are Colonel John Sartoris and Drusilla of the novel, but half-ashamed of them as creations of his pen, Faulkner tries to concentrate attention on Colonel John's boys, Bayard who is white and Ringo who is fawn-colored, and upon Bayard's Granny. For them he devises some capital adventures—a futile attempt to assassinate a Yankee officer and concealment under Granny's skirts during the ensuing search; an effort to stem the tide of freed black folks rolling towards the "River Jordan" expecting to cross; and best of all, an hilarious adventure in requisitioning mules from the Yankees on a forged order and selling them back again, to rehabilitate with the money those folk whose homes had been burned and whose property had been stolen or destroyed. Yet eventually, after the boys have tracked down and slain the renegade Grumby, who had murdered Granny, Colonel John and Drusilla gallop on the stage and usurp all interest. The neighboring ladies quite needlessly force Colonel John and Drusilla to wed; the pair keep the carpet-baggers from voting in Jefferson, and start, like Faulkner's own grandparents, to rebuild the railroad. Then, as if to demonstrate that he had not been laboring in a Southern candy-kitchen, Faulkner produces a final "unromantic" episode—after Colonel John has been shot by a partner, Bayard, summoned home to avenge him, calmly walks into the partner's office and permits the man to take two purposely wild shots at him. Drusilla leaves a sprig of verbena, however, upon Bayard's pillow to indicate that she doesn't conceive this action of Bayard's unchivalric, even if the reader does. As he smooths the substance of *The Unvanquished* between his tongue and his palate, the average reader is little likely, so it would seem, to detect any sand in the chocolate cream. The romantic Faulkner has scored a touchdown on the realistic Faulkner.

In *The Wild Palms* (1939) Faulkner, pretending misogyny, tries the experiment of running two unrelated stories of equal importance side by side, with results demonstrating that there is a better chance of securing spiritual harmony in a union of the most badly matched man and woman than there is of achieving artistic unity with such a marriage of elements. One story, intrinsically the better of the two, tells how a prison-farm convict, given a boat and instructions to rescue flood refugees when the Mississippi goes on a rampage, has the most extraordinary adventures carrying out his orders, but executes them to the letter, and is rewarded with an additional penalty as a fugitive when he eventually returns. The other narrative follows the wanderings of a hospital interne who has made off with another man's wife until they end with her death and his arrest for an illegal operation upon her. Beyond the fact that each tale is a story of drifting and the further fact that the chief figure of each ends up a prisoner of the State, the two narratives have nothing in common, and the book must be designated the poorest planned of Faulkner's novels. And though there are some passages of stormy beauty, particularly those that describe the struggle of the convict against the river and his alligator hunting, the prose is as turgid as any the author has written.

The latent humorist, sardonic and even malicious, in Faulkner emerges in his riotous tale of Frenchman's Bend, *The Hamlet* (1940), a book which must be rated only just beneath *The Sound and the Fury*. If its tangential themes are ignored, this novel is the story of the rise of Flem Snopes, the "Uriah Heep of the Canebrakes," from the insignificance of a sharecropper's son to chief man in the small community, which he invests with all his relatives as his influence grows—Eck in the blacksmith shop, I.O. in the schoolhouse, and so on. The reader of Faulkner

has met members of this verminous tribe before—I. O. Snopes as
an intimate of Jason Compson in *The Sound and the Fury*,
Senator Cla'ence Snopes as the whoreson dupe of *Sanctuary*, and
Ab Snopes as a partner of Grumby in *The Unvanquished*, but
he has not before witnessed a swarming of them over the earth.
Flem is their strong man, who builds his career on the terror
inspired in Jody Varner, storekeeper of Frenchman's Bend and
son of the leading citizen of that region, when Jody learns
that he has rented a farm to a sharecropper devoted to arson.
Jody attempts an appeasement program, offering Flem a clerk-
ship in his store, but is soon trotting to his clerk's commands,
for Flem assumes the management of the store and the cotton
gin, and the collection of mortgage money. Soon he is living
at the Varners', and after the luscious daughter of the house
has tempted the inevitable with one too many of the young men
who try her wares, Flem is glad to make her his wife, thus
legalizing a position which he has established by fear. The sale
of a herd of wild ponies, gathered in Texas while he is on his
honeymoon, symbolizes Flem's matchless skill at trade, and the
final disposition of the Old Frenchman's Place, a worthless piece
of property long held by the Varners, to the shrewdest man in
the hamlet—a feat Flem accomplishes by the old trick of "salt-
ing" the ground with "buried treasure"—makes it possible for
him to pull up stakes in Frenchman's Bend and decamp to Jefferson, the county-seat, where larger triumphs plainly await him,
though this particular sale immortalizes him locally.

Faulkner hates Flem Snopes with the hatred of the decayed
gentry, the Sartorises, towards all the upspringing members of
that class which, even before the Civil War, could be designated
Poor Whites. In the days of William Gilmore Sims, the ambitious of this class who failed to obtain a foothold in the plantation system sometimes joined one of the notorious bands of cutthroats, like Murel's Gang, to get a start in life and to satisfy
the sadism bred in them by the iron rigidity of the system which
held them down; in the New South there is no checking the rise
of these people if they have brains—as has Flem Snopes. But
the gentry may retaliate, after the fashion of the region, by

sneering at the kit and kaboodle of the relatives of the predestined man. Something of this motivation may be suspected in
Faulkner's treatment of the unsavory tribe of Snopes—Flem,
during much of the narrative, is an ominous background figure,
but the foreground of *The Hamlet* is occupied with the misadventures of two of his relatives: Ike Snopes, an idiot who has to
be broken of cattle diddling; and Mink Snopes, degenerate viper
who has to be apprehended for the wanton murder from ambush
of a worthy neighbor. Faulkner grants Flem Snopes a cunning
and cold intelligence—he will not sin against the verities by
attributing Flem's rise wholly to Dame Fortune, but he is not
loath to emphasize Flem's dirty consanguinity. It is frivolous to
deny that Flem has just such relatives; emphasis on them, however, supplants diagnosis of the springs of energy in Flem—the
only hint we get of the strange stirrings in that perverted soul is
given us by Flem's adoption of a shirt and tie the morning that
he became a clerk for Jody Varner. The cold opaque gray eyes
shut out as much from us as they do from the citizens of Frenchman's Bend. We are not sure that it is only meanness which
makes Flem withhold Mrs. Armstid's five dollars with an evasive
lie, though his motives are transparent enough when he fails to
return from Texas in time to intercede at the trial of Mink
Snopes. There is some inadequacy in the exposition of Flem
Snopes' character that indirection as a method of narrative does
not wholly conceal. But in other ways the book is magnificent:
Faulkner is strangely and even movingly poetic in his interpretation of the world through the baffled eyes of Ike Snopes, to whom
a cow was the most beautiful creature on earth; he is macabre
and terrific in describing the gross efforts of Mink to conceal his
crime; he is humorous and colloquial in giving us the point of
view of Ratliff, the sewing-machine agent; and he is epic in his
account of the Texas cattleman who manipulated the wild ponies
for Flem. Mayhap if Faulkner follows the Snopes family into
Jefferson, as he promises to do, he will come really to grips
with his protagonist. Then we shall know the wherefore of the
Bilbos and the Huey Longs. Perhaps the sequel to *The Hamlet*
will also allay the growing suspicion that Faulkner, ostensibly

the critic of Southern decadence, is gradually settling into the attitudes of the socially dominant and, unfortunately, the most decadent, class.

It has already been intimated that Faulkner has no place as a poet, despite two volumes of verse. The astonishing thing about Faulkner in this connection is that he, who is so fertile an innovator in fiction, is so imitative here. Various reviewers have indicated accurately enough how the lines of *The Marble Faun* (1924) and *A Green Bough* (1933) echo Swinburne, Housman, Cummings, and Hart Crane, but no one has indicated any originality in them. Nor is there any. In his first volume of short stories, *These Thirteen* (1931), were many original and forceful studies; the volume *Dr. Martino and Other Stories* (1931) represents a very great decline of this talent. It must not be forgotten, however, that in his early short stories Faulkner did perhaps his most artistic work. "A Rose for Emily," for example, is a much finer character study than the portrait of Miss Jenny in *Sartoris* which somewhat resembles it. Faulkner is a sort of American Thomas Kyd whose bloody inventions are packed with novelties, but who, delighting solely in invention, has perfected no one thing. The purely inventive genius always shows to advantage in the short story.

Primitivism reached its apogee and began its decline in Erskine Caldwell, who has been an apt student of all his predecessors' best accomplishment and who has lived intimately with characters designed for his very purposes. Born on December 15, 1903, near White Oak, Coweta County, Georgia, in a run-out farming region peopled particularly by a degenerate stock, he was yet separated from the land and the people sufficiently to be objective by the fact that his mother was a Virginian and his father (the pastor of a Presbyterian church) was a North Carolinian. The father's profession leading to many changes of location, Erskine Caldwell had lived in most of the Southern states before he was sixteen, when he had one year of formal schooling in the high school at Wrens, Georgia. In the next four years he had irregular employment in various Southern mills, served as reporter for the Atlanta *Journal,* and visited Mexico and Central America. After some sort of preparatory discipline in South

Carolina, he tried unsuccessfully to secure a college degree at the University of Virginia and then at Pennsylvania. He deliberately abandoned his education to write, settling in Mt. Vernon, Maine, where he discovered that he could work best on a farm. He printed two novelettes, *The Bastard* and *Poor Fool,* in 1930, and a collection of short stories, *American Earth,* in 1931—all of which he desires to have forgotten. In 1932 he published his first important and mature book, the novel *Tobacco Road.*

It is more convenient here, however, to begin a consideration of Erskine Caldwell with the collection of short stories, published in 1933, entitled *We Are the Living,* than with *Tobacco Road* or its successor, *God's Little Acre.* We are justified in doing this because some of these stories were written earlier and because they tell us more about the author's origins than do the novels. He himself asserts, "There have been no influences, I hope; development is too much of an interwoven piece for me to understand it. . . ." *We Are the Living* may be composed of many strands, but three bright ones can be distinguished in the warp and woof of it—and these three make Caldwell. They are Hemingway, Faulkner, and Anderson. The rest is merely lint. Hemingway is best seen in the short story, "Mama's Little Girl," a tale at once reminiscent of the last chapter of *A Farewell to Arms* and of "Hills Like White Elephants." It is a none-too-well-told story of a young man who has taken a girl to a mountain cabin, where they have a rendezvous with a nurse and a doctor to perform an abortion. The trick, as in Hemingway, is to avoid any mention of the operation itself; Caldwell does this, to be sure, but in a manner which shouts for recognition of what he is doing. Hemingway has written poorer stories than this, but he has also done much better.

The influence of Faulkner is seen in such a story as "August Afternoon" in which a "yellow-headed sapsucker named Floyd" takes away from "Mr. Vic" his fifteen-year-old, common-law wife, Miss Willie, without a protest from "Mr. Vic." The episode is reminiscent of the contest for Temple Drake in the early hours of her stay at the bootlegger's, but is relieved from unadulterated melodrama by Caldwell's robust sense of humor. Yet *We Are the Living* shows most the effect of reading and imitating Anderson: Caldwell's subjects are Anderson's, ridiculed rather than sentimentalized (see "The Medicine Man"), and his narrative method is Anderson's (see especially "Warm River" and "Country Full of Swedes"). One of the best-told stories in the book, "Indian Summer," which describes how two boys started to plaster a farmer's daughter with mud because she had thrown dead limbs in their swimming hole, might easily have come from Anderson's pen. Though the work here cited is in a sense imitative, it is yet original, for Caldwell has brought to his writing, as we have just said, a sense of humor, crude and masculine, which makes him more objective than any of his masters. It is in attitude rather than in method or material that he is individual.

To date, *Tobacco Road* is Caldwell's best long fiction. The novel is made to a formula supplied by Faulkner's *As I Lay Dying*. Not only does the Lester family resemble the Bundren family, but Jeeter Lester's desire to plant cotton supplies a force to *Tobacco Road* not dissimilar to that infused by Anse Bundren's determination to plant his wife in a Jefferson cemetery. The Bundren idiot boy and the Bundren pregnant girl are not prototypes of Dude and Ellie May, nor is the slow procession of the family with Mrs. Bundren's corpse comparable with Dude's mad dashes over the countryside in a new Ford, yet there lay suggestion enough here for an original and fertile mind to develop those elements which mark off *Tobacco Road* from Faulkner's novel. Of the comparative merits of the two novels, however, there is not the slightest doubt—Caldwell's book is superior to Faulkner's at every point. The theft of the turnips at the beginning of *Tobacco Road* is one of the great comic scenes in our literature; nowhere, surely, is suspense better maintained than in these pages, and after Jeeter finally gallops off to the wood with the sack of vegetables while Lov Bensey tumbles on the ground with the harelip daughter, we fear that the book must become ordinary and commonplace. The visit of the woman preacher and her sudden determination to marry Dude, whom she bribes into this arrangement by promising to buy him a new car, speeds the tale along, however, with no more than the sound of shifting gears. Yet the narrative has changed from comedy to burlesque.

Fielding has retired for Smollett, as it were, and the peregrina-
tions of Bessie and Dude are as riotous as those of the Pickle
gentleman. The result is that, as in most picaresque tales, the
story has to be ended arbitrarily, and Caldwell permits Jeeter
and his wife to burn to death in their tumble-down house. Of
course, if this ending were the only fault in the novel, it would
have a very high rank in fiction, but it is not. The tousling of
Ellie May is effective enough, but when Dude and Bessie duplicate it a little later it is tedious. Further, even if these people are
degenerate, it is melodramatic and strained to have in a bare
half dozen characters one wth a hare lip and another with a shotgun nose. Finally, the innocent residence of Jeeter, Dude, and
Bessie in a "hotel" which is really a whorehouse (copied from a
similar scene in *Sanctuary*) is also hackneyed and tedious. Nobody spends time enough these days to make a truly great book;
Tobacco Road is much better than *As I Lay Dying* because more
effort has been expended on it, yet the author could have done
much more with it.

Though Ellie May and Bessie are caricatures, and Lov and
the old grandmother are stock figures, Dude and his father
Jeeter have that vitality of drawing which is flesh and blood in
the novel. The ball-throwing, horn-blowing sixteen-year-old boy,
who has such quaint Anglo-Saxon phrases for things and who prefers to go to bed with his grandmother rather than with his wife,
plays Sancho Panza to his father's Don Quixote. He is the real-
ist; his father, the dreamer Jeeter Lester, is one of the immortals
in the American portrait gallery: victim of a despicable agricultural system, he has a tenacious love of the soil which refutes
his whining and his helplessness. There resides in his emaciated
carcase the ghost of a great race—he is the son of landowners as
well as the sire of degenerates. It is this ignored fact which
irritates Mr. Caldwell when the reviewers call Jeeter Lester a
"poor white"—a term used (so he insists) only by negroes in
the South.

Jeeter explains his earth-hunger:

"My children all blame me because God sees fit to make me poverty-
ridden, Lov," Jeeter said. "They and Ma is all the time cussing me because
we ain't got nothing to eat. I ain't had nothing to do with it. It ain't my

fault that Captain John shut down on giving us rations and snuff. It's his fault, Lov. I worked all my life for Captain John. I worked harder than any four of his niggers in the fields; then the first thing I knowed, he came down here one morning and says he can't be letting me be getting no more rations and snuff at the store. After that he sells all the mules and goes up to Augusta to live. I can't make no money, because there ain't nobody wanting work done. Nobody is taking on share croppers, neither. Ain't no kind of work I can find to do for hire. I can't even raise me a crop of my own, because I ain't got no mule in the first place, and besides that, won't nobody let me have seed-cotton and guano on credit. Now I can't get no snuff and rations, excepting once in a while when I haul a load of wood up to Augusta. Captain John told the merchants in Fuller not to let me have no more snuff and rations on his credit, and I don't know where to get nothing. I'd raise a crop of my own on this land if I could get somebody to sign my guano-notes, but won't nobody do that for me, neither. That's what I'm wanting to do powerful strong right now. When the winter goes, and when it gets to be time to burn off broom-sedge in the fields and underbrush in the thickets, I sort of want to cry, I reckon it is. The smell of that sedge-smoke this time of year near about drives me crazy. Then pretty soon all the other farmers start plowing. That's what gets under my skin the worse. When the smell of that new earth turning over behind the plow strikes me, I get all weak and shaky. It's in my blood—burning broom-sedge and plowing in the ground this time of year. I did it for near about fifty years and my Pa and his Pa before him was the same kind of men. Us Lesters sure like to stir the earth and make plants grow in it. I can't move off to the cotton mills like the rest of them do. The land has got a powerful hold on me."

Jeeter Lester, symbolic of countless impoverished farmers in the South, though they all may not be as ignorant as he, is a pitiable figure whom all the riotous laughter of the book or the play does not help one to forget. Thus early Caldwell gave indication of a social sympathy which lifts him above the other Primitivists.

God's Little Acre (1933), Caldwell's next novel, is an annoying book. It has elements of greatness, but the repetition of the *As I Lay Dying* formula is exasperating to one who had expected the author to strike out on new and bolder lines. Again the novel is held together by an old man with a fixed idea—this time Ty Ty Walden who persists in digging for gold on his farm and enlists all his family to help him. The inclusion in this company of his son-in-law, Will Thompson, who has long desired his brother Buck's wife, Griselda, leads inevitably to a fight with Buck and Shaw, another brother. Will, a "lint head" factory hand, has been able to help dig because there is a strike in the Carolina mill in which he worked; following the family row he returns to Scottsville, the milltown, and, having possessed himself of Griselda when she comes to visit, is shot as he leads the strikers in a raid on the mill. Will's death and Griselda's return to the farm are followed by a preposterous visit from Jim Leslie, Ty Ty's oldest boy, who, though married, having sighted the ravishing Griselda, is resolved to take her bodily from her husband. Buck pours the contents of a double-barrelled shotgun into Jim Leslie's chest, and the novel comes to an abrupt end with Ty Ty in one of his numerous craters, throwing out loose dirt, while he awaits the arrival of the coroner and the sheriff.

There is no great piece of characterization in *God's Little Acre*. The most convincing character in the book is Pluto Swint, candidate for sheriff and the undiscourageable lover of Darling Jill, Ty Ty's youngest daughter. In his fat helplessness, in his blushes, in his devotion, he is the exact opposite of Januarius Jones of *Soldier's Pay* and was very likely suggested by him. Ty Ty himself is merely a fictional mechanism, and the author's lack of sincerity in constructing him can be best appreciated when he is compared with Jeeter. Darling Jill, Griselda, and Rosamond seem at first clearly defined, but the similarity of their reactions to Will Thompson shows them to be one person, seen merely at different stages of animal experience. Will Thompson, the "male man," is utterly unconvincing—the irresistible loadstone for women and the visionary leader of industrial revolution!

The "talk" of the book is magnificent—racy, colloquial, virile, —but it has no particular relation to the people in whose mouths it is placed. As for the action itself, it is melodramatic throughout, as much in the switching on of the power in the mills as in the appearance of Jim Leslie to carry off his brother's wife. Little things make the honesty of the author suspect—as, for example, when his daughters urge Ty Ty to go off with a woman in Atlanta—and while a New York City magistrate cleared *God's Little Acre* of any intention of being "obscene, lewd, lascivious, filthy, and disgusting" and while there is no reason for suppressing a book under any circumstances, yet the wide and experienced reader must admit the real reason why there is no sound characterization in the book and no wholly plausible action is because the author has manured his ground too well for fibrous growth. *God's Little Acre* is not Primitivism, but a burlesque of it; like *Sanctuary*, it is caricature and not art.

Journeyman (1935) marks a broadening of Caldwell's social sympathies to include the negro. It is the story of an itinerant preacher, Semon Dye, who has moved into Georgia "to get the Devil's number, and I shall run the Devil out of this place if I do not drop dead before I'm done." Dye stays for a few days with Clay Horey, a somewhat more prosperous character than Ty Ty or Jeeter, and during that time he wins Horey's car and Horey's young wife, Dene, with loaded dice. When a negro husband finds him enjoying his high yaller wife, Sugar, and dares protest, he is shot for his pains. The preacher watches the girl drag her husband into the darkness of the hall. "They left the house by the back door and not another sound was heard from them after that. Clay knew that he would not see the Negro again until his wound was healed or his body was found. He and Sugar would go to the woods and not come back until that time." The Reverend Semon Dye is wicked and vicious, but there is no denying his vehemence—an irresistible exhorter, he gets all hearers to "come through" except the prostitute Lorene; in admiration he makes her a partner—when they drive off in Horey's car, after spending the night together, she has agreed to share her earnings with him. Yet memorable as is the portrait of this wild, ruthless creature, it is the suffering of the negroes that we retain from *Journeyman*. This would not be true unless the author willed it and his willing gives the book force.

Journeyman was followed by two books very much alike in their significance—*Kneel to the Rising Sun*, a collection of short stories, and *Some American People*, Caldwell's first non-fiction work. Both books are proletarian in sympathy, and Primitivistic only in form. Caldwell is the first of the Primitivists to abandon the doctrine of social futility and to crusade for anything in dead earnest. *Kneel to the Rising Sun* (1935) is a volume of stories

about *les misérables* of the South: the familiar starving sharecropper, the silent, resentful, close-lipped negro, the homeless
girl, the witless hanger-on, the degenerate. How any Southerner,
after reading this volume and recognizing the shameful truths
here told by a native son, can repeat the fatuous nonsense about
Southern standards and Southern chivalry, is beyond comprehension. The brutal murder of Candy-Man Beechum, the rape of
Martha Jean, the exhibition of Blue Boy, the twenty-five cent
sale of little Pearl, and the hunting of the nigger Clem are more
unforgettable than the charge of Longstreet's brigade through
the peach orchard. If literature anywhere presents coarser
brutes than the dominant white males of "Blue Boy" and "Kneel
to the Rising Sun," we are unaware of it. And what fundamental
cowards they are, as the highly diverting yarn, "The Shooting,"
reveals. We wonder what the future historian of Southern literature will say about this volume. Will he admit the high excellence
of "Horse Thief," "The Girl Ellen," "Slow Death," and
"Daughter" in addition to the other tales we have named and
pronounce this one of the best collections of American short
stories, or will he deny its patent authenticity and cite the reports
of whitewash committees to prove that the stories are not true?

Some American People (1935) is Caldwell's effort to survey
his country as Sherwood Anderson had done in *Puzzled America*.
It is a better book than its model, but not a great book. This,
however, it did not aim to be. Simple and journalistic, it concen-
trates on the plight of the automobile workers in Detroit and
on that of the tenant farmers in the South, particularly in
Alabama and Georgia. In Detroit, Caldwell found the speed-up
increased under the N.R.A., men with less than nine fingers or
over forty-five years of age unemployable, prostitution encouraged by the City Health Department and free discussion discouraged by the police; in the Georgia hills he discovered farmers whose chief fare was clay, corn-meal, and molasses—too poor
to afford anything better. The tenant-farmer generally has no
chance to voice his woes—the press of the South is conservative
and closed to him, the poll tax deprives him of political significance, and his proprietor's riders keep all outside help from
him. Unionization strikes Caldwell as one step towards better

conditions in both Detroit and the South, though he insists that tenant-farming, at least, must go. *Some American People* probably surprised most Caldwell readers by being less radical than they looked for.

To his contention that a union of sharecroppers is a partial solution of the problem of poverty in the South, Mr. Caldwell returns in the text of *You Have Seen Their Faces* (1937), an illustrated book done in collaboration with Margaret Bourke-White, the photographer, whose pictures are as moving as is the author's virile reporting. But Caldwell knows that unionization will not do everything: he allows those who believe in crop diversification, cattle raising, producing cellulose, and industrialization all to speak their pieces. Most of all, he allows defeatism its voice—the farmer who thinks that cotton planting is the alcohol of the South, the Georgia banker who can't sleep nights wondering what's going to happen. Then he himself, devoid of a thorough-going solution, pleads for a government commission to make a systematic and conclusive study of tenant-farming in the Cotton States.

Though their book produced none of the results they hoped for most, *You Have Seen Their Faces* won such acclaim from persons of artistic sensibility that Miss Bourke-White and Mr. Caldwell, now married, repeated their collaboration with another group of peasants as their subjects, the ten million agricultural folk of Czecho-Slovakia, in *North of the Danube* (1939). While this book is primarily a piece of anti-Nazi propaganda, American readers must be struck by the fact that these people, who toil as hard as our tenant-farmers, look healthier and happier, particularly the free peasants of Moravia, where they laugh as they till the earth. "We used to belong to the Baron," one said. "But that was long ago. The land is ours now. We are free." All is not equally well throughout Danubia, however, and in terse prose and eloquent photograph the collaborators expose the rotten spots which made the land so easy to crush when the Germans marched in.

Between the two experiments with socio-photography, Caldwell sandwiched in another book of short stories, *Southways*, in 1938. The sixteen stories contained in this volume are all very short—

so short, in fact, that only a few of them make a deep impression.
A year or two after reading, one remembers with an effort "The
Negro in the Well," the story of how a calloused white man bargained successfully with a colored man for two good hound dogs
because the latter had fallen into his well and could not get out
without aid; "The Fly in the Coffin," a folk story with a hero
who would not be buried with that particular insect in his box;
and "Return to Lavinia," a plausible variation on the theme of
Dark Laughter; but anthologists decades from now should be
keeping ever green "New Cabin," the real gem of the collection,
a tale of the unfaltering devotion of a seventeen-year-old girl-
wife who voluntarily follows her husband to death in a mire hole
in the pine swamp rather than surrender herself to his murderer.
The least substantial of the Caldwell volumes, *Southways* is a
noteworthy publication because it houses this faultlessly told
story.

Trouble in July (1940) is an account of a Georgia lynching
in which the emphasis is put on the psychology of all the others
involved rather than upon the terror of the victim, a guileless
colored boy named Sonny Clark. Like John Cloud in Waldo
Frank's *Holiday,* Sonny has the misfortune to be fastened upon
by a nymphomaniac, Katy Barlow, a known slut in Flowery
Bend. Yet Katy's reputation does not stay a nigger hunt for her
"raper" after Sonny has been seen in her embraces by Mrs. Narcissa Calhoun, a belligerent female who is circulating a petition
to send the negroes back to Africa. In the course of the search
for Sonny the hunters raid the negro cabins, beat a gentle colored
man and abuse his wife, and finally rape a mulatto girl. Sonny
still evading them and they not to be denied a victim, the
lynchers break into the jail and kidnap a foolish old negro, Sam
Brinson, whom they drag from a car with a rope fastened about
his body. Fortunately for Sam, before they can hang him, Sonny
Clark is brought in by a white man to whom he has surrendered
and of whom he asked protection. As Sonny's body cavorts in
the wind in a hail of bullets, Katy Barlow appears before the
lynchers screaming, "He didn't do it." Katy's few brains are
mercifully dashed out when the departing lynchers fusillade her
with rocks.

Mr. Caldwell elects to tell his lugubrious tale from the point of view of Sheriff Jeff McCurtain, a three-hundred-pound symbol of the law whose habit is to take himself off fishing whenever trouble is brewing, in order that he may not be found. Things break too fast for Jeff on this occasion, and the kidnapping of Sam Brinson, whom he likes, stirs him sufficiently to make him defy the ukase of the local Democratic boss and even to jeopardize his own reelection. The only other white man to move athwart the path of the lynchers is one Bob Watson, a plantation owner who refuses to allow his own colored workers to be terrorized while harvesting is being done. Aside from the Sheriff's tenderness towards Sam, sympathy for the blacks is negligible in Flowery Bend. The case of the farmer who captures Sonny Clark, however, is illuminating: he believes Sonny's story and is sorely tempted to aid him until Sonny himself appeals for that help— then he sets his face against him. The implication is that the lynchers act almost mechanically, or at least wholly by ritual and formula. Against these channeled responses it is all but futile to erect the feeble dams of reason—they are washed away by the spontaneous flow of Southern adrenaline at the very mention of rape. Yet the effort is not completely futile in Caldwell's opinion, or *Trouble in July* would not have been written. If conditions are ever better in the South, if the treatment of the colored man is ever more humane, we are going to owe a very great debt to Erskine Caldwell.

With Caldwell, the survey of Primitivism may well close. There are other writers employing the technique, and employing it effectively, but their work has told as yet neither in the movement nor upon the public so decisively as has the contribution of the men here studied. There are, for example, Jim Tully whose *Beggars of Life* (1924) and *Shanty Irish* (1927) are low-brow classics; James M. Cain whose *Postman Always Rings Twice* (1934) is reminiscent of both Hemingway and Caldwell; John O'Hara, a later and smarter Fitzgerald, whose *Butterfield 8* (1935) is his best novel; Henry Miller, whose *Cosmological Eye* (1939), a masterpiece of indecency, is to be ranked perhaps with any book here discussed; young Carson McCullers, whose *The Heart Is a Lonely Hunter* (1940) proves that one can be both tough and feminine; and Jerome Weidman, emergent author of *I Can Get It for You Wholesale* (1937) and *What's in It for Me?* (1938), who promises to be a first-rate man. In view of the fact that the movement has undoubtedly spent its greatest energy, it is possible to make a few summary observations about it. One thing is absolutely clear—Primitivism, despite its philosophy of despair, despite its nihilism, is a healthier and more native thing than Decadence. Although its origins can be traced back to French painting, it owes little (and that chiefly by way of encouragement) to foreign influences. Gertrude Stein and Sherwood Anderson have come nearer giving us an "autochthonous style" (so much desired by Whitman) than have any other American authors. And no school of fiction has had more definitely formulated aims than this. Reality of action and of speech have never been more arduously sought after. Further, no group of writers has been more conspicuously truthful than this: unlike Primitivists in other lands, they have not glorified the Aryan stock as such, nor any empty shibboleth. The limitations of Primitivism, however, are not wholly the limitations of individual authors. By definition, the Primitivist is interested in a low average of intelligence, and the fact that no one writer of this group has presented a character of superior intellectual powers (unless alcoholized) has dual significance: it indicates a pragmatic belief in the virtue of action merely because it is action and a corresponding lack of faith in all man's speculations. The Primitivists have almost made of action a drug, and their virtues are chiefly negative virtues—they have done no harm with their bullfighting, their popping at wild game, their carousing in aeroplanes, their literarious sexual excesses. Yet essentially these once young men are escapists—whether they choose pre-Civil War Spain, the Riviera, Africa, the blue empyrean, or a brothel, for their refuge.

Primitivism, like all anti-intellectual literary movements, makes its chief appeal to tired intellectuals who feel that the world is a dusty place and who long to go crashing among the stars merely to get their lungs full of ozone. Primitivism is a kind of Romanticism in which the reader is led to believe that the low-brow is a good fellow and that impulses are more to be trusted than ideas. "It's folks who let their head run them who make all the mess of living," Mr. Caldwell's patient and much-used Griselda tells us, and the author commends us to the direct-ness of dogs in affairs of the heart. Perhaps this has the half merit of being a somewhat more normal activity than the charac-teristic Narcissism of Decadence, yet surely it isn't much more than half a merit. The horrors of Primitivism are less loathsome but more nasty than those of Decadence; yet somehow the two seem related to each other. Is not the excessive sexuality of Primitivism the obvious result of the sterility of Decadence? To cite an interesting parallel, are not Poe's tales of sadistic horror the result of his efforts to secure an ethereal, unreal beauty in his verse? Poe combined in the range of his creative work what is the essence of two modern literary movements—Decadence and Primitivism. The chief worth of the latter undeniably is that it is a blind step away from the former. The developing social consciousness of the leading Primitivists augurs the transforma-tion of Primitivism into Communism or Liberalism and the disappearance of all but the technique from literature.

V

THE INTELLIGENTSIA

"The fact of a man being a poisoner is
nothing against his prose."—Oscar Wilde,
Pen, Pencil and Poison.

I

THE BIRTH OF PESSIMISM

THAT SUPERCILIOUS attitude towards the struggling masses of
mankind which denies to their efforts any importance and tends
to find its sole delight in the play of superior minds—in the "pure
intellectualism" of the Intelligentsia—is usually preceded by disillusionment in some dearly held idealism. Such was the case
in Germany where, as we have seen, intellectual sodomy followed the abortion of democratic nationalism. In the United
States, the way for the adoption of such an attitude was prepared
by the development of a similar disillusionment, the faintest traces
of which are visible as early as the 'fifties. The temper of American life prior to that time had been one of almost unbounded
optimism. The reasons for this are clear enough—if America
were neither the Promised Land of the Puritan idealists nor the
perfect Republic envisioned by the eighteenth-century rationalists,
it was still a land of incalculable promise, the seat of undreamed-of
Utopias, a world of unending Tomorrows. In no country on earth
were the boundaries of Time and Space (which Emerson dismissed so casually) of such little consequence as here. To be sure,
the limitations of frontier life or the meagreness of village existence at moments oppressed even the sturdiest, yet it was always
possible to laugh off any present discomfort. So America became
a nation of jokers. Behind the experiences of Seba Smith, David

Crockett, Augustus Baldwin Longstreet, Johnson Jones Hooper, Joseph Glover Baldwin, George Washington Harris, and others, one can discern much grim reality, but *The Life and Writings of Major Jack Downing* (1833), *A Narrative of the Life of David Crockett* (1834), *Georgia Scenes* (1835), the *Adventures of Captain Simon Suggs* (1845), *Flush Times in Alabama and Mississippi* (1853), and *Sut Lovingood* (1867) are riotously funny. Probably this laughter was the most convenient way available to sanguine people to dismiss their troubles.

Yet the tone of this laughter changes appreciably in the 'fifties, and to account for this change is our problem. We find our explanation of it in the discovery made by thousands of Americans in the years of the gold rush that America had definite boundaries. The effect of reaching the Pacific in droves was to discern for the first time that there were physical limits, after all, to our future, and the dreams of a thousand Utopias vanished in the ever-lurking grey mist on our watery, western horizon. Pessimism was born out of disillusionment in regard to our highest national hopes—not out of the individual's failure to find gold for himself in California. Who today can calculate the effect of the sudden realization that America, however vast her domain, could be definitely conquered and within a conceivable time might come to resemble any European nation with ills and perplexities that mere postponement would not mitigate? The "sour note" in Western humor is the first indication of a premonition heretofore foreign to American thought.

While orators and financiers in the East continued to talk of our "limitless West" and of the manifest destiny of the westward migration, the West itself began to deride the very movement which had created it. In his well-known "Musical Review Extraordinary" (1854) George Horatio Derby, writing from San Diego, where he was stationed as an army-engineer, pokes fun at the whole westward venture. The pioneers are not high-minded sires of a future race, the founders of Utopia, but rather a shiftless, shoeless lot, unwashed and unwholesome—

Suddenly we hear approaching a train from Pike County, consisting of seven families, with forty-six wagons, each drawn by thirteen oxen; each family consists of a man in butternut-colored clothing driving the oxen; a wife in butternut-colored clothing riding in the wagon, holding a butternut baby, and seventeen butternut children running promiscuously about the establishment; all are barefoot, dusty, and smell unpleasantly. . . .

To be sure that his "Review" was understood as a burlesque of the westward migration as a whole and was not taken as a satire of the movement of a particular sect, Lieutenant Derby consigned every westward-trekking family on death to Senator Thomas Benton, the special champion of our manifest destiny, author of the immortal utterance, "Through the valley of the Columbia, lies the North American road to India."

Behind the vision of America as the Promised Land lay a high moral earnestness, which the Lyceum lecturers of the 'fifties, some two hundred strong, had helped to stimulate. Emerson, the most notable of these, carried his idealism as far west as Wisconsin. It was only to be expected, then, that the cynicism of the disillusioned West should discharge itself upon the morality and culture of the East. Before 1855, Jonathan Kelly, Cincinnati editor, writing under the name of Falconbridge, had made ribald fun of the style and high moral tone of Emerson:

If Roaring Ralph touches a homely mullen weed, on a donkey heath, straightway he makes it a full-blown rose, in the land of Ophir, shedding an odor balmy as the gales of Arabia; while with a facility the wonderful auctioneer Robbins might envy, Ralph imparts to a lime-box, or a pigsty, a negro hovel, or an Irish shanty, all the romance, artistic elegance and finish of a first class manor house, or Swiss cottage, inlaid with alabaster and fresco, surrounded by elfin bowers, grand walks, bee hives, and honeysuckles.

Artemus Ward, when he began to appear on the platform in 1861, introduced himself to his already admiring public as a "moral lecturer." The public had previously been acquainted with his revolt against spelling and grammar by his contributions to the Cleveland *Plain Dealer* and to *Vanity Fair*. Yet nothing in the world was so far a cry from the well-chosen diction of the Lyceum lecturer as Artemus Ward's pretended struggle for the right word when in the rostrum. Later the London *Spectator* commented on this as one of the richest sources of his humor—

... Thus when he says that he used to sing, but not well, he stumbles in the most natural way, and is a prey to melancholy that he can't hit on the proper phrase. "As a songer," he said, "I was not successful"; and then, in a depressed and self-correcting way, conscious he had gone wrong, "as a singster I was a failure. I am always saddest when I sing—and so are those who hear me." ... So again, when he finds the seventeen young Mormon widows weeping, and asks them, "Why is this thus?" he falls a victim to the perplexity and embarrassment with which the juxtaposition of this and thus has overpowered his weak brain, and goes on helplessly, "What is the cause of this thusness?" ...

One can understand how, in the confused and anxious days of the War and of Reconstruction, the Western humorists drove the Lyceum Bureau out of existence or forced it to share a Chautauqua tent.

Ward's famous lecture on the Mormons carried him all the way to London and to the presence of Queen Victoria. Of course, in satirizing the Mormons Ward was poking fun at their greater American realism in having their wives all at once, rather than in sequence, and at American fecundity. Brigham Young, Ward averred, "don't pretend to know his children, there is so many of um, tho they all know him. He sez about every child he meats calls him Par, & he takes it for granted it is so." In London Artemus Ward was one of the nondescript horde of jesters of Yankee or Irish stock who entertained the prosperous but vulgar British middle class in the latter half of the nineteenth century. He was willing to represent the clown and oaf that the average Englishman of this class fancied an American to be. "I skurcely need inform you that your excellent Tower is very pop'lar *with people from the agricultooral districks,*" he begins his London *Punch* Letter on the Tower of London, and he puts himself in that class. Ward, who as the proprietor of a "wax works" had contended his figures were more "elevatin" than Shakespeare's plays, entertained the British public with a narrative of his visit to Stratford-on-Avon, and began—before Oscar Wilde—the fashion of under-evaluating the bard in order to raise his own stock.

Yet when one has cited all the cynical and anti-cultural elements in Artemus Ward one still has to confess to a huge delight in him. One can't quite forget remarks like "It would have

bin ten dollars in Jeff Davis's pocket if he'd never been born!"
or his recapitulation of the philosophy of the whole Gilded Age,
"You scratch my back & Ile scratch your back." It is easy, if
one is not over-critical, to slip into the mood which accepts Artemus Ward as one of the world's great showmen, a victim at
thirty-one of the Briton's hunger for his "joaks," a pathetic
symbol of an inferior people zealous to please the world's masters. But this is bosh.

Another source of cynicism in North and West was the Civil
War itself. After the War the victors had no longer so obvious
a reason for high conduct, while for the South a new and even
more harrowing struggle was just beginning. The difference in
the attitude of North and South is admirably brought out in
Miss Jennette Tandy's comparison of Bill Arp and Petroleum
V. Nasby in her *Crackerbox Philosophers* (1925). Bill Arp, the
Georgia cracker, is the voice of Charles Henry Smith (1826–
1903), Confederate soldier and military judge. "If Bill Arp has
one outstanding characteristic," says Miss Tandy, "it is pluck."
This marks his letters from the beginning of the War through
the Reconstruction period. In December, 1862, he wrote "Abe
Linkhorn"—

 . . . Mr. Linkhorn, sur, your Genruls don't travel the right road to
Richmond, nohow. The way they have been tryin to cum is through a mity
Longstreet, over two powerful Hills, and across a tremendious Stonewall.
It would be safer and cheaper for em to go round by the Rocky Mountings,
if spending time in military xcursions is their chief objek.

Three years later, in September, 1865, he wrote Artemus Ward
telling him that he was "tryin to soften down" his feelings, but
though beaten, Bill Arp is not cowed—

 . . . *I* ain't no gurilla. I've dun tuk the oath, and I'm gwine to keep it,
but as for my bein subjergated and humilyated, and amalgamated and
enervated, as Mr. Chase says, it ain't so—nary time. I ain't ashamed of
nuthin, neather—ain't repentin—ain't axin for no one hoss, short-winded
pardin. . . .

Petroleum Volcano Nasby, who erupted virulence against the
Northern Democrats all through the War and was undeniably

a great help to Lincoln in holding the Republican votes, conducted himself less commendably after the War was over. Instead of siding with the harassed Andrew Johnson who was trying, in his bungling way, to put through Lincoln's simple plan for Reconstruction, Nasby threw in his lot with Ben Wade and the other "Vindictives" of Ohio (where his creator, David Ross Locke, was publishing the Toledo *Blade*) and demanded the pound of flesh from the South. Johnson became the butt of his ridicule, and it may be said he embarrassed this President as much as he had aided his predecessor. Nasby's political cynicism in these years is matched only by his credulity in regard to Southern schemes and machinations which were largely a figment of his imagination.

It is in the "aphorisms" of Josh Billings, however, that the most complete cynicism of the school of Western humorists is found. Billings was the pen-name of Henry Wheeler Shaw, Yankee adventurer, who was by turns steamboat captain, farmer, auctioneer, and lecturer, and who, in time, travelled over most of the West. He is at once curiously sophisticated and suspiciously naïve. Possibly better than anyone else, Josh Billings represents the animal cunning, the gross shrewdness, the public sentimentality, and the hard conscience of the Gilded Age. In religion he is a superior sceptic: "Allmost enny phool kan prove that the bible aint true, it takes a wize man to beleave it" and "Christians seem to fite under cover, but the devil stands boldly out and dares the world to combat." For him, as for Daniel Drew, Jay Gould, and Jim Fiske, every man has his price: "Every man haz a weak side, and sum hav two or three." He is predatory and material: "Most of the happiness in this world konsists in possessing what others kant git." He reflects the Western attitude towards the Indian: " Musik hath charms to soothe a savage; this may be so, but i wud rather tri a revolver on him fust." Acidosis has soured his heart: "Pity costs nothing,—and aint wuth nothing." Yet he has a grim shrewdness which makes his most cynical utterance respected: "Natur never makes enny blunders; when she makes a phool, she means it." And he can even contradict himself by being sympathetic towards children: "To bring up a child in the way he should go, travel that way yourself once in a while." . . . A very dangerous man, this plausible Henry Wheeler Shaw.

Most historians of our literature treat Derby, Ward, Nasby, and Billings as unrelated to any more recent development than, say, the platform appearances of Mark Twain, while it is obvious to anyone with half an eye that the pessimism and scepticism of these rogues have spread through our thought like sorrel in a run-out field. The immediate heritors of this Western cynicism were Ambrose Bierce and Robert Ingersoll, both products of the region in which Nasby and Billings flourished, both soldiers in the Civil War. And after them came E. W. Howe and a host of others.

The securest claim of Ambrose Bierce to immortality lies in half a dozen well-told short stories. The excellence of these tales has won a reputation for Bierce that an examination of his *Collected Works* shows is wholly unwarranted. No man of taste would ever have brought together the rubbish which, in the main, fills these ten volumes. None the less, some of this stuff, while it has no artistic merit, is highly important, not only in shedding light on Bierce, but in revealing certain trends in American thought. Bierce, nephew of a hero of the Mexican War, was born in Meigs County, Ohio, into a family of limited means. Sent to a military academy by his uncle, Bierce enlisted in an Ohio regiment almost as soon as War was declared and served with proved distinction throughout the length of the contest. After the War, he entered journalism in San Francisco, writing for the *News-Letter, Advertiser, Alta California,* and *Argonaut.* In 1871, he was married to Mary Ellen Day, the only daughter of a 'forty-niner who had "struck it rich," and in April of the following year the young couple sailed for London. Bierce's London experiences were of the utmost importance to his development. An Englishman, who was a fellow-journalist in San Francisco, had taught him to respect Thackeray's contributions to *Punch,* and once in the British capital, Bierce sought and secured an appointment to the staff of the humorous weekly *Fun,* where he became associated with Tom Hood, the younger, James Mortimer, George Augustus Sala, W. S. Gilbert, and other wits. The result of this association was that Bierce deferentially polished to British taste the "aphorisms" which he printed in *The Fiend's Delight* (1872). Thus preparation was made for *The Cynic's Word Book* (1906)—a work as characteristic of Bierce as Ward's contributions to *Punch* are characteristic of Ward.

Bierce tells us that the definitions in *The Cynic's Word Book* were "begun in a weekly paper in 1881." This was probably *The Wasp,* the second journal in San Francisco of which he was editor after his return from England in 1875. Bierce used *The Wasp* for scurrilous attacks upon the prominent citizens of California, whose manners, dress, politics, or personal appearance offended him. "My trade is abuse," he confessed to a correspondent. In a single issue of "Prattle," his weekly column, so Mr. Carey McWilliams tells us, Bierce would excoriate as many as fifteen prominent San Franciscans. He frequently did this in verse, and his *Collected Works* contains pages of meaningless rimed drivel, the epitaphs of forgotten reputations. It is a wonder in those days of quick recourse to gun and knife that he was not murdered. There is little, surely, to admire in his swollen-tongued rant. His anti-clerical squibs were particularly coarse and brutal:

> . . . What a procession of holy idiots we have had in San Francisco—hot gospellers and devil-pelters of all degrees! Thick-necked Moody and Sankey of the nasal name; Hallenbeck, Earle, Knops, and all their he-harlotry of horribles. And now this grease-eating and salt-crusted Harrison from the pork regions of the northeast . . . etc.

The definitions which slowly accumulated in this paper under the head "The Devil's Dictionary" and were later transferred to *The Cynic's Word Book* rarely have, however, a personal vitriolic quality. If Josh Billings could have listened to the young wits of London excitedly discuss Pater's advice "to burn always with this hard, gem-like flame," his "Aphorisms" might have some of the quality of Bierce's definitions:

ADAGE, *n.* Boned wisdom for weak teeth. . . .
FIDELITY, *n.* A virtue peculiar to those who are about to be betrayed. . . .

Or if Oscar Wilde had had chronic indigestion instead of dubious morals and no formal education, he might have produced something of this sort. In actuality, both he and Whistler produced better things in conversation without labor. Bierce's best things smell of perspiration.

In the ninth volume of his *Collected Works* are reproduced under the head "Tangentional Views" many brief essays written over a good many years. These range from an attack on Socialism as "this wild ass of civilization" to a rather stout denial of the justice of permitting suits of breach of promise. Most iconoclastic are two essays, both done in the 'nineties, called "George the Made-Over" and "Columbus." The former is a picture of the "true" George Washington whom Bierce avers was "chokefull of the old Adam . . . loved a bottle like a brother, and had an intercolonial reputation as a lady-killer. . . ." The latter excitedly proclaims that every statue to Columbus is "a lie." Why? Oh, Leif Ericsson really discovered America. As historical researches these pieces are cribbed from obvious sources: their significance, however, is as examples of "debunking"—a kind of vilification which was to prove extremely popular a little later.

An evil fortune pursued Bierce after he quit *The Wasp,* and he suffered enough to make us pity him. His wife left him, one of his sons was killed in a shooting affray, and the other died just as a career in journalism opened to him. Before the last of these catastrophes, Bierce had become a paid henchman of Mr. William Randolph Hearst, writing first for the *Examiner* in San Francisco, then lobbying in Washington for Hearst against Collis P. Huntington, and finally contributing to *The Cosmopolitan* between 1905 and 1909. As a Hearst hireling, Bierce contributed from Washington to the *New York Journal* on February 4, 1901, the four lines (with their allusion to the unsolved murder of Governor Goebel of Kentucky) which were alleged to have inspired the assassination of McKinley:

> The bullet that pierced Goebel's breast
> Cannot be found in all the West;
> Good reason; it is speeding here
> To stretch McKinley on his bier.

In 1913 Bierce set out for Mexico, then turbulent with strife fermented by Pancho Villa. He had declared, melodramatically, "To be a Gringo in Mexico—ah, that is euthanasia!" And so it was, for he has never returned, and there has been no certain word of him.

Yet he lives because of a handful of short stories, scattered in two volumes, *Tales of Soldiers and Civilians* (1891) and *Can Such Things Be?* (1894). These are horror tales of the Gothic tradition, as Mr. McWilliams has shown. He was introduced to the work of Walpole, Lewis, and Mrs. Radcliffe by the same English friend who, in the 'seventies, acquainted him with the wits. After reading these people he rounded out his knowledge of the tale of terror by consuming those written by Mary Shelley, DeQuincey, Maturin, Ingemann, Blicher, Balzac, Hoffman, Poe, and Fitz-James O'Brien. One has only to compare his tale "The Damned Thing" with Fitz-James O'Brien's superior shocker, "What Was It?" to perceive how much Bierce owes to this tradition. Or, compare his mechanical chess-player in "Moxon's Master" with Poe's and add an examination of Mrs. Shelley's "Frankenstein" and further indebtedness is revealed. Never quite the equal of Poe, Bierce nevertheless has added some memorable pieces to the Gothic tradition: both "A Resumed Identity" and "The Eyes of the Panther" are admirably conceived as tales of terror, yet one feels their execution could be improved upon. For example, in "A Resumed Identity" some premonition of disaster should come to the doctor who attended the mad veteran before the latter's collapse and death. Bierce is at his best in "A Horseman in the Sky" and in "An Occurrence at Owl Creek Bridge," both Civil War tales in which suspense and feeling are somewhat higher quotients than in his other tales. One should not assume too hastily, however, that these are anti-war propaganda: Bierce's departure for Mexico in 1913 demonstrates that he had not got a stomachful of that ingredient. The savage destruction of war merely struck Bierce as a capital element for the tale of terror. In his greatest opportunity he remained still an Eminent Vulgarian.

To understand the tremendous notoriety of Colonel Robert Green Ingersoll one must appreciate how completely religious was the great body of American people up to and through the Civil War. Ingersoll was in no sense an original thinker; every idea on religion he had can be traced to Spinoza, Voltaire, or Comte, or better yet, to Tom Paine, whose fervent disciple he was. But whatever Ingersoll lacked in originality, he made up for in courage; however much his effect depended upon his rhetoric rather than upon his thinking, the spirit which impelled his words was fearless. For the masses, the resurrection of eighteenth-century rationalism could hardly have been undertaken by a better man.

Ingersoll combined frontier and army skepticism. Though born in Dresden, N. Y., on August 11, 1833, he was taken as a child first to Wisconsin and then to Illinois, as his strict Congregational father moved from pastorate to pastorate. Admitted to the bar in Illinois in 1854, he practiced law with success in that state until the outbreak of the war, when he recruited a cavalry regiment, of which he was elected colonel. Captured in December, 1862, in an encounter with the Confederates, he was paroled, waited in vain six months to be exchanged, then finally resigned from the service in disgust. After his return to Illinois, he entered politics and eventually become attorney-general for Illinois. His speech nominating James G. Blaine for the presidency at the Cincinnati convention of the Republican party in 1876 won him national recognition as an orator, but further political advancement was closed to him because of his skeptical views. Nevertheless he enjoyed great prestige as a lawyer and lecturer to his death, on July 21, 1899.

Ingersoll's first book, *The Gods and Other Lectures,* was issued at Peoria, Illinois, in 1874. The "Preface" of this book is a plate with two designs: the first, a picture of three crosses, one with martyrs tied in flames at its base, the other two with suspended, crucified figures—the whole captioned, "For the love of God"; beneath this is another, simpler design—three telegraph poles carrying wires to a city in the hills, entitled, "For the use of Man." The five lectures which the volume contains ("The Gods," "Humboldt," "Thomas Paine," "Individuality," and "Heretics and Heresies") are marked by a love of startling aphorism typical of the West: "An honest God is the noblest work of man"; "Even patent medicines will cure more diseases than all the prayers uttered since the beginning of the world"; "Calvin was . . . as near like the God of the Old Testament as his health permitted"; and "Heresy is a cradle; orthodoxy, a coffin." All are shot through with indignation, an anger tantamount to moral earnestness, as Ingersoll surveys the history of bigotry and fanaticism. Conceding, however, that Ingersoll is more frequently right than wrong in his condemnation of the Church, one is not forced to accept the sweeping generalizations of his book. Indeed, the very science which Ingersoll lauds (but of which he was ignorant, save in a descriptive sense) should have taught him to be less dogmatic. "Just in proportion that the human race has advanced, the Church has lost power. There is no exception to this rule." This is as ignorant a statement in its way as to assert that the Church is the fount of all that is good in the world. The growth of the Church with its doctrine of equality of souls was the first step in human history away from an order which recognized only an equality of force. It is true that attacks upon the power of Churchmen have benefited humankind, but it is also true that religious revivals, like Wesleyanism, have advanced equalitarianism and democracy. It is in the extravagance of his statement that Ingersoll is a mere iconoclast. This extravagance carried his name farther, however, than fair and judicious statement would have done and made Ingersoll one of the champions of "pure" intelligence. In distant London he was read in the Fabian Society, and he left his mark on Bernard Shaw.

There is no point in analyzing at length Ingersoll's later volumes. Such a book as the popular *The Ghosts and Other Lectures* (1878), for example, contains all the merits and all the faults of *The Gods*. It is worth while, however, to consider one or two of Ingersoll's lectures on subjects other than religion. His "About Farming in Illinois" is a shrewd preachment of the eighteenth-century doctrines of competence and thrift. Particularly sensible is his counsel to the farmers to make a common cause with industrial labor for political ends—advice which anticipates the program of Bryan by nearly twenty years. There is in it, too, a kind of Socialism which is quite the equal of Shavian socialism:

> . . . You are in partnership with the mechanics who make your reapers, your mowers, and your plows; and you should take into your granges all the men who make their living by honest labor. The laboring people should unite and should protect themselves against all idlers. . . . All laborers should be brothers.

Yet this lecture ill assorts with his speech nominating James G. Blaine for the Presidency of the United States. No friend of labor or of the farmer could describe Blaine as "a plumed knight," a "prince of parliamentarians," a "reformer," and "a leader of leaders." Robert Ingersoll as a reputation may outwear his religious iconoclasm, but he will never outlast his Republican convention address. A man does better to champion the devil than to defend a bought politician.

Related (ought one to say, "spiritually"?) to Bierce and to Ingersoll was Edgar Watson Howe, "the Sage of Potato Hill," the "Kansas Diogenes." Born in Treaty, Indiana, on May 3, 1853, Howe received some education in the common schools before going to work in a print shop at twelve. In 1872 he was publisher of the *Golden Globe,* in Golden, Colorado, and from 1877 to 1911—thirty-four years—editor and publisher of the Atchison *Daily Globe* in Kansas. Tired of running a small-town daily, he then sold out to his staff, bought a farm on the Missouri River which he called Potato Hill, and promptly began publishing a magazine to which he was the sole contributor, *E. W. Howe's Weekly.* After some twenty-two years in this venture, Howe discontinued his magazine in November, 1934. He died in October, three years later, outlasting by a few days the wife and mother of his three children whom he had divorced thirty-five years before.

Howe is remembered for his novel, *The Story of a Country Town* (1882), and for his aphorisms and sardonic paragraphs in his newspaper and weekly, some of which are collected in *Country Town Sayings* (1911) and *Ventures in Common Sense* (1919). *The Story of a Country Town* is a gloomy narrative of marital unhappiness. It is told from the point of view of the only son of the Reverend John Westlock, and concerns the hypocritical morality of that gentleman and the insane jealousy of a young man early bound to him, Jo Erring by name. Westlock, after ruling his family with unflinching severity, suddenly disappears with an unknown woman; meanwhile Jo Erring, who has romantic notions about the purity of his young wife, is suddenly (and falsely) disillusioned. Driven to madness by his brooding, he eventually murders his wife and is punished for it. For the bitterness and melancholy of the story there is a partial explanation in Howe's prefatory remarks in which he confesses that "it was written entirely at night, after the writer had finished a hard day's work as editor and publisher of a small evening newspaper. I do not think a line of it was written while the sun was shining. . . ." But this is only a partial explanation: the misogyny and misanthropy of the book are too deep to be explained away wholly on the ground of physical weariness. Underlying the book is a deep personal conviction of the relative untrustworthiness of man and the complete fickleness of woman. Permeating the writing is a conviction that all morality is pretense and that western country towns, far from being the outposts of a new civilization, are merely the latrines of an old one. *The Story of a Country Town* has immense significance as the first protest against the idealization of the village which began with Goldsmith and Miss Mitford.

The spokesman of Howe's country town is a horse trader by the name of Lytle Biggs, who is a lesser and sourer Josh Billings. Of course, the philosophy of Mr. Biggs is the philosophy of E. W. Howe, as anyone who has examined *Ventures in Common Sense,* etc., can avouch. In his own character, Howe could write, "It is a good rule to watch everybody; the honest man may be careless." As Lytle Biggs, in much the same temper, he wrote, "There is only one grade of men—they are all contemptible"; and "A man with a brain large enough to understand mankind is always wretched and ashamed of himself." This takes us directly to the sneer of Ambrose Bierce. "Only Christ ever loved all mankind." Howe is the first American to trace all morality to womankind, a Nietzschean observation, in this case, however, not derived from the German philosopher. Uttered by Lytle

Biggs, it is not far from the central idea of *The Story of a Country Town:* "Men are virtuous because the women are; women are virtuous from necessity." Poorly plotted and as melodramatic as the plays of Augustin Daly, *The Story of a Country Town* is rightly regarded by the Intelligentsia as something of a petard set off under American respectability.

A Waco, Texas, journalist, William Cowper Brann, "muscled in" on the profitable racket of shocking people much more successfully than did E. W. Howe, and as late as 1938, when his *Writings* (1898) were reissued in a large printing, still commanded a sizable audience. "Brann, the Iconoclast," as he styled himself, must have got a good deal of fun out of vituperation, if we may judge from the zest with which he wrote, before his career was terminated by an assassin in 1898. Brann, though he was looked upon in horror or disgust by religious people (and though he once remarked that society could do better without D.D.'s for a thousand years than it could without the American drummer for one day), does not appear to have been a complete agnostic. At least he differed with Ingersoll (while professing admiration for him) over the matter of revelation, and he refused to attack the vision of a Catholic girl, as he was requested to do by one subscriber to *The Iconoclast,* declaring that, although he believed the vision to be a dream, there were many mysteries in the world which he did not comprehend.

Brann was the particular scourge of sectarians and popular revivalists. He did not care for crusaders of any sort, and laid on lustily to those who appeared in his bailiwick in the Southwest. Thus the Populists, Coin Harvey, and Bryan got their trimming. In the days of the silver controversy, Brann had his own panacea—a paper currency based on national wealth. There were many contradictions in the man: he wrote with force and feeling when the Supreme Court voided the Income Tax law and when Sheriff Martin ordered his deputies to fire into the assembled miners at Latimer, Pennsylvania. He is effective in his denunciation of the American Protective Association (an organization aimed at the extirpation of American Catholicism, he claimed), and almost eloquent in his assault upon laws which set "the age of consent" at ten and thirteen years. But he is revolting in his many and obscene attacks upon "the buck nigger" and "black raper," and in his open advocacy of lynch law. His tone is so predominantly vulgar, he is so avid for the raw, cruel, sensational, and salacious, that it would not appear that he could endure save as a symptomatic writer. Nevertheless "Brann, the Iconoclast," was a jolting force in his day, and respectability quaked before him and his bad grammar.

Native iconoclasm developed into what H. L. Mencken has aptly described as the "pianissimo revolt" of the 'nineties. The intellectual leader of this revolt was Stephen Crane, who, as we have seen, was far more important as a Naturalist than as an iconoclast. Yet one who ignores the bold attacks on conventional religious concepts in Crane's *The Black Riders* (1895) misses a good deal of the significance of Stephen Crane. The youthful background of this genius was as restricted as were the parental homes of Ingersoll and Howe, and it may safely be assumed that the revolutionary lines of *The Black Riders* are more of a product of chafing under this restraint than of Crane's reading. He himself has described his poems as "many red devils" which ran out of his heart. These devils mock the gods for menacing fools and for overwhelming men with mountains. To Crane in this mood all ambition was but a futile pursuit of the horizon and one might just as well—

> Go pluck a bough and wear it.
> It is as sufficing. . . .

Crane raised his toy blunderbuss against the whole heavens, perhaps with some thought of bringing a troop of angels down, but Harold Frederic, Crane's fellow porcelain-breaker, discharged his weapon directly against the Methodist Church, then the largest Protestant sect in America. His *The Damnation of Theron Ware,* which arraigned the adventurer in religion, was the literary scandal of the year 1896. Though Comstock succeeded in persuading the Post Office Department to refuse it the mails, *The Damnation* reached a very large audience and materially undermined the influence of the lesser clergy in all Protestant sects. Frederic, a disciple of the French historical

Naturalists, Erckmann-Chatrian, drew a bold and merciless caricature of a snivelling divine and the members of his church board of trustees, then made an invidious comparison between his protagonist and the local Catholic father and his learned friends. As a result, the book is not lightly to be dismissed as agnostical—for while it filled certain Methodist bosoms with wrath, it struck more impartial readers as a just stricture on those who chose religion as a career without any inward signs of grace, and also as a bold plea for religious tolerance. Though *The Damnation of Theron Ware* is better at almost every point than Mr. Sinclair Lewis' *Elmer Gantry,* it has one glaring fault —the author's absurd notion of good taste, represented for us by the things with which a monied Irish hoyden, who takes Theron's fancy, surrounds herself in the tale. Frederic may be trusted when he draws the world he knew as a boy in upper New York State, but when he tries to impress us with his cosmopolitanism, he is far from successful. There is some good honest writing, though it is somewhat less ambitious, in his earlier tales, *Seth's Brother's Wife* (1887) and *The Copperhead* (1893). His work as London correspondent for *The New York Times* is remembered for his reports on the cholera epidemic in southern France and Italy in 1884 and the persecution of the Jews in southern Russia in 1891. Yet our respect for him is considerably diminished by his laudatory portrait of Kaiser Wilhelm in *The Young Emperor* in 1892. In London he posed as a wit and cynic and sedulously cultivated the Right People, most of whom he offended in one way or another.

"Don't try to account for anything" is the "moral" of one of George Ade's *Fables in Slang.* A kind of glandular disgust, the exuded acid of a Sedentary Life and Low Male Companionship in bars, hotel lobbies, and city newsrooms, is the effect one receives from reading the most characteristic work of this Hoosier Diogenes—*Artie* (1896), *Fables in Slang* (1899), *More Fables* (1900), *Forty Modern Fables* (1901), *Breaking Into Society* (1904) and *True Bills* (1904). George Ade was a Small Town Boy—son of The Banker of Kentland, Indiana—and he never quite outgrew that fact. H. L. Mencken, who made Ade one of his heroes in *Prejudices I,* shrewdly observes, "one would not be surprised to hear that, until he went off to his freshwater college, he slept in his underwear and read the *Epworth Herald.*" The "freshwater college" was Purdue University, from which George Ade was graduated in 1887. Newsgathering in Lafayette and selling patent medicines were the only preliminaries to a brief career as a reporter and a longer one as a columnist in Chicago, where he worked on the *Morning News* and the *Record.* His column appeared next to Eugene Field's "Sharps and Flats," and when Field died, George Ade got his desk. Possibly given direction by G. W. Carryl's *Fables for the Frivolous* (1898), Ade created the first of the *Fables in Slang,* "The Blonde Girl Who Married A Bucket Shop Man," and the demand for more made him famous.

One of Ade's less successful books, *Doc' Horne* (1899), stimulates conjectures which, if sustainable, adequately limn the man. A company of loafers is sketched, chair-warmers at the Alfalfa European Hotel in Chicago, unmarried men who have plenty of time on their hands but not the wherewithal or the strong impulse for dissipation. Each is long on talk; each affects a worldly wisdom; but all are still patently small towners, safely segregated from the experiences and temptations of the Big Town. If Ade dwelt in such a company in his early reportorial days in Chicago, and the verisimilitude of the portraits suggests a great familiarity, then the man's creative career is completely comprehensible. Ade never is cosmopolitan in his point of view: the *Fables* are "revolt from the village" and nothing more. It is their language that is deceptive; yet, on reflection, it reminds one of the brash palaver of a fellow who, after a brief excursion into the world, intends to impress home-town folk by ridiculing all that they stand for. Frequently such a fellow's talk is like his toggery: new and noisy—a sign of recent emancipation. As if by inversion, this is the type of character whom Ade himself most frequently satirizes. He is the protagonist of "What the College Incubator Did for One Modest Lambkin," "The Willing Collegian Who Was Hunting for a Foothold," "The Fable of Another Brave Effort to Infuse Gentility into our Raw Civilization," "The Fable of Handsome Jethro Who was Simply Cut Out to be a Merchant," and numerous other fables. Which, as Truthful James would say, suggests a Fearsome Awe of Arrested Development.

Yet cheerful surrender to adolescent tastes in the theatre made Ade well-to-do, his musical comedies, like *The Sultan of Sulu* (1902) and *The Sho-gun* (1904), proving no more popular than the farce hits, *The College Widow* (1904), *Just Out of College* (1905), and *Father and the Boys* (1908), whose titles sufficiently reveal their depth and the character of their divertissement. Ade has, however, a secure niche at not too giddy a height on the easiest slope of Mount Parnassus. He is almost the last of the purely indigenous humorists—above everything else he has (as Mencken remarked) the national distrust of ideas and culture. Child of Billings and Bill Nye, as his fling at Emerson proves, George Ade is a combination of drummer and literary cowboy whose one-man rodeo at the turn of the century is still remembered for the wonderful knots he tied and the loops he threw with the American language as his lariat. Despite this philological facility, so pleasing to the masses, Ade is most likely to be remembered, however, for the tones of complete finality with which he announced the Utter Futility of Attempting to Account for Anything.

Now it is to be noted that not one of the writers whom we have thus far considered, whether he posed as a Western humorist, a cynic, or an iconoclast, held himself aloof from other men. Not one ostensibly regarded himself as belonging to a privileged class of intellectuals or looked upon the craft of writing as sacrosanct. Indeed, from the deliberate bad spellers of early days to Stephen Crane, who took the view that writing, whatever its quality, is "just a little ink, more or less," each and every one of them had a tendency to scoff at literary pretentiousness. To them the concept of "the artist apart" was an alien concept, and, indeed, so it was to most of America. This idea of a privileged class of intellectuals was an importation from England, where it appears to have been an offshoot of the decline of Victorianism, when, native wit failing, the British turned to the Irish and the Irish Americans for mental pabulum, and the latter, still looked upon as inferiors by those whom they entertained, compensated by avowing themselves beyond good and evil, beyond the moral laws professed by their betters.

2

CELTIC-AMERICAN CYNICISM

Victorianism received its mortal thrust in November, 1878, and was not blown apart by a bomb in the 'nineties as Mr. Holbrook Jackson has intimated. The wits of that decade merely desecrated the corpse—one should know that from the ghoulishness of their whole proceeding. Victorianism was stabbed to death in the Ruskin libel suit, but being a body of sound flesh, transmuted beef and greens, it was able to stagger about, gasping for air for another decade, until, bled white and clammy with perspiration, it dropped from lack of ozone in the fetid 'nineties, whereupon all the little imps and pipsqueaks who had been hiding in the purple shadows rushed out, shouting they had made worms' meat of it. They would no more have tackled it living than they would have grasped lightning from the skies or broken a window in Putney to steal cakes.

Victorianism died of a lunge in tierce, administered by a trained swordsman, an ex-student of our own Military Academy at West Point. Had the fellow been graduated, doubtless he would have dropped it in its tracks. The flaw in his execution, however, was somehow typical of his whole career and afforded him as much exasperation as, through prolongation, it increased the pain of his enemies. For James Abbott McNeill Whistler, deliverer of the inept *coup de grâce,* possessed one of the finest and most delicate imaginations of the nineteenth century, yet was so hasty and mercurial that nothing he did—not even the mixing of his paints—may be proclaimed flawless, and certainly not the dispatching of Victorianism, which might well have been permitted to die of its own grossness, submerged and suffocated in layers of fat. His thrust conferred a sort of dignity upon it, wherefore it is sure to be resurrected and virtue found in it. The profound peace of that great cadaver, despite the nibbled waistcoat and cheek, the missing buttons and decorations, the pilfered pockets, and the great stain in front (fixing all eyes), wins respect. And what did Victorianism ever aim at save respect? Victorianism murdered is just as effective as Victorianism at home in slippers. In immolation and immortality there is more of a resemblance than is suggested by the spelling of the words. It is the immolator who always suffers.

Yet Whistler was so much more of a man than the claque who followed him that, if not a giant among pygmies, he at least has stature, even today. Of Irish-American stock, born in Lowell, Massachusetts, in 1834, James McNeill Whistler had looked unsteadily at a good deal of life before the celebrated libel trial of 1878. His father, an engineer, had whisked his family from Lowell, to Stonington, Connecticut, to Springfield, Massachusetts, and finally to St. Petersburg, whither he had been invited by Czar Nicholas I to build a railroad to Moscow. Seven years' effort to establish parallel rails on ice exhausted the father and he passed from his reward; meanwhile, however, his talented son had begun the study of painting in the Imperial Academy of Fine Arts at Moscow. Following Major Whistler's death, Mrs. Whistler, an anxious, Puritan lady, brought her lively Jamie home and deposited him for finishing in the Rev. Dr. Roswell Park's School in Pomfret, Connecticut. There he was properly caned for mimicking the pompous headmaster, but absorbed enough of the discipline to carry him along through three years at the Military Academy, to which he secured an appointment. He was dismissed from West Point for insisting in an examination in Chemistry that silicon was a gas, yet he bounced into a position in the Drawing Division of the Coast and Geodetic Survey. Here he learned the technique of etching which was to make him a master of copper-plate drawing; yet because he felt the lack of fancy in the drawing of the Survey maps and did what he could to make up for that lack, it was agreed that it was expedient for him to resign, and so, in 1855, he threw up this work and went to Paris to study art. Young Whistler had lived, and literally fed, upon a copy of Henri Murger's *Scènes de la Vie de Bohême* ever since its appearance in 1848; consequently he was disappointed in the actual bohemianism of the Latin Quarter, and he sought to improve upon it after his arrival, clowning it and kinging it with great zest among the grisettes and cancan dancers, so that stories of his infamy preceded him to London, whither he moved in 1860. Of course, he had had a painting rejected by the *Salon* in Paris before coming to London, but he soon had the satisfaction of seeing it hung, with five etchings, at the Royal Academy.

Duped this once, perhaps, the directors of the Academy were not to be fooled again, and they had rejected *The White Girl,* the first of his "Symphonies" in 1862. Only one explanation is possible today for the rejection of this painting. Rumor must have reached the directors (Whistler had no "private" life) that this picture in "pure" white was a portrait of Whistler's model and mistress, the beautiful Irish girl, Joanna Heffernan, and the directors must have felt the canvas a jibe at British morality. Though the drawing is not true, the angle of the rug on the floor suggesting the Flying Carpet, the painting itself is entrancing. It was the first demonstration by a modern that profusion of color, as in the current Pre-Raphaelite painting, is not necessary to the creation of a great canvas. After the Academy rejected *The Girl in White,* Whistler on invitation exhibited it with other rejected pictures in the Berners Street Gallery, where it drew much excited comment. He began and finished another study of Jo, again dressed in white, posed before a mirror, which he entitled *The Little White Girl,* "Symphony in White, No. 2." This portrait aroused the admiration of Swinburne, who wrote the verses which were inscribed on the frame when it was accepted by the Royal Academy for its 1865 show. After a trip to Valparaiso, where rumor has it he was under fire, Whistler exhibited his first "Nocturne" at the French Gallery and placed his *Two Little White Girls,* "Symphony in White, No. 3," in the Royal Academy. P. G. Hamerton, one of the lesser arbiters of British taste, pounced upon the latter picture as not strictly "white." "There is a girl in white on a white sofa," he observed in *The Saturday Review,* "but even this girl has reddish hair, and, of course, there is the flesh color of the complexion." This proved too much for Whistler and he wrote to the editor of the *Review:*

"Bon Dieu! did this wise person expect white hair and chalked faces? And does he then, in his astonishing consequence, believe that a Symphony in F contains no other note, but shall be a continued repetition of F, F, F,? . . . Fool!"

Needless to say, the editor of *The Saturday Review* did not print the letter, but that did not silence Whistler, whose tongue had become feared in London. His vigorous defenses of his "Symphonies in White" had led Rossetti to compose a limerick which further spread his fame abroad:

> There's a combative artist named Whistler
> Who is, like his own hog-hairs, a bristler:
>   A tube of white lead
>   And a punch on the head
> Offer varied attractions to Whistler.

He aided and abetted the growth of his own notoriety by affected eccentricities of dress and manners. His top hat, his dark overcoat with its three capes, his white waistcoat and trousers, his profuse black curls with the single white forelock, the white Pomeranian which he led on a leash, and the tall, slim stick on which he could rest his chin, became familiar properties in the public's image of him. Lateness as guest and lateness as host, deadliness in repartee which spared none, the habit of giving Sunday breakfasts at noon, unwillingness to modulate his laughter, made Whistler a celebrity of sorts. Yet he achieved some very wealthy patrons and was, shortly before the Ruskin trial, engaged in redecorating a dining room for one of the most liberal of these, Frederick Leyland, "the Liverpool Medici," as Whistler called him, so that the room would harmonize with a picture he had purchased—the *Princess du Pays de la Porcelaine.*

Whistler had hung his last painting in the Royal Academy, had had his first "one-man" exhibition of full-length portraits and "Nocturnes" before he showed, among other things in the first Grosvenor Gallery Exhibition, that "Nocturne in Black and Gold" entitled *The Falling Rocket* which elicited Ruskin's attack in *Fors Clavigera* for July 2, 1877:

For Mr. Whistler's own sake, no less than for the protection of the purchaser, Sir Coutts Lindsay ought not to have admitted works in the gallery in which the ill-educated conceit of the artist so nearly approached the aspect of willful imposture. I have seen and heard much of cockney impudence before now; but never expected to hear a coxcomb ask two hundred guineas for flinging a pot of paint in the public's face.

This was no impulsive comment on a canvas the critic did not like, but a deliberate frontal attack on the artist himself with the intention to check or destroy. John Ruskin was no Hamerton, no paid reviewer, but the most revered authority on art in England and the most considerable writer on the subject since the time of Vasari. Slade Professor of Art in the University of Oxford, he had already (so it might appear) demonstrated his ability to recognize worth in the new when it came along: Had he not risen to the defense of Turner's later impressionistic manner in 1843 when everyone else was attacking the painter? And had he not, when the young Pre-Raphaelites were being scourged in 1850 and 1851, written the famous letter to *The Times* that had turned the tide of opinion in favor of the brotherhood? But it is not clear that any real appreciation of aesthetic worth in the painters he championed was responsible for Ruskin's partisanship; rather, it would appear that some extraneous impulse, a fancied moral evaluation or truculent compassion for the weak and persecuted was his motive. Further, after his prolific writing on art had aroused a wide interest, particularly among the prosperous merchant class, Ruskin had felt the need of counseling caution. In his famous inaugural address at his installation in Oxford in 1869, he had forcefully restated his view that "the first necessity for the doing of any great work in the ideal art, is the looking upon all foulness with horror. . . . You can have noble art only from noble persons. . . ." He had gone on to deplore the British delight—"ever since the Conquest—in the forms of burlesque which are connected in some degree with the foulness in evil," and as examples of this "foulness" cited Chaucer and Shakespeare! Still his greatest emphasis was laid in this lecture on the dangers of traducing the bourgeois patronage of art:

We have a vast and new patronage, which, in its present agency, is injurious to our schools. . . . It is in a great measure the fault of artists themselves if they suffer from this partly unintelligent, but thoroughly well-intended, patronage. If they seek to attract it by eccentricity, to deceive it by superficial qualities, or to take advantage of it by thoughtless and facile production, they necessarily degrade themselves and it together, and have no right to complain afterward that it will not acknowledge better-grounded claims.

And he solemnly repeated the virtuous counsel of the rich man to artists that "peculiar art-skill can never be developed *with a view to profit.*"

The Inaugural Lecture was all that was Victorian, and to everything Victorian James Abbott McNeill Whistler was obnoxious: his morals were more than suspect, his training was in France (from which wicked country, through an infusion of Norman blood, Ruskin hints, the English derive their gusto for the salacious), he had wealthy patrons and patronesses, he obviously had won these by "eccentricity" and "superficial qualities," and he certainly was making a "profit" if he got the sums he was credited with getting. It was time this upstart, this Irish-American, this cockney-coxcomb was put in his place. The attack in *Fors Clavigera* was as deliberate as it was right-minded.

Far from evacuating London with his brushes and paints at this salute from Oxford, Whistler haled his foe into town and into court for libel on November 15, 1878, seeking £1000 damages. Only an impudent reliance on the Englishman's sense of fair play could have persuaded Whistler to do this; for however obvious the libel, it was almost inconceivable that an English jury would award damages against so English a gentleman as John Ruskin when it was clearly implied that English morality was somehow involved. Indeed, the defense conducted itself as though it expected every Englishman to do his duty and let its case rest there. The plaintiff took a most extraordinary line of attack: he asserted that to be competent to judge the worth of pictures one must be a painter and not an amateur; he challenged the competence of the Slade Professor altogether to evaluate art. Then the most astonishing thing happened in the annals of English jurisprudence. The jury, which knew nothing about art, was persuaded that John Ruskin knew nothing about it either, and with a nice sense of values awarded the plaintiff

somewhat less than the traditional penny—a brass farthing—
for his thought. It may be remarked, however, that the throwing
of this miserable farthing into the neatly balanced scales of
justice was enough to kick the beam and dump Victorianism out.

Not until he had got home, after stopping at the Pig and
Whistle for a pint of ale by way of celebrating, did our worthy
English juryman realize that he had sold his virtue for the
smallest price on record. He had admitted the incompetence of
anyone but the artist to pass judgment upon his art; he had
denied that art had any ethical or social values; he, the traditional lover of equality among men, had established a caste
system in the realm of the intellect—a class of "untouchables",
the artists, who were to have complete and absolute freedom to
"utter" whatever they chose, who were to be "beyond good and
evil." "You do not approve of criticism, then?" Mr. Ruskin's
counsel had asked Mr. Whistler when the latter was on the
stand. "I should not disapprove in any way of *technical* criticism
by a man *whose whole life is passed in the practice of the science
which he criticises,*" Whistler had retorted, "but for the opinion
of a man whose life is not so passed I would have as little regard
as you would, if he expressed an opinion on law." This was so
handsome a rejoinder, and so apt an appeal to the barrister's
prejudices, that he was left speechless and his case was lost. He
knew that men uttered ill-considered judgments on the law, and
he was willing to disqualify all men but lawyers from judging
whether a law was good or bad (the fundamental act of criticism) ; therefore he was willing to yield to artists the sole privilege of judging art, and by silence gave assent to Whistler's
thesis. The surrender at Yorktown was as nothing compared
with this.

Is it not apparent that if only the artist may judge art, since
his sole competence is execution, then only the painter of a particular canvas is entitled to judge that canvas and only the author
of the poem may tell us whether the poem is good or bad? It
may be objected that Whistler never contemplated any such
extension of his meaning, but unfortunately this is not true. In
December, 1878, Chatto and Windus published a brochure by
Mr. Whistler in which he amplified his views, *Whistler v. Ruskin:*

Art and Art Critics. "Let there be no critics! They are not a
'necessary evil,' " Whistler contended, "but an evil unnecessary,
though an evil certainly." It had never occurred to any Victorian
that an artist would be so bold as to claim immunity from the
judgments of his fellow men, and the very arrogance of the
claim addled Victorian wits and leveled their defenses. They
failed to retort that a desire for immunity is a revelation of
weakness and that immunity granted is privilege. They did not
realize that, when art has no meaning, this very absence of meaning has social significance. They hesitated to argue that occasionally a talent in execution might be somewhat less than a
talent in judgment, since judgment might comprehend an appreciation of other excellencies as well as the peculiar merit of the
artist. Their failure to expose the major aesthetic fallacy of their
times gave rise to one of the dominant schools of modern thought
and affected powerfully the trend of our affairs. It was through
this breach, as we shall see, that the teachings of Nietzsche, the
philosophy of a class beyond good and evil, entered and became
a part of the thought of peoples inherently predisposed against
arrogance and special privilege.

It must be admitted that the incompetence of Ruskin as a
critic of art confused men's judgments and took their eyes off the
main issue. This incapacity Whistler was able to demonstrate
with resounding effect. Not only did he do it in *Whistler v. Ruskin,* but also in the sprightly annotations to the various catalogues
of his exhibitions, and finally in the notorious *The Gentle Art of
Making Enemies* (1890), a highly amusing anthology of his
own wit. Whistler merely needed to quote Ruskin to destroy his
importance as a critic of art. Consider these lucubrations culled
by the Butterfly from *Modern Painters:*

> And that colour is indeed a most unimportant characteristic of objects
> would be further evident on the slightest consideration.
> Vulgarity, dullness, or impiety will indeed always express themselves
> through art, in brown and gray, as in Rembrandt.

Or add to them at will:

> I wholly deny that the *impressions* of beauty are in any way sensual;
> they are neither sensual nor intellectual, but moral.

Ruskin had lost the pristine qualification of the common man to judge painting—he had ceased to ask, Does this picture delight me? And to follow it with, Why? His first query had become, Ought this picture to delight me? And the answers he gave were determined by fanciful speculations on the morality of the artist. He made no attempt to find his way back to a sensible appreciation of pictures through the physiology of perception and the physics of color, or through a genuinely comparative study of canvases. He was, indeed, what Whistler described him to be, "the populariser of pictures . . . The Peter Parley of painting." By which sign, however, it is apparent that Whistler did a great service for modern painting by insisting, first, that the critic concern himself with the painting and not with the painter, and secondly, that he approach painting as a "science" (Whistler's word), that is, a body of knowledge and skill as much to be respected as any other body of knowledge and skill, and to be as patiently inquired into. Whistler here merely occupied a position previously held by Leonardo da Vinci, though he was probably unaware of this. We can rejoice in his mass slaughter of the whole class of Victorian "critics," as represented by such figures as Ruskin, Hamerton, Taylor, Colvin, Frith, Ward, Horsley, *et al.* His recommendation that Ruskin resign the Slade Professorship and accept a chair of Ethics at the University was not followed out literally, but it is true that Ruskin did resign in 1879, alleging ill health as the reason.

The Ruskin libel suit had an immediate disastrous effect upon Whistler's personal fortunes. The jury that awarded him his farthing damages did not allow him the costs of his suit, which were heavy. Further, Whistler's most munificent patron, Frederick Leyland, for the first time disappointed the artist—instead of paying the two thousand guineas for the gorgeous Peacock Room which Whistler had expected, he gave him a check for just half that sum. Whistler had laid himself under great expense in building a residence and studio; consequently his counsel fees brought his affairs to a climax, with the result that he was declared bankrupt in May, 1879. The story of his successful effort to redeem his fortunes may be briefly told. A commission to execute some etchings in Venice for the Fine Art Society was undeniably a godsend, and his election to the Society of British Artists and then to the Presidency of that society greatly aided in the restoration of his prestige. The invitation to repeat his lecture "Ten O'Clock" at the University of Oxford was not merely a conciliatory gesture but an acknowledgment of a kind of eminence as well. The most substantial proof of this eminence was furnished in 1891, when the Glasgow Corporation purchased the *Carlyle* and the French government the *Mother.* Medals, crosses, decorations, prizes followed thereafter in great profusion. Full of honors, he died suddenly on July 17, 1903, and lies in Cheswick churchyard not far from Hogarth whom he loved.

Whistler's one effort to be profound himself in the field of criticism, his "Ten O'Clock" lecture on art, is a piece of flubdubbery. He asserts that the fashioning of utensils was the first production of artists and assumes that primitive pottery and primitive dwellings were necessarily all beautiful. "And the people lived in marvels of art—and ate and drank out of masterpieces—for there was nothing else to eat and drink out of, and no bad building to live in . . . *the artist alone produced"!* Yet while accepting calmly all of the product of natural man as beautiful, he can assert (what is partially true) that Nature is not necessarily beautiful and seldom succeeds in producing a picture —without apprehending any inconsistency in his position. After the world was flooded with beauty by the artists, the tradesman saw fortune in "the facture of sham" and pushed art into the curio-shops. Whistler turns from this "tragedy" (which is too sad to contemplate) to a discussion of the critics who are "the middle-men" of art. He lumps and damns the lot—"the unattached writer," the archeologist, the professor of art, the dilettante. Then with a grand rhetorical burst, something like his *Falling Rocket,* he declares, "The master stands in no relation to the moment at which he occurs—a moment of isolation—hinting at sadness—having no part in the progress of his fellow-men." Take this statement at its face value and it could be proved that neither Whistler, nor any other painter, was a master.

That Whistler was something of a master with the brush and etching needle must be conceded, though he was far from flawless with either. His greatest weakness was an inability to draw accurately, and he himself sighed because he had never had Ingres for a master. Had Whistler himself not felt that drawing was a part of the picture, we might judge him by his color alone, but his admissions preclude this. His painting entitled, *The Balcony,* "Harmony in Flesh Color and Green," in the Freer collection is as good an illustration of his disability as any. Flopped behind a tea tray to the left of the picture is an attractive young woman in a kimono, which ample garment conceals the shocking deformity of her lower limbs—extremities shriveled to come within the bounds of the canvas. At her elbow, and back to us, stands another figure gazing out over the balcony rail, but of such diminutive proportions (so bad is the perspective) that she is plainly on the wrong side of the rail. The figure of the young lady with the musical instrument in the right foreground is that of a normal person, save that the hand on the box of the instrument has no boney structure beneath the flesh and is performing a miracle of dexterity.

Or take the picture entitled *The Yellow Buckskin,* "Arrangement in Black," reputed to be a portrait of Lady Archibald Campbell. To begin with, the lady is posed in the most awkward position conceivable, half wheeled away from us, gazing back over a raised shoulder and shot hip, for all the world like a filly glancing back over withers and rump at her master in the buckboard. Both hip and shoulder are exaggerated, and the left foot which protrudes beneath the dress has no conceivable relation to the rest of the anatomy. These may be extreme cases, but they reveal a fundamental flaw in the artist's work, traceable in his most famous canvases. Both the *Carlyle* and the portrait of his *Mother,* for example, almost lack a third dimension—the figures being more like thin bas-relief against the wall than anything else. The latter painting has had a fitting apotheosis as the design for a postage stamp.

"I don't play the piano accurately," says Algernon in *The Importance of Being Earnest,* "—anyone can play accurately—but I play with wonderful expression." Something similar could be said of Whistler's painting. Whistler's best work is in rendering atmosphere and here he is the true predecessor of Monet, just as he was himself in turn the disciple of Rembrandt, Velásquez,

Courbet, and Hiroshige. His portrait of himself in the big hat and later arrangements in black and brown show the influence of the Dutch master; study of Velásquez's infantas has aided in the portrait of little Miss Alexander, though the influence of Japanese design may be seen here, too; and Courbet dominates such paintings as *The Blue Wave, The Music Room,* and *Alone with the Tide.* His "Nocturnes" are indubitably Whistler's most original work, pure studies in color, the difficult masses, the problems in drawing all adumbrated by varying degrees of mistiness—a mistiness which made it possible for the artist to concentrate on the color and color harmonies which he loved. These are, literally, poems in paint. Curiously, of all his work on copper, stone, and tracing paper—for he is a notable etcher—it is a lithotint entitled "Nocturne" that appears the best. No one has been more successful than he in suggesting in this print the effect of half-light on water. In both painting and print it is the quality of imagination that holds us and will continue to hold us for some time to come.

Whistler was the first of all the wits who tortured John Bull in the 'sixties and 'seventies—the quickest tongue among all the lively clappers of that era, and the most incisive—the natural gadfly of the group of no-kin, Lear, Sala, Hood, Calverley, Bierce, Dodgson, Gilbert, Dobson, and Stephen. Yet perhaps it is as a precursor of the intellectual renaissance of the Irish that the painter should be remembered. This renaissance had two aspects which have not been properly distinguished. One of these might be termed the Nationalist-Decadent, while the other, with equal propriety, might be called the Expatriate-Intellectualist. Both are but different revelations of the forces set in motion by the great famine following the blight of the potato crop in 1846 and 1847, and by the defeat of the Young Ireland rebellion of 1848. Incidentally, the most radical leaders of 1848 seem to have emigrated to America, for in this country, less than a decade later, John O'Mahony founded the Fenian Brotherhood, on the model of the Jacobin Society, pledged to resort to arms, if need be, to establish the Irish republic. In 1866, some eight hundred Fenians under the leadership of John O'Neill crossed the Niagara River, entered Canada, and took Fort Erie, but were routed at Ridgeway by a corps of Canadian volunteers. Many Irishmen who fought in our Civil War, finding no easy or exciting employment when the War was over, returned to their native heath and took part in the disorders of the following years. Fenianism practically expired, however, with the Manchester murders of 1867 and the arrest of Michael Davitt in 1870, and was succeeded by the Home Rule movement, initiated by the formation of the Home Association by Isaac Butt in 1870.

Meanwhile a deep interest in Irish culture had been aroused by Matthew Arnold's lectures at Oxford and his articles in the *Cornhill Magazine,* published in book form as *On the Study of Celtic Literature* (1867). They were followed by the studies in the folklore and history of Ireland by such able scholars as O'Curry, Nutt, Hull, Joyce, Ridgeway, Hyde, and others. The movement started by Butt made few practical gains, and it was succeeded in turn by the boycott methods of the Land League, led by the released Davitt and the captivating Charles Stewart Parnell. This organization roused Irish enthusiasm to a fever heat, but a terrible debacle occurred at the beginning of the 'nineties when Parnell, who had alienated the Ulsterites by accepting Gladstone's Home Rule Bill, was involved in a divorce action, thereby offending the majority of his Catholic followers. Irish sentiment was split into factions, and as a consequence, the whole tone of the new nationalist literature had a decadent, defeatist character, plainly imitated from French Decadence, for the Irish intellectuals felt a kinship with the French, which was reinforced by the discovery of common elements in the ancient legendaries of both countries. These and other factors determined the character of the work of such able writers as William Butler Yeats, George Russell, George Moore, Padraic Colum, John Millington Synge, Lady Augusta Gregory, Lord Dunsany, James Stephens, James Joyce, and Sean O'Casey.

Well known as the writers of this school are in America and properly admired (as they should be), they are curiously less influential here than several of their kin who have been less interested in producing a characteristic Irish literature but have sought, rather, to win the respect of the English in the journals and theatres of the dominant race. A sense of inferiority, of

shame for the brawlings of their fellows and of uncertainty in
regard to their own genius, has kept most of these thinkers from
being quite genuine—they must all be poseurs and buffoons.
James Abbott McNeill Whistler, both an Irishman and an
American, poseur and wit, the first antagonist really to bring dis-
comfiture to John Bull, became their model, and his doctrine that
the artist is beyond criticism, beyond good and evil, became their
shield and buckler.

The second figure of consequence in this army in motley was
the infamous pederast, Oscar Fingal O'Flahertie Wells Wilde,
whose unhappy career was the last great scandal of the Victorian
era. Wilde, the son of Sir William Wilde, a Dublin oculist and
surgeon with an international reputation, and of Jane Francesca
Elgee, a Fenian poetess who wrote under the pseudonym of
"Speranza," was born in the Irish capital on October 16, 1852.
Poor Wilde's future was determined in part by the character and
proclivities of his parents. His papa was a very promiscuous person, and left his image in many a Paddy's cottage about Dublin,
if the biographers are to be trusted, while "Speranza" was ex-
emplary in her devotion, stoutly refusing to believe any evidence
against her husband, even when he was haled into court by one
outraged young woman. This is the more surprising since Oscar
was born to her within a year of her marriage, and she had already presented her husband with an heir and namesake. It is
said that she passionately desired a girl for her second child and
that she kept Oscar in petticoats and ribbons long after it was
decent to do so. She was an extremely artificial person, to all accounts, one of those women of masculine proportions who asserts
her femininity by adorning everything in her home with frills and
furbelows. Poor Oscar, ragged for his girlishness at Portora
Royal School, Enniskillen, and at Trinity College, retained to
the end of his days a feminine way of looking at things and of
reacting towards them, as Sherard has pointed out. His "sissy"
Vivian, in "The Decay of Lying," when invited to lie on the
grass and smoke and talk, responds, "Grass is hard and lumpy
and damp, and full of dreadful black insects." And the effeminate
Gilbert of "The Critic as Artist" when urged to talk by his little
friend Ernest petulantly insists he prefers to play the piano, "I

am not in the mood for talking tonight. How horrid of you to smile! I really am not . . ." etc. These creatures can purr and pet, and maybe scratch, but they are incapable of quarreling—and so was Oscar. It mattered not whether the rough boys at Portora upset him and broke his arm or the students at Oxford soused him in the Cherwell—they knew no better and were to be forgiven, as his mama forgave his papa. Like a good little girl, he got his lessons, and after winning the Berkeley Gold Medal for an essay on "The Greek Comic Poets" at Trinity, went up to Oxford, where he won another prize, the Newdigate in 1878, for his poem "Ravenna."

At Oxford his interest in art and aesthetic matters was kindled by the lectures of Ruskin and Pater, and on his trips from the University up to London he met and came under the influence of Whistler. It was Whistler's costume that induced him to don the Regency jacket and knee-trousers and the long silk stockings which led to his ducking. It was from Whistler that he derived the passion for blue china, flowered chintz curtains, peacock's feathers, and Japanese kakemonos. Indeed, it was from the eccentric table decorations of Whistler's eccentric Sunday morning breakfasts that he got his inspiration to walk upon the Strand bearing a lily or sunflower before him. As in Whistler's case, these affectations won him extraordinary prominence. Though never able to match Whistler in any exchange of compliments, he soon became noted throughout London society for his wit and his charm. With his unwillingness to take or give offense he was much more in demand as a guest than was Whistler, and his talk was repeated everywhere—especially in the columns of the *World*, for which his brother Willy was a writer. How much of this talk was filched from the artist none can say, but a good deal was, at first, surely. There is a well-authenticated and much repeated story to the effect that Wilde, after some thrust of Whistler's, declared enviously,

"I wish I had said that."
To which the painter retorted instantly, "You will, Oscar, you will."

Yet after he had fenced with this studio-master he easily parried the thrusts of others and needed to depend on no one for a guide. It was he who described Irving's legs, "One is a poem and the other is a symphony"; it was he who consoled Beerbohm Tree, when the latter anxiously asked his opinion of his Hamlet, with "My dear Tree—I think your Hamlet is—funny—without being vulgar." It used to be that one could write a good book about the 'nineties with an anecdote or two from Wilde as its only nucleus. His best remarks doubtless are "A cynic is one who knows the price of everything and the value of nothing" (repeated in *Lady Windermere's Fan*), "We will not go to war with France—because her prose is perfect," and his observation on coming from Reading Gaol, "If England persists in treating her criminals like this, she does not deserve to have any. . . ."

All Wilde's talent went in his first years after leaving Oxford to gain social prestige for himself, and he never was unmindful of this end throughout his life. Bernard Shaw, after remarking that Wilde's Irish charm, potent with Englishmen, did not exist for him, stigmatizes Wilde as "a very prime specimen of the sort of fellow-townsman I most loathed: to wit, the Dublin snob," and one cannot but observe how apt the characterization is. The Dublin snob is a very lofty personage in Ireland, but in England a person of very little state. The fact that Oscar Wilde dropped all his very Irish middle names before going to Oxford and the further fact that he never invited to his mother's London house any people who were not Celts are indicative of his low opinion of his own people and of his desire not to be taken for a loathsome Paddy. There is an affected "true Briton" air in his explanation of how he got the names for the characters in his plays, "I take up a map of the English counties and there they are. *Our* English villages have often exquisitely beautiful names. Windermere, for instance . . ." But generally his people are given names which are indicative only of Wilde's worship of what he thought *haut ton*: Mrs. Erlynne, Gerald Arbuthnot, Algernon Moncrieff, Gwendolyn Fairfax, etc.,—the names a shop girl would choose. Frank Harris is undeniably right in assuming that later, when Wilde became criminally involved with Lord Douglas, it was the latter's name and position that enticed him. Harris, like Shaw, insists that Oscar Wilde fawned on the socially prominent. "He was a snob as only an English artist can be a snob; he loved titular distinctions, and Douglas is one of the few great names in British history with the gilding of romance about it. . . ." This would be a matter of no consequence to us, and something lower than gossip, were it not for the fact that Wilde's snobbery is perfectly in keeping with the moral point of view—which he adopted from Whistler—that the artist cannot be judged. "There is no sin except stupidity."

Wilde's tactics were admirably calculated, however, to please his betters and to bring him the favors he sought, so that very shortly after leaving Oxford he had a host of enemies—those who hated him for his shallowness and those who envied his social success. The publication of his *Poems* in 1881 was a signal for this host to descend upon him. *Punch* flayed and caricatured him, but so far as the verses are concerned was eminently fair:

> The cover is consummate, the paper is distinctly precious, the binding is beautiful, and the type is utterly too. *Poems,* by Oscar Wilde, that is the title of the book of the aesthetic singer, which comes to us arrayed in white vellum and gold. There is a certain amount of originality about the binding, but that is more than can be said about the inside of the volume. Mr. Wilde may be aesthetic, but he is not original. This is a volume of echoes, it is Swinburne and water, while here and there we notice that the author has been reminiscent of Mr. Rossetti and Mrs. Browning. . . .

Despite the generally hostile reviews and the little merit of the book, so great already was Wilde's notoriety that this first publication of his went through five editions in the next two years. Hard on the appearance of the *Poems* and its reviews came the staging of Gilbert and Sullivan's satire of aestheticism, *Patience,* with Wilde represented as Bunthorne:

> . . . Though the Philistines may jostle, you will rank as an apostle in the high aesthetic band,
> If you walk down Piccadilly with a poppy or a lily in your medieval hand.
> > And everyone will say,
> > As you walk your flowery way,
> "If he's content with a vegetable love, which would certainly not suit *me,*
> Why, what a most particularly pure young man this pure young man must be!"

Patience was produced at the Standard Theatre, in New York City, on September 22, 1881, and set the entire New World talking about Oscar Wilde. Exactly eight days later he was cabled to give fifty lectures in America, and accepting the offer, he sailed for this country on December 24, 1881. His remark on landing, "I am not exactly pleased with the Atlantic; it was less majestic than I expected," was printed from coast to coast, and throngs of the merely curious turned out to hear him deliver his two lectures, "The Decorative Arts" and "The English Renaissance." The former, derived largely from Whistler, was his more successful talk. He said to the American yokelry in part:

> . . . You have too many white walls. More color is wanted. You should have such men as Whistler among you, to teach you the beauty and joy of color. . . . I regard Mr. Whistler's famous peacock room as the finest thing in color and art decoration which the world has known since Correggio painted that wonderful room in Italy where the little children are dancing on the walls. . . .

Though the newspapers nearly everywhere greeted him with derision, it is not true that he was not listened to or properly evaluated. *The Nation,* for example, reviewing his Chickering Hall lecture, says some very shrewd things besides observing that the same management is promoting his lectures and the tour of the *Patience* Company:

> Mr. Wilde, again, represented himself as being determined to carry on the warfare of art against Philistinism to the bitter end, but really he brings peace rather than a sword. . . . He is not an iconoclast, or in any danger of suffering the fate of a martyr. He is, we have said, spreading the true faith in Art, much as a fashionable preacher spreads the true faith in the Gospel. . . .

Incidentally Wilde's lectures probably brought most Americans their first knowledge of Whistler. Mrs. Joseph Pennell, the painter's biographer and wife of one of our best illustrators, confesses that she first learned of Whistler from Oscar Wilde. One result of the visit to America was the influence of Wilde's aesthetic theories upon the adornment of the Lyceum Theatre, built by Steele MacKaye, America's own aesthete and sponsor of the elocutionist, Delsarte. These men dreamed together of building a combination theatre and hotel at Fortieth Street and Broadway where they would produce Wilde's plays with MacKaye as director and Mary Anderson in the leads. As a matter of fact Wilde's *The Duchess of Padua* was written for Miss Anderson, but that prudish young lady, after seeing the script, refused to play in it. Doubtlessly the unvarying white costume affected by the charming Mary in all her later stage successes was suggested to her, however, by her contacts with the aesthetes. "The Dream Theatre" was never built, but after Wilde had gone back to England, MacKaye secured the necessary monies and built the Lyceum. This house, the first to employ laterally sliding curtains, electric lights, and "medicated air, charged with ozone," was described in the *Morning Journal* as belonging "to no school, unless the ultra-aesthetic—*the school of Wilde outdone by Mac-Kaye*. . . ."

Wilde's play, *Vera; or the Nihilists,* was produced at the Union Square Theatre, on August 20, 1883, with Miss Marie Prescott in the leading rôle. One turns to it in vain today if searching for any reminiscence of the talk its author must have heard of revolution in the home of "Speranza" as a boy. The piece is a trivial thing, with the heir apparent to the Russian throne a secret Nihilist and admirer of Vera Sabouroff, who, when he comes to power, is appointed to slay him. When she discovers that his intentions are to make her Empress and to right the wrongs of the People, she stabs herself "to save Russia." The moral is a little muddled. Wilde, it is clear, got his materials from Turgenev's *Fathers and Sons* (possibly the only Russian novel he ever read) and from the story of Vera Zasulich, who fired on the military governor of St. Petersburg for flogging a prisoner—and was acquitted by a jury in 1878. Wilde had no interest in politics, however, and his whole play centers on the inexplicable passion and conduct of his principals. He had hardly the courage of "Speranza," who had interrupted the trial of Charles Duffy to claim authorship of the article in the Irish *Nation* for which he was being prosecuted. The play had a very brief run, but it influenced the writing of Steele MacKaye's *Paul Kauvar* which was staged after the Haymarket riot in Chicago.

After his American tour, Wilde lived for a time in Paris, then returned to England to lecture on art and on his American ex-

periences. His remarks on America are banal, more so than the
average British comment, but his temerity in repeating Whistler
in England brought down the wrath of the painter on his head.
What does Oscar know about art? Whistler scoffed, and he accused Wilde fairly enough of "picking plums from our platters
for the puddings which he peddles in the provinces." These
charges of plagiarism led to a long exchange of discourtesies in
the *World* with Whistler the victor on every exchange. Eventually Wilde abandoned the discussion of painting and decoration
altogether. His last connection with the effort to improve wall
papers and doilies was purely nominal—as editor of the *Woman's World* from 1887 to 1889. Declaring that aestheticism
was his "second period," Wilde publicly renounced it while living
at the Hotel Voltaire in Paris in 1883 and assumed a more normal attire. In 1884 he married a Miss Constance Lloyd, of Dublin, who bore him two sons, and established himself at 16 Tite
Street, in London.

Wilde's Parisian residence, during which he met Hugo, Daudet, Edmond de Goncourt, Sarah Bernhardt, Verlaine, Bourget,
and Gide, whet anew an early taste for Decadence, which expressed itself in "The Harlot's House" (1885), "The Sphinx"
(1894), *Salome* (1893), and *The Portrait of Dorian Gray*
(1890). This was the beginning of the end of "the pure young
man" whom Gilbert and Sullivan had lyricised. "The Harlot's
House" is a hollow echo of Baudelaire—Wilde's harlot being
the sinister figure of Death who lusts for pretty girls in the
street. Even the best verses drop to earth like a "winged" buz-
zard. "The Sphinx" is so absurd a piece that one wonders at the
temerity of those who have praised it. Like a Chivers straining
to echo Poe, Wilde writes—

> In a dim corner of my room,
>   for longer than my fancy thinks,
> A beautiful and silent Sphinx
>   has watched me through the shifting gloom.

To "this curious cat" the poet puts a variety of impertinent questions ending with a query as to who is her leman. Only one suffering from poetic flatulency could write—

> Lift up your large black satin eyes
> which are like cushions where one sinks.

Not since Tupper has an English poet written so wind-given a
line as that which describes Cleopatra bending her head "in
mimic awe"—

> To see the huge pro-consul draw
> the salted tunny from the brine.

In England "The Sphinx" was looked upon as corrupting, but
how can a piece which provokes only laughter be corrupting?
"The Sphinx" is, in reality, a dreadful comment on the Englishman's sense of humor.

Wilde's *Salome,* written in French for Sarah Bernhardt and
translated into English by Alfred Douglas, has a subterranean
reputation all out of proportion to its merits—a reputation for
which the censor alone is responsible. Bernhardt had accepted
the play, and it had actually been in rehearsal when the Lord
Chamberlain conferred immortality upon it by refusing to license
it. Naturally when it appeared illustrated by the feculent but
brilliant Aubrey Beardsley, Whistler's corrupt offspring, its success was sensational, and it has continued to sell and sell. Those
who have purchased it for its illustrations can justify themselves,
but those who have insisted that it is tragedy will have to suffer
purgatory for their excess of sensibility. The play is the poorest
conceivable transcription into dialogue of Flaubert's "Herodias"; there are no motivation and no character portrayal; *Salome*
is merely coldly and dully lewd, a pederast's toy. The censor
was a fool not to have licensed it, for then it would have died
a-borning.

Undeniably *Dorian Gray* was written *épater le bourgeois,* but
for us it is primarily interesting for the recorded effect of the
diabolism of Huysmans on Wilde. Dorian, a perfection of physical male beauty, is doubly corrupted by the dissolute but witty
Lord Henry Wotton and by a yellow-covered French novel
which the latter places in his hands. This sinister volume is described at length and is easily recognized as *À Rebours.* Of
course, Huysmans' novel is not corrupting if one has wit enough

to recognize it for the deliberate concoction which it is, but for the author of *Dorian Gray* it proved to be altogether too strong meat. Wilde yielded to its influence, and not only his novel, but possibly also his life, were profoundly affected by what he apprehended as the philosophy of the book. For it must be understood that the concoction of the narrative of *Dorian Gray*—the plot of Balzac's *La Peau de Chagrin* feebly reworked—was of small consequence to the author beside his absorption in the philosophy of Lord Henry which seduced poor Dorian and his shabbier human counterpart. This philosophy is not hedonism, as described by some, but a kind of modern Satanism, important to us only in that others have perpetuated it. Such counsels gave Harry Wotton to Dorian Gray:

   . . . We are punished for our refusals. Every impulse that we strive to strangle broods in the mind and poisons us. The body sins once, and has done with its sin, for action is a mode of purification. . . . The only way to get rid of a temptation is to yield to it. . . .

   . . . One's own life—that is the important thing. As for the lives of one's neighbors, if one wishes to be a prig or a Puritan, one can flaunt one's moral views about them, but they are not one's concern.

   . . . Modern morality consists in accepting the standard of one's age. I consider for any man of culture to accept the standard of his age is a form of the grossest immorality. . . . Beautiful sins, like beautiful things, are the privilege of the rich.

Here for the first time in English is forcefully uttered the idea that current morality is always wrong, that one's vices are a private affair, and that whoever would enforce a moral discipline is either a prig or a Puritan. Here, too, for the first time the violation of convention is recommended as the most perfect demonstration of one's "culture", one's intellectual superiority, one's snobbishness.

It is profitable to examine these ideas in their primitive form before they have been smoothed and rounded by more subtle casuists. Wilde's whole attitude is built upon the assumption that modern morality is a product of bourgeois timidity. Morality may be superficially affected by the tastes and prejudices of the dominant economic class, but the roots of morality reach back to the origins of the race. Western morality has been shaped on Hebrew village laws, laws responsible for the first stable society in the Orient, the accumulation of the wisdom learned from thousands of years of error in attempting to form society without conventions. Repudiation of this natural wisdom is a denial, not a demonstration, of intelligence. Furthermore, the flat recommendation that a man of culture should make it a principle to oppose the standard of his age is about as brainless a counsel as one can imagine. Compare it, for example, with the sound advice of Descartes: "Question everything at least once in your life-time"; one is the dogma of a bigot, the other the reasonable attitude of the inquiring mind. Yet, we submit, far too many moderns, self-styled "intellectuals," have made it the principle of their empty, fruitless lives. If poor Wilde was able to convince only himself and the grooms with whom he associated that the only way to get rid of a temptation is to yield to it, other sciolists have surely found a larger audience.

Yet *The Picture of Dorian Gray* is the first thing by Wilde which has a positive literary merit. There are passages of dialogue in the book which are incontestably good, as stimulating as drink and as rich as food. The talk at dinner, for example, turns on an American girl who is to marry an English nobleman; her father, it is alleged, "keeps an American dry-goods store":

"Dry-goods! What are American dry-goods?" asked the Duchess, raising her large hands in wonder, and accentuating the verb.

"American novels," answered Lord Henry, helping himself to some quail.

This talk forecast the success of Wilde's plays, ushered in by the smashing triumph of *Lady Windermere's Fan* in 1892. The strong and weak points of this play are those of his next three successes, *A Woman of No Importance* (1893), *An Ideal Husband* (1895), and *The Importance of Being Earnest* (1895). Wilde reverted to the comedies of Sheridan for his plot, refurbished it a bit from contemporary French farce (*Punch* charged him with pillaging *Odette, Francillon,* and *Le Supplice d'Une Femme*), but then added the only element of distinction— sparkling dialogue. Wilde's plots are carpentry, his characters (with the possible exception of Mrs. Erlynne) cardboard, but his talk is so good we never consider whether it is in character or relevant to the situation. Lords quip like lackeys, and ladies like ladies' maids. A little girl sequestered all her life in the country can dash down a great lady in their first verbal tilt. The plays, for this reason, are good entertainment, but it is absurd to put them in the front rank of comedy. What have they in common with *Tartuffe, Volpone,* or *The Birds?* What with the stage version of *Tobacco Road?* Does not a comparison with Langdon Mitchell's *The New York Idea* (1906) fix their merits very definitely? When Wilde was writing his first play he remarked scornfully that it ought not to take much effort "to beat the Pineros and the Joneses"; let us admit he has done something better than to keep up with the Joneses, but let us not award the bays for a success so definitely bourgeois.

The success of his plays made Wilde deaf to the scandalous things which were being said about his conduct and indifferent to the remonstrances of his friends. Frank Harris, once anxious to place the whole burden of Wilde's corruption on Lord Alfred Douglas, dates his downfall in 1892, and Sherard concurs in this, yet they are not convincing. Languorous youths in the company of men of genius begin to appear in Wilde's dialogued essays as early as 1889, and in that year, too, was printed Wilde's notorious study of Shakespeare's sonnets, entitled "The Portrait of Mr. W. H.," in which it was asserted that these pieces were inspired by the bard's unnatural passion for a young actor named Mr. William Hughes. While this study may not justify the rumors which were even then being circulated about Wilde's private life, it does show the preoccupation of the man's mind at an early date with a subject matter later peculiarly attractive to it. *Dorian Gray* in 1890 speaks of the corrupting influence of *À Rebours* as a matter of years, and its dogma of the purification of sin through action strikes one as the conviction of a sophist in desperate need of his sophistry. It is true that *Lady Windermere's Fan,* performed in February, 1892, contains the first allusion which may be construed as referring to Douglas. The Duchess of Berwick exclaims, "My boy is excessively immoral. . . . And he's only left Oxford a few months—I really don't know what they teach them there." But there is no proof that the alliance with Douglas was Wilde's first experience in sodomy—any more than that it was his last.

It was the Douglas affair, however, which ruined Oscar Wilde. In 1894 Robert Hichens published a novel, *The Green Carnation*, which was a ruthless exposure of the Wilde-Douglas friendship. Lord Reginald Hastings, an "impure and subtle" youth, "too modern to be reticent," is refused by the wholesome Lady Locke because of his infatuation with Esme Amarinth, a wit who is wittiest when drunk. With the publication of this book the lid was off, so to speak, and Lord Queensberry, father of Douglas, attempted to break the relation of his son with Wilde by uttering charges of infamy against the writer. The "esurient Oscar," hungry for new sensations, instituted a libel suit against Queensberry, who pleaded justification and produced such witnesses in court that Wilde withdrew his suit in haste. The Queensberry tilt ruined Wilde, and to some it has seemed persecution that he was brought to trial for immorality, yet it must not be forgotten that he had ample opportunity to escape to the Continent had he chosen. Wilde was a weakling rather than a knave, and indecisive as a dumpling, he tremulously awaited his trial and inevitable conviction. No one was to blame but himself that he was sentenced to two years at hard labor—he deserved the sentence, if not for his vice, for his poltroonery. Yet there was some insufficiency in British character at this time that so few men of genius could be found to sign a petition to shorten his term. Most of the writers who refused their signatures would have done more for a dishonest jockey. Every aspect of the affair is revolting.

Wilde came out of prison apparently with the intention of leading the good life—it is said that he even refused the offer of a great sum of money from an American journalist for an account of his prison experiences. His letter to the *Daily Chronicle,* "Children in Prison," and the earlier "Sonnet on the Recent Sale by Auction of Keats' Love Letters" are the only moving things from his pen we have read. (*His Happy Prince,* 1888, and *A House of Pomegranates,* 1891,—collections of stories for children,—are too artificial for our taste, and we have never known a child pleased by them.) After he had settled himself in France, he devoted every energy to the completion of "The Ballad of Reading Gaol," his witness to the world that he had suffered intolerably and was changed. The piece has poignancy if viewed with a knowledge of Wilde's own experience, but if separated from its author and examined as a literary work, it is less satisfying. It lacks the condensation and dramatic irony of Housman's poems, from which it was imitated, and the movement stumbles and halts repeatedly. One can quote from it, however, very brief passages of excellence:

> I never saw a man who looked
>   With such a wistful eye
> Upon that little tent of blue
>   Which prisoners call the sky. . . .

Yet try to read the whole stanza in which this passage appears and the lameness of Wilde's versification is apparent:

> I never saw a man who looked
>   With such a wistful eye
> Upon that little tent of blue
>   Which prisoners call the sky,
> And at every drifting cloud that went
>   With sails of silver by.

Difficulty in marketing his works, greater difficulty in preventing piracy, difficulty attendant to effecting a reconciliation with his wife—all were factors in producing a relapse into turpitude, and very shortly he had joined Douglas again on the Riviera. After a quarrel with his evil genius Wilde lived a few sordid months in Paris, "an unproductive drunkard and swindler," before his death from disease on November 30, 1900. The stench of him, however, is likely to assail the nostrils of our children's children, for it clings to the clothing and persons of some of those who have thought his thoughts and echoed his ideas even in America.

The great repository of Wilde's ideas is not any work we have thus far examined but rather the essays which he wrote in the late 'eighties and early 'nineties, some of which were collected in *Intentions* (1891): "The Critic as Artist," "The Soul of Man

Under Socialism," "The Truth of Masks," "Pen, Pencil and Poison," and "The Decay of Lying." The first of these, "The Critic as Artist," was undeniably suggested by Whistler's attack upon criticism. The reply does not touch vitally the claim of immunity for the artist, but merely insists that the critic is also an artist. While there is validity in this claim, there is none in the corollaries which Wilde attached to it. Ernest, the interlocutor, sums up these at the end of the essay:

> . . . You have told me it is more difficult to talk about a thing than to do it, and that to do nothing at all is the most difficult thing in the world; you have told me that all Art is immoral, and all thought dangerous; that criticism is more creative than creation, and that the highest criticism is that which reveals in the work of Art what the artist had not put there; that it is exactly because a man cannot do a thing he is the proper judge of it; and that the true critic is unfair, insincere, and not rational.

The upshot of this essay, judged from this summary alone, is that, if the critic is an artist, he is entitled to as great an immunity as that which Whistler claimed for the artist. He need be neither fair, sincere, nor rational! He raises an impressionistic and immoral structure from some other creation, to which this structure of his need have no tie whatever. Indeed, by reducing criticism in its highest expression to independent creation, Wilde indicates as great a contempt for genuine analysis and evaluation as does Whistler. For him, criticism is an art if totally emasculated.

In "The Soul of Man Under Socialism" Wilde starts with the premise that Socialism is of value simply because "it will lead to Individualism." It is a consequence of this that he insists that "no Authoritarian Socialism will do" and adds some gusty nonsense to the effect that "every man must be left quite free to choose his own work"—nay, not only his work but his habits of life, for "all imitation in morals and in life is wrong." Drawing heavily from Emerson from this point on, without ever getting to the bottom of Emerson's teaching, Wilde insists that the state must give up all idea of government and the populace must relinquish all control of art. The end of life is pleasure, and "the new Individualism is the new Hellenism." The type of argument found in this essay is calculated to nettle a true Socialist, for it is political and moral anarchy that Wilde advocates; yet this essay is invaluable in revealing the self-interest of Wilde. Despite his assertion that "Individualism is unselfish," the absorption of Wilde in Socialism is altogether as a way towards complete license for the artist. The artists are to be the privileged class in his order and none shall say their works are "unhealthy" or "morbid" or "erotic." In a word, in the ideal order the public must eat the peach, scab, black spot, and rot around the stone, and never demur.

"The Truth of Masks" is a warm defense of the extravagant accuracy of costuming and stage design in the late nineteenth century—possibly as good a defense as could be made of that kind of pedantry. Yet the costumer and stage designer who insisted on picayunish detail—the proper lace for a period—seems to us today to have been peculiarly lacking in imagination and peculiarly obtuse to the *total effect* of his presentation. To secure this accuracy, Wilde held that "a theatre should be in the power of a cultured despot." Unfortunately culture and despotism mix well so rarely that even the theatre would appear to have little to gain by such a combination. One shudders at one's recollection of the Belasco sets. Against the very realism which he advocates in this essay Wilde argues with warmth in "The Decay of Lying," which is in part an attack upon "the dull facts" he finds in modern fiction. From a denunciation of Zola, Wilde moves by tortuous stages to his "final revelation" that "Lying, the telling of beautiful untrue things, is the proper aim of art." We are, perhaps, too confirmed Platonists to believe this, and our attention fastens again on the corollaries: "Nothing is more evident than that Nature hates mind," and "Egotism itself, which is so necessary to a proper sense of human dignity, is entirely the result of indoor life." We would say that nothing was more evident than that mind was the ultimate creation of Nature, and that Emerson was probably right in assuming that the rôle of Nature to the mind is that of disciplinarian. Wilde's belief that egotism is the product of indoor life reminds us of Mencken's doctrine that only the city can produce intelligence, but we cannot see that such literature as is primarily the product of indoor and urban life has increased man's sense of dignity, though it may have enormously swollen his egotism.

"Pen, Pencil and Poison," like "The Decay of Lying," proved very shocking to the sensibilities of Wilde's contemporaries. Wilde unearthed a greater rogue than himself, one Thomas Griffiths Wainewright, an early nineteenth century poisoner, and then proceeded to write a bland essay on the merits of the rascal's prose. Wainewright's defense for murdering Helen Abercrombie fills Wilde with glee, "Yes; it was a dreadful thing to do, but she had very thick ankles." Of course, had the dreadful Helen ever pretended to be a work of art, the murder would have been justified; but there is no suspicion that she ever did, and for Wainewright to kill her on the grounds he chose was hardly an act of the highest criticism, but rather a mundane business somewhat beneath the artist Wilde represents him to be. Having confounded the public judgment of Wainewright by proving the fellow an able scribbler, Wilde challenges the right of historians to express opinions on the morals of their subjects:

> . . . Nobody with the true historical sense ever dreams of blaming Nero, or scolding Tiberius, or censuring Caesar Borgia. These personages have become like the puppets of a play. They may fill us with terror, or horror, or wonder, but they do not harm us. They are not in immediate relation to us. We have nothing to fear from them. They have passed into the sphere of art and science, and neither art nor science knows anything of moral approval or disapproval. . . .

We realize that it is but a step from this point of view to sentimentalizing Tiberius and excusing his iniquities, as O'Neill does in *Lazarus Laughed,* and yet but a further step to an easy approval of monsters in the human form and the acceptance of contemporary Tiberii; wherefore we wonder if this is not a little too glib. Would it be possible for us to shudder away from Nero had he no relationship to us? Is he not, rather, an enduring symbol of an ever-present menace from which only constant vigilance will guard us? Has not Wilde (and a good many others after him) read a meaning into the "disinterestedness" of pure science which in reality is not there? The bacteriologist may delight in the growth of a dangerous culture, but his ultimate purpose is the extirpation of a disease of which the culture is a specimen. It is the ultimate social purpose which makes the growth of the culture a moral act—for if the scientist had no such end in view, we would rightly fear him and take his test tubes away from him. So, too, it would appear legitimate for the historian to keep Nero, Tiberius, and Caesar Borgia alive on the page for the extirpation of what they represent from the world. This is a moral purpose—and whoever denies us the right to exercise it is either a pervert or the enemy of man, as was Oscar Wilde, whom we attack, not as a living organism, capable any longer of pain, but as a symbol of much which is abhorrent to us.

We have dwelt unduly long on this unhappy man because we believe him the polluted source of many an inane and silly idea in current literature and thought, not because we believe his writing to have much intrinsic merit. All his work was shaping itself into a great offensive against Puritanism when he was cast down, but he labelled the Victorian opposition to his ideas Puritanism only once in his writings. Lady Windermere boasts of her Puritanism and before the final fall of the curtain on Wilde's first comedy is humiliated for it and forced to recognize the courage in one whom she had condemned. Prudery and complacency vex us more than they ever did Wilde, who was himself in a peculiar way a complacent snob; yet if we are ever to be rid of them, it is clear it will not be by lumping them with the essential morality which social preservation dictates, but by separating them and castigating them for their own nauseous character. Wilde's assault on Puritanism, so far as it developed, had, as we have seen, not only this blanket hatred of all morality, but also the selfishness of an artist clique which sought only special privilege for itself. This egocentric, immunity-seeking, anti-social sect is the Intelligentsia—the sophists of modern times.

The most vulgar of all these Eminent Vulgarians, the noisiest of all these pan-pounding anti-Puritan cavaliers was Frank Harris, Wilde's biographer and the Baron Munchausen of the moderns. Harris may have been Welsh, Celt, or Jew, according to Hugh Kingsmill, but it is convenient to regard him as an Irishman, linking together Wilde and Shaw and outdoing either in the stridulousness of his attack on British respectability. His birth-

date may be fixed anywhere between 1850 and 1860, since it is
clear it will never be signalized by public festivities, and one may
choose out of his autiobiography and the stories he told acquaintances more than a sufficient number of episodes to make up
a very full early career—though one must make a point of including some boarding school experience, a complete sexual adventure at eleven or twelve, a runaway trip to America, and
various vicissitudes in this country. The one apparently certain
fact in his early career is his registration as "James F. Harris,
Tenby, Wales," at the University of Kansas in 1874. His *On the
Trail* (1930), reputed reminiscences of his career as a cowboy,
has been shown to be so full of inaccuracies as to lead to a suspicion that he never rode a cow pony, and it may be that his
stories of his life as a bootblack and sand hog in New York and
as a hotel clerk in Chicago have as little foundation. Miss Kate
Stephens in her *Lies and Libels of Frank Harris* blows to bits
that portion of his autobiography which deals with his Kansas
experiences and puts the rest in a very bad light. Harris apparently wheedled his return passage money to England out of a
Kansas instructor who was too poor to afford this luxury. In
England he imposed on the aged Carlyle with an account of
his adventures on the plains, and the Scotchman gave him a
glowing introduction to Froude: "I expect more considerable
things from Frank Harris than from anyone I have met since
Emerson." It was with this letter, after some experiences on the
Continent, including study at Göttingen, that Harris got his first
literary work—as reviewer for the *Spectator* and *Fortnightly*.
The editor of the *Fortnightly,* according to Harris, wrote recom-
mending him as an editor to the Conservative proprietors of the
Evening News. A hypothetical account of the process of black-
mail by which Harris may have landed his first important journalistic position is probably contained in a satire, entitled *The Adventures of John Johns* (1897), by Frederic Carrel. It is said
that Harris purchased and destroyed five hundred copies of this
novel. "The sketch of Frank Harris in *John Johns* is superb,"
Oscar Wilde wrote a mutual acquaintance in July, 1897. "Who
wrote the book? It is a wonderful indictment."

As editor of the *Evening News* Harris turned that Conservative sheet into a yellow journal, with flaring headlines exposing domestic quarrels and infidelities. He kept the Conservative character of his paper by denouncing out-of-the-way riots, like the Haymarket affair in 1886, though he was later to write a novel espousing, Janus-like, the side of the anarchists. Dismissed from the *Evening News* for his handling of the Colin Campbell divorce case, which nearly involved the paper in a disastrous libel suit, Harris bounced to a marriage with a wealthy Park Lane widow, a Mrs. Clayton, and an editorship of the *Fortnightly Review.* He suddenly conceived the idea that what British politics needed was a Bismarck and offered himself as a candidate to Parliament from Hackney. This kept him from altering the character of *Fortnightly,* and even Whistler teased him about it. Hard drinking is assigned by Kingsmill as the cause of Harris' discharge from this review in 1894. In a few months he had recovered sufficiently from this blow, however, to purchase a magazine of his own—the *Saturday Review,* which he began to edit in September, 1894. Though one of the magazine's most famous reviewers, Professor Saintsbury, at once resigned, Harris was extraordinarily successful in engaging new contributors— men like H. G. Wells, D. S. McColl, Max Beerbohm, Arthur Symons, and Cunninghame Graham. His greatest *coup,* however, was to engage George Bernard Shaw as critic of the drama. When his own writing and that of his reviewers alienated all the old advertisers in his journal, Frank Harris, by devious means, filled his columns with the more lucrative prospectuses of gold- and diamond-mining companies in South Africa. He nicely gauged the proper amount of cajolery and virulence to keep the South African financiers, like Rhodes, who advertised in his columns, anxious to oblige him within reasonable limits. In the end they found it cheaper to buy him out, and this Lord Hardwicke did at a handsome figure when the conduct of the Boer War was embarrassing the Tory government. Harris wrote later of his "arduous task" of defending the Boers, but an arch-imperialist who deplored the fact that England had no Bismarck, Harris had little sympathy for the valiant Dutchmen. Indeed, shortly after selling the *Saturday Review* in 1898, Harris published a pamphlet on *How to Beat the Boer.*

It was during his early proprietorship of the *Saturday Review* that Oscar Wilde came to trial, but one looks in vain for any defense of Wilde in Harris' journal. That Harris had formerly courted Wilde and had envied him his social success there is no denying. While Wilde had social poise, the egregious Harris had only social avoidupois and suffered from the fact. "Frank Harris," said Wilde, "has been received in all the great houses—*once.*" Harris, still under the sway of Wilde's social prestige, may have defended Wilde at dinner—he was quite capable of blurting out anything—but it does not seem likely that he induced any millionaire to hold his yacht in readiness to convey the doomed man out of England. There is a certain transparency of motive in Harris' visit to Wilde in prison, in his circulation of a petition to shorten Wilde's term, and in his empty promise of financial help to Wilde later in Paris. He believed that the imprisonment had increased the monetary value of Wilde's work, and it is not unlikely that he hoped to profit from the connection. "Frank Harris," Wilde himself wrote, "has no feelings. It is the secret of his success. Just as the fact that he thinks other people have none either is the secret of the failure that lies in wait for him somewhere on the way of life. . . ." When Harris found that he could neither bully nor cajole the insensate Wilde into productivity, he abandoned him without hesitation. In his own words, he had grown "tired of holding up an empty sack."

Yet Wilde was the source of Harris' first literary success, *The Man Shakespeare* (1909), which was originally published as separate essays, beginning with an article, "The True Shakespeare," in the *Saturday Review* for March, 1898. Wilde had shocked England with his allegations of Shakespeare's immorality in "The Portrait of Mr. W. H."; taking his cue from Wilde, Harris sought a similar notoriety by dissecting the love life of the butcher's son of Avon. Of course, he could not agree with Wilde that Shakespeare was a pederast; instead he chose to represent him as a "frail sensuous singer," "a parasite," "a snob of the purest English water" who loathed his wife and became madly infatuated with a maid-of-honor named Mary Fitton. This hopeless passion Harris makes the spring of Shakespeare's work. The exposition of his thesis, however, is accompanied by a running fire of comment on those critics and professors who have made a "Puritan" out of Shakespeare. Even Coleridge, whom Harris admits has seen Shakespeare "by flashes," is not spared—

> . . . But, alas, Coleridge, a Puritan born, was brought up in epicene hypocrisies, and determined to see Shakespeare—that child of the Renaissance—as a Puritan, too, and consequently mis-saw him far oftener than he saw him. . . . There is a famous passage in Coleridge's "Essays on Shakespeare" which illustrates what I mean. It begins: "In Shakespeare all the elements of womanhood are holy"; and goes on to eulogize the instinct of chastity which all his women possess, and this in spite of Doll Tearsheet, Tamora, Cressida, Goneril, Regan, Cleopatra, the Dark Lady of the Sonnets, and many other frail and fascinating creatures. . . .

There is no point here in stressing how much Harris' book owes to some of the critics and professors, like Tyler, Brandes, Dowden, whom he condemns (Kingsmill in his two studies has brought this out adequately) ; the important thing to note is that *The Man Shakespeare* is one of the important documents on which the Intelligentsia pin their faith that one must be vicious or weak in order to write adequately about viciousness or weakness. We have little way of knowing what Shakespeare's character was, and we are probably as willing to accept the view of Harris as the view that the poet was the soul of virtue, but there is no compulsion to settle on either. There *are* both moral axioms and representations of virtue in the dramas, and it can plausibly be argued that it is as difficult to feign these things as it is to feign either viciousness or weakness without habit and experience. But to adopt either argument is to assume that Shakespeare was blind, dumb, and a blockhead. Five minutes on any street corner in the tumultuous London of his day would have acquainted his eager mind with sufficient specimens of both virtue and vice to fill a dozen plays, and there is no need of assuming that he ever preached at Paul's or lusted for the fickle Mary. As for the claim of the Intelligentsia, it does not follow that if lust produced some of Shakespeare's sonnets a comparable lust will produce anything like them. This theory was pretty much exploded in Greenwich Village in the early 'twenties. In passing, one is forced to remark that the swashbuckling vigor of *The Man Shakespeare* makes it a much more readable book then either the

Dowden or Lee studies. Harris, like Whistler, who grappled with the Slade Professor of Art, and Wilde, who sneered at the morals of Oxford, has some consequence as a baiter and destroyer of the ponderous academicians.

Harris also wrote some short fiction in the early 'nineties, collected later in *Elder Conklin* (1895) and *Montes the Matador* (1901). These books received fulsome praise when Harris was a power in the critical journals of London, but almost any number of *Western Stories* contains yarns that are quite as good, and there are forgotten people in the early collections of O'Brien who did infinitely better work. In 1908, after a trip to America, Harris published his novel *The Bomb,* which is an account of the Haymarket affair from the point of view of one Rudolph Schnaubelt, who confesses that he threw the bomb which caused the death of eight policemen and for which the State of Illinois took the lives of Spies, Fischer, Engel, and Parsons. Schnaubelt is represented as a rather guileless, good young man, from Bavaria, who proves his goodness in the book by refusing to have relations with a girl, Elsie, despite her warmest entreaties. He comes under the influence of the stout-hearted anarchist, Louis Lingg (who reminds him of the Caesar of Mommsen), just at a time when his indignation at police brutality in Chicago, which he has witnessed as a reporter, makes him putty in Lingg's hands, and he agrees to throw the bomb. Lingg helps him to escape that he may give the world a true account of the affair. *The Bomb* is far from a distinguished piece of writing—indeed, when Harris quotes from "biased" newspaper accounts of the Haymarket affair (which he frequently does) or from current magazine articles on lead and phosgene poisoning among the workers, it is noticeable how the narrative "picks up" in interest. As a tract the book is ineffective because of its hash of doctrine— Socialism, Christianity, anarchy, and hero-worship. Yet *The Bomb* is a pretty good make-shift vehicle for some of Harris' favorite dogmas: the animalism of female passion, the stupidity of formal education ("books develop memories, not minds"), and the brutality of judges. To the 1920 edition is appended a characteristic "Afterword" in which Harris, after citing an alleged remark of Flaubert to the effect that he should have criticized

Madame Bovary himself because no "fool-critic" could do it, proceeds to "dissect" *The Bomb*. He admits idealizing "Lingg beyond life size" but otherwise finds his own novel a very good job, particularly in view of "the problems" which confronted him —like rewriting the "police" pamphlet on the anarchists. We are not surprised to learn that he regards *The Bomb* as better than *Madame Bovary*.

Harris was proprietor and editor of *Vanity Fair* from 1907 to 1911; after selling this magazine, he began to write for the *English Review* in which were published in the first year of his connection as a contributor two very sensational articles from his pen—"Thoughts on Morals" and "Carlyle," the first of his *Contemporary Portraits*. "Thoughts on Morals" contains in brief form the philosophy of abandon later set forth in *My Life and Loves;* the "Carlyle" portrait gave extraordinary offense because Harris alleged in it that Carlyle had confessed to him that his marriage with Jane Welsh had never been consummated. That Harris met Carlyle is conceded by D. A. Wilson, Carlyle's biographer, but the latter believes that the whole story of the Scotch philosopher's confession is embroidered out of fancy and a "distorted recollection of what Mr. Froude had written. . . ." So, too, it may be doubted if Carlyle ever told Harris that "Heine was a dirty Jew pig." Despite all the assaults upon it, the Carlyle portrait was placed at the beginning of Harris' first volume of *Contemporary Portraits* in 1915. The five volumes (1915, 1919, 1920, 1923, 1927) which Harris filled with more than ninety "portraits" of his contemporaries would be invaluable if it were possible to accept them for what Harris represents them to be— intimate conversations on vital topics with some of the most distinguished men of his time. The "portraits" have, however, little more factual basis, apparently, than the *Imaginary Conversations* of Landor—they are highly fanciful studies in the main of what Harris presumes he might have wheedled out of his subjects provided that they surrendered cheerfully to hypnotic suggestion. Harris appears to have had two objects in view: the promotion of his own stock (he always shows to advantage over the person whose portrait he draws) and the demeaning of his "sitter" by some revelation of sexual sterility, inhibition, bigotry, or meanness. When he knows nothing about the private life of his subject, or when it is obvious that his sexual life has been complete, Harris sneers at the moral fibre of his writing, as in the case of Upton Sinclair:

> ... I have now read all of Sinclair's writings and I may as well confess it at once. There's a Puritanism in him that I can't stomach and that, I believe, injures all his work. ...

There are rare exceptions in *Contemporary Portraits* where Harris praises his subjects, but these exceptions are generally in the case of persons, like Whistler, Shaw, and Mencken, whom Harris recognized to be of his own camp, the élite among the Intelligentsia. Before dismissing these *Portraits* we should note that they are one unsuspected source of Mr. Lytton Strachey's *Eminent Victorians* (1918) and *Queen Victoria* (1921). Strachey, of course, is subtle and erudite where Harris is preposterous and infantile, but he has merely refined the reasons of Harris for his supercilious scorn of Dr. Arnold and Gladstone. And doesn't every aphorism in *Eminent Victorians* proclaim, "What a witty fellow am I"?

Harris must have been at work on the two-volume *Oscar Wilde: His Life and Confessions* (1916) when the first of the *Contemporary Portraits* was published, for he tells us that the manuscript had circulated among British publishers, who found it too sensational in its revelations, before he decided to bring it to America and issue it himself. His trip to America, incidentally, was hastened by a temporary unpopularity following a conviction for contempt of court and a short residence in Brixton Prison, after he had tried to shift the blame in his trial upon one of his subordinates. The Wilde biography perhaps should not be regarded as a biographical and critical study at all, but rather as an attempt to bait British Puritanism. Those who have found *Oscar Wilde: His Life and Confessions* prurient, however, should consult a good psychiatrist at their earliest opportunity. The book is vulgar but not obscene, and if one believes—as Harris does—that Oscar Wilde is "a tragic figure of imperishable renown" one is justified in discussing him with even greater frankness, and certainly with more accuracy, than Harris does in his book. One can fairly object, however, to the thesis that Wilde was punished for the envy he aroused in his inferiors—that "his fate in England is symbolic of the fate of all artists; in some degree they will all be punished as he was punished by a grossly material-ised people who prefer to go in blinkers and accept idiotic con-ventions because they distrust the intellect and have no taste for mental virtues." The Harris biography is not a plea for a saner treatment of the sexual pervert (Harris denounces the degener-ate Taylor who was convicted with Wilde) but a plea for the artist as a special and privileged person. Later (1925), when he accepts and prints the confession of Lord Alfred Douglas to the effect that Wilde was the chief mover in their crime, he attempts to exonerate Douglas also by finding very great merit in the lat-ter's puerile poetry.

In New York Frank Harris took over the editorship of *Pearson's Magazine,* which he made obnoxious to the authorities after we had entered the World War by virulently attacking England and defending Germany. Eventually he was forced to suspend publication. One could become quite exercised about this had one any conviction in regard to the sincerity of Harris. But Harris in 1898 had done his utmost to provoke a war be-tween Great Britain and the United States. The reader may leap to the conclusion that in both instances it was a passion for Germany which motivated Harris—but he does not know his man. Harris had, on occasion, been quite as virulent in regard to Germany; indeed, his favorite appellation for the German Kaiser was "William the Witless." The only German whom he admired steadily and whose conduct he fancied he himself emu-lated was Otto von Bismarck. As for his hostility towards Eng-land, his general attitude is well expressed in a speech which H. G. Wells puts in the mouth of Mr. Butteridge (who seems to be a satirical portrait of Harris) in his *The War in the Air:* "I lurve England, but Puritanism, sorr, I abhor. It fills me with loathing. It raises my gorge." One significant feature of *Pear-son's* during Harris' connection was the Frank Harris Brother-hood, an organization to achieve some of the ideals of Harris—

like justice for workers and the abolition of armaments. Minimum subscription to this organization was one dollar, and there was never any accounting for the funds received.

Early in 1922 Harris returned to Europe to take residence on the Riviera, where he remained for the rest of his life. In 1923 appeared the first volume of *My Life and Loves,* and subsequent volumes were issued in 1925 and 1927. *My Life and Loves* purports to be a candid account of the amorous adventures of a modern Casanova, with tested formulas for successful seduction and shirt-cuff memoranda of trial and error. In his introduction, Harris writes—

There are two main traditions of English writing, the one of perfect liberty, that of Chaucer and Shakespeare, completely outspoken, with a certain liking for lascivious details and witty smut, a man's speech; the other emasculated by Puritanism, and since the French Revolution gelded to the tamest propriety; for that upheaval brought the middle-class to power and insured the domination of girl-readers. Under Victoria, English prose literature became half childish. . . . I am going back to the old English tradition.

Lascivious details jostle one another in the first volume of *My Life and Loves,* but there is a conspicuous absence of the "witty smut" our stalwart forebears are alleged to have relished and for which we ourselves have a taste. Instead, there are drooling dialogues between Harris and his loves which make one wish that he had for ever been confined to Brixton Prison and forbidden the use of pen and ink. However glamorous his person, it is inconceivable that he ever seduced a woman worth seducing with his talk—if this is a sample. Instead of producing a rival for the *Confessions* of Rousseau, as he fancied he had done, Harris merely emitted a cheap, pornographic fiction convincing to small boys, to H. L. Mencken (before his marriage), and to Bernard Shaw. After feeling the social rebuke for his first volume ("everywhere I feel the unspoken condemnation and see the sneer or the foul sidelong grin"), Harris considerably "toned down" the subsequent volumes, to the probable disappointment of the aforementioned admirers.

The elephantine seriousness of *My Life and Loves,* the lumbering of behemoth in muck, is discarded in the "unauthorized" biography of *Bernard Shaw* (1931) which Frank Harris completed a few months before his death on August 26, 1931. The success of this spirited book is in no small sense due to the fact that Harris had to match his wits against those of Shaw whose frequent letters to him he has interpolated throughout. It is easy to say that the book is lively solely because of these letters, but that is not altogether true. Harris' remarks that Shaw's father "in spite of his abstinence" lasted until 1885, that "the naughty scenes" in Shaw's plays are "so spiceless they could hardly get into a benefit performance for the Girl Scouts," and that Shaw's letters to Ellen Terry read to him at times "like Eugene Marchbanks on a busman's holiday" give some intimation of the flavor of Harris' special contribution. Yet the critics are justified in preferring the interpolations of Shaw to the commentary of Harris, for they are without exception the better stuff. Frank Harris, lucky in life, was immeasurably lucky in death—he would have burst had he survived long enough to read the reviews of his last "portrait." The universal opinion was that the sitter had outdone the candid-camera man. As it was, Harris died content that he was the cheekiest fellow of his generation. Devious are the ways to immortality.

It is a mistake to suppose that a literary school or movement originates only with a master; bumptious and insistent little fellows who moil over the same ideas and who fulsomely puff or loudly deride each other can make quite a stir in the world if they set themselves to it in earnest. None the less, it is convenient to have one able intellect to give a movement force and vitality, and to supply the infants with quips to use upon occasion. Before the Intelligentsia discovered Nietzsche, they were very fortunate in having George Bernard Shaw for a back log and Bible, a thesaurus and jest book. Shaw, we hasten to add, seems to us to have some characteristics which set him apart from the Intelligentsia, but there is no denying that they have made most radical use of him, and that, until he can be weighed and sifted, bolted and bagged, we may count him their man. He has had for them an enormous appeal, for the very simple reason that they could turn to him for unconventional views on almost any topic—on prize fighting, art, church-going, diet, prostitution, home-rule, medicine, communism, feminine psychology, evolution,—just ask G. B. S., he has an iconoclastic opinion. Whenever a covey of fat Victorian ducks flew within range, it was convenient to pepper them with G.B.S. (Great Buck Shot), for few ever returned for a second salute. In time, however, the hunters tired of plundering Shaw—those long prefatory essays in evil print, with their captious excursions anywhere and everywhither, exhausted the patience of those who were never great readers, and they renounced Shaw unequivocally. What they had once described as richness, now they dismissed as garrulity. Shaw was an old wind-bag, a woman. . . . Moreover, it is true that Shaw, with his much talk, gave away eventually all the sources of his ideas, and a little questing proved to the bilkers that it was easier to get the stuff out of the original ore than out of Shaw. "Practically all of the sagacity of George Bernard Shaw consists in bellowing what everyone knows," cried one disillusioned American disciple of the Ulster Polonius. "I think I am as well acquainted with his works, both hortatory and dramatic, as the next man. . . . Yet, so far as I know, I have never found an original idea in them—never a single statement of fact or opinion that was not anteriorly familiar, and almost commonplace."

That Shaw has read widely and accepted cheerfully, no one who has long been an admirer of the man will deny; yet that he has made out of his reading, thanks to the graces of longevity and constitutional vigor, a fairly successful synthesis which he may call his own is not so apparent and perhaps will have to be demonstrated. The chief concern of Shaw's life has been to arrive at a settled economic outlook, and to discern why this was still a paramount issue with him even after he had achieved personal affluence one must go back to his origins. Shaw was born in 1856—the son of shabby-genteel Dubliners who had connections with the Irish aristocracy. George Carr Shaw, the father, an alcoholic with a government pension, was able to maintain his domestic establishment only by acquiescing to the presence of a boarder, one G. J. V. Lee, a teacher of singing. When Lee withdrew to go to London, Mrs. Shaw decided to follow him because of the professional opportunity the connection afforded, for she had a fine voice. Later, young George Bernard joined his mother, who had become a teacher also, and she supported him through the lean years between 1876 and 1885. "My mother," he confesses, "worked for my living instead of preaching that it was my duty to work for hers: therefore take off your hat to her, and blush." Thus early he came into possession of ideas from life which his later reading was to reinforce rather than to formulate. For example, when he was later charged with borrowing heavily from Ibsen, he used to point to the expression of similar ideas in his novels, particularly to *The Irrational Knot* (1880), written before he had heard of the Scandinavian dramatist. Ibsen's propensity to represent women as intellectual and forceful while their husbands are incompetent brought Shaw no truth which was not illustrated for him first in his father's house and not in *A Doll's House*. The fierce hatred of Shaw for poverty was derived, not from Marx, but from the scorn of the Shaw relatives for the family of George Carr Shaw. And finally, his early blushful humility, his deep sense of inferiority, which made him put his thought always with a smirk, like a guilty poacher, came from his sense that his branch of the Shaws were not quite up to the other Shaws, and that all Irishmen are inferior to Englishmen. One of the stories about Shaw which has greatly impressed us is the tale of his serious study of etiquette as a young man at the British Museum. This bespeaks a deference to the conventions of society quite out of keeping with his furious avowals of contempt for established society.

A man with a deep-seated conviction of his own worth and the justice of his cause could never have written *Widower's Houses* (1892), the first play of Shaw's to be staged. Trenchant satire though this has been alleged to be of slum ownership, it is not quite up to Mr. Shaw's experience or his convictions. At fifteen Shaw had been employed in the office of a Dublin land agent, Charles Uniacke Townshend, and had later served as cashier for the firm. In this connection he must have seen conditions far worse than those which are casually alluded to in the play, and certainly after coming to London, he must have

enlarged his slum experience. Yet there is no actual representation of these slums on the stage. Instead, we are treated to the
farcical courtship of Blanche Sartorius by Dr. Harry Trench,
his refusal to wed her when he discovers that she brings a great
dowry of rent money from her father, and his final humiliation
and acquiescence when he learns that the source of his own
income is from a mortgage given to Blanche's father on the
latter's tenements. Save for the intrusion of Mr. Lickcheese, a
rent collector out of Dickens, there is no representation in the
play of a condition of society where there are not servants. That
is, instead of a play which might be *The Lower Depths* of
Dublin, we get a serio-comic society play on the ability of a
rather crass young woman to wheedle out of her father and
lover precisely what she wants, despite the cost to their pride.
In the end, it is seen that Trench's quixotism is merely a device
to pad out the play, which is little else than a lover's quarrel
with a new type of selfish young woman as protagonist. It is
useless to argue that Shaw, being an Irishman, could do nothing
resembling what Gorki has done—Synge with humor to match
Shaw's wit gives the impression of greater integrity through
courageous realism, while Sean O'Casey (alas, a disciple of
Shaw!) outstrips both. There is merit in Shaw's play, but not
the high excellence we might reasonably expect. If one recollects
that the Ireland of Shaw's youth is the Ireland of Liam O'Flaherty's *Famine,* one has a proper measure for the limits of Shaw's
daring in *Widower's Houses.*

Shaw appears at his worst in *John Bull's Other Island* (1904)
and the "Preface for Politicians" issued with the play. This piece
was written, Shaw tells us, "at the request of Mr. William Butler
Yeats, as a patriotic contribution to the repertory of the Irish
Literary Theatre." It was not played, according to him, because
it was at that time "beyond the resources of the new Abbey
Theatre." Anyone so gullible as to be satisfied with this explanation should turn to a very small footnote in Yeats' *Collected
Works* in which he says, in regard to the failure of the Abbey
Theatre to stage *John Bull's Other Island* ". . . we felt ourselves
unable to cast it without wronging Mr. Shaw. We had no Broadbent, or money to get one." Of course a satisfactory Broadbent

could have been picked up in any pub, for only earnest Liberal convictions and not histrionic ability are necessary for the part. The Abbey Theatre had no intention of staging the play, and Mr. Shaw had no expectation that it would be performed in Dublin. He used the Dublin invitation shrewdly for awakening interest in the London presentation; if it could be suspected, as indeed it was, that Shaw had written so veracious a play on Ireland that the Irish could not tolerate it, everybody in England, whatever his views, would want to see it, and this is precisely what took place. *John Bull's Other Island,* scarcely known outside the British Isles, has been one of his most popular London productions. King Edward VII even "commanded" a special performance.

The whole episode has, however, for one who is neither an Englishman nor an Irishman, many inglorious aspects. It seems somehow dishonorable that a successful dramatist, when entreated to aid the struggling theatre of his native land, should produce a piece primarily for the delectation of his country's chief oppressor, yet that is precisely what Shaw did. It is all very well to say that Shaw was out of sympathy with the neo-Gaelic movement—his denunciation of Irish dreaming and his acid remark that, if you are to interest an Irishman in Ireland, "you've got to call the unfortunate island Kathleen ni Hoolihan and pretend she's a little old woman" are legitimate criticism—but his duty was to refuse the invitation and present his piece as an independent creation, not as something which was rather more than Mr. Yeats bargained for. The absurd pretense of the "Preface for Politicians" that the play was successful in England because it was not planned for that country but for a Dublin audience is a little too much to ask even the Shavian enthusiast to stomach. Even we, who are profound admirers, are revolted. Broadbent is nicely calculated to flatter the Englishman:—Gilbert and Sullivan had already demonstrated nothing so tickled the vanity of John Bull as a travesty of his virtues which none the less set those virtues unmistakably forth—and that is precisely what Shaw has done in this play. Is it a greater crime to represent Ireland as Kathleen ni Hoolihan than to represent England as Mr. Thomas Broadbent, Esq.? Resolve the question rather into, Is it more honorable to flatter one's country or one's country's oppressor?—and answer it as you will. *John Bull's Other Island* reveals its brilliant author as too much of a toady for us to care for the piece. There is one passage in the play, however, that seems to come from the dramatist's betrayed and bitter heart. Larry Doyle, an Irishman who has been so long out of Ireland that he sees the emerald isle realistically and cannot love it, while berating the Irish for dreaming, suddenly drops his voice *"Like a man making some shameful confidence"* and remarks bitterly on the continuous "horrible, senseless, mischievous laughter" of the Irish. Doyle is suddenly Shaw himself lamenting his long rôle as jester to the British middle class, Shaw abruptly visioning himself as the clown and mountebank he so frequently and so loudly has asserted he is. If *John Bull's Other Island* serves no other serious purpose, it at least reveals Shaw suffering from the same sense of inferiority which made more or less witty entertainers out of Whistler, Wilde, Harris, and others.

Having discovered a degree of evasiveness and a tendency to kotow in the plays *Widower's Houses* and *John Bull's Other Island,* we should not be surprised to find a good deal of shilly-shallying in Shaw's development as a Socialist—a development which has been advertised as central in his career and from which, allegedly, everything else stems. Archibald Henderson, in his official biography, has traced with care the early growth of Shaw as a Socialist, and we can follow him here. Up to the time when he was twenty-five, Shaw, aside from reading a pamphlet by John Stuart Mill on the Irish Land Question, had never approached social conditions from an economic point of view. He was full, as he explains, of Darwin and Tyndall, of Shelley and De Quincey, and of Michelangelo and Beethoven. But one evening in 1882, whether by accident or design, he found himself in Memorial Hall, in Farringdon Street, London, listening to the American, Henry George, eloquently expound "the monstrous absurdity of the private appropriation of rent." He became an immediate convert to George and soon was using the latter's arguments in controversies with friends in the debating societies in London. It was then he was told (as nearly everyone of late has been told) to read Karl Marx. There being available no English translation, Shaw read a French version of the first volume of *Das Kapital,* and became enough of a Marxist by 1885 to defend Marx against an attack by one of Jevons' disciples. This led to a meeting with his opponent, Philip H. Wicksteed, who induced Shaw to become a member of an economics club, a small organization which eventually, however, grew into the Royal Economic Society. The discussions of this club finally convinced Shaw that Marx was an able revolutionary Socialist, but an inferior economist, who had seized upon the economic theory of Ricardo as a "stick to beat the capitalist dog." The result of this conviction was a series of articles in the *National Reformer* and elsewhere attacking Marx's theory of value. These articles raised up a formidable opponent in H. M. Hyndman and finally crystallized Shaw's views in regard to Marx. He accepted the economic determinism of Marx, believed that he had the correct interpretation of history, but rejected his theory of value, his notion of the class struggle, and the need for revolution to transfer power from one class to another. The Marxist would hold, we believe, that Shaw rejected everything that is essentially Marxian.

Shaw's controversy with Hyndman was really the upshot of his decision in 1884 to throw his lot in with the Fabian Society rather than with the Social Democratic Federation, of which Hyndman was the leader. Shaw was influenced in his choice solely by "an instinctive feeling that the Fabian, and not the Federation, would attract the men of my own bias and intellectual habits, who were then ripening for the work that lay before us." Shaw's instinct was correct, for the Fabian Society was very shortly dominated by bourgeois intellectuals like himself, men of better parts than could be found in the proletarian organization of Hyndman. Shaw personally was responsible for winning over to the Fabian Society the man who was to prove its most capable member—Sidney Webb. The Federation perished in the turbulent years 1885–1887, when insurrectionism failed, and from that time forward to the First World War the Fabians dominated British Socialist thought. The program of the Fabians was to permeate all the established political parties and convert leaders here and there to "progressive" ideas. This program of permeation was most successful in the first five years of its operation under the generalship of Sidney Webb, and while never abandoned by the Fabians, was superseded by efforts to establish a genuine collectivist party. Shaw slackened his activities as an apple-cart campaigner about 1895 and more or less gave them up after a breakdown of his health in 1898. He reviewed the first two volumes of the *Works of Friedrich Nietzsche* in the *Saturday Review* in 1899 and seems to have originated about that time an amorphous theory of evolutionary socialism dependent solely upon the will.

Out of a variety of things which might be selected for the study of Shaw's development up to this point, it is convenient to choose and to concentrate upon only three—those most influential in America: the novel *An Unsocial Socialist*, completed in 1883 and serialized in *To-day* the following year; the article "Socialism for Millionaires," in the *Contemporary Review* in February, 1896; and the play *Man and Superman: A Comedy and a Philosophy* (1903). The first of these works, *An Unsocial Socialist*, is a pleasant fiction, definitely reminiscent of W. S. Gilbert, in which one Sidney Trefusis, a millionaire possessed of a Puckish personality, deserts his wife in order to be alone with his allegedly communistic ideas, but only succeeds in adding a little spice to the life of a girls' school by invading the campus in the guise of "Jefferson Smilash, Painter, Decorator, Glazier, Plumber & Gardener." To be sure, the wife dies, but in England girls are plentiful to whom this type of proletarian is appealing; hence Trefusis successfully woos and weds another, a damsel with much more social poise. "And so—" (in the words of the author) the novel ends as gracefully as a butterfly settling on a lily—

> "Jack shall have Jill,
> Nought shall go ill,
> The man shall have his mare again;
> And all shall be well."

An Unsocial Socialist is somewhat less revolutionary than a pan of biscuits which fail to rise, and less doctrinaire than a muffin. This is the more remarkable in that the novel was written

when Shaw ostensibly was a simon-pure Marxist, just before he
became a Fabian. As an afterthought, there is added to the book
a letter from Sidney Trefusis to the author, in which Shaw's
hero makes it clear that he is not a *revolutionary* Socialist (despite the fact that in the story he helps some men throw down
a wall that an arrogant landlord has erected across a common
path) but an *evolutionary* Socialist. The letter-writer is a converted Fabian, but from what is he converted? Not from his
philandering, we hope, or he would have no charm or vitality
whatever. Yet the idea that he has become an evolutionary
voluptuary instead of a revolutionary one fills us with misgiving—
we see in it the threat of the professional iconoclast which, apparently, it is possible even for an Irishman to become.

The enticing article "Socialism for Millionaires" was written
when Mr. Shaw's dialectical powers presumably were at their
best, ground, like a Sheffield knife, in the allegedly strenuous
combats of the Fabian association and as an open-air speaker
to dockhands. It does contain more than a suggestion of the gift
of the capable extemporizer in getting a laugh out of nimble
rhetoric. Pity the poor millionaire, cries Mr. Shaw; he can
neither spend on himself all he has nor give it away to his satisfaction. His personal enjoyment of his money is limited by his
physical capacity: "Can he attend more than one theatre in one
evening, or wear more than one suit at a time, or digest more
meals than his butler?" Almsgiving is a fraud, since it benefits,
not the poor, but those who should be taxed to support the poor
by relieving them of an obvious burden; and so, for similar
reasons, is the endowment of charitable associations, hospitals,
and colleges. The giving of parks raises the rent of adjacent
dwellings, whence no satisfaction can come to the donor because
of his gift, etc.

This is excellent—in fact, as an extemporaneous speech it can
hardly be improved upon: but while it leaves a smell of sulphur
in the air, so that we may tell the lightning has struck somewhere
near, it really accomplishes little more than perplexing us. Shaw
cites, for example, as proof that the endowment of hospitals is
a fraud some of the evils connected with such institutions: "irresponsibility, waste and extravagance checked by spasmodic stingi-

ness, favoritism, almost unbridled license for experiments on patients by scientifically enthusiastic doctors," etc. True, true, too true, but are the evils greater than those potential in the nationalized or state-hospital under a surgeon-dictator? Is "unbridled license for experiments on patients" a greater evil than bridled standardized treatment for each case—an almost inevitable result of the nationalization of hospitals? Reflection on Shaw's article tells us that to secure the *independence* of hospitals, schools, and other institutions, private giving must endure as a barrier against standardization until some adequate and equally competent substitute for free endowment is found—perhaps in some broad extension of the new hospital insurance system. Shaw, emerging from the period of his socialistic debates, is a piquant talker, with a plausible approach, who is quite willing to add a few millionaires to his audiences of Fabians and dockhands, provided that he can induce them to ask what immediate steps can be taken to remedy the situation. In answer, he can only advise logically the endowment of talk—

. . . Therefore, any propagandist society which knows how to handle money intelligently and which is making a contribution to current thought, whether Christian or Pagan, Liberal or Conservative, Socialist or Individualist, scientific or humanitarian, physical or metaphysical, seems to me an excellent mark for a millionaire's spare money.

Of course, the genuine Socialist would remark that such a program is merely the endowment of whimsicality and is no more likely to produce a communal society than a scheme to make the continents float on air.

Shaw's next avatar is found in *Man and Superman,* produced in 1903, and published in 1904 with an "Epistle Dedicatory" and a very important "Revolutionist's Handbook" attached. The play is an amusing adaptation of the old picaresque, Don Quixote-Joseph Andrews plot to the stage, in which a gentleman Socialist, one John Tanner, is pursued down into Spain and there held captive by bandits long enough for his pursuer, a strong-willed young heiress, Ann Whitefield, to overtake and capture him. It tickles Shaw's fancy to treat Tanner as a modern Don Juan, reader of Schopenhauer and Nietzsche, student of Westermarck, concerned for the future of the race instead of being bent upon satiating his own appetites. This conceit permits the dramatist to introduce a graceful interlude on the stage as a dream of John Tanner, in which he as Don Juan engages the Devil in dialectics and ends by lecturing him. The Don attacks with astonishing venom (considering his past) the delusion that romantic love is the highest good of man. "Invent me a means," he cries, "by which I can have love, beauty, romance, emotion, passion without their wretched penalties, their expense, their worries, their trials, their illnesses and agonies and risks of death, their retinue of servants and nurses and doctors and schoolmasters." With all the earnestness and vehemence of a Wesleyan preacher, the reformed libertine declares his conviction that a means will be found to avoid the present social consequences of passion. It will be found *because the Life Force wills it.* Though "Nature is a pander, Time a wrecker, and Death a murderer," they can all be overcome. For within Man, as within Don Juan, is working "Life's incessant aspiration to higher organization, wider, deeper, intenser self-consciousness, and clearer self-understanding." As Nietzsche would say, the Life-Force in Man aspires to produce the Superman, and it is this philosophy which Don Juan and John Tanner accept, despite the Devil's warning them against the "German-Polish madman" and berating them for deserting "my religion of love and beauty." It is thoroughly consistent, then, for Shaw in the appended "Revolutionist's Handbook" to renounce Fabianism and to declare himself for evolutionary socialism to be produced by the Life-Force:

> *The only fundamental and possible Socialism is the socialization of the selective breeding of Man: in other terms, of human evolution.* We must eliminate the Yahoo, or his vote will wreck the commonwealth.

Is it not obvious that the man who postpones Socialism until eugenics has produced a race competent to be Socialists might just as well argue that Socialism is an idle dream? We, and all those marked by our sins (even to the seventh generation), will obviously have attained to heaven before a better earthly state can be realized. We could dismiss Shaw as an iconoclast who has used Socialism merely for personal publicity (we regret the necessity of hinting anything of the sort) if *Man and Superman* were his last pronouncement on the subject, but there are also *The Intelligent Woman's Guide to Socialism and Capitalism* (1928) and *The Apple Cart* (1931) to be considered. To reach them, however, one must pass over the mountain of *Back to Methuselah* (1921), the most hortatory, arid, and tedious of all Shaw's works. No attempt will be made here to epitomize the windy oratory which rolls and reverberates through the five parts of this dramosity, representing the life of Man and Superman from the Garden of Eden to "as far as thought can reach," *i.e.*, 31,920 A.D. We will only record that Shaw manifests in this play a new term of thought, derived from Samuel Butler. The author of *The Way of All Flesh* (1903) convinced him, so Shaw declares, that Darwinian evolution is mistaken and that acquired characteristics may be inherited *provided that they are willed by the Life-Force*. In *Man and Superman* there is a hint that Shaw was reaching out for a Vitalistic philosophy which would join the teachings of Nietzsche to the science of Lamarck, in Don Juan's declaration that Nature, Time, and Death may be overcome. Yet it is certain that Shaw was not impressed by Butler's treatises against Darwinism, like *Life and Habit* (1877) or *Luck or Cunning?* (1887), when they appeared, but was converted by the posthumous novel. The earliest allusion to Butler seems to be in the Preface to *Major Barbara,* which appeared two years after *The Way of All Flesh*.

The final result of reading Butler's novel is a new ethic, only hinted at in the last sentence of the "Revolutionist's Handbook" but developed in *Back to Methuselah* in full. The "long-lived" people take the lives of the dwindling race of ordinary mortals without compunction, just as they eliminate those biological sports among their own kind who indicate a tendency to live only a normal life span. This Spartan treatment is represented as a sensible way of improving the race and of bringing about ideal conditions, though the play is lamentably weak in representing those conditions. In fact, the sexless and artless life achieved by the thoughtful "Ancients" in the year 31,920 is such a horror that flesh and blood cringes away from it "You can create

only yourself" is the sum of wisdom achieved by thousands of
years of living—a doctrine familiar to primitive Methodists in
the eighteenth century, but hardly socialistic. Aside from a highly
diverting colloquy between Adam and Eve and the Serpent in
Act I of Part I, and some pleasant ridicule of Lloyd George
and Lord Asquith in Part II, *Back to Methuselah* is perhaps the
most stupid creation by an able writer in modern times.

When Shaw descended from Sinai in 1928, after fraternizing
with Butler's ghost, he found that all but the women had deserted his camp; consequently he had to address his newest *opus*
on Socialism to them. *The Intelligent Woman's Guide* is one of
the handsomest pieces of back tracking, of apologetic scraping
and stammering, of squirming and dodging on record. Socialism
must come, for "Capitalist mankind in the lump is detestable."
Must it wait for evolution? Oh, no, no, no,—not now. "If it be
put off too long, or brought about too slowly, there may be a
violent revolution (Mr. Shaw has Russia in mind, as he indicates
elsewhere) which may produce a dismal equality by ruining
everybody who is not murdered. Only in a settled and highly
civilized society with a strong Government and an elaborate code
of laws can equality of income be attained or maintained." Consequently, *"We must build up Capitalism before we can turn
it into Socialism,"* for Shaw is now convinced that Socialism can
be arrived at best through long-term business arrangements and
extensions of the Civil Service!

The Apple Cart and its enchanting "Preface" are written to
extend and to embroider this thought. Declaring that "our
present parliament is obsolete," Shaw advocates the ruthless
scrapping of all pseudo-democratic institutions, the creation of
several federal committees in place of the legislature, and the
establishment of a central authority to co-ordinate the federal
work. In a word, friend Shaw has ended by becoming a Bureau-
crat who sees in the board of directors of a joint stock company
the ideal administrative agency for the state. This is a far cry,
surely, from what Mr. Shaw's speeches on Socialism in the debating societies of the 'eighties must have been!

Yet so far as there is a true George Bernard Shaw, he may
be said to be represented by the plays and pieces which we have

surveyed. This is not the George Bernard Shaw, however, with whom Americans are acquainted or who has most influenced our thought. Indeed, prior to this writing, we believe, no one has attempted the folly of "surveying" Shaw, of pulling him together and setting him upright to stare at, to see what the whole of him is like. More sensibly, his delighted audiences and readers have taken him simply as a scoffer, a Puritan-baiter, a wit, an iconoclast, a buffoon. And it is quite possible to get this impression from the material we have pondered. Yet American opinion of him has been formed in the main on other things, and because of this fact he does not appear to us either as a bewildered Socialist or baffled Irishman, but as an operatic Mephistopheles, the "tease" of the good and virtuous, the shocker of the moral and moderate, the cocksure diabolist. After fifteen years of Shavian drama in this country, Charles Klein could say to Montrose Moses, "I cannot see how Bernard Shaw, who denies everything from pure love to pure music, can be a public benefactor." Shaw was introduced to Americans by Richard Mansfield, who presented *Arms and the Man* at the Herald Square Theatre in New York on September 17, 1894, with more success than the earlier London performance had achieved, and who later, in 1895, opened his new Garrick Theatre with the same play. To the American intelligence of the day *Arms and the Man* was "an irreverent whimsicality" which pictured the professional soldier, Bluntschli, as a man of discretion and not of valor, and the average pretty girl, Raina, as a person without morals. It must be understood strictly that the average American playgoer was not shocked by *Arms and the Man,* but he went away from the theatre with a pleasant nervous tingle, like a boy who has been up to mischief and has just failed to be caught. His sensations were similar to those he had experienced at the Gilbert and Sullivan operas (which *Arms and the Man* so much resembles) but more clearly defined. He had got a taste of something he liked and he wanted more. And Mr. Shaw was ready to oblige him. It is evident that *The Devil's Disciple* was written especially for Mansfield and Shaw's American admirers. Introduced to an Albany audience on October 1, 1897, it proved an instant hit and was moved to New York. Mr. Mansfield played in it to full houses throughout the following season.

The Devil's Disciple fixed the reputation of Shaw in America. It is a pretty story of how Dick Dudgeon, the village atheist in Revolutionary times, permits himself to be taken for the village parson when the British are hanging the most prominent man in every hamlet to secure proper respect for the King's uniforms. Shaw (whom we have suspected of nursing a good deal of feeling towards the British) let himself go in this play, and the emphasis on the patriot's side made the play popular in the days of *Richard Carvel*. It also made palatable the severe strictures Shaw leveled at Puritan morality in the first act. Americans got a wholly new sensation from the fact that the minister's wife, Judith Anderson, plainly lapsed from her duty to her husband, lost her little head to the fire-breathing Dick, and then had to beg him in the end not to tell her husband about her dereliction. Mighty were the discussions as to whether Dick had reciprocated her feeling, and grudging indeed was the acknowledgment that he did not love her. This was the first serious attack upon romantic love to shatter the illusions of Americans. It is not surprising that the author himself came to be looked upon as the devil's disciple. This conviction was strengthened when Herbert S. Stone & Company, of Chicago, published in 1900 *Three Plays for Puritans* which not only included *The Devil's Disciple* but one of the most provocative of Shaw's prefaces. For evaluating the precise significance of this book, it is worth noting that, whereas the English reviewers concentrated angrily upon that section of the Preface entitled "Better than Shakespear?" and the play *Caesar and Cleopatra,* American reviewers chewed —one should say, Fletcherized—the section entitled "On Diabolonian Ethics" and *The Devil's Disciple.* Here many learned for the first time that Blake had pictured the devil as Redeemer and that there was such a topsy-turvy moralist as Nietzsche.

In 1898 Herbert S. Stone & Company had published *Plays Pleasant and Unpleasant.* Consumption of this volume and the success of *Arms and the Man* and *The Devil's Disciple* led, in 1905, to an attempt to stage in New York *Mrs. Warren's Pro-*

fession, which had been refused a license in England. On the second night the police, at the instigation of Anthony Comstock, raided the play. This suppression, which was wholly unwarranted, greatly increased Shaw's reputation in this country as a Puritan-baiter. Of course, *Mrs. Warren's Profession* is a highly moral play—but the censorship gave it an evil reputation and weak minds read into it what it patently did not contain. The fine characterization of Sir George Crafts, of Praed, of Mrs. Warren, and of Vivie (a rather dreadful, earnest person) and the high purpose of the author were wholly lost. Mere mention of *Mrs. Warren's Profession* is still apt to produce a leer among the cognoscenti in this country. *The Shewing-Up of Blanco Posnet* (1909) increased Shaw's following among the American intelligentsia. Not only were they attracted by the native setting of the play, but also by the obvious dependence upon Bret Harte for local color and upon Colonel Robert Ingersoll for frontier agnosticism. Shaw's long preface on the British censorship provided the American intelligentsia with ammunition for their battles with provincial prudery and comstockery.

Meanwhile, the publication of *Man and Superman* (1904) had placed in the hands of Shaw's American admirers the highly influential "Revolutionist's Handbook" appended to that play. Second only to the writings of Huneker and Mencken was this *jeu d'esprit* in winning converts to Nietzsche. Further, the maxims which it contained became the rule of action for our intelligentsia and a sort of pocket-bible for daily consumption. The sophomoric cynicism of such utterances as "Self-denial is not a virtue: it is only the effect of prudence on rascality" made a tremendous number of converts in the freshman class. The consequences of Shaw's American reputation are that his one profoundly moving play, *Saint Joan* (1923), is prized most for its pseudo-cynical, apologetic epilogue, and that his popular *Candida* (1897), whose hold upon the public is really lodged in its Barryesque sentimentalism, is regarded as important for its satirical revelation of the weakness of the ministry. That Shaw has come to prize his reputation as a modern Voltaire is revealed by the publication of the trivial *Adventures of the Black Girl in Her Search for God* (1930)—a book to be treasured, however, for its fine woodcuts by John Farleigh. One cannot see that the excellent entertainment provided by such plays as *Caesar and Cleopatra* (1903), *Major Barbara* (1905), *Pygmalion* (1912), and *Androcles and the Lion* (1915) has done more than to increase Shaw's American reputation as a sceptic and wit. But one may regret, in passing, that while Americans are generally aware of the services done Ibsen and Wagner in *The Quintessence of Ibsenism* (1891) and *The Perfect Wagnerite* (1898), too few today know "A Degenerate's View of Nordau" (1895), the best of all his destructive essays, or *The Admirable Bashville* (1901), his burlesque of blank-verse tragedy based on his own entertaining novel, *Cashel Byron's Profession* (1885). A shelf of Shaw contains other recommendable treats, but it will take much new writing on the man to offset his deeply entrenched American reputation as an iconoclast and mere wit. He will probably remain the devil's disciple so far as America is concerned, the perfect exemplar of the especially privileged artist.

3

MODERN CYNICISM

It has been the work of a group of intellectuals in recent times to introduce the cult of the privileged artist and to join the ideas of that cult to those engendered by the cynicism and pessimism already existing in America. In the van of the literary importers was Edgar Saltus, a third-rater if there ever was one, yet important as a symptomatic figure. Since, among a certain sect, there has been much lamenting of the fact that Saltus has not elbowed his way into the conventional histories of our literature, we may as well at the outset inspect his ability as a writer. Mr. Carl Van Vechten has a lyrical passage on the style of Saltus, in which he says, among other things, "It is dashing and rapid, as clear as the water in southern seas. The fellow has a penchant for short and nervous sentences which explode like so many firecrackers and remind one of the great national holiday." We have never been able to discover the passage in Mr. Saltus' works that Van Vechten had in mind when he made this observation, but there are any number of pages that it simply does not fit. Saltus wrote short sentences because he could not construct long ones without botching them. For example: "On the evening of the fourth day, a bit fatigued, the motion of the train actively continuing in his head, but in a white tie, a white waistcoat—between which two small black studs served to indicate his recent mourning—he was again in Madison avenue . . ." etc. It is easy enough to show that his fiction is trash. Let's sample *The Monster* (1912). Leilah Ogston, parting with her fiancé, asks if he will be gone long. He responds—

> "An hour or two. Apropos, would you care to leave before dinner?"
> "Yes."
> "We will dine on board, then. Is there anything in particular you would like?"
> "Yes, lilies, plenty of lilies; and pineapples; and the sound of your voice."
> Lifting her hands from his shoulders to his face, she drew it to her own. Their lips met longly. With the savour of her about him, Verplank passed out. . . .

Anyone who writes like this hasn't the semblance of a claim to be considered as an artist.

If Saltus is not an artist, what is his significance? He is the unrivalled champion of bad taste, the promoter of frippery, the hen-feathered knight of vulgarity. He did for American letters precisely what the millionaire "connoisseurs" of the 'eighties did for American art and architecture. Instead of bringing back from Europe an indiscriminate pile of plunder—Dutch tiles, Turkish rugs, French porcelain, German tankards, and whole English manors—Edgar Saltus carefully selected from the booty of the whole world only the inutile and fantastic to dump on our shores.

Born into New York leisure-class society in 1858, Saltus was educated at Saint Paul's School in Concord, N. H., before migrating to the Sorbonne in Paris, and thence to the universities of Heidelberg and Munich. Apparently first a disciple of Emerson, he was led to believe that he had a bent for philosophy— and he read widely (though never critically), first in the East Indian mystics and then in the German pessimists—Arthur

Schopenhauer and Eduard von Hartmann. To these thinkers he was converted as simply as if he had "experienced" Methodism; thus he was able to retain a sneaking admiration for Emerson and the mystics and a passion for exotic literature which he had picked up along the way: for the horror in Victor Hugo and Poe, for the effete and decadent in Gautier and d'Aurevilly, for the degenerate in Oscar Wilde and Huysmans. Similarly, a convinced misogynist because of Schopenhauer and Hartmann, Saltus took himself three wives—a rather typical act for a "connoisseur" of the last decades of the nineteenth century.

In his fiction—of which *Mr. Incoul's Misadventure* (1887), *The Truth about Tristrem Varick* (1888), *Mary Magdalen* (1891), *Daughters of the Rich* (1909), and *The Monster* (1912) are representative—Saltus has done nothing but rewrite *Dorian Gray, À Rebours,* and *Herodias.* In his rewriting, however, he has managed to rob his originals of whatever glamour they had, so that the apples of Sodom have become merely fallen wild fruit—stale and citric. Not a flash of wit illumines one of them, and the only pleasure in reading them today is to chuckle over the *gaucheries* of Saltus. Two descriptive studies of decadent society, *Imperial Purple* (1893), on the decline of Rome, and *The Imperial Orgy* (1920), a study of the Romanoffs, are delectations prepared for pampered appetites, but only a literary vegetarian would take them for meat. It is an infantile intelligence which dwells upon the glories and vices of the emperors and czars. In his so-called philosophical and historical studies the amorphous Mr. Saltus takes vague shape as an iconoclast. His first book, *The Philosophy of Disenchantment,* was published by the staid house of Houghton Mifflin in 1885. It is a descriptive sketch of the philosophies of Schopenhauer and Hartmann following a fantastic chapter on "The Genesis of Disenchantment." There is no attempt to evaluate or criticize his subjects, and in the end Saltus reaches a conclusion no more profound than that of Bierce, Ingersoll, or Howe—

. . . life may be said to be always valuable to the obtuse, often valueless to the sensitive; while to him who commiserates with all mankind, and sympathizes with everything that is, life never appears otherwise than as an immense and terrible affliction.

Having decided that the world was not worth a persimmon, Saltus proceeded in a variety of books to flout the beliefs and ideals of those who set a higher value on it. *Historia Amoris* (1906) and *The Lords of the Ghostland* (1907) are his most notorious studies of love and of religion. The former traces illicit and erotic passion from Babylon, that "bazaar of beauty," down to the time when it can be dissected by Schopenhauer. The author lingers pleasantly over the legends of Aphrodite Urania, Sappho, Aspasia, Cleopatra, Lesbia, etc., but in the end the book is merely tamely and inanely corrupt. Saltus is no Huysmans. *The Lords of the Ghostland* is an effort to confound Christians and Methodists by showing that notable features of the Christ story may be found in the legends of Brahma, Ormuzd, Amon-Ra, Bel-Marduk, Zeus, and Jupiter. The effort reminds us of Ingersoll's lecture, *The Ghosts,* and truth is, it is the same trollop with rouge and curls. We liked the wench better in her innocence. If to some, Ingersoll was Satan on the stump, to others Edgar Saltus was a very devil in the boudoirs. One blushes, however, for those who have taken him seriously.

Two other hawkers of strange wares in America at the end of the nineteenth century were Vance Thompson and Percival Pollard, both very minor journalists. Vance Thompson is chiefly remembered for his *French Portraits* (1900), a book of more or less personal recollections of young French writers, done in palpable imitation of *The Confessions of a Young Man.* The chief weakness of this sturdily bound and handsomely illustrated volume is the critic's lack of discrimination: Richepin and Bouhelier are presented to us with the same *éclat* accorded Verlaine and Mallarmé. Thompson has read widely without becoming well read. His mind may be snatched up anywhere in his book:

Life is at once too dirty and too sad. Even war can hardly make it splendid....

... Great art is always virile.

The slim pallidities of Fra Angelico belong to a day of degenerate and monkish thought.

Rubens' great blond women are the solaces of the eternal fighting man....

Nietzsche, who is cited half a dozen times in *French Portraits,* brings a gusto to Thompson's writing that his predilection for Pierre Louys and other French fairies denies. Reading this volume, however, one can understand how Vance Thompson was once regarded as standard bearer for the Intelligentsia, a position which his editorship of the smart magazine *M'lle New York* from August, 1895, to April, 1896, did much to confirm. "*M'lle New York* is not concerned with the public. Her only ambition is to disintegrate some portion of the public into its original component parts—the aristocracies of birth, wit, learning, and art, and the joyously vulgar mob" ran the Foreword.

Percival Pollard, his confrere, is as positive in his opinions, but more frequently mistaken than Thompson. In his *Masks and Minstrels of New Germany* (1911) he seeks to acquaint Americans with recent German writers as Thompson had done with recent French authors. In praising Liliencron, Hartleben, Bierbaum, and Wolzogen, he reveals his incapacity to distinguish between literature and diddling, wherefore he may be dismissed as a critic and regarded as a mere importer. *Their Day in Court* (1909) was his most read critical volume. Pollard may be measured by such a statement as, "Literature is the advertisement of one's attitude towards life," as well as by his critical judgments. To him Ambrose Bierce is "the one commanding figure in America in our time," and Edgar Saltus is a great novelist— almost as good as Robert Hichens! *Their Day in Court* is further distinguished by its attack on Brander Matthews and other professors as the "bosses" of literature and by its flattery of Vance Thompson and Huneker. Pollard, who transformed criticism into politics and back-slapping, was the first of the sect-conscious Intelligentsia.

One purveyor of European ideas to Americans in this period was both a cosmopolitan and a man of taste. This was James Gibbons Huneker, the Philadelphia Irishman of whom H. L. Mencken has written so well, not in *A Book of Prefaces,* but in the Introduction to the *Essays* which he selected and edited for Scribner's in 1929. As any one knows who has read *Steeplejack* (1918) or *Painted Veils* (1920), Huneker at the end of his critical and creative life was horribly oppressed by a sense of personal failure. In the autobiography the self-condemnation is complete and abysmal:

> ... I love painting and sculpture: I may only look, but never own either pictures or marbles. I would fain be a pianist, a composer of music: I am neither. Nor a poet. Nor a novelist, actor, playwright. I have written of many things from architecture to zoology without grasping their inner substance. I am Jack of the Seven Arts, master of none. . . .

This, says Mencken, was "the worst critical judgment in a lifetime of critical judgments." Yet he himself substantially supports Huneker's view of himself when he admits that the critic's chief defect was "excess of eclecticism." The vice was so rare, however, in the latter half of the nineteenth century in America that it is easily forgiven, and we are not inclined to believe that it alone depressed Huneker. The novel *Painted Veils* tells a different story, and to it we turn in our quest for an explanation of the funereal gloom in which Huneker shrouded himself.

Painted Veils is a narrative of the adventures of a young aesthete, "Ulrick Invern, a writer, incidentally a critic," whose well-to-do Irish father was secretary at the American legation in Paris, where Ulrick and his brother Oswald were born. Of this brother Oswald, Huneker has written a short story entitled "The Supreme Sin" which appears in that volume largely given over to the praise of Mary Garden, entitled *Bedouins* (1920). Oswald, described as a painter and diabolist in *Painted Veils*, in this short story is duped into attending a black mass at which the officiating priest, Van Zorn, is parent of the girl whom Oswald loves. When, at the height of the ceremony, Diabolus is evoked, what should appear but the beautiful image of his loved one; terrified, the young man saves himself by calling on the Son of Mary, and the vision vanishes. The last we hear of Oswald he is leading the monkish life in the deserts of Arabia. This short story, despite certain capricious involutions, comes directly from a reading of Huysmans. Its simpler outline makes it possible for us, if we are not well read in diabolism, to perceive Huneker's meaning in *Painted Veils*. For whereas the idea that the devil is a woman is treated facetiously in "The Supreme Sin," it is given much more credence in the novel.

Ulrick Invern, brother to Oswald and protagonist in *Painted Veils*, tastes only disillusionment from his sampling of women. Three ladies afford him the gamut of experience: Mona Milton, the marrying kind; Dora, a high-class prostitute; and Esther, or Istar, Brandes, an opera star. Mona, he discovers, loves him only because through him she may have the children for whom she hungers; premature birth, however, kills their illegitimate child, and she, without a pang apparently, gives up Ulrick to marry a rounder who makes her a contented mother. About Dora, Ulrick has no illusions—she loves merely professionally, and one man is as good as another. It is his burning for Istar Brandes, however, that finally destroys him. Over this young woman he presumes he has some sway because he had rescued her from an orgy of a religious sect when she was nobody, but in the end he discovers this is his greatest error. Repulsed by the crowd around her after her triumphant return from Europe and her engagement at the Metropolitan, Ulrick flees to Dora, but is pursued by Istar who takes Dora from him for her own delight, and Ulrick discovers she is the sum of his other two mistresses, a self-centered Lesbian.

One final revelation is necessary, however, before Ulrick fully understands the entire nature of feminine passion. He has had a friend throughout the course of his story, Mel Milton, who has stood by him through thick and thin,—even when Ulrick seduced his sister his friendship remained unshaken. To be sure, Milton, who is studying for the priesthood, is a tedious platitudinarian, but he has the virtue of realizing that he is tedious. Nevertheless he is concerned for his friend's soul. "A woman's heart contains treasures of affection. Don't waste them. . . . I'm a bore, but right is sometimes on the side of the stupid, and victory doesn't always perch on the banners of the intellectually elect." Mel Milton, however, is seduced in the end by Istar Brandes, and Ulrick learns several things in one crowded lesson. First, that his friend whom he has always called Milton is really named Melchizedek *(king of righteousness)* and belongs to the eternal priesthood (see Heb. 7:2). And secondly, when he calls Istar a beast, that lady informs him that she had enjoyed relations with Brother Rainbow, the negro head of the religious cult from which he had supposed he rescued her, and thus his earliest conjecture (made after reading Reinach's *Orpheus*) that the chief source of religion is fornication, is confirmed. The whole significance of the Melchizedek-Istar relationship dawns on him with paralyzing effect. Istar is Ashtaroth, symbol of all worship, who, when the final veil is removed, is seen to be sexual adoration. This is too much for the idealistic Ulrick who drinks himself to death in Paris.

Ulrick's friends never attribute his death, however, to disillusioned idealism. Alfred Stone, cynical reviewer and acquaintance of Ulrick's, has a theory which is generally accepted. According to this view, Ulrick, whose mind was "a crazy-quilt, mince pie and Chopin," failed to strike root in America because the American spiritual atmosphere was too "tonic" for his decadent ideas. "His *Fleurs du Mal* wilted. So did he. He hadn't the guts to last." Returning to Paris, he died of an evil inherited from his father ("our old enemy, Spirochaeta Pallida, I suspect," Stone sneers). This judgment is superbly ironic to the reader who knows the facts. That reader, however, cannot but see that Ulrick Invern and James Gibbons Huneker are one, and that *Painted Veils* is really an *apologia pro vita sua*—one of the most remarkable ever written. Invern acknowledges the same masters as Huneker: the Goncourt brothers, Huysmans, Gourmont, Barrès, and Nietzsche. Invern, like Huneker, had tried to practice criticism in America; both men were dismissed as fantastic and decadent. The parallels go very far—even down to Huneker's admiration for Mary Garden as a "superwoman" and Invern's early fascination in Esther Brandes. *Painted Veils,* properly appreciated, is a defense of the artist-critic as a misunderstood idealist. Huneker freely acknowledges his absorption in decadence and diabolism—but whither do these paths lead? In a preposterous epilogue Huneker maintains that the thirst of Petronious Arbiter for an absolute in evil (in the popular view the thirst of Invern-Huneker) is the same as the God-intoxicated craving of Thomas à Kempis for the Infinite. "On the vast uncharted map of mysticism extremes may meet, even mingle . . . *Credo quia impossible est . . .*"

Huneker was sixty when he wrote *Painted Veils* and he was

dying. He wanted to make his peace with the Church. In his lifetime he had condemned as the seven deadly virtues: humility, charity, meekness, temperance, brotherly love, diligence, and chastity. He had cultivated the seven arts: poetry, music, architecture, painting, sculpture, drama, and dancing. If he wished to save his soul, he must show the course of his life ultimately moral. The path of Petronius and the path of Thomas must merge in the end; the extremes of art and religion must meet somewhere in eternity. Wherefore Ulrick Invern is shown a martyr and Istar becomes "the Great Singing Whore of Modern Babylon"—the United States. But to make his allegory complete and to save his soul Huneker has to adopt a wholly medieval, but thoroughly orthodox, attitude towards woman. She is still the source of evil in the world, and if churchmen are corrupt, it is her influence. The author of Genesis, St. Paul, and Huneker are in agreement about her, but not Jesus and Pope Pius XI. *Painted Veils* is not a pretty book; in fact, it is a rather cowardly book, and we are not surprised that H. L. Mencken is discreetly silent about it. Yet it is an extraordinarily ingenious book: dependent on both Huysmans and Saltus, it is better than either, more neatly patterned, sounder in its knowledge of literature and music, more disturbing in its decadence and diabolism. As a piece of moral writing, it is quite as significant as *Mont-Saint-Michel and Chartres,* though it is inferior to it as prose. Its consequence, so far as Huneker is concerned, is to reveal his perturbation, at the close of his life, not over his eclecticism, but at his lack of moral significance and purpose.

Fortunately, James Gibbons Huneker was little occupied with his immortal soul during the course of his lifetime. There is nothing egocentric about either *Iconoclasts* (1905) or *Egoists* (1909), his most popular critical books, nor in his studies of Chopin and Liszt, nor in *Old Fogy* (1913). There is instead a joyous sampling of whatever the seven arts had to offer to a man of fine sensibility and good breeding. To understand Huneker one has to look into his boyhood home—as exceptional a home for the Philadelphia of the 'sixties as was the Dublin home of Bernard Shaw's childhood. Here congregated the artists and musicians whom his father knew; here flourished the interest in

French literature that his mother felt a necessary prerequisite for her conception of his ultimate profession of priest. It is to be doubted if any contemporary of Huneker's read, as a child, not only the sermons of Lacordaire, Bourdaloue, Madame de Swetchine, and Eugénie de Guérin, but also in the works of Pater, Arnold, Swinburne, Rossetti, Poe, Gautier, Rabelais, Montaigne, Goethe, Aquinas, Emerson, Schopenhauer, and Whitman. His runaway flight to Paris (with his parents' connivance) in 1876 seems an inevitable sequel to such a childhood. That he should have come back to teach appreciation of the seven arts to Americans is more of a miracle.

Name almost any important name in art, music, or literature in Scandinavia, Germany, France, or England in the latter half of the nineteenth century, and it is a safe bet that James Gibbons Huneker was the first to write intelligently upon that artist in America. He was the most important early crusader here for Ibsen, Shaw, Sudermann, Hauptmann, Huysmans, Stendhal, Maeterlinck, Richard Strauss, Anatole France, Barrès, Stirner, and Nietzsche. Probably his newspaper articles and his *Promenades of an Impressionist* (1910) did more to clarify in the public mind what the French impressionist painters were up to than the writings of any other critic. He believed Monet one of the greatest men of the nineteenth century, and his commendation of Monet and Cézanne gave both men an immense reputation here. Today, as we survey Huneker's work, we are perhaps inclined to see the influence of the French Decadents predominant in it, but it is doubtful if Huneker, under full sail, was more aware of the wind from that quarter than from Germany, Scandinavia or England. Yet out of two French novels on art—Zola's *L'Œuvre* and Goncourt's *Manette Salomon*—Huneker got whatever he had of method in criticism. He aimed at Impressionism, but he had such a lively curiosity about the personalities of his subjects that frequently his criticism amounted to no more than racy gossip, gossip that spread enchantment over whatever he discussed. Mencken says that his talk "made his books seem almost funereal": one has to take this as hyperbole, for it is incredible that one could talk that much better than these chatty, engaging volumes. Yet Huneker's books are not properly criticism. He was too amiable—as Mencken points out—to do a good job of critical dissection. Repeatedly he calls himself a disciple of Gourmont. "My dear friend and master, the late Rémy de Gourmont," is his tribute in *Bedouins*. But when he was charged with the lack of a unifying theme in *Egoists* and sought to defend himself by claiming that this lack of unity illustrated the practice of "dissociation," he showed that he had no clear idea of Gourmont's principle. If not a critic, James Gibbons Huneker remains the merchant prince of all the importers of European ideas at the turn of the century. Never cordial towards the Russians, whose pessimism and moral depth oppressed him, and overcautious in regard to Americans (Whistler, Whitman, and Poe are all whom he chose to praise), he selected almost unerringly people of real importance to discuss. He was, above everything else, a gifted connoisseur.

All that British and American iconoclasm had hitherto yearned for in vain was realized in the intellectual career of Henry Louis Mencken. Was Shaw garrulous and repetitious?—Mencken deduced the one inescapable conclusion from the stuttered premises of the Ulster Polonius. Did Huneker's eclecticism lead him to sample too many sweets?—Henry L. threw the confections out the window and thrust forward the spoon and bottle of bitter Rochen salts that should have been offered in the first place. He was the answer to a prayer, the culmination of a blind urge, the proof positive that desire in the Lamarckian sense can shape protoplasm to its ends. Consequently, it was to the accompaniment of ringing bells, oratorical firecrackers, and loud hosannahs that this dreadful monad escaped the placenta in bucolic Baltimore on September 12, 1880, and immediately demanded a quart of Pilsener. He was sired, it is alleged, "by a German tobacconist and sweater of cheap labor," August Mencken, who hoped to enrich the legal profession with his offspring. But the round dome of Mencken was never to nod over the labyrinthian briefs of the shysters nor to grace the solemn waggeries of our Highest Tribunal. True, as a toothless toddler he was tractable enough until he became soiled with the bilge that passed for literature in a Baltimore schoolroom. Thereupon he was unmanageable, and denounced the stout birchman who presided over his destiny as "a charlatan, a mountebank, a zany without shame or dignity." Mistaking the somewhat rhythmical tumescence and detumescence of adolescence as an urge to poetize, he determined upon a career as a Bard. The following is Specimen A of his verses, a veritable piece of *incunabula:*

> Love walks upon the waters,
>   And fares into the hills;
> Love makes himself a hiding-place
>   Among the daffodils. . . .

Here, perhaps, is shamelessly displayed a lamentable credence in aphroditean hagiography and a great innocence of physics, which, however, may be pardoned in one so young.

So badly was H. L. gnawed by the *Cacoethes scribendi* that he was soon inditing roundels, rondeaux, ballades, madrigals, and valentine verses in the best cologne-water manner of Austin Dobson and Henry Cuyler Bunner, the fruity poet-laureate of the limp hand and the flowered tie. From these worthies he pushed ruthlessly on, with his age, to imitating the hirsute Kipling, and yawped about "The Gawd that made the ocean an' painted up the sky," and ultimately—oh, ultimately, *quod maxime reris*—he imitated Robert W. Service!

> Certes the tale is a weepful one
>   Of Frederick Clarence Jones
> And how he was conned by a heartless blonde,
>   And how, in remorse, he groans,
> And tears his hair in dank despair . . . etc.

From these inklings it is obvious that he was destined to go far. Yet indubitable genius finds it ever difficult to impress its worth upon the loutish world, and Mencken saw the need of having his worth certified. Hence he, who was to be for three pious decades the scourge of the colleges, enrolled in 1898 in the Cosmopolitan University—one of the earliest correspondence schools in the country! Twice a week the rural mail man reined in Dobbin at 1524 Hollis Street in Baltimore—once to collect Henry's exercises, and once to return them blue pencilled by his "professors"—the eminent journalists Arthur M. Chase and Edward

Tyler. Over his compositions the faithful fellow sweated as earnestly as a plowman and eventually his noble industry was rewarded: he had conferred on him the embossed diploma of the university, *magna cum laude,* by Herr Doktor Professor John Brisben Walker, founder of the institution and its first president. He was now armed to slay dragons.

In passing, we pause to remark that it is impossible to over-evaluate the effect of the higher discipline of his university education upon the budding artist. The eminent caption-makers and gossip-mongers persuaded him that nothing was quite so worth imitating as current journalism: he then acquired the aptitude for perceiving in the newspaper exchanges the raw stuff which he could transmute into the unvarnished Billingsgate of his style. From the newspapers, out of pulp and glue, Billiken was formed. In the *New York World* he found O. Henry, and in the Chicago *Record,* George Ade.

The imitation of O. Henry extended beyond style to an effort to reproduce the effect of his short stories, as the tale "The Bend in the Tube" in the *Red Book* in 1904, indicates. It is style, however, that smooth green ooze, which chiefly interests us. When Mencken writes, "Now, in truth, began the winter of Boggs' discontent," he is thinking of the "clever" way O. Henry had of parodying the Bard of Avon. Thus Mercutio's death speech becomes a description of a Nashville drizzle: "It is not so fragrant as a mothball nor so thick as pea-soup; but 'tis enough—'twill serve." Later, when Mencken was to write of Dixie, "Down there a poet is now almost as rare as an oboe-player, a dry-point etcher, or a metaphysician," he was as O. Henryish as "The Gift of the Magi" or "The Hiding of Black Bill." Which author wrote, "From the Crusades to the Palisades adventurers have enriched the arts of history and fiction and the trade of historical fiction"? It sounds like Mencken, but the sentence reposes in *The Four Million.*

Yet there was not quite dash enough—or balderdash enough—to O. Henry's style to satisfy the future obiter-dictarist. By blending O. Henry with George Ade, he was able to impart the proper snort to his sentences: "One horse laugh is worth ten thousand syllogisms." From *Fables in Slang* could have come the self-conscious injunction beneath the "Preliminary Rebuke" in his first and only volume of verse: "Don't shoot the pianist; he is doing his best." This actually is, however, from one of the favorite stories of Oscar Wilde who saw it framed over the piano in a music hall on his visit to our West. From *Fables in Slang* did come the *Untold Tales* in the Baltimore *Herald* in 1901. Here are some of the titles: "How J. Catullus Braggadocia Went the Limit, and, By Putting His Stake on the Red, Won Out," "How J. Socrates Lithium Elevated the Stage and Later was Elevated Himself," "How Claudius Nero Ippolitus Rose to Eminence and Later Lost His Job." When the actual debt of Mencken to Ade is considered, we cease to marvel at the candle offerings of the Baltimore acolyte at the altar of the sainted author of the Hoosier *De Vulgari Eloquentia,* as witness *Prejudices I:* ". . . Ade is one of the few original literary craftsmen now in practise amongst us . . . he comes nearer making literature, when he has full steam up, than any save a scant half dozen of our current novelists. . . ." Yet this debt to Ade marks Mencken off permanently from the true cosmopolitan; there is always something about his writing like the awkwardness of a trans-Appalachian primate with a table fork, something that evokes visions of vapid girls, their smelly swains, and horned cattle, something native and aboriginal, like country victuals, horseflies, and dung.

With his correspondence school diploma and a style which a pop-eyed admirer has declared reached "full maturity" before 1902, Mencken was prepared to triumph in journalism. Undeniably he was better equipped than most of his fellows, and emitting ink like a squid, he quickly swam to the top of his trade. He no longer had to put together the pamphlets "of a manufacturer, of a milk-dealer, of the United Fruit Company," as he had done at the beginning of his career; at twenty-five he was belaboring the *Gelehrten* of Hopkins or the husbandmen of the Eastern Shore as Editor-in-Chief of the Baltimore *Herald;* in 1910 he was conducting the "Free-Lance" column in the *Sun.*

Yet the heights were still denied him. His university course had not supplied him with a philosophy; and whatever else he may have plucked from Ade and O. Henry, he cannot conceivably be charged with the theft of ideas from these pundits. When

Mencken tried to raise his voice from chest register to head register, a crude sort of socialism, such as Jack London stood for, was the literary scandal of the day. In this the Baltimore scholar immersed himself, reading until he reached Shaw. He found in the fragrant Irishman better browsing than the weeds and buttercups of Percival Pollard, Huneker, Meltzer, and Vance Thompson on whom he had hitherto fared in *Town Topics* and the *Criterion,* and in the first flush of his enthusiasm scribbled off an introduction to the ex-Dublinite on the model of the *Quintessence of Ibsenism,* y-clept *George Bernard Shaw: The Plays* (1905). Mencken destroyed his Shaw ledger when his account was still scarlet and has since denounced the playwright in the resounding rhetoric of an ash collector; nevertheless there is no denying that he once sat agape on the knee of this glib governess. Holy Bernard taught him self-assurance and coached him in the craft of sand-blasting his joshbillingsgate into the vigorous vernacular of the gentlemen's washroom. Between the *Untold Tales* of the Baltimore *Herald* and the *Prejudices* stand the prefaces to Shaw's plays. And (though this is a good deal to charge to the Celt) it seems likely that it was he who put Mencken's trusting hand in the iron fist of Nietzsche; for after he had finished his little tribute to Shaw, Mencken toiled like a monk with glossary, dictionary, and candle, until he had read the seer of Rocken in the original and unemasculated blonde *Deutsch* and had written the first able study of him done on this shore of the Atlantic, *The Philosophy of Friedrich Nietzsche* (1908). There was much interest in Nietzsche at this time in America—Norris, London, and Theodore Roosevelt had utilized some of his more picturesque concepts—but little genuine understanding, and Mencken's straightforward exposition did much to make the German a less amorphous monster. Yet the effect upon the expositor was greater than upon *homo boobiens* generally. He became Nietzsche's janizary in the New World, his Apostle Paul, so to speak, and like the god-intoxicated citizen of Tarsus he grievously altered the teachings of his master. There was much about the philosopher that was unsatisfactory to the Baltimore journalist: despite Nietzsche's attacks upon altruism and conscience, he was at heart an idealist and visionary, who, if he despised contemporary morality and mankind, nevertheless hoped to induce a master morality and accomplish the salvation of the race through a breed of Supermen. Mencken did not give a whoop for this part of the philosophy and scornfully rejected it as a "messianic delusion" (very much as Paul rejected the teachings of Christ in regard to women and property), but clove to all the nihilistic elements of Nietzscheism. Here were ideas enough to dazzle the yokelry.

Mencken's discipleship to the great German has many amusing aspects to the student read in the latter's philosophy and life. One of these is the Baltimorean's vague maundering about a "first caste man,"—an anaemic reproduction of the Superman. Another is his violent defense, as if it were a new thing in the world, of individualism. To one familiar with the *egoismus* theories of Fichte, the "Self-reliance" doctrines of Emerson, and the egomania of Nietzsche, Mencken reads like the comic Sunday supplement to philosophy. And then there is a farraginous litter of reference to music in all his writings, for was not Wagner the first love of Nietzsche? A genuine improvement on the German's misogynous views is Mencken's derisive, yet very sprightly, *In Defense of Women* (1918). But most amusing of all, is the apostle's desire to be known as a philologist. Nietzsche, as everyone is aware, was a deep student of comparative languages, particularly at home in Greek where he made some excellent researches. Mencken, alas! knew small Latin and less Greek, and for some time was hard put to it to follow his master's lead. At last, however, Yankee ingenuity triumphed, and we have that extraordinary philological study—*The American Language* (1919)! Yet, though inspired by the philologist of Bâle, this grand book is a monument to the cherished memory of George Ade and his drummer's idiom. Permitting himself the unaccustomed rôle of visionary and prophet, Mencken pontifically declares that the American language, the grammarless yet toothsome speech of the phonetical spellers from Billings to the present, and not English, will become the standard language of the world. English "promises to become, on some not too remote tomorrow, a kind of dialect of American." This prophecy, like others from Sinai, doubtless should be heavily discounted, yet the brief chapter of Revelations does not mar his Bible: we repeat that *The American Language* is a grand book. Somewhat less scientific than Fannie Farmer, nevertheless it has a gusto for words that leaves Otto Jespersen and George Philip Krapp yammering outside the gate.

Once Yahoo is armed at every point, the fates decree his apogee. In 1908 Mencken became literary critic for *Smart Set,* and then, after the departure of the able Willard Huntington Wright, joint editor with George Jean Nathan. This magazine, originally founded by Colonel D'Alton Mann, proprietor also of the scandal sheet *Town Topics,* had been gradually transformed from a vehicle for the vaporings of high society into a literary journal by its previous editors, Arthur Grissom and Charles Hanson Towne. It was Willard Huntington Wright, however, who gave it genuine contemporaneity and determined the outlines of the policy followed by Mencken and Nathan with such success. Yet Wright and Nathan genuflected automatically before all things European, but Mencken, who had learned the virtue of keeping his hat on in the Presence, held out for American representation among the contributors. Hence people like Ben Hecht, O'Neill, Sinclair Lewis, and Cabell eventually found their way into *Smart Set.* Mencken's growing indifference to verse, however, cost the magazine that early preeminence in poetry which had been given it by Towne and Wright.

The elevation of Mencken from the editorship of *Smart Set* in 1924 to that of the newly established *American Mercury* is comparable only to the choice of a French Cardinal for Pope. The flutter this created in correct circles, the jubilance among sophomores, the ecstasy of the Intelligentsia will be remembered in America long after the Christian Endeavor Society and the Epworth League, the Lions and the Kiwanis, are forgotten. What bellicose bawling and bellowing, what bacchanalian revelries and cavorting in the cloisters, what baying after frightened clergymen, what trumpeting on the trail of the godly, what venting down the wind! Over the verdant countryside poured a green flood of *Mercuries,* sweeping away palings, fences, and battlements, erasing marches and boundaries, wetting priest and parishman, destroying every convention, moral, and taboo. The lib-

erated masses and the ebullient bourgeoisie read together from
the same page, forgetting all class distinctions. Stenographers
went to work with the *Mercury* under their arms; millionaires
laid it aside on their blotters with regret to turn to their dreary
cozening. It became a badge of freedom, a visible symbol of intelligence, the sure sign of sophistication.

Yet in all the tumult Mencken was never quite sure of himself. There were certain points his master had not touched, and
he was sometimes forced to cast about in a hurry to supply the
deficiencies of his borrowed system. Nietzsche, for example, had
never touched on pure criticism, so far as Mencken knew. To
satisfy his followers, who clamored for an encyclical, the Pope
of Murray Hill had to make a few pronunciamentos upon his
art. In desperation he borrowed an idea from a fellow Baltimorean—long dead. In the "Rationale of Verse" Poe had written of the production of ideas by the addition of a third argument or fact, just as "in chemistry, the best way of separating
two bodies is to add a third." This became in Mencken's "Criticism of Criticism of Criticism" the famous "catalyzer" theory of
the highest art: "A catalyzer, in chemistry, is a substance that
helps two other substances react. . . . This is almost exactly the
function of a genuine critic of the arts. It is his business to provoke the reaction between work of art and the spectator." Later,
however, Mencken repented of this definition. A catalytic function ill became a first caste man. He renounced the theory, declaring significantly, it was conceived in one of his more "romantic"
moments.

Similarly, in another encyclical, seizing upon a statement by
Professor Otto Jespersen that "a good prose style is everywhere
a late acquirement," Mencken adduced that poetry belongs to the
youth of Man and is today necessarily jejune. *"Quod est poetica.
. . .* Poetry is a comforting piece of fiction set to more or less lascivious music. . . . Poetry . . . is an escape from life, like enthusiasm, like glimpsing a pretty girl." This is the first time we had
ever thought of glimpsing a pretty girl as *an escape from life*—
but let that pass. Mencken nowhere shows worse than in his discussions of the nature of poetry—unless it is in his own jingles.
However, try to square Mencken's condemnation of poetry be-

cause it is a pleasant fiction with his violent attack (in *Prejudices,* IV) upon the doctrine that art is an imitation of nature.

Mencken was more plausible when he closely dogged the footsteps of Nietzsche. The latter's denunciation of the Philistine became his tirade against the Puritan. Here he scored an easy victory over Stuart P. Sherman who was so foolish as to contend that Zeno, Christ, and Socrates were all Puritans. But it was a hollow victory. When Mencken tried to identify Comstockery with historical Puritanism in this country (in *A Book of Prefaces,* 1917), he revealed how nearly illiterate he is. As long ago as 1820 William Ellery Channing observed that Calvinism was so dead in these States that a discussion of its flaws was a more or less academic exercise. Comstockery was untheological, petty bourgeois, and definitely a product of the Gilded Age. The journalist who approached the historical issue with only a few ideas gathered from a foreign prophet could not be expected to give an account that would stand auditing. But, like the office boy who has been fired and kicks over the wastebasket in leaving, Mencken accomplished what he aimed at. The six series of *Prejudices* (1919–1927) and the ten years of the *American Mercury* (1924–1933) carried the assault on morals so far that in the latter years "Puritanism" was merely a straw horse which Mencken set up to knock down.

Though the mainspring of Mencken's animosity towards religion is Nietzsche's argument that it leads to racial deterioration and though many of his bulls against religion have been briefed for him by the German philosopher, two of his most earnest books, *Treatise on the Gods* (1930) and *Treatise on Right and Wrong* (1934), have a little of the stale, saline flavor of Edgar Saltus, whom Mencken serenaded in *Prejudices,* V. The laurels of the Almighty will not let Mencken sleep, and when he discovers that they are bay leaves, he can hardly contain himself. The Bible is a wholesale fraud, and as for its annex, the New Testament, "One might hesitate to liken it to any modern work of the first credibility, such as Boswell's *Johnson* or Eckermann's *Gespräch mit Goethe,* but it is certainly quite as sound as Parson Weems' *Life of Washington* or *Uncle Tom's Cabin.*" The second volume is the better, with certain surprising concessions to natural ethics

—evidence that in his mud fight with the moralists Mencken has now and then encountered a stone. All that is sound in moral systems may, in his belief, be attributed to instinct. His broad use of the term "instinct" to include social awareness, however, robs his volume of the punch characteristic of his other writing. He tamely concludes, "There is, in fact, such a thing as progress, and many of the new values it brings in are authentic and durable." Is it worth pointing out that *The Treatise on Right and Wrong* was published after Mencken had been chastened by the misfire of his political prophecy in *Making a President* (1932), and the tremendous decline of the *Mercury* after the débâcle of 1929?

In Nietzsche's thinking the Philistine is also the bourgeois democrat, a creature who espouses levelling and equalitarianism to protect his own inconsequence. With unexampled fury, Mencken, as a result, fell upon democracy in all his writings. The monthly "Americana" column and *The American Credo* (edited with George Jean Nathan in 1920) anthologized the blunders and inanities of obscure and distinguished personages quoted in the press from coast to coast—necessarily American equalitarians. In interviews, in editorials, in articles, and finally in a carefully considered book Mencken assaulted American democracy. *Notes on Democracy* (1926) begins with a diatribe against the ignorance, complacency, and brutishness of the democratic man. "In two thousand years he has moved an inch: from the sports of the arena to the lynching-party—and another inch from the obscenities of the Saturnalia to the obscenities of the Methodist revival." A succeeding section is devoted to the patent differences between the proclamations of democratic theorists and the practical functioning of the democratic state. The democratic process is not only "furiously inimical to all honorable motives" but it is also "even opposed to mere competence." Ability in a leader never recommends him to the democratic mass. Finally, after showing that "the common man's love of liberty, like his love of sense, justice, and truth, is almost wholly imaginary," Mencken declares that he enjoys democracy immensely: "It is incomparably idiotic, and hence incomparably amusing. . . . How can any man be a democrat who is sincerely a democrat?"

Walter Lippmann, who admirably dissected *Notes on Democracy* in the *Saturday Review of Literature,* pointed out that the book must be judged "totally, roughly, approximately, without definition, as you would a barrage of artillery, for the general destruction rather than for the accuracy of the shots." He sensed beneath Mr. Mencken's polemic a romantic yearning for feudal aristocracies, Prussian kingdoms, Bismarckian empires. He stigmatized as a "thorough-going piece of Utopian sentimentalism" Mencken's idea that complete liberty of speech is possible in a privileged, ordered, aristocratic society. Yet contemporary destructive analyses and rebuttals against Mencken's attacks on democracy had just about as much effect as pulpit fulminations against his savage assault on morality. Useless to insist that the essence of democracy is not found in provincialism, Bible Belt mores, Rotarian leadership, evangelical divinations, Prohibition, and Babbittry in general; Mencken persuaded the Intelligentsia that these were undeniably manifestations of democracy, more inevitable than a fair tally of hands in a New England town-meeting. One felt that, to be intelligent, one had to despise the body of mankind.

Future students of our intellectual history are going to be puzzled by the tremendous prestige of Mencken through the 'twenties. They will be struck by the fact that when, in the international intellectual exchange, the mark was worth virtually nothing, Mencken imported whole cargoes of German ideas, which he dispensed, like Woolworth, with Yankee sales talk. They will see that he typified, despite brilliant exposures of petty chicanery, the gross callousness towards morals which characterized the post-War years: that he led the assault on democratic ideals when democracy was the plaything of the plutocrats. On all social issues they will discover that he was singularly obtuse. Selfish, bourgeois, a rugged individualist, he is reported to have regarded success in the economic struggle wholly as a matter of luck. "Every man has both kinds. It was good luck, in large part, that made me city editor at 23—but it was bad luck that I was not owner of the paper. It was bad luck which kept some of those reporters in jobs at $15 a week—but it was good luck that enabled them to escape driving ice wagons." This view sustained him through the

early years of the depression and furnished him a vantage point
to deride the ill luck of those who in politics and finance were
trying to stem the tide. The announcements of Mr. Hoover that
we had turned the corner he found particularly amusing (as did
we all), but when the depression struck somewhat nearer home,
in 1932, Mr. Henry Louis Mencken, critic of all "right-thinking
Americans, solid citizens, patriots," began to assert (as if in
desperation) in successive issues of the *Mercury* that the depression really *was* over. He couldn't realize his luck had changed—
this aristocrat. And in this final Mrs. Partington act there was no
irony—only pathos. Then, *Jehovah jireh!* came the anounce-
ment, in 1933, that he would return to journalism. What comment will the future make on his exit? And how can historians
regard him as the champion of free speech, that some satellites
claim he is, when ten years of *American Mercuries* reveal that no
writer ever appeared in that magazine who was not content to
parrot the editor-in-chief? When Mencken resigned from the
Mercury, Harry Hansen reported that a contributor had told
him he was always astonished by his articles in print: "I saw my
articles appear in print colored with such words as *Privatdozent,
Geheimrat, Bierbruder,* and *Hasenpfeffer* which mystified my
friends because I don't know German." Whether or not Mencken
rewrote all articles which appeared in the *Mercury* (as is gos-
siped in New York) is of no consequence; what is patent is that
the material in the *Mercury* is more stereotyped than that in the
Patrologus latina. A fierce, intolerant spirit, brooking no opposition, shrewd in the knowledge that a derisive hoot is worth more
with the mob than sound reasoning, Mencken rode his age like a
yelling cowboy after a herd of stampeded longhorns. Yet, lest
the future conclude too hastily that he had no merit, let us call
attention to the fact that he could write as well as any cow-
puncher could ever ride—in demonstration of which we need call
attention merely to his destructive "In Memoriam: W. J. B.,"
the greatest piece of journalistic vituperation produced in America, and to his appreciative study of Huneker, which we have
cited before. In quite different moods these are equally effective
pieces of writing. Here is prose we can admire even if we do not
assent to the evaluation of either man.

If reading through the *American Mercury* of Mencken's editorship is today a good deal like doing penance for one's sins —that is, for an early and untutored enthusiasm, then to undertake the re-reading of James Branch Cabell is to suffer monstrously on the rack of one's innocence. We were bored with him at the outset, yet read from a sense of duty; our minds atrophy, our organs decay, our flesh shreds from our bones as we whip ourselves through him again. He is, beyond all shadow of a doubt, the most tedious person who has achieved high repute as a *literatus* in America, and only Wells surpasses him among the English. Beside the eighteen volumes pompously called "The Biography of Manuel" the Congressional Record is sprightly entertainment and the *Novum Organon* a bacchanalian revelry. Yet this is the man whom H. L. Mencken, in 1927, declared came nearer to being a first-rate artist than any other American of his time. And despite the insinuations of Mr. Cabell to the contrary, all during the 'twenties those reviewers who dissented from Mencken's estimate were in a painful minority. Today, however, literary critics as far apart as Arthur Hobson Quinn and Granville Hicks dismiss Cabell most summarily. To Hicks he is "a sleek, smug egotist . . . a fraud"; Quinn cannot understand how anyone could have taken him very seriously.

Running rather hastily over a great number of the reviews of Cabell's works during his vogue, one is struck by the reiterated admiration for his prose. "How wickedly charming the writing," chortled Mencken. "What a hand the fellow has for the slippery and narcotic phrase!" Henry Seidel Canby once declared, "Mr. Cabell has a fully matured style with body and beauty, and a perfect flow which suggests French prose as often as English." And so a hundred more. Even Quinn averred, "He had not much of a story to tell, but he had the gift, especially in his early work, of the well-chosen word, the charming phrase, and the sentence whose proportions are a delight. There were few writers of his generation who had such control over the resources of the English tongue."

Now, it seems to us that Cabell's reputation as a stylist is overblown. Once a man has been described as a stylist primarily, critics seem much more willing to accept and to repeat the tribute than to challenge the judgment. If one cites examples of down-right bad writing, they are likely to be treated with indulgence: they are exceptions in the work of the artist, "Homer nods," etc. Yet open any Cabellian masterpiece and the chances are, if you are not sleepy, you will find something that irritates you *as writing*. Here are some specimens of his "excellence":

> 1. "For all this seemed remarkably remote from my introductory re-
>   mark about Marco Polo."

Has he no ear?

> 2. ". . . and that after his departure northward, when his lieutenants
>   had failed to take Bellegarde after a six weeks' siege, Poictesme was
>   not molested further."

Would not a stylist boggle over the repetition of "after"?

> 3. ". . . and there in a snug room, with supper laid, sat Dame Lisa about
>   some sewing, and evidently in a quite amiable frame of mind."

Or would he have adorned the last page of *Jurgen* with this ill-begotten sentence?

Truth is, whoever first acclaimed Cabell as a stylist mistook as a mastery of prose writing his ability to turn an occasional sentence happily. Cabell at his best is nothing more than our honest old friend Bill Arp, grown cynical and sophisticated. He is no longer a Georgia cracker, but, after a little polishing at William and Mary, a Virginia wisecracker. "The religion of Hell is patriotism, and the government is an enlightened democracy." "In life men go wrong without dignity and sin, as it were, from hand to mouth." The rest of his writing is palpable imitation. It was C. C. Baldwin who first detected in *Jurgen* echoes from *The Playboy of the Western World* and concluded that Cabell belonged to the Irish renascence, part of which occurred in London and Paris, wherefore a Virginia manifestation was not impossible: "his matter was lifted bodily from the Irish, his rhythms from Yeats and Synge, his wit from Wilde and Swift and Moore. . . . Without George Moore there never would have been any

Cabell!" But judging from the resemblance of his prose to the work of other writers, Cabell was more eclectic than Baldwin assumes: although one should add two Irishmen—Shaw and Donn Byrne—one will detect prose which sounds like Stevenson, Harland, Hope, James, Pollard, Thompson, Barrès, France, Mencken, and Edgar Saltus! In fact, so many and varied influences intrude and there is so little synthesis of them that Mr. Cabell can hardly be said to have a style at all—not one of his many ways of writing may be said to be characteristic of him or his own. Cabell the stylist is more of a phantom than any of the mirages he has raised in his fiction.

One has to be very well acquainted with the minor British and American romantics of the late nineteenth century to perceive Cabell's origins. It is illuminating, however, to compare two of his earliest fictions, "The Love Letters of Falstaff" and "In Necessity's Mortar," both in *Harper's Magazine* (Mar., 1902; Oct., 1904), with other articles and short stories in the same periodical at that time, notably—"The Heart's Key" by Maurice Hewlett, "Peire Vidal—Troubadour" by Olivia Howard Dunbar, "The Stairway of Honor" by Maud S. Rawson, "Honfleur the Sedate" by Thomas A. Janvier, "The Maid of Landevennec" by Justus Miles Forman,—and "St. Stephen's Eve" by Warwick Deeping! Such a comparison makes it clear that one pen of no very great talent could have written all of this stuff—which appears to have been printed chiefly as an excuse to fill the magazine with the gaudy plates of Howard Pyle, the illustrator. Incidentally, as Mr. Cabell freely confesses, his connection with *Harper's* came to an end, along about 1909, when Mr. Pyle decided that Cabell's confections were too trivial for his powers as an illustrator. In point of fact, Cabell's writing is no better than that of Deeping and Dunbar, as witness the love-coo of Catherine de Vaucelles to François de Montcorbier (*alias* Villon) in his last-named story:

"My king! my king!" she murmured with a deep thrill of speech. . . .

This sentimental story of Villon suggests a relationship between Cabell and another writer who was not appearing in

Harper's—Robert Louis Stevenson. A rereading of R. L. S. with an eye attentive to resemblances between the romancer of Vailima and the romancer of "Richmond in Virginia" will bring out how derivative is the Cabellian aesthetic. Not only is there the very obvious common espousal of romantic writing and vigorous derision of realism (including a denunciation of Howells and Zola), but also, and this is surprising, there is a shared cynicism in regard to love in real life. In *Virginibus Puerisque* Stevenson remarks that the absorption with which one watches a particular peach or nectarine on which one has set one's affections as it comes around the table is "about as high a passion as generally leads to marriage." After suggesting that matrimony is "no more than a sort of friendship recognized by the police"—a suggestion which has a peculiarly Cabellian flavor, Stevenson observes that most people would die unwed if they only married when they fell in love. ". . . Love is rather too violent a passion to make, in all cases, a good domestic sentiment." On the other hand, "Once you are married, there is nothing left for you, not even suicide, but to be good." Yet *art* provides a key so that a young man may enter "into that land of Beulah which is upon the borders of Heaven and within sight of the City of Love." While Stevenson is the author of an essay on "The Morality of the Profession of Letters" and "An Appeal to the Clergy of the Church of Scotland" as well as a preface apologizing for his interest in François Villon, it is also true that he contended that "the most joyous of verses, and the most lively, beautiful, and buoyant of tales" can be made out of situations which, if not immoral, are at least "a-moral." Without any attempt at disguise (or need for it) passages from *Virginibus Puerisque,* "A Gossip on Romance," "An Apology for Idlers," "Lay Morals," etc., become the leading ideas of *Beyond Life* (1919) and *Straws and Prayer Books* (1924), Mr. Cabell's best-known dissertations upon Cabell. The innocent addition of John Charteris as expounder in one book and interlocutor in the other was curiously suggested by Wilde and Shaw; Wilde, it will be remembered, employed the pretense of dialogue in his critical essays (there is even less pretense in Cabell) and Charteris is, of course, the cynical protagonist of Shaw's least-known play, *The Philanderer.* All of which hints that an early immersion in Wilde and Shaw did little to wash away a romantic cynicism derived from Stevenson. Incidentally, the practice of printing "Tributes from the Press"—really scotching comments upon his books—begun with *Beyond Life* and imitated in the Mencken *Schimpflexion,* indicates an awareness of the technique of *The Gentle Art of Making Enemies.* Cabell, however, as a wit cannot hold a candle to James McNeill Whistler, or, we are afraid, to Oscar Wilde.

Whatever Cabell may owe to Stevenson the theorist, he cannot be said, beyond his early short fiction, to owe anything to him as a practitioner, for the Scotchman was too canny about his royalties to let his cynicism curdle the cream of his innocuous prose romances. Cabell, God wot, has written what he chose to write whether any one would buy it or not. There is a divine stubbornness, a willful wrongheadedness, about the man that wins admiration even when one's intelligence tells one that it is largely undeserved. For Cabell, after avowing that "the creative romanticist alone can engineer a satisfying evasion of that daily workaday life which is to every man abhorrent," perversely refuses to administer the very sedative which he prescribes. All his romances terminate in the disillusionment of the characters, a disillusionment which Cabell has proclaimed the inevitable upshot of any real love affair. None of his arguments, however, leads one to conclude that such an outcome is inevitable in fantasy—particularly in fantasy written with the right-worthy purpose of entertainment. Yet Cabell, no matter whither the events of his stories tend, has but one conclusion for them—as tedious as any sentimental formula—"achieving each other, we assure ourselves of eternal boredom." Too late he has seen the flaw in his own sigil. In the preface to the *Preface to the Past* (1936) he acknowledges, "I, in brief, and in dissent from my own convictions, had been betrayed, after all, into writing 'realism'. . . ."

Cabell, Puritan-baiter, predestines his characters more sternly than the God of Calvin and Knox, for these gentlemen allowed for exceptions through their doctrine of election. In Cabell's system there are never any exceptions, and therein originates the tedium of his fictions. Take such a promising yarn as *Domnei* (1920, originally issued as *The Soul of Melicent,* in 1913). Here is an extraordinarily sprightly fantasy, in which the Lady Melicent gives herself to the paynim Demetrios in order to secure the release of her lover Perion. After Demetrios has decked her out as his bride, however, he cannot consummate his marriage so long as the mind of Melicent is set upon Perion. There ensues the most engaging series of adventures in which Perion and Demetrios strive to outdo each other in combat and in courtesy, until the brave Demetrios finally gets his back broken. It is then revealed that a sinister Jew, Ahasuerus, who has long loved Melicent secretly, has contrived everything—her captivity, the death of Demetrios, and now her surrender to him by the son of the paynim. Yet, just as the reader is about to applaud a superbly planned satire of the bourgeois tradesman over the romantic hero, what happens? Mr. Cabell claps on his formula ending, like a granddame forcing overshoes over the comely ankles of sixteen, and ruins his moral. Ahasuerus, knowing that he cannot himself possess Melicent, secretly admits Perion and his men into the heathen stronghold. But Perion, achieving Melicent after years of separation, realizes—oh, dust and ashes—that she is not the Melicent of his youth and dreams. So Felix Kennaston, after an intoxicating journey into the past in slumber, in the most ingenious of Mr. Cabell's fantasies, *The Cream of the Jest* (1917), turns into "the road of use and wont" at the end of the tale. So Jurgen too, after all his dealings with Koshchei, comes back to Dame Lisa's cooking and mending.

Whence arose this dreadful imperative to subject the end of every romance to the wash-wringer? Not altogether from Cabell's reading of Stevenson, surely, for one has to pick and choose to get any accumulation of cynical utterance from the watchful Scotchman. If we suppose that Cabell read Stevenson with a selective eye, we must also acknowledge that he was in some degree a cynic before he came to R. L. S. It happens that there are the best reasons for thinking this. In his commentary on *The Lineage of Lichfield* (1922) there is a bogey-man passage on the subjection of the human race to machinery, such a passage as a feudal agrarian aristocrat might write at the threat of invading industrialism. The significance of this unguarded passage is heightened by a just consideration of *The Rivet in Grandfather's Neck: A*

Comedy of Limitations (1915), a romance of Lichfield in which Colonel Rudolph Musgrave conducts himself as he believes a Virginian and a gentleman should—even to punching a rival in the head—yet without much of the complete satisfaction that such conduct allegedly should bring. No suspicion ever enters the head of this feudal agrarian aristocrat that his life and the lives of those around him are pointless, that Lichfield is a place of well-mannered ghosts. But his wife Patricia, who is willing enough to concede that Lichfield's aristocracy—"a preposterously handsome race"—make "the pleasantest of companions," has her own verdict on Lichfield:

"A hamlet of Hamlets . . . whose actual tragedy isn't that their fathers were badly treated, but that they themselves are constitutionally unable to do anything except talk about how badly their fathers were treated."

Cabell, who as author shares this point of view with Patricia, is still a Musgrave and Lichfieldian, and in this contradiction lies both his penchant for romantic matter and his cynicism.

The most revelatory book from Cabell's pen is probably *The Cords of Vanity: A Comedy of Shirking* (1909). This fiction is a treacherous exposé of the private life of a novelist, one Robert Etheridge Townsend, of Lichfield, during his formative years. Reviewers and critics, it is to be regretted, have seen in this young man's flirtations in Virginia and Europe nothing more than an attempt to appease a gross appetite; they have failed to observe that all the charming young women whom Mr. Cabell evokes— the prettiest gallery in any piece of modern fiction—inevitably lead his Robert Etheridge Townsend back to Lichfield. His Dorian Grayish effort to be smart and cosmopolitan is never effort enough to break the cords of chivalry and gallantry. In another connection Townsend protests, "Lichfield had got at and into me when I was too young to defend myself; and I could no more alter the inbred traditions of Lichfield, that were a part of me, than a carpet change its texture." And so, too, with James Branch Cabell. Loathing the stagnant life of "Richmond in Virginia," he nevertheless will swim in no other water. He will not be guilty of romanticizing about any other place which might be compared with his native city in any way to the latter's detriment.

Hence the long "Biography of Manuel" is conveniently set in the never-never land of Poictesme. Yet because this is *an evasion,* every chocolate cream in Cabell's cellophane-wrapped box has a bit of prussic acid at its core. One can't cheat one's self without taking it out in some way on mankind. In the comedy of limitations this is an inevitable consequence.

While the future will view Mr. Cabell beyond all doubt as an important symptomatic figure because of his frustration, it must be admitted that his chief use to his contemporaries has been to teach them the lower uses of symbolism. He himself charmingly admits that "prurience gave me a leg up from oblivion." There was a time when people actually met in groups to decipher some occultism in *Jurgen* reputedly too erudite for John S. Sumner (Comstock's successor) to prosecute. Yet even this form of erudition has failed to sustain Cabell: stable boys and freshmen found low companions equally erudite without the silly circumlocutions. When his popularity waned, Cabell first tried to hold his following by being more virile. By 1924, he could congratulate himself in these elegant terms: "not many S. O. B.'s contrive to say that much unsmashed"; and emphasize it by "a request for deific condemnation of the third personal singular neuter pronoun." But when having completed the slightly scandalous and possibly blasphemous cycle with books like *The High Place* (1923), *The Silver Stallion* (1926), *Something About Eve* (1927), and *The Way of Ecben* (1929), each book less successful than its predecessor, Cabell conceded in the year of the great *débâcle* that he had never had more than a leg over the wall towards popular favor anyway, and announced his retirement as James Branch Cabell. A slighter imitator, Branch Cabell, has since written of a "nightmare" in three volumes—*Smirt* (1934), *Smith* (1936), and *Smire* (1937), in imitation of Lewis Carroll, and not of Freud; and various other small books. These have not damaged his brilliant predecessor's reputation for cleanliness nor, for that matter, affected the question of Cabell's immortality. If he survives the waning notoriety of *Jurgen,* it will be as a museum piece representing the psychology of a Virginian who would be an intellectual leader yet had not quite what it takes.

Although Cabell derisively quotes from one of Mr. Ben

Hecht's hostile reviews in the Chicago *News* to set off all his "tributes" at the end of *Beyond Life,* the two men have much in common. Both are proud members of the designated Intelligentsia, both are writers of fantasy, both have sniggered over their turpitude, and both despise democracy. "All democratic government," Mr. Cabell sneers, repeating an observation of Mencken's, "is of course based on the axiom that the man of average intelligence is in theory equal to the person of exceptional endowments, and in practise the superior by reason of numbers. . . ." Erik Dorn, Mr. Ben Hecht's most personable character, is oracular on the subject: "Bolshevism is a logical evolution of democracy—another step downward in the descent of the individual. Until the arrival of Lenin and Trotzky on the field, there's no question but what American Democracy was the most atrocious insult leveled at the intelligence of the race by its inferiors. Bolshevism goes us one better however. . . ."

Though both men have achieved about the same state of grace, their lives have run in altogether different grooves. While Cabell was born in Richmond, was tenderly nurtured, and was sent to private schools and to William and Mary before reaching maturity, Ben Hecht was born in New York City in 1893, was transplanted to the raw and traditionless Racine, Wisconsin, as a child and had become an acrobat with a road show before he was seventeen. Hard as nails at an age ordinarily described as "tender," Hecht became a reporter, first on the Chicago *Journal* and then on the *Daily News.* Consequently when he came to write he had no Lichfieldian inhibitions to overcome and was able to record his views in a bold, black chirography at the outset.

Erik Dorn (1921), Ben Hecht's first book, is to the *Cords of Vanity* what a strip-tease artist is to a member of the Junior League. True, both books deal with philandering writers, but Mr. Hecht's hero goes about his seductions with commendable directness and dispatch, and with no regard at all for the cloying amenities of speech and action. As Burton Rascoe has pointed out, Dorn, in the jargon of the psychopathologists, is "a victim of dementia praecox katatonia; he is incapable of reacting with the normal human emotion to any common stimulus." Though Mr. Rascoe says he is "without convictions of any sort," this is not quite true: Erik Dorn subscribes rather violently to the whole credo of the Intelligentsia. Morals to him are a nuisance and popular government is a menace. At thirty he can say to himself, "I am complete. This business of being empty is all there is to life. Intelligence is a faculty which enables man to peer through the muddle of ideas and arrive at a nowhere." To follow the events of his career is futile, since his desertion of his wife, his affair with Rachel, the illustrator, in Chicago, and his conquest of Mathilde, the revolutionary, in post-War Germany have no more significance than his sex adventure with a negress, *à la Huysmans,* seized in a dive in the Black Belt. The sole interest in the book lies in its evocation of character—Hecht, with no intention of being moral, has drawn a merciless portrait of one type of American journalist, the *parvenu* intellectual, the glib negationist. A perfect representative of the Intelligentsia, Erik Dorn is as well a crass vulgarian: he pictures President Wilson at the Peace Conference as "a long-face virgin trapped in a bawdy house and calling in valiant tones for a glass of lemonade." This not imperfect simile is a fair specimen of the normal venting of Erik's mind—a gray half-grown sponge clotted with stable slime —yet none the less a clearly recognizable type. The only weakness of the book is in the sentimental drawing of the women, who are represented as persons of more worth than worthlessness could make a conquest of. They are furthermore equally pliant. Yet this defect could have been made a merit had it originated in the limited vision of Erik and not that of the author, for a man of Erik's stamp is not the kind to note elements of individuality in the objects of his desire. On the other hand, in commenting on the strength of the radical Tesla, "A man of power, rooted in visions," Erik Dorn gives us a clue to his own weakness. He can absorb, but he cannot master ideas: there is no large synthesis of his thought, no will to unify, which means to select and to discard. He can trump your suit, but he cannot lead up to you, nor finesse for a grand slam. There were a good many minds like Erik Dorn's in his generation.

No other piece of realism from Hecht's pen is quite so significant as his portrait of Erik Dorn, though his stage play with Charles MacArthur, *Front Page* (1928), is more successful in re-creating the atmosphere of the newsroom than is the novel. *Humpty Dumpty* (1924) is an effort to elevate the journalist of *Erik Dorn* into a novelist, but Kent Savaron is less convincing than his prototype. In *Fantazius Mallare* (1922) Hecht recorded an erotic nightmare, yet so embroidered upon the extravagant symbolism of the Freudians that the piece was more of a naughty valentine than anything else. The illustrations in black and white were more remarkable than the text, but the two together were enough to incense the Post Office department, which destroyed the edition. This was unfortunate, for it robbed the sequel, *The Kingdom of Evil* (1924), a tract on the bondage of sensuality, of much significance. Several books of short stories and sketches, *A Thousand and One Afternoons in Chicago* (1922), *Tales of Chicago Streets* (1924), *The Champion from Far Away* (1931), and *Actor's Blood* (1936), gather material of great vitality from hither and yon, but never transform it into genuine artistic accomplishment. Hecht's most notorious short story, "The Sentimentalist," which was printed in *The American Mercury* in October, 1924, narrates with great gusto how a frightened drunkard, who has pretended to be sophisticated, refuses to go into a roadhouse but is found later asleep in a most undignified position in a small building erected for the convenience of the guests. (This was the era of the enormous popularity of Chic Sales' *The Specialist*.)

In his novel *Gargoyles* (1922) Hecht follows the career of George Cornelius Basine from the Sabbath morning in 1900 when he emerged from Madam Minnie's house of ill fame to the time when, as the result of an anti-vice crusade, he becomes a U. S. Senator and crusader for the Liberty Loan. The book is not aimed to arouse indignation that such a man should come to great power; it takes for granted that George Cornelius Basine is inevitably successful in a democracy. *A Jew in Love* (1931), Hecht's best-selling recent novel, outstrips all his other fictions in sensational sex episodes and vulgarity of expression, but these extravagances do not elevate the book even into the third rank of novels. We are frankly of the opinion that it errs in ascribing to the Jewish race the morals of its wealthy publisher-hero, Jo Boshere. When the whole of Ben Hecht's realistic fiction is considered, one perceives that his aim has been to astound and shock rather than to achieve verisimilitude. Thirteen years of reporting lurid crimes for Chicago papers are possibly poorer training for an artist than a professorship in one of the ivy colleges.

One is not done with Hecht, however, until one has considered his fantasies, of which *Count Bruga* (1926) is the best known. If some of the grosser realists and Decadents have influenced Ben Hecht, it is also true that he is a warm admirer of Arthur Machen, to whose London quarters, it is recorded, he made his sole literary pilgrimage in 1918. This is the more singular in that Machen is essentially a bookish man (despite a journalistic experience), whilst Hecht's ideas in the main have come from talk. In any event, we may attribute his writing of romance to the influence of the sceptical Welsh romancer upon him, but we will have to acknowledge that the glamor of *Count Bruga* derives in part from Hecht's still warm memory of the mountebanks and fakirs whom he met while travelling as an acrobat with Costello's road show. The tale is delightfully preposterous: Enrico Panini, "the World's Greatest Magician," arranges his suicide so that divers people, including a Mr. Winterbottom, Latin teacher and Puritan, are suspected of murdering him. Our moving eye in this is Julius Ganz, *alias* Count Hippolyt Bruga, a vagabond poet whose amorous adventures eventually lead him to the grave of Panini's young woman assistant, whom he had hoped to seduce. *Count Bruga* is Ben Hecht's most artistic production, marred only by the author's consciousness that he is a professional iconoclast, a doctrinaire:

"No," Hippolyt replied savagely. "I think exactly what I say. All wives are alike. All tell the same lies and exude the same poisons, and have for their objective the corruption and ruin of the unsuspecting fools they call their husbands."

Strindberg is no greater misogynist than the Count. Yet, in the main, the story trips along merrily with this load. All of which leads us to wonder whether the Ben Hecht who sets off stink bombs is not more of a poseur than the graceful literary acrobat who performs the flips and handsprings of which *Count Bruga* is made up.

Neither the fantastic adventures of Dom Manuel nor the sky-larking and tumbling of Count Bruga approach the experiences of the godmother of the Intelligentsia, that munificent patron of cubist art, Mrs. Mabel Dodge Luhan, as they are soberly chron-icled in *Winter in Taos* (1935) and in the *Intimate Memories* of which four volumes have appeared: *Background* (1933), *European Experiences* (1935), *Movers and Shakers* (1936), *Edge of Taos Desert* (1937). Mistress of a Fifth Avenue salon just around the corner from Greenwich Village, Mabel Dodge entertained the great, the near-great, and the never-would-be-great in the exciting years just before our entrance into the First World War. Probably there had never been such a mingling of art, sex, politics, spiritualism, cold meats, and lettuce sandwiches as occurred at her parties, and reverberations from them were longer drawn out than those which rolled from the conflict over-seas. Though the utter freedom to eat and talk did not attract everyone (Floyd Dell has written, "I had a proletarian and puritanical prejudice against rich women who gave tea and sand-wiches to poor young artists and tried to boss them about their careers"), they brought together characters as diverse as E. A. Robinson and Bill Haywood, Margaret Sanger and Lee Simon-son, and are undeniably an episode in our intellectual history. Mrs. Luhan's memoirs have an equal appeal to the scandal-monger and the cultural historian, whence their immortality is assured. Though she made many mistakes in her shopping after genius, she came eventually to appraise men and women with a hard eye; and while her narrative, after all, is Mrs. Mabel Dodge Luhan's story, nevertheless this acquired objectivity allows her to see her guests half humorously and half critically, which is clear enough for all purposes we can think of. Her salon was a *marché des puces* for the exchange of ideas—ideas eagerly appropriated whether they harmonized with the philos-ophy of the appropriator or not. And if the hawker's cries ex-ceeded the value of their wares, what difference? Somebody got sold and the publicity helped everybody.

One of the most welcome guests at 23 Fifth Avenue when Mabel Dodge resided there was Carl Van Vechten, who has sketched the famous salon and its mistress in *Peter Whiffle*

(1922). Mr. Van Vechten is a native of Cedar Rapids, Iowa, where he was born on June 17, 1880. His boyhood in Iowa, before he went off to the newly-founded University of Chicago to be educated, is pleasantly recorded in *Sacred and Profane Memories* (1936) and again, more pleasantly, as the youth of Gareth Johns in *The Tattooed Countess* (1924). In 1906 he became music critic for *The New York Times*, a position he held down to 1913, with two years out as Paris correspondent for the paper. His work as a music critic is best represented in the volume *Interpreters* (1920), which contains studies and reminiscences of Olive Fremstad, Geraldine Farrar, Mary Garden, Feodor Chaliapin, Mariette Mazarin, Yvette Guilbert, and Waslav Nijinsky. These essays are marked by the sympathy of the critic for the interpreter, who is so often compared unfavorably with the composer of music; and by the critic's sharp preference for artists trained in France over those trained in Germany. They are informative and graceful, without being as vigorous as Huneker's or as penetrating as Rosenfeld's.

Outside the field of music, where he writes with authority, Van Vechten is less happy. Such a volume as *Excavations* (1926) is marred by extravagant estimates of Ouida, Saltus, Shiel, and even lesser people. The book contains two excellent pieces of special pleading, one for the later work of Herman Melville and the other for a proper recognition of the prose of Arthur Machen. Van Vechten is at his best, however, in his introductory and valedictory essays, "On Visiting Fashionable Places Out of Season" and "A Note on Dedications." His vice is a headlong passion for collecting curios (it is said that he even cherishes unusual book jackets), and in these essays he raises it whimsically into a virtue. Carl Van Vechten belongs to the Intelligentsia by his undiscriminating eclecticism, more than for any other reason. It has made his career as an intellectual peculiarly pointless, which result the clan generally applauds as the highest merit in its membership.

Yet it would appear that *Peter Whiffle: His Life and Works* was begun as a satire of a youth with so many aesthetic enthusiasms that they efficiently cancel each other out and leave their sponsor a perfect zero. "If there has been one set purpose

in my life," Peter Whiffle confides to his prospective biographer,
"it has been not to have a purpose. That, you alone, perhaps,
understand. . . ." The novel, however, fails completely as an
anatomy of negation. In loading his protagonist with ten thousand enthusiasms Van Vechten commits the inevitable error of
sharing too many of them with Peter Whiffle. We forget whether
it is he or Peter who has the astounding collection of catalogues
of laces and perfumes, the albums of designs used by the masters
of tattoo in the Bowery and at Coney Island, the passion for the
works of Huysmans, Saltus, and Cabell, and the queer erudition:
"The cocottes of the period were wont to wear very large bell-
shaped hats. Lily Elsie, who was appearing in *The Merry
Widow* in London, followed this fashion and, as a natural consequence, these head-decorations were soon dubbed, probably
by an American, Merry Widow hats." The result is, nevertheless, convincing portraiture: Peter Whiffle is plausible and adorable—that is, adorable if you have not toiled on Washington
Square for fifteen years and bought tea and toast for a whole
generation of Peter Whiffles and listened to their enthusiasms.
Then it palls a bit, as it does not in the story, where Peter, the
sum of them all, is quite the male enchanter. Like *The Confessions of a Young Man,* though a more readable book, *Peter
Whiffle* acquainted hordes of young intellectuals with what they
should taste and what they should abjure.

Shifting enthusiasms explain each and all of Van Vechten's
novels. The vogue of the flapper and the popularity of Fitzgerald produced his most frothy fictions, *The Blind Bow-Boy*
(1923) and its sequel, *Fire-Crackers* (1925). When Hollywood
was discovered as literary material, first by the French, perhaps,
who applauded Charlie Chaplin, Van Vechten brought forth
without a single labor-pang *Spider-Boy* (1928), his one complete
failure in the novel, a failure due to lack of substance and to
triviality. When "the revolt from the village" was a glib phrase
on every tongue, he wrote *The Tattooed Countess* (1924). This
novel, however, has a perdurable quality which the fictions just
enumerated lack. It is the story of Countess Ella Nattatorrini,
a handsome, passionate woman of fifty, who, after being duped
by a twenty-two-year-old tenor in a travelling operetta troupe,

conceives the idea of returning to her birthplace, Maple Valley, Iowa. This confusion of heartache and nostalgia on her part has one happy consequence: in Maple Valley she fastens upon another youth, one Gareth Johns, a dreamer whom the crassness and dowdiness of the town keep painfully awake, and when Maple Valley is just about ready to pronounce dreadful judgment on this attachment, she carries her new prize off to Europe with her. We know of no seduction in modern fiction more praiseworthy than this; *The Tattooed Countess,* which strangely suggests the story of Isabelle Archer in theme, is, on the whole, a more convincing book. Gareth has much more reason to cleave to the Countess than Isabelle has to return to Gilbert Osmond; furthermore, one knows this is not final. *The Tattooed Countess,* capable of provoking the risibilities of the urbane quite as much by its gentle satire of its principals as by its broad thwacks at the Iowa "peasantry," is destined to have a secure place with lovers of well-written books for some time to come.

A different mood animates *Nigger Heaven* (1926), a study of Harlem made just when the Intelligentsia discovered its night life potentially more thrilling than the night life of highly commercialized Greenwich Village. Van Vechten's interest in the negro life dates from a somewhat earlier time, as his familiarity with his material suggests, and may have been aroused by his acquaintance with Miss Stein, although his writing in this book is not imitative of her prose. *Nigger Heaven* is a very sympathetic handling of the lives of two superior negroes, Mary Love, a librarian, and Byron Kasson, a writer, who cannot free themselves from the lower and more animalistic members of their race. The Prologue to the novel is Van Vechten's best piece of fiction: it is a thumbnail sketch of Anatole Longfellow, alias the Scarlet Creeper, the murderer for whose crime Byron Kasson is arrested—and, we assume, executed—at the end of the tale. What this stud-nigger represents, so Van Vechten implies, is just what limits the destiny of so fine a character as Mary. *Nigger Heaven,* despite its sympathy, is in no sense sentimental—Van Vechten has no more patience with negro pretense to culture than he would have with white pretense, as his delineation of Orville Snodes and Hester Albright shows. Earnest treatment of what to him is an insoluble problem makes *Nigger Heaven* take a place with Langston Hughes' *Not Without Laughter* and Miss Stein's "Melanctha" as one of the best fictional treatments of the negro in American letters. Incidentally the book is enhanced by the songs and snatches of Blues contributed by Langston Hughes. *Nigger Heaven, The Tattooed Countess,* and *Peter Whiffle* justify the claim Mr. Van Vechten has never made to being the best creative artist among the American Intelligentsia, even though the sum of these three produces no consistent attitude towards life and no philosophy.

Once it might have seemed that greater range and superior abilities would give first rank among the Intelligentsia to Elinor Wylie, the thrice-married poetess, whose fiction was as well known as her verse. Elinor Hoyt Wylie was born in Rosemont, Pennsylvania, in 1887, and passed her formative years in private schools in Bryn Mawr and Washington, D. C. Though she had previously experimented with verse, she did most of her publishing after becoming acquainted with William Rose Benét, who in 1923 became her third husband. Four volumes of verse—*Nets to Catch the Wind* (1921), *Black Armour* (1923), *Trivial Breath* (1928), *Angels and Earthly Creatures* (1929)—and four volumes of prose—*Jennifer Lorn* (1923), *The Venetian Glass Nephew* (1925), *The Orphan Angel* (1926), *Mr. Hodge and Mr. Hazard* (1928)—were prepared for the press before her untimely death in London, on December 16, 1928.

A decade has shaken most of our values and destroyed many of our reputations, wherefore it is not surprising to find Elinor Wylie nearly forgotten. Her poetry seems the preparation for a career rather than the product of one; only two of her fictions are memorable, and these apparently only in the minds of oldsters. One poem alone finds infrequent quotation, the piece called "Let No Charitable Hope." Its bitterness and cynicism have made a more or less indelible stain upon the racial cortex, but none can quote more than the second stanza. It is of the "O-God-the-pain-girls" school:

> . . . I am, being woman, hard beset;
> I live by squeezing from a stone
> The little nourishment I get.

Two other pieces make the definition of Elinor Wylie complete. The little poem called "Beauty" instructs us to—

> Say not of Beauty she is good,
> Or aught but beautiful. . . .

while "The Eagle and the Mole" adds the stern injunction to—

> Avoid the reeking herd,
> Shun the polluted flock. . . .

The two pieces make clear her preciosity, her connections with Decadence, and her contempt for the commonality. Further reading in her verse adds only a sense of oppressive literariousness— she is not a mole grubbing under ground, but a bookworm. Many poets are echoed in her verses, but most frequently Blake ("I saw the Tiger's golden flank"), Housman, Conrad Aiken, and especially Marianne Moore. The influence of Miss Moore is most clearly seen in "Demon Lovers," "Castilian," "Minotaur," "King's Ransom," "Chimera Sleeping," and in the sonnet beginning absurdly—

> You are the faintest freckles on the hide
> Of fawns. . . .

With the exception of "Castilian," a romantic evocation of the spirit of Velásquez, no one piece from Miss Wylie's pen seems to us completely beautiful, but there are lovely lines and images—

> My soul, be not disturbed
> By planetary war . . .

We wonder, however, why she should deliberately reproduce something as familiar as—

> He wanders lonely as a cloud. . . .

One cannot but conclude, after turning thoughtfully the heavy, watermarked pages of her *Collected Poems* (1932), that she chose to cultivate too narrow a plot of ground, the soil of which was pretty much worked out before she undertook to till it. It is further apparent that the cross-fertilization of her reading had produced very few poetic plants up to the time of her death which a more vigorous cultivator would not have discarded.

Elinor Wylie's first novel, *Jennifer Lorn,* was more or less a finger exercise in preparation for her later fantasies. The graceful runs and arpeggios do create an insubstantial picture of the British gentry produced by the plundering of India in the time of Warren Hastings. Something about *Jennifer Lorn* vaguely suggests Joseph Hergesheimer's *Balisand,* but Richard Bale is of much more solid bone and flesh than the Hon. Gerald Poynyard. Miss Wylie was a good deal taken in by her reading, we fear, for no undeluded person would ever present the Hon. Gerald in so favorable a light. Her next novel, *The Venetian Glass Nephew,* succeeds precisely because it does not even make the pretense of reality. The old Cardinal Peter Innocent Bon longs for a nephew such as the other members of the College possess; hence for a good price one is made for him through the combined arts of a necromancer, Monsieur de Chastelneuf, and a glass blower, Alvise Luna. The product is Virginio. The fragile nephew, with his pale blue eyes, transparent skin, cold hands, and golden hair, falls promptly in love with a healthy, bouncing Italian girl, named Rosalba. So great is the danger to his fragility and so much does Rosalba love him that she consents to being baked into a perfect mate at Sèvres by M. de Chastelneuf. Of course the tale is irreverent—but if one must have irreverence one prefers it in this form to public exhibitions by blasphemers in which they conceitedly ask the Almighty to take time out to strike them dead. *The Venetian Glass Nephew* is as fragile and pretty as anything ever blown out of glass. In its way it is such a thing as Marianne Moore describes in "An Egyptian Pulled Glass Bottle in the Shape of a Fish." There ought to be a special shelf somewhere for the preservation of such pieces of *virtu,* which are scarcely substantial enough to survive by themselves.

In *The Orphan Angel* Elinor Wylie attempted to fictionize the career of a typically Romantic poet, say Shelley, but the very responsibility of her task weighed her down, and her sole distinguishing trait in fiction, light evasiveness, is lacking. *Mr. Hodge and Mr. Hazard,* her last work of fiction, is her best. Mr. Hazard, whose person contains the pale souls of Byron, Shelley, Trelawny, and Leigh Hunt, has the temerity to return to England in 1833 after long exile. His very un-Victorian conduct gives tremendous offense to Mr. Hodge who, if he is not the soul, is at least the body of Victorianism. Hazard is at length willing enough to let Hodge pack him out of England, though before he departs he must send to Lady Clara a little intaglio showing a lion with its teeth sunk in the shoulder of a flying stag. The only difficulty that the modern reader finds with *Mr. Hodge and Mr. Hazard* is its failure to arouse in him much enthusiasm for the amorphous Mr. Hazard. Such a reader recognizes that by 1833 the Romantic spirit is sickly and overworn —Scott, Byron, Shelley and Keats are dead and Southey has become poet-laureate: to take sides with Hazard is to indulge in a sentimentalism almost as dangerous as to applaud the hard sense of Hodge. Still, a qualified surrender to Miss Wylie's mood shouldn't carry one so far that he could not regain his feet again nor enjoy his experience.

With the coming of the depression the Intelligentsia lost their grip upon the reading public when in most instances their own anxiety betrayed their cynicism as a brittle and friable veneer. Yet the Intelligentsia made their contribution to the younger generation of wits who supplanted them. Though this latter generation owes as much to such genial humorists as Don Marquis and Franklin P. Adams as it does to the Mencken set, it has inherited from the Intelligentsia a scorn of feeble good intention, which would be wholly admirable if it were only matched by caustic self-analysis. "The sophisticated humorist in America," Gilbert Seldes has observed, "still jeers at the stupidities of the stupid, and seems not aware of the fact that a prime object of satire is the stupidity of the intelligent." Despite this defect, *The New Yorker,* which has been the chief organ of expression for the younger wits since its founding in 1925, is a better humorous magazine than such predecessors as *Puck, Life,* and *Judge,* simply because *The American Mercury* revealed the sentimental limitations of these periodicals, and a better critical journal than the *Mercury* itself simply because the columns of Don Marquis and Franklin P. Adams taught its contributors an urbanity which Mencken as a writer never possessed.

Singularly enough, the newer generation of wits was nearer to complete fulfillment when it began to be heard than it is today, for most of the wits appeared as parodists. Robert Benchley's travesty of Dickens' *Christmas Carol,* Donald Ogden Stewart's overturning of the Wellsian omnibus in *A Parody Outline of History,* and Dorothy Parker's extreme statement of Elinor Wylie's *Weltschmerz* are nearer to criticism of the intellectuals than are, respectively, *The Treasurer's Report and Other Aspects of Community Singing, Mr. and Mrs. Haddock Abroad,* and *Death and Taxes* by these authors. Yet it should be noted that it is the kind of intellectualism in which the bourgeoisie believes that is parodied. The leading ideas of our time are rarely treated to the bastinado. Perhaps one reason why Samuel Hoffenstein never got fairly inside the periphery of the circle of wits is that in *Poems in Praise of Practically Nothing* he was a little indiscriminate in his parodies—yet it is also true that his later work lacks urbanity and sophistication. But consider the fact that the most original of all *The New Yorker* group of contributors, Peter Arno, an artist as sure of immortality as Thomas Nast, is absolutely limited by his style to the satire of stupid pomposity, and the limitations of the whole group are revealed. Yet, though time works greater havoc with the reputation of wits than with that of any other human performer, burlesque artists not excepted, some of the work of this group has as perdurable a quality as most of that of the Intelligentsia. Dorothy Parker's short stories, with their especial sympathy for ineffectuals, learned from Ring Lardner and F.P.A., are examples, as are Leonard Q. Ross' *The Education of Hyman Kaplan* and Arthur Kober's *Thunder Over the Bronx.* James Thurber's *My Life and Hard Times* and *Let Your Mind Alone,* Thurber and E. B. White's *Is Sex Necessary?* and White's "I Paint What I See" are the most conspicuous assaults upon revered intellectualism, though these men have gauged their attacks to fall always upon a floundering foe. Some few readers will cherish, it is hoped, even at a fairly distant time what Mr. Seldes calls very appropriately the "lunatic over-tones" of meaning in the writings of S. J. Perelman. Essentially ephemeral and topical, this stuff should wear as well as that of Cabell and Hecht and longer than that of Pollard and other Intelligentsia.

As one reflects upon America's literary Intelligentsia one is struck by the fact that so many of them are escapists, so many are singing sailors on a magic carpet bound for never-never land. Mr. Saltus with his yachts and salons constructed out of purple adjectives, Mr. Cabell with his castles and enchantresses blown out of metaphor, Mr. Van Vechten with his apotheoses of giddy-brained youths, Miss Wylie with her fumigated and dry-cleaned Romantics, Messrs. Huneker, Pollard, and Thompson with their unreal ethics and their soap-bubble aestheticism, and even Mr. Mencken with his handsome delusion of a Bismarckian aristocracy—all seem singularly detached from the twentieth century, vague and shadowy spirits, or genii of the lamp, drifting in some upper, scented ether, whither not even the all-pervading blare of the radio can reach them. They are fairies, fantasts, dreamers, speculators, abstractionists, daisy-gatherers among the stars. They have no kingdom on this earth, and we fear that with the sinking of tonight's sun they will be evanishéd forever. Truly, we bleed, for some of them flew with the grace of gulls over this old ferry, albeit yawping unmelodiously each to the other.

4

SCHOLASTICISM

Idolatrous worship of the pure intellect and its fanciful constructions is one of the ties that bind a large group of American scholars to the other contingents of the Intelligentsia and creates American scholasticism. Devotion to the technique of research without much concern as to the utility of their results is typical of these scholiasts and suggests their kinship with that cult of privileged artists of whom Whistler and Wilde are representative. It is their privilege to be beyond good and evil, but not, in any vulgar way, like throwing kisses at the bishop's wife; rather, in judging their own results and in denying the right of society to hold them to an accounting. Properly understood, American scholasticism is completely a-moral. Pure art and pure scholarship are sisterly narcissans under their translucent skins.

American scholasticism is, of course, of German origin. The fame of German institutions of learning reached this country early in the nineteenth century, and provided an excuse for George Ticknor, Edward Everett, Joseph Green Cogswell, George Bancroft, Henry Wadsworth Longfellow, John Lothrop Motley and other bright young gentlemen to go abroad. No harm, surely, was imbibed by these dilettante revelers in *Werther*, who improved their fencing and horsemanship fully as much as they widened their knowledge at Göttingen, Weimar, Heidelberg, Munich, and elsewhere. The German university, so far as American students were concerned, was a very pleasant place between 1816 and 1832, the dates respectively when Ticknor and Motley took first residence at Göttingen. Ticknor wrote Channing on June 16, 1816:

A man of science here lives entirely isolated from the world, and the very republic of letters, which is a more real body in Germany than it ever was in any country, has no connection with the many little governments through which it is scattered without being broken or divided. From this separation of the practical affairs from science and letters to the extraordinary degree in which it is done in Germany, comes, I think, the theoretical nature of German literature in general, and of German metaphysics in particular.

German scholarship, however, was not to keep its otherworldliness. With the emergence of Prussia, the unification of Germany, and the spread of pan-Germanism it was totally to change its character and become subservient to German political hopes and dreams. The studies in comparative philology of Rasmus Rask, of Franz Bopp, and of Jacob Grimm, which established firmly the connection of the German language with Sanskrit, were suddenly given political significance when the Aryan myth was born. Grubby Teuton historians and political scientists—men like Carl Hegel, Von Mauer, Hassen, Meitzen,

Nasse, Waitz, Erdmannsdoerfer, and Johann Kaspar Bluntschli
—bent their whole energies towards showing that certain German political institutions (notably, the village moot) are as definitely an Aryan heritage as are their snuffling vocabularies.
These industrious persons were not Treitschkes; nevertheless
they were useful propagandists in teaching the German people
to look backwards and southeastwards over the paths of racial
migration. Their work was as much a part of the new German
self-consciousness and imperialism as the operas of Wagner, the
politics of Bismarck, the Caesarism of Mommsen, and the philosophy of Nietzsche.

Naturally young American scholars, treading in the footsteps
of a previous generation of gentle cosmopolitans, came under
the influence of the new "science." Of these young Americans,
the two who were to prove most important, Herbert B. Adams
and Albert S. Cook, were trained respectively in political science
and in philology. Herbert Adams took his doctorate *summa cum
laude* at Heidelberg in 1876, four years after his graduation
from Amherst. He at once received a call to Johns Hopkins
University, where President Daniel Coit Gilman, out of the
largesse of a defunct grocer and distiller, was building America's first graduate school on the German model. Adams organized an historical seminary and probably was responsible for
the suggestion to President Gilman that Edward Augustus Freeman, author of the *History of the Norman Conquest* (1867–76),
be invited to lecture here in 1881.

Of the three great British historians of the generation—
Stubbs, Bryce, and himself—all of whom came under the influence of German mythology and methodology, Freeman was the
most complete convert. His *Norman Conquest* was an effort in
many volumes to establish the fact that British institutions were
essentially Anglo-Saxon in character (i.e., ultimately Germanic
and Aryan) rather than Norman. He was eager to come to
America, for, as he said later, "The institutions of Massachusetts or Maryland . . . are not simply institutions of Massachusetts and Maryland. They are part of the institutions of the
Teutonic race, and those are again part of the general institutions of the whole Aryan family." To his mind there were "three

Englands,"—Germany, England, and the United States,—and when he came to this country in the fall of 1881 on the joint invitation of Johns Hopkins and the Lowell Institute, he came with a mighty resolve to knit up the racial consciousness. In doing this, he was, for the moment, eminently successful; furthermore his lectures roused interest in native history such as no other event had done. On the model of certain German publications, Herbert Adams initiated the Johns Hopkins University Studies in History and Political Science in 1883, the first volume of which, *Local Institutions,* contains an introduction by Freeman. To this, and to subsequent volumes, Herbert Adams contributed three articles in the Aryan tradition: "The Germanic Origin of New England Towns," "Norman Constables in America," and "Saxon Tithingmen in America." A sentence from the first of these essays reveals the character of them all: "Town institutions were propagated in New England by old English and Germanic ideas, brought over by the Pilgrims and Puritans, and as ready to take root in the free soil of America as would Egyptian grain which had been drying in a mummy case for a thousand years." In an effort to rally all right-thinking Neo-Teutons, Herbert Adams called attention to Americans who had already taken some feeble steps in the direction in which all American historians should go. There was Henry Adams up at Harvard whose seminar students had made some original researches in Anglo-Saxon law; there was William F. Allen, of the University of Wisconsin, who as early as 1870 had noted the resemblance between American and Anglo-Saxon communities; and there was Professor George E. Howard (German trained), of the University of Nebraska, who was leading his seminar students through a comparative study of institutional history. It was probably under this impetus that the American Historical Society was founded in 1884, with Herbert Adams as its first secretary—an office he held until 1900.

The foundation of the American Historical Society marked the end of Neo-Teutonism, however, in the study of American history. Our historians were very shortly absorbed in local matters and forgot the wandering and brawling drunkards (as Taine had correctly characterized them) of primitive Germany. When Frederick Jackson Turner read his famous paper on "The Significance of the Frontier in American History" before the historical association in 1893, the victory of the local sons was complete. It might be added that those who seriously considered the conceptions of the Aryan historians rejected them on the good ground that Bluntschli, Freeman, and their ilk claimed altogether too many things to be of Aryan origin. Granting that the village moot is the fount of democracy (which is dubious), it is difficult to believe (with Bluntschli) that feudalism—its opposite—was also introduced to England "by Saxon thegns." Today the philosophy of Aryanism is accepted by no historian of consequence outside of Germany. Boas, in *The Mind of Primitive Man* (1927), and Margaret Schlauch in her little brochure, *Who Are the Aryans?* (1937), have ridiculed various aspects of the Aryan legend.

Yet Aryanism, completely rejected by one body of scholars, was completely accepted by another and much larger body—the teachers of literature. The reasons for this are clear enough— as graduate schools were organized in Baltimore and elsewhere on the model of the German universities it became apparent that there would be no place for literature in the curricula of these schools unless it, also, could be studied "scientifically." Sidney Lanier, who was lecturing at Johns Hopkins, bent his frail energies to the solution of the problem and produced *The Science of English Verse* (1880). This book (which is largely unintelligible to the average teacher of literature) is merely a suggestion that poetry is best scanned by a system of musical notation—and hardly served as the beginning of a "science" of literature. Albert Stanburrough Cook, student of philology at Göttingen, Leipzig, and Jena, called to organize the department of English at Johns Hopkins in 1879, solved the problem. The graduate study of literature would be the study of philology, or what was generously termed "Anglo-Saxon literature." So, despite the fact that there was hardly a piece of writing in Old or Middle English before 1370 that had as much aesthetic merit as *Ten Nights in a Bar Room,* the scientific analysis of this stuff was begun. Cook went from Baltimore to the University of California, and then, in 1889, to Yale, carrying his methodology with him. Meanwhile another very important event had happened—Mrs. F. C. Conybeare had translated, in 1883, Wilhelm Scherer's *Geschichte der deutschen Literatur*. Scherer's book was such a compilation of "facts" about literary men and pieces of German writing, such a demonstration of how literary history could be turned into a process of *Quellen-forschung,* that it opened whole new vistas to the sadly limited graduate teachers of literature. Out of the "factualism" of Scherer and the philological science of Cook that curious thing termed "pure scholarship" was born. Pure scholarship is the morphology of everything connected with literature which has no aesthetic merit. In the first flush of enthusiasm for this new "science" the Modern Language Association was formed in 1883.

One cannot ignore the weight of Freeman's essay, "Race and Language" (1885), upon the efforts of these pure scholars. His praise of philology and his use of it as a test of nationality tickled the egos of these new scientists who fancied that their researches would be of the utmost consequence to society. Further and further back into German forests, up Scandinavian fjords, and over Icelandic barriers they pushed their quests for the origin of words. Now, while it is true that the commonest words in English speech have Anglo-Saxon originals and these in turn have Gothic counterparts, not one of these scholars has demonstrated that the ideational content of these limited Northern vocabularies was a heavy burden for the intellect of a moron. Words like *the, is, have, sleep, drink* and *eat* represent the profundity of primitive Anglo-Saxon thought. Pundits, of whom the revered Walter W. Skeat, Litt.D., LL.D., D.C.L., Ph.D., F.B.A., of the University of Cambridge is typical, have laboriously traced *Ha* (interj. E.) back to Old Friesic *haha* (to denote laughter!) and to German *he;* but it is said that Caligula quite unethically uttered a similar sound when he ordered Pomposo, the philologist, thrown to the lions. In all the Northern vocabularies there are no equivalents for such words as *democracy, politics, morals, aesthetics,* and—horror of horrors— *scholarship!* The wolfish pursuit of moronic vocabularies and the ghoulish unearthing of the kennings and pennings of the Northern barbarians diverted young students from the true historical fount of wisdom—the Greek and Roman classics, which fell into the greatest disuse in Western history. There was treachery, alas, among the teachers of the classics themselves; for under the leadership of Basil Gildersleeve (educated at Berlin, Bonn, and Göttingen, though a graduate of Princeton), who was appointed Professor of Greek at Hopkins in 1876 and editor of *The American Journal of Philology* in 1880, American classical scholars turned away from the teaching of concepts to the venal study of syntax and word origins. Before long there were no classical scholars in the old sense in America but only philologists, papyri readers, and robbers of tombs. On every front save that of history the triumph of *Kultur* over culture was complete.

Then what crimes were committed in the academies in the holy name of literature! Harvard, never content with a secondary rôle, soon excelled Hopkins in the new discipline. Francis James Child, son of a Boston sailmaker and student at Göttingen and Berlin, was elevated in 1876, after twenty-five good years of theme reading at Harvard, into a professorship, and between 1883 and 1893 brought out his five volumes of *English and Scottish Popular Ballads*. This heroic piece of collecting has been inordinately praised in academic circles, but it is on the whole a monument to the simple credulity of a good man in the current dogma of Primitivism. Child thought the ballads to be survivals of one of the earliest forms of Anglo-Saxon literature, a pure poetry gushing out of primitive communal life. In recent times Miss Louise Pound has punctured this bubble by showing that the pieces were largely of fifteenth century composition by individual authors of very unequal abilities. Child was soon succeeded at Harvard, however, by the most influential of all the Aryanizers, George Lyman Kittredge, who was appointed to the staff in 1888, and who dominated the English department, the university, and American literary education from 1894 to 1936. Kittredge taught Old Norse, and Old and Middle English, which had previously been taught at Harvard, and introduced courses in Icelandic, Germanic mythology, and the history of English grammar. He took over from Child the teaching of Shakespeare, which he turned into a word-by-word analysis of the plays, and the conduct of the doctoral examinations. In his regime the form of the dissertation—a device for killing the last spark of sensibility in the future teacher of literature—became as standardized as the *American Mercury* under Mencken. His students spread out over the land and occupied for a time most of the major positions in teaching. Noteworthy and typical of these are the late John Manly, recently chairman of the department of English at Chicago, Karl Young of Yale, and John S. P. Tatlock of California. The precise contribution of these gentlemen to our culture is worth considering. Professor Manly is chiefly known for a card index, compiled at great expense, with a subsidized staff, of every line of Chaucer's writings in every known manuscript in every library in the world. What this index has done, however, to increase our knowledge or our appreciation of Chaucer is not apparent. Certainly the Manly and Rickert six-volume edition of *The Canterbury Tales* (1939), made out of it, has been a disappointment even to the followers of the Chicago teacher. Professor Young is the author of two tremendous tomes, heavy enough to hold down a tent in a Kansas cyclone, on *The Drama of the Medieval Church,* in which he has painstakingly catalogued and discussed every antiphonal scrap of Latin song he could lay his hands on; yet when he is confronted by a genuine dramatic piece, like the *Jeu d'Adam,* his only comment is that it is "transitional." Professor Tatlock, in addition to discovering "Muriel, the earliest English poetess" (of whose writing not one line exists!), is the joint compiler of a concordance to Chaucer—a clerical task notable chiefly for its dimensions. When the work of this triumvirate is considered, one is sorely tempted to ask if there was ever such a multiplication of zero by nothing, ever such a preoccupation in history with the absolutely meaningless, as this. Yet the students of Kittredge and his disciples are legion—they are spread not only throughout the institutions of higher learning, but through their offspring and through their text-books they exercise still a dominant influence upon the secondary schools. Is there anything under heaven more appalling than the spectacle of some recent girl graduate teaching *Midsummer Night's Dream* in a country high school word by word (as the Notes and Teaching Plan suggest) in the manner of the great Kittredge? If there is, it is found only in the graduate schools themselves in the spectacle of young men and women wasting their lives in an arid discipline. The chairman of the department of English at Columbia University reported in 1938 that the average time spent by doctoral candidates before standing for their examinations in that institution is ten years. What a dehydrating process that must be! If the purpose of American education is to take young men and women out of circulation, the monastic discipline of factualism and of philology has much to commend it; if, however, the purpose of our higher institutions is cultural, then let us get back to men of the stamp of James Russell Lowell as quickly as possible.

Robert Maynard Hutchins, the young president of the University of Chicago, whose ideas are best examined in *The Higher Learning* (1936), holds that the educational system must perform the dubious monastic service of taking more Americans out of circulation, but he would exclude factualism and philology from the university. He cleaves, however, to the medieval division of studies into a quadrivium and trivium: he recommends that the study of grammar, rhetoric, logic, and mathematics be confined to the junior college (a division created out of the last two years of high school and the first two of college), and that the natural sciences, social sciences, and metaphysics be the total substance of the university curriculum to which he would submit all qualified students. The higher learning lacks, in his opinion, most of all, unity and a fixed content. Theology gave the medieval university unity, but Dr. Hutchins ruefully admits we are not sufficiently orthodox as a people to restore theology to the curriculum: the best substitute is the study of "first principles"—of metaphysics. If one of the first principles of metaphysics is the existence of God, as the author implies, the kind of unity he would give to the university would still be the theological and medieval. And with his insistence on a fixed content not merely the university but the junior college as well would take on a medieval air. President Hutchins' attack upon what he calls "the service station conception of a university" (the idea that the university should make itself felt in the community, should serve the community), his insistence that institutions need to be completely free from public regulation and attempts at control, and his declaration that "the people . . . do not believe in the cultivation of the intellect for its own sake," make him one of the extreme advocates of scholasticism as a life apart. Under his unimpeded direction the new monasticism, one fears, would create a small and privileged society completely cut off from the world. He forgets that his medieval model functioned also as "a service station."

The monastic character of American higher education is suggested not only by the trivial pursuits of their thousands of scholars; but the huge endowments of some of these schools— Harvard, $128,827,068; Yale, $95,838,568; Columbia, $69,-226,412; Chicago, $59,478,903; etc.—also suggest the tremendous accretions of wealth by the ecclesiastical establishments of England before the Reformation. The comparison is enhanced, furthermore, by the absurd efforts to transform American colleges and universities into specimens of Gothic architecture. In part this is due to the eloquence of John Ruskin and Henry Adams, but the most active single agent of this false aesthetic credo is Ralph Adams Cram.

Cram is, in many respects, one of the most remarkable men of our time in America. Son of a Unitarian minister, he has become the most important American Anglo-Catholic; undecided between a career in architecture or in letters, he has distributed his talents rather evenly between both. Though as a creative artist we believe him to be less original and independent than Frank Lloyd Wright (yet not altogether medieval and mistaken, as his solution of the architectural problems of Rice Institute in Texas reveals), we cannot but admire some of his great creations, however anachronistic they are—the Post Headquarters at West Point, the Refectory at Princeton, the nave of the Cathedral of St. John the Divine in New York, and the East Liberty Presbyterian Church, in Pittsburgh. No one will come to harm by these things, and many who cannot afford the grand tour may come to a sense of the grandness and solemnity that imagination working through stone, wood, and glass can achieve.

Possibly after Europe has been reduced to rubble by constant warfare these will be the only monuments to suggest the grandeur of the Middle Ages—which will be ironical enough.

To Ralph Adams Cram we also owe the gift of Henry Adams' book *Mont-Saint-Michel and Chartres* to the general public, for he persuaded Adams to let him publish it. It was he, also, who was the chief moving spirit in the foundation of the Catholic layman's magazine—*The Commonweal,* which, under the editorship of Michael Williams, became possibly the best Catholic periodical in the world. Again, Cram was prime mover in the formation of the Medieval Academy of America, organized for the study of Latin literature in the Middle and Dark Ages. Whilst this organization through its quarterly *Speculum* has to date given altogether too much attention to the less important, it is possible that it may became one instrument through which the modern world is reunited with the classical. This can be brought about, not by the study of medieval Latin as a language or by excavations at Cluny, but by the study of ideas. What relation has the polity of Augustine and the philosophy of Aquinas with classical polities and philosophies? These things need to be taught, for if there is anything young men and women need today it is a sense of the continuity of all that is best in the world —a sense broken by the nineteenth century's junketing expedition into Aryanism. Henry Osborn Taylor, who came under the influence of the "new" history, has shown the way in many volumes but notably in his magnificent work, *The Medieval Mind* (1911), yet his essay on the continuities, *A Historian's Creed* (1939), is all but too tardy.

Cram is a propagandist for the medieval way of life in such books as *The Nemesis of Mediocrity* (1918), *Walled Towns* (1919), *Towards the Great Peace* (1922), and even in his autobiography, *My Life in Architecture* (1936). Yet Cram, the medievalist, is curiously offset by Cram, the advocate of rugged individualism. He has extravagant notions about the "liberty" which he alleges existed in the hierarchial society of the years between 1000 and 1500 A.D. And his statement that "the lines of demarcation (in that society) were fluid and easily passed" is completely false. He need not have perused the laws of Charlemagne, nor Bracton's *Legibus et Consuetudinibus Angliae;* any elementary history would have acquainted him with the character of the Statute of Laborers of 1351 or the attitude of the Church towards bastards, who surely were not responsible for their condition. We wonder what he thinks caused the Jacquerie or the Peasants' Revolt of 1381—both events considerably earlier than Luther and Calvin on whom he places a share of the burden of destroying the society which he admires. His conviction that the "progressive abandonment of religion" and the "dismemberment of the Church during the Reformation" were responsible for "the abrogation of the old ecclesiastical inhibition against usury" and the rise of the bourgeoisie has just enough semblance of truth to deceive the ignorant—but unfortunately the greed of churchmen was prior to and responsible for the evils which beset the great institution to which they were false.

First and last, the Middle Ages of Mr. Cram's recounting are a period of time as remote from earthly calculation as the kingdom of Mr. Cabell's Dom Manuel. On the other hand, Mr. Cram knows very definitely what he wants. The obstacles, as he sees them, to the development of "a right society" at the present are "the enormous scale in which everything of late has been cast" and the doctrine of equalitarianism. In attacking the concentration of people in "megalopolis," he anticipated some of the articles of Mr. Stuart Chase on the topic. Cities of more than 100,000 are to him "a menace"; when they exceed 1,000,-000 "a crime." The only equality that Cram will admit among men is a spiritual equality. Although in the sapiency of his youth Cram was a royalist and belonged to a Jacobite society in Boston called "The Order of the White Rose," he is curiously a vociferous advocate of decentralization in government, "with a return to the States, the civic communities, and the individual citizens of nine-tenths of the powers and prerogatives that have been taken from them in defiance of abstract justice, of the principles of free government, and the theory of the workable unit of human scale." He is possibly the original sponsor of the proposal to divide the country into provinces or districts for the more efficient administration of government and the curtailment

of central power which Mr. Franklin Roosevelt adopted in part
and with different emphasis in his plan for national reorganization. One sees in it, however, so far as Mr. Cram is concerned,
that balancing of power between the throne and the barons
typical of medieval England, just as one sees in his hatred of the
metropolis (whatever special justification his arguments have)
a personal pique because its sky-line dwarfs his particular kind
of architecture. All Cram's thinking is intensely egocentric—
wherefore we like to please our imaginations by placing so recalcitrant an individualist back in the hierarchial society he touts.
Always the dream ends with the protagonist affected by apoplexy.

Cram, we have said, symbolizes for us the monastical tendency in our institutions of higher education (never forget he has
been Professor of Architecture at Massachusetts Institute of
Technology); on the other hand, the New Humanist Movement of the late 'twenties symbolizes for us the pathos of a
purely academic revolt from that monasticism. Paul Elmer More,
one of the leaders, had taught Sanskrit at Harvard and Bryn
Mawr—and should have made an excellent Aryanist; but a venture into the world between 1900 and 1909, when he served successively on the *Independent,* the *Evening Post,* and the *Nation,*
half converted him away from the current academic discipline.
Irving Babbitt, another leader, though he took two degrees from
Harvard, received a measure of enlightenment during a sojourn
at the Sorbonne, before returning to the States to teach French
at Williams and at Harvard. Had these gentlemen really broken
with the prevailing discipline, they might with justice have called
their movement the New Humanism. But beyond accepting
Plato's description of the dual nature of man, they betrayed
little real interest in classical ideas. Even in his search for a
word, Babbitt was philological—*Humanism* comes (he explains)
from a special use of the word *humanitas* in the late Latin
writer Aulus Gellius:

Humanitas, says Gellius, is incorrectly used to denote a "promiscuous
benevolence, what the Greeks call philanthropy," whereas the word really
implies doctrine and discipline, and is applicable not to men in general
but only to a select few—it is, in short, aristocratic and not democratic
in its implication.

The complete arrogance of this attempt to give to *humanism* a special meaning is quite typical of academic dogmatism: it ignores the fact that Humanism with a broader meaning was already an established concept in the Western World. What, one might ask, has Mr. Babbitt's use of the word to do with the career of Erasmus, who, to the Western mind must always stand as an example of the Humanism of the Renaissance? Babbitt's insistence on the importance of distinguishing between *humanism* and *humanitarianism* has merit only in the understanding of the ideas of himself and his clique—it has no applicability to the teachings of Erasmus, or Plato, as a reading of the *Republic* would have shown him. "Our object," says Socrates, "is not to make any one class preeminently happy, but to make the whole state as happy as it can be made."

Because he was fundamentally a pedant, the nearest approach to Scaliger the New World has seen, Babbitt was totally ineffective in his single blast against current education, *Literature and the American College* (1908). By using a spade and generously excavating, one can discover that this book has an animus against the philologists, but on the surface it is the most amazing hodge-podge of pedantry and personal pique ever delivered at the general public. Babbitt had one of those minds which Oliver Wendell Holmes called *jerky*—"Their thoughts do not run in the natural order of sequence . . . their zigzags rack you to death. After a jolting half-hour with one of these companions, talking with dull friends affords great relief. It is like taking the cat in your lap after holding a squirrel." *Literature and the American College* bounces from topic to topic in such a fashion that one is almost justified in saying that the chapter headings merely indicate what is not discussed in the chapters. If there is a model for this kind of writing it is a German dissertation. The book is really a *Quellen-forschung,* a search after the sources of what is wrong with the American college—and, bless us! if Babbitt doesn't trace all our evils back to Bacon and Rousseau! The most cogent part of the dissertation is an attack on President Eliot for his advocacy of the elective system (a device almost *aboriginally* American), which Babbitt sees as derived from Rousseau. Through Kant and German philosophy in some

mysterious way (so Babbitt claims) Rousseau has affected the
"Baconian" science of philology. Out of this farrago not even
Babbitt's learned colleagues got much of anything save a suspicion that Bacon and Rousseau were merely symbols for crude
child fears. We know not in what superstitious eighteenth century sectarianism Babbitt was reared, but his lack of salivary
control at the mere mention of *science* or *democracy* suggests
the rural hymn singer and sermon note-taker, rather than the
cosmopolitan. Had he read his Aristotle, he would have been
prepared for Bacon, for he would have seen that philosophy and
literature are built upon the science which he condemns. How
could any but rustics rally behind such a leader?

Both Babbitt and More were by instinct pulpit thumpers and
rhetoricians, with a disheartening burden of scholarly lore and
an almost complete unfamiliarity with the major ideas of their
times. When reason failed, they became authoritarian and invoked Christ, without regard to His teachings, to support their
parochial dogmatisms. More, for example, wrote that Christ
"never for a moment contemplated a religion which should rebuild society. His kingdom was not of this world, and there is
every reason to believe he looked to see *only a few chosen souls*
follow in his footsteps. . . ." They were horribly incensed with
the outspoken creative writers and at the rumors of the conduct
of city folks as they filtered into their parishes. Like a beneficed
clergyman berating the squire's simple dependents, or a dean
scolding a freshman, each turned to lecturing his countrymen,
using antiquated concepts and a pulpit jargon gathered from
every whither. Mencken particularly incensed them, and on his
head they poured the vials of their wrath. This is all the more
amusing because they had not a little in common with Mencken
—they at least shared his respect for an hypothetical aristocracy and for property. "There has been a convincing uniformity
in the way in which wealth and civilization have gone together,"
avers Mr. More. Property, the same thinker declares, is worth
more than human life; society, more than the individual. Both
Mencken and More agree on the validity of "a natural aristocracy." Yet Mencken knows nothing of "decorum" and there is
more than a suspicion that his vigorous biological equipment is

devoid of an "inner check." Wherefore the dons denounced him. Aside, however, from issuing polemics against the moderns the sole activity of the New Humanists was to drift rather strongly in the direction of Neo-Thomism. Thus, in the end, the New Humanist revolt circled back to a kind of monasticism more ambiguous and more desiccated than that from which it had originally departed.

Yet if Babbitt was too pedantic and jerky ever to achieve literary distinction, the same cannot be said for More. In those studies in the *Shelburne Essays* (1904–21) which are not polemics against humanitarians—notably in such pieces as "Lafcadio Hearn," "Henry Adams," and "The Spirit and Poetry of Early New England"—there is displayed such an aptness in choice of phrase, such an urbanity of expression, that we are reconciled to the lack of psychological penetration and sharp analysis. The pontifical style has great merit when the pontiff is not angry, and no one has better exemplified that style in critical writing in America than Paul Elmer More. "If W. D. Howells was the dean of our fiction," wrote Stuart Sherman, "Mr. More is the bishop of our criticism," and we see no reason to dissent from that rather guarded praise.

The connection of Mr. Stuart Sherman with the New Humanists was at once his making and his ruin. It was his making because Babbitt, under whom he studied at Harvard, filled him with a disrespect for the philological learning of Kittredge (witness the charge of bird shot he levelled at the bowels of Kittredge in *Americans*) and because More curried and disciplined him when he was just beginning to write. But the penalty for this was a concern with morals when the chief issue was aesthetics, with history when the case might have been decided by looking about him. The result is that Sherman's early books, like *On Contemporary Literature* (1917), *Americans* (1922), and *The Genius of America* (1923), are authoritarian and dogmatic, narrow and unyielding in their outlook. In his critical exchanges with Mencken over Puritanism, he was badly worsted, as we have previously pointed out. Then came his real escape from the influence of the dons, with his resignation from the chairmanship of the department of English at the University

of Illinois, and his acceptance of the editorship of the newly
established *Books* in 1924. In the two short years he was destined to live (he was accidentally drowned in the summer of
1926) he outgrew and discarded his New Humanism. *The Emotional Discovery of America* (1932) contains essays which show
a sympathy and understanding of what contemporary writers
were trying to do that neither More nor Babbitt was ever capable
of. Death came too soon, however, to Stuart Sherman for him
to arrive at a fixed position in philosophy and criticism that
would have lasting meaning for Americans. He was one of the
victims of our intellectual advance, a writer who reveals how
an academic background makes difficult the sane appreciation
of contemporary letters.

Another writer tremendously confused by an academic back-
ground and too much connection with the schools is Thornton
Wilder. Son of the editor of the *Wisconsin State Journal,*
Wilder was born in the university town of Madison, on April
17, 1897, went to China to 1906 when his father was appointed
consul-general at Hong Kong, and remained there eight years.
His high school education at Chefoo was interrupted when his
father returned to the States in 1914; he finished it in the
Thacher School in California. After two years' work at Oberlin,
Wilder joined the Coast Artillery Corps in 1918; in 1920 he
was finally graduated from Yale. The next year was passed in
study at the American Academy in Rome, and, in the fall of
1921, he became a housemaster at the Lawrenceville School,
where he remained for seven long years until *The Bridge of
San Luis Rey* (1927) made him famous. After two years away
from the cloisters, Wilder became a lecturer at the University
of Chicago, a position he held until 1936.

Thornton Wilder is the author of two good books and of
half a dozen poor ones. *The Cabala* (1926), first of his novels,
was undoubtedly suggested by reading Norman Douglas' *South
Wind.* Like it, *The Cabala* describes a small group of people,
not upon an island, unless it be a social island in the waters of
Roman life, not affected by a simoon but by a common ambition
to restore the political power of the Church (a Cramish theme),
a group of conservatives—rich, intellectual, powerful—who have

elected to live altogether in the past. It is a completely decadent group, though the narrator of the tale, a young New Englander, is not thoroughly aware of it until he has become very intimate with its members. Wilder's book is a better narrative than the one from which it is drawn, largely because it is simpler, there is more action, and the characters are dealt with one at a time and not in conjunction. Yet the great virtue of *South Wind* is altogether lacking from *The Cabala;* in Thornton Wilder's book we do not see the characters subtly adjusting themselves to different kinds of dissimulation as they encounter different members of their society. It is to be doubted if Wilder is capable of this sort of analysis. Yet if this virtue has to be paid for by Norman Douglas' long-winded Victorian dullness,—George Saintsbury, inured to hard reading, is the only critic to praise effusively *South Wind,*—it is a virtue we can get along without.

If one can put *South Wind* completely out of mind, the story of "Marcantonio" seems an original, as it certainly is a dramatic, narrative. Our young New Englander is induced to go out into the country to "hold down" the young Prince Marcantonio whose dissipations have alarmed the Cabala. Both Miss Grier and the Cardinal warn him to do the boy no harm, and the latter especially advises him not to attempt to do anything against the bent of human nature. Yet after he is thoroughly acquainted with the dissipated little fourteen-year-old, and has the boy's confidence, the American cannot forbear reading him a violent lecture. The results are reformatory beyond his expectation. Young Marcantonio, excited into committing incest again with his sister, takes his own life afterwards in revulsion of conscience. His body is found in the garden by Frederick Perkins of Detroit, who had got up that morning very early in order that he might "crash the gate" and secure through his American acquaintance inside an introduction to the titled aristocracy.

Now, though this is admirable and Wilder's best piece of writing, it is done all wrong. We never hear the young prince speak, nor his sister, nor the horribly misguided young American. Even Mr. Perkins, when he tumbles off the wall, is speechless. On the other hand, we are permitted to hear the faintest tremolo of the brook and the fountain which so ravishes the author that he can think of no less hackneyed comparison than orchestra music. This isn't narration; it is description—description strained through the gauze of a bookish intellect. And the most admirable description in the world is a poor substitute for the direct telling of a story. Mr. Thornton Wilder is an aesthete on whose eye and ear the rhythms of action and speech fall harshly and discordantly: he prefers tableaux and soft music.

The enormous popularity of *The Bridge of San Luis Rey,* which came a year after its publication in 1927, is better explained from popular psychology than from the merits of the book, for the positive values of the novel are not those which ordinarily appeal to the public—pattern and style. One cannot applaud the ingenious framework of this story without regretting that Wilder's use of it has precluded its employment by an abler artist— who, however, might never have thought of it. And despite the fact that Wilder condemns style as "the faintly contemptible vessel in which the bitter liquid (of the author's heart) is recommended to the world," style is one of the positive merits of *The Bridge of San Luis Rey.* On the other hand, the talk and action of the book are poor. Brother Juniper, the Marquesa de Montemayor, Esteban, Uncle Pio, and Camila are described to us; they have no real existence. They are notations for characters— their breath would not disturb a feather.

It is a rather singular thing that Wilder's people move like figures swathed in chlorine, for the drama has apparently always fascinated him. In the Foreword to *The Angel That Troubled the Waters* (a collection of little plays, 1928) he confesses to have begun composing one-act plays when he was fifteen and to have written more than forty of them, excluding *The Long Christmas Dinner* (1931) which has since appeared. Yet an examination of such of these as have been published shows the same deficiencies we have noted in the novels; these plays were not preparations, nor have they been to date correctives. They seem more like charades than anything else. Walter Prichard Eaton, who knows his theatre, observes correctly that "they lack any real bite." Yet the good copybook maxim, "Persistence has its rewards," has worked out its proof in the successful stage plays *Our Town* (1938) and *The Merchant of Yonkers* (1938), and it may be that the lessons here learned will show up in the novel, if Wilder ever reverts to that form.

The success of *The Bridge of San Luis Rey* was rather a bad thing for Wilder, for the New Humanists at once adopted him. They were delighted to discover a novelist with a "sense of form and values" and a respecter of decorum. They could not have read Part Five, "Perhaps an Intention," of *The Bridge* very carefully. Yet it did affect the novelist to have such a body of unsolicited admirers of they knew not what. Their acclamation of him as a prophet in literature was disconcerting, since he had never been too sure of himself. Before he knew it, he found himself admitting he was "religious in that dilute fashion that is a believer's concession to a contemporary standard of good manners." Equivocal as this is, it satisfied the New Humanists, and the flattered author drew the substance for his next novel, *The Woman of Andros* (1930) from classical literature, that is, all save the first paragraph which still reads like Norman Douglas. *The Woman of Andros* is Wilder's weakest novel: its reworking of the theme of the *Andria* of Terence reminds one of the kind of digests that are prepared for readers who want a short-cut to the World's Great Literature.

Apparently Mr. Wilder suddenly came to the realization that he was keeping poor company with the New Humanists. Perhaps he was helped to this realization by the savage critical study made of his work in the *New Republic* by Michael Gold. *Heaven's My Destination,* out in the first week of 1935, is nothing if it is not Mr. Wilder's declaration that he belongs to his times and his country. The hero of this novel, George Marvin Bush, is a salesman of educational textbooks; of devout religious convictions, he writes religious mottoes on hotel blotters, reproves a young woman who smokes, and tries to convert chance acquaintances. Wilder hates this man so much that he leads him from being thumped to being drubbed so rapidly that the reader pants in pursuit. Indeed, the fervor with which Wilder pursues him is suspicious: we suspect he is flaying demons out of a figure which somehow symbolizes his own immediate past. As a novel, *Heaven's My Destination* is a poor thing, yet technically nearer what a novel should be than Wilder's better-written earlier books. One perceives, however, that in it Wilder has not quite caught up with his times—American novelists were blistering the poor addled religioso a good decade earlier. The question now is whether Thornton Wilder will ever catch up—or will he be content to produce out of his reading further miscellaneous books?

The strange parallel of Mr. Wilder's case with that of Mr. Van Vechten—both workers in fiction—completes an unsought and unpressed parallel between the literary and academic Intelligentsia. Both camps have pursued ideas of syllogistic excellence but of little social worth. Their thinking has been destructive in the main. While some of them have venerated, and others have denounced, Nietzsche, they all have been contemptuous of the struggling, troubled democracy, to which they have suggested codes of action so extreme as to exhaust either flesh or spirit. They have demanded much more attention indubitably than they are worth, for of all our thinkers, they have brought us the least. The future may draw from such diverse figures as Mencken and More the Emersonian axiom that thought is never truth until it is tested by action. The Intelligentsia—all types and kinds— lived too much out of the world to instruct the world in much of anything. Just as German scholarship did nothing to save Germany, so our Intelligentsia have done nothing for us. We shall muddle on—with, or without, them.

VI

THE FREUDIANS

> "If there is anything you do not under-
> stand in human life, consult the works of
> Dr. Freud."—Sherwood Anderson, *Dark
> Laughter.*

I

WOMAN IN BONDAGE

HAVELOCK ELLIS in his first book, *The New Spirit* (1891), celebrated "the rise of women" as one of the three great movements reinvigorating the "degenerate civilization of the nineteenth century" and producing that "renascence of the spirit" which we call contemporary thought. Few men have ordinarily used words with a more precise knowledge of their full content and all their possible implications than did Mr. Ellis, yet in uttering his *cliché,* he added weight to an idea very much in need of dissociation, in Gourmont's sense, today. Ellis himself notes that there are three aspects to woman's alleged advance: the right to education, political enfranchisement, and freedom to work. It is to the third aspect of that "rise"—freedom to work —that we would direct attention. Was the station of woman improved when she was lured into competitive employment? To be sure, the development of machines which women could operate and the development of the single standard of economic competence reduced the sex differentiations of centuries almost in the twinkling of an eye. Economic necessity in the guise of economic opportunity sent man and wife to work in the same mill, or to tend counters in the same shop, and brought them quickly to the same level, but did this for the woman constitute a rise?

The question can be answered only by a brief survey of some of the consequences of that employment. One result of setting women to work was the removal of the fundamental check upon the sexual life of the lower classes. If girls could be employed as readily as boys—and never forget that spinning, the first of the major industries to develop, employed chiefly women—child bearing was less of an economic hazard than in the days when the birth of a daughter meant merely one more mouth to feed. Indeed, a worthy man married to a fertile wife might even achieve economic independence through propagation of his kind, could the children be induced to bring home their weekly earnings from mine, field, and factory. Hence women who did not secure the freedom to work won the greater freedom of bearing more children than previous mothers had borne in the history of the race. The population of the globe, estimated at 850 millions in 1800, more than doubled itself in the next hundred years. The "rise of women" in the nineteenth century apparently was from child-bed to child-bed, and before this fact the legal and educational concessions made the sex seem extraordinarily trivial.

As a matter of fact, human "proliferation" for economic purposes began in America with the founding of the colonies. Fifty years before Samuel Pepys wondered what employment he could find for his idle wife, that is, in 1629, Francis Higginson was writing home to England:

> In our Plantation we have already a quart of milk for a penny. But the abundant increase of corn proves the country to be a wonderment. Thirty, forty, fifty, sixty are ordinary here. Yea, Joseph's increase in Egypt is outstripped here with us. Our planters hope to have more than a hundred fold this year. . . .
> *Little children here, by setting corn, may earn much more than their own maintenance.* . . .

Reports of this sort, like the preaching of the Middle Ages, started what might fairly be called the Second Children's Crusade, that mighty effort to populate America, which raised a handful of settlers in Virginia in 1607 to one hundred and thirty-odd millions of people in 1940. Truly America had, as Crèvecœur remarked in 1782, "one of the finest systems of population which has ever appeared." As early as 1767 Governor Moore of New York had written enthusiastically to the Lords of Trade, "every home swarms with children, who are set to spin and card"; but when the superstition got abroad that residence in America increased the fertility of the race, so salubrious was the climate, Benjamin Franklin sought in his mild fashion to give a more plausible reason, which he did in his essay *Observations Concerning the Increase of Mankind and the Peopling of Countries* (1751):

> The great increase of offspring in particular families is not always owing to the greater fecundity of nature, but sometimes to examples of industry in the heads, and industrious education by which the children are able to provide better for themselves, and their marrying early is encouraged from the prospect of good subsistence.

Early marriage was the rule in America, so much so that John Lawson in *A New Voyage to Carolina* (1709), after noting the frequency with which girls of thirteen and fourteen married, asserted that she who stayed unwed till twenty was "reckoned a stale maid," and this was true on the frontier far into the nineteenth century. Lyman reports that "Some persons tell of having found married women in the woods of the Columbia playing with their dolls."

Adam Smith's observations on the relation of American fecundity to early marriage and the employment of children were well known throughout Europe and are said to have influenced the migrations of thousands of widows with their children to America:

> . . . Those who live to old age, it is said, frequently see there from fifty to a hundred, and sometimes many more descendants from their own body. Labor is there so well rewarded that a numerous family of children, instead of being a burden, is a source of opulence and prosperity to the parents. The labor of each child before it can leave their house, is computed to be worth a hundred pounds clear gain to them. A young widow with four or five children, who among the middling or inferior ranks of people in Europe would have so little chance for a second husband, is there frequently counted as a sort of fortune. The value of children is the greatest of all encouragements to marriage. We cannot, therefore, wonder that people on North America should generally marry very

young. Not withstanding the great increase occasioned by such marriages there is a continual complaint of scarcity of hands in North America.

In New England women were gainfully employed in manufacturing, according to Edith Abbott, almost from the foundation of the colonies. There is an early, undated record of women sewing shirts for the Indian trade at eight pence the piece. In 1656, John Hull in his *Diary of Public Occurrences* records that "twenty persons or about such a number, did agree to raise a stock to procure a house and materials to improve the children and youth of the town of Boston (which want employment) in several manufactures." William Molineux petitioned the legislature in 1770 to aid him in his plan for "manufacturing the children's labour into wearing apparel" and for "employing young females from eight years old and upward in earning their own support"; and the public of his day commended him because, in the words of a contemporary, "The female children of this town . . . are not only useful to the community, but the poorer sort are able in some measure to assist their parents in getting a livelihood." A linen manufactory employing one hundred people was established in Philadelphia, possibly as early as 1764, while in 1775 the "United Company of Philadelphia for promoting American Manufactures" was employing at least four hundred women who worked in their homes. Samuel Slater built the first cotton mill in Rhode Island in 1789, and the first power loom on American soil was set up in Waltham, Massachusetts, in 1814. Alexander Hamilton, in his famous *Report on Manufactures* (1791), gave it as his considered opinion that "In general women and children are rendered more useful by manufacturing establishments than they would otherwise be"; while Matthew Carey, the economist and publisher, supported the employment of young women on the same grounds that Franklin had, namely, as "an inducement to early marriages" and as leading generally to "the welfare of society." In 1810 Albert Gallatin estimated that 87.5% of the employees in the cotton industry were women and children, and the Convention of the Friends of Industry, meeting in New York City, in 1831, proudly boasted that at least 39,000 women were employed in cotton manufactures. The classical economist F. W. Taussig guardedly admits that, until the influx of the Irish after 1846, the employees in the Massachusetts mills "were chiefly women who came to the factories for a year or two in order to accumulate some savings."

Both the moralists and the popular magazines encouraged girls to work. Thus William A. Alcott in 1840 in *The Young Woman's Guide to Excellence* wrote:

. . . Every healthy young woman ought to be so trained, as to be able to make her own way through the world without becoming its debtor . . . every American young woman ought to be able, in the common language of the community, to support herself through life.

Even the liberal *Democratic Review* in 1844 congratulated the poor man on his "half score" of blessings in little children who could be profitably employed.

Literature echoed these and similar sentiments. Indeed, there is in American letters in the nineteenth century what might almost be termed the "Cult of Fecundity." Most of the leading men of letters contributed to it, but it was Whitman who became the high priest of that Cult. It was he who came—

Singing the song of procreation,
Singing the need of superb children and
therein superb grown people. . . .

The fear of being thought scatological has kept critics and scholars from assigning Whitman his true place in our literary history—the natural voice of breeding and prolific America, the Priapus of the new continent. If there is one poem that is central, from this point of view, in all his writing, one poem that ties him most completely to his times, it is "Thou Mother with Thy Equal Brood." In what is perhaps a copy or an elaboration of some notes he prepared on painting, at about the time he gave his single lecture to the art students of the Brooklyn Art Union, on March 31, 1851, Whitman wrote:

to Picture Makers

Make a Picture of America as an IMMORTAL MOTHER,

surrounded by all her children young and old
—no one rejected—all fully accepted
—no one preferred to another. Make her
seated—she is beautiful beyond the beauty
of virginity—she has the inimitable beauty
of the mother of many children—she is
neither youthful nor aged—around her are
none of the emblems of the classic goddess—
nor any feudal emblems—she is serene and strong
as the heavens.
    Make her picture, painters! And you her
statue, sculptors! Try age after age, till
you achieve it! For as to many sons and
daughters the perfect mother is the one where
all meet, and binds them all together as long
as she lives, so the Mother of These States
binds them all together as long as she lives.

This painting, of course, was ultimately made to the satisfaction of all America by James McNeill Whistler, whose portrait of his mother is the one canvas revered by all his countrymen for whom it symbolizes the worn maternity they know.

Having given up the idea of being a lecturer, Whitman later made a note to use the same idea in a poem:

In Poems—bring in the idea of Mother—the idea of mother with numerous children—all, great and small, old and young, equal in her eyes—as the identity of America. . . .

Thus the poem "Thou Mother with Thy Equal Brood" was eventually born in 1872, the one piece of writing which perfectly sets forth the apparent desire of Americans to breed a race filling these shores in the least time possible:

Beautiful world of new superber birth that rises to my eyes,
Like a limitless golden cloud filling the western sky,
Emblem of general maternity lifted above all,
Sacred shape of the bearer of daughters and sons,
Out of thy teeming womb thy giant babes in ceaseless procession
                                                    issuing,

Acceding from such gestation, taking and giving continual strength
and life,
World of the real. . . .
I merely thee ejaculate!

Census returns of the decades that this poem was in gestation
(1850–1870) show that phrases like "new superber birth,"
"teeming womb," and "babes in ceaseless procession issuing" are
cold, precise expository statements, rather than the "loose, lewd
babble" they are sometimes described as being. Well might Whitman "merely ejaculate" or exclaim over such pregnancy.

The saddest of all the writings over which one may pore if
one chooses to pursue this topic are those of the young girls who
fancied they were doing something for their sex when they went
into the mills to work. "The girls who toiled together at Lowell,"
wrote Lucy Larcom, who began watching bobbins on the spinning frames at eleven, "were clearing away a few weeds from
the overgrown track of independent labor for other women.
They practically said, by numbering themselves among factory
girls, that no real odium could be attached to any honest toil
that any self-respecting woman might undertake." That courage
faltered and that vision sometimes grew dim Miss Larcom substantially admits in her story of the overseer who confiscated all
the Bibles he found among these Yankee working girls until he
had a desk full. She thought she had a right to the Scriptures,
for "if we needed them anywhere, it was at our work. I evaded
the law by carrying some leaves from a torn Testament in my
pocket." Bolstered by faith and Holy Writ, these innocents fancied they were engaged in a crusade for the freedom of womankind. And to whose advantage was it to undeceive them? Yet the
plain facts in Lucy Larcom's case were that her mother could
not make sufficient profit out of the Company boarding house
she ran for working girls (where meals cost $1.25 a week), and
she was forced to put her two little daughters into the mill.
Another one of these girls, a Miss Farley, actually wrote an article which appeared in the *New England Offering* lamenting the
fact that some of her companions would be enticed into the
"Great West, with all this clamor for teachers, missionaries, and
wives" following the discovery of gold in 1849.

Expanding industry and the "clamor for teachers, missionaries, and wives" in the West gave the United States, as has been implied, the highest increase in population in the world. To bear him children, a man frequently had three wives, if not at one time (as had the realistic Mormons, whom it is stupid to cite as very exceptional), then in succession as he buried them from early deaths brought on by excessive child-bearing, hard work, crude obstetrical practices, and abortions. From 1800 to 1900, according to the census returns, the increase of population in the United States was 1,331.6% as compared with 204.3% in Belgium, then the fastest growing of European countries, and with 155.9% in the British Isles. Inasmuch as in no decade did the number of immigrants exceed 8% of the total population, and in most decades was less than half of this, it is clear that the greatest increase was due to births. The United States was the most prolific nation on earth, and perhaps in the history of man. It seems natural to suppose that this unusual activity, quickly followed by sharp checks (as the rapidly falling birth rate from the late 'eighties onwards indicates), should be strongly reflected in our thought. And, as we shall see, so it is.

2

TRANSITION

If "freedom to work" was not a path to an improved condition for women, but rather the *via dolorosa* to premature marriage, many children, and early death, what did serve to elevate womankind? Unquestionably the sex occupies a better position today than it held in 1800. What brought this about? Doubtless there were many factors in the "rise of women," but three appear to transcend the others in importance and these three wrought their chief effects in the early twentieth century rather than in the course of the nineteenth. They are the dissociation of the idea of love from procreation, chiefly accomplished by modern literature, the advocacy of birth control, and the payment more generally to the emancipated women of a subsistence wage.

No American writer of consequence risked a frontal attack

upon the ideal of Romantic Love, the ideal of fidelity to conjugal ties (always rewarded by its brood of happy cherubim in
the literature of the day), in the course of the nineteenth century. Yet among intellectuals there was apparently some questioning, though very restricted, of the procreative tendencies of
the age. Of the sixty-two communal societies established in
America in the nineteenth century, by far the majority looked to
some form of birth limitation, and the great appeal of these
communities to women was undeniably on the score that they
offered something other than the lusty breeding of the day.
New Harmony, founded by Robert Owen whose eugenic ideas
were well known, attracted twice as many women as men; and
when, right on the crest of popular interest in that community,
Robert Dale Owen published in New York his *Moral Physiology*
(1830), which frankly discussed methods of contraception, one
can understand why it went through many editions. Prior to that,
Fanny Wright, founder of the "gradual emancipation" community of negroes at Nashoba, Tennessee, had written an article advocating birth control to protect the resources of America
from the danger of too rapid growth in population, which appeared in the *Free Enquirer* on July 22, 1829. Later, on March
5, 1831, in the same magazine she wrote warmly endorsing
Owen's *Moral Physiology*. At the Oneida Colony, John Hum-
phrey Noyes preached the twin doctrines of "scientific propagation and true Christian Communism." His advocacy of "stirpi-
culture" aroused much moral indignation and eventually Noyes
had to flee to Canada; nevertheless his little tract, *Male Continence,* apparently found its avid readers. In view of the covert
and overt expressions of interest in birth limitation on the part
of these leaders in social experimentation, one is puzzled that
there was so little scientific interest in birth control. It is surprising to find among American physicians (who saw all the ills of
frequent child-bearing) only one courageous advocate of contraception. He was Doctor Charles Knowlton, a respectable
practitioner in Massachusetts, whose pamphlet giving birth control information, *The Fruits of Philosophy,* was published anonymously in New York, in January, 1832. For circulating his
pamphlet, however, Knowlton was fined in Taunton, and im-

prisoned in 1833 in East Cambridge at hard labor. Suppressed here, *The Fruits of Philosophy* sold in excess of 40,000 copies in England.

Population figures make clear that these scattered small publications on contraception reached an unappreciable audience. Other records indicate the need which the people of that day had for a sane approach to the whole topic of sex relationships. Congestion of young women immigrants who could not find work in our great cities during hard times produced the first serious moral situation for the nation at large in our history. The "poverty, wretchedness, and vice" of the "Five Points" in New York had aroused the loathing of Charles Dickens on his famous visit in 1842, but the general social degradation of our large cities and their low moral standards in the 'fifties are better reported in B. K. Pierce's *A Half-Century with Juvenile Delinquents* (1869) and in Charles Loring Brace's *The Dangerous Classes of New York* (1872). Both of these men, who had devoted their lives to philanthropy (Brace founded the Children's Aid Society in 1853), knew whereof they wrote. It is significant that the first American *History of Prostitution* was published in 1857. Its author, Doctor William W. Sanger, made a study of the situation in New York City, in 1855, with the aid of the police, who questioned 2,000 prostitutes. Of these women 61.09% were foreign born, girls who had come to the United States looking for work. It is to be doubted if the police could round up and question that number of prostitutes today in New York, though the city is more than six times as large as it was in 1855. The Dewey investigation in 1936 did not disclose anything comparable. The Bohemian crowd in the *Saturday Press* frequently alluded to the situation, while William Allen Butler in his Beppoish "Nothing to Wear" mocked the wealthy young women, the McFlimsies of Madison Square, who fretted about their clothes when their sisters on the back streets were nearly naked.

The discovery of gold in '49 had moved the center of population westward more rapidly than the moral discipline could travel, with the result that vice was rampant in the mushroom towns of the West, and soon reflected in the East, when returning prospectors sought a freedom the mining camps had accustomed them to. Conditions in the Far West are best revealed by Bret Harte, whose Cherokee Sals, Mother Shiptons, and Duchesses have every air of being drawn from life. With the Civil War came a general breakdown of moral control, though by no means so openly acknowledged as was that of World War I. When the city of Memphis was crowded with soldiers, regulation of prostitution, accompanied by medical inspection, was first tried in America by the Confederate authorities. After the War impetus came from both Europe and the West for the licensing of prostitution. The situation was so bad that the step seemed warranted to many. No future historian of our times will be able to call such a roll of dives and houses of prostitution as does Herbert Asbury in his chapter, "When New York Was Really Wicked," in *The Gangs of New York,* describing conditions in the metropolis following the Civil War. (Incidentally that chapter shows how well-deserved was Whitman's epithet for Manhattan—"City of Orgies.") In January, 1866, Bishop Simpson of the Methodist Episcopal Church made a speech at Cooper Union in which he asserted prostitutes were as numerous in New York as Methodists, and later fixed the number at 20,000. This, John A. Kennedy, Superintendent of Police, denied, but admitted that the records of his department showed 3,300 public prostitutes, 621 houses of ill-fame, and 99 assignation hotels. In 1867, the New York Legislature ordered an investigation of the feasibility and desirability of licensing prostitution. A bill for legal regulation passed the legislature in 1871, but died through pocket veto. When the State Committee on Crime reported again in favor of licensing in 1875 and 1877, all legislation was killed through the weight of a petition prepared by the Women's Social Education Society of New York. Aaron M. Powell in *State Regulation of Vice* (1878) presents some of the effective arguments used against the proponents of the system. Venereal disease is admitted to have increased in Paris under licensing; the system enslaves women of the lower class, and is class legislation, etc. With particular relish Powell quotes Alexandre Dumas, "O, besotted nation, to turn all these lovely women who should be our companions in life's work, wives, and mothers, into *prostitutes!*"

In one instance legal regulation of prostitution fared better in the West. In 1870, on the basis of an amendment made to its charter by the legislature, granting the city power "to suppress or regulate houses of ill-fame," St. Louis began an experiment with the licensing system. Four years later, however, a body of citizens, led by Dr. Eliot (grandfather of the poet), of Washington University, forced repeal of this legislation. In 1871 the women of Chicago were largely responsible for defeating an attempt to establish the licensing system there, and in 1874 the same thing happened in Cincinnati. If prostitution continued, it continued without legal sanction.

The increase of prostitution in the United States between 1850 and 1880 was but one symptom of a growing evasiveness in the country in regard to the assumed responsibility of producing many children. The appearance of all sorts of abnormal sexual conduct at the same time was also a symptom of this evasiveness. There exists a more definite record of these aberrations than most Americans suppose. Phrenologists, like Dr. Benjamin Fowler and John Cowan, who had established themselves as champions of large families, were quick to note any variation from the norm of lusty breeding. Cowan, who detected abnormality when a woman lavished affection on a pet, issued a significant rebuke to Americans in his *Self-Help* (1870) when he wrote:

. . . The great primary object of the sexual element is reproduction and *reproduction only,* and when this divine purpose is thwarted *or ignored,* so sure as day follows night do misery, sorrow, unhappiness, and premature death result. . . .

In 1852, in *The Blithedale Romance,* Hawthorne treated with disapproval a situation resembling that in *The Captive,* a French drama banned from Broadway in 1925, and in the same year Melville, in his frenetic novel *Pierre,* reviewed some rather startling relationships growing out of what he politely called "the moral ambiguities." Three years later Walt Whitman compiled in *Leaves of Grass* a complete list of all the abnormalities known to modern psychology—and plainly compiled them from his observations. It was the situation in America, as well as the interest aroused by the Bradlaugh-Besant trial in England in 1877, which led a group of physicians in the Harvard Medical School, including that wise and sane American, Dr. Oliver Wendell Holmes, to initiate the reprinting of Dr. Charles Knowlton's book on contraception, *The Fruits of Philosophy*, which this time appears to have had a wide circulation. Mrs. Besant's *Law of Population* (1879) and Doctor Allbut's *The Wife's Handbook* (1887) were likewise issued in this country; and a translation of Max Forel's study of sex had considerable circulation.

Yet all contraceptive literature had to make progress against the censor. Knowlton, Besant, Allbut, and Forel were beyond the reach of the American police, but their publishers and distributors were not. Neither were Americans who desired to write on contraception. Anthony Comstock, though he was himself one of ten children, was most ruthless, as special agent of the Post Office Department and head of the New York Society for the Suppression of Vice, in his persecution of those who attempted to disseminate information on birth control. Undeniably he hounded several well-intentioned but stubborn visionaries to death. Indeed, after he had caused the suicide of Miss Ida C. Craddock, author of *The Wedding Night,* the Reverend Doctor Rainsford wrote him, "I would not like to be in your shoes. You hounded an honest, not a bad woman to her death. I would not like to have to answer to God for what you have done." Among Comstock's other victims were Ezra H. Heywood, freethinker and author of a book on love and marriage, called *Cupid's Yokes* (1876); De Robigné Bennett, elderly publisher of an organ called *Truth Seeker* who incurred Comstock's wrath by offering to send *Cupid's Yokes* to all who wrote in for it; and Moses Harman, who struggled against Comstock for twenty years, receiving many fines and sentences for printing contraceptive material in his journal called *Lucifer*. Yet it is not to be supposed that Comstock and his aides kept people, particularly those in the upper classes, from getting in devious ways the information which they desired; the advocates of birth control made some progress, and even ineffectual methods and efforts at continence began to have results for the census taker—towards the end of the century the birth rate began to fall off.

Although birth limitation was begun as a practice in the Gilded Age, there was still much talk in the press and elsewhere about the virtue of large families. The thing which, more than anything else, put an effective damper on such talk was the publication in 1875 of Richard Louis Dugdale's famous report of the Prison Association, entitled *The Jukes, a Study in Crime, Pauperism, Disease, and Heredity*. Dugdale, born to English parents in Paris in 1841, came to America ten years later, and after attending public school and Cooper Union, obtained employment as a stenographer. His deep interest in social problems and his acquaintance with many influential social reformers led to his appointment in 1868 to the executive committee of the Prison Association of New York. While serving on yet another committee in 1874 to inspect county jails, Dugdale was struck by the fact that so large a number of the inmates were interrelated, and desiring to push his observation further, he secured private backing to investigate carefully one large family connection, to which he gave the name of "Jukes". Of the estimated lineage of 1200 persons born to two sons of "Max" (a Dutchman, born between 1720 and 1740, described as "a hunter and fisher, a hard drinker, jolly and companionable, averse to steady toil") who married two of the "Jukes" sisters, Dugdale was able to investigate 540 people, together with 169 of other strains. Of these 709 persons, 180 had either been lodged in the poorhouse or had received "outdoor relief" for a total of 800 years, 140 had been convicted of some criminal offense, 60 were habitual thieves, 7 had been murdered, 50 were known prostitutes, 40 venereally diseased had infected at least 440 persons, and the "Jukes" line as a whole had cost the State of New York at least $1,308,000.

Dugdale studied not only the family itself but its "ancestral breeding spot," a rocky inaccessible area, where the people are backward and degenerate, an area which he stigmatized as "one of the crime cradles of the State of New York." The investigator himself did not believe that heredity was wholly responsible for the character of the "Jukes" family. Indeed, in his essay

"Further Studies in Crime" (1877), he summarized *The Jukes* in this surprising fashion: "In *The Jukes* it was shown that heredity depends upon environment, and that a change in environment may produce an entire change in the career." But this was not the lesson that the general public drew from the book. For the average American reader Dugdale's book was a study in the determinism of degeneracy, and he commenced to wonder if those persons of low social rank should breed the most children. While hitherto there had been many encomiums in our literature on the large, happy families of the poor—encomiums reminding us of the spirit of Burns' *The Cotter's Saturday Night* —these suddenly dwindled. Now, when a literary person represents the sodden poor, the floors of their dwellings are crowded with children, and there is an implied stricture of the sire of these *misérables*. A good example of this is seen in Alice French's short story, "A Communist's Wife" (1887), which incidentally depicts the radical Bailey as the father of more children than he can support. The attitude is general, however, in all American fiction since 1875. *The Jukes* is a genuine landmark in American social history.

If the poor bred too many children, it was patent that "the old lines" were breeding too few. The new science of Darwin and Dugdale taught this, before Theodore Roosevelt began to preach against race suicide at the end of the century. If our better families had the normal desire to perpetuate a name or tradition, that desire became an imperative command with any wide understanding of the doctrine of selection. The psychological effects of this are all but incalculable, yet if incalculable, still capable of illustration. The career, the "education," the mind of Henry Adams, are at least partially explicable from this point of view and he is our illustration. But he is also our illustration of American Protestant mariolatry—the worship of the wife-mother—at its apogee.

Henry Brooks Adams was born in the shadow of the Boston State House, on Mt. Vernon Street, on February 16, 1838. His father, Charles Francis Adams, was the son of John Quincy Adams and the grandson of John Adams; his line, most Americans would agree, was one of those most worthy of perpetuating in the United States. It had not in any sense been weakened by marriage; while the wife of John Quincy was never to be as famous as Abigail Adams, the resourceful and brilliant wife of John, she was deservedly respected in the Massachusetts capital. Abigail Brooks, Henry's mother (the "Queen bee," her son called her), was the daughter of the man reputed to be the wealthiest in Boston. Yet Henry Adams bore little resemblance to his substantial and illustrious forebears: their robust vigor was absent; their intellectual muscularity was wanting. This was the heritage of his brothers, particularly of Charles, who promised to follow their father. Effeminate in appearance, idle by habit, and empty of purpose, Henry Adams must have been a source of anxiety to his parents, who doubtless tried to impress upon him all the responsibilities he was heir to. Of his mental endowment they had no suspicion: an attentive eavesdropper to the spirited conversations in his father's house—Dana, Palfrey, and Sumner could be found there as frequently as at home, Henry knew answers to questions never raised in Mr. Dixwell's school, where he was in perfunctory attendance. From these friends of his father, all Anglophiles whose love for British society was intensified by local ostracism (a result of their anti-slavery views), he received an impression of the charm of that existence which was to remain the fondest delusion of his life. Instinctively he began to cultivate the graces and to read in desultory fashion the poets and historians of the eighteenth century as preparation for some fancied rôle as wit or autocrat in an American *haut monde* of the future. Harvard College gave him no higher ideal, and he made no attempt to distinguish himself there and was graduated in the middle of his class.

What he needed, he reflected, was a career in which social position, such as the Adamses enjoyed, had value. In the raw republic perhaps only literature combined with teaching provided such a career. With no very clear idea of what his choice entailed, Henry Adams announced to his family his intention to study Civil Law in Germany and was surprised to secure parental approval. Thus the Grand Tour was his without his really having asked for it. In November, 1858, he went to Berlin, ostensibly to begin his studies. These never went very far; he registered for courses in Berlin and, later, in Dresden, but failing to acquire any fluency in German through want of application, he got nothing from the lectures (which he rarely attended) and made the universities merely foci for pleasant excursions in Central Europe. In 1860 Adams drifted down into Italy. Garibaldi's redshirts were then outside Palermo and the young American managed to interview the Liberator. Two letters to the Boston *Courier* describe his impressions, but his sympathies were not enlisted—as were those of Margaret Fuller—in the Italian cause. He appeared to be accomplishing so very little that his father summoned him home in November, 1860, and possibly in order to keep him under *surveillance,* made him his private secretary.

At the outbreak of the Civil War the elder Adams was appointed Ambassador to the Court of St. James, and though Henry expressed a desire to enlist, his father ruled that he must accompany him to London, still in the rôle of private secretary. Politics kept the American minister from being popular in the British capital, though Charles Francis Adams gradually gained the influence which he desired. Meanwhile Henry hovered, an eager butterfly, on the periphery of that society which seemed to him the most cultivated in all the world, and in his leisure read De Tocqueville, Comte, and Mill, quite possibly to satisfy his father. Earnest being demanded of the seriousness of his intentions in literature, he dashed off an essay on Captain John Smith for the *North American Review* and followed it by two more solid articles on British finance. It is plain now that Henry Adams might have made a name for himself in the field of economics had he persisted: he was shrewd and discerning; moreover, he was fearless. But he had gained his entrée into society, at least into secondary circles, and had been elected into a club on St. James Street. His letters become choked with trivialities—the round of entertainments tires him, yet it is a joyous fatigue.

He had, however, sufficiently satisfied his family as to his intentions and abilities as a writer, so that, when the Adamses returned to the United States in 1868, he was permitted to establish himself alone in Washington to pursue a career in journalism. There seems to have been some idea that, in this way, he could support his brother Charles in politics. But Henry's dilettantism reasserted itself; he did little important writing, and what he did—especially the "Session" articles—subjected him to vicious ridicule. A Senator from the West described him as "a begonia," an epithet which rankled in Adams' mind for more than forty years. The family became disturbed at the reputation he was acquiring and decided to give his career new direction.

Charles Francis Adams had attained considerable influence at Harvard and he induced President Eliot in 1870 to invite his wayward son to teach medieval history at the College and to conduct the *North American Review*. It mattered not that Henry's only qualifications for these appointments were his fliers in journalism and his facile talk about the English historians whom he had met in London through his friends Palgrave and Gaskell. John Quincy Adams had taught rhetoric and oratory at Harvard, hence the step could not be regarded as one downward in Henry's career. To the teaching of medieval history he brought the prejudices of the Palgraves against the Aryanizing tendency of the German historians and their English followers, but he lacked the equipment for a frontal attack upon the new school. He had to content himself with heckling reviews of Stubbs, Maine, and Freeman in the journal of which he was editor. But in the end, possibly due to the growing prestige of Johns Hopkins University which had adopted the German methodology, Adams had to come into line, and with a good deal of outside assistance he and the students in his "seminary" produced an excellent study in Anglo-Saxon law in which is utilized the technique of Sohm, Mommsen, and Curtius. It had looked like surrender or perish, and Adams had chosen to surrender.

Meantime he had been routed on another front. Attempting to give a cosmopolitan air to the stodgy society of Cambridge, he had produced only scandal by giving champagne parties, which brought ladies to his chambers. Possibly a good many people were relieved when Henry Adams became engaged to and married Marian Hooper, of Boston, daughter of the well-to-do Doctor William Hooper and Ellen Sturgis Hooper, an heir to the Sturgis shipping fortunes. Katherine Simonds, who in her article "The Tragedy of Mrs. Adams" has done much towards illuminating our subject, makes it clear that this vivacious young woman was a person of great charm and exceptional taste. Her elder sister was described by Henry James as the "exquisite Mrs. Gurney of the infallible taste, the beautiful hands, and the tragic fate"; her brother, Edward William Hooper, treasurer of Harvard College for twenty-two years, was, like Henry Adams, a collector of Chinese paintings. Henry, it seemed, could hardly have done better for a wife; indeed an acquaintance pronounced theirs "a marriage of similarities"—with what accuracy, however, only time could show. Granted a year's leave of absence from his academic and editorial duties, Adams took his bride abroad in 1872–1873.

There was no real reason why the Henry Adamses should return to Cambridge where no amount of stimulation could overcome the provincial suspicion of the amenities and where limited purses restricted the evolution of society. To establish a salon which should give direction to American politics and an edge to American taste, as had those of London, required a location nearer the heart of things, and Henry naturally fastened his eye on Washington. Yet he did return to Harvard for a brief period before moving to the national capital. One announced advantage of the transfer was the proximity to the Congressional Library, where Adams found available more source material for the apologetic history he contemplated writing.

In Washington the Adamses became the most discriminating and exacting hosts in the city. Entertainment became their object in life. "We generally have the latch up from five o'clock till bedtime," Mrs. Adams writes, "and we learn more out of books than in." Yet they gained no real influence, save with a small group, really a clique, including John Hay, William Evarts, and Clarence King, who were as much outside things as themselves. This group became the baffled critics of the Gilded Age, Adams contributing anonymously the novel *Democracy,* in 1880, and Hay, *The Breadwinners,* in 1883. Hating particularly that element in current politics called "Western," Adams drew in *Democracy* the portrait of a typical, corrupt politician, Senator

Ratcliffe, from that vast, vague territory, then called "the West."
It is interesting to note, however, that most of the salient details
of Ratcliffe's character were drawn from those of the Honorable
James G. Blaine, of the state of Maine. From our point of view,
Democracy is chiefly instructive for the rôle which Henry Adams
assigns its heroine, the widowed Mrs. Lee. This lady, losing
her taste for both New York society and for charitable enterprises, elects to establish a salon in Washington because "she
wanted to see with her own eyes the action of primary forces;
to touch with her own hand the massive machinery of society. . . .
What she wanted, was *Power."* When one reads the half-
innocuous letters of Mrs. Henry Adams one cannot ascribe to
her any such self-derived ambition, but it is not impossible to
see in Henry's portrait of Madeleine Lee a prescription for the
rôle he expected his wife to fill in Washington. At first blush, the
most flattering position conceived by an American for a woman
up to that time, being a salon mistress with a national influence
might have its lugubrious aspects—there were always the Rat-
cliffes to deal with—and a sensitive woman might flinch at some
of the duties of the rôle. Was this the reason why the Adamses'
salon exerted only a limited influence? Aside from stirring up
speculations of this sort, Adams' novel has little merit, and
another book, called *Esther,* published under the pseudonym
"Frances Snow Compton" in 1884, consoles the reader to the
fact that Adams wrote no more fiction.

Yet this novel *Esther,* if we follow Miss Simonds, determined
Adams' future, for Esther is a portrait of his wife. The novel
itself is trivial—the story of a woman who loves a popular minister but, being a sceptic, cannot marry his church or submit to his
faith. It is the severity of the portrait that stuns. Esther, or
Marian Adams, is revealed as a creature of a "gaiety almost too
light," a person who, according to Adams, "picks up all she
knows without effort, and knows nothing well, yet she seems to
understand whatever is said." Though she has "a style of her
own," the author can never make up his mind whether he likes
it or not. She appears to him to have too little conviction about
anything to survive the ordinary tests the spirit is put to:

... I want to know what she can make of life. She gives one the idea of a lightly sparred yacht in mid-ocean unexpected; you ask yourself what the devil she is doing there. She sails gaily along though there is no land in sight and plenty of rough weather coming.

One cannot say, however, that the portrait has no loving touches; on the contrary, *Esther* appears the product of an exacting love, the love that demands perfection in the object adored; a love calculated to fill that object with despair.

And this may have been the effect of *Esther* on Marian Adams, who does not seem to have been aware that her husband was writing another novel, though she herself has supplied some of the minor detail in *Democracy*. Even Miss Simonds has not unriddled the full purport of the book for the wife of the author. She fails to remark that the Reverend Mr. Hazard, who resembles Henry Adams in most details physically, has his "knack of fixing an influence wherever he went," and is absorbed in special topics interesting to Adams (for example, in the art of the thirteenth century), is steadily exerting an "impalpable" pressure to shape the heroine to his end. From this "tyranny" there is no escape for her, since "to be steadily strong was not in Esther's nature. She was audacious only by starts and recoiled from her own audacity." Though the influence over her might be "feminine in appearance," its persistence conceivably could be terrifying.

Added purport is given the portraiture when we note that Esther, chid for being a "Puritan," is alleged to resemble Hawthorne's "Esther Dudley," irrational defender of the *ancien régime* in Boston. Was Marian Adams reluctant to admit new types of American into her circle? And then the cruelest, or perhaps the most thoughtless, touch of all: Esther, like cracked old Esther Dudley, is made fond of children, but, as she complains, she is good only for telling them stories. Doubtless Adams meant to make his heroine less angular by posing her favorably among the infants; but if one were distraught, the passage could be taken as a rebuke: the Adamses had been married twelve years and were still childless. A woman acquaintance says, "Not having any was a greater grief to Mr. Adams than to her," yet this is not certain, for a great change had come to Marian Adams. As a young girl, we are told that, "She did many kind and generous actions," yet later, "she had a reputation for saying bitter things and of unsparingly using her powers of sarcasm whenever an opportunity presented. She was feared rather than loved." Furthermore, Mrs. Adams within a few months after the publication of the book was to lose her long-doomed father, to whom she was greatly devoted. In Adams' novel Esther likewise loses her parent, a man who, after his retirement, "amused the rest of his life by spoiling this girl." Esther's father, dying tries in vain to bolster his daughter's courage and strengthen her faith:

> "It is not so bad, Esther, when you come to it." But now that she had come to it, it was very bad; worse than anything she had ever imagined; she wanted to escape, to run away, to get out of life itself rather than suffer such pain, such terror, such misery of helplessness.

Who can doubt that here was the suggestion for suicide, and that Mrs. Adams' death on December 6, 1885, from cyanide poisoning must have appeared to the author of the book as the one inevitable result of the portrait? Yet she took her life at a time which she ordinarily gave to writing letters to her father, and it was of him that she was probably thinking then rather than of her husband, the author of *Esther*. Adams had no assurance of this, however, nor could he be certain that his disappointment in regard to children was not a factor in his wife's rash act. Mrs. Whiteside, close enough to Marian Adams to refer to her by her nickname "Clover," evidently thought that the suicide was partly chargeable to the Adamses' yearning for children, for she wrote—

> How often we have spoken of Clover as having all she wanted, all this world could give, except perhaps children. And now at forty years old down comes a black curtain and all is over. . . .

To Henry Adams the death of his wife under these circumstances was a final blow, the culmination of a series of defeats in the Adams family fortunes. John had fairly won the Presidency, John Quincy had got in (so it was charged) on a political bargain, Charles Francis had never achieved his political aims, and a political career had been completely closed to Henry. His brothers had no longer aspirations in the field, and he, the truest representative of the line, was without heir or the prospect of heir. Nor could he longer hope to influence national politics even indirectly. The times were chaotic and the best blood was thinning out. Small wonder that, for Henry Adams, civilization seemed on the wane and even the cosmic forces ebbing in strength.

The major work of Adams' Washington residence, for which ostensibly he had left teaching at Harvard, was a *History of the United States during the Administrations of Jefferson and Madison* (1885–91), in one way a polemic in conception, since the author attempted to vindicate John Quincy Adams for breaking with the Federalist Party. Though the book is chiefly concerned with politics, the early chapters of the history treating economic and social conditions at the beginning of the nineteenth century are more comprehensive in their plan than any that had been written up to that time in this country. They show that Adams understood and accepted the challenge of Henry Thomas Buckle "to link ideas" and to study history in terms of force, and not to regard it, as Macaulay had done, as "antiquarianism and anecdotage." While he was in the full swing of this work and daily supervising the erection of a new home in Washington, Mrs. Adams' death occurred, and the history, begun with so much zest, was pushed to a conclusion without enthusiasm. The loss of his wife resulted in a search for Nirvana, for complete peace and forgetfulness, rather than for new interests. History could not absorb a man who felt life emptied of meaning.

Picturesque Japan, the atolls of the South Seas, the companionship of LaFarge and King hardly brought Adams forgetfulness; hence philosophy enticed him. In 1863 he had written his brother Charles of his conviction—a conviction to which Comte and Buckle contributed much—that the same laws govern man as govern Nature; idly now he speculated on these laws. Eventually he reached the conclusion that "Chaos is the law of nature; order the dream of man"—a conclusion startlingly different from his original premise. Surveying all modern history, Adams found but one period on the long scroll which was at all unified—one century in which man's dream of order came somewhere near realization. This was the first great period of peace in the West, roughly that century between 1170 and 1270 when the French, under the influence of the Virgin Mary, "built eighty cathedrals and nearly five hundred churches of the cathedral class, which would have cost, according to an estimate made in 1840, more than five thousand millions to replace" or more than a billion dollars. Fascinated, not by this one solid fact of men's fervid devotion to a single ideal in this period, but by the thousand evidences he found of it, Adams bent upon the century his full analytical powers. The result was a book entitled *Mont-Saint-Michel and Chartres,* privately printed in 1904, and after wide circulation and discussion, given to the general public in 1913.

Before we can examine *Mont-Saint-Michel and Chartres,* we must understand how Adams abandoned his view of the dominance of law in Nature and in the life of man, and decided that Nature is lawless and order a dream of man. One thing is perfectly clear, Mrs. Adams' death was not immediately responsible for this change. As late as 1894, Adams addressed a letter to the American Historical Association, of which he was the absentee-President, urging that Association to seek a science of history, though that science should overthrow all the existing institutions —capitalism, state, and church. It is a bold and vigorous letter from a man who still believes that science holds the key to man's future, and that that key *must* be used. Though this letter comes from Guada-C-Jara, Adams had begun some reading in Paris, three years before, that was to influence him profoundly. His efforts to write fiction had shown him his deficiencies in this field, but had not cured him of interest in it. Hence we find him in January, 1891, trying to absorb the French Naturalists. "Imagine my state of happiness," he writes to Elizabeth Cameron, "surrounded by a pile of yellow literature, skimming a volume of Goncourt, swallowing a volume of Maupassant with my roast, and wondering that I feel unwell afterwards. These writers have at least the merit of explaining to me why I dislike the French, and why the French are proper subjects for dislike. . . ."

Yet by his process of reading at least a volume a day, Adams came to Joris-Karl Huysmans, an author who may have repelled him, but in whom he maintained an interest for at least twenty years. Huysmans' career was to have certain parallels with his own, parallels Adams could appreciate better than any one else, and he had treated, and was to treat, certain subjects of especial interest to Adams. Huysmans, as we have noted earlier, began his career as a Naturalist, a believer in Positivism and a follower of Goncourt and Zola. He had, at the outset, as firm a conviction in the value of science as Adams. Then came the sophisticated and audacious satire of the Decadents in *À Rebours,* a volume which plausibly may have appealed to Adams because of its cynical tone and its profession of admiration for what is decadent. At the time when Adams was reading yellow-backed novels in Paris, however, the Huysmans book which was most likely to fall into his hands was *La Bas,* over which Paris was still agitated, though the volume had appeared in 1884. *La Bas* has three threads of interest: the hero Durtal's researches for the book he is writing on the infamous fifteenth century sadist, Gilles de Rais; Durtal's desire to see the Black Mass performed and his eventual accomplishment of this desire; and, finally, Durtal's affair with Hyacinthe, wife of Chantelouve and the former mistress of the foul Canon Docre, the defrocked priest who celebrates the loathsome mass. *La Bas* is a disgusting book, an effort to pile refuse on the High Altar; and while its scepticism may have appealed to Adams' mood, we are not of the opinion that it was this which permanently attracted Adams to the book. There is, first of all, in *La Bas* a hatred of the nineteenth century; even occultism, Huysmans insists, has degenerated since the Middle Ages. "The people," one character says, "grow from century to century more avaricious, abject, and stupid." And again, "Society has done nothing but deteriorate in the four centuries separating us from the Middle Ages." *La Bas* denounces the "Americanisms" that Henry Adams detested in the America of Grant's administration. The Catholic general, Boulanger, so much like Grant, is arraigned for "American" methods of self-advertisement; Huysmans even insists that Gilles de Rais' death at the stake is to be preferred to an "American lynch-law" death.

Very important in the book is Huysmans' attack upon Joan of Arc. If Joan had only stayed with her mother, France would not have become a heterogeneous nation; the Charles she saved was the leader of Mediterranean cutthroats, not Frenchmen at all, but Latins—Spaniards and Italians. Without Joan, Northern France and England would have remained united, a homogeneous nation of Normans. Now this is a most important passage for the development of Henry Adams' thinking. When we are invited by the author to visit Mont-Saint-Michel, it is on the score that, if we have any English blood at all, we are also Norman, with an hypothetical ancestry of two hundred and fifty million in the eleventh century, ploughing the fields of Normandy, rendering military service to the temporal and spiritual lords of the region, and helping to build the Abbey Church. Adams was inordinately proud of his Norman ancestry, and in that highly personal poem "Prayer to the Virgin of Chartres," which was found among his papers after his death, he even fancies himself "an English Scholar with a Norman name" returning to France in the thirteenth century to study in the schools and worship at the shrine of the Virgin. Finally, Adams found in *La Bas*—though he may not have been immediately attentive to it—a scepticism in regard to science more deeply felt than Huysmans' hostility towards the Church. In the nineteenth century, says Huysmans, speaking through the character Gévingey, "People believe nothing, yet gobble everything." Positivism, the first love of Huysmans, is roundly denounced. Barbey d'Aurevilly had prophesied after reading *À Rebours* that Huysmans would choose either "the muzzle of a pistol or the foot of the cross," and to the discerning this choice was possibly even more apparent in *Las Bas*. To Henry Adams, however, it must have come as something of a surprise to find that the sacrilegious writer who had fascinated him in *La Bas* had set off in 1892 to be converted at a Trappist monastery. He read the story in Huysmans' novel *En Route* (1895); and followed it through the highly symbolical novel *Le Cathédral* (1898), from which he several times quotes in *Mont-Saint-Michel and Chartres;* reaching finally *L'Obtat* in 1903. *Les Foules de Lourdes* (1906) with its discussion of the many shrines erected in Southern France to the Virgin, which, to the casual reader seems most like Adams, came out too late to have exerted any influence upon him. If Adams interpreted the writing of *La Bas* as an act which drove Huysmans back to Catholicism in contrition, he could not but realize another parallel between himself and the Frenchman— both had written a novel of which they repented.

If we give Joris-Karl Huysmans the credit for turning Adams' thoughts to the Middle Ages and to religion, we must admit also that Adams went beyond this eccentric in his thinking. He discovered the revival of Catholicism in Belgium and France, and came under the influence, so far as it was possible for a Protestant to do so, of the great Pope, Leo XIII. Though Leo was a many-sided man, interested in education, in improving the conditions of the working classes, and in politics, it was his revival of scholasticism that most affected Adams. Immediately upon coming to the Papal throne, Leo had issued an encyclical, *Aeterni Patris,* on August 4, 1878, in which he urged the Catholic world to return to the philosophy of Saint Thomas Aquinas. He declared—and this won wide attention—that scholasticism could live on friendly terms with the natural sciences, nay, could even supply them with directives. At his urging, the University of Louvain established a chair of Thomist philosophy—a chair first occupied by Canon, later Cardinal, Mercier, a man who not only was thoroughly grounded in Thomism, but also well read in Positivism and the English and French psychologists. From this radial center, Thomism (or Neo-Thomism) spread over the world. It became a philosophical force—Jacques Maritain is its best contemporary representative in France, and a political one, since *L'Action Française* (probably without much justification) pretends to derive its ideas from Thomism.

Now Adams plainly did not share the sanguine views of Leo XIII about the compatibility of modern science and scholasticism, but the concluding essay in *Mont-Saint-Michel and Chartres,* devoted exclusively to the implications of the philosophy of Saint Thomas Aquinas, remarks at the similarity of method of Thomism and Science: "the quality that rouses most surprise in Thomism is its astonishingly scientific method." What Adams admires in Thomism is the unity of the plan. Saint

Thomas' "sense of scale was that of the great architects of the age." The *Summa* is like a cathedral; theology and science have become adornments in it. "Both the *Summa Theologiae* and Beauvais Cathedral were excessively modern, scientific, and technical, marking the extreme points reached by Europe on the lines of scholastic science. . . . The essence of it (this science and art)—the despotic central idea—was that of organic unity both in the thought and in the building." But, Adams adds, "From that time the universe has steadily become more complex and less reducible to control." Modern science, instead of showing that all the lines of the universe converge, as the thirteenth century believed, shows that they diverge from every imaginable center of unity. Adams has no hope, apparently, that a revival of Thomism will restore a sense of unity in the world, yet he is all admiration for what the passion for unity created in art, architecture, and theology in the thirteenth century. Adams can accept Thomism in the thirteenth century but not in the twentieth. Chaos is now too deep for any dream of unity to order it.

Mont-Saint-Michel and Chartres more ostensibly is a contrasting study of two centuries—the warlike eleventh and the peaceful thirteenth—as they are exemplified, not in generalship, not in statecraft, but in the typical architectural structures they raised, —in the fortress-like island Abbey of the Normans, completely masculine, from its thick piers and battlements to the figure of the Archangel Michael on the summit of the tower; and in the "child's fancy, the toy house to please the Queen of Heaven," the magnificent Cathedral at Chartres. These two great churches are an expression of the energy of their time. The same force which conquered England in 1066, and which produced the *Chanson de Roland,* erected a granite shrine in the grey sea to its patron, Saint Michiel de la Mer del Peril, protector of the Church militant. Here is not beauty, but power; no suggestion of peace, but rather of eternal vigilance. This is not what any man seeks, Adams implies, and he turns his attention inland and southward to Chartres, where the Virgin Mary has gathered a greater following than ever the Protector of the arms of Normandy could number. As *a force* she excels not only Saint Michael, but all the other forces the world has ever known. This was because, as

Adams has made clearer than any one else, the Virgin was to the thirteenth century a very real woman, a genuine queen, the Queen of Heaven, differing from living queens only in the infinitely greater majesty and refinement of Her Presence, yet more approachable than they. Ten thousand people were at any time to be begging for her favors. Surveying all the works inspired by her, Adams concludes she was the greatest artist, musician, philosopher, and theologian who had ever lived on earth, with the exception of her Son, who at Chartres is still an infant, like Saint Louis, under her guardianship. The popular conception of Mary in the thirteenth century, Adams concedes, had little relation to the orthodox Church conception of the Virgin. The Church, however, impelled by self-interest and the insistence of court and crowd, accepted the popular view of her and established her on a throne beside Christ, the Judge. Even this, he indicates, did not satisfy the times which would have been content to see the Trinity absorbed in her. She was not intercessionary, but *absolute Power*. That is why great nobles and petty bourgeoisie invested in her: they were satisfied their investment would be repaid with interest in the life to come. That is why they could not do enough for her; that is why France blossomed with her cathedrals and churches in a single century, why monies unequalled were spent on them and her clergy.

Mont-Saint-Michel and Chartres is one of the most eloquent tributes to the power of Woman ever penned by man. For whatever she may have meant to the thirteenth century, and whatever she continues to mean to the devout, the Virgin symbolized for Adams Woman Enthroned. He writes with scarcely less eloquence when he treats of the three great queens of France, Eleanor of Guienne, Mary of Champagne, and Blanche of Castile, at whose courts poetry and courtesy were born. They brought to the political and social world the order and unity Adams so much admired. Whether he writes of the legendary windows or of Nicolette and Marion, it is the feminine influence on glass and "chante-fable" that interests him. *Mont-Saint-Michel and Chartres* surpasses, in our estimation, as a tribute the statue that Saint Gaudens carved for Arlington Cemetery at Adams' request, and its necessary connection with the author's personal history cannot be overlooked. Robert E. Spiller has indicated that Adams' portrait of the Virgin is a consequence of his portrait of Esther, but no one has observed that Henry Adams is still exerting in *Mont-Saint-Michel and Chartres* an almost "impalpable" pressure to induce American women to shape American society. Accompanying him on his pilgrimage to the shrines of the thirteenth century and in spirit into that century itself (for all his explanations are made for her) is an American "niece"—some unattached Daisy Miller, whom Adams hopes to teach the great truth that, if she will absorb the lesson of that century, she can go back to her own country to create a society, even a matriarchy, which she can dominate through her sex. This is the meaning of her presence and a revelation of Adams' deepest purpose in writing the book. It is his last effort to give to the society of his country the quality he so much admired in that of the British and Continental capitals.

Yet even when we understand the seemingly incongruous presence of the niece in *Mont-Saint-Michel and Chartres,* the passages addressed to her are so unnatural and self-conscious that we feel they mar the book. Though they are the most annoying flaw in that splendid composition, they are not the only one. It may be altogether doubted if the thirteenth century possessed in actuality the unity Adams fancies that it did. In *First and Last Things* H. G. Wells remarks, "It seems to me one of the heedless errors of those who deal with philosophy, to suppose all things that have simple names or unified effects are in their nature simple and may be discovered and isolated as a sort of essence by analysis." Adams has too much simplified his century. If we were living in the time of the Crusades, if we saw our king captured by the Mongols and were forced to ransom him, if our queen were divorced by the king and married to a foreign potentate, if the great ones over us were always intriguing for power—to mention only a few of the things which actually occurred in Adams' unified century—we should probably think our times very chaotic, indeed. Today we look upon the nineteenth century, which was so meaningless to Adams, as simple and unified. But this is a tendency that the trained historian should seek to avoid. The book *Mont-Saint-Michel and Chartres* should not be looked upon, possibly, as an historical study, but rather as a cathedral of words

—various, complex, and beautiful, yet designed to give a single impression—a cathedral erected by Henry Adams to the glory of Womankind.

Though Adams makes it clear enough in *Mont-Saint-Michel and Chartres* that he believed it was mariolatry and not religion which was the great force in civilizing France in the thirteenth century, he did not state his idea boldly and fully until he came to reflect upon it in *The Education of Henry Adams,* privately printed in 1907. This latter book was undeniably prompted by the former: it sets off one man's total failure to find any principle of unity in contemporary times, and it contrasts this chaos, this "multiplicity," with the simplicity which the previous book had revealed. It is not an autobiography, nor a string of anecdotes. It is a record of confusion which seemed to Adams, at least, to promise to increase rather than to diminish. Against this confusion only one force had ever prevailed, and that was the force of the Virgin Mary. Yet with all their love of force—as exemplified by his friend Langley's enthusiasm for the Dynamo—Americans, so Adams felt, would never recognize the potency of the single force which might unify life for them. It was a "problem in dynamics" which gravely perplexed him. "The Woman had once been supreme; in France she still seemed potent, not merely as sentiment, but as force. Why was she unknown in America?" The only answer Adams can give to his own question is that Americans, because of their Puritan background, regard Woman as something to be ashamed of. ". . . Anyone brought up among the Puritans knew that sex was sin. In any previous age sex was strength." The Virgin, like Venus, was a symbol of sex, and until America can understand and worship this force— at least such is Adams' implication—only chaos will prevail here.

This passage, which ends with a denial that an American Virgin or an American Venus can ever exist, this passage which contrasts the accomplishments of the force of sex as civilizing agent with those of the Dynamo, the most impressive of man's recent mechanical triumphs, then humming purposelessly in an exposition hall where Adams viewed it, this passage has been the most influential in all of Adams' writing. It said for the first time impressively what we were soon to hear from all sides: we had no

culture, no literature, no art, because, hamstrung by Puritanism,
we were powerless to move under the compulsion of the great
force of sex, the force which had created the culture and literature and art of the Old World. This was not particularly true,
but Adams, of all Americans, because of the tragedy of his life,
was to feel that it was true. And the prestige of an Adams was to
give this view great force in American letters, as we shall see.

Because Henry Adams in the closing chapters of *The Education* played with the idea that the Dynamo is symbolic of a force,
the force of Science, the idea has somehow got abroad in the
world that he felt this force might eventually mean as much to
the world as did once the Virgin of Chartres. Yet a careful reading of *The Education* would have told the critics that Adams
repudiated altogether the hope that Science could elicit either
unity or meaning out of the chaos which is the modern world. In
the poem entitled "Prayer to the Virgin of Chartres," found, as
has been stated, among Adams' papers after his death, Adams
reviews Western history since the Reformation. Protestantism he
condemns without a single reservation, since it has dethroned
Father, Son, and Virgin, and has led man first to self-idolatry and
then to the worship of pure energy:

> Ourselves we worship and we have no Son.
> Yet we have gods, for even our strong nerve
> Falters before the Energy we own.

Though we are confused as to whether we are masters of our
science or our science masters us, we adore the symbols of our
science and raise our prayers to the Dynamo as we once raised
them to the image of the Virgin. Adams sees the futility of this
and, like Huysmans, turns his back upon Positivism and Science,
resuming the veneration for the Gracious Lady his ancestors had
revered seven hundred years before. He believes that when man
has all that Science can bring him, he will have but "power above
control." Then he, too, will take the path back to the Virgin.
"The Prayer to the Virgin of Chartres," without any of the
crude speculation on the Virgin as a symbol of Sex, but with
much feeling for her as Mother and Intercessionary, shows that

Adams, at the close of his life, without ever becoming a communicant, but surely having done his penance, was as close to the fold of the Catholic Church as pride would let him go.

Yet is not this proximity tell-tale and everything? In choosing the Virgin as his symbol of Sex, Adams emphasized in particular the fructifying aspect of that force. She is not merely the Mother of God, but Creatress of all the works of wonder of the Middle Age. At best, his allusions to the Sapphic aspects of sex are but casual jibes at American reticences. He is at one with the nineteenth century in expecting the Woman to be fruitful, and there is nothing in all his writing so filled with pain as that line in his "Prayer" on the barrenness of Protestantism with its inescapable double-entendre, *"Ourselves we worship and we have no Son."* In this bit of last, honest self-recrimination is the epitome of Henry Adams.

Adams' reaction to the forces acting in America and the world at the end of the nineteenth century was a highly personal one, yet he reflects so much and was so influential that even this extended treatment of him must seem cursory and brief. Some of his contemporaries may be dismissed with more dispatch. That period which Thomas Beer has called "the Mauve Decade" was, from the point of view of its attitude towards sex, one of the worst in our history. With all free discussion limited by censorship and with the sale of contraceptives restricted to "bootleg" supplies, prostitution was about the only solution left. Furthermore the "wild oat" theory gained a prestige it had not had before in America. This was because of the sanction of a new idle class, the sons of well-to-do people, who were popularly called "the Gilded Youth." George A. Baker, Jr., devotes an essay to these youngsters in *The Bad Habits of Good Society* (1886). He has "met him in supper rooms, where all have fled dismayed from his energetic elbows, and champagne disappeared before him like snow wreaths in the sun." He is about 19 years old. Further—

He has not even the semblance of an occupation. Being the only son of wealthy parents, he enjoys an ample allowance. He dresses in the most extravagant fashion, and indulges in unlimited neckties, ponderous watch chains, low shoes, silk stockings, linked sleeve buttons, and colored ribbons on his hat. His language is a mixture of the lowest sort of American slang, and such Anglicisms as he can cull from the pages of third-rate English novels. His manners are a combination of the awkwardness of the hobble-dehoy and the impudence of the Prince of the powers of the air. His accomplishments are a thorough mastery of the intricacies of draw poker and an unapproachable skill in handling a billiard cue. He knows nothing, reverences nothing, and cares for nothing but himself. . . .

Yet after thus berating this child of the Gilded Age, Baker adds, ". . . We believe there is nothing bad about him. He is only a boy, who by accident of wealth, and a total lack of proper train-ing, has been led to think himself a man, and who does his best, according to his light, to act like one. It is not his fault that he is a gilded youth. It is the fault of a business-engrossed father and a foolish mother. . . ." The Gilded Youth were innocent enough, but complete freedom and tolerant parents led inevitably to vice. The Van Bibber stories of Richard Harding Davis and the Horse Show yarns of David Gray reveal an innocuous, charm-ing youth, but stories like Frank Norris' *Vandover and the Brute,* written in 1895 at Harvard, reflect some of the horror these young men felt as a result of their experiments with sex, both with seduction and prostitution. Allowing for a good deal of exag-geration, there is a note of genuine feeling in *Vandover* we can-not close our ears to.

Of course, these Gilded Youth became models for other young men in less easy circumstances. There is, in George Ade's *Fables in Slang* (1899), one fable which reveals perfectly the perplexity of parents in training children during this period. Entitled "The Fable of the Parents Who Tinkered with the Offspring," it tells the story of the double failure of a Married Couple who possessed two Boys named Joseph and Clarence. Joseph was brought up under the "sheltered life" plan, his mother reading to him "about little Rollo, who never lied or cheated, and who grew up to be a Bank President. She seemed to think that a Bank President was above Reproach." But Joseph ran away with a waitress. Failing with Joseph, they resolved to "give Clarence a Large Measure of Liberty," thus acquainting him with "the Snares and Tempta-tions of the World while he was Young"; they made a point of keeping liquor on the sideboard. But Clarence "stood in with the

Toughest Push in Town" and came out no better than his brother.

It was all very confusing, and when those who read turned to books, they got no help from that quarter. The English novels on which Baker's Gilded Youth modeled his speech were generally insincere and nasty. They were such sensational things as Sir Rider Haggard's *She* (1887), the story of a passionate young Englishman who falls in love with an African sorceress; George Du Maurier's *Trilby* (1893), a fantastic story of how an Austrian Jew, Svengali, controls the destiny of an artist's model through hypnotic powers and makes a great singer out of her— a novel so popular in America that the sculptor Saint Gaudens remarked, "Every other woman you meet thinks she could be an artist's model." A list of many titles could be drawn up of books that were subtly seductive in character, depicting impossible situations where more could be read into the relationships than even the author intended, which is saying a good deal. Of course, these produced American imitators, of whom Robert W. Chambers was the most notorious and successful. If one were to make a list of the most subversive fiction published in America, it would be crowded with titles popular in the Mauve Decade. That these had an effect upon the morals of the youth was inevitable.

3

THE EMANCIPATORS

There were those, however, who struggled against the bad taste and low morals of the time. In 1883 Madame Helena Modjeska tried to introduce Ibsen to the American public, but *A Doll's House* failed to interest and had to be withdrawn. Mrs. Fiske, who played her first Ibsen rôle, that of Nora, in 1894, persisted in presenting the great Norwegian until Americans were fairly familiar with his best work. Yet singularly, Ibsen has not been very important in the development of American thought and his influence in the drama has come to us diffused through the work of other European dramatists. This is the more singular because, thanks to these two great actresses, America saw Ibsen earlier than certain European audiences. *A Doll's House,* for example, was not seen in London until 1889 and in Paris until 1894. The reason why Ibsen has been less influential here than one might suppose would appear to be that, when interest was finally aroused in him, more novel thinkers were already at hand to elbow him out. William Archer once explained the difficulty connected with the British, American, and French reception of Ibsen by asserting that his plays seemed old-fashioned and commonplace, so rapid was his own development—and we presume the growth of those influenced by him—by the time these audiences were acquainted with him. Nora, certainly, did not impress American audiences as a "new" woman; a fair guess is that they misinterpreted her desertion of her husband and child as a purely capricious act of a woman of means. The elaborate sets used for *A Doll's House* put Nora in a class of women from whom Americans expected only "selfish" acts, and neutralized the effect of the play.

Only one American dramatist can be said to have been directly influenced by Ibsen, and this was James A. Herne, author of *Hearts of Oak* (1879), *Drifting Apart* (1888), *Margaret Fleming* (1891), *Shore Acres* (1892), *Sag Harbor* (1900), and other plays. Herne, whose real name appears to have been Ahearn, was born at Cohoes, N. Y., on February 1, 1839, but had his most important early theatrical experience in the West, as stage manager, first of Maguire's New Theatre in San Francisco in 1874, then of Baldwin's Theatre in 1876. At the Baldwin Theatre, he became associated with David Belasco, with whom he first collaborated on a play, an adaptation of Gaboriau's *Within an Inch of His Life,* in 1879. Before going to California, Herne had married in 1866 the actress Helen Western. After one season in her company the pair had separated by mutual agreement. Now Herne was attracted by a gifted young actress, Katharine Corcoran, whom he married in 1878. A. H. Quinn is of the opinion that the importance of this second marriage upon Herne's career can hardly be overestimated, since most of his plays were written with Miss Corcoran in mind as the leading woman. But it is also worth remembering that his separation from Helen Western provided an experience which probably taught him as much as he could learn from *A Doll's House.*

The collaboration with Belasco carried the Hernes eastward, but the purchase of Belasco's rights in the play *Hearts of Oak,* which was later very successful, made independent production possible.

After trying his hand at several plays, Herne produced *Margaret Fleming,* the best of all his plays and the only one certainly written under the influence of Ibsen. Philip Fleming, a small manufacturer, has an affair with a girl who proves to be the sister of his wife's maid. When the girl dies, Philip's infidelity is disclosed to his wife who unwittingly had gone to her on a mission of kindliness impelled by the maid. The shock of this discovery brings blindness to Margaret Fleming, who had been suffering from incipient glaucoma. Philip proves a coward, runs away and even attempts suicide, before returning to Margaret to beg forgiveness, which, of course, is freely granted him. The first two acts of the play, dealing realistically with Philip's business and domestic life, are well handled, and the characterization of Philip and Maria is convincing; but Margaret Fleming so conspicuously fails to measure up to Nora that the play falls off at just the point where she is meant to rise above her husband. Herne has made the mistake of sentimentalizing her when the theme, as well as justice to her sex, demanded that he endow her with a commanding intelligence. It may be, however, that Margaret Fleming and Nora Helmer represent altogether too well the difference between the American conception of the perfect wife and the Scandinavian ideal of the free woman in their day; Americans were pleased that Margaret forgave her husband, for the American tradition emphasized that as her duty.

The American tradition, however, was going into the discard very rapidly, and the change may explain why another Scandinavian dramatist, August Strindberg, had a much better reception here than Ibsen, and is far more important in the development of American thought. Between the Civil War and the end of the Gilded Age, that is, between 1865 and 1890, the number of divorces for a given unit of population exactly doubled, and by 1906 more than 72,000 decrees of separation were handed down annually—a figure twice as large as that reported in the same year from the rest of the Christian world. One need concentrate on no other figures to realize that, with tightening economic conditions forcing the limitation of families and with no thoroughly disseminated knowledge of the methods of contraception, friction in the marital relationship was widespread. To a people baffled by frustration and disharmony the teachings of Strindberg had at least a plausibility, and in the decade just before they turned to Freud, they gave to his analyses of feminine psychology an attentive ear.

Strindberg's personal life, despite its neurotic aspects, had some elements that the more harassed of his American auditors could understand and appreciate. The dramatist was born into an impoverished Stockholm family on January 22, 1849. His father, a steamship agent, had had three children before he was legally wed to their mother, a poor barmaid, two months prior to August's birth. In a few years, despite frequent funerals, the three rooms of the Strindberg home housed eleven persons. Among these the sensitive future poet and dramatist was buffeted about —"life, a terrible, depressing burden weighed down upon me every day." It was an experience that at once frazzled his nerves, making human proximity torturous to him, while it stirred deeper longings for a truly sympathetic companionship. He was fortunate in escaping the hard lot of his brothers and sisters when a Jewish physician, taking a fancy to him, turned patron and sent him to the University of Upsala. Declining to study medicine, Strindberg attempted to become an actor. We need not dwell upon his discouragement with minor rôles, his attempt at suicide, and his first ventures into the writing of historical dramas; more important is the fact that the king, personally impressed by *The Outlaw* which the critics derided, granted the young author a stipend to finish his university course and then gave him a position in the Royal Library. Thus the underling was brought with the highest approval into a society where, though still an underling, he could meet the bright creatures with whom he had peopled his dreams. While he mastered the Chinese language in order to pose as an authority on Oriental subjects and while he scribbled away on a satirical novel, to be published as *The Red Room,* he found time to have a grand affair—with the wife of Baron Wrangel. After her divorce in 1877, Strindberg was married to her. With Sigrid Wrangel he lived in a "happy, erotic state," by his own admission, for the first few years; then his jealousy led to quarrels, and the quarrels to infidelity. It is all painfully and shamelessly set forth, from his point of view, in *A Fool's Confession* in 1888. Strindberg and Sigrid were legally separated in 1891.

Though by then Strindberg was indelibly on record as a misogynist, the hunger for an understanding companion was not satisfied. Accordingly, he married again, this time a young Austrian writer, Frieda Uhl, whom he met in Germany. Their union lasted only a few years, and their separation was attended by great bitterness. Strindberg gave up writing and plunged into chemistry with some fantastic notion of proving the transmutability of the elements. Fond dream gave way to delusion, mystical states to insanity, and he fled to a private sanitarium in Sweden, kept by an old friend. In 1897, deeming himself of sound mind, he resumed his literary work, and within three years was once more engaged to be married. His last union, with the brilliant actress Harriet Bosse, was his most normal: the couple quietly separated in 1904. The remaining eight years of the author's life were passed in seclusion in Stockholm, where he died of cancer of the stomach on May 14, 1912. In death he needed no biographer, for everything he had written was autobiographical—the record of an unhappy, bigoted nature, blind and yet not blind, sensitized to catch the dark and elusive facts of human action, but less capable of receiving the light of good intention. No man has ever suffered more—nor left a longer account of his sufferings, over a hundred volumes in all. Yet the labelled autobiography—the three volumes of *The Bondwoman's Son* which describe his youth, *The Author, A Fool's Confession, Inferno,* and the poignant *Alone* of 1903—indicate the psychological instability of the author clearly enough to throw doubt upon his accuracy as an observer. *Inferno* reveals him as a pathological case, suffering from delusions both of persecution and grandeur. "To search for God and to find the Devil! that is what happened to me," he reports in this book; the reader may find plenty of evidence of the results of this quest, but none at all of its original purpose.

Yet this beset spirit and unstable genius did not want, the last three-quarters of his life, for a world audience. Thrice shipwrecked in marriage, he could still render an account of the relations of man and wife which the world, no matter how much it disapproved of him personally, must gravely ponder before it could proceed in its old brutal, nonchalant way. For here was more than the account of petty bickering or noisy brawls with which some authors chose to adorn their tales; here was the assertion that sex is a fatal magnet drawing together two venomous antagonists armed with secret knives—that in this duel the spiritually inferior, the woman, is the stronger because more realistic and unscrupulous. Held by varying degrees of conviction and horror, readers and playgoers, Americans as much as the rest, deliberated Strindberg's thesis long enough to have their own thoughts, their own constructions of life, affected by it, as we shall see.

Strindberg arrived at his conception of the "war of the sexes" by slow stages: it did not come to him as a full-blown idea, probably, during his first quarrel with Sigrid Wrangel. The fact that the author was wed always to what are euphemistically termed "superior women" may have had something to do with convincing him that the woman has every advantage in an encounter with the male, particularly the nineteenth century male with his chivalrous notions of womanhood (learnt from his mother, who is the first to betray him); but the conquests which Strindberg himself made of these superior women can just as certainly be cited as the source of his idea that the person of low birth, who hasn't the handicap of chivalrous associations, easily dominates women of the upper class—an idea he developed in *Miss Julie*. Strindberg formed certain ideas which were to germinate his mature philosophy before he had even met his Countess. In the early 'seventies, when he was working in the historical drama, he turned to Henry Thomas Buckle's *History of Civilization* for subject matter, but found there instead a scientific method used with materials which had hitherto been approached only romantically. Buckle's antiromanticism and Buckle's determinism profoundly affected him, and whetted his appetite for further reading in popular philosophy. The whole cast of his thought was given a darker color by his careful study of Eduard von Hartmann's *The Philosophy of the Unconscious*. The "Unconscious" is the Universal Soul, whose interests are opposed to ours, but for whom we live. It would be to our advantage not to live, but the "Unconscious" has planted in us an unreasoning desire to live and has filled the world with illusions to persuade us to do so. Particularly compelling to Strindberg, probably, were Hartmann's views of love and marriage. Not only is all happiness an illusion, but especially is the happiness which love offers "a chimera . . . and its pains greater than its pleasures. . . ." As for marriage, "there is, at most, but one disagreeable woman in the world; it is only a pity that every man gets her for himself." This pessimistic philosophy, with its attendant misogyny, won complete conviction with Strindberg, and with little modification remained his the rest of his life.

There were periods, however, when its expression was confined merely to smart turns of phrase. In the early, "happy, erotic" years of his first marriage, during which he did his only truly popular work, things like the fairy-play *Lucky Peter's Travels,* Strindberg was content with a kind of Chinese firecracker display of his philosophy. Yet the resentment aroused by the flippant irony of *The Red Room,* by the scandal of the Wrangel divorce, by the satirical tone of his work, even of *Lucky Peter's Travels,* was enough so that Strindberg and Sigrid decided to leave Stockholm for Paris and Switzerland in the early 'eighties. In 1884 he published the first fruit of his foreign residence, a collection of Naturalistic short stories called *Marriage.* The book, which was felt to outrage public morals in Sweden, was confiscated and its publisher arrested. Strindberg, induced to come to the latter's rescue by friends, rushed home and stood as defendant in the case. The jury acquitted him and the liberal youth of the land made him their hero. The leaders of the militant feminist movement, however, incensed at his Naturalistic and flippant portraits of women (and ignoring the fact that they were identical with his treatment of men), abused him in speech and print. This attack by the feminist group with whom he identified Ibsen (object formerly of his veneration), fully as much as his subsequent unhappy relations with his wife, led him ultimately to the position in regard to women for which he is best known.

Strindberg's rage at the feminists, at the bluestockings, at those who sought to purge marriage of its physical values and, ignoring obvious biological handicaps (as he felt), to place

women on an equal plane with men, vented itself in a new volume
of short stories, again called *Marriage* (1886) as if offered as a
corrective to his first book. The second volume of *Marriage* is
Strindberg's own, while the first might have come from the pen
of Guy de Maupassant; it cannot be said, however, that the
stories of the second volume are superior in quality to those of
the first—indeed, the objective Naturalism of the earlier studies
is on the whole more convincing, if less provocative. The key narrative in the 1886 volume is a tale called "A Doll's House." In
this story a naval captain is represented to have maintained for
his wife over six years the adoration of a lover while she has
played, childlike, at being his mistress. Their letters and their talk
are full of the twitterings that Ibsen had ridiculed in the talk of
Helmer and Nora in the first act of his play. Then, at the captain's suggestion, the wife invites into her home a companion who
is supposed to instruct the children, but who teaches their mother
instead. Ottilia even induces the wife to read Ibsen's *A Doll's
House,* thereby producing the latter's "emancipation." In vain
the captain dissects the drama for his wife; in vain he storms at
the bluestocking who has come between them:

"Ottilia! Ottilia! . . . What she wants is a taste of the handspike.
Send the witch to the lower deck and let the mess loose on her behind
closed hatches. One knows what is good for an old maid."

Things go very badly with the once ardent lovers, the captain and
his wife, until the latter's shrewd old mother gives the husband
some advice. She suggests a flirtation with Ottilia. The captain
proves very adroit at this, with the result that his wife banishes
Ottilia and harmony is restored in "a doll's house."

Strindberg's story is, by itself, an amusing and instructive tale.
His picture of Ottilia is not an impossible one: old maids have
derived a perverse satisfaction occasionally by revenging themselves upon the husband of a happy pair with whom they have
come in contact. As a portrait of a warped character whose motivation can be traced directly to a frustrated sex life it must be
among the early inventions of this sort in modern literature. Yet
one cannot acclaim Strindberg's satire as a good burlesque of

Ibsen's play. Mrs. Linde of the drama is not an Ottilia. Ibsen's
Helmer, furthermore, is such a self-infatuated ass that Nora is
justified in escaping him on purely emotional grounds. Strindberg's captain is obviously no Helmer. Finally, Strindberg has
grafted on to *A Doll's House* a weakness the play does not have:
Nora needs no assistance in arriving at her conclusion that she
must leave her husband. If the satire, however, is ineffective, it is
still important historically in Strindberg's development: it shows
how much the feminists infuriated him and carried him onwards
towards his conviction of the fiendishness of women in conjugal
relationships.

We need not consider all of the work in which Strindberg elab-
orated his view of the character of woman nor all in which he
built up his conception of the sex duel. Aside from *Marriage,* the
work of Strindberg which has been influential in America is confined definitely to five or six plays, and these are all that we need to
examine: *The Father* (1887), *Miss Julie* (1888), *The Creditors*
(1889), *The Stronger* (1890), *The Link* (1897), *The Dance
of Death* (1901), and *The Dream Play* (1902). *The Father*
pictures a cavalry captain, who has continued to live with his wife
for twenty years merely for the sake of his daughter, now goaded
to madness when he opposes his wife's wishes in regard to the
child's education. The play is extraordinarily effective, granted
that a character could be as diabolically possessed as the wife. On
the stage this wife is convincing as Svengali is convincing—a fascinating study of a sadist, yet few would be willing to generalize
about the whole sex from her, as Strindberg does.

Miss Julie (known only as a one-act play in America) is undeniably one of the best pieces of theatre of modern times; it is
a triumph of dramatic art to get an hour of breathless entertainment out of one setting and only three characters—two of them
servants. Who had accomplished this before Strindberg? The
play expounds one of his favorite ideas: that in the encounters of
aristocrat and plebeian, where the former is reduced to equality
by sentimentality, the latter always triumphs. Neurotic Countess
Julie (Strindberg, too, had had his Countess) dares to flirt with
the man-servant, John, and after being taken by him, can think
of no satisfactory way of escape (since there is the other servant

Christine to consider, who is John's mistress and will betray what she knows of this affair), until John at the end of the play puts a razor in her hand and directs her to the door. No work of Strindberg shows better than this how women (as he contends) survive in the sex duel only because the chivalric code protects them; once Julie has sacrificed this protection she has no will to oppose the brutal implicit command of her servant-master.

Again, in *Creditors,* Strindberg tries to demonstrate that woman, though inferior to man in intellect, is his superior in the inevitable struggle between them because she regards the code as a mere convenience and is completely lacking in moral sense. Tekla, the fantastic vampire who dominates this play, is the epitome of evil, a compound of all the horrendous traits that Strindberg imagined could ever occupy the tenement of woman. *The Stronger,* shortest of all Strindberg's dramas, is a monologue in a café during which the wife, with growing sureness as she senses her victory, asserts her superiority over the other woman, who does not get a chance to reply before her antagonist sweeps out and the curtain falls. This one-act play is a milestone in the evolution of the experimental drama and deserves full praise from the standpoint of the theatre, even if the meaning of the play wholly changes with different actresses in the rôles—so indefinite is the characterization. *The Link* sets the stage with a divorce court—a sensational case in which a local baron and his wife are to be separated is on the calendar. Even in the face of the dissolution of their legal bond the couple are bound together by their common anxiety to spare their child, for whose future they have already made arrangements. The clumsy conscientiousness of the young judge leads the woman to vilify her husband, and the baron to retort, so that before they can check themselves, they are wrangling in the open court—with the result that the judge takes from them their child and places him under a stupid guardian, offensive to both. Inferior as theatre to *Miss Julie* and *The Stronger, The Link* is much more convincing than either. Even the railing at Heaven, so apt to be melodramatic, coming at the end of a tragedy, seems consistent with the overwrought condition of the principals as the curtain falls on this play.

The Dance of Death—a tedious, two-part play covering long years of bickering and mutual loathing—gets its title from the fact that both husband and wife, unwilling to appeal to the divorce court in this instance, wait for the release of death which the husband's failing health seems to promise. Yet perhaps the supremely ironical passage in Strindberg is found at the end of *The Dance of Death*—when the wife, who has exulted over the fallen and dying man, admits he was good and noble, and with her hatred no longer to sustain her, feels her own dissolution near. It is the Unconscious, so it would appear, who is the true enemy of both. As soon as these puppets fall from the strings, new figures will be attached, and the dance will begin all over.

It is one of the extraordinary things in modern literature—a thing for which Freud has an explanation—that every writer who has been peculiarly absorbed by sex has also been much concerned about God. Strindberg is no exception to this generalization and his *Dream Play,* a fantasy governed by chance association in which even the characters split or multiply, blur or vanish, is his thesis in divinity. Brahma, the World Soul, has been prevailed upon by the World-Mother, Maya, to propagate himself —and as a result of this heavenly sin, the mating of Spirit with Matter, and of Idea with Sense, the world is born, filled with creatures who vainly aspire to free themselves from matter. Every joy is checked by pain. Strindberg, to be brief, has elevated woman into a force responsible for all the evil in the universe. This is a pretty myth, and as plausible as any, yet if it were absolutely true, not to be given human credence, since it frees the male sex altogether of any responsibility.

It would seem impossible to thrust the critical scalpel between the man and his work in judging Strindberg. Unfortunate in love and indubitably chiefly at fault in this, he judged all womanhood from the women whose lives he helped to warp; hypersensitive, he recorded more accurately than anyone else the vindictive responses of the woman to whom love was still a subtle whip: and the accuracy of his reporting is responsible for the great power of his plays. His tortured Baronesses, his Alices, and his Julias convince only the prejudiced that they are representative of their sex; their obvious sickness moves Strindberg's audiences to compassion, which lends force to his plays. As a dramatist he is to be condemned for the capriciousness of his action, which is plausible only with warped characters, and for the generalization implicit in the action. No man ever labored harder than he (Was he trying to convince himself?) to make the exception seem the rule. And few men, surely, have brought more art to the business.

Yet, in final justice to Strindberg, it should be pointed out that, in a limited way and through a distorted lens, he reflects social conditions in the Sweden of his day. It was in that country that, after the general increase in population typical of all Europe, the birth-rate fell earliest and most abruptly; it was that country which had the highest rate of illegitimacy of any European nation in Strindberg's day. One cannot assume from these two facts that marital conditions were the happiest in Sweden, or that Strindberg did too great violence to them. And was it not predictable that, when economic conditions put a check on the legal sexual freedom of the nineteenth century, some one should voice the wrath of the frustrated male? That this anger should first take the form of an unchivalrous vilification of woman would seem natural, too. The credence which Strindberg won would seem to indicate that he twanged a few responsive chords, and it is possible that his plays were an adequate release for many of their own unholy emotions. In his more violent attack upon the feudal conception of woman, Strindberg paradoxically did far more than Ibsen to destroy the romantic ideal of the sex—a piece of iconoclasm necessary, it would seem, if woman were ever to be treated as the perfect equal of man. In sum, for all his perversion, Strindberg was a liberator.

This correspondent of the "War" between the sexes was more fortunate in his introduction to Americans than was Ibsen. Though his first presentation here was not until 1912, and then in the little theatre, his ideas had already begun to permeate American creative work, largely through the influence of the novelist Robert Herrick. The Chicago author is not wholly a disciple of Strindberg; Ibsen and Tolstoi have likewise influenced him; and perhaps what is best about him is not a foreign heritage at all, but native liberalism. In technique, he is a follower of William Dean Howells. Herrick was born in Cambridge, Massachusetts, on April 28, 1868. He is the son of William A. Herrick, a Boston lawyer and writer on legal subjects, and Harriet Emery Herrick, through whom he is distantly related to Hawthorne. Like Henry Adams, Herrick did not care for Cambridge, and just as Adams preferred Quincy, so Herrick preferred Boxford, where he spent his summers. After his graduation from the Latin School, he attended Harvard College, where he was one of a set of brilliant young men—Norman Hapgood, William Vaughn Moody, Robert Morss Lovett, and George Carpenter. He was editor of the Harvard *Advocate* and of the newly-founded *Monthly*, which he nearly wrecked financially by publishing the first translation of Ibsen's *Lady from the Sea*. After taking his degree, Herrick taught English for three years at the Massachusetts Institute of Technology, and then, at twenty-six, he was invited to organize the English department of the new University of Chicago on the Harvard plan. He was soon relieved of many teaching and administrative duties, however, in order that he might devote more time to his writing. He had proved his abilities by having short stories published in the *Atlantic* and *Scribner's* before going to Chicago.

The *cursus* of Herrick's novels would strike the average fiction reader of today as hard, if not downright dull, reading. The reasons for this are quickly discoverable by opening any one book. Herrick has made no concessions to his readers—there are no colorful collocations of words, no epigrams, no attempt at fine writing, no memorable descriptions, no telltale marks or traits by which characters may be distinguished, no terrific emotional surges, no completely breath-taking events. Yet it is not incapacity that is responsible for this amazing lack of fictional amenities: it is deliberate choice. Herrick has chosen not to write down to his readers. He has a definite conviction, apparently, that concessions are no part of the game, that narrative writing should consist of talk, action, and characterization, that attention to writing *as writing* in fiction is, well, almost unethical. Within limits, of course, and as practiced by Howells who wrote beautifully while giving most attention to clarity, this theory is sound, but Herrick has applied the theory with some of the rigidity of a Puritan judge. A blind man writing between copper wires is not more confined than he is at times by his convictions. Detachment, aloofness, and modesty in statement are traits of the man himself (or in the portrait Harry Hansen has drawn of him), yet these traits, admirable in the person, are not the ones to make his fiction popular. Even the experienced reader, used to hard going, is apt to feel that, as a writer, Robert Herrick has too much schooled himself.

The Man Who Wins (1895), Herrick's first novel, has an ironic title, for Doctor Thornton is kept from devoting himself to research because of the frivolous demands of his wife and her family. Here is the familiar friction between the sexes of Strindberg's writing, made more plausible, however, by the fact that Herrick does not represent the wife as diabolically motivated, but rather, as petty, selfish, and thoughtless. She cannot really appreciate her husband's endeavors, her passion is for society, a passion which Herrick, in a review of Mrs. Wharton's writing, was to describe as "the pathological absorption of American women." In *The Gospel of Freedom* (1898) Herrick aligns himself with Strindberg as a critic of the Ibsen position of complete and purposeless independence for women. Freedom, in his view, does not mean irresponsibility, and he has no sympathy for the selfish woman who, with means and education, can find nothing in European travel or in an American marriage to absorb her. *The Web of Life* (1900), which follows the career and amorous entanglement of another physician, Doctor Sommers, is less important. *The Real World* (1901, originally entitled *Jock o' Dreams*), is a study of one man's effort to escape the dream world that most men create for themselves (compare Farrell) and to find a genuine world in which he can function with satisfaction to himself. Jack Pemberton's childhood was sufficient cause for him to ensconce himself in a dream world,—his family was poor and his parents were constantly bickering. He escapes his home as soon as he can, and while engaged as a clerk in a summer hotel, makes the acquaintance of a pretty materialist, Elsie Mason, who arouses his ambitions for worldly success. Jack Pemberton's summer hotel experience, and his later attendance at Harvard College, remind us of Howells' *The Landlord of Lion's Head*, but it is Elsie Mason who is most like Jeff Durkin and not

Pemberton, for it is she whose utterly frivolous character is finally revealed in a mercenary marriage. Pemberton emerges a finer person from this affair and from his love for Isabelle Mather, whose name suggests her more conservative character. The "real world" is the world of ethical principle and unselfishness.

The Common Lot (1904) is the best of all Herrick's novels, a quaint book which insists on the value of integrity and the cleansing power of the admission of guilt. Jackson Hart, the "favorite" nephew of the millionaire Powers Jackson, who has given him an education at Cornell and a training in architecture at the Beaux Arts in Paris, is left at the old man's death with only ten thousand dollars out of three millions and a good deal of resentment. The bulk of the estate goes to found a workingman's industrial school in Chicago. Hart would have protested the will had he not desired to appear well in the eyes of Helen Spellman, a worshipper of his uncle and the recipient of a small legacy from him. With his ten thousand dollars and a private commission to draw plans for a wealthy widow's home—a commission he should hardly have accepted while still employed by another architect,—Hart decides to set up for himself. Yet his nature is such that he cannot make the sacrifices nor undergo the penury necessary to honest success. Shortly married to Helen Spellman, whose tastes are altogether different from his, he lives beyond his means, accepting jobs that are no challenge to his ability and conniving with contractors to defraud his customers. His most unfortunate connection is with a builder named Graves, for whom he first designs apartment houses in a manner to permit the latter to defeat the building code. When, finally, the trustees of Powers Jackson's estate are ready to build the school, Hart, through the use of undue influence, secures a contract to draw the plans and supervise the building. Before the award of the contract he has borrowed money from Graves to recoup stock market losses, and as a result is forced to make the specifications such that Graves is the successful bidder for the actual construction. In order that Hart will consent to the use of inferior materials, Graves makes him treasurer in a dummy corporation to build an apartment hotel—an arrangement which promises to put seventy thousand dollars in Hart's pocket. The architect's old resentment at his uncle's will makes him eager to get "his slice" of the old man's fortune in this roundabout way. Unfortunately for their schemes one of the trustees of the school fund is a scrupulously honest person, who hires an engineer to check on the work with the consequence that the fraud is exposed.

It is at this point that Helen, long unhappy at her husband's course, has revealed to her accidentally the suspicions of the trustees, and when she interrogates her husband and he refuses to answer her categorically, realizes that her fears are well grounded. His refusal to rectify wrongs committed or even acknowledge them forces her to leave him and go with their children to a Vermont farm. The action here is grounded in Ibsen, but Helen's reasons for separating from her husband are clearer than those of Nora. After his wife's departure, Hart drinks more than he should and eventually drifts around for consolation to Mrs. Phillips, the pretty widow who gave him his first contract. He has agreed with her that a European trip would do him good, when the "fireproof" Graveland hotel burns with a loss of life to seventeen persons. This disaster brings Hart to his senses. He resolves, to the terror of Graves and city building inspectors, to tell what he knows and to acknowledge his own guilt to the Grand Jury. Before doing this, however, he goes to his wife and confesses the error of his ways. Helen and the children return with him to Chicago to face the disgrace. As a result of his testimony his career as an independent architect is ruined and he faces the prospect of imprisonment for manslaughter. Political influence, no part of his conniving, removes this latter danger, and Hart, with clear conscience and the complete love of his wife, resumes work as an employee in the draughting office of the architect who first employed him, a large-hearted man willing to give him a chance to redeem himself.

The substance of *The Common Lot* is excellent, though one could desire that the character of Jackson Hart were a bit more fully developed at the outset, so that his conversion in the end would seem completely plausible. Just what qualities make him first successful with Helen Spellman is not clear, though it is apparent that these are the ones which make his transformation possible in the denouement. Helen, herself, is fairly well drawn. Herrick, in portraying her, made use of the hesitancy of the women of the day to inquire into their husband's business affairs to support his characterization, but one wishes that we understood better her relations with her husband. Mrs. Phillips, who pities Hart for his "unimaginative" wife, is the selfish woman of Herrick's earlier novels, a character he derived from Strindberg. ". . . She considered all men base,—emotionally treacherous and false-hearted, and would take her amusement wherever she could get it." To her daughter, Venetia, is attached an interest that has nothing to do with the novel, in which she is a minor character. Venetia is a portrait of a girl who is seeking complete freedom, and, to the consternation of the "veranda tabbies," does not hesitate to break the conventions of the day. She smokes, drinks, lets men kiss her, and visits dubious parts of Chicago unchaperoned late at night with intoxicated young men as her guardians. And this in 1904! The general loosening of American morals and the changing of conventions in regard to the conduct of women are ascribed to the First World War, but here in this portrait is evidence of earlier beginnings for these changes.

Herrick's next novel, *The Memoirs of an American Citizen*, deserved more attention than it got when it was issued in 1905. It is a study of Van Harrington, meant to be typical of the successful figures of the Gilded Age. Van Harrington came up to Chicago as a young man, eager and honest, but found, as did so many of his associates, that there was nothing to live for in Chicago in that day but Success. Van Harrington made his "pile" in the packing business, with which he first became associated as a teamster in the 'seventies. The crowning glory of his life was his election as senator of the State of Illinois. Van Harrington tells his own story, and as he narrates with pride his deals and schemes, his coups and his frauds, one is struck (as Herrick intends) by the total unmorality, the almost innocence, of the opportunist. Van Harrington is not only a preeminent citizen of the Gilded Age—he is also a *typical* citizen, as the title of Herrick's book suggests. Yet, because he has seen so much of life flow by, Van Harrington, incapable of thought before action, in reflection realizes his earlier deeds were not always above reproach. An unforgettable illustration of this is his recollection of the Haymarket bomb trial in which he served as a juror and his comment on that judicial massacre, of which he had once been proud:

> ". . . The only connection the lawyers could establish between those eight men and the mischief of that night was a lot of loose talk. His Honor made the law—afterward he boasted of it—as he went along. He showed us what sedition was, and that was all we needed to know. Then we could administer the lesson. Now that eighteen years have passed that looks to me like mighty dangerous law. Then I was quick enough to accept it.
>
> ". . . The pity of it all was—that our one motive was hate."

After this excursion into historical morals, Herrick returned to the contemporary scene, and in *Together* (1908) wrote a satirical study of marriage. It is singular that this novel should have enjoyed a good sale, for it is one of the most difficult of Herrick's books to read. Probably its great pertinence at the time had much to do with its success. Matrimony, in this book, "becomes an interplay of wills, a jockeying for advantages and a game of spurring the husband on to greater efforts at money-making to meet the extravagant demands of the society in which he lives." Isabelle Prince, whose marriage to rising John Lane opens the book, unconsciously sets the pace for all her friends, whose wedded lives are singularly unhappy. Lane's absorption in business matches his wife's extravagance, but after he is made the scapegoat in court for the railroad of which he is vice-president, he and his wife resolve to begin a new partnership on a different footing. But Isabelle and her husband are very much the exception in their discovery of the need for different values in marriage than the times extol, the author insists. "From the prairie village to the city tenement, the American woman sees in marriage the fulfillment of her heart's desire,—to be a Queen, to rule and not work. Thus for emancipated Woman."

Together is a poor novel, because it is more polemic than fiction, and a poor polemic because it passionately overstates the case. Women in America, in 1908, are free "as never women were before." Yet—and we are reminded of Theodore Roosevelt's recent attacks upon race suicide—yet "they have lost their prime function: they will not or they cannot get children." Herrick demands of this free woman (melodramatically) what she has done with the souls of men given into her keeping.

> ... The answer roars up from the city streets,—the most material age and the most material men and the least lovely civilization on God's earth. No longer the fighting companion at man's side, but reaching out for yourselves, after your own desires, you have become the slave of the Brute as you were before, and a neurotic slave. For when Woman is no longer comrade of man in the struggle, she is either Nothing or a—but blot the word!

Blot the whole paragraph, or the chapter rather, for this writing is almost as absurd as Strindberg at his worst. No one has ever given into the keeping of woman the souls of men, and that Herrick should harbor such an idea suggests that somewhere in his nature is a fondness for the typically American notion that woman is a pure fountain to which grubby man returns every now and then to get cleansed. It makes her a part of the best sanitary system in the world! Yet *Together,* despite all its nonsense, is a valuable document in the history of the confusion which followed the changes in the sexual habits of the nation. Ideas current in this book were current in America at the time. Some of them, unfortunately, live on.

Herrick's later books are of less consequence to us than these on which we have centered attention. This does not mean necessarily that they have less value as fiction, though *The Master of the Inn* (1908) is a piece of sentimentalism with a deliberately popular appeal. *A Life for a Life* (1910) is a good story of a clash between a banker and a power trust, marred, however, by a sloppy prologue and epilogue, nor was it quite necessary, on the score of reality, for the banker to love the daughter of the power magnate. *The Healer* (1911), very much like *The Man Who Wins* and *The Web of Life,* is the story of another physician, Doctor Holden, whose professional purposes are thwarted by the social desires of his wife. *One Woman's Life*

(1913), a study of a capricious, selfish, destructive, yet winsome girl, Milly Ridge, is also in line with Herrick's earlier work, but has profited by notes taken on the feminine personality—taken by Mrs. Wharton. *Clark's Field* (1914) is second only to *The Common Lot* among Herrick's fiction. It tells with feeling the story of Adelle Clark, orphan, whose whole destiny is delivered up to the fortune in real estate she fortuitously inherits. Adelle's arrival at the dignity of complete womanhood after all her misadventures is a satisfying and logical outcome to the story. It is Herrick's best character study. Incidentally, there is some excellent satire of private schools in the book, as well as revelatory material about the sex life of the prisoners of such institutions. When, after the First World War, which absorbed his energies as a propagandist, Herrick again turned to writing fiction, he did a very similar thing to *Clark's Field* in *Homely Lilla* (1923), which narrates how Lilla made her own way successfully after others sought to control her destiny. Lilla's mother is the first study of a sexually repressed woman in Herrick's work, the first indication of the effect of the new psychology upon him.

Waste (1924) is the only pessimistic novel that Herrick has written, though the theme is that of *Together*. A neurotic, pleasure-seeking woman wastes the love of an engineer, Jarvis Thornton, whose professional experience leads him to see the great wastage of national resources and to connect the two psychologically. No one who considers the general effect of the University of Chicago upon American intellectual life can regret the thinly veiled satirical history of that institution which Herrick wrote in *Chimes* (1926), a book which also reveals the moral abandon of the youth of the day. The most astonishing of Herrick's books is *The End of Desire* (1932), for it is an attack upon the obsession of contemporary thought with sex— as if that had not been one of the major interests of his own work and as if it were not in the novel itself, which represents the cooling passions of two physicians, Arnold Redfield and Serena Massey, both nearing fifty. A none-too-happy Utopian romance, called *Sometime* (1933), allows Herrick freedom to express some of his views on economics and eugenics. In a some-

what nebulous Socialist state, the government controls the production of children as well as other economic goods. This is for
those who like it. The weakness of his later novels should not
blind us to the fact that Herrick, historically, is a very important
person. Through him the influence of Strindberg seeped out to
other creative writers, particularly to the Chicago school. The
themes of marital unhappiness, of the dominant woman, and of
the clash of the sexes in the later Dreiser, Ben Hecht, Anderson, and even in the *Spoon River Anthology* (note "Molly Mc-
Gee," "Daisy Fraser," etc.) derive probably from Herrick's
early works.

Informative as are the novels of Robert Herrick in regard
to the relations between the sexes in our country before the First
World War, there is one dark area to which he alludes only
casually. That is the growth in the early twentieth century of
commercial prostitution, which for the first time was organized on
a national and international scale. The general ignorance of the
American public is attested to by the fact that we sent no representative to the international white-slave-traffic congresses of
1899 and 1904. The preliminary call for the second congress in
1902, to be held in Paris, touched upon the importation of girls
to the United States for immoral purposes and aroused some
public opinion in this country. A committee of fifteen, with W.
H. Baldwin as Chairman and Professor Seligman as Secretary,
investigated conditions in New York City with the very able
aid of George J. Kneeland, and published a stirring report, *The
Social Evil,* at the end of 1902. It is interesting to note that this
committee did not put legislation first, but advocated changing
the economic situation which led to prostitution—the prevention
of overcrowding in tenement houses and the improvement of
"the material conditions of the wage-earning class, and especially of young wage-earning women." This may account for the
fact that the report led to no legislation.

President Taft proclaimed the White Slave Treaty of the
unattended convention of 1904, four years later, but as we had
no federal police or means to enforce his proclamation, this had
merely the effect of stimulating interest. Reformers finally succeeded in securing the passage of the Mann Act against inter-

state traffic in girls in 1910, and between 1911 and 1915 practically every state enacted laws against commercial vice. Of great importance to the Middle West in this campaign was the publication of the 399-page report of the Vice Commission of Chicago, entitled *The Social Evil in Chicago,* with its picture of the plight of farm girls in the lake metropolis. George J. Kneeland was again investigator for this commission. It was one of the triumphs of Comstockery that this report, published by the city, was forbidden the U. S. mails. Identical facts, however, received the widest circulation in articles which Miss Jane Addams published in 1911 and 1912 in *McClure's Magazine* and later gathered in her spirited book, *A New Conscience and an Ancient Evil.* Other informative work developing out of this crusade and written largely by crusaders includes George J. Kneeland's *Commercialized Prostitution in New York City* (1913), Maude E. Miner's *Slavery of Prostitution* (1916), and H. B. Woolston's two-volume work, *Prostitution in the United States* (1921).

While the reminiscences of Theodore Dreiser, Floyd Dell, and others shed light upon the extent of prewar vice, the best study of the life of the prostitute is David Graham Phillips' *Susan Lenox: Her Fall and Rise,* a novel completed in July, 1908, but not published until 1915, when it appeared serially and aroused much indignation. Sumner and the Society for the Suppression of Vice secured the withdrawal of the novel when it was issued as a book in 1917, but permitted its re-issue when certain objectionable passages (as they thought) were deleted. Phillips, whose short life was filled with turmoil, was spared the tumult his best book aroused. A crazed violinist, Fitzhugh Coyle Goldsborough, who, in 1911, fancying that Phillips had used his sister for a model in one of his many society-indicting books, fired six shots at close range into the novelist's chest, thereby stopping a heart which Robert Chambers has described as that of a paladin. Phillips, if a paladin, was paladin of the press, for he was from first to last a reporter, rarely transcending the limitations of the able journalist, and it is as a more or less faithful reporter he is to be prized.

Phillips was born in Marshall, Indiana, 1867, attended Princeton University where his friendship with Albert J. Beveridge gave his life direction, and entered journalism in Cincinnati. At twenty he left the Halstead papers for New York, where he secured a position on Dana's *Sun,* to be graduated three years later to the *World,* where he became one of Pulitzer's favorites and even enjoyed the doubtful privilege of travelling with his chief in Europe. Phillips used Joseph Pulitzer, however, for his first muck-rake novel, *The Great God Success,* a study of journalism, published in 1901. Ten years later, when, at forty-four, the murderer's fusillade put an end to his labors, Phillips could claim the authorship of twenty-six books, most of which were more than 100,000 words in length. These books flay political rottenness, the fraudulent manipulation of insurance companies (in the time of the Hughes prosecutions), the dominance of Wall Street in American life, and, joining forces with Herrick's novels, satirize the new woman as parasitic and vicious. The best of them are *The Reign of Gilt* (1905), *The Palm Tree* (1905), *Light-Fingered Gentry* (1907), *The Second Generation* (1907), *Old Wives for New* (1908), and *The Husband's Story* (1910). Phillips' courage won him many admirers who were extravagant in their praise of his work: as late as 1927 Frank Harris could write an essay entitled "David Graham Phillips, the Greatest American Novelist," and in all seriousness could declare, "I would rather have written *The Hungry Heart* and *Light-Fingered Gentry* than *Anna Karenina.*"

Despite the fact that interest still endures in some of these books, David Graham Phillips can hardly be taken seriously as a creative writer. His characters are formularized and unconvincing (even when based on real persons), his descriptions are news-descriptions, and his reflections are sophomoric. Discard all for which the great novelist is admired and there remains of Phillips' writing an unworked body of fact—fact fused with fire so that a lava-like deposit is left, containing petrified remains of the decade in which the journalist was most prolific. These remains belong to socio-political and economic history, rather than to literature.

Quite as lively as his fiction, but possibly less accurate as reporting, is the series of articles written for the *Cosmopolitan* magazine, attacking Senators Depew, Aldrich, Knox, Foraker, and Platt for their connections with Big Business, called "The Treason of the Senate." It was this series which led the "pirouetting" Roosevelt to turn upon the busy young fact-finders of *McClure's, Everybody's, Munsey's, Cosmopolitan, Collier's,* and the *American* and to fasten upon them the term "muck-raker," borrowed from the wretched figure of Bunyan's *Pilgrim's Progress* who was so busy raking in the muck for straws he had no notion of the glories of the heavens above him.

Roosevelt's epithet supplied a certain generative force in the creation of Phillips' best book, *Susan Lenox,* for its pattern is vaguely that of *Pilgrim's Progress,* to which the novelist several times refers. Susan's career, like Christian's, compasses most of the events which could conceivably come to a person of her circumstances; indeed, it should be regarded as a *progress* through these events. Susan is a child born out of wedlock; therefore expected "to go wrong" by her aunt who takes her into her home and conceals from her the facts of her origin. The girl is apparently caught in that wrong when she falls in love with a young man from Yale and meets him without prearrangement in a graveyard. Susan is so badly used that she runs away to Cincinnati, which act is taken as final evidence of guilt, with the result that, when she is traced, she is given in marriage to a coarse young farmer to save her name. The horror of a night with him weighs upon her mind for the remainder of our acquaintance with her. Again, she flees and, befriended first by a young newspaper man and later by a showboat proprietor, once more reaches Cincinnati.

When this second friend falls desperately ill and all their money is exhausted, Susan, after trying in vain to find work to cover his hospital expenses, sells herself for the first time. After his death, without extraordinary expenses, she tries to make a living in a box-manufactory and in good times barely makes a go of it by clerking in a bakery in the evening. When hard times come and the bakery is burned, Susan is forced back into prostitution. Lucky with some wealthy boys from the University of Michigan, she attempts to repay Roderick Spenser, the young newspaperman who had earlier aided her. This leads to her becoming his mistress and going to New York with him; Spenser's jealousy drives her from him and she secures a position as a cloak model. A huge order from a Chicago buyer for her firm hinges upon her favors to the buyer after her day's work is done. Susan aids her house but is so nauseated by the experience as to quit her job. All that is left are the sweat shops where she can earn less than five dollars a week, but to these and to tenement life (which Phillips regards with the investigators as one of the commonest sources of prostitution) she turns.

Half starved, ill-clad, beaten, she resorts to street walking when she can stand no more. She is lured into the clutches of a young gangster, Freddie Palmer, who makes his living from girls by establishing them in rooming houses under his control. Though he takes a personal fancy to her, Susan is unable to give up drink as he orders and he threatens to break her of the habit by having her arrested. To her mortification this occurs once, but without effect, and the gangster fixes on a longer term. The fear of this leads her to escape from the Tenderloin district to the lower East Side. Here, however, she is drugged by a "cadet" and put in charge of a "madame" in a house. She escapes by a ruse, reestablishes herself in a cheap hotel, but is sinking down again when her discovery of the drunken Spenser in a barroom gives her a new motive for recovery.

In the kaleidoscopic action of the last pages of the novel Susan Lenox manages to set Spenser on his feet as a playwright, studies acting under the personal direction of Robert Brent the great dramatist, and goes abroad on a "salary" with Freddie Palmer, now a successful "boss" with social ambitions. In Paris, again encountering Brent, she realizes that she loves him; when her actions betray this to Palmer, he has Brent murdered but he cannot hold Susan who, as Brent's heir under his will, is at last free to realize her ambition to become a great actress, and at last "hard" enough to encounter life without losing.

Many things about *Susan Lenox* are preposterous: that the heroine should keep a certain purity of character through all her adventures challenges the credulity of the reader no less than the fact that her experience brings her into no contact with the social diseases. It is difficult to follow Mr. Phillips in his con-

tention that her career has been ennobling and some descent
into the depths was necessary if she were ever to reach the
heights. We cannot believe that even Continental tailors could
design clothes that would bring out "all the *refinement* of feature
and coloring" of Freddie Palmer, the tenement-graduate
gangster, or that Susan should feel that this thug who had lived
off stranded girls was "a big man and a big man couldn't be
possibly a bad man."

Phillips, after the Hardy-set fashion of his day, is also too
fond of the "ironies" to be convincing. It is a satisfying "irony"
that the baby Susan had to be saved for her career as a prostitute through the great resourcefulness of the doctor who
attended at her birth and her mother's death; yet when these
"ironies" multiply—as, for example, when Susan sells herself
for the first time to save her friend Burlingham only to discover,
when she goes to the hospital, that he was already dead, or
when she learns from Gideon that he would have placed his
order with the cloak and suit firm whether she had given herself
to him or not—we are irritated. Admit weak characterization
and a badly manipulated plot, admit bad writing (is "nervifies"
worse than calling the Parisian cafés "the official temples of
Venus"?), enough remains in *Susan Lenox* to make it an important sociological document. Phillips has canvassed most of
the possible employments for homeless young women in his book,
and canvassed them thoroughly. Nowhere else is there a better
picture of what these young women had to endure than here.
To be sure, this is a reporter's triumph, but it is fairly won and
should be fairly recognized. The detail of *Susan Lenox* is more
moving than the report of the committee of fifteen on *The Social
Evil* in New York; the novel is the better report.

Susan Lenox was seventeen when she began her career; the
Yale youth whose dishonorable intentions started her along her
way was scarcely twenty—and the pair are meant to be symbolical of the way in which the double standard of morality
of the turn of the century and the "wild oat" theory were involving "mere children" (only in America are youths of their ages
looked upon as adolescents) in moral difficulties. Had not the
ignorance of parents been abysmal in regard to youth, remedies

would earlier have been applied to the evils. Although Charles Darwin in an article contributed to *Mind* in 1877, the "Biographical Sketch of an Infant," began what must be regarded as the first objective, detailed, and careful study of child behavior, the first psychologist to venture into this important field was the German, W. Preyer, friend of Wundt, whose *Mind of the Child* (*Die Seele des Kindes,* 1881) was for fifteen years the only authoritative book in the subject—yet a book literally unknown in America. In 1891, G. Stanley Hall, who had been a student at Wundt's laboratory in Leipzig, founded the *Pedagogical Seminary,* a journal with a very limited circulation devoted to child psychology. Three years later he published his first important psychological study, with the not-very-attractive title *The Contents of Children's Minds on Entering School* (1894). Meanwhile, certain progress had been made in England. Sully had established the British Association for Child Study in 1893, and in 1895 he printed his influential *Studies of Childhood.* In 1896 the first Psychological Clinic for maladjusted children was opened in Philadelphia by Witmer, who was in charge of the psychological laboratory at the University of Pennsylvania. Though this event aroused no great interest at the time, J. C. Flugel was to write of it in 1934, "The foundation of Witmer's original clinic nearly forty years ago was, however, a step indicating remarkable insight and courage and marks an epoch in the history of applied psychology." The event which meant for Americans a new era in their attitude towards youth was the publication, in 1904, of G. Stanley Hall's *Adolescence,* though immediate results were impossible from it since the general public was not ready for it and college students who were assigned it had to mature to appreciate it.

Granville Stanley Hall was born in Ashfield, Massachusetts, on February 1, 1844, a farm boy who attended the district school, the local academies, and finally was graduated from Williams College, in 1867, with the conviction that he belonged in the ministry. With this in view he entered Union Theological Seminary in New York City, undertaking at the same time to support himself by teaching in a private school for girls. In the evening he was employed as a sort of holy "cadet" by the City

Missionary Society to invite street walkers to attend the midnight mission. Discovering that he was unsuited to the ministry, he appealed to his friend Henry Ward Beecher, who found funds to send him to Bonn and Berlin for two years. When he returned to America, he could not secure the teaching appointment he desired; hence he decided to finish his theological course. Whether or not administrators considered this the right salt for German philosophy is not clear, but at any rate, Hall was appointed to the teaching staff of Antioch College in the fall of 1872. While in Yellow Springs, he read the first volume of Wundt's *Physiological Psychology* (*Grundzüge der physiologischen Psychologie,* 1873) and then and there resolved to return to Europe to work under this great pioneer. It was not until 1878, however, that he accomplished this; meanwhile he had moved on to Harvard, having secured an instructorship there, and had studied under William James, taking his doctorate in the year of his second excursion to Europe.

In his *Life and Confessions of a Psychologist* (1924) Hall admits how little taste he had for America on his return, how much it depressed him: ". . . the narrow, inflexible orthodoxy, the Puritan eviction of the joy that comes from amusements, from life, the provincialism of our interests, our prejudice against continental ways of living and thinking, the crudeness of our school system, the elementary character of education imparted in our higher institutions—all these seemed to me depressing, almost exasperating. I fairly loathed and hated so much that I saw about me that I now realize more clearly than ever how possible it would have been for me to have drifted into some, perhaps almost any, camp of radicals and to have come into such open rupture with the scheme of things as they were that I should have been stigmatized as dangerous, at least for any academic career, where the motto was Safety First." Hall was saved from this descent by a trial lectureship appointment at the new Johns Hopkins University in 1881, which became a full professorship in Psychology the following year. Here he established the first American laboratory in psychology in 1882; here he trained such important people as John Dewey, J. McKeen Cattell, Joseph

Jastrow and James Hyslop. In 1888 he was persuaded to resign his professorship to become the first president of the proposed Clark University in Worcester, Mass. In its founder, Jonas Gilman Clark, millionaire wagonmaker and mining machinery manufacturer, Doctor Hall encountered a man who was to exhaust his patience, thwart his educational aims, and waste his valuable energy for the next twelve years. Despite his trials, Hall found time for the development of his studies, for editorial work, and for the foundation of the American Psychological Association, in 1892, of which he was the first president. Clark's death, despite the litigation over his will, released the tired university president from the rôle of scapegoat and he was able to turn to the writing of books he had long contemplated. In 1904 the two-volume study of *Adolescence* was brought to completion; this was abridged in 1906 as *Youth, Its Education, Regimen, and Hygiene*. In turn these were followed by *Aspects of Child Life and Education* (1907), *Educational Problems*, 2 vols. (1911), *Jesus, the Christ, in the Light of Psychology*, 2 vols. (1917), *Morale* (1920), *Recreations of a Psychologist* (1920), and *Senescence: The Last Half of Life* (1922).

Adolescence, despite the fact that it is a "scientific" book written more than thirty years ago, still contains more of truth than of error. This is because, in the first place, despite its provocative presentation of ideas, it is a fairly conservative book— a fact on which scientific authors desiring immortality through the word may well ruminate. This is not to say, however, that the times in which *Adolescence* appeared so regarded it, but we must remember those were the days when any matter-of-fact statement about sex instantly stilled conversation. An author, however, who could whole-heartedly commend the study of Plato for the great philosopher's portraits of youth and enthusiastically expatiate on the Platonic dialogues for their pedagogical method and their "noble love of adolescent boys" was hardly a dangerous radical. Indeed, the chapter on "Adolescence in Literature, Biography, and History" is one of the most stimulating excursions into literary criticism of the first decade of the twentieth century. The fact that American schools of "Education" have not been able to do more with Hall's suggestion that "ephebic literature" is a real province for study is a greater stricture on them than any that can occur to one off-hand.

Adolescence presents, not like the books of John B. Watson, wholly the results of the laboratory research of Hall and his students, but presents that research in its proper relation to that of other workers in the whole field, qualified and amended. Though Hall considered the writings of Freud "genetic and vital" and although it was he who invited Freud to America in 1909 to lecture at Clark University, his scientific caution is shown in the fact that Freud is cited only three times in *Adolescence*. This is in line with Hall's later refusal to accept any of the psychological "intelligence" tests as very valuable for determining mental capacity. The work is an orderly presentation of what workers in laboratories all over the world had discovered in regard to the physical and organic growth of boys and girls, the normal expression of these changes in action, the abuses and ills peculiar to juvenile development, the sensible adaptation of knowledge and custom to the physiology and psychology of youth, and the relation of adolescents to society as a whole. It may be said that these topics were as thoroughly canvassed as was in any way possible in 1904, and that so far as Hall's statements are in need of modification today, it is on the score that improved devices and techniques have made measurements more accurate, but that his conclusions are in the main not materially affected. One broad generalization is more open to challenge than the others: that is his conclusion that in play the child passes through a series of phases or epochs corresponding to the cultural phases of the race, a hunting period, a building period, and so on. Yet thus far the only rival hypotheses about play are those of Herbert Spencer, who makes it merely a manifestation of surplus energy, and of Karl Groos, who looks upon play as Nature's preparation of the child for its future activities. In the present state of our knowledge Hall's culture-epoch theory seems to be quite as good as these, though one should hesitate to subscribe to any one of the three. James Mark Baldwin in an earlier book, *Mental Development in the Child and the Race* (1895), had likewise sought for parallel phases in the development of the individual and of the race. Probably the idea has more poetic worth than scientific validity.

Hall sensed a weakening of moral fibre in America that filled him at times with deep concern. With more vision than anyone else he prophesied the moral chaos into which America was headed in 1904. In his Preface to *Adolescence,* he predicts what has euphemistically been called "the revolt of modern youth" and lists the forces which even then (as he felt) were at work to produce this unwelcomed result:

Never has youth been exposed to such dangers of both perversion and arrest as in our land and day. Increasing urban life with its temptations, prematurities, sedentary occupations, and passive stimuli just when an active, objective life is most needed, early emancipation and a lessening sense for both duty and discipline, the haste to know all and do all befitting man's estate before its prime, the mad rush for sudden wealth and the reckless fashions set by its gilded youth—all these lack some of the regulations they still have in older lands with more conservative traditions. In a very pregnant psychological sense ours is an unhistoric land. Our very Constitution had a Minerva birth, and was not the slow growth of precedent. Our literature, customs, fashions, institutions, and legislation were inherited or copied, and our religion was not a gradual indigenous growth, but both its spirit and forms were imported ready made from Holland, Rome, England, and Palestine. To this extent we are a fiat nation, and in a very significant sense we have had neither childhood nor youth, but have lost touch with these stages of life because we lack a normal development history.

We know now how right this prophecy of moral confusion was; but when G. Stanley Hall viewed the developing situation, it was merely an emotional chaos: it had no ideology; it was completely nihilistic. Ideas were supplied to the younger generation of experimenters and rebels, contrary to general opinion, by their elders. Of the ideologists influential in America the most important, of course, was Sigmund Freud, whose visit in 1909 literally caused an earthquake in public opinion. Mark Sullivan in *Our Times* records that after 1910 the newspapers were packed with references to Freud's doctrines and that in the next decade more than two hundred books were written on Freudianism. The reaction of the mature American was horror; consequently the immature generation in revolt against its elders took up the banner of Freud. He became their "philosopher," for, as Thomas Mann insists, Freud is more important as a thinker than as a scientist, and certainly this is true so far as his influence in America is concerned.

Viewed critically, Freud has aspects as an ideologist which suggest the love-lorn German sentimentalist-poet of the early nineteenth century. In him not only Goethe and Schiller live again, but also Herder, Tieck, and Uhland. Love holds all captive, that Erl-King's daughter; in chains she leads them through her realms; but she is invisible, and though her captives, they sigh for her, and defy the gods, who stand for the proprieties. It was in a feudal Vienna where the German Romantics were still cultivated and Goethe and Schiller were still the popular dramatists in the Burgtheater that Sigmund Freud (born in Freiburg, May 6, 1856) grew to manhood, and here that fame came to him after he was forty years of age. Like many of the important innovators of modern times (Marx, Bergson, Einstein), Freud was a Jew. The amazing range of literary allusion in his work is accounted for by the fact that, sensitive to rebuffs as a child, he early sought solace in books. According to his own confession, Freud turned to science, when he had to make a choice of a profession, through the influence of a *Fragment upon Nature* penned by Goethe when the latter was thirty-three. The *Fragment* is a transcendental dithyramb in which the seer of Weimar proclaimed that Nature's "crown is Love. Through Love alone does one draw near to her. She creates gulfs between all things and everything will swallow itself up. She has set everything apart in order to draw all together. With a draft or two from Love's cup she compensates for a life of toil and trouble. . . ."

Of course, this passage is not the germ from which grew the teachings of psychoanalysis, but there is much like it in Goethe; and Freud's lasting absorption in the German poet (not only does he admit to dreaming of riding and talking with Goethe, but also he has shown his great admiration for the poet by solemnly declaring, after he was awarded the Goethe prize for 1930, "This was the climax of my life as a citizen.") explains better than anything else the peculiar limitations of his "science" and his "philosophy." In Goethe, Freud found expounded the enormous importance of the *intuitive* approach to Nature rather than the *inductive*. Psychoanalysis is a system of intuitions—and this Freud would have insisted upon—rather than a scientific system. The great value of the intuitive method obviously is that by conjecture it can supply "truths" much faster than they can be arrived at inductively—and sometimes they are just as good. One cannot help reflecting on the startling contrast afforded by the tons of Freudian literature and the meagre accumulation of Behaviorist pamphlets—in the latter case not much more than conditioned stimuli and responses (the work of Bechterev and Pavlov) proved and undisputed. Yet how difficult for the sake of comparison would be a quantitative analysis of the two!

Goethe's *Die Natur,* then, set Freud at work in the preliminary studies of botany and chemistry in the medical curriculum, carried him on through the physiological laboratory under Brucke, and established him as a research student in the Institute for Cerebral Anatomy. Limited finances forced him to give up research, and he became a clinical neurologist, eventually achieving the rank of Docent in Neuropathology at the University. In 1884 Joseph Breuer, a Viennese physician, related to Freud how he had cured a stubborn case of hysteria in an eighteen-year-old girl by inducing the patient to recollect its causes in an hypnotic state. Freud, having received a medical scholarship, went to Paris the next year to study under Jean Marie Charcot, the eminent neurologist, whose associate, Pierre Janet, was even then working upon his theory that the personality in hysteria is invaded by alien or unconscious ideas. Janet, however, did not trace these ideas to an origin in a vast unconscious life nor postulate a subconsciousness or an Id; that remained for Freud to do long after he completed and published some important papers on aphasia and cerebral paralysis in children. At length, in 1893, he persuaded Breuer to print the record of his case and collaborated with him in *Studien über Hysterie* in 1895. Jastrow, critic of Freud, seems to attribute most that is fundamentally important in psychoanalysis as a form of therapeutics to Breuer, but the fact remains that it was Freud who substituted "free association" for hypnosis in the "cathartic" treatment of hysteria and postulated the conflict between the consciousness and the subconsciousness to which he gave the name "repression." Only the most stubborn minds deny the genuine therapeutic value of psychoanalysis in the majority of cases—indeed, centuries of the confession in the Roman Church have demonstrated its worth— but there is probably a legitimate criticism of psychoanalysis in the charge that "free association" is sometimes less free than it seems, that the analyst possibly suggests situations and states which never existed, that he may occasionally plant confusion as well as eliminate neuroses or repression.

For the next decade Freud labored alone at psychoanalysis, developing it in two directions: as a technique for the treatment of the milder neuroses, and as an account of the unconscious mental processes, as a "depth psychology." It is the latter development which has attracted the most attention and which has most absorbed the poet-ideologist. The Freudian epic of the Unconscious is contained in *The Interpretation of Dreams* (1900), *Psychopathology of Everyday Life* (1904), *Wit and Its Relation to the Unconscious* (1905), *Three Contributions to the Theory of Sex* (1905), *Five Lectures on Psychoanalysis* (1910), *Totem and Taboo* (1913), *Beyond the Pleasure Principle* (1920), *Group Psychology and the Analysis of the Ego* (1921), *The Ego and the Id* (1923), *Collected Papers* (1925—), *The Future of an Illusion* (1927), *Civilization and Its Discontents* (1930), *New Introductory Lectures on Psychoanalysis* (1933), *The Problem of Anxiety* (1936), and *Moses and Monotheism* (1939).

The Freudian epic, as extended by the disciples, begins before birth, but stops at the grave, where even the Unconscious apparently ceases to function and "the death instinct" triumphs. Yet the epic includes our absent-minded periods and our sleep. For Freud, citing Plato's *Republic* to the effect that the virtuous man "contents himself with dreaming that which the wicked man does in actual life," presents the dream as evidence, not alone of the existence of the unconscious mind (which had been conjectured before he began his studies), but of the major importance of that mind to the whole life of man. It is no mere lumber room to which are relegated oddments that the mind cannot immediately use: such a storehouse Freud calls "the Preconscious." The Unconscious is the deeper reservoir where abides the primordial force of our natures, the fundamental drive of life. Dreams reveal that the Unconscious is wholly or almost wholly preoccupied with sex, for every element in a dream is susceptible of sexual interpretation. "The interpretation of dreams," writes Freud, "is the *Via Regia* to the knowledge of the Unconscious in mental life." Other evidence is available for proof of the existence of the Unconscious—post-hypnotic suggestion, for example, is regarded as evidence of a psychical zone beneath consciousness and memory (preconsciousness), yet no evidence is quite so conclusive as that of the dream for the sexual monism of the Unconscious. Freud finds, however, confirmatory proof of this monism in day dreams, fantasies, and hallucinations, in slips of speech, misspellings, absentmindedness and the chance associations of wit, and finally, in the success of psychoanalytical therapeutic treatments based on the assumption that his hypotheses are true. Yet the value of the dream is twofold: it is a universal phenomenon, a normal activity of normal people; and secondly, its evidence is reducible, as we have seen, to one meaning.

Because in dreams the consciousness is thus invaded by materials and images of one character, Freud argues that at other times some sort of *censor* functions either to repress, or to regulate, suggestions from the unconscious. The chief reason for this censorship is that free expression of the fundamental concern of the Unconscious, that is, the sex urge or *libido,* is at times incompatible with the occupations of the consciousness, which are dictated by the outside world—a world of taboos, moral codes, parental authority, and Christian discipline. The result of inhibiting or controlling the *libido,* however, is to create intrapsychical conflict, for life is unharassed and natural only when the movement of the *libido* towards a love-object is free. In a sense artificial and even dangerous is the deflection of libidinal energy into social purposes (Freud calls this process "sublimation"), for such a deflection calls for "sacrifices in the gratification of the primitive impulses." The thwarted *libido* may seek relief in a variety of ways—in self-love, in fixation on an immature object, in regression, and in repression. Since any one of these results is undesirable, it is patent that censorship is a very dubious activity of the Psyche.

Yet just what the *censor* is, Freud never made sufficiently clear. Figuratively it was, in Freud's first writings, a sentinel posted in the Preconsciousness to defend the consciousness from unwelcome ideas originating in the Unconscious. Later efforts to locate this sentinel and yet another on the borders of the psychical zones did not satisfy Freud, and he decided to rechart the mental topography of man, which he did, dividing the Psyche into the Super-Ego, the Ego, and the Id. The necessity for this new delineation of mental areas was very apparent to Freud. His early, simpler scheme of division into consciousness, Preconscious, and Unconscious was inadequate because his conception of the *censor* was inadequate. Freud does not believe in the will, and repeatedly refers to the "illusion of free will." Yet, as Crichton-Miller points out, "it seemed as though Freud, strenuously denying freedom of choice to the individual, came very near to reinstating it in the censorship."

Though Freud did not acknowledge it, his reconstruction of the Psyche was an effort to buttress the weakest point in his system. In his new description of the mental life the Ego acts as repressor of suggestions from the Id, the well-spring of *libido,* at the bidding, however, of the Super-Ego, which now stands for all the ideas of social discipline which are lodged in the Psyche. Yet the areas of the Ego and the Super-Ego lie in unconscious, as well as in preconscious and conscious, zones. This is a very important conception, for Freud believed it protects his idea of repression as instinctive and not a matter of choice. It would seem now that the Ego functions unwittingly to repress the *libido* since Freud postulated that the Super-Ego is a "moral critic who maintains in the Ego an *unconscious* guilt sense." It is important to note, too, that Freud conceived the Super-Ego to have but a small portion of its area in the conscious zone, while the Id is wholly unconscious. Yet while this description conveys Freud's idea of the Ego as an intermediary, governed by logic and expediency, between the instinctive force of the Id and the inhibitive power of the Super-Ego, and while it is a much more plausible account than his first version, it still leaves much to be explained, as we shall see, before Freud's determinism can be accepted. If any part of the Super-Ego is conscious, it would seem that in repression the functioning of the will would have to be conceded. Further, the Ego, admittedly conscious of reality and in a sense self-sufficient, would seem to be a freer agent than Freud makes it out to be. Yet in sinking inhibitory control into the unconscious zones, Freud (if he was right) made man out to be more of an automaton than he did formerly.

Freud's studies in sex are not confined to the mature man but begin with the once "innocent" child. It was, as a matter of fact, his account of the sexual life of the very young which aroused hostility to his work and led to the excited discussions which spread some of his theories broadcast among people who, to this day, have never read a word in his many books. The *libido* is always present: the infant derives a sexual satisfaction from the stimulation of nursing, but in time other erotogenic areas, the anus and genitals, furnish delight until at five a sort of maturity is developed in what Freud calls the stage of "phallic primacy." Then, after a period of "latency," this series of oral, anal, and genital eroticism is repeated in adolescence. If the child or adolescent experiences unusual pleasure or frustration in any one of these stages, it is likely to affect powerfully his character. A child who has particularly enjoyed the oral experience is liable to be an optimist, while he who has been peculiarly thwarted is prone to be querulous and exacting. Similarly orderliness, frugality, obstinacy, and pessimism are products of the period of anal erotization.

Now just as there are three stages in the localization of eroticism, so there are three successive ways in which the *libido* expresses itself in the development of the child and adolescent. These are called auto-erotic, narcissan, and allo-erotic. In the first stage the child is at once lover and loved-one, deriving satisfaction purely from stimulation; in the second, he develops (with the growth of the Ego) self-love; while in the third, he detaches his love from self and directs it toward a love-object. The transference of libidinal interest may not be to an object in one's own generation, but is more likely to be to some one near of an older generation, notably one's parents. This results generally in what is termed the Oedipus complex, in which the son loves his mother and envies his father, or in its converse (once called the Electra complex) in which the daughter loves the father and is jealous of the mother. Though there are other complexes, Freud regarded the Oedipus complex as most important: everyone apparently passes through the Oedipus situation; those who do so successfully achieve a normal love life; but a great number fail to do so and repressions, neuroses, and psychoses may be traced to this failure. The notion that the love of a child for a parent of the opposite sex had a libidinal content was apparently very shocking to Americans, for writers were to exploit this complex beyond almost any other aspect of Freudian psychology; yet however shocking was this idea, it has become very widely accepted.

Acceptance of Freud's psychology meant for Americans acceptance of his philosophy as well. Always implicit and frequently stated in his writings is the conflict between the "natural" urges of man and the conventions of the society in which he finds himself. In this conflict surrender to blind force, to primitive desire, seems the expedient thing, for resistance opens up a prospect of punishments that are subtle and appalling. Indeed, one of the first results of the spread of Freudian doctrine in America was to bring about an awkward revolution in the technique of seduction. Lovers took to urging their companions to forget their "repressions." The cult of the primitive got an extraordinary foothold on this continent and the purveyors of the philosophy of pessimistic determinism discovered their most powerful ally. All the entrancement of erotic pleasure added to the conviction that Freud gained, while to resist his doctrines was to arouse the suspicion that one was inhibited or neurotic, and paradoxically, to excite *social* condemnation. If Freud could have witnessed some instances of the practical working out of his teachings in America in the late 'teens and the 'twenties, he would have been somewhat hesitant about assigning all repression to the influence of society upon the individual.

To the appeal of the Primitivism and Naturalism of his philosophy Freud added, almost as an annex, the appeal of Decadence. Ignoring altogether the teachings of biology, he postulated, in

Beyond the Pleasure Principle, a "death instinct" in all living cells to return to an inorganic state. We are not surprised to find that *Civilization and Its Discontents* is an attack upon Culture, or that the conclusion of the book is ". . . our so-called civilization itself is to blame for a great part of our misery, and we should be happier if we were to give it up and go back to primitive conditions . . ." No other thinker combines so many of the subversive trends of contemporary thought in his philosophy as does Freud, and this may explain his profound influence upon, and diffusion through, the intellectual life of America. Up to the time he made his appearance our thinking on sex relationships was sufficiently confused, but it had the merit of being pragmatic; since Freud it has been Decadent mid-European: sentimental-romantic, Naturalistic, and Primitivistic. Freud determined the conduct of one generation of Americans and has probably influenced that of generations yet unborn.

Lay-criticism of Freud was once regarded as impossible, and probably would not have been convincing even had it been very thorough. The generation which received Freud was in no mood to be persuaded by his opponents. He was attacked at points where he was strongest, for example, in his development of infant and child sexology. American youths checked back on personal experience and came to the conclusion that Freud was more right than his critics. This was warrant enough for them to accept his philosophy. The critics were "Puritans," as writers other than Freud had already suggested. The later "speculative" writings have done something, however, to shake our faith in Freud. His silly venture into fiction in *Beyond the Pleasure Principle,* in which life is described as "a struggle between Titans"—the Eros instinct and Death instinct—must have opened many eyes to his romancing. Yet it was singular that a generation which owed so much to the scientific method should have accepted his intuitions at the outset. Freud himself has incautiously admitted the validity of the inductive method in *The Problem of Anxiety.* Criticizing Otto Rank's theory (in *The Trauma of Birth,* 1923) that persons become neurotic who on account of the severity of birth have never succeeded in abreacting it, Freud wrote: "The principle objection to be raised against it (i.e., the Rankian theory), however, remains the fact that it hangs in mid-air, instead of being based on a verified observation. . . ." A very great deal of Freud hangs in mid-air and has never been verified.

Take the all-important evidence of dreams as to the nature of the Unconscious. Let us suppose that dreams when they occur are filled with materials generally susceptible of sexual interpretations as Freud contends (though this has been disputed and cases of war-neuroses somewhat shook Freud's own convictions). Does this fact necessarily supply the proof Freud thinks it does? It is a physiological fact that dreams are provoked by heavy drinking and eating, both of which, because of the close relationship of the digestive and procreative mechanisms, would be apt to give dreams the content Freud describes. Dreams, it is also known, do not occur in the deepest sleep; indeed they frequently result in the dreamer's wakening. Do, then, dreams reveal anything about the Unconscious or its total content? Isn't the very fact that dreams have a narrative orderliness suggestive of their conscious origin in that period of wakening when the Ego adjusts to outward reality? We would not controvert Freud but rather suggest the inconclusiveness of his evidence. It must not be forgotten that his other evidence in regard to the character of the Unconscious is gathered entirely from abnormal circumstances, where sexual maladjustment is freely admitted.

The most dubious of Freud's doctrines is the completely evil character he assigns to all libidinal control. Freud, singularly enough, does not appear to have adequately considered the relation of control to satiety. It is possible that the Frenchman who says, "Je suis tres ennui," to the persistent courtesan might cohabit with her, but it is also true that he may refuse her with results less harmful to the Psyche than over indulgence. Freud writes of the *libido* as though it had no physiology and was inexhaustible. Benjamin Franklin's rule of chastity, "Rarely use venery but for health or offspring, never to dulness, weakness, or the injury of your own or another's peace or reputation," makes its bow to conscience, to be sure, but it cannot be contended that the only element of control in it is social. Freud's effort to deny the possibility of the functioning of the will in these matters is far from convincing.

There is seeming inconsistency in Freud's assertion that all literature and art are sublimated products of the *libido* and his attack upon culture, so created, for repressing the *libido*. Freud, however, did not believe in evolution and could not conceive that man can be compensated by other pleasures as partial substitutes for libidinal release. Yet it is possible that man is evolving so that some social approval will be as satisfying ultimately to the Psyche as libidinal indulgence, and that in time, so solaced, neurotics may diminish rather than increase. The neurotic, perhaps, should be looked upon as one of the present proper costs of evolution and civilization, and in this respect it must be said that Freud has done mankind a great service in making us sympathetic towards those who pay so heavy a price for the pleasures of civilization that the rest of us enjoy. Indeed, psychoanalysis itself is presumably part of the destructive "culture" which Freud deplored. Yet Freud probably would not have admitted that psychoanalysis (whatever its immediate effect upon the younger generation in America) is more of an evil than a good. It must be so regarded, however, if all things of social consequence are to be condemned. Thinking Freud through inevitably gets one into a monstrous tangle, and this is mainly because he made no effort in his system to adjust to the known facts in related fields. Despite his Naturalism, Decadence, and Primitivism, he was an anarchist in philosophy and science, one whose entire offering will have to be completely revalued at a little more distance in time. We must content ourselves to record merely its chaotic effect on American thought. Jastrow appears to be right in accusing Freudianism of doing more wrecking than salvaging so far as America is concerned.

Two of Freud's disciples, later in revolt against the master, are very well known in America. One of them, Alfred Adler, has evolved a system of psychology very much like the philosophy of Nietzsche and will be discussed elsewhere. It is convenient, however, to interpolate the work of Carl Jung at this point. Jung accompanied Freud to America in 1909 and likewise lectured at Clark. His chief distinctions at that time were that he had developed a method of plumbing the Unconscious quite different from Freud's and that he had originated the concept of the "complex," taken over by Freud. Jung penetrated into the Unconscious through the method of word associative reaction. A subject, given a list of words and requested to react to them in the briefest possible time, either reveals through his responses or his failures to respond (or even through variations in reaction time) a good deal, so it is claimed, about the content of the total Psyche. This method has the advantage over the "free association" method of Freud in that the personality of the investigator is not placed in quite so influential a relation to the patient. Its success, however, depends wholly upon the correct reading of the word reactions, which allows for about as much arbitrariness as does Freud's interpretation of dreams. Yet Jung, studying the countless reactions he obtained, decided that the *libido* had not quite the character Freud had given it, and consequently broke with Freud about 1912. To distinguish his work from Freud's he gave to his writings the name "analytical psychology."

For Freud, the *libido* is the sum total of the "component instincts" entering the sexual urge; Jung makes the *libido* the sum total of all impulses—a force very similar to Bergson's *élan vital*. Jung shares with Freud the belief that the Unconscious is greater than the Conscious; indeed, he extends the Unconscious to include a "Collective" as well as a "Personal" "Unconscious"; but apparently he is of the opinion that the relative importance of Conscious and Unconscious is subject to change in the advance of the race, since he holds that the Unconscious is that part of the Psyche not adapted to reality. Evolution, denied by Freud, is with Jung the development of unconscious mind into consciousness. It is when Jung turns to charting the *terra incognita* of the Unconscious that he loses his air of scientific respectability and becomes more like the great romancer, his master. Indeed, both of these boys, in their reports of that nebulous region which as yet no man has visited, remind us a little of Marco Polo and his fabulous stories of the East. They are chiefly valuable for offsetting each other and in warning us to wait for the report of a true Columbus, a Magellan, a Matthew Ricci. Jung's notion of a Collective Unconscious which is archaic, impersonal, and universal— a sort of compounded racial and ancestral memory—fills us with scepticism. That there exists as a separate entity a Personal Unconscious which selects elements for its use out of the Collective Unconscious seems absolutely indemonstrable. On the other hand, Jung's contention that much of the lumber of the Unconscious is non-sexual, or rather *desexualized,* has some appeal, perhaps merely because it is less dogmatic than Freud's assertion of sexual monism. Though we possibly have no right to argue from the analogy, it is true that the stuff of the Consciousness is at any time apt to be very complex: should not, then, the Unconscious with its postulated greater area and depth contain a greater variety of stuff?

Central in Jung's conception of the Unconscious is the idea that it functions in a sort of compensatory way to the Conscious. The Conscious has a face it presents to the world, which Jung calls the *persona* after the mask which the Roman actors wore. Any extravagant expression of the *persona* is immediately compensated for by the development of an opposite expression in the Unconscious. This opposite presses to seek expression in the Conscious to correct the exaggeration of the *persona.* In simple statement this seems reasonable. We know the blusterer to be a coward at heart whose inner weakness will betray him. It is in some of the extraordinary applications that Jung makes of this principle that he is unconvincing; for example, his notions that the Ego throws a "shadow" in the Unconscious, and that the *persona* of the Conscious is offset by an *animus* in the buried mind. In man, the masculinity of the *persona* is offset by the femininity of his *anima,* etc. Every Samson apparently has his own Delilah, which he has created more or less as Jove begot Minerva. And every demure little puss innocently conceals a cave-man *animus* in her Unconscious.

A very important development in analytical psychology was the elaboration of a theory of types. In 1914 Jung distinguished two psychological types into which he believed all human beings could be classed, the extravert and the introvert. The extravert is a person whose feelings strongly predominate, while the introvert is a person whose thought processes mostly absorb his energies. In the extravert the potentialities of thought are buried in the Unconscious; in the case of the introvert feeling is similarly engulfed. When life situations demand of the extravert thought, or of the introvert feeling, the conflict in the Psyche may lead to neuroses. By 1923, when he published *Psychological Types,* Jung was dissatisfied with this simple classification. Deciding that every individual possesses four functions—thinking, feeling, intuition and sensation, he proceeded to subdivide his original classification into the following types: the introverted thinker, the extraverted thinker, the introverted feeling type, the extraverted feeling type, the introverted intuitive type, the extraverted intuitive type, the introverted sensorial type, and the extraverted sensorial type. By way of illustration, Flugel indicates that Kant would be an example of the thinking type, when introvert; Darwin, when extravert. The poet Blake would be an example of the introverted intuitive type, while the politician Lloyd George would serve as an illustration of the same type extraverted. All of this is very interesting, but not very conclusive. One remembers that during the Renaissance men were classified by their "humours," and that such a classification seemed then very satisfactory to the majority, but that it was soon abandoned as specious and futile. In all likelihood individual men and women are too complex for any such classification, except for purposes of satire.

Jung's later subdivision of types has made very little impression in America, but a strange thing occurred here when knowledge was first gained of extravert-introvert classification. Jung, it must be remembered, did not point out that either of the types is preferable to the other, though it is true his earliest use of the word "introversion" was very close to Freud's conception of repression. But the idea of the introvert, who suppressed his feelings, through chance proved more obnoxious to Americans than the idea of the extravert. The reason for this was that all America was giving rein to its feelings at just the time the idea of introversion was introduced. Those little mouse-trap minds, the "educators," seized upon the popular reaction and introduced a noble campaign to make everybody into extraverts. They were particularly successful during the late 'twenties when extravert traits were at a premium and they so completely devalued the reflective personality that thought itself was held in derision. It is because of this fact that the teaching of Jung did almost as much harm in America as the teaching of Freud, though his philosophy has none of the subversive elements found in Freud.

Another sex-revolutionary whose ideas produced a profound effect upon young America was Edward Carpenter, British lecturer and Socialist. Carpenter, born in Brighton on August 29, 1844, planned to enter the Church, and acted for a while, after his graduation from the University, as curator of a Cambridge church. Tremendously stirred up, according to his autobiography *Days and Dreams* (1916), by reading first Walt Whitman's *Leaves of Grass* and then his *Democratic Vistas,* he resigned his curacy in 1874. After a trip to Italy, he became an extension lecturer for the University of Cambridge and had occasion to visit British industrial towns. This led to his meeting both workers and Socialist leaders. His early books of verse were unsuccessful, but three books on the interrelations of social subjects and politics were widely read in England: *Towards Democracy* (1883), *England's Ideal* (1887), and *Civilization: Its Cause and Cure* (1889). Carpenter's strangely compounded Primitivism and Fabianism is best seen in the last volume where he argues at once for "individual freedom and Savagery" and "a complex human Communism . . . in some sort balancing and correcting each other, and both visibly growing up within, though utterly foreign to, our present day civilization. . . ." This view of society was perhaps a result of an effort to reconcile the teachings of Herbert Spencer with those of Walt Whitman, whom he crossed to America to visit in 1884. His meeting with the bard of Camden is described in *Days with Walt Whitman* (1906). Carpenter died in England on June 28, 1929.

None of the volumes from Carpenter's pen thus far mentioned has been much read on this side of the Atlantic. This is not true, however, of Carpenter's little book, entitled *Love's Coming of Age,* which he printed at his own expense in 1896 after failing to find a publisher. For *Love's Coming of Age,* after being published here with great success by Mitchell Kennerley in 1911, was reprinted in several series of cheap tracts and had the widest success. It was one of the most influential volumes with the younger generation, particularly with those who had strong social instincts but were as uncritical as youth is wont to be.

Love's Coming of Age has many points of merit. There is in it a healthy hatred of prudery, and when Carpenter cites Max Müller for leaving in the original Sanskrit the passages relating to sex in his translations of the Upanishads, one is inclined to applaud. Yet it is puzzling to find these assaults on prudery offset by statements (many of them reminiscent of a similar confusion in Whitman) which seem as prudish as the prudery condemned; for example, "Sex today throughout the domains of civilization is thoroughly unclean. Everywhere it is slimed over with the thought of pleasure." Why thoughts relating to sex should not be pleasant one cannot see. Again, Carpenter's chapter on "Woman: the Serf," in which he attacks the nineteenth century middle-class ideal of leisured dependence of the wife in marriage as "the festoon" theory, has much to commend it. On the other hand, his notion that "the subjection of sex relations to legal conventions is an intolerable bondage," coupled with his notion that such a bondage is "inescapable as long as people are slaves to a merely physical desire," shows a muddiness of thinking and a lack of critical realism little short of appalling. The most pernicious aspect of *Love's Coming of Age* is its ambiguity and indefiniteness, its austere precepts and its endorsement of unhampered sex expression. His picture of "a marriage so free, so spontaneous, that it would allow of wide excursions of the pair from each other . . . yet would hold them all the time in the bond of absolute sympathy . . ." is marvelously seductive, but just as false as it is seductive. It led to too many "spontaneous" adolescent marriages in the mayor's office, and to far too much promiscuity after the couple had solemnly pledged eternal fidelity to each other. Carpenter was a perfect representative of that type of well-meaning person, who, possessed of half a truth, does an inconceivable amount of damage in the world. *Love's Coming of Age,* utilizing perfectly the abundant idealism of youth, prompted young Americans to all sorts of ill-considered action which led to infinite confusion and pain.

The American publication of Carpenter's *Love's Coming of Age* fell between the appearance of two books by Ellen Key, the Swedish feminist, in American editions—*The Century of the Child* in 1909 and *The Woman Movement* in 1912. Miss Key's

contributions to the feminist magazine *Idun* and her lectures to
young women materially aided in the emancipation of her sex in
Sweden, as did the publication of *The Woman Movement* here;
but her reading of Nietzsche and her adoption of his hostility to
morality, which finds ecstatic expression in *The Century of the
Child,* probably offset all the good that she did in the world. For
while *The Century of the Child* has as its main thesis that the
parents are equally wrong if they act as though the child existed
only for their benefit or if they assume they exist only for the
child's benefit, this thesis serves merely as a spring board for
Miss Key to plunge into matters much nearer her heart. Moral
compulsion, in her view, is a hideous thing; objective laws must
be replaced by subjective desires. Ethics must spring from character. Consequently a marriage enforced by legal regulation and
religious approval is to be avoided. "Marriage . . . offers no guarantee that the proper disposition towards the relations of the two
sexes is present. This can exist as well outside of as within marriage. Many noble and earnest human beings prefer for their
relation the freer form as the more moral one . . ." When *The
Century of the Child* appeared in America, it was the boldest
presentation of *laissez-faire* sexual morality with which the generality of readers could readily become acquainted and its specious arguments wrought incalculable harm.

Granting that "voluntary fidelity is a sign of nobility," one
cannot believe that a workable ethic for society can be produced
by the free exercise of individual desire. Free exercise is surrendered, and must be surrendered, when man enters society, which
is an artificial thing and must have a degree of artificiality in its
laws. Noble and earnest human beings, if they are at all social
minded, should be able to endure the irk of artificiality in legal
marriage unions, since society, either by legal or moral force,
inevitably guarantees as a consequence the protection of these
unions from outward assault. The total experience of mankind,
whatever may have been asserted to the contrary, shows the practical worth of legal union, as the studies of Westermarck, Malinowski, and others have proved. Morals, furthermore, cannot
originate with the individual, though they may be enforced and
illustrated by his actions. Morals are definitely a "social" prod-

uct, the result of a joint desire of at least two individuals (one of whom may be hypothesized, but just as surely exists) to perfect a code whereby they may get on harmoniously. Indeed, the modern discoveries of the tribal origins of morals give them a force for the modern man quite equal to their former influence as heaven-sent laws. What Miss Key desired was moral anarchy, and what she produced among her fervent feminine followers was something very close to what she desired. With Carpenter she was one of the most effective advocates in America of free union, an experiment somewhat freely tried here in the 'twenties, with none too happy results.

At about the time the general public became aware of Freud, Carpenter, and Ellen Key it became aware of Havelock Ellis as an "authority" on sex. Singularly enough, a good case could be made to support the argument that Ellis belongs more to America than to England, which is his home. For when Ellis published *Sexual Inversion* in 1897 and the London bookseller was arrested and the edition confiscated, Frank A. Davis of Philadelphia volunteered to publish that and subsequent volumes on sex, provided that the sale was confined to doctors and lawyers. This was agreed to, and Davis eventually published the entire seven volumes of the *Studies in the Psychology of Sex*. These books were not given to the general public until 1936, when Random House brought out a handsome four-volume edition; but long before that, through the retailing of the privileged purchasers, but more especially through slighter, popular essays and books which exploited some of the materials, the main ideas of the *Studies* were well known. Ellis, indeed, had been before the general public here as a seer in the field of sex since about 1910 when he began writing prefaces for Ellen Key and others. Yet his most available book was the *Little Essays of Love and Virtue* published in America in 1922.

Before the work of Ellis in the field of the psychology of sex can be evaluated, it is necessary to know something of his life and methods of research. The son of a sea-captain, Henry Havelock Ellis was born in Croydon, Surrey, on February 2, 1859. He made one trip with his father to Australia at six and another at sixteen. The second journey led to a four-year sojourn in the bush, during which he did much tutoring and school teaching. It was at this time that, puzzled over the phenomena of sex, he reached his fine resolution to spare other adolescents the confusion which was his:

> ... I determined that I would make it the main business of my life to get to the real natural facts of sex apart from all the would-be moralistic or sentimental notions, and so spare the youth of future generations the trouble and perplexity which this ignorance had caused me.

To prepare himself for this wholly legitimate end, he returned to London and enrolled as a student of medicine at St. Thomas' Hospital, where he remained eight years, until 1889, when he was given his medical diploma. He had already, however, shown his abiding interest in literature and science by editing two series of books, one called *Contemporary Science* while the other was the famous *Mermaid* series of Elizabethan dramatists. Torn between his duty to practice medicine and his desire to write, he appealed to his friend, Olive Schreiner, who advised him to abandon medicine.

He made a long visit to Paris with another friend, Arthur Symons, before publishing his first book, *The New Spirit* (1890). This visit led to meetings with the French Decadents whom Symons admired—Mallarmé, Huysmans, Verlaine, Moréas—and to a lasting attachment to one of them, Rémy de Gourmont, as omnivorous a reader as Ellis himself in the varied fields of literature, anthropology, psychology, and sex. Out of this visit and friendship grew Ellis' lasting interest in Naturalistic and Decadent French literature which he, with Swinburne, Wilde, Symons, and Dowson, helped to make a vogue in England. There is no sign of this in *The New Spirit,* however, with its five studies of Diderot, Heine, Whitman, Ibsen, and Tolstoi. This book is one of ecstatic hero-worship and mysticism: "To pronounce the names of such men is of the nature of an act of worship." Defining religion as "the sum of the unfettered expansive impulses of our being" (surely one of the most extraordinary definitions of religion ever given, though the prompting of Whitman is clear enough), Havelock Ellis discovers that religion is the driving force of all his heroes:

. . . It is strange: men seek to be, or seem, atheists, agnostics, cynics, pessimists; at the core of all these things lurks religion. We may find it in Diderot's mighty enthusiasm, in Heine's passionate cries, in Ibsen's gigantic faith in the future, in Whitman's not less gigantic faith in the present. . . .

The total effect of this is to deny the possibility of being irreligious, and to suggest that unqualified strong emotion—no matter what its character, provided that it is sufficiently unfettered and expansive—is itself somehow sacred and to be respected. This heresy would not be worthy of belaboring if it did not reappear so frequently in the author's later work. The extraordinarily popular book *The Dance of Life* (1923) is permeated with it. Here it is argued that all the creative activity of man, including his literature and his religion, is rhythmical, like the dance, which Ellis uses effectively to symbolize what for him is the rhythm of the universe. The reader may inquire what harm lurks in so pretty a conceit. The answer is, none if properly understood, but the tendency of man is to take all figures of speech too literally. To identify religion, which must be either the highest intellectual and spiritual exercise of man or nothing, with primitive urges, frenzies, ecstasies, rhythms, orgasms, deliriums, into which the (perhaps futile) effort to achieve self-abnegation and rapture may break over, is as mistaken as to assume that the waste products in the manufacture of radium are every whit the equivalent of radium itself. Scepticism is more logical than this, and on the whole has done less harm in the world.

About a year after the publication of *The New Spirit,* in December, 1891, Ellis was married to Miss Edith Lees, a former secretary of the New Life Association, a fanciful outcropping from the first Fabian group, the Progressive Association. Mrs. Ellis, a novelist and essayist legitimately bent upon a career of her own, was apparently responsible for the form of this union, which she described as the "Semi-Detached Marriage." Husband and wife had separate residences, outside friendships, and diversified interests, but appeared to maintain a strong affection for each other as long as Mrs. Ellis lived. This illusion was shattered, however, by Ellis himself in his autobiography, *My Life* (1939), a book which whittled the sage down to a small man more effectively than all the hostile criticism ever directed at him.

The union appears to have been of the sort properly reported under abnormal attachments in *The Studies in the Psychology of Sex,* without either respect or affection to grace it. One other lamentable lack in Ellis' life was children, for the psychologist, so earnestly bent on knowing all aspects of sex, could never report authoritatively on that culminating experience, parenthood, which (say what you will) crowns all relationships. (Where, in the *Studies in the Psychology of Sex,* is there any mention of the simple fact that children are sometimes born as a result of sexual union and have to be cared for?) In passing, it seems proper to remark that literarious people generally are better reporters on marital miscues and irregular conduct than they are good counsellors, for if not neurotic themselves, their very genius denies them the average relationship. Ellis, himself, is far better at satirizing unfortunate situations and wrong-headed attitudes in sex relationships than he is at developing a program of happy conduct. This is well illustrated in *Man and Woman* (1894), in which Ellis, comparing the sexes, successfully maintains that many of the differences are not biological, but merely superstitions, grounded in the traditional attitudes of society. Yet, in the end, he admits the "conservatism of Nature" a more imponderable thing than the "conservatism of man," and allows that his investigation has merely shown us "in what state of mind we ought to approach the whole problem." It is a negative victory.

Even less than Freud, is Havelock Ellis a laboratory scientist. His method is synthetic: he has read the letters or listened to the verbal accounts of hundreds of people about their sex life, has absorbed the reports of anthropologists and the conjectures of psychologists, and has meditated the whole to produce the bulk of the *Studies in the Psychology of Sex.* Yet Professor Parshley, by no means an easily satisfied critic, has approved of the method as sufficiently "scientific." Whether one should go as far as Dr. Parshley and affirm that the *Studies* are "in each case an orderly, documented, intelligible and illuminating picture that affords at once a clear understanding of the phenomena in question and a firm basis for determining future action, whether personal or social" seems highly dubious. It would be wiser to regard Havelock Ellis as an extraordinarily capable compiler who has arranged a great mass of chaotic material so that genuinely scientific work on it could be begun—that is, as soon as the physiologists and zoologists are ready to recapture that field (plainly theirs) which the psychologists have usurped. It should be pointed out, however, that Ellis, in his very character of compiler, has been more willing to consider the evidence of science outside his field than has Freud. For example, while restating Freud's theory of childhood sexuality, Ellis imposes a cavil by citing Matsumato's proof that hormonic activity begins at puberty. In the end science may reject less of Ellis than of Freud, for this reason, though Ellis is much less the original thinker. Ellis had a share, however, in developing the ideas of auto-eroticism and of narcissism before they were exploited by psychoanalysis, and it is claimed for him, on the basis of his essay on Casanova, that he anticipated Freud in describing the creation of literature as a form of sublimated sex activity.

Parshley is amused that Ellis should consider the *Studies* too "cold and dry" to interest the "non-scientific frivolous reader." He points out that, not only has the subject matter a fascination of its own, but "unfortunately" the author has "underestimated his charm of style, which is far from being 'cold and dry.' " Indeed, as early as the publication of *The New Spirit* Ellis showed himself a master of prose style. The man wrote so much better than the average critic that few reviewers have had the temerity to analyze his thought. It is doubtful, with all our tendency to truckle, if any British author has had such uniformly favorable American reviews. We have taken up Ellis and coddled him, as the English do occasionally one of our authors. Yet the reviews say but one thing, "how exquisite the style." Supple, sinuous, and effective it surely is: there are no better-written passages in contemporary English than some of those in the series of *Impressions and Comments* (1914–23) and in that superb little volume, *The Soul of Spain* (1909), which first sent Gertrude Stein, Waldo Frank, and Ernest Hemingway down into the Iberian peninsula. Our favorite passages in these purely literary books are those on Milton's love of olives and the Spaniard's love of noise. How one could say better what Ellis says in these we cannot conceive. Yet Ellis' mastery of style not only has given him immunity from criticism, but has lent seductiveness to whatever he has said. He and Freud had a pervasiveness, one from style and the other from image, almost unrivalled in the early 'twenties.

Although he clung to his early Fabian belief in "advancement," hence was not like Freud on this score, Ellis shared the Vienna master's hostility towards social morality and authority. This is more often implicit in his work than explicit, for example:

> . . . We cannot have too much temptation in the world. Without contact with temptation, virtue is worthless, and even meaningless. To face temptation and reject it may be to fortify life; to face and accept temptation may be to enrich life. . . .

It is but a step from this to argue that vice should be condoned, since it is plainly put into the world for a good purpose. Youthful America was half prepared to accept this dogma, if we are to believe G. Stanley Hall; further, our youngsters were carelessly eager to accept temptation as a way of enriching life. Those who had read Boccaccio had doubtless forgotten his ironical treatment of this ethic, or were too naïve to suspect the irony.

It was the naïveté of the generation which read Ellis (a fault which could hardly be charged to him, even if he shared it) that made him a dangerous writer and books like the inexpensive *Little Essays of Love and Virtue* incendiary volumes. This particularly popular book was prepared with the hope that it might "come into the hands of young people, youths and girls in the period of adolescence," who Ellis thought should decide "whether the book is suitable to be placed in the hands of older people." *Little Essays,* like Ellen Key's *The Century of the Child,* frankly makes its appeal to the Younger Generation by arraying it against its elders. "The world is not dying for lack of parents." The nineteenth century is depicted as building up a "harsh tyranny" of "duties," "reticences," and "subserviences." The United States, as a result, is more given to "solitary sexual indulgence" than any other nation. Jung and Freud are cited to win conviction that other and worse punishments are impending for the continent. "It is passion, more passion and fuller, that we need." While there is an admirable treatment of what Ellis terms "the play function of sex" in the book, and an altogether proper insistency on eugenics and a single standard (not of morals, but of freedom) for men and women, the approach to the subject and the emphasis are all wrong. The flattery of youth and the conviction of righteousness given them by the volume reveal an irresponsibility and immaturity hardly consistent with Ellis' reputation as "a thinker." In the last analysis, whatever Ellis may have contributed to "science," it is plain that he is one of the chief exponents of the *laissez-faire* morality which was to sweep America between 1915 and 1930.

The final foreign intellectual impulse towards moral chaos is perhaps the hardest to define or calculate. It came from Bertrand and Dora Russell, whose actual writings on sex and marriage are too late to have been a formative force in America. Bertrand Russell, grandson of Lord John Russell, and heir, in 1931, to his title of Earl, has long been, however, a familiar figure to Americans, with whom his interviews in the press and his actions have been as influential as his more measured words. After graduating from Cambridge University, he was married in December, 1894, to an American, Alys Pearsall Smith, of Philadelphia, and began the studies which were to make him one of the world's great figures in mathematics and philosophy. His pacifist views, expressed with great ardor and courage in the midst of recruiting in England for World War I, resulted in his dismissal from his lectureship at Cambridge and in a heavy fine. When he attempted to come to America to lecture at Harvard College, the military authorities forbade him to do so; and in 1918 he was sentenced to six months in jail for his anti-war propaganda. In 1920 he went to China to lecture at Peking University, fell ill with pneumonia, and was reported dead by American newspapers. During his absence from England, his first wife, who had refused to divorce him until she learned that another woman was about to bear him a child, now secured her separation, and in September 1921, he was married to Dora Black, thus legitimatizing his son. Dora Russell, a graduate herself of Cambridge and an ardent feminist, published her first important book on sex, a critique of the feminist movement, called *Hypatia,* in America in 1925. In it she announced that the movement lacked vitality because it dared not to cry out that women had bodies. "To me," she said, "the important task of feminism is to accept and proclaim sex." Especially did she proclaim against legal marriage. "As a Labour Minister is corrupted by Court dress, so is a free woman by the marriage contract. Nothing but our desire for children would make us endure it." These, and like views, received even greater emphasis in Dora Russell's *The Right to Be Happy,* a sensational plea for a primitive, instinctual life for women, which, published here in 1927, resulted in her being banned as a lecturer at the University of Wisconsin the following year. At a later time her experience became her husband's when the authorities of City College in New York cancelled Mr. Russell's contract to teach there in 1940.

Dora Russell's views of marriage were shared by her husband, and after receiving some newspaper exploitation as a result of interviews during his visits to lecture in America in 1924 and 1929, were finally incorporated in his book *Marriage and Morals* (1929). He holds that every man and woman should have perfect freedom to live together without legal ties until the woman becomes pregnant. Even then, divorce should be possible, though he urges parents to avoid it if possible, pointing out that adultery, if permissible, would relieve most marital tension! "Americans," he boldly counseled us, "should indulge in marital infidelity to preserve their homes. . . . Marriage is not the culmination of romantic love as is conventionally supposed. It should be primarily a system whereby a home may be provided for children— and making a home has nothing, or very little, to do with sexual love." The only comment necessary upon this view of the highest human relationship is to point out that the union of Bertrand and Dora Russell, both of whom practiced the infidelity they preached, ended in a most muddy and bitter divorce trial in 1934. One suspects that there are values in "romantic love" never apprehended by the Russells, and on the whole that it makes a better basis for marriage than a purely sexual attraction which at times can be sensibly resisted. Yet the views of the Russells probably had considerable force in some American circles just prior to the economic débâcle of 1929, when an effective non-legal restriction was suddenly imposed on our gay philanderers.

4

THE NEW FREEDOM

One cannot believe that the ultimate effect of the views of Freud, Jung, Carpenter, Key, Ellis, and the Russells will be evil, for free discussion of any subject aerates it, and if any subject needed discussion in America in 1915–25 it was sex relationships. Yet the immediate effect of these philosophies of release was a comfortable relaxing of the moral standards between 1925 and 1929. In part, the causes for this had been accurately set forth by G. Stanley Hall, as we have seen, in 1904. There was not sufficient moral discipline among the youth of America to receive such strong meat as the propagandists placed before them. Other, and very important, causes have been enumerated by the Lynds in *Middletown* (1929) .and by Frederick Lewis Allen in *Only Yesterday* (1931). They list, besides the Freudian gospel, post-war disillusion, the automobile which carried youngsters far from parental chaperonage, prohibition which made excessive drinking fashionable, the tremendous growth of the sex and confession magazines, erotic motion pictures and songs, and finally, the new status of women. All of these enumerated causes are so obvious as to need no exposition here, save the last. By "the new status of women" the Lynds and Allen mean woman's new legal status— she had won the suffrage in 1920—and her new freedom from domestic responsibilities. Allen, for example, points out that by 1920 housekeeping duties had been reduced to a minimum— families were moving into small apartments, living more and more on canned goods, bakery, and delicatessen products, using more freely laundries, and doing the work which had to be done with electrical devices: vacuum cleaners, washing machines and electric irons. But even this does not cut deep enough.

The "new status of women" in 1920–30 meant, above everything else, their new economic independence. This had been brought about in a variety of ways. General Spinner, U. S. Treasurer under Lincoln, had succeeded in introducing some 1,500 women into government clerical positions, despite considerable opposition, when male help was scarce. Yet women clerical workers in all businesses numbered only 7,000 by 1880. Then the invention of the typewriter, first exhibited at the Centennial Exposition at Philadelphia in 1876, effected a revolution. There were 120,000 women in clerical positions by 1890, 250,000 by 1900, and then, in response to World War I, 2,000,000 in 1930. Meanwhile women had gradually been elbowing men out of the department stores, out of teaching positions, and out of the telephone exchanges. Captain Rowland H. Macy not only employed more than 50% women in his very successful establishment, but also a certain Margaret Getchell, as store manager. Though women had always had a share in teaching from the time of the "dame school," it was not until 1870 that women outnumbered men about two to one in education. Men were the first telephone exchange operators, but in 1878 Miss Emma Nutt, hired as "an experiment," opened the way for the great vanguard of "hello-girls." *Fortune* magazine, which collected these interesting facts, believes that the unrivalled employment of women between 1920 and 1930 in no small measure produced the great business boom of those years. The 11,000,000 women who were gainfully employed by 1930 were, in less than half of the cases, supporting relatives, and this was particularly true of the clerical workers. The result was that they spent their earnings on luxuries: silk stockings, new styles, cosmetics, cigarettes, women's magazines. National advertising changed in order to appeal to them. But this is not the whole story. *Fortune* neglects to summarize the effect produced by the growing tendency of men to will their property to their wives and to make them the beneficiaries of their insurance policies. Life insurance, issued by less than a dozen companies in the 1840's, became a more secure investment following scandals at the turn of the century and the new legislative enactments, with a result that, just before the 1929 crash, some 300 companies were issuing policies. Mary Sydney Branch, in *Women and Wealth* (1934), points out that the beneficiaries of 80% of the eighty-seven billion dollars of life insurance then in force were women. It is asserted that women controlled better than 60% of the nation's wealth between 1920 and 1930. The significance of all this is, so far as we are at present concerned, that women were in America, perhaps for the first time in the

history of the race, free to experiment in the field of sexual relations. While hitherto the wayward girl had to dread being thrust
from home if she erred, there was no particular danger in that
threat now. Further, the matron who had tired of the marital
relation and had some sort of inherited competence was likewise free to do more or less as she chose.

Economic freedom would have been a bitter jest to the promiscuous woman had it not been that, almost simultaneously, she
received a degree of freedom from nature's check upon promiscuity—the fear of pregnancy. The courageous woman who gave
her this new freedom, Margaret Sanger, had no intention of
benefiting her primarily. Mrs. Sanger aimed to free womanhood
generally of the tyranny of the unwanted baby and of the abor-
tionist. Her own mother, after bearing eleven children, had died
when only forty-eight. Her father, an Irish stone-cutter by the
name of Higgins, though a kindly, well-disposed man of liberal
views, had never entertained any thought of family limitation.
He, however, lived till he was eighty. From her crowded home
where study was difficult, Margaret Higgins was sent to Hudson
River Institute; later she studied nursing and soon was a graduate nurse in New York City. Married to William Sanger, an
architect, she bore him three children, but then, being able to
commit their care to her mother-in-law, she took up again the
profession for which she was trained. Constant contact on the
East Side with families burdened with unwanted children, with
mothers who settled into despair or took to drink, and with
horrifying cases of abortion, aroused in Margaret Sanger's breast
a resolve to do something for these people. A summer on Cape
Cod in 1913, among a congenial group of social rebels—people
like Mary Heaton Vorse, Hutchins Hapgood, and "Big Bill"
Haywood—fixed her resolution, with the result that in the
autumn the Sanger family sailed for Paris, Mr. Sanger to study
art and Margaret to gain what knowledge she could of contraceptives. Amply fortified, she returned to America with her
children early in 1914 to challenge the power of Anthony Comstock.

The challenge took the form of a monthly magazine, *The
Woman Rebel,* of which six numbers appeared between March

and August, 1914. Four of these issues were forbidden the mails, though they contained no contraceptive information, being designed merely to open up the subject of family limitation; then, in August, Mrs. Sanger was arrested. Because it appeared to her that there was a determined plan, under the cover of the War, to give her a long penitentiary term, she decided not to appear at her trial and, under an assumed name, fled to England. In the next three years, she was to become intimately acquainted with some of the great leaders of her cause in the world: C. V. Drysdale and Dr. Alice Vickery (British leaders of the Neo-Malthusian League), Marie Stopes, Havelock Ellis, and Dr. Rutgers of the Dutch Neo-Malthusians. She was repulsed only by Dr. Aletta Jacobs, first woman doctor in Holland and founder of the world's first birth control clinic in 1878, who, however, later regretted her act.

News reached Mrs. Sanger in 1915 that her husband had been arrested when one of Comstock's agents had begged of him a pamphlet, *Family Limitation,* which she had prepared, but had not distributed, before leaving for England. Mr. Sanger had never given out any pamphlets hitherto and did so on this occasion when the agent represented that he was a friend of Mrs. Sanger's and desired it for his own personal use. Yet he was convicted and sent to prison. This brought Mrs. Sanger home to stand trial. Though a National Birth Control League had been organized during her absence, under the leadership of Mary Ware Dennett, Anita Block, and Clara Stillman, it remains to the discredit of this organization that it at first refused to do anything in Mrs. Sanger's behalf. The death of her daughter, Peggy, shortly before the trial, touched public sympathy and resulted in an unsolicited defense fund. But more important than this was the deluge of letters received by the trial justice, protesting the indictment. The result was that, after several postponements, the government entered a *nolle prosequi* in the case on February 18, 1916, and the first victory for birth control was won.

After a stormy lecturing tour, Mrs. Sanger turned to what she deemed an imperative step in her program—the opening of free birth control clinics such as she had seen in Holland. Despite the existence of a state statute which forbade even doctors to give contraceptual information, Margaret Sanger, Ethel Byrne, and Fania Mindell opened in a poor section of Brooklyn, at 46 Amboy Street, on October 16, 1916, the first American birth control clinic. All three women were arrested; Mrs. Byrne, sentenced to the workhouse, began a hunger strike which eventually forced an executive pardon. Mrs. Sanger herself served quietly thirty days in the workhouse.

Appeal of her case afterwards resulted in an interpretation of the law by Judge Crane to allow for the operation of the clinics. Meanwhile Mrs. Sanger herself had come to the realization that, if she desired her work to succeed, she must appeal to women of more political influence than the mothers of the poor. As a result, she opened an office on Fifth Avenue and began the publication, in February, 1917, of the *Birth Control Review,* which aimed "to render articulate the aspiration of humanity toward conscious and voluntary motherhood." The sale of this magazine—which contained no contraceptual information—on the streets resulted over a period of years in numerous arrests for Mrs. Sanger's volunteer helpers, yet spread awareness of her cause. Meanwhile Mrs. Sanger was quietly divorced from her husband. Though she was faced with disheartening financial worries, she managed to carry on and was rewarded by seeing birth control organizations spring up all over the United States. Mrs. Mary Ware Dennett withdrew from the National Birth Control League, founded the Voluntary Parenthood League, and carried the first unsuccessful fight to Washington to repeal the Comstock laws. In 1920 the New York State Federation of Women's Clubs voted to endorse favorable legislation—the first proof that Mrs. Sanger was succeeding with that class which she had hoped to reach with her new tactics. Scores of prominent people came to her aid, and her two books, *Woman and the New Race* (1920) and *The Pivot of Civilization* (1922), carried to thousands the most cogent arguments for voluntary parenthood. The American Birth Control League was founded on November 10, 1921, but the attempt to hold a National Conference in the Town Hall, New York City, in the same month was thwarted by the police, at the instigation of Cardinal Hayes. This led, however, to wider dissemination of birth control information, since the metropolitan dailies took up the suppression of the conference as an act against freedom of speech. By 1922, if any citizen in America did not know that birth control was a possibility, he or she was beyond the reach, not only of the press, but of ordinary gossip.

Yet the enemies of birth control failed to appreciate what general popular approval the movement had. As late as March, 1929, the Clinical Research Bureau at 46 West Fifteenth Street, New York City, was raided, its records seized, and the doctors arrested. Public indignation forced dismissal of the case, demotion of the policewoman leading the raid, and a censure of police tactics employed. Although an important bill to place the control of contraceptive advice in the hands of doctors was permitted to expire in a Senatorial committee in 1931, the birth control leaders won a great popular victory when the United States Circuit Court of Appeals ruled, on December 7, 1936, that physicians might send contraceptives by mail—a decision which rendered practically innocuous the infamous "Comstock laws." Previously, in 1930, the New York Academy of Medicine had endorsed birth control, and in May, 1931, the Federal Council of the Churches of Christ in America had given it, through its Committee on Marriage, official sanction.

The triumph of birth control was slow beside the spread of contraceptual knowledge which was beyond the limits of any conceivable control at the outset of the 'twenties. Unfortunately, this knowledge, however, was not of practices that had medical approval or much scientific justification; indeed some of the methods were dangerous to the health of the women employing them. Worse yet, knowledge good and bad was widely disseminated before any proper moral codes were evolved for the governance of human conduct in respect to the new freedom. Mrs. Sanger, herself, much as she is to be praised for her services to mankind (and one must place her in the company of Dorothea Dix, Mrs. Stanton, and Mrs. Stowe), was sufficiently vague as to the moral effect of her program. Much influenced by Havelock Ellis, she writes in her otherwise thoroughly sound book, *Woman and the New Race,* of the "new morality" that is to be created by womankind. But of only one aspect of that morality is she conscious—its freedom. ". . . The new standard will be based upon knowledge

and freedom while the old is founded upon ignorance and submission." Freedom, that was what the 'twenties wanted and it
was what the 'twenties tried out, only to end in bitterness and
disillusionment. Hedonism, wrote Walter Lippmann in *A Preface
to Morals* in 1929, had "never before been tested out under such
favorable conditions." Yet he could not see that it was proving
itself more triumphant in the modern world than in the ancient,
where it had been regarded as the "persuader to die." Moral
standards seemed about as necessary to Mr. Lippmann, then, as
they had ever been. Indeed, there was a sort of inverse ratio
to the need. "Just because the rule of sexual conduct by authority
is dissolving, the need of conventions which will guide conduct
is increasing." Yet Lippmann could merely indicate a way to
approach the problem; he had no solution.

But it was only after a decade of Hedonism that Walter Lippmann ventured his criticism. Our task is to show the effect of that
Hedonism on American thought, to discuss the influence of the
"Freudian" philosophy under conditions which were ideal for
its practice—generally prosperous times, an absence of moral
restraint, and a technique for avoiding physical consequences.

Among the innovators of the "new" or modern attitude towards love must be reckoned Sara Teasdale, whose most important book of verse, *Rivers to the Sea,* was published as early
as 1915. Miss Teasdale was a fellow townsman of T. S. Eliot,
having been born in St. Louis on August 8, 1884. She was the
daughter of John Warren and Mary Elizabeth Willard Teasdale, both of whom could trace their families back to Revolutionary ancestors. Indeed, on her mother's side Miss Teasdale could
claim Major Simon Willard, one of the founders of Concord,
Mass., as a progenitor. Privately educated, she early became interested in poetry, forming for the verse of Christina Rossetti
her first passion. Yet her earliest efforts to versify were translations of Heine. After her studies were completed in 1903, she
made her first trip abroad, and later became very much of a
traveller. Her poetry reflects visits to, and residence in California, Arizona, Greece, Egypt, Palestine, Switzerland, Italy,
France, and England. In 1914, Miss Teasdale was married to

Ernst B. Filsinger, of St. Louis, vice-president of the Royal Baking Powder Company; she was divorced from him in 1929. On Sunday morning, January 29, 1933, Miss Teasdale was found dead in her apartment, at 1 Fifth Avenue, New York, apparently a suicide. She had been in ill health since the previous summer when she had had to abandon a biography of Christina Rossetti on which she was working.

Sara Teasdale's first two volumes of verse, *Sonnets to Duse* (1907) and *Helen of Troy and Other Poems* (1911), are chiefly remarkable as the work of a young woman who was trying desperately to find other women interesting, whence earnest verses on the great Italian tragedienne, on the immortal Helen, and on Beatrice, Marianna Alcoforando, Erinna, and Guinevere. There are, to be sure, verses for Colin and Pierrot, who are innocuous enough males, and a sonnet, "For the Anniversary of John Keats' Death," yet one finds nothing truly arresting till he has all but put the volumes aside. On the last pages of *Helen of Troy,* however, there are not only some sharply etched "City Vignettes," but there is also (oh, the daring of 1911!) a little piece, "Vox Corporis," which represents human passion as an elemental, jungle thing over which the mind must watch. The poem closes thus:

> ... The beast to the beast is calling,
>   They rush through the twilight sweet—
> But the mind is a wary hunter;
>   He will not let them meet.

It is in *Rivers to the Sea,* four years later, that Sara Teasdale at once achieved stature as a poet and voiced what must be regarded as the characteristic attitude of the intellectual woman of her generation towards love. She insists, first of all, on her equal right to a completely passionate experience. She is not sorry for her soul, that it must go unsatisfied; she adopts instead an attitude that heretofore had been regarded as traditionally male:

> I am not sorry for my soul,
>   But oh, my body that must go
> Back to a little drift of dust
>   Without the joy it longed to know.

Nor will she be put by with "sublimated" substitutes. Though powerfully moved by the beauty of the fog in the park, "the drowsy lights along the paths," she feels that the world has no substitute for passion.

> . . . O, beauty are you not enough?
> Why am I crying after love?

On the other hand, she asserts as equal a right to experiment in love as the other sex has ever known. Thus in "The Flight," while begging her lover to hold her on his heart, she can suggest that this is no complete surrender by asking, "But what if I heard my first love calling me once more?" In "New Love and Old," the situation is reversed; after a new love has entered her heart she ponders a dilemma:

> . . . Old love, old love,
>> How can I be true?
> Shall I be faithless to myself
>> Or to you?

Yet, with all her "new freedom," she demands a fidelity and completeness in love that woman had hardly expected of man before—

> Love me with your whole heart
> Or give no love to me . . .

> You must love me gladly
> Soul and body too,
> Or else find a new love,
> And good-by to you.

It was this note in *Rivers to the Sea* which made it a tremendously exciting volume in 1915, rather than the exquisite music, or the happy turn of phrase. It is significant that the reviewers ignored altogether the long and labored pieces, Miss Teasdale's most ambitious "From the Sea" and "Sappho." And to tell the truth, Sara Teasdale could not manage a long line: her blank verse fails to move and her sonnets are mere exercises. She was effective only in the most lyrical forms, and now that her theme has no novelty, there is something tragic about her pretty little verses, as there is to fallen cherry blooms on the carpet.

Love Songs (1917) won both the Poetry Society and the Pulitzer awards, but no one, thumbing its pages today, if he is at all candid, will admit to being greatly moved by the volume. The poem "Refuge," which speaks of her "spirit's gray defeat," may catch the eye, for it has a poignant note in its almost fierce recourse to poetry in the failure of her hope—

> If I can sing, I still am free.

Aside from this there remains only the generally admired lyric called "Barter," which begins:

> Life has loveliness to sell
>   All beautiful and splendid things,
> Blue waves whitened on a cliff,
> Soaring fire that sways and sings,
> And children's faces looking up
> Holding wonder like a cup. . . .

Though the first two, and the last two, lines of this stanza are marvelously beautiful, the others make us aware of Miss Teasdale's greatest fault as a poet—her willingness to be content with conventional imagery to fill out her pattern. Though the coiner of many beautiful images, Miss Teasdale was never notably prolific in imagery, and her poverty forced her to rely more and more on the traditional, to the ultimate damage of her reputation. While she never knew caustic criticism in her lifetime—and for this we may be thankful, since she appears to have been too delicate a spirit to have borne it—she could not conceal from herself her own deficiencies, and a growing awareness of these may be responsible for the increased melancholy of her later volumes of verse, *Flame and Shadow* (1920), *Dark of the Moon* (1926), and *Strange Victory* (1933). Furthermore, she was primarily a love poet, and as she never turned again after *Rivers to the Sea* with full abandon to this theme, perhaps for reasons that lie hidden in her private life, the writing of verse had to be something of a perfunctory exercise for her. Certainly the poems written on various places and those composed on the stars (for boys and girls in *Stars To-night,* 1930) suggest this. Of her later verse, the better pieces are "I Have Loved Hours at Sea," "Pain," "There Will Come Soft Rains," "At Midnight," "A December Day," and "To the Sea." Yet in all of these is the note of frustration and defeat. For those who would trace this to its source one would suggest that the poem "Pain" and the poem "At Midnight" contain as complete an answer as could be desired. For one in ill health, to whom love was not, as for Miss Millay, a convenient spur for rhyming, but a passion, the wreck of love was the end of poetry. So Sara Teasdale. . . .

The rebellion of iconoclastic youth and womanhood found its second coherent lyric utterance in the poetry of Edna St. Vincent Millay. "She gave voice," writes Hildegarde Flanner, "to a new freedom, a new equality, the right of the woman to be as inconstant in love as the man and as demanding of variety. To what extent it was actually applied as a new ethic by Miss Millay's very numerous admirers one hesitates to say. It was, however, a timely statement of intellectual and biological equality, an aspect of feminism for the first time put into poetry of audacity, lyric quality, and vogue."

A more complete summary of *A Few Figs from Thistles* (1920), Miss Millay's second volume of verse and the one which appealed most to the younger generation, would be hard to find. It is doubtful if adolescents since the time of Byron have repeated any poems (without compulsion) as frequently or as enthusiastically as the youth of the 'twenties recited "My candle burns at both ends" and "Safe upon the solid rock. . . ." And as late as 1930 one was hearing matrons repeat, with what F. P. A. was to describe as a sort of "fallen archness," such sentiments as,

> . . . I would indeed that love were longer-lived,
> And vows were not so brittle as they are,
> But so it is, and nature has contrived
> To struggle on without a break thus far,—
> Whether or not we find what we are seeking
> Is idle, biologically speaking.

How much this attitude was really that of a child pretending to maturity, as G. Stanley Hall would have explained, is indicated in such poems as "Grown-Up" and "The Penitent." In the former a girl plainly in her 'teens complains that she feels "domestic as a plate" for being sent to bed "at half-past eight," while the "wicked girl" in the latter concludes, after trying in vain to feel remorseful for an unnamed Sin, that—

> ". . . If I can't be sorry, why,
> I might as well be glad!"

If some of the other verses, like "She Is Overheard Singing," ostensibly express the ideas or experience of a person older in years, the point of view is the same, and the diagnosis must be "arrested development." That *A Few Figs from Thistles* was once described as "sophisticated" seems today astonishing, no less than the once tremendous vogue of the book, for the confidence and wisdom are those—to twist Emerson's figure—of a girl overheard talking in the parlor. The book is assured a sort of immortality, not as poetry, but as symptomatic of the times which produced it. Naughty innocence, sophisticated naïveté, is pressed between its leaves like a flower, the flower of our youth.

Yet the lilting lines and the affected callousness of *A Few Figs from Thistles* conceal the hardship and poverty of the Bohemian life from which they were produced. The few vignettes of Greenwich Village in the book scarcely reveal this at all. Miss Millay was, however, at the time of writing *A Few Figs,* struggling, undetermined between poetry and the stage, for fame with hundreds of others, her age and younger, in the Village. She had come first to New York, to attend Barnard College, from Maine, where she was born in Rockland, on February 22, 1892. She had transferred from Barnard to Vassar, had won a cup in the Intercollegiate Poetry Contest, and had attracted wide attention with her contribution, "Renascence," to the anthology *The Lyric Year* (1912). After leaving Vassar in 1917 she returned to New York to live meagrely in the Village, and to act and to sing in the Provincetown plays. Floyd Dell in *Homecoming* has a good picture of her in these years, and it is one of a person of pluck, as well as of charm, undiscouraged by the continued rejection of her poetry by the magazines. Incidentally there is much resemblance between Miss Millay's poetry written at this time and some of Dell's. Here is a single verse from the pen of Floyd Dell which Miss Millay set to music and sang in *Sweet and Twenty:*

> I had clean forgot what my mother did say,
>   April—May!
> But I learned it all and I learned it soon.
>   May—June!

It was in the Village that she met the divorced husband of her undergraduate idol, Inez Milholland, Eugen Jan Boissevain, who was later to become her own husband, and it was in the Village that notoriety came to her with the publication of *A Few Figs from Thistles.*

Fame, which even in America may not necessarily mean rich rewards, had come with "Renascence," again kindly greeted by the critics in Miss Millay's first volume, *Renascence and Other Poems* (1917). Louis Untermeyer pronounced this "possibly the most astonishing performance of this generation." It is a poem of soaring imagination which instructs us that reality is fixed only by the individual heart; if it quails or wilts, the bounds of life contract accordingly—even the sky threatens to fall on him whose soul is flat. Despite its "counting-out rime" beginning, it has the quality of high seriousness which we associate only with the best poetry, and nowhere else with the work of a woman poet. The sheer power of expansion of the most meaningless setting, described in the prosiest language "three long mountains and a wood," into all the experiences which the dreaming mind may seek is one of the most adroitly managed things in modern verse. Only one who had imagined great events and had fought against the bitter monotony of village surroundings could so graphically describe the sky descending or the horizon closing in like a rubber band. How true psychologically are the lines—

> I screamed, and—lo!— Infinity
> Came down and settled over me. . . .

With this hysterical release comes the quieting realization that her thwarted individual desire is a universal thing wherever genius is confined and trapped. The language at once becomes

warmer, the phrases more romantic, the imagery suggestive of
Coleridge:

> A man was starving in Capri;
> He moved his eyes and looked at me;
> I felt his gaze, I heard his moan,
> And knew his hunger as my own. . . .

Yet it is necessary that the soul perish and rot before it achieves
rebirth. Most effective are the lines in which the poet describes
the overpowered spirit settling into the earth and then crying in
the rain for regeneration. More convincing is this than Henley's
"Invictus" of the last resources of the spirit and the will. Since
the prayer to God to live is a sign of the will to do so, the grave
is washed away by the rain, and the soul is restored to its former
surroundings, fortified, however, by the knowledge of its own
strength. While "Renascence" is totally at variance with the
spirit of much of Miss Millay's poetry, it is based upon a truth
which her own struggle for recognition illustrates, and demonstrates for us again that the best poetry is a reworking of the
poet's experience, and not a synthesis of what others have written
or said.

Though "Renascence" is the star poem in the volume which
houses it, there is other verse of merit in the same book. "God's
World" is a companion piece, in which the poet finds in autumnal
beauty a glory and such a passion "as stretcheth me apart." This,
we fancy, is the genuine Millay, though long since forgotten.
Slighter, but still with its background of Maine reality, is the
picture of the old woman who does not like the winter cold in
"When the Year Grows Old." This poem suggests how much
Miss Millay derived from the ballads which were the delight of
her childhood.

> I cannot but remember
> When the year grows old—
> October—November—
> How she disliked the cold!

In only one poem in *Renascence and Other Poems* is there even a
hint of the Millay of *A Few Figs from Thistles*. This is in the

last sonnet of the five in the book, in which, imagining the death of an imaginary lover first learned of from a newspaper on a subway train, she tells how she would read with studied care—

> Where to store furs and how to treat the hair.

Yet here the callousness is merely affected to cover how vitally she has been hit, not cultivated for its own sake, as in the later verse.

The complete sincerity of *Renascence* Miss Millay was never wholly to recover. In all her later volumes there is a sort of deference to what the readers of *A Few Figs from Thistles* might think, an effort to keep the front they might expect. Very few will be found to contend that this has done Miss Millay any good. In her later work she has struggled to elevate insouciance into cynicism, and has been more successful than we could wish, yet she never again has been quite natural, and this is too great a forfeit to pay.

Second April (1921) is the first book of Miss Millay's to be definitely imitative in some of its effects, and here most frequently are heard echoes from *A Shropshire Lad*:

> Boys and girls that lie
> Whispering in the hedges
> Do not let me die,
> Mix me with your pledges. . . .

Later the poet was to make considerable use of Housman's *Last Poems* as well. When E. A. Robinson once was asked what he thought of Miss Millay's poetry, he replied to praise it, but deplored the fact that she wrote so much about rain and death. Both topics were dear to Housman, and Miss Millay's natural tendency to be dampish became "watery wet" under this influence. This led to Samuel Hoffenstein's parody of "Burial" in this volume:

> I want to drown in good salt water,
> I want my body to bump the pier,
> Neptune is calling his wayward daughter,
> Crying, "Edna, come over here."

It must be admitted that a good many of Miss Millay's later poems, like "Passer Mortuus Est" in *Second April,* are both imitative and mawkish, yet the best section in the volume is that devoted to the memory of a Vassar friend with lines directly traceable to several easily detected poets. What raises this section above the rest of *Second April* is, however, its admixture of original lines marked by genuine feeling, as in the little four-line dedication, ending—

> . . . With hands that wrote you little notes
> I write you little elegies!

Probably everyone in America who knows poetry and loves it can quote part, or all, of that exquisite poem beginning—

> Let them bury your big eyes
> In the secret earth securely . . .

Its magic recapitulation of the voice of the lost friend denies altogether Miss Millay's assertion that her voice shall never again be heard and washes the poem of its inherited pessimism. That this, however, is the only thing of complete excellence in *Second April* is indicative of the effect of writing *A Few Figs from Thistles* on its author.

In the same year that *Second April* appeared, Miss Millay published three verse plays, later gathered in one volume: *Two Slatterns and a King, Aria da Capo,* and *The Lamp and the Bell.* The first of these is a very trivial thing which relates how a King sought the most meticulous housekeeper in his kingdom for a spouse, and how by chance he chose Slut instead of Tidy, who for the first time in her life, through a series of accidents, could present neither a clean kitchen nor a neat person. *Aria da Capo* is more ambitious, being intended as a satire of war. Its allegorical picture, however, of Thyrsis and Corydon erecting a paper boundary between themselves and quarreling over their small possessions would hardly keep two sisters from scratching each other. *The Lamp and the Bell,* a five-act, blank-verse tragedy vaguely reminiscent of the several treatments of Francesca da Rimini by Boker, Phillips, and D'Annunzio, is infinitely superior to Miss Millay's other two pieces despite its romantic material and conventional characters. One may feel it a pity that the poet, with her connection with the experimentation of the Province-town group, realized no compulsion to do a more original, real-istic thing for the Vassar girls, yet one must concede that *The Lamp and the Bell* is palpably well done in its outworn vogue. The verse is not strong and compelling, as blank verse should be, but rather, satisfying because of its fresh imagery. Thus Carlotta, a conventional choleric woman, is sometimes worth listening to, even if the plot is never advanced through her:

> *Carlotta* . . . The woman stirs me to that point
> I feel like a carrot in a stew,—I boil so
> I bump the kettle on all sides!

A most effective use of the minstrelsy of Fidelio is made in the play, yet the feature that makes the more lasting impression in *The Lamp and the Bell* is the author's treatment of Platonic love, which, she insists, can be as strong a thing between women as between men. Of course, the argument is weakened by the fact that the women are royal persons in a Never-never land, but it is a good argument none the less.

The Harp-Weaver and Other Poems (1923) won the Pulitzer prize. Had the award been made for a single poem in the book, the sonnet "Euclid alone has looked on Beauty bare," it would have been fairly won. There is no other contemporary sonnet, no sonnet written in English in fifty years, to compare with this. And there are few poems more completely satisfying. When a person who has devoted his whole life to the study of letters and has read so much that the acclaimed masters fill him with boredom finds in fourteen lines an ever-fresh stimulation to wonder and delight, no matter how frequently he returns to them, he is as-sured—despite the fact that he does not care for the general tenor of the poet's work—that these lines are great poetry. "Euclid alone has looked on Beauty bare" is one of those supreme things that have the power "to tease us out of thought as doth eternity."

"The Ballad of the Harp-Weaver" itself is Miss Millay's best use of the folk rimes and themes that are echoed in her verse. It is her tribute to the maternal devotion which, while it may not have made "king's clothes" for her, is in some way responsible for her success. The sonnet "I know I am but summer to your heart," and scattered lines through "The Ungrafted Tree" series, like—

> She filled her arms with wood, and set her chin
> Forward, to hold the highest stick in place . . .

and—

> Toward morning, if a dog howled, or a mouse
> Squeaked in the floor, long after it was gone
> Her flesh would sit awry on her . . .

—would seem extraordinarily good were they not in such company. Yet the best in *The Harp-Weaver and Other Poems* is almost muted by the worst in it—dictated immorality to the younger generation. Thus the lad in "The Betrothal," who for his consolation knows that he is but a substitute for "the dark head" the lady loves yet may not have, is told—

> I might as well be easing you
> As lie alone in bed. . . .

and a more "distressed" woman, having surrendered to a physical passion, avers—

> . . . I find this frenzy insufficient reason
> For conversation when we meet again.

To persuade ourselves that these sentiments are purely rhetorical is easy enough, yet Miss Millay must have been aware, after the profound effect of *A Few Figs from Thistles,* that they were chaos-working sentiments nevertheless. Those who mouthed these verses were not mature enough to see the contradiction between the dedication of *The Harp-Weaver,* "To my mother," and the lines—

> Who builds her a house with love for timber
> Builds her a house of foam. . . .

It would appear that the poet carelessly contributed—as did others—to the moral chaos of the 'twenties.

The King's Henchman (1927)—the libretto for an opera by Deems Taylor—done under contract, is a poor play, almost redeemed, however, by a good third act. Though the setting is the tenth century and the play opens with the recital of an alliterative epic lay at a banquet scene out of a Vassar sophomore's study of *Beowulf, The King's Henchman* is a reworking for the thousand and first time of the Tristram story. This is peculiarly unfortunate, since it suggests an immediate comparison with other poetic treatments of the legend, to many of which Miss Millay's version is undeniably inferior. It will not hold a candle, for example, to Robinson's. Yet this is not enough: Miss Millay uses as a dramatic device the heroine's discovery of her loved one through a charm on All Hallows Eve, a thing which reminds us instantly of Keats' "The Eve of St. Agnes" and forces comparison of the two as poetry—a comparison decidedly not to Miss Millay's advantage. Indeed, there is little quotable verse in *The King's Henchman,* though some of the chants in the play are very effective in dramatic presentation. As has been indicated, there is an unexpected "lift" in the third act, an unlooked-for tightening of dramatic intensity, when Æthelwold asks his beautiful wife to stain her face and appear the hag he had described to Eadgar, the king, who had sent him to court her as future queen of England. When Æfrida, persuaded by her nurse, appears in her finest robes in breath-taking beauty Eadgar and Æthelwold's deception is revealed, a suspense is achieved that is magic in its character. Miss Millay's solution of the situation is to have Æthelwold commit suicide, have the king praise him for his noble character and curse his wife—somewhat illogically. What better ending the play might have is not our problem; it is sufficient to point out that the existing one is weak.

In September, 1928, Miss Millay printed another volume of verse—*The Buck in the Snow and Other Poems*—the least distinguished of her volumes. From Housman (see "Moriturus," "Hangman's Oak," "West Country Song," etc.) she has turned to Decadence, a new and devastating theme in her poetry. In a sonnet entitled "On Hearing a Symphony of Beethoven" she writes:

> Sweet sounds, oh, beautiful music do not cease!
> Reject me not into the world again.
> With you alone is excellence and peace,
> Mankind made plausible, his purpose plain. . . .

Then begs that she may live until death as—

> . . . A city spell-bound under the aging sun,
> music my rampart, and my only one.

This is the mood of Poe, Baudelaire, Mallarmé, and Eliot; and, inexplicable in the outward circumstances of Miss Millay's life, in indicates a search for new materials to eke out a dwindling subject matter. The interest in Baudelaire was publicly acknowledged by the translation, done with George Dillon, in 1936, of Baudelaire's poems. To offset partially this new Decadent mood and to keep our faith in Miss Millay is that courageous poem, "Justice Denied in Massachusetts," a caustic comment on the outcome of the Sacco-Vanzetti case. Yet it should be noted that Miss Millay, who joined the protesting marchers, got no feeling of hope from the numbers and idealism of the protestants, but only bitterness and the taste of death from the event. The electrocutions made Massachusetts a wasteland:

> . . . The sun that warmed our stooping backs and
> withered the weed uprooted
> We shall not feel it again.
> We shall die in darkness, and be buried in rain . . .

Baudelaireism permeates the fifty-two sonnets of *Fatal Interview* (1931) which, however, have other qualities that lift them into a notable achievement in verse. Descriptions of Love as "This beast that rends me in the sight of all," the "extreme disease," "the sick disorder in my flesh," etc., the preoccupation with death, and declarations like "night is my sister" are all out of Baudelaire. Indeed, one can cite passages from *Fatal Inter-*

view that are more like the French poet than are most translations of his verse, as for example:

> . . . all in good time, my dear,
> We shall be laid together in the night.
> And ruder and more violent, be assured,
> Than the desirous body's heat and sweat
> That shameful kiss by more than night obscured
> Wherewith at length the scornfullest mouth is met. . . .

The theme of these sonnets is the brevity of human love, to which
Miss Millay seeks to give more permanence, or the effect of permanence, by heightening the intensity. The result is that natural
passion seems denied and a sort of nymphomania, a diseased love,
substituted. Beginning with *A Few Figs from Thistles,* the poet
had stressed the transiency of love—a thing to endure "only until
this cigarette is ended"; now come to a greater wisdom, but
robbed of naturalness by her affected cynicism, she cannot sing of
the calm, unruffled, set current of an abiding passion. In denying
love in youth, Miss Millay, like her generation, is the inheritor
of unhealth in maturity; as she undershot, now she overshoots
her mark:

> . . . in me alone survive
> The unregenerate passions of a day
> When treacherous queens, with death upon the tread,
> Heedless and wilful, took their knights to bed.

To illustrate the intensity of her burning, it is permissible, we
suppose, for a poet to write of taking Jove to bed (Sonnet XII),
yet it does seem a trifle ridiculous. If these sonnets suggest an
aphrodisiac passion, however, there is no element of falseness in
their building: technically flawless, they are verbally rich and
musical. Sonnets XIII, XXII, XXVIII, XXIX, XXX, XXXI,
XXXIX are unsurpassed in her work save by the great four-
teener in *The Harp-Weaver,* and how beautiful are single lines—

> My kisses now are sand against your mouth

The manuscript of *The Princess Marries the Page* (1932), a
one-act play performed at Vassar College in May, 1917, was

long misplaced; it was discovered and the play again produced (with such an able actor as Dudley Digges in the part of the King) by the Cosmopolitan Club in Philadelphia in 1930. Its reception possibly has something to do with Miss Millay's desire to see it in print, for she has no illusions in regard to it. "It was unmistakably a youthful work, and very slight, but I thought it rather pretty. I had a desire to see it among my published books. So here it is." In print immediately after *Fatal Interview,* its artificiality troubles us less than the unnaturalness of the later book, for it belongs to the category of a whimsically-kept fondness for colored story books; it is of a piece with Miss Millay's early love for folk and counting-out rimes which bred poetry in her.

Wine from These Grapes (1934) is a volume of verse executed in precisely the temper of the lines from *The Buck in the Snow* from which the title is taken:

> Wine from these grapes I shall be treading surely
> Morning and noon and night until I die. . . .

It is verse professionally turned out to meet the publisher's expectation of a periodic volume from a poet of proved success. The promise that we shall have more of these dully-trod pieces does not whet the appetite. The high point in the book is an "Apostrophe to Man," in which the indignation is plainly whipped up, as the feeble vituperation, *"Homo* called *sapiens,"* at the end clearly shows. The fifth section, "Epitaph for the Race of Man," contains only two fairly good sonnets, No. VI upon the kings of Egypt, and No. XVI upon the greed of man, and the latter is far from musical. Sonnet III is full of harsh dissonances, and its final rimes are disagreeable: "core, coos, store, ooze, shore." There is a dearth of captivating image in the volume, and worse yet, a lack of music for the first time in Miss Millay's career. Horace Gregory notes a "straining toward unrealized vitality" which we could only feel was inevitable when Miss Millay first turned to Decadence, revealing thereby the spent imagination. Gregory has a final word to say on the poet, provoked by this volume and by *Fatal Interview,* which is just:

I am inclined to believe that the symbol of "poet" created by Miss Millay will in time resemble the immortality reserved for Elizabeth Barrett Browning. Miss Barrett leaving Wimpole Street upon the arm of Robert Browning was a signal of revolt in the same terms that attracted women readers to the legend of Edna Millay. I think her future reputation will be measured in the same terms that now apply to the work of the Victorian poetess, and that her merits will be preserved within the poems where she is least conscious of a possible immortality.

Conversation at Midnight (1937) is Miss Millay's late effort to be timely and yet to remain non-partisan so far as the issues she raises are concerned. She is very adroit at concealing her own views, but needless to say, she does not quite succeed. Six men besides the host assemble in the evening at Ricardo's: Merton, a stockbroker, with the tastes of a connoisseur in painting and poetry, but equally fond of horses and hunting; John, a gifted but unsuccessful painter, defeatist in his outlook; Pygmalion, a successful writer of short stories for popular magazines and an utter cynic with a racy, flippant tongue; Carl, a poet, a communist, and the irrepressible baiter of Merton; Father Anselmo, musician and Roman Catholic priest, whose convictions about the impermanence of the material and eternality of the spiritual worlds cannot be shaken; and finally, the immature Lucas, an advertising man, at present much in love, who must have a formula for everything. Ricardo, the host, is a cosmopolite, the son of an Italian petty nobleman and a rich American mother (both dead); his wealth and urbanity make him a charming host to very different types of people and conceal his negative, decadent outlook. These men talk, somewhat better than an equal number of real people would, for several hours, and then part without blows, no one of them affected in any way by their talk, each with precisely the same view that he brought to the party. Of course, this was intended by the author, but it is one of the weaknesses of her piece. Unwilling to grant anyone a victory, she unwittingly implies that they are all without eloquence or force. In particular are they all adamant about the major issue of their evening's talk: Resolved, that the United States should become a Soviet Republic as quickly as possible. It is conceivable that Carl and Merton, each representative of a society which hates the other, should each remain uninfluenced by the other's opinion, but that the other gentlemen present should stick to a predetermined position in each case is more debatable. The reason why this happens, however, is obvious enough: Miss Millay wants to give the impression that she is thoroughly cognizant of what is going on in the world, but she does not want to risk her popularity by throwing her lot in with either camp.

Yet she does commit herself. A sheaf of reviews shows the critics divided as to whether she speaks for herself through John or Ricardo, but not one reviewer names any other than these two as representing her outlook. At bottom, John and Ricardo are very much alike: they are decadents, who, however, prefer the *status quo* to a society in which they would have to rub elbows with their fellow men, break bread with them, or smell the foul smell of their bodies. Bourgeois (they claim to be Liberal) in politics, they have a Flaubertian and aesthetic disgust for the bourgeoisie. Carl fairly senses the enemy in them, as is revealed by his shot at Ricardo, "You talk too well. . . . What about . . . a sturdy, inarticulate GOOD IDEA?" The same challenge could be thrown to Miss Millay. She loves to whirl gracefully in the circle of flame, but let the flames mount a bit and she will forget her pirouetting and get out of the circle as quickly as possible. The Liberal world, which is her protection, gains nothing when she and her John and her Ricardos come back into the fold; indeed it is chiefly weakened by such dependents, the flirtatious "intellectuals" of the Latin quarter and Greenwich Village. Miss Millay will find it safer to write on love and death than on politics. Besides communism, dogs, and horses, *Conversation at Midnight* treats also the ideas of men about the other sex, and some very witty things are said; but it should be pointed out that men never talk like this about women unless there are women present to enjoy this kind of disguised flattery. Eavesdropping has done Miss Millay no good; someone has guessed that she was behind the screen or portiere, or in the closet, and the talk has been tempered to the ewe lamb. The only character whose speech she has perfectly recorded is Pygmalion, the self-centered, profane and garrulous short-story writer, who is always the same, whether there are women present or not. And as for poetry, *Conversation at Midnight,* though it contains much experimentation, including an effort to mix the verses of Maxwell Anderson with those of Ogden Nash (which have about as much affinity as oil and water), it is significant that there are no quotable lines.

Huntsman, What Quarry? (1939) is a better book because of Miss Millay's unchallengeable excellence whenever she is "in voice." Love exacts its heavy tribute, as usual, and we should add, *as is just,* since it is the poet's religion:

> As God's my judge, I do cry holy, holy,
> Upon the name of love however brief.

To be wholly consistent, Miss Millay should have written "however *long.*" We do not need to tally here the particular excellence of this ballad or that sonnet (though we do want to note the excellence of the group of poems in memory of Elinor Wylie) ; but since a part of our concern with Miss Millay is with her as an influential intellectual, we should note that, with wholesome liberalism, she is with the Chinese in their fight for independence and with the Loyalists, even in defeat, in Spain. This does a good deal to redeem the evasiveness of *Conversation at Midnight.*

Her all-aid-to-France-and-Britain poem, *There Are No Islands Any More* (1940), written just prior to the downfall of France and issued separately in September, is primarily an attack upon the isolationists in something not much better than doggerel. One needs to feel strongly and sanely that democracy is worth saving, not frantically and spasmodically. A more enduring love for it would have produced harder-hammered lines. Poems like "Underground System," read before the *Herald Tribune* Forum, and the *President with a Candidate's Face,*" contributed to the *Herald Tribune* to defeat F. D. R., if possible, lead one to speculate on how much honest, sober thought Miss Millay, in her present dither, has really given to the issues of the day. Certainly she hasn't spent much time in perfecting her verses recently if these are fair samples of what she is doing. Her announcement that she is going to become a poetic journalist, as reported in an interview in the *World-Telegram* (Nov. 15, 1940), whatever the cost to her verse, in order to save democracy doesn't fill one with an unbecoming enthusiasm. On the whole, one would rather be able to place her as a Decadent of parts than a pop-off liberal. Democracy to endure will have to be built for a long time and so, too, should the poetry that will sustain it.

The poetic hedonism of Sara Teasdale and of Edna St. Vincent Millay was at once a transcript of, and an inspiration to, the living hedonism of the gay "flappers" and their trailing "jellybeans" of the late 'teens and the early 'twenties. Pure photography was the early work of F. Scott Fitzgerald, *This Side of Paradise* (1920), *Flappers and Philosophers* (1920), *The Beautiful and the Damned* (1922), and *Tales of the Jazz Age* (1922). A stenographic record of the conversation of the "revolting youth" would be less satisfactory as an historical document than this fiction, for Mr. Fitzgerald plumbed deeper and recorded the "thoughts" of his generation as well. How infinitely well satisfied with itself it was—

A simple healthy leisure class it was—the best of the men not unpleasantly undergraduate—they seemed to be on a perpetual candidates list for some etherealized "Porcellian" or "Skull and Bones" extended out indefinitely into the world; the women, of more than average beauty, fragilely athletic, somewhat idiotic as hostesses but charming and infinitely decorative as guests. Sedately and gracefully they danced the steps of their selection in the balmy tea hours, accomplishing with a certain dignity the movements so horribly burlesqued by clerk and chorus girl the country over. It seemed ironic that in this lone and discredited offspring of the arts Americans should excel, unquestionably.

Despite Mr. Fitzgerald's fond hope that his sophomoric hedonists might go on dancing for ever, his generation was soon complaining of stomach ulcers, boredom, and sexual infidelities. Ironically, there is hardly more hint of this outcome in Stephen Vincent Benét's *The Beginning of Wisdom* (1921), Percy Marks' *The Plastic Age* (1924) and Warner Fabian's *Flaming Youth* (1925), Mr. Fitzgerald's imitators, than in Mr. Fitzgerald himself.

Received as almost identical in spirit with the poetry of Miss Teasdale and Miss Millay and the fiction of Fitzgerald was Floyd Dell's novel *Moon-Calf* (1920). Yet while this book treated with engaging frankness the sexual adventures of its hero,

Felix Fay, and of the girls who entertained him, the resemblance was merely a superficial one. The publication of its unsuccessful sequel, *The Briary-Bush* (1921), made painfully apparent the fact that Felix Fay did not "belong"—he was not "collegiate," he would never be tapped for "some etherealized 'Porcellian' or 'Skull and Bones,'" he was not a member of the too simple "healthy leisure class"—and his dancing was wretched. Though *The Briary-Bush* was quite as well written a novel as *Moon-Calf* and a very necessary commentary upon it, it did not please the age which liked Teasdale, Millay, and Fitzgerald; *The Briary-Bush* swept aside too quickly the veils of rosy illusion hung by the young hedonists. The idea of doubting, in 1921, that the "balmy tea hours" could be protracted indefinitely!

How completely misunderstood *Moon-Calf* was is apparent from some of the contemporary reviews of it. Even five years after its appearance, Stuart Sherman could write of it as though it were an unqualified brief for utter and complete sexual freedom, with no view at all of the consequences of this freedom. Sherman asserts that Dell's vision of the happy life, and the end of every man's desire, is—

... to be one of two children playing in a garret, two comrades who can sit down, and first having told the story of their lives, *i.e.* their previous love affairs, recite poetry to one another, talk about art, perhaps write a poem or two and a one act play about what happened to the children after the piper led them into the hill, and then exchange many kisses of happy and irresponsible comradeship.

Now this is unfair to Dell and a gross misrepresentation of *Moon-Calf.* The novel is, in reality, a study of adolescence in which the hero, a poor boy whose ideas have been formed from books borrowed from free libraries, gradually acquires a more realistic way of looking at life and love. Mr. Sherman pretends to have found the essence of the book in a single episode, Felix Fay's first clandestine meeting at twelve years with a girl slightly older than himself, an episode so distorted by Mr. Sherman that it is all but unrecognizable. Felix, the bookish younger brother of a tom-boy sister, has scarcely dared look more than covertly at the girls, for his natural timidity has been increased by the joking of his family and his fear that he cannot act in quite the knightly way of his book heroes. The meeting, when it occurs, is painfully innocent: Rose Henderson, who lives with her grandfather in the same "double-rent" with the Fays, takes the initiative in bringing about a *rendez-vous* with Felix in the attic, where they do *not* "recount their previous love affairs," but where they do read poetry to each other. When they are discovered, the child Rose is badly treated by her grandfather, and Felix hasn't the courage to meet her again, though she waits for him there. "The Fays moved again, and school reopened, and Felix read books, and forgot. . . ." There is something monstrous in Mr. Sherman's distortion of the episode.

It is natural that Felix's next friendship, formed when he is in high school, should be a Platonic affair with another omnivorous reader like himself, Stephen Frazer, who introduces him to Ingersoll and Atheism. A summer job in a candy factory where there are many girls results in Felix's deep emotional attachment to one of them, but he is still too much the moon-calf to declare his feelings. He becomes articulate again in the presence of the other sex only when a patronizing librarian takes an interest in him, but his rush of talk about Housman, Heine, and Verlaine and about his own poetry leaves him with "a strange sense of bafflement and hurt." Encouraged by a male companion, Felix "picks up" a girl at an amusement park; but when, in his ignorance and uncertainty, he makes no progress with her, he turns abruptly to Socialism, quite unconscious of his inner reasons for doing so. Through intellectual friends, he secures a job on a local newspaper, narrowly misses being enticed into an affair with a married woman seeking a thrill, and, all the time maturing, finally arranges his first real "date" with a girl whom he takes for a stenographer in the outer office of a man whom he is sent to interview, but who proves to be the man's niece. It is Felix's affair with this Joyce Tennant, an expelled Oberlin student, which probably gave the reviewers the notion that *Moon-Calf* belonged to the literature of hedonism. It is true that Felix and Joyce talk the solemn talk of the young people of the 'twenties about "freedom," but the author manages to convey (without too much subtlety for the reviewers, it would seem) his own scepticism as

to their sincerity. For example, this is clearly revealed when Joyce
tells Felix that she can be her real self with him and he replies
that it makes him very happy to hear it and Joyce cannot but
wonder—

"Happier than—than to hear me say I love you?"
"Yes," said Felix. (He lied—for there was a note in her voice when she
said those words that went tingling all through his body. But he was not
going to admit it.) "Any two people can be in love," he said. "It's a rarer
thing to be free. . . ."

Yet when Felix tries to conduct this vital affair, in which his
heart is really engaged, by the prescriptions found in the modern
novels he has been reading, when he insists that he does not believe in marriage, he loses Joyce whose iconoclasm, after all, is
merely experimental. Too late he discovers that she desires a conventional marriage and fidelity in her husband. Thus *Moon-Calf,*
if read with half an eye, is not only a study of adolescent love—
its hesitancies, fears, and confusions—and a good study at that,
but also a rather pointed satire of the new hedonism. The most
admirable thing about the book is the skill with which the author
has maintained the point of view of maturing youth throughout
the narrative. He is as successful in portraying the anguished self-
consciousness of a very small boy as he is in depicting the obstinate intellectualism of twenty. Dell really made his years of study
of child psychology and sex—he had published *Women as World
Builders* in 1913 and *Were You Ever a Child?* in 1919—count
for the utmost in *Moon-Calf.* A decade older than Fitzgerald,
and maturer than the women poets, he was able to see the revolt
of the 'twenties objectively and yet be sympathetic towards the
revolutionaries—from whom Mr. Sherman was *two* decades removed. *Moon-Calf* may not be a great novel, but it is a very
good novel. One cannot name a better book which attempts to do
the same sort of thing.

The Briary-Bush takes Felix Fay from small-town reporting to
Chicago, where he eventually becomes dramatic critic for one of
the great dailies. The novel is not focused, however, either upon
the newspaper experience or upon Felix Fay's studio married life.
He and his wife, Rose-Ann, the willful daughter of a small-town

clergyman, attempt a union in which neither surrenders anything, in which each is perfectly free of the other. This works beautifully until Felix falls in love with an ardent young worshipper of independence, is repulsed by her, and attempts to compensate with an actress. Rose-Ann leaves him for a career of her own in California before he realizes he cannot live without her. After kicking a while at his pride, Felix goes to the Coast to persuade Rose-Ann to rejoin him, and the novel closes with her forgiveness and their plans to build a house. No more apposite comment upon the sex discussions of 1921 than *The Briary-Bush* is discoverable, but the novel said what no one wanted to hear, and Dell was through as a popular novelist with his second novel. Nevertheless his history of Felix Fay remains not only his most solid achievement, but a dispassionate commentary upon the limitations of human experiment in a field where lasting happiness (not the hedonist's "moment") is the ultimate goal.

Those who have read *Home-Coming* (1933), Floyd Dell's autobiography, are aware that the history of Felix Fay owes its vitality to the fact that it is definitely a sifting of Dell's own experience. In fact, the combination of *Moon-Calf* and *The Briary-Bush* gives a much better effect of authenticity than does *Home-Coming,* though the latter is valuable for its anecdotes of the many people of literary consequence whom Dell has known. Floyd Dell was born in the small town of Barry, Illinois, on June 28, 1887, when his father, a former cavalry soldier in the Civil War, was forty-eight years old, and his mother, an Irish school teacher by the name of Kate Crone, was forty-one years old. His two brothers and sister were much older than he; consequently, like Felix Fay, he early sought the companionship of books. His boyhood was almost nomadic, for the elder Dell, pugnacious and more or less incompetent, moved his family from place to place in vain effort to find a secure niche for himself in the economic order. Floyd was forced to work during summer vacations ("I was the sort of boy who could always get a job, if there were jobs to give; a bright-looking boy.") and did a variety of things, of which working in a candy factory left the most indelible impression. He and his father were reading together all sorts of radical literature, from socialism to nihilism, and while still in his 'teens, he became an active member of the Socialist Party. In Davenport, Iowa, Floyd Dell got his first journalistic experience, working on local papers from 1905 to 1908, and in this city became infected with the bohemianism of his first genuine literary friends, George Cram Cook, Mollie Cook, and Susan Glaspell.

In November, 1908, Dell went up to Chicago and, when his money was almost gone, secured a position as reporter on the *Chicago Evening Post.* He was soon assisting Francis Hackett, editor of the paper's Friday *Literary Review,* and when Hackett resigned in 1911, Dell succeeded him. Though only twenty-three at the time, Dell demonstrated his competence by making the *Review* the best critical journal in Chicago in the next two years. Meanwhile he had impulsively married, he and his wife agreeing to the sort of union Felix Fay and Rose-Ann had tried to maintain. He admits that his own infidelities were responsible for the failure of his marriage—for the couple separated in 1912.

In that year Dell severed his connection with the *Post* and moved to New York City. Contributions to radical papers led to his being invited to assist Max Eastman in editing the *Masses* from 1914 to 1917. He was, of course, one of those tried for sedition when the magazine was suppressed, and there is an entertaining, but inadequate account of this in *Home-Coming.* When more or less the same group established the *Liberator,* Dell again served as an editor from 1918 to 1924. From his first coming to New York, he was a resident of Greenwich Village and active in the bohemian life of that colony. One-act plays of his were performed by the same amateur casts which later participated in plays staged by the Washington Square Players and the Provincetown Players. More definitely hedonistic in character, but ephemeral at best, these plays have been variously published and forgotten (*The Angel Intrudes,* 1918; *Sweet and Twenty,* 1921; *King Arthur's Socks,* 1922). In 1919 Floyd Dell was married to Berta-Marie Gage, of Pasadena, California, and afterwards went to live in Croton-on-the-Hudson. She was probably responsible for his finishing *Moon-Calf,* which he had been dilatorily engaged in writing for six years. A review by Heywood Broun "made" the novel.

Though one may justly admire Mr. Dell's first two novels, one need not conclude that he is well cast as a novelist. His later fiction is, on the whole, disappointing. He has written historical romance, *Runaway* (1925), *Diana Stair* (1932), and *The Golden Spike* (1934); he has glanced at a variety of sex relations, *An Old Man's Folly* (1926), *An Unmarried Father* (1926), and *Souvenir* (1929); he has descanted humorously on Greenwich Village in *Janet March* (1923) and *Love in Greenwich Village* (1926); and he has reworked the theme of his first two novels in *Love Without Money* (1931)—but none of these books quite convinces. They are entertaining, yes; but memorable, no. The subjectivism which makes the drawing of Felix Fay convincing keeps Dell from creating other successful characters, who must be seen objectively to live.

Some of Dell's non-fiction may not be treated quite so summarily, though books like *Looking at Life* (1924) and *The Outline of Marriage* (1926–27) are shoddy enough. The biography of Upton Sinclair (1927) was a good service to an early radical, but it hardly did complete justice to the subject. Historically more important was a little guide-book for the intelligentsia, called *Intellectual Vagabondage* (1926), in which Dell appears the perfect Villager he was taken for when *Moon-Calf* was published in 1920. He himself does not describe it as a guide-book, but as "a plea in defense of that generation of intelligent, sensitive and more or less creative young people to which I and most of my friends belong." Yet it prescribes definitely what one must believe in to belong to the Intelligentsia, while informing the reader what clever people the Intelligentsia are. The chief interest at this date in the book lies in the record it preserves of the rebellious mind of the 'twenties. After a condemnation of all that the nineteenth century stood for (which leads him to conclude that even Darwinism, seemingly at first a "Tong-War" with Religion and Science bent on exterminating each other, was in the end "nothing more than a lively advertising campaign between rivals to whom competition is indeed the life of trade"), Dell turns to writing "A Spiritual Autobiography of my own generation in Its Literary and Social Aspects." The autobiography is an account of progress from Ingersoll and atheism, through Whitman and aimless freedom, Fitzgerald and hedonism, Ibsen and the discovery of "a Glorious Playfellow" (meaning the New Woman), Stirner and the release of the Ego, Carpenter and new sexual conduct, Kipling, Carman & Hovey and a "joyous" vagabondage, Whistler and a new art (as seen through George Moore's *Confessions of a Young Man*), Wells, Shaw and the hope of a Future Utopia—despite a desperate Present, to Marx, the Russian Revolution, the repudiation of the idea of freedom —and "bankruptcy!" A dreadful hodge-podge, the reader may say, none-the-less it is the intellectual history of Mr. Dell's kind and generation. While Dell is conscious his generation will achieve nothing, he is sanguine in regard to his successors. He neatly avoids telling us what the successors will achieve, but apparently it will be some form of Socialism, for his criticism of the nineteenth century has a Socialist cast. Byron, Shelley, Keats, Landor, and Browning "left England because they could not live in England; and they could not live in England because England was the foremost capitalist country on earth." Lincoln, he avers, was "accurately designated the servant of Northern capitalism," etc.

This raises the issue of Dell's radicalism and of his precise contribution to radical thought. Sinclair Lewis has called him "a faun at the barricades," while Stuart Sherman declared that Dell is "about as much of a Socialist as J. P. Morgan." "At no time was Floyd Dell a real revolutionist," Michael Gold contends in *The New Masses*. "At all times he had a distaste for reality, for the strong smells and sounds and confusions of the class struggle. He had none of the contacts with workingmen and strikes and battles that John Reed had. He was a Greenwich Village playboy. Even in those days his main interests were centered in the female anatomy. . . ." Bemused, scornful, and angry critics deny him much force as a radical, yet all seemingly admit he played some sort of rebellious rôle in the 'twenties. We have seen that his chief creative work, the history of Felix Fay, was really conservative, cautionary in its counsel if not reactionary. Was his rôle no more than that of tramp in the realm of ideas, as *Intellectual Vagabondage* suggests? Dell, like all the Intelligentsia, has been extraordinarily footloose, yet so far as Socialism is concerned, he has repeatedly turned his steps back to this idol. He is no revolutionist, but neither is he precisely a faun. His Socialism has been more or less of the Fabian variety, a program-less faith in the inevitable, a typical pre-War product. Yet, while never evangelical, it has a sort of insistency in most of his books which certainly has not been entirely negative in its effect. Such a thing is hard to gauge, but our guess is that the accumulation of small passages, scattered insinuations throughout Dell's work (let's discount his youthful efforts and the *Masses* trial), did about as much for Socialism in America as Jack Reed up to 1929, but of course infinitely less than the Jack Reed legend since the depression. This, of course, is less than what Norman Thomas accomplished in the same period.

In *Love in the Machine Age* (1930) Floyd Dell has written a book which might have been designed by Havelock Ellis, save that it has a broader sociological base than any of Ellis' books. It is a study of the sex relations and problems of adolescents, but not an original study, rather a synthesis of Dell's reading of Freud, Malinowski, Frazer, Adler, Watson, and the files of *Mental Hygiene*. Incidentally, it contains a tribute to Ellis which should be set against any summary of the man's deficiencies. "There is not a sexual oddity which he has not labored to make us understand as an exaggeration of some aspect of normal human emotional life," writes Dell. "He has thus become *par excellence* the teacher of tolerance to our generation." The main thesis of *Love in the Machine Age* is that, since our morals were formed by a patriarchal society which is disappearing, knowledge of sex forces is necessary for happiness in a transitional age which has no absolute code for guidance. The book disseminates as knowledge such doctrine as Dell has accepted from the investigators he has read. Yet the chief interest of *Love in the Machine Age* is its attack upon what Dell terms "ideological over-compensations." These are, in his view, a product of overzealousness in the "cultural campaigns against patriarchalism, in favor of a variety of concepts of modernity." Prominent among these ideological overcompensations which he is completely successful in discrediting are arguments for the abolition of the family, Watson's dogma of disinterested child care, work as a substitute for love for women, and sex as amusement. Unfortunately he does not treat any of Freud's ideas as overcompensatory, nor while attacking the idea of sex as amusement does he tell us that Ellis is chiefly responsible for the spread of this doctrine. Yet, in a negative and critical way, *Love in the Machine Age* is a good book, and in line with the best work of Dell's career. Better informed than many who used the materials of sex relations as subject matter in his time, Dell has a place as a more or less able commentator on extreme tendencies and chaotic urges.

Another contemporary whose experience was much wider than Dell's, though his reading appears to have been much more limited, was Ben B. Lindsey, for twenty-seven years judge of the Juvenile Court of Denver, Colorado, whose proposal for the legalizing of "companionate marriages" created a tremendous stir in the middle of the 'twenties. Lindsey is a full-fledged Progressive of the old school. Born in Jackson, Tennessee, on November 25, 1869, and equipped only with a public school education, he was admitted to the Colorado bar when he was twenty-four years of age. Angered because he and his partner lost workmen's damage suits against the Colorado corporations through jury fixing, he first declared war on the trusts in the late 'nineties by getting a three-quarters jury vote decision law through the legislature. When the Superior Court declared the law unconstitutional, he engaged the trusts on other fronts. These battles of his youth are told in *The Beast* (1910) and in *The Rule of Plutocracy in Colorado* (1912), the first done in collaboration with Harvey O'Higgins. After forcing juvenile court laws through the legislature, Lindsey was appointed administrator, and then judge of the Juvenile Court of Denver in 1900. He attracted international attention through his success in handling juvenile delinquency while on the bench. In 1906 he was defeated as candidate for governor, and in 1912 he served as a member of the Progressive National Committee, though he had entered politics as a Democrat. The temper of the man may be gauged from the Rooseveltian title of his autobiography, *The Dangerous Life* (1931).

The books which caused the tumult in the 'twenties were *The Revolt of Modern Youth* (1925) and *The Companionate Marriage* (1927), both done in collaboration with Wainwright Evans. In the former book Lindsey maintains that the check on prostitution (which, we have seen, was exerted between 1911 and 1915) has resulted in modern youths turning "to girls of their own class, a thing they had seldom done in the past." Arguing that "the crude sex hunger, like the food hunger, should be governed and controlled, not by legal fiat and moral compulsion, but by the educated wisdom, self-control, and good taste of the individual," Lindsey advocated a "hands-off" policy and even suggested the possibility of "trial marriage" for youngsters as a solution for irregular sexual conduct. Two years later, he retreated from this hazarded opinion, remarking that "trial marriage" is merely Free Love that avails itself of a legal form. He found that sophisticated people "were enjoying, through birth control and collusive divorce, a more practical form of union," which he termed "Companionate Marriage." He proposed legalizing this sort of union to make it available for all. "Companionate Marriage is legal marriage, with legalized Birth Control, and the right to divorce by mutual consent for childless couples, usually without payment of alimony."

One is impressed by the healthy equalitarianism behind Lindsey's idea to extend the freedom of companionate marriage to all. Yet one questions if Judge Lindsey has quite gone to the bottom of the matter, or has understood all the implications of his proposals. "The right to divorce by mutual consent" strikes us as incorporating the doctrine of complete *laissez-faire* in marital relations. In effect, it reduces marriage to the coupling of dogs. The fact that certain "sophisticates" have fallen into such a relationship does not make it desirable for all. Separation on the grounds of "mutual consent" is a vastly different thing from separation on the grounds of incompatibility, though to the thoughtless it may not seem so. The plea of incompatibility recognizes the social responsibility in marriage, even though the marriage is childless. The plea of incompatibility is a plea of failure in a relation in which society has a right to expect a high average of success. To free on these grounds, however, is reasonable, yet this is as far as liberalism should ever go. And, of course, the evidence for incompatibility should be satisfactory to the state.

Lindsey's proposal to void the right of woman to alimony if

she "were in good health, and able to work, and to support herself" shows that he views alimony wholly as a compulsion (which, in part, it is) to continue the marriage relationship after any other incentive is dead. That he should so view it is not surprising in light of the scandalous alimony awards of our courts, yet the theory of alimony—an economic compensation to the woman for a real loss she has sustained in an unfortunate union—is good. Though Lindsey is modern in scoffing at "romantic love," he certainly is a little romantic himself to suppose that society looks upon a divorced woman (who has successfully practised birth control) with the same favor it regards a virgin. There are chivalrous and romantic individuals who do well at this, but society generally does not. Until society changes its view, alimony is a necessity. Furthermore it is clear that, with the tendency to cheapen womankind, now that America demands less of her reproductive powers, large alimony awards will decrease, and even the right to any award is likely to be challenged. The most promising remedy for the alimony situation probably lies in the training and employment of a woman judiciary for divorce cases.

Lindsey is cogent and may be understood; so too may all the writers who dealt specifically with youth—Fitzgerald, Teasdale, Millay, and Dell. But the times produced a large number of writers who were incoherent largely because they sought to justify sexual release, not on frankly hedonistic grounds but by assuming the false rôles of mystics and philosophers. Their occultism is easily explained on the ground that they were too timid to be honest, and too shrewd to be plain. Their philosophies and their mysticism may all be reduced, without serious loss to the thinking world, to eroticism. Such a reduction is necessary, however, if we are to understand the mental unhealth, as well as the vigor, which is a part of the intellectual life of America. Expose a sore to the sun and the healing process begins.

In any summary of American incoherence, to judge from the reviews of his work, Waldo Frank stands first. Joseph Warren Beach, who has analyzed Joyce, Mrs. Woolf, and Proust with success, writes of this author, "I find myself incapable of evaluating the work of Waldo Frank in the whole. I do not know whether it is sound, whether it has significance on which one can rest as on something solid. . . ." Critics generally have given him up as too difficult to understand, which has led, inevitably, to extraordinarily diverse estimates of his importance. Even well-intentioned friends flounder in evaluating him. Paul Rosenfeld, who carefully avoids saying what the themes of Frank are, insists that his intelligence would make him distinguished in France, while "in Manhattan such mental equipment towers." Let the reader try to reconcile this flattering estimate with Mr. Rosenfeld's later statement in regard to Frank, "None of his more ambitious works exhibits the direct and well-sustained application of the intelligence to the materials of art," before accepting it as a final evaluation of the importance of Waldo Frank. Let the reader also examine Mr. Rosenfeld's devastating analysis of Frank's failure in characterization (the contention is that the people of the novels are all alike) and speculate why he paid so handsome a tribute to Frank without casting up his account.

Waldo Frank might well be called, in no derogatory sense, the Wandering Jew of American literature. The pattern of the quest is the invariable one of his novels, and his life has been so diffusive that this may be said to be its pattern also. Son of an able, well-to-do lawyer, Julius J. Frank, and of a gifted Southern woman, Helen Rosenberg, Waldo Frank was born in Long Branch, N. J., August 25, 1889. After attending the public grammar schools and De Witt Clinton High School, in New York City, as well as a private school in Switzerland, Frank was entered at Yale College. Here, in 1911, he won both the B.A. and M.A. degrees and a Phi Beta Kappa key, while serving, in his last year in New Haven, as dramatic critic for the *Journal-Courier*. After his graduation, Frank struck off for Wyoming, where for a few months he worked on a ranch, and then swung back to New York. In the metropolis he had a brief term of employment on the *Evening Post* and the *Times*.

In 1913 he went to Europe, beginning the travels that were to take him ultimately to Germany, Spain, Russia, and South America. The following year he was back in New York as a free-lance writer. In 1916 he helped to launch *The Seven Arts* and was married to Margaret Naumburg, founder of the Walden School, of New York City, where psychoanalysis was first applied in education in America. Divorced from her, after the birth of their son Thomas, Frank was married to Alma Magoon in 1927. Meanwhile, in 1917, he had published his first novel, *The Unwelcome Man,* had made a critical study of his country in *Our America* (1919) and had returned to the novel in *The Dark Mother* (1920). He was among the few young men who registered as conscientious objectors on our entry into the World War I. To his critical work and novel writing, he added editing, translating, and lecturing. In addition he became a contributing editor to *The New Republic, The New Masses,* and various French and South American journals. His diffusiveness is shown in his later book titles: *Rahab* (1922), *The Novel of Tomorrow* (1922), *City Block* (1922), *Holiday* (1923), *Chalk Face* (1924), *Salvos* (1924), *Virgin Spain* (1926), *Time-Exposures* (1926), *The Re-Discovery of America* (1929), *New Year's Eve* (a play, 1929), *Tales from the Argentine* (ed., 1930), *America Hispaña* (1931), *Dawn in Russia* (1932), *The Death and Birth of David Markand* (1934), *In the American Jungle* (1936), and *The Bridegroom Cometh* (1938).

Waldo Frank's first novel, *The Unwelcome Man,* is a study of the boyhood and adolescence of an "unwanted child," Quincy Burt, domineered by brother and sister, father and mother, and even coached and directed by the girls and women in whom he later betrays a half-hearted interest. His quest for twenty-two years is to be normal and conventional, a goal against which, however, his genius rebels. Despite the agony of loneliness which drives Quincy to his frustrated efforts to conform, an antithetical stubbornness makes him perform little acts of defiance, like keeping a dirty handkerchief, running away from home, and refusing to participate in athletics at college. Only just before the climax of the tale, when he loses the girl whom he is not sure he loves, does Quincy realize that to be conventional, even if successful, is to fall into a sort of oblivion, to be swept away by a stream:

"Most people succeed in America, not because they have brains or shrewdness or luck, but because the current is too strong to let them sink."

Quincy hasn't quite the vital force in him to press the trigger of
the pistol he has bought, so his story ends abruptly with his slipping into the deadly current of normal American life:

> The history of Quincy is lost in the Stream's clotted pressure. He is one
> more molecule, replenishing its substance. . . . The Stream's source is
> Quincy. Quincy's epilogue is the Stream.

The Unwelcome Man is a much more intense book than
Moon-Calf, yet the objectivity Dell attained is here altogether
lacking; not only is the subject matter adolescence, but the point
of view is still adolescent. Psychology should have taught Waldo
Frank that health for his character meant some sort of adjustment to life. *The Unwelcome Man* is valueless, not because Quincy
Burt fails to adjust, but because Frank looks upon suicide apparently as preferable to adjustment. In spite of the book's fidelity
occasionally to youthful emotional states, one cannot but feel
that its total effect is chaotic. The vision of the wise counselor,
a rôle the novelist assumes whether he wills or not, is lacking.
What could either youth or maturity get from this book? Yet, in
passing, one should not fail to note that *The Unwelcome Man,*
whatever its faults, is a pioneer novel in its use of the new psychology.

The search for a way to escape the Stream of American life
becomes the theme of Frank's later novels. Let us consider those
interrelated stories, *Rahab* and *City Block,* which give us the
career of one of Waldo Frank's most original characters, Fanny
Dirk Luve, prototype of O'Neill's Cybel, though by turns an
exalté extraordinary. Mr. Eric Estorick has done an admirable
job of interpreting Fanny in *Trend,* and we will follow his
analysis though we may not reach his conclusions. Frank's idea
for *Rahab* came to him from a comparison of the two short passages in the Old and New Testaments touching the harlot Rahab:

> And Joshua saved Rahab the harlot alive . . . because she hid the mes-
> sengers which Joshua sent to spy out Jericho. (*Joshua,* 6:25)

> Likewise also was not Rahab the harlot justified by works . . .?
> For as the body without the spirit is dead, so faith without works is
> dead also. (*Gen. Epistle of James,* 2:25-26)

Fanny Dirk Luve becomes a modern Rahab when her husband, Harry Luve, returns from a philandering career a convert to religion to discover that she has had "a mystically-elevating relationship," *i.e.,* has committed adultery, with a Jew. Driven from her home and child by her fanatical husband, Fanny is first the mistress of her boss in New York, whom she leaves for some mythical fear that she will "heal" herself, and then—after an interlude in a sweat shop and an illness—a prostitute and eventually the madame of a house of prostitution. Here she accomplishes her "salvation" through "works"—not only serving the men admirably, but caring for her girls (so that one of them declares, "Only a woman can love a woman"), till finally, when she refuses to let her house be used in framing a completely worthless Jew, it is "pulled" by the police, and the book of *Rahab* ends. Even in this catastrophe Fanny, according to Mr. Estorick, achieves a sort of triumph: "And yet my soul was One. It was unchanged. It moved through the broken sea of my Disaster, it knew it was One. . . ." She has retained her individuality, a Whole Consciousness; she has not yet fallen into the Stream. Plausible or not, the characterization has real appeal, and one does not put *Rahab* aside without the impression that it has been used somehow effectively in shedding a kind of light into stygian gloom, for the novel otherwise is oppressively sordid.

Fanny Luve, still plying her trade, reappears in *City Block.* In the first episode, "Accolade," she supplies drunken Clarence Lipper, who has wasted or lost all his money, with a silver brush and comb to take home to his wife as a Christmas present. This is another *act,* of course, by which she shall be saved. Since acts and faith are inseparable in the Epistle of James, Mrs. Luve again appears in the fourth episode ("Faith") preaching confidence to a patrolman who has taken as a mistress a young English governess whom he picked up in the Park. But Patrolman Pat Broaddus thinks of his wife, his children, and his Duty, rather than of her words—

". . . For God's sake, *take* her. Take her decent. She's lovely, man. How dare you hide her in a hole-and-corner. Take her out to the sun, where the two of you belong!"

Fanny Luve herself forces the issue by refusing to let them have her room any longer, but the s⁺ratagem fails: Pat is of the Stream and falls back into it.

City Block is systole to the diastole of *Rahab*. Fanny Luve discovers the Wholeness of giving herself completely, but *"City Block* is the story of characters (tenants) starved for love, suffering from the fruits of loveless unions (which bear soulless fruit), suffering from disharmonic familism, from broken and disrupted families, suffering from the tragedy of the incompletenesses of existences that would be more than ordinary." The novel really has two concluding chapters, "Ecclesia Sanctae Teresae" and "Beginning," each of which recalls an earlier episode in Frank's fiction. Mr. Estorick reminds us that the first conclusion has its relation to the story of Fanny Luve, though she does not appear in it:

> . . . Clarence Lipper's wife comes to Father Luis Ajala Dennis saying: "I love him too (meaning her husband). And that is it, Father Dennis . . . It is Christmas Eve. I want to give him something." (She is with child and she feels that she has not given her husband the experience of sin: the test of love in Christ). "But how can she give? How can she break the bonds except through Sin?" For thus she would mar and test his unconscious happiness: she would make him less happy. And Father Dennis, who is suffering from incestuous dreams, thinks unto himself: ": . . And white straight healing that she is. And Sin? What is Sin but a lack, a great Hunger? What if I am sinning in my holy state . . . dreaming incestuous dreams that all my blood and all my entrails blanket from my mind? What of it? Who cares about sin? Not Christ, surely not St. Paul! Not our holy Mother Church that blots sin out, insignificant and mean, before a word . . . for a candle!" But all that is resolved by the great white healing that is Mrs. Lipper. They embrace under the very image of Christ, and there is a mutual release . . . and Mrs. Lipper feels that she is healed, that she can go to her husband bearing the gifts of healing, wholeness, and holiness. "I have something new to give at last to my husband!" Thus, Mrs. Fanny Dirk Luve, who had shown the light to Clarence Lipper, has wrought a miracle through the instrumentality of Mrs. Lipper and Father Dennis. And so Rahab justifies her life and work and faith. . . .

Though the relation of the encounter of Mrs. Lipper and the Castilian-Irish priest to the mystical adultery of Mrs. Luve and the Jew is not cited, this strikes us as an admirable inter-

pretation and close to the author's meaning. But what of the last
section in the book, entitled "Beginning"? Here we shall have
to make out for ourselves. We plunge into the thought stream
of fifteen-year-old Paolo Benati, the unsmiling bootblack who
has penetrated mystically into the lives of all the tenants in the
block and who has given their stories to the novelist, a being
like himself, one of those "sacrificed and consumed." Yet Paolo
is admitted greater than his "scribe", for in the night he dwells
"with the Presence, holy and awful," and when he has made plain
to the novelist the meaning of all these lives, he buys a pistol and
goes out to the park and shoots himself—thus escaping (where
Quincy Burt could not) the Stream, thus achieving a Beginning.

A "Beginning" in suicide does not commend itself to most of
us as much of a "Beginning." Yet we are meant to feel that the
miserable exaltation of the boy is somehow akin to spiritual
translation—Paolo Benati is a saint in the hagiography of
Waldo Frank, and Fanny Dirk Luve wears a nimbus brighter
than that which glows about Saint Teresa. Paolo is a sort of
prophet of Christ, and the acts of Mrs. Luve are ever in emula-
tion of Him. What means all this mystery? What holy secret
does Waldo Frank possess? What light has he seen? Though
Rahab and *City Block* are enforced throughout by Scriptural
allusion and though Fanny has absorbed the essence of the Bible
by lying with it spread open on her breasts, the reader does not
need to be persuaded that the hedonism of Waldo Frank has
anything more than the most tenuous connection with the teachings of Christ: its true reference (of which Frank perhaps is
wholly unaware) is to the decadent hedonism of the Cyrenaic
school—a school which started with the premise that pleasure
is the end of life, but at length despairing of any satisfaction in
positive enjoyment, concluded to renounce all external things,
just as Frank abjures the Stream of American life and fastens his
attention on death. The most significant episode in *Rahab* and
City Block is none of those cited by Mr. Estorick. It is the
Dance of Death which Fanny Luve performs in her house of
prostitution to the chant of a dissolute visitor: "The Western
World is dying . . . Death creeps up, Death creeps down . . .

etc.,"—she, who had just been thinking, "Our world unfolds
... leaping toward God"!

Another unintentional travesty, though more legitimate perhaps, of Christian story is contained in *Holiday*. In a town,
significantly named Nazareth, in the deep South a white girl,
Virginia Hade, and a black man, John Cloud, are propelled
towards each other by gnawing sex hunger, but convention keeps
them from physical union: wherefore there will be no birth of
Love, healing the rawness between the two races, in Nazareth.
After John is gone, Virginia Hade wounds herself with his
knife, and these wounds displayed provoke the lynch-mob to hunt
John Cloud. Trembling, she lies in bed while they burn him in
the Square, and then she sleeps. Yet when his body had been
stripped, the women watchers had been sucked forward, and a
little black-frocked man had cried, "O Christ . . . O Christ!"
And ". . . with the world sinks Nazareth into the well of night."
Here Frank's thesis that physical love might prove the *aqua
regia* to melt the hard hatred of black and white, that a Saviour
might have been born of miscegenation, is lost sight of in the
intensity of the drama, the fatalism of John Cloud, and the compulsion of Virginia Hade—all plausibly managed. Yet we must
not forget that the night that settles on Nazareth is the "Death
of the Western World."

Waldo Frank has made a sincere, but abortive, effort to throw
off his decadent hedonism in *The Death and Birth of David
Markand,* written, after fourteen years, as a sequel to *The Dark
Mother*. The earlier book, the novelist's only dull effort, is the
story of David Markand's release from his dangerous friendship
with Tom Rennard, whom Frank implies is of the Stream. This
release is effected by Tom's sister, who, loving David herself,
yet introduces.him to the girl whom he marries. This might have
been a better novel had there been any other episodes than the
various phases of David's mooning in it, or had Frank really
defined the relationship of the three people in the story. That
he should think enough of his early novel to write a sequel to it,
thus calling especial attention to it, indicates that he does not
know how complete a failure *The Dark Mother* is.

The Death and the Birth of David Markand, on the other

hand, is a very readable book, more closely approximating the conventional Naturalistic novel in form than the other books of this unconventional writer. Startlingly enough, it is dedicated "to the American worker who will understand." What Frank thinks the American worker will get out of his novel is certainly a puzzle. *The Death and Birth of David Markand* is the travelogue of a confused and wealthy neurotic who, deserting his wife and children, wanders over America in his insatiable quest for sexual adventure, which Frank curiously confuses with spiritual release. Markand's last act before leaving home is to impregnate his wife, but neither his knowledge of the pregnancy, the birth of her child, nor the death of his son draws him back to her. His whole justification is that he is trying to find himself —a purpose which results in as flagrant an exhibition of egocentricity as our literature affords. Frank tries to persuade us that the "scientific" character of the quest elevates Markand's explorations above ordinary lechery. How this can be viewed as anything other than casuistry is inconceivable:

And Ted . . . yes, face the truth! . . . the impersonal possession of Ted was a substitute for Helen (his wife). . . . Not an ecstasy real in itself? No! Unreal. Leaving, therefore, no trace, compelling its own endless and hopeless repetition. His sexual relationship with Ted, perfect because unreal, has been a substitute for his imperfect because real relationship with Helen. . . .

During his wanderings Markand handles freight, serves as a bar-tender, and works in a packing plant (where the work makes him sick). He is for a short time connected with a Farmers' League movement on the Middle Border, and—towards the close of the book—is represented as the spiritual companion (nothing more) of John Byrne and his mistress, who are heroically trying to unionize the coal miners of Howton. They tolerate him for reasons that are not sufficiently clear, though Frank apparently thinks that David is a revolutionary, for he has a girl tell him, despite his protests—

". . . But you *are* a revolutionist. Even though you don't know it. You have been, you big boy! You have been, ever since you walked away from your home."

This adolescent confusion of realities leads to Markand's being present as a captive when poor Byrne and his Jane are brutally murdered and he himself is properly bruised. In this night, according to Frank, the old David Markand dies and a new David is born. Yet we are not convinced of this, nor does David's return to his wife (page 542!) add to our conviction. It is not the murder of the labor agitator which is the most vivid incident in the book, but rather a hideously repulsive episode in which the experienced lecher plays upon the body of a young girl, who, despite the fact that she is a prostitute, has never been sexually aroused until he places his hands upon her. Her terrible hatred of him when her orgasm is past strikes him between the eyes, though the glass she hurls at him misses. This is a type of experience which converts the gross sensualist into the decadent hedonist, but in this case makes him wish to reach out for something more. Yet one suspects the social reality which David Markand fancies himself possessed of is mere delusion—it is an emotional substitute for sex for the person of jaded appetite. Much good it will do the workers of America if a legion of David Markands—the Big Boys!—enlists in their behalf!

In *The Bridegroom Cometh* Frank came nearer doing what he had aimed at in *The Death and Birth of David Markand* than in the earlier novel: if we are correct in assuming that he meant David's "birth" to be the realization of a Spinozistic union among all men. His heroine, Mary Donald, is one of two sisters —Martha and Mary of Christian antithesis—who grow up in a New England small town, where they imbibe religious clichés with their meals, eating to sustain the spirit. A curiously mixed young person who fervently hopes to be ready when the Heavenly Bridegroom comes but who cannot always suppress the vagrant thought, "what if I were naked when he came," Mary is rescued from her plan to become a missionary by friends who take an interest in her and send her to Winant College. The girls in this school and her work in a summer hotel let a meagre light filter into her brain, but the dismissal of her favorite teacher, Doris Solberg Granes, from the faculty for an indiscreet talk on Russia does more for Mary than anything else. She leaves Winant, not a convert to any doctrine but to the woman.

Education becomes more intensive for Mary Donald when she goes to live in New York with Mrs. Granes and her husband Peter, a successful columnist and seducer, while attending "New Amsterdam" College. Her first shock is to discover that Doris Granes has a lover, and her first test is to keep this from Peter at Mrs. Granes' instruction. The Graneses' emancipated friends and their talk cause explosions in her mind, but still its underlying stratum is intact. When her sister, who has married a racketeer and come to New York, has an abortion, she is more shaken than by her engagement to the pure young man, Willem Taess, or by her job in the children's aid society (in which she proves good only as a filing clerk, failing as an investigator). Both she and Willem are afraid of sex, but Willem, who is still under the dominance of his mother, a Dutch Jewess who hates her daughter-in-law, has the greater fear. Before their marriage goes to smash, they try to give one party like those that Doris and Peter Granes give. When it becomes bacchanalian, Mary drives the drunken revelers from the apartment as Christ drove the money-changers from the Temple.

Telling her husband that she needs a chance to think, Mary slips away with her sister for a vacation near their old home. Martha is inconsolable over the loss of her man, who had been slain when attempting to muscle in on a racket in Chicago. One sexual surrender to a person for whom she does not care and Martha's suicide in the lake teach Mary that Willem will never satisfy her yearning for love. She breaks with him utterly, and moved by the remembered words of Dolg, a Communist purchasing agent of the Soviets in this country, on the wholesomeness of the workers, she attempts to become a working girl. After a great variety of experiences in which she learns how the working girl is beset from every direction, she finally becomes fixed as an operator in the E-lite Collar Company in Long Island City and joins the Communist Party. When the leaders dissolve a "Sunday school" of indoctrination for small children which she had helped to organize and when they order her good friends Kurt and Lida to marry and go to Howton, Tennessee, to direct a strike there —not because they are the best people to do this but because the Party needs some martyrs and they will surely be slain, Mary revolts. Her outbreak against the leaders who "do not love enough" brings her censure and threat of worse. Then the ubiquitous David Markand, who had arrived unannounced several chapters earlier to help Mary throw off the influence of a psychoanalyst, inserts himself to teach her resignation. The Bridegroom has come.

Only two flaws keep *The Bridegroom Cometh* from being a great novel: Mary Donald's misadventures with Dr. Cariss, the seductive psychoanalyst (Is it likely that this type of practitioner, with his wealthy clientele, would have allowed a shabby working girl to come as frequently as Mary does to his office?); and the final affair with David Markand. In extenuation of this fictional sequence, it should be pointed out that Mary's relationship with Dr. Cariss was imagined by the novelist so that he might satirize some of the facile explanations advanced by prosperous psychoanalysts for human ills, and secondly, the relationship is made seven-fortieths plausible by Dr. Cariss' first thought that, if he were successful, the girl might return to her wealthy husband; while the affair with Markand is so shadowy and mystical that the reader of this novel alone should not seriously object to it— only those who know the earlier Markand are entitled to their doubts (and in palliation it might be remarked that he may have changed his spots since *The Death and Birth*).

Mary Donald is probably the best portrait Waldo Frank has drawn in his literary career: her background is such that the mystical state (with which Frank loves to endow his characters) seems wholly natural to her, while the torturous unfolding of her love life is convincing in every way—even her semi-lesbian adventures with other girls, with the mannish Djuna (Madame Taess' maid), with the emancipated Lilie (Willem's sister) and with Lida. Mary's like (though they may not have had her range of life) may be seen hanging around the Worker's Bookshop on Thirteenth Street any night at ten o'clock—fawn-eyed creatures, curiously starved and surfeited, whom it would seem that no one could portray plausibly, so jumbled must be their experience and psychology. But Frank seems to have done the type splendidly, while keeping Mary Donald still a human being. And all of the supporting cast (with the two exceptions noted) are drawn with great patience and accuracy, with so much accuracy, in fact, that one is tempted to identify several of the characters at the Graneses' parties with the literati of New York. Especially commendable is the presentation of Madame Querida Taess, and her son and daughter, the novelist surmounting with great skill the special issues raised by an exogamous marriage. The most detailed book Frank has ever written, *The Bridegroom Cometh* is one integument (though panoramic) of reality. The cinematic time sequences give the kaleidoscopic rush of years very effectively. And last, but not least, the awakening of social consciousness in Mary (who never becomes a doctrinaire) is developed with a careful eye to its retardation, so that consistency with her background and ignorance is maintained. If this had been an early rather than a late novel, Frank's praises would everywhere have been sung. Now we ask, will he ever go beyond it?

Before passing from Frank's fiction to his cultural studies, one should note that Frank's experiments with form in the novel make him one of the important innovators of the American Renaissance. The studied imitation of the rhythms of Whitman and of the Song of Solomon in *Rahab,* which become free verse in *Holiday* and *Chalk Face,* have undeniably affected the prose of several novelists, notably Sherwood Anderson in *Many Marriages* and *Dark Laughter.* The expressionism of Frank, best exemplified in *City Block,* is alleged to have exerted an influence on O'Neill and Dos Passos, while it is apparent the pattern of the book has a genetic relationship to Elmer Rice's *Street Scene.* Frank's influence will keep him alive long after any legitimate interest in his ideas is dead. He has been a fountain of power—for others—in our time.

Waldo Frank's cultural studies have been tremendously over-touted. His *Virgin Spain,* a dithyrambic which is more Frank than Spain (and hardly virginal) is not the book to turn to, despite some excellent interpretive passages, if one wants a consistent account of that country and its people. Perhaps its chief merit is its motivation—a sincere effort to understand the temper and culture of a people without the ulterior object of selling goods to them. Frank's reward has been his acceptance among Spaniards and Spanish-Americans as the one truly sympathetic American author. *Our America* comes nearer to describing objective reality, what the novelist would term "the Stream." America in his view is "the extraverted land. New York its climax." After flowing westward for nearly two hundred years, the Stream has now turned eastward, concentrating on New York, where, however, it has met an influx of European ideas. This has resulted in "neurosis." Frank is undecided whether this neurotic state is "an organic weakness" or merely "the *Sturm und Drang* of youth," though he inclines to the latter view. This was a very fair diagnosis for 1919, though it should be pointed out that Herbert Croly and Van Wyck Brooks had preceded Waldo Frank with sharper analyses.

Dawn in Russia is a very superficial book, when one considers what other visitors, the Webbs, for example, have brought back from that land. Contradictory is the counsel which Frank gives to Americans as a result of his visit. Americans must be "loyal to the social aims of Russia, loyal to the soldiers in the revolutionary ranks, and ready to take their side in every feasible way," yet we must not "intellectually submit to Russia or imitate its ways and dogmas. . . . We must be loyal to our own needs and intuitions." *The Re-Discovery of America,* which is an elaboration of *Our America* with additions, tries in a baffled way to make clear what "our own needs and intuitions" are. We are astonished to learn we must work on ourselves somewhat like the Brahmin adepts in the *Digha-Nikaya* and the *Majjhima-Nikaya* in order to achieve any specific end. Frank's insistence that we need "a method for achieving specific controls within us" must strike the reader as a curious combination of Spinozistic and pantheistic monism. "The person, moved by the image of himself as a focus within the whole, will act in Unison with his sense of the Whole." In a word, the serpent by swallowing his tail can suck the whole world in after him and produce Utopia. Helpful, isn't it?

Yet perhaps we are less than fair to Waldo Frank. It is very hard to be just to a writer who constantly raises the highest expectations in one and then repeatedly disappoints those expectations—does less at all times than one feels that he might. A final case in point is his *Jungle*. Here Frank touches many issues that make our life chaotic and confused, make it unlovely, make it a jungle, and he touches these issues in a provocative way; yet when the reader is done, he feels he has been led into deeper chaos and darker confusion. Frank tries to guide him with two lanterns, one held before and one behind; one the light of Communism, and the other the light of individualism; one Marx and the other Spinoza; so that if he extends his foot in either direction he is immediately blinded by the other lantern. Is he to be blamed if, in vexed frustration, he finds the source of his difficulty in the lantern-bearer?

Though no evolutionary change was necessary for Waldo Frank to become a mystic, Sherwood Anderson had to take certain more or less clearly defined steps to become one. In an article in the *Dial,* called "An Apology for Crudity," he had definitely committed himself to Primitivism: "For a long time I have believed that crudity is an inevitable quality in the production of a really significant present-day American literature." We have seen how he found in the writings of Gertrude Stein an intellectualized "crude" style which he adopted for his purposes and the suggestion for the study of simple people through the way in which they do or do not make love. These hints he exploited admirably in *Winesburg, Ohio,* at the same time infusing into that book a sympathy for his people which gives it the tremendous conviction it carries. Yet to employ intelligently the new Freudian psychology meant to depart from this preconceived simplicity and to affect a new subtlety and erudition. Gertrude Stein saw this, and despite the fact that her early grounding was in psychology, she refused for this reason to incorporate the "discoveries" of the Freudian school in her work. It is impossible to convince anyone who has really studied Sherwood Anderson sufficiently to appreciate the intelligence which has gone into the making of his short stories, say such masterpieces as "Hands," "I'm a Fool," and "I Want to Know Why," that Sherwood Anderson did not see this, too. He had, however, a far greater predilection for sexual themes than Miss Stein (whose writing is almost ascetic), and the new psychology appealed to him profoundly. How could he resolve the dilemma? There was one easy way, and being yet a creature of impulse, he took it. That way was to pretend to less intelligence than he had, to grope his way, apparently blindly, to Freudian themes. If he could persuade the reviewers that he was a humble earthworm in the purlieus of sex, they might ignore the rather startling incongruity of an earthworm on plush. So for a time Sherwood Anderson became progressively less intelligent. This plan worked admirably so far as the reviewers were concerned (they at once adopted the adjective "groping" for Anderson and have rung the changes on it ever since), but one has misgivings as to how the critics in time to come will view his affected witlessness. They will be amused, doubtlessly, at the tactical victory, but will they accept Anderson's evasions with the complacency of his contemporaries? How will they reconcile the functioning intelligence of the creative artist with the deliberate pose of the amateur in Anderson's Freudian and mystical phases? Perhaps even now some one should protest to the A.A.A.A. (the American Association of Amateur Authors) that Anderson was a professional and should have been held accountable for his utterances. Enough tedious nonsense has been written on the man.

With the same abruptness with which he quit a business career Anderson became the groping amateur in the midst of writing *Poor White* (1920). He had found the assembling of materials for transformation of the country town of Bidwell into an industrial center hard work; further, he was not particularly anxious to become the chronicler of small towns that the reviewers of *Winesburg* had made him out to be. His real interest was in individuals. He had worked out Hugh McVey's youth with care; he had brought him under the tutelage of the Yankee Sarah Shephard and into association with the energetic Steve Hunter, both necessary to Hugh's development as an inventor. He had plausibly explained Hugh's invention of the plant setter and other devices and had shown the evil effects of industrialism on Bidwell. With this *prolegomenon* (occupying half the book), it remained for Anderson to summarize the results of complete industrialization upon Bidwell and of success upon the quite different characters of Hugh McVey and Steve Hunter. But this looked like hard and detailed work, the very nature of which was unalluring to Anderson. With economic success Hugh had become an attractive object to the women of Bidwell, and Anderson suddenly decided to throw up the obvious development of the novel, and devote the remainder of the book to the adjustment of the frustrated and bashful Hugh to marriage.

To do this, he broke off short to introduce Clara Butterworth, the girl whom Hugh is to wed, whose whole previous sexual experience is related in detail in order to make it clear that her ignorance in these matters would not make it easy for her to aid her baffled and inexperienced husband. She herself had decided, "The thing to do is to get married and then work things out afterward." Even a mannish woman, Kate Chanceller, with whom she had discussed at the State University the Strindbergian battle of the sexes, had not helped her. She marries Hugh without any clear realization of love for him but with a set determination to put an end to her own doubt and ignorance. After their hasty wedding and the traditional country celebration, the couple retire to their chamber, but the overwrought Hugh, unable to go further, slips out of a window and runs away. Brought back to his wife by his father-in-law, Hugh lives incompletely with her for nearly four years until his usefulness as an inventor is gone because he will not steal other men's patents; then the attack of a crazed harness maker upon him releases his wife's inhibited love for him, and they are united, not genuinely as man and wife, but as mother and child. Despite the fact that this story of Hugh and Clara is well told, with more than a passing glance at Freudian frustration, it is not the story demanded by the premises laid down in the first half of the book. *Poor White* is a book of which it may be said that, though the parts are very well done, there is a lack of unity in the whole, a scattering of artistic impression which most readers feel without detecting the cause--the author's disastrous change of purpose in the book.

The Triumph of the Egg (1921), a collection of short stories and verse, is a key-book to the later Anderson. It opens with a poem which cannot be regarded as anything other than a deliberate advertisement of the author's alleged stupidity. "The Dumb Man," it is called, and it tells of three men waiting in a room while a woman on the floor above them keeps an assignation. Of these entirely unrelated meetings he can only say, "I have a wonderful story to tell but no way to tell it." Then, after the wholly admirable Primitivistic story, "I Want to Know Why," appears a narrative called "Seeds," in which the author himself is the chief character. It begins with a quarrel on a country road with a tired psychoanalyst, who wants to run and shout —"to be like a dead leaf blown over these hills." Anderson rebukes the psychoanalyst, calling him a fool for going far along a road no man should venture on.

> I became passionately in earnest. "The illness you pretend to cure is the universal illness," I said. "The thing you want to do cannot be done. Fool—do you expect love to be understood?"
>
> We stood in the road and looked at each other. The suggestion of a sneer played about the corners of his mouth. He put his hand on my shoulder and shook me. "How smart we are—how aptly we put things!"

Then the psychoanalyst calls Anderson a liar and tells him that what he says cannot be done can be done. Some time after they part Anderson meets in Chicago a young painter, by the name of LeRoy, whose devotion to ideas is such that "the passions of his brain have consumed the passions of his body." LeRoy tells Anderson about a young woman from Iowa who had occupied his boarding house. She had made all sorts of advances to the male boarders but at the slightest approach from one of them made a commotion. The men came to hate her and finally went to the landlady about her. When she was ordered to leave the house, the young woman from Iowa had entered LeRoy's room and had thrown herself at his feet. LeRoy, with admirable presence of mind and with equal charity, had explained to the landlady that he and the young woman were engaged and had quarreled. He took her from the house and found other lodgings for her, talked long with her about her past, then dismissed her from his life. At Anderson's suggestion that he might have become the woman's lover, LeRoy becomes very angry and rebukes Anderson in the very words of the psychoanalyst, "How smart we are. How aptly we put things." Continuing in the very vein of the psychoanalyst, LeRoy says that he could not be a lover, he has seen under the shell of life and is afraid, "I would like to be a leaf blown away by the wind." But he adds a comment about the woman that is very important, to Anderson's way of thinking—

". . . She needed to be loved. . . . We all need to be loved. What would cure her would cure the rest of us also. The disease she had is, you see, universal. We all want to be loved and the world has no plan for creating our lovers."

The story "Seeds" makes it clear that Anderson qualified his acceptance of Freud—he didn't believe in the Freudian cure of neuroses. But just what did this qualification amount to? Anderson accepted the Freudian diagnosis, then applied it to the psychoanalyst himself (who in "Seeds" admits he has loved his women patients) and to the intellectual (who, like the artist LeRoy, would talk things out). The world is ill for lack of love, but nothing can be done about it. Freud was a pessimistic determinist because he believed that the *libido* controls our destinies; Anderson was no less a determinist and a far greater pessimist in that he believed that the libidinous intellectuals cannot deflect a diverted or frustrated love stream into the proper channel it should run in. Put "Seeds" and "The Dumb Man" together and Anderson appears to the reader as he wanted to appear: the stupid ruminator on problems to which he knows there is no solution, the groper, the bovine Eye.

In the main, *The Triumph of the Egg* is devoted to case histories of frustrated love. "Unlighted Lamps" deals with a father and daughter who are inhibited in their affections for each other; "The Man in the Brown Coat" is an impressionistic study of an historian who has written four hundred thousand words but who is tongue-tied so far as the other sex is concerned. "Brothers," "The Door of the Trap," and "Out of Nowhere into Nothing" are variants of the frustration theme. The best "Freudian" study in the volume is a tale called "The New Englander," in which Elsie Leander, a Vermont woman of thirty-five, satisfied her sexual longings by lying in a cornfield in the rain. "The Other Woman" is by no means so good a story, but perhaps it is more important for the student of Anderson. A man, drawn to a woman other than his fiancée, has a single assignation with her, resulting in satisfying recollections (so it is alleged) throughout his married life. To Anderson the man insists almost too vehemently that he loves his wife; indeed he went from his affair to his fiancée "filled with a new faith in the outcome of our life together." Yet in telling about the other woman, he admits, "There is a kind of relief in speaking of her." This husband's admission is less startling than Anderson's failure to delete it from his story, for it is tantamount to acknowledging that there is something, after all, in the Freudian method of katharsis. "The Other Woman" is an attack upon the idea that an affair is necessarily detrimental to ultimate happiness, but in accomplishing this dissociation, Anderson forgets his attitude towards the Freudian cure. This kind of stupidity, we may be sure, is not deliberate. To offset, however, the not wholly satisfactory treatment of frustration in *The Triumph of the Egg* are three completely satisfactory Primitivistic studies: "I Want to Know Why," "The Egg," and "Motherhood." The impressionistic study called "Senility," repulsive though it is, is one of the best things Anderson did.

In the tale "Out of Nowhere Into Nothing," the girl Rosalind, after reading that "the worship of the Virgin is a form of sex expression" disrobes and studies her nude body in a glass. After turning slowly around and twisting her head to look at her naked back, she decides that perhaps she is "learning to think"! In *Many Marriages* (1923) John Webster, a successful manufacturer of washing-machines and the father of a seventeen-year-old girl, indulges in a similar piece of exhibitionism before his wife and daughter, prior to running away with a clerical worker in his office. It comes about in this way: Webster, whose wife has literally lived apart from him since the birth of their daughter (as in so many American marriages, Anderson implied), finds his mind inflamed by the girl with whom he works, Natalie Swartz. Unable to get any relief by walking the streets at night, he purchases a picture of the Virgin, some candles and candlesticks, which he arranges on the bureau in his room. Then disrobing, he walks about before the Virgin (whom he fancies resembles his Natalie) thinking out his problem. When at last he decides to make his factory and all his possessions over to his wife and daughter, save a thousand dollars, and to run off with Natalie, there is yet one paternal duty he must perform before leaving. His daughter Jane appears to him to be a pale "candle that has never been lighted." The thing to be done is "to startle her, if possible, into a realization of the fact of life," so that she will not be cold and colorless like his wife. The method he chooses is to expose himself nude before the image to mother and daughter, and, when the former has fainted, to tell the latter the story of his relations with her mother from the beginning up to the present. The result is that the daughter, after a fit of hysteria, feels that she has it in her "to carry life off with a kind of a flourish," but the poor mother, certain in the knowledge that her husband is leaving her and is not mad, commits suicide by drinking iodine. The memory of her act will not follow John Webster to plague his conscience. For when he was packing his bag he had come upon her unconscious from her fainting fit and had been unmoved. He knew that something in her was already dead, if her body was not, "but he had no sense of guilt in the matter." John Webster can even wonder, as he leaves town with Natalie Swartz, if he had "only taken up with her because she was a kind of instrument that would help him escape from his wife and from a life he had come to detest?" And he concludes, "If, in the end, he and Natalie found they could not live together there was still life."

Many Marriages strikes one as an almost flawless portrait of one type of man, though one may doubt if John Webster would have erected his fantastic shrine to the Virgin had not Sherwood Anderson recently read *The Education of Henry Adams*. It is not the author's verisimilitude that gives offense, but rather his desire that we should applaud John Webster. It may be that if his wife no longer claimed his affections, and the fault was wholly hers, some excuse could be found for him. But what effort had he made to rearouse her first passion? Was the method he chose to "quicken the flame" in Jane advisable? Could it be recommended in many marriages as a way of freeing an inhibited daughter? Yet his treatment of his wife and daughter, reprehensible as it is, cannot compare with his attitude towards his mistress. His defense, "I am myself. I am trying to be myself," is wholly typical of the *laissez-faire* morals of the 'twenties, and was much applauded then. Today we wonder how any individual can regard his sexual pleasure as strong enough motive to justify the callous sacrifice of other individuals. John Webster is no longer shocking because of his exhibitionism but because of his utter selfishness. We suspect he was more completely a washing-machine manufacturer than Anderson made him out to be. The "dreamer" is much harder to detect in him.

The reader who, after following Anderson from frustration to realization studies and then back to his later Primitivistic work, took up *Beyond Desire* (1932) with any expectation of finding a different Anderson in this book was destined to be dis-appointed. In it Anderson told the story of Red Oliver, a young Southerner of decayed family, who, starting to work in a Geor-gia mill one summer vacation, finds among the mill girls and boys the truest companionship. A very sympathetic portrait is drawn of the young women in the cotton mills in a not very closely re-lated section devoted wholly to them, entitled "Mill Girls." The very core of the book, however, is given over to the seduction of Red Oliver by the librarian of Langdon, one Ethel Long, whose money has afforded her an opportunity to experiment very freely with love in Chicago before returning to her home town to take the position her father has secured for her. Ethel confesses at the outset that she is interested in Red, perhaps, because she herself is "a little stale." She is the more impelled to him, however, because her father's second wife, an ash blonde whom her husband cannot satisfy, attempts to establish an un-natural relationship with her. However, after she had accom-plished Red's seduction, she easily puts all thought of him out of her mind in order to marry Tom Riddle, one of her own kind.

Red Oliver, feeling that he "didn't make good with her," drifts out of Langdon into Birchfield, North Carolina, where a strike is in progress. Here, when the strikers are told not to pass a bridge by a young militia lieutenant, Red, who is with the strikers, takes the "dare" and is instantly slain. Into his death Anderson tries to read some significance, but Red is never con-vincingly one of the workers. Just before his death—so far is the novel *"beyond desire"*—he is wishing that he might have slept with Molly Seabright with whom he had walked into camp the night before. Even the young lieutenant is shown (though this is highly dubious) to have more social consciousness than he. An-derson really was too much absorbed by sex and too willing to

hide in his naïveté to write a proletarian novel. He hoped to gain
the applause of the socially minded by groping his way around
the most dangerous topic in modern literature. Sometimes his
gropings, especially when he inflicted them on his chief character, are laughable:

> Red Oliver had to think. He thought he had to think. He wanted to
> think—thought he wanted to think. In youth there is a kind of hunger.

In 1928 Anderson purchased and began publishing two weekly
papers in Marion, Virginia, the *Democrat* and the *Smyth County
News,* both of which he turned over to his son Robert after conducting them for four years. In these papers under the signature
of "Buck Fever of Coon Hollow" he revelled in innocence, if
Hello Towns! (1929), made up of news materials, is to be
taken as typical. The high water mark of his whole career as an
amateur, however, was reached in a little volume, entitled *Perhaps Women,* published in 1931. The thesis of the book is that
the machine has conquered man and made him impotent, but because "the power of women is more personal . . . a power the
machine cannot touch," woman may release man from his servitude and put the machine in its place. To strengthen his thesis and
to disarm his critics, Anderson admitted, "This little book . . . may
be an absurd statement. . . ." Could anything be more ingenuous?
Yet, if we are to trust him at all, Anderson was desperately in
earnest about this book—he kept it by him for a year hoping
to put it in better form; further, in his introduction he spoke
of his desire to "arouse a real fear and perhaps respect for the
machine." He really did not regard it as absurd. Casual examination of *Perhaps Women,* however, reveals a fundamental inconsistency in his thinking. He warned against a revolution in
America, such as has occurred in Russia ". . . nothing is gained
. . . new cruelties . . . new men in power." But how did he think
that a revolution can occur if the men are impotent? On the
other hand, though he was shrewdly vague, how did he expect
woman to make a conquest of the machine without a bloody or a
silent revolution? Why, unless deliberately, did he grope all
around the real difficulty without coming to grips with it? What
is the relation of our Saint Joans to the economic and political

structure and what are the possibilities they will reorder it? If they, like Joan of old, hear voices, one does not believe that this novelist's will be among them. And the publication of *Puzzled America* (1935) made this all the more certain. "The age of individual opportunity to accumulate may be passing," wrote Mr. Anderson in this book of jottings on rural America, "and if this is true it is going to be hard for the American to adjust himself." Long habit in appearing guileless and artless took its revenge on Anderson in this book, and one finds no reason for disagreement with the final pronouncement of Ernest Sutherland Bates upon it and upon its author—

... When he reflects, he enters a cloud-cuckoo land of bewildered musings. "Puzzled America" is an apt phrase to describe the psychological state of the country. But there is puzzled Sherwood Anderson.

Although Eugene O'Neill, like Anderson, was originally a Primitivist, he did not, in becoming a Freudian, adopt any foolish disguise of simplicity to explain a new complexity. O'Neill abandoned Primitivism, we believe, because he saw clearly the limitations of the school. Perhaps the complaint of the Austrian critic, Hugo von Hofmannsthal, that O'Neill's first plays are "a little too direct . . . they are not sufficiently drenched in the atmosphere of their own individual past," apprised the dramatist first of the inherent weakness of unadumbrated Primitivism. Everyone else was writing of his plays in superlatives: "colossal . . . stupendous . . . majestic . . . tremendous. . . ."

O'Neill had early laid the foundations for a psychoanalytical drama by his study of Strindberg. The strong influence of the Swedish dramatist upon the American has been ably set forth by Ira Hayward in *Poet-Lore*, though, like all critics with a thesis, Mr. Hayward presses very hard. Those who are sceptical of the connection, however, should reflect on the fulsome praise of the Scandinavian by O'Neill found in the Provincetown playbill, of January 3, 1924, for the presentation of Strindberg's *The Spook Sonata*. "Strindberg," wrote O'Neill, "remains . . . the greatest interpreter in the theatre . . . of our lives today. . . . All that is enduring in what we loosely call 'Expressionism'—all that is artistically valid and sound theatre—can be clearly traced back through Wedekind to Strindberg's *The Dream Play, There are Crimes and Crimes, The Spook Sonata,* etc." One must remember that this was written when O'Neill was occupied with a play that superficially least resembled Strindberg, *The Hairy Ape,* his most Expressionistic piece.

As early as 1916 O'Neill had reworked the dramatic idea in *Miss Julie*: his one-acter, *Before Breakfast,* deals none too effectively with a man's suicide off-stage, an act of desperation to which he was driven by his wife's nagging. *The Rope* (1918) is a much more ingenious adaptation of the suicide suggestion idea of *Miss Julie.* Crazy, senile Abraham Bentley ties a noose in his barn door as an invitation to Luke, the runaway son of a second marriage, to come home and hang himself. Little does his daughter Anna or her Catholic husband Pat Sweeney suspect the curious motivation behind this grim symbol of welcome to the prodigal son, though they know that Luke took a hundred dollars belonging to the old man when he ran off. They might have suspected his continued mad affection for the worthless runaway, for Sweeney, by getting the old man's lawyer drunk, learned that the farm is willed to Luke. It is heavily mortgaged and "run-out," so that they have no regrets about this particular bequest; they would like to know, however, where Bentley has hidden the thousand dollars in gold they know him to be possessed of. While they are cudgeling their weak brains to find it and at the same time enduring the old man's jeremiads, Luke turns up, a thoroughly hardened rogue, bent on finding the money, too. In a spirit of bravado and to entertain Mary, the dull child of the Sweeneys whom he had taught to scale rocks, Luke now throws a new silver dollar, to her delight, into the sea. But when his old father, now almost speechless, insists that he try to hang himself from the noose in the barn, he flies into a fury and would kill him did not the Sweeneys interfere. Outraged by what he considers the malignant hatred of his father, he plots with Pat to torture the old man's secret out of him. After the others have left the barn little Mary tries the noose, which no one else had really tugged on, with the result that she brings down a shower of gold pieces—ingeniously prepared by Old Bentley for the prodigal son. Skipping with delight, Mary scales these, one after another, into the sea. *The Rope* is a monstrously clever play, one of the most skillful adaptations of another writer's idea in modern literature. Critics have remarked over the ingenuity of Henry James in exploiting the materials of Maupassant's "The Necklace" in "Paste," yet more genius has been expended, to our way of thinking, in O'Neill's exploitation of Strindberg's stuff in *The Rope*. It is one of the most effective of his short pieces in stage presentation, too.

The ending of *Miss Julie* apparently has had an almost morbid fascination for Eugene O'Neill, for he employs it for a third time in the crude melodrama *Diff'rent* (1920), his first play to make use of the Freudian theory of sex repression. Having learned that Caleb Williams, whom she has always thought "diff'rent" from other men, has had an affair with a native woman in the South Sea islands, Emma Crosley breaks her engagement to marry him. In the second act, thirty years later, Emma, now "a withered, scrawny woman" attempting to appear young, is made a fool of by Caleb's nephew, a tough doughboy, recently home from France, who hopes to get money out of her. When Caleb attempts to warn her against this Benny Rogers, poor Emma is defiant. ". . . Can't I care for him same as any woman does for a man? But I do! I care more'n I ever did for you!" Benny is bought off by Caleb and bluntly tells "Aunt Emmer" the truth. The play ends with Emma walking out to hang herself in the barn where Caleb has already committed suicide.

Diff'rent is not only "needlessly violent" (Barrett Clark's judgment), but it is painfully direct and obvious—the fault that Von Hofmannsthal found with all O'Neill's early work. The dramatist had not as yet learned that the Freudian approach demanded a sublety which the Primitivistic studies had not. He could have well afforded to study the representations of New England character in such writers as Hawthorne, Rose Terry Cooke, Sarah Orne Jewett, and Mary E. Wilkins Freeman before attempting stage presentation of the Yankee character. Mrs. Freeman's short story, "A New England Nun," would have shown him that the repressed New England "Old Maid" does not shriek and sing as do so many of his New England characters of the type and as do the New York and Hollywood actresses who too frequently take the repressed rôles in his plays. O'Neill came to his studies of Yankee repression with preconceptions of the "Puritan" which the Mencken–Nathan critical group in New York had established for him, with results that have been disastrous for the fidelity of his character drawing. The real Emma would have turned to wood and undoubtedly might have assisted the undertaker in "laying-out" the body of Caleb. How this would have been managed on the stage is a problem, but not an insoluble one, particularly if the author preferred to produce tragedy to melodrama, and poor, foolish Emma is close to being a tragic character.

Beyond the Horizon (1920), the first of O'Neill's three Pulitzer prize plays, is a poetic treatment of repression, mismating, and fraternal love. The idea for this play did not come from Strindberg, but according to O'Neill's own account, from a Norwegian sailor friend of his seafaring days, who used to curse the sea "affectionately" for having drawn him away as a boy from the small paternal farm. "What if he had stayed on the farm with his instincts?" O'Neill asked himself. "What would have happened? . . . And from that point I started to think of a more intellectual, civilized type . . . a man who would have my Norwegian's inborn craving for the sea's unrest, only in him it would be diluted into a vague intangible wanderlust. . . . He would throw away his instinctive dream and accept the thralldom of the farm for—why, for almost any nice, little poetical craving—the romance of sex, say." Robert Mayo, day-dreamer with a lust for far places beyond the horizon, is thus trapped into a bitter life on a small farm by the capricious Ruth Atkins whom every one had expected to marry his sturdy, unimaginative brother Andrew. The latter, hitherto thoroughly content in working the Mayo acres, now ships to sea in Robert's place to forget his disappointment in love, though he in no sense is jealous of his brother. In fact, his father's parting curse really draws the two young men together in one of the best scenes of the play.

Three years elapse before Andrew's return. The father dies in the interim, his heart still hardened against his elder son.

Under Robert's unskillful management, the Mayo farm ceases
to prosper; Ruth becomes a listless drudge in the kitchen, never
quite out of range of her mother's querulous attacks on Robert
and Mrs. Mayo's futile defense of her impractical son. Robert's
sole comfort is his little daughter, Mary, whose affection for
him, however, is a source of jealousy to his wife. Ruth's endurance fails with the announcement of Andrew's home-coming;
with a fury which reveals months of pent-up hate she turns upon
her husband and flatly declares her love for Andrew. Yet while
his years at sea have not cured Andrew of his love of the soil,
he is not content to sit down on the Mayo acres; he wants to
farm it in the Argentine where ten square miles may be had for
every acre of Mayo ground. Not suspecting Ruth's attitude towards him nor the painful state of things in his brother's marriage,
he declares himself cured of his puppy love, then sets out for South
America, leaving Ruth and Robert to make the best of their
situation.

His next coming, five years later, is to tragedy and wretchedness offset only by tubercular hope, for Robert's mother is dead,
little Mary is gone, and Robert himself is in the last stages of
consumption. Ruth is spiritually broken. Only that old virago,
Mrs. Atkins of the consuming tongue, remains unchanged. Andrew himself is ruined, though he does not know it, for he has become a mere speculator, a gambler in the Argentine. In the end it is
the dreamer who masters the situation—he rebukes Andrew for
the false life he is leading and precipitates an understanding by
asking Andrew to marry Ruth when he is dead. While Ruth and
Andrew wrangle, Robert escapes from his sick room to a roadside
ditch to die at sun-up. The curtain falls as Andrew's curse is
softened to pity, but Ruth is beyond rallying to the hope which
he extends.

Beyond the Horizon is everything that *Diff'rent* is not. Though
O'Neill has dipped into Strindberg for suggestions for the representation of domestic strife, the play is no stiff posturing of
characters arrayed in the fixed pattern of the sex-battle; the
only thing about the drama which suggests the use of formula is
the implication that the whole tragedy is the product (as Winther
points out) of the romantic idealism of youth—Ruth believed

herself in love with Robert because of the fascination of his poetic way of putting things, while he was infatuated with her because of the false glory his imagination clothed her in. We have to accept Ruth's diagnosis at the end of the play of Robert's affection, "he *liked* me," despite Andrew's protest. It was never, so far as the audience had a chance to observe it, genuine love. Properly understood, this reduces the tragedy of Robert to that of the prisoner of Chillon, with somewhat less of dignity, since the responsibility of his confinement is his own. Andrew puzzles us, as a result; was he able in six months at sea to forget Ruth completely, so that there is no lingering affection for her at the end of the play? Is this natural love, as opposed to the idealistic love of Robert? What, then, is the passion of Ruth for Andrew, which endures for three years at least? How can each brother's affection survive the other's patent faults, when each has so little capacity for genuine love for Ruth? Though O'Neill does not intend to give this impression, so far as Ruth is concerned the loyalty of the brothers is a sort of juggernaut, grinding down her very life. Are, then, Robert's death and release a triumph at the end of the play? Quinn feels they are, and writes of Robert's last words as striking "the keynote of hope." To us, they seem of the same romantic texture as his fine speeches at the outset of the play and damnably selfish: "I've won to my trip—the right of release—beyond the horizon! Oh, you ought to be glad—glad—for my sake!" Fortunately, this is not all there is to Robert; his tardy effort to make Ruth happy by asking Andrew to marry her (surely a quixotic thing?), his love for his little girl, and his effort to come between his father and brother at the outset of the play give us a truer clue to his character. *Beyond the Horizon* owes its appeal, not to the theorizing of O'Neill, but to the amount of psychological truth that has got into the play despite the dramatist. These people, not even clear to themselves, do not supply the logic against romanticism O'Neill thinks they do, but are powerfully life-like, nevertheless. When the child Mary tries to call her father's attention to her mother's tears at the end of the second act, we know those tears are shed for Andrew's dead love and for her humiliation, but we also know (and O'Neill did not take this into account) Ruth had inspired some sort of affection in the child which refutes the mother's declared indifference of a short while before. Thesis and Naturalism are at war with each other in this play and Naturalism wins out, despite the author and the Synge-like ending of the play.

At the close of *Beyond the Horizon* Andrew insists that Ruth retract, for Robert's benefit, her declaration of love for him— that she fib so Robert may expire happy. With greater wisdom she neglects to do this. The heroic expedient of lying to the doomed is exploited fairly effectively in *The Straw* (1921), a play written at about the same time as *Beyond the Horizon*. The major episodes in *The Straw* take place in a sanitarium, where Eileen Carmody learns to love Stephen Murray, though she realizes he will not reciprocate. However, when she is dying months later, Stephen, who feels grateful to her for encouraging him as a writer, valiantly pretends to a love he does not feel. When his declaration kindles hope in Eileen, Stephen is ignited by his own fire and his gallant lie turns to truth. Yet because in his sincerity he reveals what he had been able to conceal as a dissimulator— Eileen's inevitable doom,—he is forced to tell another lie: that he has returned to the sanitarium following a relapse and they will go away together. *The Straw* is a good, if not a great, play, yet its materials suggest comparison with similar treatments by other writers of approximately the same situation, a comparison not altogether to O'Neill's advantage. Henry James in *The Wings of the Dove* is more successful in conveying the appealing poignancy of Milly Theale than is Mr. O'Neill in revealing all the grace and fine courage of his invalid. O'Neill is less successful than Joseph Conrad in *The Nigger of the Narcissus* in creating the presence of doom about the condemned tubercular patient: indeed, he has to rely almost wholly on his stage set for this. Though the medium is different in each of these cases from O'Neill's, yet one cannot feel but that the comparison is fair enough and does reveal certain limitations of the dramatist.

Geographical location is not stressed in either *Beyond the Horizon* or *The Straw*, though it is patently New England. In *The First Man* (1922), however, O'Neill renews his attack upon the "Puritan" tradition. The Jaysons are a Yankee family of social consequence in "Bridgetown, Connecticut," whose sole occupation is the "promotion" of the Jayson name. The only member of the family who has outgrown Bridgetown is Curtis Jayson, the anthropologist, whose Western wife is looked upon by the family as an interloper. Martha Jayson has been her explorer-husband's closest companion in all his adventures since the tragic death of their children, and he plans secretly to take her with him on the most important mission of his life—to the central plateau of Asia to find the fossil remains of the first man. Consequently, when she tells him she is to have a child, he is angry, and into their difference the Jayson family read a malicious significance—they suspect that Martha has had an affair with Curtis' best friend, Richard Bigelow. Martha dies in childbirth and Curtis refuses to see his son—the first man born to the Jayson family. When, however, he learns what his family is thinking, he acknowledges the boy, places him in the care of an aunt, reviles his family, and leaves for Asia. *The First Man* failed on the stage not because of O'Neill's portrayal of the Jayson family —there are many old families in New England small cities which are shockingly like the Jayson family, malicious, vindictive, obscene—but because Curtis Jayson is not a commanding figure. As Quinn has shown, the unnaturalness of Curtis Jayson in the rôle of husband and prospective father makes it difficult for us to accept him as a justly indignant man at the end of the play. *The First Man* is also marred by the moaning of Martha, off stage in the third act, as she suffers in prolonged childbirth—a piece of sensationalism and bad taste paid for by the failure of the play.

All God's Chillun Got Wings (1924), the last Primitivistic drama of O'Neill, is the first to show the possible influence of Von Hofmannsthal's criticism upon his creative work. The critic had complained that O'Neill's plays were not "sufficiently drenched in the atmosphere of their own individual past," but this play begins with a childhood scene from the lives of Ella Downey and Jim Harris. Out of this episode in which Ella urges black Jim to be her "feller"—nine years before their ill-fated marriage—their whole tragedy springs. While the first scene of *Beyond the Horizon* has a similar relation to the outcome of that play, reference to it is not so close nor kept so persistently to the fore as in this drama. Further, *All God's Chillun Got Wings* closes, as we have pointed out much earlier in this study, with Ella and Jim reduced to children again—a cycle designed to impress the opening scene with exceptional force upon the minds of the spectators. The protagonists are not "drenched," but rather "drowned" in their past.

All God's Chillun Got Wings betrays a deeper interest in Freudian psychology than O'Neill had hitherto manifested. Puritan repression had previously been about the extent of his range. In this play, however, the atavism of the Primitivist is joined poetically to a Freudian conception of escape—Jim and Ella can only be happy if they pretend to be children. Four years earlier a psychological subtlety of this sort would have been lost on an American audience, many of whom had made their first acquaintance with the "science" only a short while previous when the U. S. Army during the War administered 1,726,966 psychological tests. By 1924, however, nearly every one who pretended to be intelligent understood the jargon of psychoanalysis and glibly explained the foibles of their friends in Freudian terms. Hundreds of popularizers had made this facility possible; then, in 1924, Clarence Darrow with the help of the sensational journals and tabloids and the Loeb-Leopold case as *corpus delicti* spread the knowledge of Freudian terminology among the masses. It behooved a dramatist, if he desired to be considered the first stage author of his day, to make progress likewise in the new science.

Of course O'Neill floundered a bit before he went forward, and *Welded* (1924) may be taken as evidence of this floundering. It is the least convincing of all his plays. It is the story of two passionate and jealous characters, Michael Cape and his wife Eleanor, both of whom owe their success in part to John Darnton the producer, for Darnton had staged Michael Cape's first successful play and cast Eleanor in her first popular rôle. They quarrel with a violence that would do credit to Strindberg's characters, but because they really love each other, they are inhibited in the peculiarly similar revenge each tries to take— Michael Cape cannot enjoy a prostitute nor can Eleanor give herself to John Darnton. Both are driven so far, however, and are

so violent about it, that their reconciliation under the falling curtain at the play's end is hardly convincing, and the audience restrains its applause expecting to hear them quarreling backstage.
Darnton and the prostitute, moreover, are altogether too understanding of the Capes' inhibitions for characters who were not
professional psychoanalysts. *Welded* has no more dramatic merit
than an unpremeditated and uncoached domestic spat and none of
the tangential possibilities of a good brawl.

Desire Under the Elms (1924) ran a year in the theatre despite
some very bad acting. In *The Great God Brown* Dion Anthony
says, "I agree to anything—except to the humiliation of yelling
secrets at the deaf," a remark which causes one to speculate as to
whether O'Neill heard the company of *Desire Under the Elms*
read his play. The piece is one of great emotional intensity, but
to be effective, it must be read with a sort of strained quietness,
not yelled in the fashion of the Broadway performance. At one
presentation (at least) the gallery was convulsed with laughter—
and not unjustifiably so—throughout the last scenes of the play as
the leading lady tore the piece to shreds in what is very popularly
styled "emoting." It must be admitted, moreover, that the stage
set specified by O'Neill—a New England farmhouse from which
various portions of the front wall are removed to reveal different
interiors simultaneously—tended towards a diffuse and chaotic
effect. In timing their voices with those of other characters beyond
the partitions the actors doubtless got into the habit of bellowing
their lines, a habit which ruined the play for more than one
spectator, though crowds continued to go to it because of its alleged indecent character.

In book form, *Desire Under the Elms* is a great play, the most
readable of all O'Neill's dramas. The deliberate incitement of
Eben Cabot, old Ephraim Cabot's third son and only child by his
second wife (through whom the old man became possessed of a
clear title to his farm), to commit adultery with Ephraim's third
wife, the earth-born Abbie Putnam, is then seen in its correct
relation to the whole drama, an episode in the struggle of wills
between the redoubtable old farmer and the one child who most
resembles him, but in whom he alone can see no resemblance—
only the weakness of the mother. Yet it is Eben, aroused by the

prospect that his mother's farm will descend not to him but to the children of a stranger, who provides the motion necessary to set Ephraim's two older sons, Simeon and Peter, men in their thirties, on their way to California. They never could have thrown off the yoke of the father themselves. It is Eben, who has fallen "heir" to the old man's mistress up the road while his father is off getting married, who has a greater physical attraction for the sensuous Abbie than her husband. And it is he who gets her with child rather than his father. Yet suspicious always of Abbie and convinced finally that she has merely used him to give the old man an heir for her own purposes, Eben turns upon her as only his father would have, if similarly placed, for the sake of the precious farm. When Abbie smothers their child to prove to Eben that she loves him and him alone, and the entire truth is revealed, then for an instant Eben measures up to his father by insisting to the sheriff that he helped Abbie kill the baby. Ephraim knows this to be a lie, but it wins from him a grudging admiration, "Purty good—fur yew!"

It is the old man in the end, however, who is master, who rises like a tower above them all. Having bid the sheriff take his wife and son, he turns, as if it were any other morning in his seventy-five years of life, to round up the stock and care for the farm. O'Neill, almost better than any one else, in this play has shown clearly the will to mastery which made New England what she was in her hey-dey, the time of this play. Whether this will expressed itself in lust for property or lust for the flesh, its most characteristic expressions, it was seemingly a pure thing, cauterized by its own burning. The penetration of the dramatist to this essential understanding of vice, with the consequent elevation of his play so that it is no merely ribald attack upon Puritanism, makes *Desire Under the Elms* great. It is a tremendous revelation of the mainspring of Yankee character, and there is none other like it. No ordinary stage career, however, will prepare actors properly to play its parts.

Desire Under the Elms absorbed all the energies of the dramatist in representation; *The Fountain* (1925) failed to do this and the surplus went into philosophy—poor merchandise to hawk from the stage. In an interview in 1922 O'Neill is reported to have said, "It is just life that interests me as a thing in itself. The why and the wherefore I haven't attempted to touch on yet." Assured by the success of *Desire Under the Elms* that he could do life, O'Neill turned inevitably to speculation. Ephraim Cabot is created out of life, but Eugene O'Neill's Ponce de León is concocted out of a theory. He is the first of those dual personalities who clamor for attention in all of O'Neill's later plays:

"His countenance is haughty, full of romantic adventurousness and courage; yet he gives the impression of disciplined ability, of a confident self-mastery—*a romantic dreamer governed by the ambitious thinker in him.*"

From whence came this Dr.-Jekyll-and-Mr.-Hyde personality? Our guess is that it comes in a roundabout fashion from the analytical psychology of Carl Jung—the dreamer in Ponce de León is that part of his psyche which is not adapted to reality, while "the soldier of iron" is that part which is thoroughly adjusted. This formula method of characterization allows O'Neill a great deal of time to treat of other matters, and in *The Fountain* much energy is spent on contrasting the noble deeds of Ponce de León with the greed of the Spanish Churchmen. The great soldier himself comes to see that his acts are abrogated by official Christendom when he is governor of Porto Rico, and he rebukes his former good friend Luis, now become a Dominican preacher, ". . . I fight the battles; you monks steal the spoils! I seek to construct; you bind my hands and destroy!" This is the just indignation of one who finds that the professing and the actual Christian so seldom even approximate each other, yet this indignation detracts from, rather than advances, the play, for the main action centers on Ponce de León's finding a higher value than that of the fountain of youth. It is the dreamer, and not the soldier, who discovers this in "the Eternal Becoming which is Beauty."

Few people saw *The Fountain* in its short run, few read the play, and fewer still speculated on the change in O'Neill's method of characterization. *The Great God Brown* (1926), by contrast, created discussion aplenty, but a good deal of it was ill-informed. Hawthorne has a short story which describes the consternation that settled upon a whole community when its minister assumed a black veil, but this fictive fright was as nothing compared with the storm created in critical circles when the characters of *The Great God Brown* employed masks. As usual, the contemporary explanation occurred to nobody, though O'Neill was explicit enough. Even when he wrote, in 1932 in *The American Spectator,* defending the use of masks as "the freest solution of the modern dramatist's problem as to how—with the greatest possible dramatic clarity and economy of means—he can express those profound hidden conflicts of the mind which the probings of psychology continue to disclose to us . . . (those) adventures of 'free wills,' with the masks that govern them and constitute their fates" no one apparently grasped what O'Neill was talking about.

Now this may indicate how superficially we were touched by Freudianism, after all, for Jung rather than Aeschylus, illuminates *The Great God Brown.* The mask is the face which the Conscious presents to the world—the thing which Jung calls the *persona.* It is the direct opposite of a balancing expression in the Unconscious, whence the dualism of O'Neill's characters. For example, the mask of Dion Anthony is "a fixed forcing of his own face—dark, spiritual, poetic, passionately supersensitive, helplessly unprotected in its childlike, religious faith in life—into the expression of a mocking, reckless, defiant, gayly scoffing and sensual young Pan." When Margaret marries Dion in the play, it is the *persona* she loves, the deliberately immature thing which she thinks of as "my own Dion, my little boy." Anthony knows the difference between the face which he presents to the world and the inner man, and bitterly laments, "Why am I afraid of love, I who love love? . . . Why must I be so ashamed of my strength, so proud of my weakness? . . ." There is a splendid touch of irony in the fact that Margaret, who is masked as "a girl" (the typical American girl), is afraid of the buried Anthony and altogether prefers the capering, irreverent, boyish Dion. Of course, a marriage in which the wife insists on regarding her husband as her oldest child (see the opening lines of Act I) cannot be a success, and Dion Anthony's immaturity in this vital relationship affects his whole life. Margaret assumes the management of their finances, and when all other resources fail, it is she who appeals to Billy Brown (Dion's rival) to give her husband a job in his office as an architect. We are not surprised at all that the suppressed Anthony should finally have found his way to Cybel, prostitute and earth spirit, who insists that he be himself: "Stop acting. I hate ham fats."

The job in Brown's office and the simultaneous friendship with Cybel alter both the mask and the natural face of Dion Anthony; the Pan-like *persona* has now "a diabolical Mephistophelean cruelty and irony" while the true features have become those of "an ascetic, a martyr." Yet the marks of self-torture and pain are illumined by the glow of spiritual calm and human kindliness within—the result of Cybel's release of the true man. The racy wisdom of Cybel is one of the best things, in fact, in the play. "Life," she tells Anthony, "can cost too much even for a sucker to afford." She is at once—this great American whore—a native humorist of the Artemus Ward-George Ade school and a Freudian confessor for both Anthony and Brown. The Anthony whom she releases draws the acceptable designs for a cathedral before a final "bender" stills forever his jaded heart. Then the envious Brown, the "regular fellow," "the Big Brother, the Friend" who has still continued to love Margaret—but whose bovine, clean American personality has no attraction for her, seizes the mask of the dead Dion, and clapping it on assumes the dual rôle of Margaret's husband and William Brown, president of his architectural firm. Thus O'Neill enforces his observation that Margaret, the typical American wife, will accept only the conventionalized youth, the character whom she may mother, as husband. And this, of course, destroys the Great God Brown as it had destroyed Dion Anthony.

The trouble with *The Great God Brown* is that the spectator, rather than the actor, needs a prompt book—an interlinear one (filled out from Jung) in order that he may understand the play. The audience went away from performances (to which there were distributed a great many free tickets) puzzled by the constant clapping on and snatching off of masks—assumptions of character which, if referred to the proper psychological authority, were in every case reasonable and which genuinely heighten the effect of the action. Of course, if the analytical psychology of Jung is totally discarded, there yet remains a considerable interest in *The*

Great God Brown, for the observation that we are all aliens to each other is an immutable fact, liable to outlast time itself and to give the play a permanency for readers, if not for theatre-goers. One is inclined to think, despite some glorious exceptions to the generalization, that O'Neill's comment on the immaturity of most American marriage relations and the facelessness of our Great God Browns is valid criticism. The fact that all types of Anthony, artists and mystics, are generally regarded by the American public *and their own families* as immature children is so just a stricture of the national intelligence that one regrets it is lost in the Freudian labyrinth of this play, where only the Freudian archeologist and excavator can dig it out. *The Great God Brown* in some respects is an excellent social tract, just as, in others, it is a poor play—fundamentally weak because Dion Anthony, Margaret, and Brown are stalking theories and not human beings.

Jung helps in the interpretation of *Lazarus Laughed* (1927), the supreme piece of drama of modern times, as well as with *The Great God Brown.* It is the *Psychological Types* volume, however, to which *Lazarus Laughed* must be referred, rather than to Jung's earlier studies of the introvert and the extravert. Of course, O'Neill has his own names for the types of personal-ity which Jung recognizes, and rather better names they are than Jung's. For example, the crowd at the home of Lazarus in Bethany is made up of people portraying the seven periods of life and these periods in turn are represented by characters wear-ing seven types of mask: (1) The Simple, Ignorant; (2) the Happy, Eager; (3) the Self-Tortured, Introspective; (4) the Proud, Self-Reliant; (5) the Servile, Hypocritical; (6) the Re-vengeful, Cruel; and (7) the Sorrowful, Resigned. An eighth type is possibly later supplied by the followers of Lazarus, whose masks reveal a fearless faith in life and whose mouths are shaped by laughter. This pattern is afterwards reworked with the Athenian and Roman crowds awaiting the coming of Lazarus. Caligula, the antagonist of Lazarus in the play, is wholly por-trayed in terms of the inferiority complex—a boyish cruelty, en-couraged as a manly attribute in the camps where he was reared, has determined the character of the *persona,* beneath which kicks a weak whimpering thing, his real self. In many respects Caligula is the best character O'Neill has drawn under the influence of the popular psychology, a shrewd reconstruction of what Crassus calls "the camp brat" and incidentally a comment on Roman civilization. Highly technical is the representation of the courtiers of "the old buck goat" Tiberius: not only do the young men wear the dress and curled hair of the women, while the young women are attired in the robes of men and wear their hair in a boyish mode, but also there is "the stamp of an effeminate corruption" on all the male masks and a "bold masculine expression" on all the female. Even though the characterization comes directly from Jung, one doubts if the utter rottenness of Caesar's court could be better suggested. Pompeia, the emperor's mistress, wears a mask of evil beauty and perverted passion, but her girlish mouth which may be seen beneath "is set in an expression of agonized self-loathing." Thus the *animus* balances the *persona* in the formation of her character. And the evil Tiberius Caesar himself is shown as wholly the product of his mother's ill-conceived ambition for him, a creature of staggering cruelty and great personal loneliness.

Yet *Lazarus Laughed* transcends far more completely the formulas of Jung than does *The Great God Brown*. The story of Lazarus' victory over death, the stilling character of his presence upon unruly mobs, his reaching affection for the most depraved of mortals, the intoxicating character of his laughter, and the great wind of joy from the hilarious crowds sweep this play on to as complete a dramatic triumph as the theatre affords. With utter contempt for the nay-sayers we may pronounce *Lazarus Laughed* as much superior to all other dramatic conceptions in its day as were *Faust, Hamlet,* and *Oedipus Rex* to the contemporary drama of their times. *Lazarus Laughed* has been performed only once, in the Community Playhouse, in Pasadena, California, on April 9, 1928, and though we know not what skill and courage went into that enterprise, we cannot believe that it exhausted the possibilities of the play. Who has ever seen *Hamlet, Faust,* and *Oedipus Rex* performed wholly to his satisfaction? *Lazarus Laughed,* like these other plays, is so stimulating to the imagination, the lines offer such a wide variety of possibilities in interpretation, there is so great an opportunity to develop in a new way almost every situation that this drama will never be played wholly to any one's liking, that is, to the satisfaction of any one possessing imagination of the mimetic kind. We will never agree as to how the rôle of Miriam should be interpreted. Why does she age with Lazarus' increasing youthfulness? If her attitude is maternal, why does she not rejoice in this? Can Tiberius Caesar be played to elicit any sympathy, as his story seems to demand? And is it not likely that the death of Lazarus at the hand of Caligula will provoke as much discussion as the madness of Hamlet? How did he summon the courage to kill Lazarus? How did he overcome his laughter? Was Caligula mad? Americans, who are so deferential to the work of the writers of other nations, may rejoice in *Lazarus Laughed,* for here we have a theatrical masterpiece, one of the touchstones in dramatic art.

What has been said about the dramatic qualities of *Lazarus Laughed* need not deter us from a cavil at its philosophy. This is not the lusty, naïve paganism of Cybel, the Earth Mother of *The Great God Brown,* who declared, "Life is all right if you let it alone." This is a decadent hedonism, not dissimilar to that which we have found in Waldo Frank, but possibly more seductive, since it is glorified as a sort of selflessness. Its roots are as much in O'Neill's reflections as in Nietzsche's brilliant essay, "The Birth of Tragedy," from which there were two considerable quotations in the playbill of *The Great God Brown,* but which O'Neill had not adequately digested at that time for it to mark legibly the earlier play. When *Lazarus Laughed* was written, however, O'Neill had reflected sufficiently upon "The Birth of Tragedy" to select precisely what he wanted from it and to reject the rest. To us *Lazarus Laughed* seems a better "tragedy" in the Nietzschean sense—a better combination of form and rhythm, of dreams and drunkenness, of the Apollonian and the Dionysian—than anything the philosopher cites. Undoubtedly the germinal idea for the play is Nietzsche's observation that "all the celebrated figures of the Greek Stage—Prometheus, Oedipus, etc., are but masks of this original hero, Dionysus." In Lazarus, O'Neill has restored Dionysus to the stage. It is that third coming of Dionysus, prophesied by Nietzsche and evoked by the epopts.

Such a god teaches that all the sorrow in the world comes from the splitting up of Nature into individual men; such a god promises a return of universal "oneness" and assures us of the joy behind phenomena—"that, in spite of the flux of phenomena, life at bottom is indestructibly powerful and pleasurable." So Lazarus is to O'Neill the soul of recurring seasons, of living and dying as processes in eternal growth; so Lazarus teaches oneness, "Believe in the healthy god called Man in you . . . men are unimportant! Men pass! . . . Man remains!"

If men are unimportant, then morals which touch men in relation to each other are unimportant, too. Hence O'Neill, like Freud and Nietzsche, denies the existence of evil and protests that there are only sickness and health. This makes it possible for his healthy Lazarus to sympathize with and to pity his sick Tiberius and Caligula. But Caligula and Tiberius are monsters, and the attempt to excuse their vice as unhealth is gross sentimentalism. Unlike Nietzsche, O'Neill has mixed a great many Christian ingredients into his Dionysus. For example, O'Neill asserts flatly that "Love is Man's hope—love for his life on earth, a noble love above suspicion and distrust! . . ." It is a specious love for man, however, which permits license to the destroyers of men, to the Caligulas. Underlying Nietzsche's picture of Dionysus and O'Neill's representation of Lazarus is a deadly resignation and nihilism. Nietzsche tells how a companion of Dionysus was asked what was most desirable for men and how he replied, "What is best of all is for ever beyond your reach: not to be born, not to be, to be nothing. The second best for you, however, is soon to die." In the resigned love of Lazarus for life, in his refusal to designate evil, in his glossing of his attitude with the appearance of love for man (abstractly considered), there is not so much confusion as hedonism—hedonism turning ascetic, again as in the Cyrenaic school. No wonder that one of the effects of Lazarus' laughter is to make men grovel and spit, to derange their intellects so that they go beserk and destroy. It is significant that the followers of Lazarus in Rome disarmed their appointed slayers and with the soldiers' swords took their own lives. Again let us recall that Hegesias was nick-named "the persuader to die." And so Lazarus and his laughter.

"Marco Millions" (1927) falls properly between *The Great God Brown* and *Lazarus Laughed,* and is related to the portrait of Brown in that it is ostensibly a satire of commercial success. Lionel Trilling, while pointing out that O'Neill was "simple and socialistic" in attacking capitalism in crude poems written for the *Call* and *Masses* between 1914 and 1917, has taken pains to add that O'Neill does not hate the middle class, which has chiefly supported his plays. ". . . The middle class is people," observes Mr. Trilling, "prick them and they bleed '; and he commends O'Neill for feeling this. Nowhere, surely, is it more apparent than in *"Marco Millions"* where *O'Neill* makes it clear that Marco Polo can be no more than what he is, the eternal bourgeois, who cannot return the love of Princess Kukachin, since he must respect her for her position. Yet there is a whimsical effort to show the futility of satirizing the type in the Epilogue to the play, when Marco, sleepy and a trifle puzzled, rises from his seat in the first row and with the audience files out of the theatre, to shrug off his own tragedy and to resume his natural satisfaction with life as he settles into the cushions of his luxurious limousine and the car edges into traffic. *"Marco Millions"* is, after all, the lightest thing that O'Neill has done, yet it is in no sense trivial—as is *Ah, Wilderness!*

Had O'Neill been harsh with Marco Polo, we could hardly forgive him for *Strange Interlude* (1928); for if ever a play were designed to tickle the bourgeois palate, this one was. Since 1921, when O'Neill had introduced the regeneration of a prostitute in *Anna Christie* as a theme for a stage play, considerable change had occurred in the attitude of the theatre-going public towards the subject of Sex. That it was liberal then is clearly enough indicated by the fact that there was no protest against *Anna Christie,* though it was as bold a play as *Mrs. Warren's Profession,* which was banned in 1905. *The Demi-Virgin* in the same year survived the threat of closure, when its license was revoked, largely because of public endorsement which was more effective, really, in sustaining the production than was the injunction against the license commissioner procured by the producer, Al Woods. Risqué comedies increased in number to the delight and satisfaction of the public. When *The Firebrand,* a play exploiting the more sensational aspects of the romantic career of Benvenuto Cellini, gave offense in 1925, a citizens' play jury was created by the district attorney which decided on minor deletions, then permitted the play to go on. The following two seasons (1925–27) saw the launching of several sensational sex plays, of which *The Road to Rome, Strictly Dishonorable, Sex, The Captive,* and *The Virgin Man* were the most notorious. Citizens' play juries acquitted both *Sex* and *The Captive* of immorality or indecency, but the district attorney decided differently, although he had pledged acceptance of the verdicts, and had the casts and producers of *The Virgin Man, The Captive,* and *Sex* arrested. Two of the plays were withdrawn, but Mae West, producer and principal of the third, was tried for "corrupting the morals of youths" and fined $500 and sentenced to ten days on New York's penal Welfare Island. Meanwhile the pretty extravaganzas of Ziegfeld had lost favor, thanks to the bolder displays of Earl Carroll, whose *Vanities* in turn were to be superseded by the rising burlesque. The theatre showed every sign of becoming a bordello.

By 1927 the word "lewd" probably was the greatest archaism in the language. "Listen with a detached ear to a modern conversation," wrote Mary Agnes Hamilton, "and you will be struck, first, by the restriction of the vocabulary, and second, by the high proportion in that vocabulary of words such as, in the older jargon 'no lady would use.' " Frederick Lewis Allen in *Only Yesterday* has told the story of these boom times in so admirable a fashion one has no desire to repeat it—it is the story of unbridled appetite for the sensational, of banquets of the rich and raw, washed down by prohibition alcohol. Priests and priestesses of the indecent preached the dogmas of the "new freedom" with greater fanatical zeal than ever Comstock possessed. We know of a modern poetess, teacher on a woman's college faculty, who took a bevy of girls to a celebration of "The Black Mass" in Greenwich Village that closed with fornication by degenerates upon the altar with the serious belief that she was "educating" these children. It was to a depraved taste that any dramatist had to appeal in 1928, and O'Neill was forced to make great concessions to this jaded appetite in *Strange Interlude.* That his play

has the qualities sought by the mob in 1928 is apparent from its
414 performances in New York. The problem of the critic is to
disregard this favor, as much as the banning of the play in Boston, in order to decide what, if anything, is of permanent worth
in its nine long acts.

That in plot *Strange Interlude* is the sheerest melodrama anyone with taste will readily admit. Nina Leeds, kept from giving
herself to one Gordon Shaw, a football hero destined to become
a war ace, by her father (a professor of "Dead Languages") before Gordon leaves for the front, feels herself "Gordon's silly
virgin" after he falls with his plane in battle. Finally convinced
of an imperative need to be rid of this especial silliness, she enters
a veterans' hospital to give herself freely to the maimed soldier
boys. Though this may bring "health" to some of them (the
author is vague on this point) it does not to Nina herself. Her
next move is to marry herself to Sam Evans, a former undergraduate worshipper of Gordon Shaw and now her idolater, because he arouses the maternal instinct in her and affords her a
sort of emotional release. Doctor Edmund Darrell who maneuvers for this marriage is unaware of one thing—the curse of hereditary insanity in the Evans family. So, when Nina is pregnant and
her own mental difficulties promise to abate in motherhood, Mrs.
Evans is forced to reveal to her secretly this family skeleton and
to urge abortion upon her.

Because Mrs. Evans does not wish her son to be apprised of
the insanity he is heir to, she herself suggests to Nina that she
have a baby—after the abortion—by another man. The "healthy
male" whom she selects to father her next child is, of course, the
"dispassionate" Doctor Darrell. The first result of this experiment could have been easily foretold: Nina becomes contemptuous of her husband, Sam Evans, and infatuated with Darrell.
He, however, plagued by conscience—for Sam is his protégé—
refuses to accept the "romantic" idea that he loves Nina and assumes a detached, scientific pose towards her. It is not a pose he
can successfully maintain, and after trying to forget Nina in
dissipation in Munich, he rushes back to her to suggest that she
divorce Sam. Nina in the interim has adopted his point of view—
she admits loving Darrell, but she will not break with Sam and

ruin his life. The experiment must be carried further. So Darrell continues a safe relation with Nina and puts up money in order that Sam may prosper in business. Darrell's biting comments on Sam, however, at last cause his boy Gordon to flare up against his real father in the defense of his official parent. This is the first sign that his mother's affair with Darrell has turned the boy's affections to Sam. Nina makes a last desperate effort to hold Gordon to her during the boat race of his senior year in college; she attempts to tell his fiancée who is watching the race from the Evans' yacht that she must not marry Gordon because there is insanity in his family, but Darrell, who shrewdly suspects her intent, thwarts her. Sam dies of a stroke of apoplexy, and Gordon, angered at the thought that Darrell will now marry his mother, insults his father, then immediately apologizes and urges the pair to wed. After the drone of his plane overhead tells them that he is gone, Darrell proposes to Nina, who refuses him as he directs (because it will give immense satisfaction to Gordon). Then Charlie Marsden, the inhibited novelist who, throughout the drama, has kept up the pretense of being Nina's "Uncle," leads her off, to assume, we understand, a proprietary paternal interest in her for the rest of her life. The only thing which conceivably might happen that does not occur in this play is for the second Gordon to fall from the skies in his plane in order to crash upon the stage and begin the dreadful cycle all over again. The only reason O'Neill left this out was doubtless the expense of smashing a new plane each performance. Otherwise *Strange Interlude* is singularly complete—even redundant.

Yet it may be questioned whether a dramatized textbook of all the neuroses discoverable by psychoanalysis is great or enduring theater. Each character in *Strange Interlude* is not a human being but a prescription. Marsden is a figure kept puerile by a strong-willed mother, and inhibited by a revolting initiation stunt of his college days. Evans, another adolescent, is the product of the enforced coddling of mother and wife, who successfully keep his tainted heredity from him; his later success is wholly dependent upon this protection. Gordon Evans, reared in the sticky legend of Gordon Shaw, is an artificially quixotic person whose life is colored by what he supposes to be his mother's Platonic friendship for Darrell. Darrell, in turn, is a man inhibited by a scientific attitude and a sense of honor in conflict with his sexual desires. And Nina runs the whole gamut of neurotic experience. One is aware from the success of Ben Jonson's *Every Man in his Humour* that a play with strictly formularized characters may be effective drama, but no one has ever been convinced that it was great drama. Further, the strictly patterned play, as Restoration Comedy shows, is always good entertainment, but not memorable action. *Strange Interlude* is not an original dramatic composition, but a case history. There is not a single break in the pattern: the web is complete, but it has not much more individuality than a net of regular squares.

Yet there is one admirable thing in *Strange Interlude*. The play embodies O'Neill's most forceful attack upon romanticism. It is a legendary Gordon Shaw, after all, who wrecks the lives of Nina Leeds and of the four men who love her; yet she gives birth to and rears his very counterpart in Gordon Evans, the chivalrous prig of Acts Seven and Nine. The skill with which O'Neill brings home the fact that Gordon Shaw, despite his athletic prowess and Apollonian features, must have been a good deal of a wooden image is immeasurably satisfying to one who is tired of handsome football heroes and war aces and is looking for deeper riches of character. On the other hand, it is hard to see that Darrell's desire to be honorable is of quite the same stuff, as O'Neill implies. O'Neill's treatment of Darrell as the experimental physician is a little unworthy of the dramatist, but beyond a doubt can be explained as the natural hostility of the Freudian convert to the traditional enemy of his school—the intuitionalist arrayed against the man of science. Nina Leeds in one of her most oracular moments and in one of her best speeches sneers, "Did you ever know a young scientist? . . . He believes if you pick a lie to pieces, the pieces are the truth." And Marsden, after the death of his mother, curses all doctors as "a pack of God-damned ignorant liars and hypocrites!" Darrell is shown as "human, all too human," just such a hypocrite, incapable of maintaining his rôle of scientific propagator, willing in the end to forswear medicine for biology, where he will never have to deal with life in more than one cell. This is grossly unfair to Darrell whose "experiment," after all, was prompted by no medical theory but by the Freudian dogma that to be the father of a son would be Sam Evans' salvation—and so it was. O'Neill's thinking around this point is more than a little fuzzy.

Hardest to accept is what might be called the theology of the play. Life, Nina tells us after having tasted pretty much the whole of experience, is a strange dark interlude "in the electrical display of God the Father." Opposed to this capricious, egocentric ruling force in the universe is the life force of God the Mother, the "something in one cell that does not need to think" to reproduce itself and to die. Death (which O'Neill, like Nina, seems to feel a desirable thing) means "reunion with Her, a passing back into Her substance, blood of Her blood again, peace of Her peace!" *Strange Interlude* brought to the jaded New York audience which witnessed its long run but one hope, for Nirvana, which apparently has always become the most intense desire of a civilization wholly pleasure-bent, as was ours from 1925 to 1930. Yet perhaps the thought of self-annihilation is the last conceivable delight to those who pander wholly to the senses, whence its fascination for the hedonist to whom the idea of eternity, linked with the conception of God, is unendurable. When *to be* is mere sensation, the craving for escape or death once the senses are satiated is inevitable. It is to be regretted that O'Neill, who was more or less forced to supply his 1928 audience with sensational episode, did not resist complying with the ultimate demands of that audience for the theology it wanted, also.

Whoever ignores the banning of *Strange Interlude* in Boston in 1928 misses an important clue to O'Neill's next plays. It is not Puritanism alone which has imposed a censorship in the Hub on such varied things as *The Children's Hour, The American Mercury, A Farewell to Arms,* and *Lady Chatterley's Lover,* but Irish Catholicism allied to Puritanism. With *Strange Interlude* one wonders whether the promiscuousness of the heroine gave quite so much offense as did the strange theology of O'Neill to Boston's Irish Catholics. It must have been a grievous blow to O'Neill—the harshest of whose plays somewhere reveals a touch of the sentimental Irishman—to have received this reproof from his own race, for it seems clear that he offered the unsuccessful *Dynamo* as an explanation and an apology.

Dynamo (1929) is unredeemable melodrama—unredeemable, because after it failed in Guild performance, O'Neill revised it in an effort to redeem it, but in vain. The play meant much more to O'Neill than it did to those who saw it or who have read it since. Not only was it announced as the first drama in a trilogy on the subject "What is God?" (of which the other dramas were to be "Without Ending of Days" and "It Cannot Be Mad"), but it was meant to *redeem O'Neill himself* in the eyes of those of his faith and race. *Dynamo,* obviously parodying or satirizing New England's most important speculative mind of recent times, Henry Adams, boldly attacks as well bigoted Yankee Protestant-ism (which the Boston Irish, with some justice, hate) and sci-ence (which they, with less justice, fear). *Dynamo* tells the story of Reuben Light, son of a fundamentalist clergyman and his somewhat pagan wife, who in his father's eyes commits a treach-ery by falling in love with Ada Fife, the daughter of an atheist living next door. Ramsay Fife, quite as fanatical in his atheism as the Reverend Hutchins Light in his sectarianism, through a trick destroys Reuben's faith at once in God and in his own mother. As a result, Reuben denounces both, addressing the Deity as the "Old Bozo" and daring Him in a thunderstorm to strike him dead. After knocking about in the world for a while, Reuben returns home to find that his mother is dead. She expired repeat-ing the words, "Don't be a fool," which he had frequently sent her on a postcard during his absence from home, mocking the religion he had been taught. Since these words were said to his broken father, Reuben assumes that in the end his mother came around to his view of things, that "Electricity is God." Conse-quently, through Ada he secures a position with Fife in the local light and power company, and begins to worship the Dynamo as the "Divine Image on earth" of "the Great Mother of Eternal Life, Electricity," with ritual and prayers that are a travesty on the famous passage on the dynamo in *The Education of Henry Adams.* When he cannot rid his mind of the adultery he has com-mitted with Ada Fife, he assumes that this is because he has desecrated the shrine of the Dynamo. Therefore he shoots Ada to death in the powerhouse and immolates himself upon the desecrated altar.

In *Dynamo,* for the benefit of Catholicism, O'Neill renounces "God the Mother" to whom he paid lip service (if not more) in *Strange Interlude.* In this play it is demonstrated that worship of this Mother Force (here, Electricity) leads only to murder and self-destruction. This is as satisfactory an attitude towards Adams' suggestion that one might pray to the Dynamo as any devout Catholic could desire. Yet there is some fairness in the late Percy Hammond's complaint that "Eugene O'Neill seems less than just to Science." The powerhouse he draws is an uncanny place of eerie incandescence and weird sounds—"altogether unlike the same ministrations of a Westinghouse or Bylesby unit." "In the mad operations of this booby-hatch," wrote Mr. Hammond, "electricity is not given a chance to make good as a deity."

Most of us are not interested in having electricity "make good as a deity," but we do, like Pope Leo XIII, believe that science is an ennobling enterprise, and we are puzzled to understand how Reuben Light who, by his own confession, has studied "a lot of science," has failed to arrive at a wholesome attitude towards it. Why has it not purged him of his immaturities and follies? Why, during his absence from home when he worked in and around electrical plants at every opportunity, did Reuben Light fail to find that emotional release, which, according to the Freudians (in whom O'Neill still trusts, if we judge from the character delineations), would have made a normal life with Ada possible for him? Not only is O'Neill less than just to science; he understands neither science nor pseudo-science. His Reuben Light is no more a convert to science than was Doctor Darrell; worse yet, his Reuben Light does not even develop according to the canons of the Freudian psychology to which O'Neill subscribes.

Though Robert Littell holds that O'Neill is no more fair to religion than to science in *Dynamo,* we can understand and forgive the motives which led to the merciless caricature of the Reverend Hutchins Light. O'Neill, long a student of Synge and a follower of the Abbey Theatre, knew that the Irish of Dublin had ignored more blasphemous (though less dangerous) dia-

logue than that contained in *Strange Interlude*. Why were the
Boston Irish so severe with him? Why, unless their whole character had been changed and blunted by contact with the Puritan?
So all the hatred of O'Neill concentrated on the Yankee Protestant—of whom the Reverend Hutchins Light is the worst type.
To contrast the admirable drawing of Ephraim Cabot in *Desire
Under the Elms* with the caricature of this weak fundamentalist
is to gain some conception of how fierce a hatred of the Yankee
the Boston censorship aroused. Yet this hatred defeats its own
ends: so fierce an attack wins sympathy for the victim—and
Hutchins Light, cowering from the thunderstorm, muttering
prayers behind drawn shades, is a pitiable figure rather than a
villain! The play *Dynamo* does not suggest the soundless, beautiful mechanism, but the destructive force of the electrical storm.
Here is power but no control.

His fierce hatred of the Yankee impelled O'Neill to write one
of the great plays of his career in *Mourning Becomes Electra*
(1931). Occasionally, to be sure, this hatred vents itself in pure
spleen, as, for example, when O'Neill describes Mrs. Borden as
*"a typical New England woman of pure English ancestry, with a
horse face, buck teeth and big feet, her manner defensively sharp
and assertive."* Generally, however, he keeps his anger well in
hand, with a result that his portraits of the Mannons and their
neighbors are completely devastating. Provided that he has the
technical skill, a repressed and directed fury in a dramatist, if allowed to surge through violently opposed characters, as in this
play, is likely to produce something of consequence; and if *Mourning Becomes Electra* is not of the first consequence, there is no
modern drama at all, and our faith in the contemporary theatre
is mere delusion.

Mourning Becomes Electra is the boldest play that Eugene
O'Neill has written, in that he dares comparison with the finest
work of antiquity. Representation of Clytemnestra's infidelity to
her husband, of the indifference of Agamemnon to all warnings
and of his murder, of the revenge of his father's death by Orestes at his sister's urging, and of the pursuit of the matricide by
the furies was first attempted (so far as we know) in the trilogy
of Aeschylus—*Agamemnon, The Choephoroe,* and *The Eumeni-*

des, then in part in the *Electra* of Sophocles, and finally in the *Electra,* the *Orestes,* and the *Iphigenia* of Euripides. Some comprehension of the feat attempted by O'Neill may be gathered by those unacquainted with the works of Greek tragedians from Professor Gilbert Murray's assertion that, "As far as we can speculate, there is not the faintest probability of any poet ever setting to work on, let us say, the essential effect aimed at by Aeschylus in the Cassandra-scene of the *Agamemnon* and doing it better than Aeschylus. The only thing which the human race has to do with that scene is to understand it and get out of it all the joy and emotion and wonder that it contains." Yet O'Neill has repeated what is essential in that scene, by uniting the characters of Cassandra and Electra, in his drama. Is the result a travesty upon the original or a challenging creation of comparable magnitude?

Let us grant at the outset that the prose of O'Neill cannot compare with the poetry of the Greeks, no more than can the sniggering Yankee neighbors of the Mannons, who comment on their pride and destiny, compare for dignity with the stately choruses of Aeschylus. Yet it is a mistake to assume that O'Neill's failure to employ verse totally disqualifies the play from comparison with Ancient tragedy, just as it is obviously stupid—since the purpose was satirical—to lament that O'Neill's gossiping Yankees are not more dignified. The problem is not whether O'Neill is the equal of Aeschylus as a poet, but rather, does he challenge comparison as a dramatist? It is our thesis that on the score of motivation—all that makes action essentially sound—he does. Our answer will irritate classical scholars from here to Oxford, but their ire ought not to force us to blink the truth.

When we consider the motivation of Clytemnestra, as elucidated by Aeschylus—

> "What I did, I did
> Not with a random inconsiderate blow
> But from old Hate, and with maturing Time"—

we must be struck by one fundamental weakness. The hatred of Clytemnestra for her husband originates in the sacrifice of her daughter Iphigenia by Agamemnon at Aulis. Now, this act cannot be conceived a crime against the mother, since it is fully explained by the conventional beliefs of the time and Clytemnestra is nowhere made out a liberator of the Greeks from superstition. It is merely an unreasoned device to set the wife's hatred in motion, yet it endows that hatred with the quality of madness. We are inclined to forget this when later the queen appears to have a better justification in her jealousy of Cassandra, the prophetic captive of whom Agamemnon has made a concubine. Sympathy for Clytemnestra, however, is a modern sentimentality, and the Greeks looked upon her undeniably as a wicked person deserving punishment. There is a mere physical clash in the *Agamemnon*, therefore, and not a spiritual struggle between equally justified characters.

Contrast this with the motivation of *Mourning Becomes Electra*, where the hatred of Christine Mannon for her husband has a double justification. First, there is the strong physical repulsion originating in a brutal wedding-night attack that destroyed totally her love for Ezra Mannon. There is, secondly, the subtle growth of her hatred towards him, because he and his ally, the daughter Lavinia, were partially responsible for forcing her son Orin, on whom she had fixed her frustrated love, to enlist as a lieutenant in the Civil War. Freud has supplied roots for the growth of a thorny tree of hate which in Aeschylus is merely a canvas property. When Christine fixes her love on Captain Adam Brant, the justification is not lasciviousness, but the modern doctrine that each human being is entitled to a genuine love. It should be noted, however, that the proper motivation of Christine does not make out of General Ezra Mannon a mechanical villain. Inhibited by his strict Puritan upbringing (his father had driven his brother from the house for an affair with a Canadian French maid), he is incapable of the tender passion necessary for the gentle cultivation of the love of Christine. O'Neill achieves one of his finest effects by having General Mannon, who genuinely loves his wife, declare his remorse for his share in creating the unhappy marital relationship, on his return home from the War, having discovered in that holocaust of hate and death the value of a tender love. Yet too late, for the heart of his wife, pledged to Captain Brant, is now fixed on her husband's death. Acquainted with the fact that General Mannon is suffering from heart's disease, Christine, on the very night of their reunion, provokes a fainting fit by declaring her true relation to Brant, and when her husband calls for his medicine, administers a fatal potion she and her lover have prepared. After the General's death, this episode is given superb ironic touch when one sniggering Yankee suggests to another that the husband has died from *angina pectoris* in the ecstasies of renewed love. "It was love killed Ezra!"

With the death of the General (Agamemnon returned from the wars) and the revelation to Lavinia of her mother as a poisoner the tragedy of *The Homecoming,* the first play in Eugene O'Neill's trilogy, comes to an end. The second play, *The Hunted,* deals with Lavinia's successful effort to avenge her father through the feeble instrumentality of her brother, Orin, the Orestes of the modern trilogy. Here again it appears to us that O'Neill has surpassed the ancient dramatists on the score of motivation and here again he has done it with the aid of Freudian psychology. In all the Greek originals the motivation of Electra is excessively simple—treated as a slave by her infatuated mother, she honors her treacherously slain parent and evokes the unwritten code to her purpose, which is the punishment of Aegisthus, her mother's lover. Indeed, her instrumentality is very slight since Orestes is determined on revenge before encountering his sister. Lavinia Mannon, on the other hand, from childhood has been jealous of her mother, who has denied her a natural love, since she was conceived on that fearful wedding night. The Electra-complex, however, is not offered as a complete explanation of Lavinia's desire to avenge her father. At the direction of Christine, Captain Brant has paid false court to Lavinia to distract her from spying on her mother. When the truth is revealed to Lavinia, she has this secret insult to avenge as well as General Mannon's murder. "The fury of a woman scorned" propels her as much as justice to her father. The agent for her revenge, however, the deluded Orin, is bound to her mother by all the fatal coils of the Oedipus complex. Indeed, the first words he utters in Act I of *The Hunted* (when we meet him for the first time) are, "Where's mother?" No sense of duty to a father whom he did not love can arouse Orin Mannon to action. Yet when he reveals a dark jealousy of his mother's lover, his implacable sister uses that as a spur to goad him to the murder of Captain Brant. Still burning with the fury of his hatred of the interloper in his mother's affections and determined to see her suffer, Orin, in his only display of independence, tells her that he has slain her lover and precipitates her suicide—an act more comprehensible than the murder of Clytemnestra by Orestes.

The Hunted moves with a tragic swiftness and certainty which outpaces the tempo of *The Homecoming*. The action throughout is tremendously elevated by the struggle for dominance between Christine and Lavinia. Christine, who, in *The Homecoming,* attains to something of the dignity of Lady Macbeth, shrinks in this play pitifully before the relentless attack of her daughter upon her security, upon her dream of bliss, even upon her hope of flight. There is something of the remorselessness of Strindberg's women in these two—the frenetic fury of the sex turned upon itself—as they lash out at each other, and there is achieved suspense of the highest tension as Christine and Lavinia play for control of the hapless Orin, who, however weak and indecisive, may become, with the proper stimulation, as dangerous as Orestes armed with an axe. Had he not, hysterical from killing, walked laughing, like O'Neill's Lazarus, towards the enemy's bastion at Petersburg, leading his men to perform what his own father described as one of the bravest acts of the War? And had not his dangerous head wound made him more susceptible to murderous suggestion? Two contestants wrestling for a dagger on the ground could not freeze the attention as do these women in their contest for this instrument. Christine has one of the best speeches in the modern theatre at the end of Act II, when, exulting over Lavinia because the Mannon pride will keep her from taking her father's murder to the prosecutor and Orin's declaration of hatred for his father seemingly makes him unfit as the tool for Lavinia's revenge, she suddenly breaks down and begs her daughter not to tell Orin about Adam Brant, thereby giving direction to that cruel purpose, with the result which we have described.

In *The Choephoroe* of Aeschylus, Clytemnestra, before she is dispatched, threatens her son with the furies which wait on matricide, and *The Eumenides* depicts his pursuit by the Erinyes, sped on by her ghost, until by the judgment of Athena, the tormented son is acquitted. Granting the complete faith of the Athenian audience in the involved mythology (which the motivation of *Agamemnon* places in doubt), we see that the trilogy of Aeschylus rises to a grand climax in *The Eumenides* wherein all await the foreknown judgment of the goddess. Although O'Neill achieves a wholly adequate climax for his trilogy at the end of *The Haunted,* his third play, when Lavinia, having renounced her lover and accepted the fate of the Mannons, turns on her heel and marches into her ghost-filled home, O'Neill's action breaks badly before it sets towards its goal. This is because he has taken too easy a path with Lavinia, whom, despite the admirable drawing of *The Homecoming* and *The Hunted,* he does not wholly understand. Her characterization, furthermore, is enfeebled by a dramatic necessity which O'Neill does comprehend. He realizes that his sea will break with a more terrific roar if it can draw back before the final, devastating lunge. Lavinia must herself catch some vision of rapture before she surrenders to her doom. The weakness of the vision supplied mars the drama. Lavinia, when *The Haunted* opens, is expected back from a trip to the Orient whither she has gone with her brother. When she returns, we are startled at the transformation in her—the grimness, the statuesqueness which reminded us of her military father, are gone, and in their place are a youthfulness and a sensuousness reminiscent of her mother, a reminiscence enforced by the dramatist's insistence on a physical resemblance of Lavinia to the Christine of Act I of *The Homecoming.* If this were mere psychoanalytical nonsense, we could endure it; but whatever the Freudian overtones, this new Lavinia's resemblance to the old Christine has moral and aesthetic indications we cannot ignore. We are told that Lavinia, during a sojourn with her brother on a coral isle, has become infatuated with the conception of pagan love, stimulated by the attentions of an adoring native chief. That is, she has virtually accepted her mother's philosophy that sensuous passion is the one categorical imperative of life. It is easy for O'Neill, with his conviction of Yankee hypocrisy, to accept this change in Lavinia as natural, but it is not easy for anyone who really knows New England to accept it. Electra, who merely touches the sword of Orestes in Euripides' play, dares scarcely hope for any joy thereafter. She will have to placate the furies as much as will Orestes.

> "And whither, to what country shall I fly,
> Wretch that I am? What nuptials shall be mine?
> What husband lead me to my bridal bed?"

Yet what are the implacable Erinyes to a New England conscience? Orin Mannon is faultlessly portrayed as gnawed by the furies and as craving relief in confession. Yet Lavinia has come back from her South Sea adventure, not only bent on happiness, but washed of any sense of guilt. This is incredible. Hawthorne, who doubtless overshoots the mark, pictures the New England conscience as so powerful an agent that one of his characters, Hilda of *The Marble Faun,* can have no spiritual peace until she has revealed the agents in a murder in which she had no other share than that of innocent witness. How then has Lavinia purged herself of the murder of Captain Brant and of her mother's suicide? The character of Lavinia suddenly disintegrates, for the author has reconstructed her out of theory and prejudice, and not out of her known and adequate past.

O'Neill introduces a theme into *The Haunted* which is not found in his Greek originals but which had been treated by Robinson Jeffers in *The Tower Beyond Tragedy* in 1925. Orin Mannon, mentally unbalanced by his sense of guilt, tortures his sister with his desire to confess, but when she offers to pay any price for his silence, he proposes (what Shelley described as the most powerful dramatic motive) incest as a solution for both of them. When Lavinia, in her new rôle of innocence, is revolted by this, Orin shoots himself. Though Peter Niles, Lavinia's fiancé, will carry out his pledge to wed her despite his family, Lavinia realizes her way is marked with death and, allowing Peter to believe the worst of her, she sends him from her. Thus in the end she reachieves that tragic greatness the dramatist momentarily robs her of. Like Ephraim Cabot, she transcends defeat, accepting life as her punishment for being born.

> "O Atreus' seed!
> How hardly, after many labors past,
> Art thou come forth to liberty at last,
> Through this new trial perfected indeed!"

Thus in the end, almost in spite of himself, but with an aesthetic conscience which transcends private considerations and makes all motives pure, O'Neill does final justice to the race of Mannons and the detested Yankees! Thus he answers affirmatively the question Walter Prichard Eaton tells us he asked in his diary, in 1926: "Is it possible to get modern psychological approximation of the Greek sense of fate into a play which an intelligent audience of today, possessed of no belief in gods or moral retribution, could accept and be moved by?"

The audience which sat through five hours of *Mourning Becomes Electra* left the theatre with some sense of katharsis, but the writing of his trilogy apparently did as much to cleanse the emotions of the dramatist as the performance did for those of his audience. There is no sign of malice in O'Neill's next play, *Ah, Wilderness!* (1933), though the setting is a small Connecticut city. At least three reviewers were struck by the resemblance of this piece to Booth Tarkington's *Seventeen*. Apparently concocted for a depression audience, *Ah, Wilderness!* is a good genre comedy of the pre-War type, describing at once sympathetically and humorously the brief and frustrated rebellion of adolescence against convention. The Miller family are about as near the dead level of "decent" folk as any represented in either our drama or our fiction. The chief merit of *Ah, Wilderness!*, however, was that it convinced the sceptical of O'Neill's marvellous facility. It is true that Ibsen and Strindberg couldn't (or possibly wouldn't) have written it.

Days Without End, O'Neill's second play of the 1933–34 season, failed in presentation. It is obviously the second member of the trilogy on "What is God?", announced in 1929 as *Without Ending of Days*. As theatre, it is a poorer thing, even, than *Dynamo,* the trilogy's first member. It will survive, however, for the peculiar light it sheds on its author, who, one would guess, is represented by the protagonist of the play, John Loving. Indeed, *Days Without End* strikes us as a sort of *Education of Eugene O'Neill* on the model of Adams' book, which he had read for *Dynamo*.

John Loving is a schizoid personality, represented by two actors in the play—John and Loving. John is the man of fine sensitivity, poet and idealist, suppressed by Loving, the sneering cynic, the follower of all the fashions in contemporary thought. The latter's intellectual past is very like O'Neill's: he has been, according to Father Baird, atheist, atheist-socialist, atheist-anarchist, and disciple of Nietzsche. The same commentator tells us that Loving is now a Bolshevik, largely because the Russians have abolished love and marriage and have substituted the State for God—"the most grotesque god that ever came out of Asia!" John is working on a novel into which his particular devil, Loving, inserts all the iconoclastic parts. When John reveals the plot of his novel to his devoted wife, Elsa, he little understands that he is also confessing his infidelity to her; for not only does she properly identify the novel's hero with her husband, but a mutual friend, the woman with whom John has had relations in his character of Loving, has told Elsa enough of the story (naming no names) for her to piece out the rest. Distraught, she rushes into the winter night and contracts pneumonia. While she lies at the point of death, John and Loving struggle for mastery in her bedchamber. John finally decides to go out to the Church of God for help, and Elsa, believing him about to commit suicide, rallies and forgives him. In the sanctuary Loving dies, and from his body, which symbolically forms a cross upon the floor, the whole John Loving, no longer a split personality, rises to receive the blessing of Father Baird. He, we are assured, has found the meaning of life.

Autobiographical or not, *Days Without End* marks the most complete retreat of O'Neill's creative career. It may be eminently satisfying to those who, like Arthur Hobson Quinn and Richard Dana Skinner, see that career wholly in terms of a poet's quest for spirituality; but it is a renunciation of the hedonism of *Lazarus Laughed* and of the pagan "natural right" to love by which O'Neill has tried and condemned New England morals in *Dynamo* and *Mourning Becomes Electra*. It is not easy, either, to reconcile its tardy endorsement of the Church with Ponce de León's recognition of the "enemy" in the Churchman, whatever his guise. No, *Days Without End* is hardly a logical capstone to the work of O'Neill: it is, however, a symbol that he has rejected the philosophy of his creative work (as proceeding too much from his ingenious Loving devil?) and is ready to reaffirm his faith in traditional things. And this means more than Roman Catholicism, for John identifies "pig wallow" morals with a loss of national idealism, a belief in America. There is, it would seem, reason for both delight and anxiety in *Days Without End:* joy because O'Neill has rejected a palpably false philosophy of life, and fear that the acceptance of tradition may ruin the dramatist. Is Eugene O'Neill such that only a Promethean position is possible for him, if he is to do creative work? Is he one of those who need to feel themselves in opposition to the gods, to do work beneficial to man? Let us recognize that, however wrong-headed his plays have been, they have been provocative of thought on matters few of his contemporaries have consistently touched. Can we spare this Promethean fire for candle-light? Bernard DeVoto, who rendered "a minority report" when O'Neill was awarded the Nobel Prize for 1936, apparently is of the opinion that we can, but many more of us are anxious over the result. We would not care to see a string of plays like *Ah, Wilderness!* or a sequence of historical dramas. Yet our concern is wholly for the artist; we agree that the man has found himself.

Only one other contemporary can compare with O'Neill, as we shall see, for his use of Freudian material, but many writers between 1920 and 1930 treated sex themes with a freedom hitherto unknown in literature. Some of this writing will survive for its craftsmanship, but more, probably, for its social significance. If we are to take altogether literally his word that his poem *Two Lives* "was substantially written in the autumn and winter of 1913," William Ellery Leonard is obviously the first person to consider in this category, though *Two Lives* was not printed until 1922 and was not given to the public until 1925.

The most important episode in Mr. Leonard's life, according to his none-too-plausible autobiography, *The Locomotive God* (1927), was a fit of terror, experienced when he was only two and a half, on the platform of a Plainfield, N. J., railroad station, because an on-rushing locomotive bringing home his minister-father, appeared to be coming directly at him. In his infantile horror he saw the mechanism as God. He asserts that because of this episode he has all his life long been a victim of a "distance phobia"—a neurotic condition, it may be added, unique with him. *The Locomotive God* will be remembered primarily, we will venture, as an illustration of the strange ills persons fancied themselves subject to after reading Freud. Mr. Leonard, being a person of some imagination, has increased by one the neurotic conditions hypothesized by the Viennese physician.

Despite his "distance phobia" Mr. Leonard has done considerable travelling. After receiving his A.B. in 1898 from Boston University and teaching Latin there for a year, Leonard became principal of the high school at Plainville, Mass., and commuted to Cambridge to work on his M.A. at Harvard. Later he studied at the German universities of Göttingen and Bonn. At Bonn he saw Kaiser Wilhelm and was impelled to write ". . . The Kaiser comes—and every inch a King!" Returning to the United States, he was in residence a year at Columbia University before receiving a doctorate degree for the dissertation *Byron and Byronism in the United States* (1905). He was appointed an instructor in English at the University of Wisconsin in 1906 and became a full professor at that institution in 1926.

Professor Leonard is the author of many books, among which, however, are only two of any consequence. His translation of Lucretius' *De Rerum Natura* (1916) into English verse is the best translation of that solemn determinist with which we are acquainted—and we do not forget some of the paraphrases of Spenser and Dryden. Leonard's renderings of *Fragments of Empedocles* (1908) and of *Beowulf* (1923), on the other hand, miss by a considerable margin the spirit of their originals. It is for his autobiographical poem, allegedly treating his first marriage in 1909 to Charlotte Freeman, of Madison, who died in 1911, that William Ellery Leonard will be remembered, if at all.

Two Lives is the story of a man who against all auguries and counsel married a woman tainted with hereditary insanity. His courage might have won out had not the couple ill-advisedly gone to live in the home of the bride's father, where the wife had constantly to choose between her duty to her querulous parent and to her jealous husband. The upshot of the experiment was that the wife, in a period of depression, took poison to escape her unhappiness. There is no denying that *Two Lives* is a graphic case history and a well-posted warning against attempting this sort of experiment under precisely these conditions. But it is a history and a warning *in verse*—in 205 sonnets to be exact—and must be examined as poetry. First should be noted the technical mastery of the poet: despite the very difficult form chosen, the story flows out as easily as if it were written in prose. Leonard's masters are easily guessed at: only the thorough student of Byron, the lover of *Beppo* and *Don Juan,* could have managed as effectively the bitter, satirical touches of the poem; and only the convert to Lucretius could have given the poem its weightless yet terrible compulsion forward to tragedy. A mirthless, wicked Byron draws the portrait of the brother-in-law playing billiards at the club, while an awed, but modern Lucretius acknowledges the sway of Venus over the life of woman:

> Lo had begun again for her the time,
> The cyclic time (through Nature's fixed decree),
> That woman in her large fecundity
> Shares with the barren moon in every clime. . . .

Yet one re-reads *Two Lives* with diminishing enthusiasm: it is not like those pieces of first quality to which one returns ever to freshen one's appetite—the whole was apprehended at the first reading as in some superior piece of journalism. Worse yet, there are no memorable lines which the poetry-lover unconsciously repeats betimes when he thinks his mind is otherwise occupied. When one reflects that none of Leonard's other poetry is moving, from *Sonnets and Poems* (1906) to *A Son of Earth* (1928), one begins to apprehend that it is as a *raconteur* and not as poet that the author of *Two Lives* is arresting.

Evelyn Scott is another writer whom we value more for her personal experience, as recorded in *Escapade* (1923), than for her creative work, though there appears to be merit in the novels *The Narrow House* (1921) and *Narcissus* (1922). Mrs. Scott is a native of Tennessee, where she was born in Clarksville, in 1893, and where (as she tells us in *Background in Tennessee,* 1937) a case of boils produced an inferiority complex that made her a writer while still a child. At fourteen she had short stories published under a pseudonym. She is reputedly the youngest student ever to have entered Tulane University, and she was only twenty when she ran away to live for three years in Brazil with the artist Cyril Kay Scott.

When her account of her Brazilian adventure was published in 1923 as *Escapade,* it was the frankest account, written for general public consumption, of a woman's feelings and thoughts during pregnancy. But what particularly enhanced that account was the fact that its author was placed in such unusual circumstances—an exile in a land where she understood only the hostile eyes and where the most earnest efforts of her companion could barely provide subsistence for them. The man she defended was, she knew, accused of running away with a mere child, while her conviction was that he and she were entitled to their love, though he had deserted a wife in order to bring it about. *Escapade* is full of the defiance of the 'twenties, bold in its refusal to count the cost, but frank in revealing the inconveniences and penalties attendant to breaking conventions. Another virtue of *Escapade* is that its author is never wholly unaware that she is a bit of a *poseur*—"there is something Byronic in my sadness," she flatly states. Hence the book has a real place, both in the literature of adventure and in any summary of the attitudes that rationalization forced Americans into in the 'twenties.

The novels of Evelyn Scott have grown steadily in bulk but not in consequence. As has been intimated, *The Narrow House* and *Narcissus,* published at the beginning of the 'twenties, remain, with the exception of the autobiography, her best work. They deal with the neurotic Lawrence Farley, his weepy, sickly, morbid first wife, his worse second wife and her lovers, his pathological parents, his sister Alice (who is a sex-repressed old maid with a bitter tongue), and some unhealthy children. Each character is engrossed with his own sickness within the confines of a "narrow house" which forces contiguous pain upon pain, so that the total effect, in the words of Alice, is that of "a moral cellar." The author succeeds well enough in making us realize the relationship of her characters, but she does not succeed in making us care. She has tried to get what she calls the "psychological essences" of her characters—and she has succeeded too well. Her people are mere

types of disease, and we are no more sorry when they are tortured and destroyed than we are in seeing a plague wiped out.
This great deficiency in the novelist is responsible for her successive failures to convince, despite indefatigable industry, much
well-chosen naturalistic detail, and a variety of subject matter in
The Golden Door (1925), *Migrations* (1927), *The Wave*
(1929), *A Calendar of Sin* (1931), *Eva Gay* (1933), *Breathe
Upon These Slain* (1934), and *Bread and a Sword* (1937).
Where, in all these books, is a vital character? Mr. Joseph Warren Beach has fixed with deadly certainty upon another fault of
Mrs. Scott's, when he writes of "the large freight of exposition
which the author carries, rather clumsily." Mrs. Scott is a slave
to the new psychology; she dares see people only in its terms. She
is afraid of being "unscientific." But she is not afraid in other
regards, as her courageous denunciation of fascism and communism in the preface to *Bread and a Sword* reveals. Perhaps she
will yet score again as she did in *Escapade*.

A convert to Freudianism was Harvey O'Higgins, the Cana-
dian-born Irish journalist, who became an American citizen during the World War and served as Associate Chairman of the
Committee for Public Information. It was he who had shaped up
in *The Beast* Judge Ben Lindsey's crusades for social reform in
Colorado. Between 1920 and 1924 O'Higgins published in various magazines a number of Freudian analyses of important
American figures, then, in the latter year, gathered these studies
into a volume called *The American Mind in Action*. The thesis
of this book is that any American may be interpreted adequately
by determining how much his inner life is one of Puritan "psychic
anxiety—of soul-fear." From Henry Adams and Van Wyck
Brooks, Harvey O'Higgins inherited a distrust of the alleged
Puritan repression of sex, and from Freud the theory which
makes this repression a complete explanation of American character. Unfortunately, he cannot cite the ideas of any historical
Puritan on sex, and has to content himself by quoting Saint Paul
and Henry Adams, neither of whom is a very satisfactory historical Puritan. The letters of Margaret Winthrop (who was a
third wife) to her husband indicate a high degree of bliss in at
least one Puritan marriage, and there is other evidence which

could be cited. A far better explanation seems to be that the Puritan, with no attempt at birth control, with his large family, and not infrequently his succession of wives, had adequate sex expression and saw no need to write or to discourse on the subject. Ideas get into print only under pressure. It was with the economic checks of the post-Civil War period that the sex life of America became restrained and the need for expression in print (admittedly now a radical thing, in view of the traditional silence) genuinely imperative. Yet for O'Higgins nearly every American is some kind of Puritan, in one way or another badly adjusted to reality. Thus, "Lincoln showed it in his melancholy, Mark Twain in his despair, Emerson by his introversion, Comstock by his fanaticism, and Barnum by his attempt to escape from the reputation which, like a jocular hair shirt, he had himself assumed in his autobiography." Andrew Carnegie, the adopted American, shows the same maladjustment, for "the Scotch Calvinists, from whom he derived, were the brothers in faith of the New England Puritans."

As one reflects on the Americans whom O'Higgins analyzes as spiritually unwell, one cannot help thinking that a little maladjustment to one's environment may be a good thing. Yet one would be unwise to seek, on the basis of Mr. O'Higgins' evidence, spiritual unhappiness as a key to greatness. Take the case of Emerson. "His psychology," we are assured, "may perhaps be accepted as typical of his kind in the American environment. . . . He was a clear and unadulterated product of Puritanism. . . ." But who, in heaven's name, were Emerson's *kind?* Who would concede that Emerson was *typical* of anybody but Emerson? Said Lowell of him, comparing him to Carlyle—

> That he's more of a man you might say of the one,
> Of the other he's more of an Emerson.

And beyond that there doesn't appear to be much more to say. To assume that Emerson was an unhappy introvert, as O'Higgins does, because Emerson's mother was undemonstrative and his father, a "somewhat social gentleman, but severe to his children," who tried to force a rough adjustment of the boy with the world by pushing him off a wharf or bathing house into salt water (to teach him to swim!), seems to us a trifle absurd, particularly when Mr. O'Higgins glibly reverses the formula with Andrew Carnegie. The student of Emerson knows that he was aware enough of what was going on about him in the world—

The Cossack eats Poland like stolen fruit,—

and he admits that Emerson suffered from amnesia at the close of his life, without accepting this as the inevitable result of being pushed off a wharf as a boy—

To the new psychology, he appears, in fact, as a timid, dependent, introverted recluse who retired within himself and shut out reality until he ended in amnesia and the inability to remember even the names of things.

On the basis of the best medical knowledge we have today and in lieu of positive evidence such as only an examination could give, we would be inclined to attribute Emerson's general amnesia to physical causes—the overtaxing of a none-too-rugged physical equipment in the lecture tours that he extended further and further west as he grew older. No man could write more frankly of waning bodily vigor than does Emerson in "Terminus." And how that strength was taxed by the daily stream of visitors who came to see "the recluse" of Concord only one knows who has read, not only Emerson's journals, but the memoirs and recollections of his neighbors and acquaintances, in Concord and outside. Merely because Emerson expressed himself occasionally as envious of the contemplative life which he had so little opportunity to live, one must not assume that he was an introvert. Mr. O'Higgins' study of Emerson—and one could show this study to be *typical* of others in *The American Mind in Action*—is convincing only to those who like handsome generalizations or who have some especial interest in destroying our intellectual traditions.

The best application Mr. O'Higgins made of his method is not contained in this book, but in an essay, "Alias Walt Whitman," which appeared in *Harper's Magazine* three months after the author's death from pneumonia, on February 28, 1929. Here is cited much evidence to show that Whitman was sexually abnormal and that the treatment of sex in his poetry was dictated by an urge towards exhibitionism. The case is a very strong one and can be further strengthened by evidence which Mr. O'Higgins did not cite and apparently was unaware of. Yet what about Whitman's earnest desire to give expression to "the forbidden voice"? Could a Narcissan (Mr. O'Higgins' word) be thus conscious of his exhibitionism and remain abnormal? If one is troubled by the evidence of Whitman's alleged abnormality, as collected and displayed by the various analysts, one should know that Whitman's mind ran more deliberately to sex in print, apparently, than out of it. His various notebooks, which since his death have been unearthed and printed, and his talks with Horace Traubel are relatively reticent on the subject, considering the expression it receives in *Leaves of Grass*. Proved or not proved, however, the Freudian analysis of Whitman in *Harper's* is the best example of this type of criticism in our letters and deserves fame or notoriety as such.

Harvey O'Higgins was the author of two novels, *Julie Cane* (1924) and *Clara Barron* (1926), and a volume of fictional sketches, *Some Distinguished Americans* (1923), in addition to being a critic with a Freudian thesis. Both novels are studies of girls who are the products of unhappy marriages. In each case the husband is early discredited in the story: Julie Cane's father set her mother's bed afire by placing in it a hot-brick, while Clara Barron's sire swam away from his wife and daughter after upsetting a canoe and leaving them to be rescued by the gardener. In the first instance, the father compensates by forming an alliance with the daughter; in the second, the daughter dominates the mother and drives the father out of the home. *Julie Cane* degenerates after a good beginning into a sort of Harry Leon Wilson-Mary Roberts Rinehart romance, while *Clara Barron* is awkwardly finished off as a tragedy. The sketches in *Some Distinguished Americans* complete the proof that O'Higgins had only a formula with which to approach fiction—his characters cannot kick themselves loose of the Freudian situations in which he places them or develop properly within the restrictions he imposes.

Very similar in his development to Mr. O'Higgins, but much more prolific as a writer, is Ludwig Lewisohn, who likewise is an

American by adoption, for he was born into a German-Jewish family in Berlin, on May 30, 1882, and came to the United States first when he was eight years old. For three years his father struggled to run a store in a small South Carolina town, then gave it up and moved his family into Charleston, where Ludwig entered high school when he was only eleven. Graduated from the College of Charleston in 1901, Lewisohn took an M.A. degree at Columbia University two years later, but found that he could get no teaching appointment because he was a Jew. Rather than continue with his doctorate to no purpose, Lewisohn left the university (despite the protests of Professor Trent) and took a reader's job with Doubleday, Page & Co. He was married to Mary Arnold Crocker in 1906, and began to turn his hand to any sort of writing which would bring in money—reviews, articles, short stories. He confesses to selling six serials, so false to life that they eventually turned his stomach, and he was forced to do a serious book out of justice to the artist in him. *The Broken Snare* (1908) was thought well of by Dreiser, who read it for the publisher, but it had no luck with the general public. The plates for Lewisohn's next novel were seized by Anthony Comstock and destroyed. The author was plunged into the deepest abyss of his career:

> . . . I was beaten, broken, breadless. I was a scholar and forbidden to teach, an artist and forbidden to write. Liberty, opportunity. The words had nothing friendly to my ear.

He was forced to go back to Columbia to beg help in securing a teaching appointment. Although Professors Lawrence and Trent did their utmost for him, it was finally through William Ellery Leonard that he secured a position, not in English as he had hoped, but in German, at the University of Wisconsin. It is Lewisohn's belief that he was turned down at the universities of Virginia and Minnesota, and at Princeton, where there were vacancies, because he was a Jew. After serving as an instructor at Wisconsin for a year, Lewisohn received an appointment as assistant professor of German at Ohio State University, where he remained from 1911 to 1919. In 1916, before we entered the War, Lewisohn had been so rash as to publish a book entitled

The Spirit of Modern German Literature, in which, while insisting upon the survival of the spirit of Goethe in modern Germany, he had contended that Nietzsche was "indisputably one of the great masters of prose." True, this volume was offset in 1918 by his book *The Poets of Modern France* (containing some of the best translations that we know), but the fact he had put himself in print as an admirer of some things German and the fact that he was reputed to defend German culture to his students were too much for the ignorant official defenders of America, and he was "investigated." Feeling was so high in Columbus that Lewisohn availed himself of a sabbatical leave due him and did not return.

His early reviewing, his book *The Modern Drama* (1915), and the interest of Oswald Garrison Villard resulted in his being appointed to the staff of *The Nation,* which he served from 1919 to 1924, as dramatic editor and then associate editor. His marital affairs had reached a crisis in 1923; he felt that he had married a Gentile under persuasion of "the false liberalism of the nineteenth century" which his father radiated and that his marriage was a mistake. He deliberately gave his wife grounds for divorce by seeking the companionship of one of his own race. With "Thelma" of *Mid-Channel* he went abroad to live and to study in 1924, and remained there, except for periodic visits, until after the depression began, when he took up his abode in Burlington, Vermont. In February, 1940, he was wed to Miss Edna Manley, a Rochester, N. Y., newspaper woman, while being sued in the courts for a settlement by "Thelma" and her son. Since 1923 he has been one of the prominent leaders in the Zionist movement, the case for which he stated most completely in *The Answer* (1939).

Lewisohn has written his autobiography in *Up-Stream* (1922) and *Mid-Channel* (1929). The first is undeniably an important book, both a moving human document and a fearless tract for racial equality. One is stirred to indignation that a man must suffer so much humiliation and injustice as is painfully set down in *Up-Stream* merely because his blood is not that of the dominant stock in America. One does not believe, of course, that Lewisohn was always so discriminated against as he thinks he was.

For example, we doubt if "Brewer" of Columbia hated him because he felt in him "the implacable foe of the New England dominance over our national life" or because he was a Jew. But that Lewisohn had sufficient reason in other instances to see malice behind any choice that involved himself is sufficient commentary on the existing racial prejudice to disturb any liberal American. And the record of national hostility during the war-hysteria to all things German—even in our universities—is mortifying, so painful, in fact, that we revert to it only under the moral compulsion that the memory will do us good. *Up-Stream* is the perfect antidote, with its broad cosmopolitan reference and its passion for universal culture, for 100% Americanism.

How, then, shall we view *Mid-Channel* which is the direct antithesis of *Up-Stream*? In the earlier book Lewisohn had insisted that he could take no refuge in the spirit or traditions of his own people. "My psychical life," he says, "was Aryan through and through." After this was written, however, he separated from his Gentile wife and took a Jewish mate; further, he made an intense study of the cultural traditions of the Jews, learning Hebrew and Yiddish of which he had hitherto been ignorant, and he consorted with leaders of his race in Germany, among whom the Zionists made the strongest impression on him. The result was a trip to Palestine and a conversion to Zionism, which he preached in *Israel* (1925) and to which he recurs more movingly in *Mid-Channel*. Assimilationism was the impractical ideal of the nineteenth century Jew; nationalism is the practical ideal of the twentieth century leader of his race, according to Lewisohn. That is, the national race consciousness which he finds objectionable in Americans in *Up-Stream* he now advocates breeding among his own people. Furthermore, though Lewisohn derides "German-Jews" and "American-Jews" and declares himself for "Jewish-Jews," it is not at all clear on just what model he would form his people. Who are the Jewish-Jews? Certainly not the bourgeois-Zionistic rabble of Jerusalem today, who no more resemble the ancient Hebrews, to whom Lewisohn reverts, than a lyric by Irving Berlin resembles a psalm of David. Is Mr. Lewisohn a Jewish-Jew? Nonsense. Mr. Lewisohn is an American, and there is no evidence in *Mid-Channel* that all his reading of the Torah and the Prophets has changed him one iota from the sort of person he was in *Up-Stream* when he could see no Jewish elements in his own psyche. *Mid-Channel* is not only unconvincing because of its twentieth century nationalism, but also because it is too apologetic in regard to the broken marriage. The author's self-pity and his excuses are tedious, and his new assumption that he is an introvert is contradicted by his reporting on what is about him. There is a moving passage in *Mid-Channel* on the St. Valentine's day massacre of the Jews in Strassburg in 1349, and some good satirical writing on wealthy Jewish ladies who make it a principle to receive in their salons only such Jews as do *not* associate with Jews, but that is all.

As narratives, Mr. Lewisohn's autobiographical studies are better reading than his fiction and, we are inclined to think, more important. Yet while Lewisohn's abilities as a writer of fiction are greater than those of Mr. O'Higgins, we do not feel they are such as to warrant full discussion of his novels here. In all his novels he carries a heavy burden of expository matter and his tendency has been to reduce dialogue and action appreciably with each new book. *The Island Within* (1928), Lewisohn's best novel, devotes more than a hundred pages to the ancestry of his hero before he himself is introduced. This antecedent material tells the story of the sufferings of a Jewish family in Europe from 1840 to the Great War, yet as a representation of persecution it is far less effective than similar material in Abraham Cahan's *The Rise of David Levinsky*. Cahan has felt his experience, while Mr. Lewisohn's is obviously a piece of reconstruction. When he finally gets down to his study of Arthur Levy, son of an American furniture manufacturer, who is driven from a medical internship in a public sanitarium, because he cannot stand the abuse accorded Jewish patients, into psychoanalysis as a career, Lewisohn becomes really effective. Doctor Levy's infatuation with Elizabeth Knight, daughter of a Methodist minister, leads to a hasty marriage when she becomes pregnant, though Mr. Lewisohn takes pains that the doctor should declare his intentions before Elizabeth can reveal her condition. After the birth of their son, a fine Jewish boy in appearance, Doctor Levy and his wife drift apart. She scores her first success as a writer by pillaging his special knowledge of psychoanalysis for magazine articles, then discovers a knack for writing stuff that publishers snap up. Lewisohn makes it clear that Elizabeth is in no sense an artist and intimates her writing is a form of sex release—a necessary gratification since she is inhibited towards her husband because he is a Jew. Eventually, they part peacefully enough. She completes the book which will outsell all her others, and he, after identifying himself again with his people through volunteering his services to the Beth Yehuda Hospital, is induced to go on a mission in their behalf in Rumania. Elizabeth agrees to alimony only for the support of the boy.

Artistically considered, the novel is weakened at the end by the introduction of a long manuscript on a massacre in 1096 of the Jews of Worms which Arthur Levy reads prior to accepting the mission to Rumania. The remorseless drawing of Elizabeth could be more cheerfully applauded if Arthur Levy were less of a saint. Small episodes in *The Island Within* are much better handled than those which advance the plot: the futile effort of Elizabeth to get a good room for herself and her son under the name of Levy in an Adirondack hotel, and Arthur's success in reconciling his sister and her husband after their marriage has gone awry. Of course, *The Island Within* raises the issue of whether or not happiness is possible in an exogamic marriage. Lewisohn is plainly convinced that it is not. We would agree, if the persons involved were so differently endowed as to sensibility and intellect as were Arthur and Elizabeth—but this is not a fair case. They could hardly have made a go of it were they of the same race. Special pleading spoils the case. On the other hand, Mr. Lewisohn convinces us that there is less psychological strain and soul-searing for the weak in the harbors provided by racial colonies within the large cities. Further, we like his idea that the culture of any racial group is worth perpetuating.

Stephen Escott (1930), which followed *The Island Within,* is by no means so earnest a book, but it displays a wit and sardonic humor, lacking in Lewisohn's earlier novels and not recaptured in *The Last Days of Shylock* (1931), *The Golden Vase* (1931), or in *An Altar in the Fields* (1934). The two great defects of *Stephen Escott* are its lack of unity and its narrative method. The book has three parts, though organized as five; we follow Stephen through a precipitate marriage to a "pure" Wisconsin girl to his blessed release after too many years through the death of his wife from uremic poisoning; next, we find him in France trying to make up for years of sex-starvation with a rich woman who lives wholly for her sensations; when that episode comes to an end, we follow him back to America where he is a mere spectator, while his law-partner, an able and brilliant Jew, works to free the protagonist in a love-murder from a sadistic district attorney. Each unit in this novel would make a whole, or all of them might have been harmoniously joined had Lewisohn been able to make more of his theme of the broadening effect upon a rather narrow Yankee mind of a partnership with a Jewish intelligence. There is some great stuff in *Stephen Escott*—especially the portrait of Dorothy Escott, but the novel reminds one more of an over-turned basket of vegetables than a horn of plenty. Lamentable, moreover, is the prosy expository method.

Marred, too, in the telling, is *Trumpet of Jubilee* (1937), a story of a Jewish refugee woman and her son, Gina and Gabriel Weiss, who fled the Third Reich, after the murder of Kurt, Gina's husband, to seek hospice with relatives in a small town in the American mid-West. Anti-semitism in Germany raises a righteous wrath, but when Mr. Lewisohn makes Gina's American cousin Julian go mad, for not much other reason than his opposi-tion to Zionism, and when he presents the now mature Gabriel as a splendid knight in shining armor fighting for Zionism and Brit-ish imperialism (in a war which he placed in the late 'forties), we simply have to surrender our critical faculties to coast along. *Trumpet of Jubilee* is a very strange book.

With the exaggeration of sex in the 'twenties it was inevitable that someone should write a history of American letters from the Freudian point of view. Freudian studies of individual authors had filled the magazines and two interesting books, one by O'Hig-gins and one by D. H. Lawrence, before Ludwig Lewisohn com-pleted his *Expression in America* in 1932, which he had begun in 1927. Despite the fact that Mr. Lewisohn had had a seminar in American literature with Professor Trent when he was at Colum-bia years before, the greatest weakness of *Expression in America* is the author's obvious unfamiliarity with his material. It is irritating to have him call Emerson's "Hamatreya," "*Mamatreya*," and Sarah Orne Jewett's "Marsh Rosemary," "*March Rosary.*" Yet we could dismiss little slips of this sort, even though numerous, did the author show a general familiarity with historical material. Such a section, however, as the second in his volume entitled "The Polite Writers," allegedly treating "that entire group of writers, from Longfellow to Brander Matthews," demonstrates Lewisohn's unfitness for his task, since it betrays not only an abysmal ignorance of the authors cited, but also an unwillingness to examine the material. It is nothing more than a wild harangue against a number of people in no sense related (Joaquin Miller is lumped with Longfellow, Sill, and Lanier) whom Mr. Lewisohn suspects of perpetuating the "Puritan" tradition, which he believes to have been stultifying. We do not know what the "Puritan" tradition was since the author dismisses the colonial writers with a wave of his hand. If the force of Puritanism was as evil as he thinks it, it deserved a more adequate study than he has accorded it.

Although *Expression in America* is valueless as an historical study, it is at times stimulating as social and literary criticism. There is, for example, a good passage on the German pietists and poets of Pennsylvania in colonial days. The attack upon Franklin's "venery for health" is soundly indignant, but strange from the lips of the castigator of Puritanism. There is pertinency in his observation that genteel Boston of 1884 "was so disgustingly 'pure' because it was so violently sex conscious," and his citation of the blushes of Irene when Silas Lapham indicated where her bedroom would be in their new house is apt. One is delighted with his insistence that Howells, so generally neglected or derided in the 'twenties, is important: ". . . the more one reads him the surer one is that in the fine sense of Jules Lemaître, he exists —he and his works, and can never wholly fade from the cultural landscape." The high-water mark of the book is the tenth section, "The Great Critical Debate," dealing with the battle-royal between Babbitt and More on the one side and Mencken and his constituency on the other. Here Lewisohn draws upon a wide reading in comparative literature to enforce his points, and his page is rich and nourishing. More of this and less dogmatism, and *Expression in America* would have been a great book.

Puritanism, an inhibiting, anti-cultural force to O'Higgins and Lewisohn, is a cruel, fear-inducing tyrant to Vardis Fisher, the Idaho novelist, whose semi-autobiographical tetralogy *In Tragic Life* (1932), *Passions Spin the Plot* (1934), *We Are Betrayed* (1935), and *No Villain Need Be* (1936) is a monolithic pile to that "soul fear" frequently alluded to in *The American Mind in Action*. The son of Mormon pioneers, Vardis Fisher was born in Annis, Idaho, in 1895, and had the painful childhood and bitterly won education which he describes. After taking his Ph.D. at the University of Chicago, Fisher taught English in the University of Utah and at New York University, before leaving education to write. He lives with his second wife, Margaret Trusler, whom he married in 1929, on his father's ranch near Ririe, Idaho.

Prior to beginning the tetralogy, Mr. Fisher published two novels, *Toilers of the Hills* (1928) and *Dark Bridwell* (1931), which he himself thinks deserve the condemnation that his Chicago mentor, Robert Herrick, laid on them. They are the work of a sort of inferior but more intense Hamlin Garland. With *In Tragic Life* Vardis Fisher first showed signs of power. The title for this novel is taken from a passage in George Meredith's *Modern Love,* as are the titles for the three other novels in the tetralogy:

> . . . I see no sin:
> The wrong is mixed. In tragic life, God wot,
> No villain need be! Passions spin the plot:
> We are betrayed by what is false within.

The rotten core of himself Vridar Hunter (the protagonist of the series) finally decides in *No Villain Need Be* is his romantic idealism, which has made a blind prig out of him. We are not conscious of this idealism, however, until we reach the second volume, *Passions Spin the Plot,* and find Hunter horribly disillusioned with the university training for which he has struggled, and tortured because his Idaho sweetheart, Neloa Doole, cannot attain to his vision of love. In the volume *In Tragic Life,* this idealism is timidity and sensitivity which make the grim life in the crude farm shanty almost intolerable. Coarse jokes, the necessary brutality of branding and butchering, the accidents of the farm—as when his mare Alice becomes impaled on a stake in trying to leap a fence, all these leave their mark on the morbid adolescent, until the conquest of his fear becomes the imperative need of his life. Conquer it he does, but success is achieved through masochism and sadism, which are but different aspects of a mad idealism. Despite suspicion and abusive treatment, despite his infidelity, his wife Neloa, whose smaller failings rouse his jealousy, clings to him until (at the end of *We Are Betrayed*) he tells her he prefers another woman, then she kills herself. Too late, Vridar Hunter realizes it is Neloa whom he loves and needs. In the final volume of the series, he comes to a full realization that self-pity is his nemesis, and throwing that off, is able to marry Athene, a companion who has been "a kind of mother to five years of grief." Indeed, it had to be a woman's bosom or the madhouse for Vridar Hunter, since further struggle in the world was impossible without annihilation.

Within the limits of the unadorned method of telling, inherited from Herrick, Mr. Fisher's tetralogy is compelling narrative—but narrative of a peculiarly lonely soul. In fact, the most important question raised by the tetralogy is not whether its intense action is melodrama, but whether that action has any general significance. Are there ten Vridar Hunters in the world? Nay, is there any other Vridar Hunter? Is there not a sort of sterility to the series, as Margaret Cheney Dawson suggests, because Mr. Fisher's vision bends inward with such fierce intensity? Vridar Hunter is Vridar Hunter only, and not an eye through which society may be glimpsed or evaluated. Yet in presenting his hero, Mr. Fisher may have achieved a katharsis necessary if he is to do important work on the novel, which high seriousness qualifies him for.

The publication of *Forgive Us Our Virtues* (1938), a polemic for a newer, freer love, was not encouraging to the author's supporters, but his epic of the Mormon migration and settlement, *Children of God* (1939), restored confidence. It is to be doubted if anyone could have penetrated further than Mr. Fisher has into the psychologies of Joseph Smith and Brigham Young or could have handled more convincingly the emotions which the activities of these two men engendered in others. Yet more than his handling of conjugal episode and mob scene, the author is to be praised for the anecdotage and wry humor of his book. Perhaps definitely he has passed beyond Vridar Hunter.

The hectic quality of the Fisher tetralogy is typical of much literary creation originating in the 'twenties, particularly with books carrying the heavy freight of sex. Constant preoccupation with the subject, perpetual striving to imagine more fantastic sex situations, led inevitably to the personification of the sex force as a god—not Cupid but Priapus, a spiteful but whimsical dæmon. This progress may be traced through the work of Mr. Louis Bromfield, who once was looked upon as a writer with much promise. He began as a sober critic of Puritanism, so sober as to be almost dull, in the trilogy *The Green Bay Tree* (1924), *Possession* (1925), and *Early Autumn* (1926). From the inhibitions of his characters in these books, he turned to the ranker meat of the Oedipus complex in *A Good Woman* (1927). Though Emma Downes, the domineering mother of the tale, sometimes stands clear of all encumbrances, this novel leaves us with the impression that the author is all but mastered by his material. The complete collapse of his creative abilities occurs in *The Strange Case of Miss Annie Spragg* (1928), a fantastic story involving the incarnations of the god Priapus in the persons of Cyrus Spragg, a Mormon "prophet" of 1840, and his thirteenth daughter, Annie, whose pleasure it is to walk the hills with a black he-goat and who, at the outset of the story, is found dead with stigmata. The novel is dedicated to "R. Thornton Wilson" and feebly imitates the method of narration found in *The Cabala*. The different "evidences" of the supernatural phenomena are held together by the interest of Mr. Winnery, correspondent for the *Ladies' Own World* and resident of Brinoe, who is plainly as impotent as J. Alfred Prufrock. The only value of the novel is symptomatic—it reveals the ascendancy of Venus in the American heavens as nothing else does. In the year of the great bull market she was threatening to pull everything into chaos. Mr. Bromfield's novel is of a piece with the effort to glorify Mae West in marble.

The use of the Oedipus complex in *A Good Woman* suggests

that superior treatment of the theme by the very versatile play-wright, Sidney Howard, in *The Silver Cord* (1926). Mr. How-ard had done considerable writing for the theatre before attempt-ing his Freudian theme. Born in Oakland, California, on June 26, 1891, he went to Professor Baker's "47 Workshop" at Har-vard to study dramaturgy, after taking his B.A. degree at the University of California in 1915. Before America entered the World War he was driving an ambulance on the Western front; later he was a captain in the Aviation Service. In 1919, he joined the staff of *Life,* and in 1922 published his first book, *The Labor Spy,* a good piece of journalism in the field of industrial relations, which secured for him the job of special investigator for *Hearst's International Magazine* in 1923. Incidentally, his signature ap-pended to a manifesto for William Z. Foster, in 1932, indicated strong leftist convictions, which, however, never are voiced in his creative work. He was, moreover, a member of the Willard Straight Post of the American Legion and helped that post to be "a thorn in the side of the national organization." His first drama, an heroic play in a rather loose free-verse form, entitled *Swords,* was produced with the actress (who the next year be-came his wife) Clare Eames in the leading rôle of Fiamma, in 1921. Early in 1924 was produced a romantic concoction called *Bewitched,* into which both Howard and Edward Sheldon had stirred ingredients—chiefly confectioner's sugar.

Howard scored his first success with *They Knew What They Wanted,* which won the Pulitzer Prize for 1924. Singularly enough, this is a reworking of the old Francesca da Rimini theme, with a happy, rather than a tragic, solution. Tony Patucci, an Italian wine grower in the Napa Valley, California, and a man past sixty, has successfully courted by mail Amy, a waitress—but the letters which did the trick were written by Joe, his young American helper, and were accompanied by Joe's picture. Natu-rally, when Amy arrives she finds her husband repulsive to her and seeks solace with Joe. This is made easy because Tony is in-jured on his way to the station to meet her. When, months later, Amy's infidelity is revealed, Tony does not kill Joe, but permits him to drift out of their lives, for by now he has won the affection of Amy and really desires as his own the child she will bear. Joe, despite all his toughness, is revealed as a very shrewd analyst of the human heart, and his voluntary exile has a kind of mixed idealism about it that wins our regard.

Mr. Joseph Wood Krutch remarks on what an opportunity Sidney Howard had in this play "to expound a paradoxical morality, to define Love, to explain the Case for the Unmarried Mother, and, in general, *épater les bourgeois*"; and he finds a high merit in the fact that Mr. Howard has bent every energy towards characterization and refused to be *doctrinaire* at all. It is true that the chief excellence of the play is its characterization, but it also is true that the characters work out their solution because they are simple people who have learned what is essential in life and have no "honor" or pride to protect. *They Knew What They Wanted* affords a sort of commentary on American intellectuals in the 'twenties who plainly did not know what they wanted. With what, by ordinary standards, was a much more "difficult" situation than that, say, in *The Silver Cord*, Tony, Joe, and Amy avoid tragedy without particular effort, while Mrs. Phelps and her boys cannot. But we get ahead of our story: *Lucky Sam McCarver* (1925) and *Ned McCobb's Daughter* (1926), one the study of a big-hearted night club proprietor and the other a demonstration that the will can triumph over roguery, were both produced before *The Silver Cord*. Neither is of much consequence, though the characterization of Carrie McCobb, the Yankee mistress of a roadside Spa, shows that Sidney Howard did not share the prevalent literary antipathy to the New Englander.

The Silver Cord is built upon Mrs. Phelps' endeavor to control completely the destinies and affections of her sons. David, the elder, a "steady" unimaginative type, is married to Christina, a Western girl who is a research biologist; Robert, his brother, is engaged to Hester, a frail, nervous girl who has recently been ill. Mrs. Phelps, "pretty, distinguished, stoutish, soft, disarming," is wholly Victorian in her pronouncements about a wife's relations to her husband, especially to the two girls, but while disguising her purpose as their best interest, implacably presses to rule her sons without any consideration of the young women. In Christina she meets her match, for when pushed to it, Christina can reveal the springs of the older woman's selfishness with the skill with which she can perform a laboratory dissection. And this she does eventually, forcing David to decide between his mother and his wife. David, despite the fact he is no Alexander, cuts the silver cord, but his weak young brother Robert, with no such powerful ally, surrenders his bride-to-be and resigns himself to his mother for ever. Christina wins, but it is a rather hollow victory, for the audience feels that neither Robert nor David is worthy of the effort made in the play to save them. The one weakness of *The Silver Cord* is that it leaves us with so little faith in David: a compelling young woman has taken him away from his mother, but we have no sense of his ability to gain manhood afterwards. We wonder how he won Christina, how she consented, even with certain stipulations about her own career, when he pressed his suit for the third time. Aside from this qualification, we have only praise for *The Silver Cord*: the characterization of Mrs. Phelps is superb—she rises again to dignity, at least in Robert's eyes, after her defeat by Christina, intoning, "mother love suffereth long and is kind; envieth not, is not puffed up, etc." The dialogue is swift and natural, despite double-entendre and malice. Psychological subtleties are elucidated so clearly that the unread are informed in the theatre. In fact, *The Silver Cord* is a better exposition of the Oedipus complex than any discussion by Jung or Freud.

Of the later work of Sidney Howard, three plays have merit without bringing anything new to the theatre or to American thought. *The Late Christopher Bean* (1932) is an able and amusing resetting of René Fauchois' *Prenez Garde à la Peinture*. Mr. Howard's adaptation of Sinclair Lewis's *Dodsworth* (1934) is primarily interesting as revealing how much more competently the dramatist can organize than can the novelist; and finally, *Yellow Jack* (1934), an expansion of one of the best-told narratives in Paul de Kruif's *Microbe Hunters,* is deserving of praise as an effort to keep in the public eye the sacrifices of medical science for human betterment when increasing fees remind us only of the physician's commercialism. In passing, proper mention should be made of the share of Laura Hope Crews in the rôle of Mrs. Phelps and of Pauline Lord in the rôles of Amy and

Abby in making Mr. Howard's dramas successful on the stage.
The author could hardly have desired better actors in the parts,
yet the plays read so well that it is conceivable lesser people
might have carried them off.

As a lone swallow may sport against the black of an onrushing
storm, so Robinson Jeffers, above the chaotic tumult on sex in the
'twenties, used the mad currents and eddies of discussion to support his flights of unforgettable narrative verse. Close, several
times, to being overwhelmed, he has nevertheless come through
the storm, and, like O'Neill, awaits the judgment of posterity.

Robinson Jeffers, the first son of Dr. William Hamilton Jeffers, classical scholar and Presbyterian minister who was fifty-
two years old at the time, was born in Pittsburgh, on January 10,
1887. His mother, then only twenty-five, was a good musician.
The family traveled extensively, and Robinson Jeffers began his
education under the tutelage of his father. From twelve to fifteen
he attended schools in Vevey, Lausanne, Geneva, Zurich, and
Leipzig. At sixteen he enrolled in the Western University of
Pennsylvania, but when his family moved to Pasadena, he transferred to Occidental College, where he was a mile runner and
long distance swimmer. His first poem, "The Condor," was published in the *Youth's Companion,* on June 9, 1904, when Jeffers
was seventeen. After taking his B.A. degree, he spent some "desultory years" studying at the universities of Zurich, of Southern
California, and of Washington, first medicine and then forestry,
but he wasn't "deeply interested in anything but poetry." At
twenty-five, he received a modest legacy from a maternal cousin
for whom he had been named, and in 1913, he married Mrs. Una
Call Kuster. Their intention was to live in Europe, but the outbreak of the War made them abandon this plan and they settled
instead at Carmel Beach, California, where eventually they built
Tor House and Hawk Tower, Jeffers rearing the latter structure
out of stone with his own hands. Here, with their twin sons, they
have lived quietly ever since; Jeffers devotes his mornings to
verse and his afternoons to swimming or solitary walks.

Robinson Jeffers' first published volume was a collection of
love songs and lyrics, somewhat in the Shelley-Byron manner,
called *Flagons and Apples* (1912). Four years later, a much

stronger volume, *Californians,* was published, without arousing, however, much interest. A similar neglect apparently awaited *Tamar and Other Poems,* which was issued in 1924 by an obscure New York printer, Peter G. Boyle; but James Rorty, who had come across Jeffers' verse when editing with George Sterling an anthology of California poetry, was determined that this should not happen. He himself wrote an enthusiastic review of *Tamar* for the *New York Herald Tribune Books* of March 1, 1925, and he induced other reviewers to pay a proper respect to the volume. As one result of this, Boni & Liveright issued in 1925 *Roan Stallion, Tamar, and Other Poems,* the first volume of Jeffers' poetry to reach the general public.

It is well to understand the purposes motivating the poet before examining Jeffers' work, for otherwise one might reach the too hasty conclusion that Mr. Jeffers is either hopelessly morbid or is cheaply bent on merely shocking middle-class sensibilities. One could conceive Jeffers, of course, as primarily *a poet,* "beyond good and evil" insofar as his subject matter is concerned—using human situations for their dramatic and poetic possibilities solely—if Jeffers himself were willing to take refuge in that aesthetic fortress. But Jeffers is the heir of Shelley, no "bright ineffectual angel," but a modern Platonist, bent on informing man of the continued worth of absolute values. "I have," wrote Shelley in his Preface to *Prometheus Unbound,* "a passion for reforming the world. . . . But it is a mistake to suppose that I dedicate my poetical compositions solely to the direct enforcement of reform. . . . Didactic poetry is my abhorrence. . . . *My purpose has . . . been simply to familiarize the highly refined imagination of the more select classes of poetical readers with beautiful idealisms of moral excellence; aware that until the mind can love, and admire, and trust, and endure, reasoned principles of moral conduct are seeds cast upon the highway of life which the unconscious passenger tramples into dust, although they would bear the harvest of his happiness. . . ."*

If one turns to Jeffers' "Ode on Human Destinies," the best piece in *Californians,* one perceives how much this Shelleyan pronouncement of purpose informs the work of the Western poet. Indeed, the "Ode on Human Destinies" sounds back, like a sunset cliff, echoes of the immortal music of the "Hymn to Intellectual Beauty," the "Ode to the West Wind," and "Prometheus Unbound." Jeffers' choice of his "beautiful peninsula" for setting, his Promontory of Stones, reminds us what sublimity the writings of Shelley partake from "earth, ocean, air, beloved brotherhood!" The wildest aspects of nature contrasted with her most intransitory stones—the West Wind, fierce spirit moving everywhere, Mont Blanc piercing the infinite sky, broken rainbows that "lean out of clouds and vanish"—these are ornaments to verse dear to both poets. Yet to presume they are mere ornaments is to miss the whole relation of man, the immutable, to his environment, to "the inveterate stability of things" which both poets ask us to adore. For Shelley, writes Professor Herford, Prometheus "stood for man creating and enduring, endowing the gods themselves with wisdom and strength, and suffering their vindictive rage. But, for Shelley, no symbol of humanity could suffice which excluded the perfected man of the future he confidently foresaw." Consequently, his Prometheus, who symbolizes humanity, survives the overthrow of Jupiter. The regeneration of man is completed when the love that is "blindly wove through all the web of being" melts into the love-pervading nature, and makes "one harmonious soul of many a soul." So, when the Earth, which is no more than "a drop of dew that dies," threatens to fall into the abyss, it is saved by the love and the hope of man.

> . . . to hope till Hope creates
> From its own wreck the thing it contemplates;
> Neither to change, nor falter, nor repent;
> This, like thy glory, Titan, is to be
> Good, great and joyous, beautiful and free;
> This is alone Life, Joy, Empire, and Victory.

Just as, for Shelley, Prometheus is more noble than the Jupiter, who is overthrown, so for Robinson Jeffers the fate of man has a majesty that needs "nor God nor goal." Indeed though Death will reap at last all the heritage of man, Death cannot alter the character of man.

> Man will change not, though all Gods
> Utterly change. . . .

Man is the "work and will," the "child and slave, of constant Fate"—a Fate which has fixed his need for love, love for friend, for mate, and for forms of natural beauty. This Beauty is a "Holy Spirit" from eternity, as in Shelley's hymn, the purest loveliness which Plato tells us is one with Goodness and Truth. It is this ideal, which Jeffers, being man and poet, must serve:

> . . . I, driven ahead on undiscovered ways
> Yet predetermined, do not fail to see,
> Over the fog and dust of dream and deed,
> The holy spirit, Beauty, beckoning me.

To familiarize the imagination of the more select classes of poetical readers with the ideals of Truth, Beauty, and Goodness is no such simple task, as Jeffers conceives it, in the twentieth century as it was at the beginning of the nineteenth. For man, even the man who formerly had the "highly refined imagination" of which Shelley speaks, has become horribly self-centered, or "introverted." "There is no health for the individual whose attention is taken up with his own mind and processes; equally there is no health for the society that is always introverted on its own members." Consequently, "humanity is the mold to break away from" and "humanity is but the start of the race." Unless we can break away from sentimentalizing ourselves and our destiny, we shall never perceive the perfected man, the Prometheus Unbound, envisioned by Shelley and Jeffers. Indeed, the rise of science has doubled the difficulty for man between Shelley's time and ours, for now "he's bred knives on nature [and] turns them also inward"—medicine and psychoanalysis which have increased his "self-love and inward conflicts." The task of the poet is to help humanity break its mold, to gain a sense again of immortality, to find absolute values. And the way is obviously to fix attention on what is *in*human, both in nature and in man. Jeffers himself has found peace in this way, as he tells us in his latest volume, *Such Counsels You Gave to Me* (1937):

> I wish you could find the secure value,
> The all-heal I found . . .
> The splendor of inhuman things. . . .

Though Shelley's audience comprehended no such introverted thing as the modern man, the imagination of Shelley bodied forth a monster surpassing him. This is Count Francesco Cenci, who in his youth "thought of nothing else but pleasure . . . and fed on honied sweets" till he grew tired, then still insatiate, turned to the practice of cruelty for his delight until invention palled. When we encounter him first in *The Cenci*, he is contemplating—

> a deed to act
> Whose horror might make sharp an appetite
> Duller than mine.

Yet despite the fact that he has "no remorse and little fear" he doubts if *manhood* still remains "to act the thing I thought." Act it he does, adding to his mountain of crimes the culminating horror of incest with his daughter Beatrice. The effect of this is to destroy the last touch of humanity in him:

> I do not feel as if I were a man,
> But like a fiend appointed to chastise
> The offenses of some unremembered world.

So Beatrice, plotting with her mother, destroys the fiend and not her father, "dislodging a spirit of deep hell out of a human form." From this unnatural crime, this parricide for which she is arrested, tried, and condemned, she rises austere and beautiful, the only genuine tragic figure in nineteenth century British drama. Her parting words to her brother reveal her spirit triumphant over fear and pain:

> Be constant to the love
> Thou bearest us; and to the faith that I,
> Tho' wrapt in a strange cloud of crime and shame,
> Lived ever holy and unstained. . . .
> . . . And never think a thought unkind
> Of those, who perhaps love thee in their graves.
> So mayest thou die as I do; fear and pain
> Being subdued. Farewell!

Contemplation of *The Cenci,* the power of katharsis he may have felt in that great tragedy, and the realization that a mon-

strous crime broke the common mold of humanity for both
Beatrice and Count Francesco Cenci, all had something to do
with Robinson Jeffers' choice of themes for his narrative poems.
Of course, his thinking was reinforced by his knowledge of Greek
drama, which is possibly as thorough as was Shelley's. Aeschylus,
Sophocles, and Euripides all use extreme forms of violence to the
purpose of revealing the potentialities of the human spirit—a
purpose which is always Jeffers', no matter how revolting the
incident.

Tamar, Jeffers' first essay to startle the more poetical imaginations from self-love, is a narrative poem of more than two thousand, long, sonorous, unmeasured lines. These lines toll off, however, one of the most torturous narratives in English, a story
rivalling the legend of the house of Atreus for brutality, a tale in
which a living girl—a fiend rather—pursues the ghosts of her
family and will not let them rest nor their crimes be forgotten.
The "idyll" opens with a relatively trivial incident: young Lee
Cauldwell, coming back drunk from whoring in Monterey, spurs
his pony over a sea cliff, killing the little beast and breaking the
bones of the greater one. Nursed by his sister, Tamar, Lee decides to give up his dissolute life and live quietly at home, despite
the warning of his father, "better dance your pony down the
cliffs again than close young life into a little box"—a warning
reminding us of Jeffers' theory of the disease of introversion.
Tamar, motherless, with no chaperon save an aunt (who is
brooding the past) and an idiot sister, is thrown wholly into the
company of her brother, by his decision, and the pangs of sex
stirring in her, begins incestuous relations with him. When, however, she becomes pregnant, she thinks of her lover, Will Andrews, whom Lee had driven off the place in his first paroxysm of
virtue. If she can induce him to have relations with her, the world
may make him the father of her child. Although Andrews is inhibited by a sort of adolescent idealism, Tamar seduces him only
to discover that he is revolting to her after her other lover; none
the less she arranges for him to come regularly on signal to her
chamber. Meanwhile she learns through the prophetic talk of her
spiritualistic aunt and the jibberings of her sister of a trap baited
to catch her before the granite foundations of the world were

laid: she by her act has merely perpetuated the incestuous history
of her family. Her mother was betrayed by her own sister, Helen,
who had relations with Tamar's father before her death. Mad
with a desire to produce an abortion, Tamar goes down to the
shore with her Aunt Stella and foolish Jinny, to where the Indian
women used to dance the dance of pregnancy. When her aunt falls
into a trance, Tamar is able to converse with the dead Helen,
toward whom she conceives a dreadful hatred for the treachery
to her mother. Though the ghost of Helen tells her that "Sin
never buys anything," she swears to be revenged upon the ghost.
A delirious dance she performs, the fancied giving herself to the
ghosts of the braves, and the horror she has undergone produce
a miscarriage. Old Cauldwell curses his son who vows never to
look upon his face again and enlists to go to the war in France.
But Tamar, pursuing a diabolical scheme of vengeance, wrests
her father from the ghost of Helen, and waking his youth with
the sight of her body, makes him her third fleshly lover. Then
her poisoned brain conceives the destruction of her three lovers,
adoring her, as the final triumph of her mad career. Lee is told
that he was not her first lover nor the father of their child, and
Andrews is summoned by Tamar's window light to an ambuscade; when he appears and Lee quails from the new crime, Tamar
manages to imply that Lee and her father have produced an
abortion of Andrews' child while beating her for being pregnant.
Hence a bloody quarrel ensues, during which the three men and
the girl, entangled with each other, are wrapped in flame, like
Laocoön, when silly Jinny fires the house.

Of course, *Tamar* cannot be judged by ordinary standards of
criticism. We may insist that the characterization of the girl is
incredible, but to no point, however, since Jeffers has deliberately
sought to embody more than a human wickedness in Tamar; she
is transcendent; she is a fiend. *Tamar* must be judged for what
the author intended it, a violent antidote for introversion. That
the poem has a compelling horror all its readers will agree, but
whether this horror produces katharsis or merely pain is the
moot question. We have no hesitation in saying that *Tamar* fails
as a dramatic specific. The protagonist of the piece never wins
through to tragic composure such as Beatrice attains to at the

end of *The Cenci*. Jeffers thinks she does, and he has her proclaim:

> "If I have done wrong it has turned good to me, I
>   could almost be sorry that I have to die now
> Out of such freedom. . . ."

But he is not convincing. Even after this alleged serenity, she has to invent lies to bring the action to its "fated" conclusion. This is not only bad drama, but also poor evidence of the "freedom" of the heroine. Further, all her schemes succeed, and this mitigates all her pain, even her final shift of fire. No absolute truth is discovered in the poem: the beauty revealed is fragmentary and does not infuse the whole, as the presence of Beatrice elevates *The Cenci*. Nevertheless *Tamar* is a failure which prepares us for the later successes of Robinson Jeffers, since only a poet of magic powers could tease beauty of the kind that marks the scattered passages into being. Unforgettable bare beauty of Tamar in the cool secluded pool, baroque beauty of wounds and whip welts, oriental beauty of fire. And the final malignant beauty which breeds the horrific and the loathsome, as "the intolerably masculine sun" breeds centipedes and worms in the Cauldwell house ("their phalloid bodies cracking underfoot with a bad odor").

Artistically *Roan Stallion* is as complete and satisfying as *Tamar* is not. Even if this tale were told in prose, it would be a gem surpassing in brilliance Wilbur Daniel Steele's "Blue Murder," which it brings to mind, for all the elements of good narrative are in it—plausible situation, proper motivation, adequate characterization, and an inevitable solution. Verse adds a plus to this, like a rich, well-chosen dessert at a banquet, but not an overplus of emotion. It is said that Jeffers, in composing the narrative, was influenced partly by the Leda myth and partly by a statue in Turin of a horse whose lover was a woman. However, such Greco-Italian origins are completely obliterated in the telling, for *Roan Stallion* belongs more to California than anything else that Jeffers has written. The principal actor is a woman, nobly formed, though begotten out of a Spanish-Indian half-breed by a Scotch sailor twenty-one years before the first line of her story is sounded. Named California by her father, she is married to an odious, smirking, and wasted Dutchman, called Johnny, to whom she has borne a pale and meagre child. Her husband, with rioting in Monterey, has forgotten the child Christine and the two days to Christmas, though he has come home leading a great stallion which he has won gambling. California plans to go to town the next morning to purchase presents for the child, but Johnny, waking, delays her to satisfy his desire (which she yields to with pretended eagerness though she long had felt no need), with a result that, on her return the next evening, she finds the ford so swollen with the day's rain as to be all but impassable. In answer to her prayer, the Christ child appears in great white light, illuminating the ford, so that she and the mare may cross by swimming.

In April a man brings a mare to breed to the stallion, and California, who has convinced herself that she hates the stallion for its uselessness, suddenly finds herself trembling with desire. After Johnny goes off with the man (with a coarse promise for his return) and she has put Christine to bed, California slips out to the corral, and in the grip of insatiable longing, rides the great beast up into the hills where she lies on the turf till her fever has cooled. When Johnny returns the following night the thought of him is revolting to her and she runs away to hide. Warmed by his wine he sets the dog after her and follows like a faun after a wood nymph. California slips into the corral, and the stallion turns on dog and man. Christine at the house has wakened and brings a rifle to her mother. California's first shot brings down the dog; she does not fire again until hooves of the horse have pounded the life out of Johnny and then "some obscure human fidelity" prompts her to pump three shells into the stallion—

> And the beautiful strength settled to earth: she turned
>   then on her little daughter the mask of a woman
> Who has killed God. . . .

Roan Stallion is magnificent as story, a round whole in construction, with every detail patiently attended to, so that even the miracle of the ford (unlike most modern clap-trap of this type) is soberly satisfying. Here, too, is beauty, nay splendor, of storm and moonlit countryside. Yet is the piece tragedy? Or is it a new

and (because of its beauty) rather lasting sensation? Let us say
emphatically that it does all it aimed to do. We feel that the sex
power of the stallion is something wholesome and good beside
the dirty lust of Johnny; indeed, not since Swift have we had
brought home to us quite so forcefully that horses may be better
than men. Yet does Jeffers aim quite high enough in *Roan Stallion?* Is there not something in us that keeps us from identifying
the horse with anything god-like, an "obscure human fidelity" if
you will, but enough of a natural barrier so that the poem does
not become tragic? We must pity the stallion to derive any absolute value from the poem, and this is psychologically impossible.
The attitude demanded is the romantic sentimentalism of the sex-
hungry lone cowboy toward his pony, which sobs through his
ballads. The unconscious effort to dignify it is abortive. Weakness
makes the *Roan Stallion* native and "Western" more than anything else.

Yet to dare greatly is American, too, and in *The Tower Beyond Tragedy* Jeffers has reworked the story of the House of
Atreus, as told by Aeschylus, thus defying comparison between
himself and the Greek. This is a bolder thing than O'Neill attempted in *Mourning Becomes Electra,* because the comparison
is in terms of poetry, where the Greek is most secure. Jeffers'
variations in the ancient story are to enforce motivation, which,
we have indicated, is the weakness of the Grecian tragedy. Unfortunately, while elaborating the character of the queen, Jeffers adopts the sacrifice of Iphigenia as the principal alleged motive of the murder of Agamemnon by Clytemnestra. This sets at
naught the masculine characteristics with which he endows the
queen and confuses her relationship to her paramour, Aegisthus.
His conception of the queen holding at bay the vengeful soldiers
until Aegisthus can come to her relief by the device of slowly exposing her person to them is melodramatic and quite beneath
Clytemnestra's defiance in the *Agamemnon* of Aeschylus:

> Threaten, then,
> Even as ye list; but so as, being assured,
> That force must win the day. If so ye win,
> I yield. . . .

It is indicative of the greater sex fascination of our times. The forcing of Cassandra by the ghost of Agamemnon and the speaking of that ghost through her teeth is ingenious but sensational, while the disappearance of Electra and Orestes is less plausibly managed than the departure of Orestes in *Agamemnon* and the meeting between him and his sister in *The Choephoroe*. Jeffers clarifies the queen's intentions towards her son and daughter, but he does not strengthen thereby her character. He has contributed a definite improvement to the tragedy by having Electra urge on the son's arm against his mother. One of the weakest points in Aeschylus is the appeal of Orestes to his friend Pylades as to whether or not he shall slay his mother. The calm citation by Pylades of Apollo's stern command indicates a faith in the gods which Clytemnestra's grief over the sacrifice of Iphigenia belies. The root of the difficulty was probably scepticism, as the later plays of Euripides indicate, but none the less the lack of firmness injures the dramas. On the whole, however, Jeffers' version of the story up to the time of Clytemnestra's death is weaker than the handling of Aeschylus. This is understandable, for Jeffers' sole interest in the early tragedy is the effect of matricide upon Orestes. The slaying of one's mother is so unnatural an act that it places one out of the human order of things and Orestes becomes the Prometheus of Jeffers. When Electra recognizes this and offers him her body as an opiate so that he may return and govern as Agamemnon, he rebukes her, telling her that she has too much of her mother in her. Orestes has no desire either to mend the pattern he has broken or to fit himself back into it. "I will not waste inward upon humanity," he declares. Instead he falls in love *outward*—with the contemplation of something beyond the sidereal universe.

> ... Orestes walked in the clear dawn; men
> say that a serpent
> Killed him in high Arcadia. But young or old, few
> years or many, signified less than nothing
> To him who had climbed the tower beyond time, consciously, and cast
> humanity, entered the earlier fountain.

If Electra is understood to represent the present day absorption of society in power and in sex (which it is by no means clear that she does), then the withdrawal of Orestes is more explicable. There is in the calm survey of man's fate and of eternity—so it seems to Jeffers—the best remedy for these twin evils. Orestes denies society in order to teach its superior members the way to health, to all that is noble or sublime. In society Jeffers is not interested, for as Cassandra prophesies, creeping frost from the two poles will put an end to all institutions, and man only will survive the death of his world. It is good to be reminded of this fate, and individuals with it in sight bring society the example of an austerity and selflessness which is purgative; yet death is nearer each man than the eternal snows to society, wherefore a concern about the fate of man seems less idealistic, less selfless, more introverted than a passionate interest in the improvement of society. Perhaps both have their place, and Jeffers' being the rarer passion in our time, the more worthy statement. In passing, it must be remarked that the statement could be improved: Orestes does not dominate the whole action as does the protagonist of *Prometheus Unbound*. For our purpose it is unnecessary that the whole story of Agamemnon and his return and murder should be played out. This is poor art and poor art never enforces a philosophy. This does not deny, however, some beautiful, hammered lines in the early portion of the poem, notably in the passage where the ghost of Agamemnon speaking from Cassandra's lips searches for a word to shrivel his murderess.

In *The Women at Point Sur* (1927) Jeffers himself lost all sense of austerity. He became more interested in being inhuman than he did in finding any values beyond the immediate interests of society. Conspicuously among his poems *The Women at Point Sur* is the shilling shocker. Its long, involved story of how the Reverend Doctor Barclay denounced his congregation, resigned his pastorate, deserted his wife, and went forth to roam over dry gullies to find ultimate reality—in forcing his daughter after trying the women of Point Sur—need not be recounted in detail here. As art, only the Prelude and first canto of the poem have merit. A part of the difficulty lies in an ill-digested reading of Nietzsche whom Jeffers allows in this poem to dictate to his true masters, Shelley and Aeschylus. Nietzsche is a great idol-smasher and altar-desecrator, yet the darkness he creates hardly aids our poor eyes to see the never-too-sharp outlines of truth. Then, undeniably, Jeffers was persuaded into perpetrating this piece by the monstrous, orgiastic character the "introversion" of society took on in those hectic years just before the great débâcle of 1929. *The Women at Point Sur* should be looked upon as a sort of bomb exploded in a bordello: it was not Jeffers' fault that the tumult was already so great that a bomb merely enforced the new tempo, like the thunderous crash of a jazz orchestra announcing a new rhythm. If he thought that any word picture of a father raping his daughter would startle America in 1929, it is plain that he was unacquainted with the daily fare of the mob in the tabloids. It is not even certain that he provided Americans with a new sensation. In a mad world, his was merely a milder madness. We frankly doubt, moreover, whether the Barclay of the fine denunciation of the first canto could ever quite have become the monster of the later passages of the poem. Jeffers might well have taken counsel of his teacher Shelley, "No man has a right to do an evil thing that good may come," and "Expediency is inadmissible in morals." Jeffers is less than Shelley for not having suffered sufficiently before seeking his eyrie on the Pacific Coast. Situations in *The Women at Point Sur* show that he has not felt pain.

Cawdor (1928) is likewise touched by the windy madness of Nietzsche and the diabolism of the late 'twenties, but it is merely touched. Whatever the poem has of strength and majesty is drawn from that example of Greek tragedy which Aristotle proclaimed the masterpiece of the theatre, the *Oedipus Tyrannus* of Sophocles. Amplified by countless tellings of trivial episodes, such as occur when persons of strong will and emotion live close together, *Cawdor* is nevertheless relatively simple and fiercely direct in plot. When Fera Martial, the nineteen-year-old bride of Cawdor, who is fifty, fails by every device known to her to arouse Hood, Cawdor's son, to commit adultery with her, she revenges herself horribly, after several ineffectual trials, by persuading the father that Hood has taken her against her will. After Cawdor murders his son by throwing him off a cliff, Fera begins the long

and subtle task of persuading Cawdor that Hood was innocent.
When again she succeeds, Cawdor gouges out his own eyes with
a piece of flint. The poem closes magnificently with Cawdor complaining afterward—

> It was mere indulgence.
> The punishments are a pitiful self-indulgence.
> I'd not the strength to do nothing. . . .

Cawdor awes us: blind Oedipus achieves to no more, whatever
the ages may have thought of him. Cawdor is not less noble,
surely, for not being a king. The imperial quality of will in Cawdor, his power to transcend pain, remind us of the dauntless spirit
and supreme courage of those pioneers whose westering feet beat
out the paths of thought and commerce across our nation. Is it a
mad dream to fancy that one of these, or one of his sons, might
rise to all the dignity of a king of a small Grecian city? No, a
thousand times no. Cawdor convinces, not alone because he breaks
the web of humanity, but because we recognize in him the matchless quality of will which spun the web of humanity across the
continent. Even in the end, Cawdor is no Titan, but a human, but
such a human as our country knows no more, sample of a kingly
race, now dead. That he is used by Fera does not unking him:
her wicked, ingenious mind is match enough for him and nobility
is easily victimized; further, we are content, now that Nature is
no longer his opponent, for his qualities to be brought out by
action on a smaller scale—they ring as true as ever. *Cawdor* succeeds where much of Jeffers fails, because we are apprised
(whether the author wills it or not) of the grand resources of
human character. We are led to feel, despite the poet, that the
race may yet redeem itself before the end of time.

On the other hand, *Dear Judas* (1929) is one of those
descents into sentimentality and bathos which genius apparently
requires to spring up again. The naughty boy who suggested in
Cawdor that post-mortal consciousness is merely the cell-chemis-
try of disintegration now guesses that Judas sold Jesus, not for
thirty pieces of silver, but because he wished to prove the divinity
of God and was taken in by a fakir. This is a thoroughly legitimate theme, provided that the author can endow Judas with as

great idealism as the Scriptures endow Christ, but Jeffers fails to do this. Judas appears merely as a fool, taken in by a quack, and we cannot but prefer the Jew who sold his master as a person of more character. Had Jeffers dealt with *him* the poem might have more significance than a mud-ball shied at conventional beliefs. The realization of the Messiah, not as God, but as a man swollen with conceit of himself and his powers, grown hard towards suffering, is not without merit. Singularly enough, the volume containing *Dear Judas* also holds one of the most beautiful of Jeffers' poems, *The Loving Shepherdess*. That Jeffers meant this poem should also be a "shocker" is indicated by the jacket-blurb which the publishers take from a letter of his to the effect that the shepherdess "has committed self sacrifice," is "a saint . . . going up to a natural martyrdom." Not only does the blurb flaunt the Christlike selflessness of the shepherdess, but the poem itself insinuates a comparison between the virtues of Jesus and those of the simple girl Clare Walker, who, after being exonerated of her father's murder, wanders with her dwindling herd of sheep northward, solacing every hungry man with her body although she knows that pregnancy, because of a physical defect, will bring her death. Looked at in this light the poem is merely a ribald comment on chastity. The weakness of it as satire, however, is that Clare, though of fixed purpose, is not really wilful. She is to us a sweet character, blameless because not conscious of her unmorality, banefully plotted against by outward and inward circumstance. She is the only woman of Jeffers' creation to elicit a tender sympathy. The anxiety over the loss of her sheep, her resigned telling them off, move us only less than her terrible death in travail, alone and unattended, in a willow thicket on the banks of the San Joaquin. It is good to see character drawing triumph over ill-conceived purpose, as it does in this poem, for Jeffers' resolute insistence on fidelity to character is what really defeats and ennobles his work here.

The sixteen poems which make up *Descent to the Dead* (1931), a product of a trip Jeffers made to the native Ireland of his immigrant grandfather, have no especial interest for the student of Jeffers, save as they suggest a vague awareness of the supernatural work of Yeats, but *Thurso's Landing* (1933) must be reckoned one of Jeffers' masterpieces. This poem owes its greatness to precisely the same qualities which elevate *Cawdor*— the resources of character which violent action reveals the descendants of pioneer stock to possess, here splendidly studied, and the assurance that an indomitable will is one of the chief glories of man. It is the will of Reave Thurso which finally awes and wins the pity of his wife, the Helen of destructive beauty, who hates him for bringing her back after an elopement with a Western Paris, one Rick Armstrong, a road builder and "dynamite man." Home, after a year with her lover, Helen has to endure the hatred of Thurso's old mother and the exasperation of the inhibited lust of Reave's brother Mark, who is going slowly mad from his visions of the restless ghost of their father. To lay this ghost, Reave takes himself to the head of the farm quarry to cut down a great cable which hangs over them all, tethering their lives to the father's failure and suicide. When the cable snaps, Reave himself is caught by it and cruelly crippled so that, living, he is helpless but in constant pain. Now all the hatred of Helen melts to love before his fierce will to live and to endure.

Of humanity Jeffers writes in *Thurso's Landing*:

> It is rather ignoble in its quiet times, mean in its pleasures,
> Slavish in the mass; but at stricken moments it
> > Can shine terribly against the dark
> > magnificence of things.

Back-broken, in a sweating agony most of his interminable conscious moments, stricken if ever a man was stricken, Reave Thurso shines like a god in the gloom of his gathering fate. When Mark fails to persuade Helen to let him lie with her and hangs himself, Reave compels his mother, wife, and a farmer-helper to carry him to the rock head above the house, so that he may "taste air." There, in a quarry shed, Helen cuts his throat in a strange mixture of passion and compassion, then swallows contraceptive pills to accomplish her own death. Dying, she is forgiven by Reave's old mother, who at last understands the depth of Helen's love for her son and her utter fitness for a hero's mate, even in destruction. In *Thurso's Landing* no one character wholly triumphs at the cost of the others, but dispassionately the author deals a kind of nobility to each in turn after his deserts, to Reave and Helen at length equally, to the old mother, and finally, but not negligently, to the mad brother. Thus we see, for the only time in Jeffers, how a great will may work on others, infecting them with purpose, compassion, and dignity. Well might Jeffers declare, of *Thurso's Landing,* "It . . . seems to me to be the best thing I have yet written . . .; the persons seem to me to be a little more conscious of the moral implications of what they do. . . ." The 'twenties were over; it was no longer necessary to shock in order to produce an impression; and Jeffers, tasting the clean fresh air of better moral times, could write with more of human sympathy, like Sophocles, rather than madly and badly, like Nietzsche, or remotely and austerely, like Aeschylus. Reave Thurso's will to suffer glorifies life, however far it may impel his spirit over the Lethean ooze. All of our heroisms and sacrifices are made of the same stuff as this, and it is proper to celebrate it in verse as potentially a moral force, the highest attribute of man.

Jeffers followed *Thurso's Landing* with a study of conscience —almost the last thing one would expect from him—in *Give Your Heart to the Hawks* (1933). Catching his brother Michael making love to his wife Fayne during a drunken picnic, Lance kills him, then instantly regrets it and would confess but for Fayne. Though the crime is taken as an accident, Lance cannot reenter the human world, and violence becomes a necessity with him. Eventually he takes his own life, ending a debate between Fayne and himself which apparently stems from the plagued mind of Raskolnikow in *Crime and Punishment.* Though the poem has its moments, it never quite convinces: Jeffers can evoke the furies but not remorse. The suffering of Lance is curiously vicarious, from the pain he causes rather than in the pain he actually feels, and even his suicide is a sort of cheat. Lance gets beyond good, in the Nietzschean phrase, but not beyond evil. Jeffers' sentimental interest in him, Jeffers' desire to give his life moral significance, does not ennoble him; Lance is a mean character, his killing of his brother is impulsive and his later violence merely disgusting.

The volume containing the story of Lance and Fayne also

contains a poem on Helen of Troy, entitled "At the Fall of an Age," which is the first indication of a tendency in Jeffers to turn to decadence. In *The Tower Beyond Tragedy* Jeffers had allowed the ghost of Agamemnon to enter the living body of Cassandra, in lust but not for lust, to speak to his soldiers to urge revenge for his murder. In this new piece, however, imperishable Helen is ravished by the ghost of Achilles, in a fashion which suggests the wakening of a dormant necrophilism in the poet, a delight in the sensational contact of the warm and fair with the cold and dead. Surrounded by dead soldiers, Helen seeks Polyxo, her old friend, who, jealous of all beauty, hangs her. Yet Helen, hanged, is more beautiful than ever. If the poem means what it seems to mean, beauty is all that survives ancient times, our sole heritage from Greece. But this beauty is neither Shelleyan nor Platonic: it is the beauty of dead and sterile things, it is the beauty of *The Waste Land.*

"At the Fall of an Age" must, of course, be evaluated in relation to "At the Birth of an Age," the introductory poem in the volume *Solstice* (1935). This piece, with its clarifying preface, reveals Jeffers' conviction that Christianity is the chief evil of modern civilization, an Oriental religion superimposed on hostile Western blood. Though dying as a faith, Christianity flourishes still as an ethic, "manifesting itself as generalized philanthropy, liberalism, socialism, communism, and so forth." The age which Christianity created, beginning at the end of Greco-Roman times, has about reached its peak, in Jeffers' estimation, and shortly will begin its decline. He can sum up this Christian age, therefore, as "the most bewildered and self-contradictory, the least integrated, in some phases the most ignoble, that has ever existed." While Jeffers' prophecy of the inevitable decline of this our age reveals his decadence, his facile summary of nearly two thousand years of history exposes merely his incompetence as a thinker. The great weakness in his speculation lies in his acceptance of the exalted acts of Greek tragedy as typical of Greek life (which it is plain they were not, from no more evidence than the choruses offer), wherefore he has postulated an assurance, an integration, and a prevalent nobility in ancient times, that he cannot see in his own day, where he does not consult literary masterpieces at all, but rather the evidence of life around him. How much assurance the Greeks had is seen in the contradictory attitudes towards the gods found in Aeschylus, as we have pointed out, and in the bewilderment and terror of the characters of Euripides. The nobility of the Greeks is admirably suggested in *The Agamemnon* where they are faced down by a woman. Just what Jeffers means by "integrated" is not clear, but if he means the Greeks shared a common morbidity, he is sound enough. Homosexuality, the common practice of abortion, the fascination of abnormal sex themes in poetry, the gross representation of sex in comedy point to as completely an "introverted" life as ever a people shared in this world's history. Mr. Jeffers hardly does well to cry up the Greeks and cry down the moderns as he does in "At the Fall of an Age" and in "At the Birth of an Age." If his own verse reveals anything, it is the probability that modern American life has some of the unhappy constituents which gave ancient Greek literature its character.

For narrative substance, "At the Birth of an Age" has the vengeance of Gudrun, wife of Attila, upon Gunnar and Hoegni, his brothers, for the slaying of her former husband Sigurd—an episode found, as everyone knows, at the end of the *Nibelungenlied*. The "self-contradiction and self-frustration" of Gudrun stem from the new Christianity, which so affects Gudrun's serving-woman, Chrysothenius, that she is martyred for her faith, being buried alive in Gudrun's grave by Attila's order. The folly of this is meant to be shown when Gudrun's spirit meets the ghost of Christ, who admits he is "perfectly fooled in the end." We are reminded of the imperishable Helen when Jeffers sniggers at the close, "His beauty redeems his acts. . . ." Gudrun, cleansed of folly, is eager to live once more, "willing to eat of whole serpent again." Despite the resemblance (which Babette Deutsch points out) to Yeats' lyric "Dialogue Between Self and Soul," the piece is one of Jeffers' poorest—a confused, bedlamite thing, with a labored contrast between the resignation of Jesus and the acceptance of Prometheus. In order that we may miss none of the implications of the poem, Attila the Hun listens to the servile plea of the Christian Bishop Lupus of Troyes to spare his town, while stopping at a ruined Roman villa on the walls of which is painted the torture of Prometheus. Of course, the Greek god and the fooled spirit, Jesus, have to contend for Gudrun after her death. "At the Birth of an Age" is followed by a sadistic piece, weakly imitated from the Medea story, in which Madrone Bothwell cuts her children's throats rather than surrender them to her divorced husband as the law allows. Jeffers is unable to endow Madrone with anything more than utter savagery: she appears mad rather than wilful, and the acts of madness are not tragic. The poem gives its title to the volume *Solstice,* but from it we may conclude Jeffers' sun has crossed its southern line and is about to set.

Such Counsels You Gave Me (1937) borrows for its title-poem stuff out of *Oedipus Tyrannus,* but its medical student protagonist is no Greek king, and after a period of dictation from his mother, finally surrenders to the law to put a period to his pain and to the reader's. The volume, like the last several of Jeffers' books, contains many short pieces, chiefly argumentative and prophetic. He had aroused resentment among the thoughtful by prophesying in "Ave Caesar" (in *Solstice*) some Sicilian tyrant for Americans until a real Caesar could arrive—from which the reviewers guessed accurately enough his potential, incipient Fascism. In this book he is equally oracular, predicting the same bitterness—

> I see far fires and dim degradation
> Under the war-planes and neither Christ nor Lenin
> will save you . . .

But he does hold out again the cup of hemlock which he offered at first and from which his contemporaries may drink such con-solation as—

> The old wound opens its clotted mouth to
> ask for new wounds. Men will fight
> through; men have tough hearts. . . .

Through to what? Why, to ultimate dignity and austerity to fit them to be matched against the universe.

While one turns from a protracted immersion in Jeffers' poetry

with relief and while it is clear that the bulk of it lacks the elevation of tragedy, it must be granted that twice his narratives discover the ultimate reserves of human character—in such Americans as Cawdor and Reave Thurso—and bring katharsis, and
that once he stirs us to deep pity, with *The Loving Shepherdess.*
His long line is never far from prose, as William Benét has
pointed out, yet some of the verses form themselves on the
tongue without our conscious effort in tranquillity and we know
the flavor of real poetry. We may deplore his lack of sympathy
with our problems—his first idol Shelley found as much in humanity as ever he in man—yet at his best Jeffers enriches our
thought by demonstrating the glory and beauty of an imperious
will, our sword and shield, possibly, in other circumstances than
he has imagined. At his worst, Jeffers is still symptomatic of the
moral confusion of his time, its mirror and mouthpiece. If the
future chooses to judge us by Jeffers' most abortive work, the
future will not go far wrong. There are other aspects, chronicled
by other men, but who is so indicative of our sickness as he?

Americans generally came to the conclusion that they had become foolishly introverted (though not quite in Jeffers' sense)
after the depression failed to yield to psychoanalysis. The great
panacea for every ill during the 'twenties, it was the first patent
medicine thrown out of our closet in the 'thirties, and the hand
that removed it, threw Behaviorism after it, and threatened to
follow that with everything named Psychology. Mr. Sidney
Howard's play *Half Gods,* opening in the winter of 1929, was
apparently a little premature, for Americans were not quite ready
to accept wife-beating as a substitute for psychoanalysis. The
publication of the "symposium to end symposiums," *Whither,
Whither or After Sex What?,* and of Messrs. Thurber and
White's delightful satire of our absorption in sex in *Is Sex Necessary?,* both in 1930, were the first books against "introversion"
to win public favor. In a much discussed article in *Harper's* for
December, 1932, "Lo, the Poor Introvert," Dorothy Canfield
defended introspection and subjectivity as essential to the highest
life and belabored the "extravert" as typical of formula-made
society. In the same magazine, shortly afterwards, Mr. Ludwig
Lewisohn recanted and asked, "Is Love Enough?" He felt

America tyrannized over by dogmatic people, like Bertrand Russell, whom he termed "sex-radicals," and he went on to point out "it is a fact, which sexologists will bear out, that over-anxious and highly self-conscious sexual vigilance, undiverted by the normal easements and preoccupations of a properly embodied marriage, is in itself a powerfully inhibitory element." And many concluded, after Mr. Lewisohn, that we had given too much thought to love. So complete was the reaction, in fact, that Grace Adams could write an excellent article in the *Atlantic,* for January, 1934, on "The Rise and Fall of Psychology."

Of course, this reaction to the sex absorption of the 'twenties did not solve all our problems. Lest anyone think that it did, let him consult the facts that Doctor Edward Westermarck has gathered on this country in his book *The Future of Marriage in Western Civilization* (1936). The London sociologist concludes we have the highest divorce rate of any country on the globe, with the possible exception of Russia, that adultery outside marriage is alleged to be committed by one out of four partners, while homosexuality is rampant. This is not quite the national distinction we would seek, but after our tremendous growth in the nineteenth century had established habits of freedom, which were roughly checked, and the whole current of our thought (filled with foreign flotsam and jetsam) was to eddy about the subject of sex and to concentrate on it, this result is not surprising. The cure for the situation lies in less emphasis on the subject, in better economic conditions permitting earlier marriages and the freedom to bear children, but to limit reasonably their births, and finally and perhaps most important, as Mr. Walter Lippmann has pointed out in *A Preface to Morals* (1929), in the rediscovery of values and ideals. Towards this discovery Emily Newell Blair and Donald Culross Peattie have already written thoughtful and stimulating essays, and this has been the whole tenor of the writings of Professor Ernest Groves (*Social Problems of the Family,* 1927; *Wholesome Marriage,* 1927; *The Marriage Crisis,* 1928; *Wholesome Childhood,* 1931; etc.), who in the early 'twenties introduced at Boston University the first course taught in America on marriage and its problems.

Let nobody carp, however, and say that the revolt of the

'twenties was wholly in vain. Though the overriding of taboos brought pain, and sin, and death, it is also true that it brought a measure of free discussion such as the world has not had in a long time. One cannot but regard the famous decision of Judge Wooley on *Ulysses* in 1933 as one of the landmarks in our intellectual freedom, but this decision would have been impossible unless the tide of battle had not set previously this way. One can realize best what this freedom means by reading Mr. Joseph Wood Krutch's article in *The Nation* on the closing of the New York burlesque shows in 1937. While admitting the method was deplorable, Mr. Krutch pointed out that the shows were incontestably dull and stupid. Once an intellectual would have had to defend this dullness and stupidity for the sake of freedom, but that condition exists no longer—save in alien Boston. Another great victory, really a product of the battles of the 'twenties, was signalized in the United States Circuit Court of Appeals decision of December 6, 1936, which ruled that physicians might send contraceptives by mail. This made dispensation of the knowledge of birth control legal and tended to place the methods under the supervision of the proper scientific authority. We may look forward to the day of improved contraceptives—if the American Medical Association understands its duty—and the elimination of harmful and dangerous alternatives. Eugenics, conceived by Galton, may be revived as a science.

Let no one maintain, either, that our vagrant sexual history is not responsible for some great literature, the range being from Whitman, the poet of fecundity, to O'Neill, the dramatist of frustration and inhibitions. High merit surely is exhibited in the prose of Henry Adams and the verse of Robinson Jeffers. Later generations will appreciate the work of Dell, Anderson, Miss Millay, and others, but to no generation will any of these people mean as much as they do to ours. They set us free.

ENVOI

"But from that spell, I burst again, as all
the Past smote all the Present in me."
—Herman Melville, *Mardi.*

WHATEVER OTHER impressions one has formed in traversing these many pages, this impression he must share with all: rarely in history has there been such a release of the creative spirit as there has been in our time in America. Here admittedly is but a partial view of the forces at play in our era: yet here enough to satisfy even the querulous on this score. Not all of the contributors to our intellectual Renaissance are of equal importance, yet the reflective person would hardly discuss any figure in fewer words than have here been grudgingly expended: it is a fair wager that, if he differs with the presentation offered, it is in regard to the adequacy of some one evaluation or the omission of a worthy figure. Rare the age that has produced so many indispensable intellects. In this, our time resembles that of the Elizabethans where not a figure can be spared, not even a Drayton or a Nashe, without a sense of loss.

Yet why are the men and women of our time so indispensable? Though we may have learned from them a respect for things as diverse as the appetites of the natural man and the pure creations of his spirit, their philosophies are generally too alien for more than sufferance here. In a word, these brave creatures are not indispensable because they have been carriers of the infections and distempers of Europe. It is the peculiar pleasure we take in the lustre of each special spirit that makes us prize it. More than anything else, the richness and variety of personality which the period has displayed entitle us to term these times in America a Renaissance. No common mind without somewhere its bright affinity; hence such an awakening as we have never had before in America.

Out of the muck the flower fair and perishable: perennially renewed and rendered perdurable by the imaginations of men. Four centuries ago the invention of printing and gunpowder made the pillage of Church and heavy galleon possible: reckless distribution of this wealth sent a swarm of favored young intellectuals down into Italy to plunder its decadent culture: then the intellectual quickening of England resulted in a demand for a new society, plans for which were drafted by native intellects—by Hobbes and Harrington, by Filmer and Locke. Similarly the invention of the automobile and radio released a golden flood in America, some of which, lavishly expended, sent our youths to pillage the decadent culture of Europe, with results that this volume has partially set forth, the chief of which was a new birth of mind—a prodigious quickening of intellects. Yet with the rare, and even holy, divertissements (from the point of view of us who worship Apollo) provided by our once-youthful and saucy vendors of Old World wares, we cannot be ultimately and completely satisfied: the play, we now feel, is not quite concluded with their graceful epilogues, many of which were spoken in haste about 1929, many of which, no more convincing, still remain to be spoken. The stage slowly fills with other characters, some of whom we might have discerned before, though they are joined by new figures from either wing. Two hosts they seem, frowning on each other. What foreboding have we? Their whole act's immutably decreed, rehearsed by them before their sires' sires crossed the ocean. New Hobbeses and new Harringtons, new Filmers and new Lockes, will they bombard each other only with tracts, so that out of the torn pages of *Leviathans* and *Oceanas,* of *Patriarchias* and *Essays on Liberty* we may piece together new Constitutions for the mutual good of men, or must the ultimate document be written in their mingled blood? They are fairly on the stage, these totalitarians and individualists, these patriarchists and libertarians, and it is certain that they shall never retire till the issue is joined. We neither want nor expect it. We are keyed to the issue—let it come. Meanwhile let us scan the combatants, let us study *the contending forces,* to know our good, if good there be, from each. Then our study becomes no cenotaph reared to American democracy, but a book opening on the glorious future (these are Elizabethan words) of our race.

Index

(To fundamental definitions and to persons of consequence mentioned in the text.)